CHRONICLES

OF THE

Scotch-Irish Settlement

IN

VIRGINIA

EXTRACTED FROM THE ORIGINAL COURT RECORDS OF
AUGUSTA COUNTY
1745-1800

BY

LYMAN CHALKLEY

COMPLETE IN THREE VOLUMES

VOLUME I.

Southern Historical Press, Inc.
Greenville, South Carolina

Originally Published 1912

SOUTHERN HISTORICAL PRESS, INC.
PO BOX 1267
Greenville, SC   29601

ISBN #978-1-63914-096-1

Printed in the United States of America

FOREWORD.

In the year 1745, all that portion of the Colony of Virginia which lay west of the Blue Ridge Mountains was erected into a County which was named Augusta. In December of that year, the County Court was organized and held its first sitting. Prior to that time it had become the refuge and abiding place of a strong body of Scotch-Irish immigrants. The bounds of the new County were limited on the north by Fairfax's Northern Neck Grant and the boundaries of Maryland and Pennsylvania to the westward of Fairfax; on the east by the Blue Ridge Mountains; on the south by the Caroline line. On the west its territory embraced all the soil held by the British without limit of extent. For about twelve years the County Court of Augusta was the only Court and repository of records within that district. From the end of that period, at frequent intervals, its jurisdiction was restricted by the erection of other Counties as the demands of the settlers required. Its original constitution embraced all Virginia west of the Blue Ridge (with the exception of the Northern Neck Grant, whose southern boundary was in the present County of Shenandoah, and western, through the Counties of Hardy, Hampshire, and northward to the Potomac); the whole of the present state of West Virginia; a portion of the present Western Pennsylvania, including Pittsburgh, which was, at times, the seat of the County Court; and the lands on the waters of the Ohio and Mississippi Rivers.

The value of this compilation of notes and abstracts will be determined by the extent of its contribution to the history of the early settlement of a great country and the acceptability of its form. It is not claimed that it is of equal value with the records themselves, or that it is perfect as a compilation. Nor does it constitute a history in the accepted sense. Yet, as the progressive record of the daily life, the needs, the trials, the struggles, the efforts, the labors, the implements and tools, the occupations and amusements, the aids and obstacles, the aims and longings, the achievements and failures, the forming and shaping, the beauty and ugliness, the riches and sordidness, the risings and declinings, the moral, physical, and spiritual evolution of an offshoot and a nucleus of a people whose characteristics have ever been truth, honesty, simplicity, singleness of purpose, and courage, it is believed that it presents history in its truest, most reliable and most attractive form. There is much in it that will be found to be of no direct import; much that cannot be classified; much that cannot be reduced to a generality; much that cannot be made to point to a moral. But every item has its value, each has its place in the picture, each gives a touch or different shade of color, each limits, or broadens, or enlightens its own surroundings. The vista unfolds by grades and steps, and truth becomes plain, as it always does, through growth and development. The story is told by those who act the play. Nothing is added by commentator; nothing is colored by bias; nothing is affected; nothing the result of self-consciousness.

To present the bare facts has been the purpose of the compiler. Each reader will weave his own story, with his own coloring and atmosphere.

PREFACE.

These abstracts of the original Court Records of Augusta County, Virginia, compiled by Judge Lyman Chalkley, were purchased by the National Society of the Daughters of the American Revolution in 1905.

The Twenty-first Congress, National Society of the Daughters of the American Revolution, held in Washington, D. C., April 15–20, 1912, by a unanimous vote, presented these records as a gift outright to Mrs. Mary S. Lockwood, Honorary Vice-President General, National Society of the Daughters of the American Revolution, who has prepared them for publication, with the assistance and co-operation of the following Publishing Committee:

Miss Grace M. Pierce (Chairman), Registrar General, National Society, Daughters of the American Revolution, 1909–1911.

Miss Aline Solomons, Librarian General, National Society, Daughters of the American Revolution, 1905–1907.

Miss Julia McBlair, Librarian General, National Society, Daughters of the American Revolution, 1899–1903.

Mrs. Edward B. Rosa, Librarian General, National Society, Daughters of the American Revolution, 1903–1905.

Mrs. Short A. Willis, Librarian General, National Society, Daughters of the American Revolution, 1909–1911.

Miss Catherine Brittain Barlow, Secretary, Dolly Madison Chapter.

Miss Delia Jackson, Member, Amsterdam Chapter.

Miss Mary E. Barlow, Member, Dolly Madison Chapter.

Mrs. George A. Beach, Regent, Monticello Chapter.

Mrs. Sarah Hall Johnston, Member, Mary Washington Chapter.

Miss Zillah Solomons, Member, Mary Washington Chapter.

Miss Lesley Jackson, Member, Mary Washington Chapter.

EXECUTIVE COMMITTEE

Mrs. Charles W. Fairbanks, President General from 1901–1905.

Miss Virginia Miller, Regent, Mary Washington Chapter.

Mrs. Eleanor Washington Howard, Vice-President General in charge of organization, 1899–1901.

Mrs. Della Grame Smallwood, Regent, Patriots' Memorial Chapter.

Mrs. Joseph S. Wood, Honorary State Regent of New York.

Mrs. John Buel, State Regent of Connecticut.
Mrs. Mary Stilson, State Regent of California, 1910–1912.
Mrs. James G. Dunning, State Regent of Massachusetts.
Mrs. George M. Sternberg, Regent, Army and Navy Chapter.
Mrs. Sara T. Kinney, Honorary Vice-President General.
Mrs. J. J. Estey, Vice-President General of Vermont, 1903–1907.
Mrs. Charles Warren Lippitt, State Regent of Rhode Island, 1902–4, 1908–10.
Miss Isabella Forsyth, Honorary State Regent of New York.
Mrs. Samuel Verplanck, Honorary State Regent of New York.
Mrs. William Cumming Story, Honorary State Regent of New York.
Miss Sophie Waples, Vice-President General of Delaware.
Mrs. John M. Horton, Regent, Buffalo Chapter.
Mrs. J. Heron Crosman, Vice-President General of New York, 1900–1904.
Mrs. John C. Hazen, Vice-President General of New York, 1905–1907.
Mrs. Frances W. Roberts, Honorary State Regent of New York.
Mrs. M. B. Tulloch, Vice-President General in charge of organization, 1909–1911.
Mrs. Henry F. Blount, Historian General, 1892–93.
Mrs. Willard S. Augsbury, State Regent of New York.
Mrs. William G. Slade, President, Daughters 1812.
Mrs. N. Taylor Phillips, Member, Knickerbocker Chapter.
Mrs. Drury C. Ludlow, Vice State Regent, District of Columbia, 1911.
Miss Mary Wilcox, Regent, Colonel John Donelson Chapter.
Miss Janet Richards, Official Reader, Continental Congress, 1900–1909.
Miss Dorinda Rogers, Recording Secretary of Mary Washington Chapter.
Mrs. M. E. S. Davis, Regent of Deborah Knapp Chapter.
Mrs. Sarah Croissant, Regent of Katherine Montgomery Chapter.
Mrs. Leonard Mattingly, Regent of American Chapter.
Miss Mary L. Goddard, Regent of Manor House Chapter.
Mrs. Frances Barton Millard, Member of Omaha Chapter.
Mrs. Jessie Barton Christiancy, Member-at-Large.
Mrs. Charles Russell Davis, Member, Saint Paul Chapter.
Mrs. F. W. Yates, Vice-Regent, Irondequoit Chapter.
Mrs. Velma Sylvester Barber, State Treasurer of the District of Columbia.
Miss Sallie L. Yewell, Treasurer, Jacksonville Chapter.
Mrs. Frank Greenawalt, Regent, Ruth Brewster Chapter.
Mrs. William H. Wanamaker, Regent, Potomac Chapter.
Mrs. Ellis Logan, Regent, Mary Breed Chapter.
Mrs. Sarah C. Guss, Regent, Continental Dames Chapter.
Mrs. Oscar Roome, Regent, Thirteen Colonies Chapter.
Mrs. Charles L. Merwin, Member, Sarah Franklin Chapter.
Mrs. Margaret Moore, Regent, Marcia Burns Chapter.
Miss Mary Perry Brown, Treasurer, Mary Washington Chapter.
Miss Bertha M. Wolfe, Regent, Wendell Wolfe Chapter.
Mrs. Corra Bacon Foster, Member, Emily Nelson Chapter.
Mrs. Gilbert M. Husted, Regent, Louisa Adams Chapter.
Mrs. Redwood Vandegrift, Regent, Margaret Whetten Chapter.
Mrs. Joseph Arnold, Vice-Regent, Patriots' Memorial Chapter.
Mrs. Arnold W. Spanhoofd, Member, Dolly Madison Chapter.

Mrs. De B. Randolph Keim, Honorary Vice-President General.
Miss Minnie F. Mickley, Registrar General, 1902–1903.
Mrs. Grace P. Hopkins, Historian, Louisa Adams Chapter.
Mrs. William A. Smoot, Vice-President General, 1908–1910, Virginia.
Mrs. Frank Bond, Member, Cheyenne Chapter, Wyoming.
Miss Virginia Fairfax, State Regent, Louisiana.
Mrs. Frank D. Callan, Regent, Mohawk Valley Chapter.
Miss Edith M. Tilley, Member, William Ellery Chapter.
Mrs. John Campbell, Vice-President General, Colorado, 1909–1911.
Mrs. John Lloyd McNeil, State Regent, Colorado, 1907–1909.
Mrs. Orlando J. Hodge, Vice-President General of Ohio, 1905–1907.
Miss Mabel Louise White, Regent, Continental Chapter.
Mrs. Charles B. Bryan, Vice-President General of Tennessee.
Mrs. Sarah Adsit Clemons, Regent, Little John Boyden Chapter.
Mrs. Julia Washington Harbaugh, Regent, Sara Franklin Chapter.
Mrs. James E. Mulcare, Registrar, Sara Franklin Chapter.
Mrs. Ida B. Winter, Secretary, Sara Franklin Chapter.
Miss Ethelwyn B. Hall, Regent, John Hall Chapter.
Mrs. Adelaide K. Lowe, Secretary, District of Columbia, 1911–1912.
Mrs. Henry B. Patton, State Regent, Wyoming.

AUGUSTA COUNTY COURT ORDERS.

These notes are from the Order Book of the County Court, which contains the entries of the proceedings of the Court at its daily sittings during the terms. The terms were held monthly. The reference is in each case to the Book in which the order noted is contained, the date of the order and the page of the Book where it will be found.

DECEMBER 9, 1745.

Page

(1) County Court formed—First Justices: James Patton, John Buchanan, Peter Scholl, Robert Campbell, Robert Poage, Thomas Lewis, Robert Cunningham, Richard Woods, Robert Craven, Adam Dickinson, John Anderson, John Lewis, George Robinson, James Bell, John Brown, John Pickens, Hugh Thomson, John Finla, John Christian, James Kerr, Andrew Pickens.

(1) James Patton qualified Sheriff. William Thompson surety.

(2) John Madison qualified Clerk.

(2) John Buchanan and Henry Downs qualified Deputy Sheriffs.

(2) William Russell, James Porteus, Gabriel Jones, John Quinn, and Thomas Chew qualified Attorneys.

DECEMBER 10, 1745.

(2) Thomas Lewis qualified Surveyor.

(3) Sheriff ordered to summon guard to keep prisoners and to provide shackels, bolts, handcuffs and fetters of iron.

(3) Prison to be built and C. H. repaired.

(3) Mathew Edmondson, James Carter and John Finla to open a road from Andrew Hamilton's in calf-pasture thro' Jennings Gap to John Finla's.

(3) James Trimble to be Deputy Surveyor.

(3) Gideon Marr qualified Attorney.

(4) James Lesley appointed Constable vice William Baskins in Geo. Anderson's Co.

(4) Daniel Dennison appointed Overseer Road vice John Pickens.—Bridges to be repaired.

(4) William Right appointed Constable vice David Edmondson in Saml. Gay's Co.

(4) John Rusk—Constable vice Andrew Pickens Cap. Wilson's Co.

(4) Motion Margaret Lundey, Robert Craven and John Stinson appd. guardians of Thomas and John Leviston, orphans of Robert Leviston.

(4) Thos. Harrison, Wm. Williams, Jeremiah Harrison, Hugh Douglass—appraisers of Jo. Levenson.

(4) Robert Young—Constable—vice John Kerr in Richard Woods's Co.

(4) James Greenlee—Constable—vice William Moore in Benj. Borden's Co.

FEBRUARY 10, 1745/6.

(5) Samuel Wilkins—Ordinary License at his house. Thomas Story surety.

(5) Petn. Samuel Wallace—Road ordered from William King's to the C. H., thence to Samuel Gay's.—Wm. King, Morrice Ofrield and John Trimble to lay off 1st part.—Wm. Hutcheson and James Trimble, the residue.

Page

(5) John Grymes—Overseer Road in calf-pasture (vid p. 3 supra) on other side the Ridge and Ro. Armstrong, this side.

(5) John Hawkins and Henry Downs—Under Sheriffs qualified.

(5) Daniel Griffeths committed by James Kerr for stealing a horse from Edward Franklin of Orange, acquitted.

(6) John Newport, Timothy Holdway and Ro. Looney to value improvements of Christian Zimmerman on 400 acres.

(6) Wm. Linwell committed and fined for being drunk.

(6) Andrew McCord bound to peace towards James McCleary.

(6) David Davis—to show cause against paying William Morrison freedom dues.

(7) John Newport and Obadiah Merriot quald. Attorneys.

FEBRUARY 11, 1745.

(7) Benjn. Pendleton qualified Attorney.

(7) Ann Jenney Usher chose James Knox guardian.

(7) Daniel McAnaire and Hannah ackd. deed to Gardner.

(7) Same as above to James Trimble.

(7) John Nichols and Wm. Wright quald. Attorneys.

(8) James McCune ordered to be committed for speaking treasonable words.

(8) Wm. Henderson, Wm. Long, James Alexander, Jno. Black to appraise Ro. Wilson's estate.

(8) Wm. Pierce and Adam Miller to view a road from top Blue Ridge at head Swift Run to Cap. Down's place, formerly Alexander Thomson's.

(8) Wm. Smith and Ro. Gay—Overseers Road from David Davis Mill to top mountain above Wm. King's.

(8) Daniel Holdman and Saml. Wilkins—same from Benj. Allen's mill to North River.

(8) Wm. Magill and Thos. Stinson—same from North River to John Anderson's.

(8) John Anderson and Andrew Lewis, same from Anderson's to C. H.

(9) James Clerk spec. bail for Saml. McGaw.

(10) Silas Hart spec. bail for Robt. Renix.

(11) John Carre (Kerr) spec. bail for Hugh Martin.

(11) James Biggs, Philip Jones, Thomas Moore, garnishees.

(12) John and David Harry, Ro. Crockett and John Boil (a miller) garnishees.

FEBRUARY 12, 1745/6.

(13) Robert McClenachan—Ordinary license at Co. Ho. David Stewart, Sty.

(13) John Hutchison—same.

(13) Andrew Pickens, Peter Scholl, Richard Woods recommended coroners—and Pickens to act until appt.

(13) Wm. Thomson, security for Alexr. Thomson.

(14) Enis Young, security for James Davis.

14

(14) Wm. McCandless security for Ro. Galloway.

(15) Robert Seyers security for John Patterson.

(15) Moses McClure vs. George Hall—Judgt. for Deft., suit "dismist and the bill sued on be damned and shall not be given out of this office."

(16) Robert Cunningham fined 5 sh. for being drunk.

(16) William Morrison to have his freedom dues paid out of the attached estate of David Davis.

(16) Andrew Pickens—Admr. Joseph Martin—and John Trimble, Wm. McFeters, Saml. Wallace and John Brown, Appraisers.

(17) Thomas McCullogh—Ordinary license—his house.

(17) Attorney interrupting another or speaking when not employed forfeits 5 sh.

(17) William Smith fined 5 sh.—being drunk.

FEBRUARY 19, 1745/6.

(17) For Proof Public Claims and Propositions and Grievances.

(17) Claim Richard Woods—Losses by Indians.

(17) Claim John Mathews—Losses by Indians.

(17) Claim Henry Kirkham—Losses by Indians.

(17) Claim William Henderson— for assisting of. with arms and ammunition.

(17) Claim David Edmondson—

(18) Claim Benj. Borden and Magdalen, Admx. John McDowell—Losses by Indians.

(18) Claim Francis McCown—Losses by Indians.

(18) Claim John Buchanan and others—for patrolling.

(18) Claim Joseph Lapsley—Losses by Indians.

(18) Claim Mary Doughert—Losses by Indians.

(18) Claim Patrick Martin—taking up a slave, property of Dr. Hopkins.

(18) Claim Andrew Myrtin—Losses by Indians.

(18) Claim Isaac Anderson—Losses by Indians.

(18) Claim Joseph Coulton—Losses by Indians.

(18) ClaimJohn Walker—Losses by Indians.

(18) Claim Dominick Berrall—Losses by Indians.

(18) Claim Jno. Wilson et als—patrolling.

(19) Claim James Walker—Losses by Indians.

(19) Claim Thos. Black et als—patrolling.

(19) David Edmondson makes oath the men mentioned in his list were pressed by him and served the time mentioned.

MARCH 10, 1745/6.

(19) Ordinary Rates Regulated.

(20) Mark Evans, William Kervine, John McFarron, James Mc Gomerie appd. Overseers of Road Blazed by Orange Co. from inhabitants of Roanoke to top Blue Ridge at bounds of Brunswick Co. and Cap. Robinson and John Mills are to lay off precincts and tithables.

(20) James Patton, John Lewis, John Pickens, Recd. Sheriff.

Page

(20) Nathan McClure—Constable—vice Wm. Moore, Burden's Co.

(20) Wm. Kervine—Constable—vice Simon Acres—Geo. Robinson's Co.

(20) Thos. Gardner committed for disturbing John Buchanan in his office.

(20) John Graham and James McGaw—same as to John Hawkins.

(20) Thos. Scot—continued Overseer from Top of Ridge to Alexr. Thomson's.

(20) Andrew McCord discharged from recognizance—Br. Peace.

(21) Ephraim McDowell committed to answer Roger Keys.

April 14, 1746.

(21) Abraham Strickler's widow refuses to administer—Jeremiah Sutton, Randolph Mack, John Spittler and Paul Lung, Appraisers.

(22) John King dismissed from complaint Peter Sholl—John not being a legal constable.

(22) Robert Scot qualified Captain of foot.

(22) Wm. Finley qualified Captain of foot.

(22) Robert Craven—Ordinary License.

(23) Thomas Moffet's petn. to be levy free—Dismissed.

(23) Andrew McNabb—child sworn to by Martha Allison.

(23) William Thomson—Spec. Bail for Alexr. Thomson.

(23) John King—garnishee.

April 15, 1746.

(24) John Nicholas, Depy. Atty. having refused to officiate Gabriel Jones recommended.

(24) Elizabeth, wife of Robert Poage—deed to Robert Gamble.

(24) Margaret, wife John Lewis—deed to James Robertson.

(25) John Graham—special bail for Saml. McGaw.

(26) Petn. Margaret Lundey—her clothes and goods taken by David Logan Constable on attacht. vs her decd. husband Thomas Lundey at suit of Daniel Harriss, be returned.

(28) Mary Perry to be bound to Wm. Thompson until she is 18.

(28) Clerk to have presses for Records made.

(29) Geo. Cathey vs John Quin—Pl. nonsuited and makes oath that he never employed Thos. Chew to bring suit and Judgt. vs. Thos. for costs.

(31) John Harrison Spec. bail for Saml. McGaw.

(31) Petition John Risk for a road—Rejected.

(32) Carr vs. Smith — £4 Penna. Curcy.= £3 Cur. Money, Va.

(33) Erwin Patterson—appd. Constable on Roanoke near the Great Lick.

(33) John Robinson—same on Fork of Roanoke.

(33) James Hervey (or Hewey)—same on James River.

(33) William Scott—appd. Constable on Cutabough Creek.

Page

(33) Christopher Zimmerman—valuation of improvements returned and John Newport having made oath that it had not been before valued, recorded.

(35) Charles Berry, surety for John Pattison.

(35) Isaac Anderson, surety for Saml. Davis & Edw. Boyle.

(35) Erwin Patterson, sp. Bail for James Greenlee.

(36) Borden vs. Isaac Anderson—Ejectment—350 acres.

Borden vs. John McPharron—Ejectment—319 acres.

(36) Alexander vs. McClure—Plt. produced deft's. bill with endorsement, which was read out by James Patton without the Court's orders—Gabriel Jones ordered to indict him—and suit is dismissed.

(37) Mathew Mitchell—garnishee—also Jane Burnett—Joseph Reid and Andrew Russell — £15, 2, 7 Penna.= £11, 6, 11 Current money.

(37) William Morrison's freedom dues—£3, 10 Current money.

(42) Sam'l Lockhart and Wm. Linwell—garnishees.

(42) Wm. Thompson vs. Saml. Lockhart—Ejectt.—400 acres.

(42) Silas Hart, John Mathews, Charles Burk, Benj. Borden, John Ruddle, Joseph Lapsley, Ebenezer Westcoat, and James Montgomerie recomd. Justices.

MAY 12, 1746.

(43) Thomas Black—appd. Constable. Cap. Christian's Co.

(43) Gabriel Jones—quald. Depy. Attorney.

(43) William White, William James. Wm. Carroll, Morgan Briant—Appraisers John Dobikin's Estate.

(43) A grand jury sworn were immediately dismissed because 25 were sworn.

(43) Alexander vs. McClure—Thomas Chew asks permission to withdraw the bill in order to bring suit which is denied until the charge vs. Col. Patton is tried. Judt. in this case, page 184 infra 20 March, 1746—Look it up.

(43) Abraham Job—appd. Constable at Masaunting.

(43) William Taylor appd. Constable fr. Benj. Allen's to lower end of Co.

(43) James Robinson—appd. Constable fr. Linville's Cr. to North Gap.

(44) William Carroll appd. Constable fr. Smith's Cr. to Cap. Allens and Cap. Dobins's bounds.

(44) Adam Miller—same on North River and below Peaked Mount.

(44) James Hogshead—same at North Mountain.

(44) Saml. Stuart—same Head Linville's Creek.

(44) Wm. Guy—same Calfpasture.

(44) Michl. O'Dugherty—same Capt. Woods's Co.

(44) Robert Young—same vice John Risk.

(44) Charles Hayes—same vice James Trimble.

(44) John Lynn—same vice George Colville.

(44) John Preston proved his importation; Elizabeth, his wife; William, his son; Lettice, Margaret and Anne, his daughters, immediately from Ireland into this Colony.

17

(44) Simon Acres appd. Roadoverseer vice Wm. Kerwin.

(45) Jost Hite vs. Thomas Linville.

(45) Nicholas Brock summoned on complaint of Val. Sevear.

(45) Robert Armstrong appd. Overseer Road from Jenning's Gap to Daniel McAnaires—thence to John Finla's Cooper—thence to the Court House—all tithables within 4 miles on each side to work the road.

(45) Joseph Russell and John Smith make affidavit—Roger Mallory's account not sworn to.

(45) Road ordered from the Great Lick in the cowpasture at Col. Lewis's land to Andrew Hamiltons in calfpasture. Andrew and George Lewis Comrs. to mark it off.

(45) Robert Gwin appd. Constable at head of Great Calfpasture.

(45) George Anderson appointed Constable South River vice David Logan.

(45) Robert Kirkham quald. Admr. Michael Kerkham.

(46) Richard Woods, Joseph Lapsley, Henry Kerkham and Peter Wallace—appraisers.

(46) Edward Boyle sentenced to stocks and fined for damning the Court and swearing 4 oaths in their presence.

MAY 13, 1746.

(46) Henry Downs, under sheriff, ordered to get a house for a jail.

(46) Wm. Lusk's petition for turning the road around his place is granted.

(47) William Wright appd. Constable vice David Edmondson.

(47) Thomas Lackey appd. Road Overseer vice James Gill from North River where James Gill dwelt to the South River.

(47) Adjourned till 3d Wednesday in June according to late Act of Assembly for altering the same.

JUNE 18, 1746.

(47) Gabriel Jones qualified Attorney.

(48) James Hogshead, Thomas Black, William Wright, William Guy, Robert Gwin, Charles Hays, George Anderson, Adam Miller, James Robinson, Thomas McCulloch, appd. Constables last Court qualified.

(48) Order for securing prisoners at last Court contind.

(48) James and John McCune, on testimony of John Risk and James Lockhart, committed for having spoken treasonable words.

(48) Margaret McCowen's privy Exn. (wife of Francis?)

(49) Robert Young qualified Constable.

(49) Elianor Roork, servant of Mathias Seltzer—run away.

(49) William Brock to be bound to Valentine Sevear.

(49) James Porteus—certified that he is a man of probity, honesty, diligence, good demeanor and a fair practitioner in order to be "examined according to law."

(49) Daniel Richeson, Michael Stump and Benj. Hardin, to view road petition of Richard Crunk.

Page

(49) John Wilson—leave to build water grist mill.

(49) Morrice Offield, John Trimble and Wm. King to make remainder of the road from top of North Mountain to said King's and thence to Co. Ho.

JUNE 19, 1746.

(50) Aaron Jackson—above 14—chose Wm. Hutcheson his guardian.

(50) Commission to Orange for privy examination of Elinor, wife of Robert Green.

(51) Same as to Margaret, wife of Robert McKay.

(51) Henry Spears and Mathias Seltzer appointed road overseers over road from Thorn's Gap from South River to county line.

(51) Wm. King—permission to dig a race thro' John Trimbles land to his mill.

(52) James Biggs, Philip Jones, Thomas Moore, garnishees.

(53) Samuel Wilkins vs. Robert Scott—First Jury.

(55) William White, witness.

JUNE 20, 1746.

(63) Thos. Cresap vs. Jno. Johnston } One John Johnston appeared and on oath declared that he was not the person indebted and non suit.

(64) £2, 13, 4 Proclamation Money=40 sh. Current Money.

(65) William Miller, an idle vagrant person and a man of loose behavior—with George Hall, surety-bond.

(66) Order to summon Robert Young for bringing a woman into the County who is likely to be chargeable to the Parish, renewed.

(67) Cap. John and Jonas Denton—overseers from County line

(68) to Stoney Creek, and Griffith Thomas and John Ruddle, Sr., from said Creek to the new road.

(68) Alexr. Herrin—overseer from Robt. Cravens to Saml. Wilkins's, and Thomas and Jeremiah Harrison from Craven's to the Indian Road— Cap. Scholl to lay off the precincts.

JULY 16, 1746.

(68) New Court—Commission dated 13 June, 1746: James Patton, George Robinson, Robert Cunningham, James Montgomery, Wm. Jameson, Saml. Gay, John Lewis, Peter Scholl, John Wilson, Silas Hart, Richard Burton, Wm. Thompson, John Buchanan, James Bell, Thomas Lewis, Henry Downs, John Christian.

(69) Henry Downs to be Sheriff and qualified, and John Hawkins and Henry Downs, Jr., qualified Under Sheriffs.

(69) Commission to prepare a deed from Beverley for 25 acres according to an order of Council.

(69) Wm. Woods, Thos. Williams, Michael Finey, appointed Constables in Fork of James River.

Page

(69) Law books provided for each justice, Webb's Justices and Mercer's Abridgements.

(70) James and John McCune brought before the Court for speaking treasonable words—evidence heard—both took the oaths and gave bond for good behavior.

(70) John Maxwell and William Thompson to make road from the Co. Ho. to Tinkling Spring.

(70) Robert McMahon and Samuel Lockhard being bound over to this Court for misbehaving themselves towards William Thomson in killing his hogs, horses, etc., and William saying he feared further damage—they gave bond for good behavior, George Anderson and Wm. Pierce for Lockard, James Givens and Geo. Cathey for McMahon.

(71) John Buchanan qualified Coroner.

Peter Scholl qualified Coroner.

John Buchanan qualified Under Sheriff.

(71) Road ordered from Co. Ho. to Clerk's Office, and tithables of John Madison, William Nut, James McCorkle, Robert McClenachan and James Armstrong clear it.

AUGUST 20, 1746.

(72) Petition of Henry Downs—Road to be marked from the road that leads off the mountain near Alexr. Thompson's to the lower Meeting House and Wm. Thompson, Jr., Saml. Givens and John Campbell mark and lay off the same.

(72) Valentine Sevear—Ordinary license. Edward Hughes, surety.

(72) James Porteus qualified Attorney.

(72) Licenced by Peyton Randolph, St. Lawrence Burford, Esqrs., and Wm. Nimmo and Stephen Dewey, gentlemen.

(72) Report as to road from top North Mountain to Wm. King's and thence to C. H.—Robert Davis appointed overseer. The following tithables to work it: George Kill Patrick, James Young, James Mills, Robert McClellan, Andrew Pickens, Jacob Lockart, John Trishell, Hugh Young, Samuel Kinkead, William Mills, William McFeeters, James Clark, Henry Cristwell.

(73) John Brown to be overseer of same road from King's to C. H. with following tithables: Hugh Spears, John McKenney, Thomas Peary, John Bartley, Patrick Martin, James Phillips, James Bell, George Vance, James Montgomery, Thomas Kill Patrick, John Spears, Saml. Wallace, Wm. McClintock, John Davis.

(73) William Thompson to be overseer from Court Ho. to Tinkling Spring, already viewed, with these tithables: John Lynn and his three sons, John Henderson, John Ramsey, John Preston, Wm. Palmer, David Stuart, James Coile, Joseph McClelhill, Alexr. Thompson, John Mitchell, John Hutchison, Andrew Russell, Geo. Caldwell and his two sons.

(73) James Montgomerie and George Robinson — a comn. to notify Lunenburg Court that a road had been built in Augusta from the part of Roanoke in this Co. to the top of the Ridge adjoining Lunenburg and ask to have it continued in Lunenburg.

Page

(73) John Buchanan, Patrick Cook, Alexr. Walker—to mark and lay off a road from said Buchanan's to Co. Ho.

(74) John Graham to be overseer from James Carter's mill to the Co. Ho. as far as the first ford above Bell's land—and all tithables from head of the river to John Miller's work it.

(74) Cap. Daniel McAnaire to be overseer of above road with following tithables: Samuel Wallis, Alexr. Crawford, John Elliott, David Trimble, John Hogshead, Alexr. Gardner, Sampson Archer, Alexr. Gibson, Robt. Davis, Thomas Gardner, Walter Trimble, John Sixby, David Stuart, Ro. Renix, Francis Gardner, John Trimble, Thomas Beard, Ro. Gilkason, John Archer, James Bell, James Mills, James Dyer, Charles Clendening, Wm. Hogshead, Ro. Ralstone, John Moffet, Saml. Lusk, James Phillips, Danl. Brealey, Mathew Edmonston, James Trimble, John Ferguson, Wm. Anderson, John Spears, John McKenney, Wm. Brady, Ro. Armstrong, James Miller.

(74) James McCune to be overseer vice Francis McCune.

(75) John Elswick charged with murdering Wm. Cape. Not guilty of murder, but killed by chance.

AUGUST 21, 1746.

(75) Sheriff to provide weights and measures.

(75) Order for Sheriff for securing prisoners—continued.

(76) James Allison, assignee of Hugh Boil ⎤ Pl. not an inhab-
                 vs. ⎬ itant of this
David and Alexander Gibson ⎦ country.

(76) James Patton qualified Coroner.

(77) John Quin qualified as Attorney—having been licensed under former law.

(77) Henry Downs, Jr., qualified Captain of Foot.

(77) Wm. Thompson qualified Lieutt. of Foot.

(79) John Hammond, garnishee—£28, 10 sh. Penna. Cury.= £21, 7, 6 Current money.

(80) Thomas Chew, Att'y, made to pay all costs because of his neglect in not summoning the witnesses on his side.

(81) Jury—John Moffet, William Bates, Thomas Stinson, Edward Hughes, etc.

(81) John Bartley and Lofty Pullin ordered immediately before the Court for disturbing it while sitting.

(82) James Finla was removed out of the Colony.

(83) Petition of John Holmes vs. Thomas Chew for neglectg. his business as an attorney is dismissed.

(83) Gabriel Jones adjudged guilty of a misdemeanor in interrupting Richard Wainscut in giving his evidence.

AUGUST 22, 1746.

(84) £4 Penna. Money = £3 Current Money.

(84) Moffet vs. Graham. Jury—John McMasters, Alexr. Duglas, etc. No appeal to be granted on a general verdict without errors being filed first.

Page
(84) John Trimble to be overseer vice Robt. Young.
(85) Daniel Deniston, Jr., to be Constable vice Thos. McCullock.
(86) Robert Patrick to be overseer vice Cap. Gay.
(88) Ewell vs. Briant—Verdict, "we find for defendant." Atty. filed errors in arrest of judgment—referred to next Court.
William Pickins, witness in above suit.
(89) Edward Hughes, witness in above suit.
Richard Wanscot, witness in above suit.
Margaret Sherrill, witness in above suit.

AUGUST 23, 1746.

(95) £3 Penna. Money = £2, 5 Cur. Money of Va.
£5 Penna. Money = £3, 15 Cur. Money of Va.
(98) Rob. Cunningham, Gent., in action, ejectment by Beverley, insisted on his privilege as Burgess, setting forth that he was served with the Declaration within the privileged time.
(102) Philip Lung—garnishee.
(102) James Patton et als. made their return on the order for viewing and receiving the Co. H. lot—

We, subscribers, being appointed 16 July, 1746, to view and receive the 25 acres laid out by Beverley according to an order of Council, having viewed the land as laid out by Thos. Lewis, etc., etc., find the land entirely ill convenient and useless, being most part of it on a barren hill or mountain where the County cannot pretend to sell one lot if the said land be received nor fall into any way or method to raise the quitrents, it affording neither firewood nor water, no spring being included in the whole 25 acres, though several are nigh and adjacent.—Advise non-acceptance unless it be so laid off that the Co. Ho. be in the center, and when so laid off ⅔ will be barren hills without timber and of little or no use to the County.
A Copy ordered to be certified to Beverley.

SEPTEMBER 17, 1746.

(105) Hart vs. Thompson. Jury—George Cathey, John Stinson.
(106) Roger Keys bound to peace towards James Greenlee.

SEPTEMBER 18, 1746.

(107) John George Bonsley, same towards his father Jacob.
(108) Jurymen—Daniel Holdman, John Hood, James Armstrong, John Rutledge, Adam Dickerson, James Armstrong, Ro. Gibson, Thos. Cotner.
(108) Pet. Robert Foile vs. Edward Erwin is rejected.
(110) John Hite of Frederick—a witness.
Robert Warf of Frederick—a witness.
(111) Watkin Vaughan Ellis qual. Att'y.
(111) Mary Cafferty, indented servant, vs. her master, Robert Young.
(111) Motion James Greenlee—added to list of tithables.
(111) Motion Silas Hart—added to list of tithables.
(112) John Lynn, Jr.—witness for John Lynn.

Page

(112) Thomas Coleman, juror.
(112) Alexr. Thompson bound to peace.
(112) Uriah Chadwick—witness.

SEPTEMBER 19, 1746.

(113) Clerk to transmit a copy of the answer to Col. Beverly. Letter to this Court to him and require a positive answer against Nov. Court.
(113) Complt. of James Patton that James, Ezekiel, Wm. and Patrick Colhoon were divulgers of false news to the great detriment of the Inhabitants of this Colony—to be committed for Nov. Court.
(113) Benj. Borden, Samuel Woods, added to tithables.
(118) Judgt. vs. John Mayfis of Co. Salem, wheelwright, for £4, 4, 2 money of New Jersey = £3, 3, 1½ Cur. Money.
(126) Jane Robinson no inhabitant of this Colony.
(127) £2 Penna. Money = 30 sh.
(129) Jacob Dye } Deft. moved the suit be dismissed because he had
  vs. } not been aiding and helping Sigismund Henley
  John Homan } away, who was present in Court—Court adjudged
that as the principal debtor is in Court and ready to stand suit, and the deft. was only sued as one aiding and abetting him to run away, that it be dismissed.

NOVEMBER 19, 1746.

(129) John Preston—Ordinary license.
(129) Grand Jury—Nathan Patterson, Ro. Dunlap, John Holmes, and others—grand jurors.
(130) John Wilson, late a servant to Francis Beatey, received a discharge setting forth his honesty, etc.
(130) Joseph Lapsley qualified Cap. of Foot.
(130) Road ordered from North Fork of James to Looney's Ford on So. Fork James—with all tithables except John Boyr, Jos. Long and Jno. Peter Sallings's families.
(130) Road ordered from Reed Creek to Eagle Bottom and thence to top of Ridge that parts waters of New River and those of So. Fork of Roanoke, and these are to work it: George, Ezekiel, William and Patrick Colhoon, Bryant White, Wm. Handlow, Peter Rentfro and his two sons, George the Tinker, Jacob Woolman and two sons, John Black, Simon Hart, Michael Claine, John Stroud, Saml. Starknecker and all the Dunkers that are able to work on the same and all other persons in that precinct. James Colhoon and Charles Hart to be overseers.
(130) Road ordered from Adam Harmon's to the River and No. Branch of Roan Oak—Adam Harmon, overseer, with these workers: Geo. Draper, Israel Lorton and son, George Hermon, Thos. Looney, Jacob Hermon and three sons, Jacob Castle, John Lane, Valentine Harmon, Adren Moser, Humberston Lyon, James Shaggs, Humphrey Baker, John Davis, Fredk. Stering and two sons and all other persons settling in the precincts.
(131) Road ordered from the Ridge above Tobias Bright's that parts the waters of New River from the branches of Roan Oak to the lower ford of

23

Catabo Creek. Tobias Bright, overseer. Wm. English and two sons, Thos. English and son, Jacob Brown, George Bright, Benj. Oyle, Paul Garrison, Elisha Isaac, John Donahu, Philip Smith, Mathew English and the rest of the tithables as nominated by George Robinson and James Montgomery.

(131) Road ordered from Ridge dividing waters of New River from waters of So. Br. Roanoak to end in a road that leads over the Blue Ridge—James Cambell and Mark Evans, overseers. Old Mr. Robinson and his sons, Thos. Wilson and his two sons, Wm. Beus and his brother, all the Ledfords, Saml. Brown, Henry Brown, Saml. Niely, James Burk, James Bean, Francis Estham, Ephraim Voss and servants, Francis Summerfield, John Mason, Tasker and Thomas Tosh, John and Peter Dill, Uriah Evans's sons, Mathuselah Griffiths and sons, John Thomas, Peter Kender.

(131) Wm. Long to build water grist mill.

(131) Saml. Earley complains of his master, Saml. Bly.

November 20, 1746.

(132) County Levy:—To Ro. McClenahan to find small beer, candles, to keep Court House in order and to find stableage for Justices', Attorneys' and Officers' horses, 1,600 lbs. tobacco, 961 tithables at 34 lbs. tobacco each, or 2 sh. 1 d.— Current Money.

(132) Prison to be secured by guard until finished.

(133) Hugh Thompson and Thos. Stinson appd. overseers from Wm. Thompson's to the Meeting House.

Wm. McGill appointed Constable.

(133) Court House to be repaired.

(133) John Brown, charged with failing to return his list of tithables, says he neglected to set up advertisements before the 10th of June or to take the list—ordered to be prosecuted.

(134) James Clark allowed to build a water grist mill.

(134) Surveyor to lay off 10 acres with Co. Ho. in center as prison bounds and set a stake at each corner.

(134) Grand Jury presentments.

James Bourk—common swearer.

(134) David Bryans, Israel Robinson, James Bullock and James Houston—being vagrants, hunting and burning the woods.

(134) John Hays and John Hawkins—swearing.

(134) Humberston Lyon and Susan, wife of Wm. Mires—for Adultery.

November 21, 1746.

(135) John Peter Sailing qualified Captain of Foot.

(135) Adam Miller and Ludwick Francisco appointed overseers from Alexr. Thompson's to Swift Run Gap and all tithables from Jacob Cober's to Saml. Scot's at upper end of Peaked Mountain clear it.

(136) Jurymen—Wm. Hall, John Macom.

(138) John Francis—witness.

(140) John Hutchison to build a water grist mill.

(141) Cresap vs. Johnson.

£13, 6 Maryland Money = £7, 4, C. Money, Va.

Attacht. on 3 wooden bowles, 6 pewter spoons.

24

Page
(142) Commission to examine records.
(142) Posts of directions to be set up on roads.
(142) Road ordered from Co. Ho. to Timber *Broge* (Ridge?).
(144) James Fowler vs. Saml. Givens.
  Deft. pleaded—Plaintiff's own assault.
  Plt. replied—Defendant's own wrong.

FEBRUARY 18, 1746/7.

(151) Ro. McMahon—garnishee.
(151) James Connerly, charged with felony in stealing deer skins—acquitted; but convicted of killing 38 red deer contrary to law and fined, and being a vagrant person, put under recognizance. Joseph Lane and Baptist McNabb securities.
(151) Andrew Baxter, nearly eighty, to be levy free.
(151) Robert King to build a water mill.
(151) John Ruddle to build a water mill.
(151) Henry Guy to build a water mill.
(152) James Allison, to build a water mill.
(152) John Stevenson qualified Lieut. Foot.
(152) Adam Harman qualified Captain Foot.
(152) John Edwards qualified Under Sheriff.
(152) John McCown, Michael Finney, Thos. Williams, appointed Constables in Forks of James—precincts to be laid off by Richard Burton.

FEBRUARY 19, 1746/7.

(153) Baptist McNabb qualified Ensign of Foot.
(153) Adam Dickerson to build a water grist mill.
(153) Wm. Aylett, John and Henry Guy to appraise Crockett's estate.
(153) Abraham Drake chose Thomas Grubbs guardian.
(153) Administration of Abraham Drake's estate committed to Thos. Grubbs, guardian of Abraham Drake, son of Abraham Drake. John Davis, Alexr. Mathews, Daniel Stover and George Leath, appraisers.
(153) Ro. McClenahan—Ordinary license in County.
(154) Catherine Cole, servant of David Stuart.
(154) Wm. Aylett, Thos. Symster, Wm. Ayler and John Guy, appraisers.
(154) Ulrich Kyhner to build a mill at the narrow passage, rejected.
(154) John Hodge, leave to build a mill.
(154) Catherine Quin, recognized on charge petty larceny.
(155) Lucus Morgan (servant of Wm. Miller) imported from Ireland under 19 years and in this Colony above 6 months.
(158) Jurymen—Wm. Elliott, Joseph McClelhill, Andrew Nutt.
(159) When Church Wardens are chosen they are to bind out Wm. Anderson.

Page

(161) £14, 2 Penna. Money = £10, 11, 6 Cur. Money, Va.

(162) Jurymen—Wm. Beus, Ro. Brown, James Price, John Lynn.

(163) James Wright, dead over 30 days without will, has very small estate and Sheriff ordered to sell it.

(163) Report on Clerk's Office—favorable.

(163) Christian Boyter—witness.

(164) Margret Sherrill—witness.

(164) John McClewrath—garnishee.

(167) John Hunter relinquished his right to qualify on estate of his mother, Elizabeth Hunter, in Lunenburg Co., who died lately intestate in said Co., to Wm. Hunter, his younger brother.

(167) John Rutledge and James Bell produced deeds from Thomas Galesby, but Henry Downs claimed that he was Galesby's security for £50, and Court refused to record deeds.

(167) Robert Renix qualified Lieut. of Horse.

(167) John Ramsey qualified Constable in Cap. Thompson's Co.

MARCH 18, 1746/7.

(168) James Montgomerie qualified Coroner.

(168) Road ordered from lower end of cow-pasture to Carter's Mill, and Adam Dickenson, James Scot, Wm. Galespy, James Simpson, Wm. Dowerty, Andrew Maldrough, Hugh Coffey, John Donerly, Alexr. McKay, John Mitchell, John Moore, Ralph Laverty, John Cockmill, James Huy, Wm. Hugh, James Stewart, James McKay worked it.

(168) Road ordered from Caleb Jones's mill down to County line, James McKay, Moses McKay, Henry Harding, John Hill, Philip Crine, Thos. Land, Wm. Hursh, Thos. Burk, Wm. Harrel, Thos. Grubbs, Wm. Hawkins, Zachery McKay, Joshua Job, James McNeal, Adam Cunningham, Jacob Sterrell, Charles Coxe, Charles Burk, Ephrm. Leech, Caleb Job.

(168) Road ordered from Top of the Ridge to John Terrald's and James Beard's, with these tithables, John Bomgardner, Jacob Harmon, Robert and Saml. Scot, John Stevenson, Robert Hook, Wm. Burk, Mathew Thompson, Charles Duel, Nicholas Noel, John Lawrence, Jacob Pence, Henry Dickens, Valentine Pence, George Scot, John Viare, Jacob Harmon, Sr., Mathew Sharp, John Harmon, Ro. Frazier, James Beard, Mathew Thompson, John Robton, Stiffell Francisco, Wm. Lamb, Samuel Lockard, Ro. Smith.

(169) Daniel Kidney acquitted of stealing Indian fodder from Henry Christwell.

(169) Saml. Wilkins to keep an ordinary.

(169) John Archer required to deliver up to Catherine Quin her child, and James Carter and Ro. Davis, arbitrators.

(171) James Burk (greatest creditor) Admr. Isaac Bean.

MARCH 18, 1746/7.

(172) Appraisers of John Jennet's estate.

(173) Wm. Burk complains that Torance McMullen has a horse the property of the widow Fulsher of Orange.

March 19, 1746/7.

Page

(173) Liquors rated.—Ordinary keepers required to abide by these rates, and if any sell bad liquor, he is to forfeit his license.

(173) John Bramham qualified Under-Sheriff.

(175) David Davis and John Smith to lay off a road from the Co. Ho. to top Blue Ridge, near Rockfish Gap, and from thence to Falls of James River and Fredericksburg.

(177) Sarah, wife of Robert Allen, a witness from Frederick Co.

(179) John Newport, Assignee of Ogullion vs. Joseph Wait } Three days work, six shillings.

(181) James Campbell and John McCown appd. Constables.

March 20, 1746/7.

(181) Court for proof of Public Claims and Receiving and Certifying Propositions and Grievances.

(181) A Proposition and Grievance from this County concerning a place to fix the Court House on—it is ordered to be certified that a copy of the order of Council and all Col. Beverley's letters to this Court concerning the Co. Ho. and letters from the Court to him be sent to Genl. Assembly, and that Beverley never made any answer to the last letter sent him by this Court. Court adjourned.

April 1, 1747.

(191) Examination of Rebecca Buchanan for murder. She was so sick, trial deferred until May Court.

(191) Mary Ann Campbell, Ruth Buchanan and Rebecca Buchanan, the other criminals, be committed for trial till May Court.

(191) Rebecca Hays, Isabella Taylor, Sarah Paxton, Elizabeth Davis, Mary McClung, Agnes Gray, Esther Lyle, Agnis McClure, Catherine Mc-Nabb, Jane Hall, Prudence Campbell, Elizabeth McCroskie and Hannah Miller appeared and their husbands recognized that they appear at May Court to testify against Rebecca Buchanan, Jr., and Senr., Mary Ann Campbell and Ruth Buchanan. John Carmichael also recognized.

May 20, 1747.

(192) Trial of Rebecca Buchanan, Jr., on suspicion of murder, and Rebecca Buchanan, Sr., Mary Ann Campbell, Ruth Buchanan, alias Carmickell, on suspicion of being accessories. All acquitted except Rebecca, Jr., who was committed for trial at Williamsburg.

(193) Thos. Paxton, James McClung, Isaac Taylor, Gilbert Campbell, Wm. Hall and Andrew McNabb recognized that their wives, as above, appear as witnesses: William Lusk in behalf of Agnis Grey; Saml. Davis in behalf of his mother, Eleanor Davis; Moses McClure in behalf of his mother, Agness McClure; Andrew Hays in behalf of his mother, Rebecca Hays; Silas Hart in behalf of Esther Lyle. Acknowledged themselves as above. Wm. Henry also acknowledged as above.

Page

(194) David Kinkead and Winifred, his wife, witnesses.

(195) On petition of Abraham Drake, Sr., Admr. of Abraham Drake, his decd. son granted him during minority of his grandson, Abraham Drake, Admn. to Grubs is revoked.

(196) George Wythe qualified Attorney.

(196) Sarah Hays, widow of George, Adm'tes on George's estate.

(196) Admn. of Joseph Watson granted to his widow, Elizabeth.

(196) Admn of John Taylor granted to Peter Dyer, greatest credr.

(196) John Davis a runaway servant.

(196) George Gabriel, horse thief.

(197) Andrew Muldrough, John Donerly, Alexr. McClary, and Hugh Coffie, appraisers of John Watson.

(197) Martin Coffman, Peter Roughenough and Jacob Burnet, appraisers of Abraham Drake.

(197) Thomas Williams and John McCowen qual. Constables.

(198) Michael Finey, qualified Lieut. Foot.

(198) Saml. Delap appd. Constable, vice Nath. McClure; John Spear, Constable, vice Jno. Trimble; James Galespy, Constable, vice Wm. Wright; Ro. Ramsey, Constable, vice Thos Black; Alexr. McCroskie, Constable, vice Charles Hays; John Erwin, Constable, vice James Hogshead; James Hogart and Wallace Ashton, Constables, vice James Maies; Thos. Cohoon and David Miller, Constables, on Roan Oke; Archd. Hamilton and David Stevenson, Constables, vice Danl. Deniston; James Slone, Constable, vice James Hony; Geo. Draper, Peter Rentfro and James Cohoon, Constables, vice Humb. Lyon; John Ramsey, Constable, vice Wm. Guy; James Beard and John Maggot, Constables, vice Adam Miller; Andrew Scot, Constable, vice John Ramsey; John Campbell, Constable, vice Ro. Givin; John Leath, Constable, vice Elisha Job; Valentine Sevear, Constable, vice Wm. Carroll; John States, Constable, vice James Robinson; Ro. Montgomerie and John McClintin, Constables, vice Wm. Scot.

(199) Wm. Russell neglected his duty as attorney.

(199) Road ordered from Fork of the New Road, near Jumping Run, or Colletts, to the Co. Ho., and John Dobikin, John Smith, Jacob Dye, Thomas Moore and William Brown lay it off.

(199) Grand Jury Presentments: Col. Thomas Chew, common swearer; John Bramham, sheriff, common swearer; John O'Neal and Mary Corbit, alias Smith, adultery; James Kerr, disturber of common peace by carrying lies and as a common lyer; Valentine Sevear, swearing six oaths; Ro. Harper, being drunk and swearing three prophane oaths; John Bramham, for prophanely desiring God to damn George Robinson and his company; Robert Young, breach of Sabbath; James Kerr, breach of Sabbath; James Burk, common swearer.

(200) Daniel Curlew, breach of Sabbath; James Burk, prophaner of God's name by common swearing.

(200) Road from Co. Ho., formerly laid off by Wm. Thompson, be re-laid off by David Stuart and Andrew Russell.

(200) Robert Trimble exempted from levy for infirmities.

Page

(200) John Allison have license to keep a ferry from his landing to Herbert McClures.

(200) Road to be repaired from Alexr. Thomson's to top of Ridge leading to Louisa, and Wm. Thomson, Jr., with the tithables from the So. Mountain across by the Peaked Mountain to North Mountain and from So. Mountain by Ro. Turk's across by John Anderson's to North Mountain assist.

(202) Sheriff ordered to ask Orange Court to connect a road with the road near Swift Run Gap to Top of the Ridge.

(202) John Edmondson, leave to build a mill.

MAY 22, 1747.

(202) Samuel Black, a dissenting minister, took all the oaths.

(204) John O'Neal died at house of John Preston and his estate so inconsiderable—none will admr., and sheriff ordered to sell.

(206) John Maycomb—a witness.

MAY 23, 1747.

(213) Saml. Blythe to be summoned—petn. Mordecai Early.

(214) Rob. Caldwell appd. Constable, vice Val. Sevear.

(215) Thos. Cotner refused license to sell liquors. Wm. Watkins and Alice, his wife, witnesses; Ruben Franklin, witness; Adam Miller and Barbara, his wife, witnesses.

JUNE 17, 1747.

(216) John Johnson acquitted of being a runaway slave.

(216) Lewis Morgan, servant boy of Martin Coffman, to learn blacksmithing.

(216) Administration upon John Young granted to James Young (his brother.)

(217) Thos. Waterson appd. Constable, vice David Stevenson; Wm. Carr appd. Constable, vice James Gillespy; Andrew Fought, appd. Constable, vice Rob. Finley; John Spear, James Beard, Archd. Hamilton, Andrew Scot, qualified Constables.

(220) Isaac White—Garnishee.

JUNE 18, 1747.

(221) John Westvall qualified Constable.

(221) James Coburn, Michael Harness, James Simpson, Michael Shef, appraisers John Bogard's estate.

(221) James Porteus neglected his duty as attorney.

(221) £7, 11, 8, Penna. Money = £5, 11, 9, Cur. Money.

JUNE 19, 1747.

(239) Robert Patterson and James Allen to view a road from John Pickens' Mill to Lower Meeting House, and Andrew Lewis and Ro. Poage view a road from said mill to the Co. Ho.

Page

(240) Thos. Linville ordered fined for not attending as a witness.

(245) John Windlekite fined for swearing in presence of the Court.

August 19, 1747.

(246) Daniel Gawen, a servant boy of Saml. Doak, adjudged to be 12 years old.

(248) John Pickens and Wm. Bell to be overseers of the road (see p. 239 above) from Co. Ho. to Picken's Mill, with these tithables: Wm. Lewis, James Robertson, Thomas Gordon, Wm. Baskins, James Lasley, James Wallis, Danl. Deniston, Daniel Deniston, Jr., William Bell, Jr., John Poge, Geo. Crawford.

(248) Wm. Hines appd. Constable, vice Andrew Foughlet.

(249) John Harvie qual. attorney.

(249) Saml. McGaw put under recognizance of peace.

(250) Geo. Lewis—leave to build a mill.

(250) Ro. McCutchon—leave to build a mill.

(250) Petition of James McCown for road from the crossroad below Patrick Hays's, also the road that leads by Edward Hall's to their meeting at the foot of the mountain.

(251) George Lewis fined for swearing four oaths.

(251) John Holms appointed Constable, vice David Stewart; Mich. Dougherty, appointed Constable, vice Thos. Williams.

(251) Thos. Gardner ordered arrested for resisting arrest in the Court House. Stephen Holdston—same.

August 20, 1747.

(252) Vestry ordered to divide the Co. into precincts and appoint processioners.

(252) Wm. Priore qualified Under-Sheriff.

(252) Thomas Gardner fined. See p. 251, supra.

(252) Church wardens to bind Walter Sorrell, son of Richard Sorrell to Joseph Tees.

(252) James Porteus to pay costs in a suit which he had brought wrong.

(253) Jurymen—John McFarron, Wm. Carroll..

(253) John Patterson, aged and infirm. Comn. to take testimony.

(253) Elizabeth, wife of Rob. Looney, aged and infirm. Comn. to take testimony.

(253) Margret, wife of John Buchanan, relinquished dower.

(254) Robert Ralston added to Cunningham's list of tithables; Alexr. Gibson added to Cunningham's list of tithables; Wm. Frazier added to Hart's list of tithables; Jno. Bomgardner added to Hart's list of tithables.

(254) Thos. Carson fined and put in stocks for swearing and abusing the Court.

(254) Stephen Holston recognized to the peace.

(254) Alexr. Thompson qualified Captain of a Company.

(255) Andrew Gaghagen ordered to be recognized to the peace, especially towards James Davies.

(255) Catherine Coleman, servant of James Armstrong.

(255) John O'Neal ordered to be recognized to the peace, especially towards Danl. Harrison.

(255) Robert Cravens and Saml. Wilkins appointed overseers from the Co. Ho. to the Indian Road, near said Cravens', vice Alexr. Herrin, Thos. Harrison, Jeremiah Harrison.

AUGUST 21, 1747.

(257) Arthur Watts sues for freedom dues from Charles Hays, £3, 10.

(257) John Peary petitions that Saml. McGraw has taken his wife and child. Constable ordered to pursue Saml. and return the child to John.

(257) Benj. Borden ordered to be prosecuted for using false receipts for quitrents.

(257) John Graham ordered under arrest for abusing and threatening the life of Rev. John Hindman.

(257) Andrew Campbell complained that Saml. Gay has abused him and threatened to put him in the stocks and whip him. Saml. acknowledges his fault and is discharged.

(259) Mary, widow of Saml. Cunningham, administers on his estate.

(261) Son of Philip Smith to be bound to John Buchanan, Admr. of Philip, and one daughter be bound to Thos. English and one to Jacob Harmon.

(261) Andrew Gaughagen gives recognizance of peace.

AUGUST 22, 1747.

(286) Thos. Carson to be set at liberty out of jail.

SEPTEMBER 16, 1747.

(286) Called Court for examination of Patrick Burk and Bridget O'Dowland, convict servants belonging to Robert Bratton, for horse stealing—convicted.

(287) Thos. Gilaspy, about to remove an orphan boy of Wm. Humphrey's decd. out of the Colony—ordered that he deliver the orphan to the Church Wardens.

(288) Road from the Cross Road below Hays on No. Side So. River to the ridge be cleared, and Thos. Stuart and Wm. Christian be overseers. George Caldwell and his son to be added to the tithables.

(289) Mathew Young bound to the peace towards Michl. Brady.

SEPTEMBER 17, 1747.

(289) Called Court for examination of John Brice for beating Charles Quails—acquitted.

(290) Thomas Landrum—appraiser.

(290) John Anderson and Valentine Seviar appointed Inspectors of pork and beef.

(291) Robert McClenachan moves for counter security against Mary, wife of Andrew Mitchell, late widow of Saml. Cunningham, who stated they

were leaving the Colony immediately. Counter security ordered and appeal taken. Robert McClenachan appointed guardian for (Margret, see p. 310; Andrew Mitchell appointed.) Mary Cunningham, dau. of Saml. Cunningham.

(294) Juryman—Wm. Pierie.

(298) Saml. Wilkins convicted of selling liquors without a license in a booth or stall at the Court House.

(299) James Carter is going to leave the Colony.

(302) Philip Chittam surety for Saml. Chew.

SEPTEMBER 18, 1747.

(303) Road ordered from Tinkling Spring Meeting House to Col. Patton's Bridge, these to work it: James Patton's tithables, Robert Gibson's, Edward Hall's, Sam'l. Davies's, Wm. Thomson's, and Geo. Caldwell's tithables.

(303) Road ordered from the Court House to where the church is to be built and thence to the Timber Grove.

(303) Robert Foile bound to good behavior.

(303) Jurymen—John Speat, Henry Patton, Robert Foile.

(316) Clerk ordered to make copies of letters from and to Col. Beverley, also the charges the Co. has been at for yunkling and dawbing the Co. Ho., and represent how unfit the Co. Ho. is to hold Court in this winter—all to be laid before the Council.

NOVEMBER 18, 1747.

(318) Jennet Steel, widow of David Steel, qualified Admx. James Caulton, &c., and John Mitchell appraisers.

(318) Wm. McFeeters has leave to build a mill.

(319) Ro. Ramsey and David Mitchell to mark a road from Timber Grove to where the church is to be built, and that James Lockhart and Wm. Ledgerwood lay off and mark a way thence to the Co. Ho.

(319) John Elswick—grand juryman.

(319) County Levy.

NOVEMBER 19, 1747.

(320) County Levy continued.

(321) To James Patton and Ro. Cunningham, for expenses in attending the Council and going down. 1670 tithables at 23 lb. tobacco, at 3 farthings per pound = 1 sh. and 5 pence.

(321) James Brown—license to keep ordinary at Co. Ho.

(321) Lettice Brackenridge chose Robt. Brackenridge guardian.

(321) Ludwick Freedly complains that John Sisigmund Hanley has clandestinely carried out of the Colony his dau. Magdalene Freedley, about nine years old. The girl had been bound to John Harmon, son-in-law of Hanley, and Harmon had lately died intestate in this Colony and no person has administered. Hanley required to enter into bond for producing the child in May next.

Page
(322) John Michael Miller acquitted for enticing away from Isaac Smith a servant man named John Smith.

(322) John Bruce is in jail as escaped from Louisa jail.

(322) James Trimble has leave to build a grist mill.

(324) James Huy, a juryman.

324) Thos. Renix complains that Saml. Scot had abused him in the court yard, and Saml. bound to the peace.

NOVEMBER 20, 1747.

(325) Ro. McClenachen and James Huey qualified Under Sheriffs.

(326) Jurors—Joshua Hickman, James Gilmore.

(328) Jurors—Wm. Aylett, John Macom.

(329) Andrew Erwin and wife summoned for abusing the children of James Patterson, decd. and to account for the estate left by Patterson to the said children.

(331) Grand Jury Presentments: Henry Speer, overseer, for not keeping road in repair; Geo. Campbell and Jno. Ellison, breach of peace; Jno. O'Neal for swearing three oaths.

(332) John Bruce for forging hand of John Gillison; Joseph Milligan, for adultery with Martha Milligan, and Martha for adultery with Joseph; Gabriel Jones, for swearing one oath; Ro. Bratton, for swearing one oath; Courthouse and Prison not sufficient.

NOVEMBER 21, 1747.

(334) John Zetter, convicted of gambling and cheating at cards.

(334) John Preston has leave to keep ordinary.

(334) Wm. McClean bound over as idle and vagrant.

(335) Abram Clements, same.

(335) McCuney vs. George Forbush and Olive, his wife.

(335) Thos. McCullock, charged with detaining goods of Wm. Burk, acquitted.

(337) Mary Yeates, Admx. of Abraham Yeates, decd.

(340) Andrew Mitchell fined for abusing the court.

(344) Josh. Walker has license to keep ordinary.

FEBRUARY 17, 1747/8.

(344) John Lewis granted leave to build a mill.

(344) Patrick Finley convicted of aiding Utis Perkins and George Steel to escape.

(344) Ro. Breckinridge qualified Under Sheriff.

FEBRUARY 18, 1747/8.

(345) Ro. Cunningham complains that Samuel Gay has indulged Utis Perkins in several things after he had apprehended him; ordered under bond; John and Wm. Anderson securities.

(346) John Brownlee appointed Overseer of the Indian Road, vice Patrick Campbell.

Page

(346) Wm. Plumer, witness; also Wm. Hines.

(346) Wm. Christian—Ordinary license.

(346) Robert Erwin—Supernumerary on acct. of sickly and infirm.

(347) Curators appointed for estate of Wm. Skillern and for his orphan children.

(347) Elizabeth Anderson, late Elizabeth Skillern, and Robert Black, Jr., bound to the peace towards Thomas Turk.

(347) John Cartmill and others to value the improvements on the land bought by Ralph Laverty from John Lewis made thereon by one Joseph Wadle.

(348) Patrick McDonald fined and recognized for being drunk and drinking the Pretender's health.

(356) Thos. Stinson appd. road overseer from Henry Downs, Jr., to the Meeting House.

(356) Widow Elizabeth, qualifies on John Preston's estate.

(356) Robert Foyle exempted from levy, being a cripple and unable to labor.

MARCH 16, 1747/8.

(357) John Lewis—Ordinary License.

(357) Henry Witherington, servant boy of John Stevenson, adjudged to be eleven years old.

(357) Petition of Ute Perkins is rejected.

MARCH 17, 1747/8.

(360) John Pickens appointed road overseer, vice Danl. Deniston.

(360) Liquor rates.

(361) John Miller and Robert Black to take the estate of Wm. Skillern, heretofore committed to James Patton, and sell the same for the use of Skillern's orphan children.

(361) Joseph McClelhill and Jane, late widow of Randolph McDonall, to give counter security.

(361) Catherine Quin declares Archibald McMullin, decd., was indebted to her.

(361) Benj. Borden convicted of using false receipts for quitrents.

(362) Patrick Finla convicted for allowing Ute Perkins to escape.

(362) John Teel—witness.

(362) John Barclay charged with disturbing the Court.

(363) A horse, supposed to be stolen by Utes Perkins, delivered to Sheriff.

(363) John Briant appd. overseer, with Robert Cravens, of the road from Craven's to the Indian Road.

MARCH 18, 1747/8.

(364) Saml. Gay acquitted of charge above concerning Ute Perkins.

(365) Thomas Waterson—juror.

Page

(368) Thomas Burk—witness from Frederick.

(368) Jacob Darnell—Witness from Frederick.

(368) Jacob Harrell fined for not attending as a witness.

(373) Mary McCullough makes oath that the goods levied on at suit of Saml. Gay vs. Thos. McCullough, her son, are the goods of herself and her grandchildren, and not those of Thomas.

AUGUSTA COUNTY COURT RECORDS.

ORDER BOOK No. II.

March 29, 1748.

(1) John Flanagan committed for horse stealing.

April 20, 1748.

(2) William Hoopwood, servant of Valentine Sevier, to be returned to his master.

(3) Ann Brackenridge, wife of George Brackenridge.

(3) Wm. Waldon, John State, Geo. Forbush and Chas. Daley, appraisers.

(3) Rebecca Steel chose Nathaniel Steel her guardian.

(4) Robert McMahon bound to the peace on application of his wife, Joan, towards herself and her children.

(4) John Sloan appd. Constable, vice James Huey.

May 19, 1748.

(11) Eleanor Murry, step-daughter of James Renold, to be bound to Isaac Taylor until she is eighteen.

May 20, 1748.

(15) Eleanor, wife of William Davis.

(17) Ordered that the Clerk by (of) the Court of Claims make a copy of all accounts relating to the County levy, as also the order of this Court for one of the members to attend the Governor and Council.

(20) Rev. Mr. Andrew McKay took the oaths of allegiance.

(20) Certified that Presbyterian meeting houses have been built at Timber Ridge, at New Providence, and Falling Spring.

(22) John Preston—dead.

(24) John Patterson—dead.

May 21, 1748.

(32) Erwin Patterson to deliver up a horse supposed to have been stolen by Ute Perkins.

(34) Presentment vs. Court House, giving dimensions, built of logs, chinked with mud, but cracks 4 to 5 inches wide and ____ feet long, two windows cut but no glass in them, &c, &c.

Page

(43) Samuel Gay, justice of this County, now removed to Carolina.

(44) Petition of justices and others for quarterly courts certified to General Assembly.

AUGUST 17, 1748.

(47) John Sowell, a servant, petitions to be free, which being rejected, he is given 25 lashes for his false complaint.

(48) Thomas Taylor bound to peace towards Jude Stoner, neither appearing—dismissed.

(49) Halbert McClure (by Halbert McClure), an orphan boy not above eleven years, to be stricken off the list of tithables.

(49) Doctor Luin (Quin?).

(50) David Edmiston appd. overseer of road from Tinkling Spring to Stuart and Christian's Road, with these: James and John Campbell, Archibald Stuart, Chas. Dallis, James Hamilton, Richard Pilsher, David Henderson, George Vance, Robt. McCutchin, Saml. McCune, Robert Moody, John Frazier, John Thomson, Wm. Johnson, Alexr. Henderson, Saml. Henderson and Samuel Farguson.

AUGUST 18, 1748.

(52) Mary, widow of Alexr. Smiley, summoned to administer on Alexander's estate.

AUGUST 19, 1748.

(58) Saml. Lockhart to be added to list of tithables, Robt. Smith to be added to list of tithables, Wm. Craig to be added to list of tithables, also Robert Craig, James Craig, and John Craig.

(59) James Porteus proved his importation direct from London.

(59) Patrick McDonald proved his importation direct from Ireland.

AUGUST 20, 1748.

(60) A proposition from sundry inhabitants of this County for having the dissenters turned out from being Vestrymen was received and ordered to be certified to the General Assembly for allowance.

(61) John Warnock having made oath that he was not in this County the 10th of June, 1747.

(61) £8, 18, 7, Penna. Currency = £6, 13, 11, Va. Currency.

(63) Robert and Wm. Christian to lay out a road from Black James Armstrong's to Wm. Long's mill, thence to James Alexander's fence, with these workers: James Armstrong, George Rutlidge, Thomas Rutlidge, James Caldwell, James Armstrong, James Frain, William Robb, John Christian, James Alexander, John Black, John Wilson, Anthony Black, Wm. Wright, and Wm. and John Robinson.

(64) John Row proved his importation directly from England.

(64) Robert Phillips, son of James, stricken from list of tithables, being under 16.

Page

(65) James Beard added to tithables.

(65) Iron collar about neck of William Shaw, servant of Daniel Morley to be taken off.

(67) Saml. and Jacob Brown on Roanoke.

FEBRUARY 15, 1748.

(68) Swain Rambo, son of Barbara Rambo.

(69) Jonathan, son of James Coburn.

(69) Ann Mary Freedley, widow of John Lewis Freedley.

(72) John Lewis qualified Justice.

(72) Robert Fowler and others allowed to build a house of worship near David Edmonson's, and another at Piney Spring, near the North River.

FEBRUARY 16, 1748.

(76) James Robinson qualifies as admr. of his father, James Robinson, the widow and the heir-at-law having refused.

(76) Rev. Alexr. Cummings, a dissenting minister, took the oaths required.

(77) The meeting house built near John Brown's ordered to be received as a place of public worship.

(78) John Hutchison petitions on behalf of his son, John Hutchison, Jr., late a servant of John Oliphant, to be paid his son's wages out of Oliphant's estate.

(78) Henry Downs petitions for counter security from Jane McDonald, widow and admx. of Randol McDonald (admn. granted in Orange), now the wife of Joseph McClallan.

(83) John Patterson, dead.

FEBRUARY 17, 1748.

(86) William Elliott intends to leave the Colony; John Ramsey intends to leave the Colony; Philip Walker intends to leave the Colony; Thomas Thompson intends to leave the Colony; Saml. Gay intends to leave the Colony; James Gay intends to leave the Colony.

(87) Robert Gay intends to leave the Colony.

(100) John Craig, son of Jane Craig, late a hired servt. of John Oliphant, an infant, allowed his wages out of Oliphant's estate.

(100) The Sheriff ordered to arrest all such as have behaved in a riotous manner and bring them before the Court tomorrow.

FEBRUARY 18, 1748.

(102) Wm. Shurley, Thomas Fitzpatrick and Valentine Sevier, arrested as above, begged pardon of the Court and were discharged.

(102) John Davis, carpenter, garnishee.

Page

(104) Eleanor Draper appd. Admx. of George Draper during the non-age of her son, John Draper.

(105) Jacob Castle, being charged by Adam Harmon with threatening to aid the French—ordered to be arrested and brought before a called Court on next Monday.

(112) Last will of John Patterson presented, but not allowed to be proved, because the Exr. Francis McCown was a witness, thereupon admn. c. t. a. was granted to Agnes Patterson, the widow.

(117) Robert Patterson petitions to be reimbursed for his trouble in burying Daniel Corlet—rejected.

(119) Samuel Hulls presented for breach of the Sabbath by singing prophane songs.

MAY 19, 1749.

(125) John Graham petitions for relief a security for Jane Graham, widow of William Graham.

(126) Overseers of the Indian Road from Frederick Co. line to Toms Creek be continued until they put up sign posts.

(127) A commission from Gov. Gooch, dated 9 May, 1749, to James Patton et als., being read, the gents then present refused any further to act. Then new justices qualify.

MAY 20, 1749.

(129) Israel Christian's, at South River.

MAY 22, 1749.

(130) Jacob Castle acquitted of charge of treason in going over to and assisting the French.

(148) Court adjourned until 4th Tuesday in August, according to Act of Assembly.

AUGUST 22, 1749.

(149) New Commission.

(151) Rosemond Hughs, a servant of Mathew Thompson, petitions for freedom dues.

AUGUST 23, 1749.

(154) Morgan Brown, servant of Andrew Lewis.

(154) Andrew Franster (?) added to tithables.

(154) Josiah Richards added to tithables.

(154) Arthur Duff, servant of Wm. Carroll.

(155) John Windleheefer, charged with forgery, escapes and disappears.

(155) Mary Brown, servant of John Smith.

(155) Mary Elliott, servant of Wm. Williams.

(156) Michael Grady added to tithables.

AUGUST 24, 1749.

(158) Settlement of John McDowell's orphans's estate set out in full.

Page

(159) John Campbell, orphan of John Campbell, decd., settlement by guardian in full.

(159) Robert Renix intending immediately to leave this Colony.

(160) Richard Brown, servant of John Lewis.

(161) Robert Moffet added to tithables.

(161) John Patterson added to tithables.

(161) John Rosemond added to tithables.

(161) Ann, wife of George Breckinridge, relinquished dower in deed, Breckinridge to Mathew Erwin.

(162) William Hopwood, servant of Valentine Sevier.

(264) William Parks's 2464 acres on So. Br. Potomac to be valued by Geo. Sea, Martin Stroup, John Knight Owells (O'Neils), Henry Kerr, John Skelton, John Patton, Jr., James Rutledge and John Smith.

August 25, 1749.

(264) Robert Renix added to tithables.

August 26, 1749.

(274) John Beaty added to list of tithables.

September 7, 1749.

(286) George Young, alias Hughes, committed for housebreaking and larceny.

November 28, 1749.

(287) Fourth Tuesday—Not enough justices and adjourned to tomorrow.

(287) New Commission.

November 29, 1749.

(288) Thomas Black added to tithables.

(288) William Johnston added to tithables.

(288) Patrick Cannon added to tithables.

(292) Margaret McGill, relict of William McGill, renounced all benefit or advantage under her husband's will.

November 30, 1749.

(294) John Stevenson added to tithables.

(294) Wm. Armstrong added to tithables.

(296) Catherine Christian, Sarah, Peter, and Catherine, orphans of Peter Kinder, to be bound by Church Wardens.

December 2, 1749.

(302) Thomas Godfrey, a servant of John Bomgardner.

FEBRUARY 27, 1749.

(311) Six pounds tobacco to be collected from every person that has not delivered in his crows heads or squirrels scalps, according to law.

(313) John Brown, security for James Knox, guardian for Anne Genny Usher, prays counter security.

FEBRUARY 28, 1749.

(320) George Willson arrested on hue and cry.

APRIL 7, 1750.

(352) New Commission.

MAY 22, 1750.

(360) Church Wardens to bind out Jane O'Neal, Margaret O'Neal, and George Wiley, orphans of John Wiley, decd.

(362) William Bishop, servant of Charles Campbell.

MAY 23, 1750.

(365) Isaiah Harrison, admr. of Joseph Harrison, removed to Carolina.

(365) William O'Briant, servant of John Harrison.

(366) Sarah Wilkins, wife of Samuel Wilkins, relinquished dower in deed Saml. W.—to Alexr. Herron.

(371) Road ordered from Ezekiel Calhoun's to Wood's River, thence to Top of Ridge between Wood's River and the South Fork of Roanoke. John McFarland and Joseph Crockett to be surveyors of former, and Wm. Crisp and Wm. Pellam, of latter part, with tithables, and the following: Henry Batton, Mordecai Early, John McFarland, Jacob Goldman, John Downing, John Goldman, Charles Sinclair, Nathaniel Wilshire, Wm. Sayers, Jacob Goldman, Wm. Hamilton, Humbertson Lyon, Frederick Carlock, Robert Norris, James Miller, James Cave, Saml. Montgomerie, Steven Lyon, John Conley, Andrew Linam, James Willbey, Saml. Stanlick, James Maies, Robert McFarlin, James Harris, John Vance, John Stride, Robert Miller, Alexr. Sayers, John Miller, Jacob Castle, Robert Alcorn, John Forman, Wm. Miller.

MAY 24, 1750.

(373) Road ordered from County line to John States' mill.

(373) Joseph How directed to set up sign posts and keep it up with these: John Elswick, Andrew Viney, John Dunbarr, William McBride, Francis McBride, Robert Denton, James Thomas, James Scot, James Hamilton, William Miller and Valentine Sevier.

(374) Robert Young petitions that Benj. Borden be not allowed to acknowledge any lands to him without his consent—allowed.

(377) Robert Harrison, son of Daniel Harrison, owned 230 acres on Dry Forks of Smith's Creek.

(379) Contract for jail to be relet.

Page

(384) Catherine Smith, orphan of Philip Smith, to be bound to Thomas Engles; Elizabeth, ditto, to Adam Harmon.

(384) James Edmondson and Sarah, his wife, admx. of George Hays, decd.

(393) Overseers of Roads, Rivers and Creeks continued in office until May next.

MAY 26, 1750.

(393) William Englis reports that County funds collected by him had been consumed in his house by fire.

(393) Catherine Cole, servant of Thomas Scot.

(400) James Greenlee, being unable to read or write, is released from being Constable.

MAY 28, 1750.

(410) Montgomery vs. John Shite, the Helmn.

AUGUST 28, 1750.

(414) Hugh Campbell added to tithables.

(415) James McNeal, Wm. Overall, Josiah Parent, Ephraim Leath, Abraham Ciler, Benjamin Gugar, Steven Philips, John Hawkins, Wm. Jackson, Thomas Dodson, John Little, Bernard Agen, Henry Netherton, Richard Waters, George Leath, John Davis, Robert Boyd, added to list of tithables.

(416) Wm. Hamilton, George Scot, Jacob Cooper, Wm. Ralston, with two others, Wm. Dunlop, Robert Ralston, David Ralston, added to list of tithables.

(416) Rose Ticton, relict of Richard Ticton.

(418) John Watling servant of Edward Hall.

(419) Hugh Lawson, Ludwick Bakon, David Stokes, Roger Dyer, Wm. Dyer, Moses Campbell, John Patton, Wm. Stevenson, Saml. Patton, Alexr. Crockett, Matthew Patton, added to list of tithables.

(420) David Evans, John Smith, Peter Horse, Henry Horse, John Eby, Hans Eby, Michael Props, Mark Swattle, John Brown, Postley Hover, Michael Stroud, John Walker, (above, to Wm. Dyer, added on motion Alexr. Crockett), Henry Henry, Windell Brown, Peter Creson, Alexr. Skoot, Saml. Skoot, John Skoot, James Skoot, added to list of tithables.

(421) Benj. Skoot, John Knowles, Joel Hornback, John West, Thomas Crawford, George Baffenbarger, John Christian Carlock, David Craig, John Walker, Jr., George Say, George Say, Jr., Simon Say, John Cunningham, Wm. Cunningham, Henry Landcisco, John Colley, Burket Reager, Henry Carr, Daniel Richardson, Nathaniel Clearey, added to list of tithables.

(422) Landred Hyard, Landred Hyard, Jr., Rudy Hard, Martin Job, Jacob Job, Luke Collins, Jacob Peters, Jacob Peters, Jr., Martin Peters, John Dunkill, George Dunkill, Peter Moore, Jacob Siver, George Muse, Henry Faney, George Dove, Thomas Dove, Jr., George Yockham, Henry Spear, Samuel Henderson, added to list of tithables.

Page

(423) Abraham Vanderpool, Mathew Uter, Abell Westfall, Anthony Bogard, George Osburn, Jeremiah Osburn, Jeremiah Osburn, Jr., John Osburn, James Simson, Jacob Westfall, Leonard Neiff, John Westfall, Hermanus Skout, Anthony Reger, Anthony Reger, Jr., Michael Rhyne, Peter Reed, George West, Thomas Iax, Robert Graham, added to list of tithables.

(424) Robert Carscaden, added to list of tithables.

(424) Effee Brock, orphan of Rudy Brock.

AUGUST 29, 1750.

(425) James McKay and John Wilkins added to tithables.

(425) Patrick Croskey, servant of David Stuart.

(426) John, James and Mary, orphans of John Campbell, to be bound out.

(429) Eleanor Dryden, dau. of David Dryden.

(430) Jean Rutledge renounces her right to adminr. on estate of her husband, James Rutledge, and Hugh Parker qualifies.

(431) James Patterson, added to list of tithables.

(432) William Sandford, servant of Robert Young.

(432) Mary, wife of John Maxwell, relinquished dower in deed John M.— to Robt. Breckinridge.

AUGUST 30, 1750.

(436) Wm. Edmondson, added to list of tithables.

(438) Robert Wiley, added to list of tithables.

(440) David Caldwell, Saml. Lusk, John O'Neal, Benj. Haws, added to list of tithables.

AUGUST 31, 1750.

(441) John Lawrence, William Acres, Thomas Acres, Uriah Acres, added to list of tithables.

(443) George Hutcheson, John Hutcheson (son of above), James Hutcheson, John King, added to list of tithables.

SEPTEMBER 1, 1750.

(456) Robert Carlile, John Carlile, added to tithables on motion of Ro. Breckinridge; Benjamin Posey, added to tithables on own motion; Wallace Estill, Loftus Pullin, Richard Bodkin, added to list of tithables on motion of Ro. Breckinridge.

(457) Mathew Harper, Hans Harper, added to tithables on motion of Ro. Breckinridge.

(464) John Sherman, Attorney.

(471) John Daniel, charged by Ro. Breckinridge with speaking treasonable words, committed to next Court.

(483) Catherine Cole, servant of James Armstrong.

(483) Francis McBride summoned to give account of estate of his deceased brother, Benjamin McBride.

SEPTEMBER 21, 1750.

(484) James McDonall, alias John Dolphin, committed on charge of stealing from Rice Price of Lunenburg.

NOVEMBER 27, 1750.

Page
(486) County levy—numerous wolf heads.
(488) Francis Hughes—one old wolf head.

NOVEMBER 28, 1750.

(490) Saml. Davison, Saml. Lockhart, added to tithables, own motion.
(493) Ute Perkins and his followers—property supposed to belong to them to be delivered up to the offices.
(494) Robert Moore, late servant of Andrew McCord and James Walker.
(495) Jacob Coger presented for driving hogs over the Blue Ridge on Sabbath.

NOVEMBER 29, 1750.

(501) Rev. John Todd, a dissenting minister, took the oaths.
(501) James Calhoun qualified Captain of a Troop of Horse.
(502) Sarah Thorn petitions for permission to keep her child, Hannah Bogard. (Had Sarah, wife of Anthony Bogard married Thorn?)—allowed.

FEBRUARY 26, 1750.

(516) Elisabeth, relict of Asabel Hodge, refuses to admr.

FEBRUARY 27, 1750.

(522) John Harrison's petition to be reimbursed out of the estate of William Young, who was killed in attempting to rob John Harrison, granted.
(531) David Evans summoned for not providing for his children in a decent and Christianlike manner.
(531) Jennet Cowdon—same.

MARCH 1, 1750.

(539) Susannah, relict of Henry Carson, summoned to qualify on the estate.
(547) John Patton, orphan of John Patton, decd., to be bound by Church Wardens.

MARCH 2, 1751.

(556) Commissioners appointed to inspect the beer sold at every Court, and if it appear that the same is not at least one month old, well hop'd, then they presume not to ask more than one penny a quart for it.

MAY 28, 1751.

(565) Edward Davis, servant of John Gilmore of Albemarle, died at the home of James Brown, near the Court House, in the town of Staunton, leaving goods and money supposed to have been stolen from Saml. Dunlop of Isle of Wight.
(569) James Frame presented for breaking the Sabbath in unnecessarily travelling ten miles.

(569) John O'Neal and his son, Thomas, presented for larceny.

(571) Road ordered from Caleb Job's to James McKay's, crossing the river at a place called the Brush Bottom Ford, and so along the river by Henry Spears' plantation, and that the said Spears, with Mason Combs, John Sallers, Richard Sheitz, William Hurst, William Overall, Thomas Hues, Zachariah McCoy, Torrance Carroll, Wm. Dickenson, Steven Philips, Alexr. Gunnod (?), James McNeal, John Hawkins, Benj. Grider, Ephraim Leath, Charles Williamson, Josiah Parent, Wm. Parent, Thomas Parent, Edmond Bollen, Adam Coningham, Francis Grubbs, keep it in repair.

(574) Road ordered from John Davis's mill to Wood's New Cleared Gap, and John King, with Andrew Erwin, John McGill, Wm. McGill, Robert Fowler, Hugh Campbell, John Erwin, Edward Erwin, Robert Carscaden, Francis Erwin, Edward Erwin, Wm. Frame, Benj. Erwin, Charles Campbell, Robert Campbell, Wm. Brown, Michael Dickey, Robert Brown, Henry Smith, Hugh Diver, Charles Diver, David McCummins, John Davis, Danl. Smith, James Anderson, John Francis, Wm. Alexander, Robert Gamble, Andrew Combe, James Patterson, Francis Brown, Gabriel Pickens, keep it in repair.

(577) Francis Hughes appointed road surveyor.

(578) William Riley, a servant of Richard Hall, under 16 years, petitions that his indenture is void, which is opinion of the Court, whereupon William chooses Rev. Mr. Robert Rose his guardian, who qualifies.

(579) George, Mary, Agnes, James Alexander, orphans of William Alexander, to be bound out; Thomas, orphan of Wm. Pritherock, ditto.

(580) George McSwine has recorded that his indenture time expired about the middle of last March.

(580) Road ordered to be cleared and kept in repair on the cowpasture by these inhabitants: Wallace Estill, Robert Carlile, John Carlile, Loftus Pullen, Richd. Bodkin, Saml. Ferguson, Mathew Harper, Thomas Wright, Michael Harper, Hance Harper, John Miller, William Price, James Anglen, James Hall, Philip Phegan, John Shaw, Herculus Wilson, William, and John Carlile.

(580) Henry Netherton, servant of John Stevenson.

(580) Thomas Mann, orphan of John Mann, to be bound; James and David, orphans of Wm. Graham, ditto.

(582) Road ordered from Huy's Fulling Mill to Timber Ridge Meeting House.

May 30, 1751.

(585) John David Wilpert petitions that he has been at considerable expense in coming from the northward and settling here, and had rented three lots in Staunton, through which runs a good and convenient stream of water for building a mill, prayed leave to build a grist and fulling mill on one of said lots, there being no other mill on said stream of water, rejected, because John Lewis states he is about to build a mill which he had already begun within less than one mile.

(585) James Mays publishes his intention of leaving the Colony for Carolina with several horses, and Court certifies that he is a freeholder and has behaved himself honestly.

Page

(586) Joseph Love, clothier, has leave to build a fulling mill on Roan Oak.

MAY 31, 1751.

(594) Sheriff complains that Anne (wife of James Brown) had abused him; summoned.

(596) William Beus, a juryman. This name appears frequently.

(597) Margaret, relict of Wm. McGill.

(597) On motion of Robert McClenachan, on behalf of his servant, Alexr. Fullerton, stating that Valentine Severe detains several books, the property of Alexander, ordered that Severe be summoned.

(599) Mary Elliott proved her importation direct from Great Britain into this Colony.

(600) Francis McCown, guardian of James McCord, summoned to answer complaint of Andrew McCord that Francis is about to send James to Carolina.

JUNE 1, 1751.

(602) Shields
vs.
Wilson and Gilmore
} Verdict stayed because jurors, Walter Davis and Malcolm Campbell, the one ran out of the Court House, the other jumped out of
the Co. Ho. window, separated themselves from their fellows and talked with other persons.

(604) Love
vs.
Wright
} Pl. for want of evidence has leave to withdraw a juror and cause continued.

(609) Daniel Harrison appointed next friend to his son, Robert Harrison

(609) Daniel Harrison appointed next frient to his son, Robert Harrison in order to bring suit vs. John O'Neal.

AUGUSTA COUNTY COURT RECORDS.

ORDER BOOK NO. III.

On the fly lead is the following:

"Memorandum.—That Saturday, the 6th of February, 1747/8, was the coldest day yet known in America."

JUNE 11, 1751—AUGUST 27, 1751.

(176) This book begins August 1749, but there are no orders but those of suits and actions until August 27, 1751, when a new Court was organized under a commission from the Hon. Lewis Burwell, President of Virginia, dated 11th June, 1751, directed to James Patton, Peter Scholl,* Robert Cunningham, Wm. Jameson, David Stuart,* John Lynn,* Erwin Patterson,* Thos. English, Benj. Borden,* Joseph Kenady, John Denton, Wm. Christian, Robert Breckinridge, John Lewis,* Silas Hart, Andw. Lewis,* James

Rutledge, Alexr. Wright, Ro. McClenahan,* Robert Campbell, John Wilson, Richd. Burton, Patr. Martin, James Lockhart, John Mills, Ro. Ramsey, Richd. Woods, John Anderson, John Ruddle, Thos. Stuart, John Lyle, John Buchanan, Thomas Lewis, Archd. Alexander, John Mathews, Adam Dickenson, Mathias Seltzer, Wm. Harbeson. (Those marked (*) qualified.)

AUGUST 27, 1751.

(176) Robert McClenachan qualified Sheriff and
(177) Ro. Breckinridge, his deputy.
(177) Patrick Frazier appointed surveyor of road.
(178) Joseph Love sumd. by his servant, John Butler.
(178) Andrew Johnson has absconded.
(178) John Black and his son, Saml. Black, added to the list of tithables.
(178) Joseph Love bound to the peace towards his wife, Margaret.
(179) Road ordered to be viewed from John Anderson's to the Co. Ho. by John Poage and James Allen.
(179) Wm. Harrold appd. overseer of road, vice Wm. Hurst and James McKay, and tithables on west side So. River to Fred'k Cy. and on Goody's Run—keep it in order.

AUGUST 28, 1751.

(180) Fredcriek Sea quald. Admr. of George Sea.
(181) Robert McClenachan's servant, Alexr. Fullerton.
(181) James Lockhart reports that Wm. Williams is .about to remove to Carolina and take with him Mary Lundey, orphan of Thomas Lundey; order to bind Mary out.
(181) Daniel Richardson, John Coningham, Joel Hornback, and John Sea, appraisers of Alexr. Scot's estate.
(181) Francis Hughes complains that Ro. McClenachan has taken him up as a runaway servant and seized his horse; order Francis to be released, but to pay Robert 10 sh. for keeping and feeding his horse.
(182) Thomas Lewis qualified surveyor.
(182) Andrew Lewis qualified dept. surveyor.
(183) James Trimble qualified dept. surveyor.
(183) Robert Lusk chose Andrew Hays guardian.
(183) Margaret Bell chose John Moore.
(184) John Graham to deliver a horse to John Man.
(184) Henry Witherington, a servant of John Stevenson, is in jail and has an iron lock around his neck with a gag in his mouth—ordered to be taken off.

AUGUST 29, 1751.

(184) Wm. Thompson, guardian of Joseph and John Campbell, orphans of John Campbell, ordered to settle his accounts.
(185) John Graham appointed guardian of James and David Graham, orphans of Wm. Graham.
(186) John Justice has built a water grist mill for Wm. Wilson, and same is not properly built.
(186) Vestry to divide the County and appt. processioners.

Page

(186) Peter Cartner complains that Mary Freedly, admx. of her decd. husband's estate, is since married to Nicholas Brock, and they waste the estate. Counter security ordered.

(186) James Brown complains that John Harmon has abused him and his wife.

(186) James Leeper to Nicholas Leeper. Margaret, wife of James.

(187) John Stevenson vs. his servant boy, Henry Witherington, ordered to serve 58 days for runaway time and expenses in taking him up at the rate of 1½ months for every hundred pounds.

(187) James Berry, guardian of John Berry, orphan of James Berry, complains of John Jones, in whose custody the orphan is, that he abuses him.

(187) Road from So. Branch to Swift Run Gap, accepted; Ro. Craven and James Batley, surveyors.

(188) William Morrison married the widow of John Davison.

(189) Lucretia Griffith, admx. of her husband, is since married to James Burk.

(189) John Smith committed for aiding Jean London in breaking jail.

(190) John Bryan, Cornelius Bryan, Thomas Bryan, Wm. Rinkens, added to tithables.

(196) William Hughes, a runaway servant of Thomas Dansie, of King Wm. Co.

(196) James Lockhart qualified Justice.

(197) John Coningham—ordinary license.

(197) Ducking stool ordered to be built.

(197) David Kingkade to make such alterations in the jail as are necessary, and were not included in his contract for the building of it.

September 4, 1750/1 (?)

(197) Called Court on Jane London—not guilty of the felony, but bound to the peace towards Bryce Russell and Alexr. Walker.

October 1, 1751.

(198) Called Court on Day Thoroughgood, on suspicion of the murder of his master, James Connerly; confessed and sent on for trial before the General Court.

November 26, 1751.

(198) David Stewart qualified Sheriff; John Lewis and Wm. Lusk quald. Under Sheriffs.

(198) Robert McClenachan, Wm. Horbeson and John Mills, qualified Justices.

(200) John Campbell—license for ordinary; Wm. Bethell—license for ordinary.

(200) John Davis and Saml. O'Dell, to view a road from Thorn's Gap to Henry Netherton's.

(201) Paul and Nicholas Lung, Henry Dickens and David Loudeback, appraisers of John Windlekite; John Gum and Michael Waring, appraisers of Cornelius O'Bryan.

Page

(202) David McClewer added to list tithables.

(202) Grand Jury—James Trimble, James Caldwell, Wm. Baskins, Wm. Henderson, Robert Patterson, Alexr. Thompson, Andrew Russell, Mathew Armstrong, Archibald Hamilton, Thos. Gordon, Wm. Bell, James Robinson, Patrick McCullow, James Callison, Alexr. McFeeters, Thomas Waters.

(202) John Harrison petitions to be levy free; rejected.

(203) Daniel Stringer, Robert Craven and John Craven to value James Wood, Gent, improvements on 400 acres on Muddy Creek.

(203) Thomas Bird, servant man of Joseph Robinson.

(203) County levy: To various persons for wolves' heads—in all 225 heads. This list is interesting.

(206) John Butler complains vs. his master, Joseph Love.

(206) John Hogshead's improvements to be valued.

(206) Robert Renix's improvements to be valued in Forks of James—241 acres.

(206) Grand Jury Presentments: Elisha Job, swearing more than four oaths; Owen Crawford, for drinking health of King James and refusing to drink to King George; James Shaw, swearing three oaths; Robert Armstrong, a common swearer; John Grems, a common swearer.

(207) Francis McCown, charged by Andrew McCord with sending James McCord, an orphan, out of this Colony, dismissed for non-appearance of Andrew.

(207) Elizabeth and Catherine King chose John Archer and John Pickens their guardian.

(207) Robert Craven, Michael Warren and Alexr. Herron ordered to value John Harrison's improvements on 400 acres on Dry Forks of Smith's Creek.

NOVEMBER, 28, 1751.

(207) Robert Breckinridge qualified Justice.

(208) Patrick Lynch and John Butler summoned for aiding David Dundass to escape from jail.

(208) Sarah Lynn relinquished dower in 269 acres conveyed by her husband, James Lynn, to Andrew Lynn.

(208) Andrew Lewis and Robert McClenachan to convey lots in the 25 acres conveyed by Beverley to the Co.

(208) John Mathews, Richard Wood and John Lyle quald. Justices.

(208) Adam Dickinson, David Davis, Peter Wright and Joseph Carpenter, lay off a road from Wright's Mill to the Cow-pasture near Hugart's or Knox's.

(209) James Nealey, Richard Hall, Thomas English and Tobias Bright, appraise estate of James Connerley.

(209) James and John Scott, Wm. McMurry, James Simpson, James Frame, Robert Montgomerie, James Montgomerie, Hugh McDonall and Wm. Galespy, to lay off a road from the lower cow-pasture to Burden's tract.

(211) Archibald Crockett chose Robert Bratton and James McCorkle guardians.

(211) Above guardians complain that John Ramsey, who married Margaret, relict of Robert Crockett, father of Archibald above, are wasting the estate.

NOVEMBER 29, 1751.

(213) Power Att'y. from Wm. Mills to John Mills allowed to remain for further proof.

(216) James Brown—ordinary license.

(216) Wm. Jameson—qualified Justice.

(216) Daniel Harrison—qualified Under Sheriff.

(217) Frederick Fitzjarrill proved his importation immediately from Great Britain into this Colony—50 acres.

(217) Joseph Roberts—the same as above.

NOVEMBER 30, 1751.

(217) Henry Down's estate attached.

(218) Richard Woods, Joseph Lapsley and James Davis to value David Cloyde's improvements on 2 tracts, 400 acres each, on Cedar Creek of James River.

(218) James Montgomery, Joseph Robinson and Tobias Smith, same, 2 tracts, 400 acres, and 260 acres, on Possimmon Run.

(219) Benjamin Borden's improvements on a tract on a branch of Shannando, near a place called the Chimney Stone.

(222) Saml. McClenery—a witness.

(222) Nathaniel Woodroff—a witness.

(225) John Madison to have made books and presses for the preservation of the books and papers of the Co'ty.

(225) John Warwick—a witness.

(225) James Berry, guardian of the orphans of James Berry, decd., complains that John Jones, who married the widow of James Berry, is wasting the estate.

DECEMBER 2, 1751.

(226) James Brown asks admn. of estate of Edward Davis. Benj. Borden says admn. was already granted in Genl. Court to James Dunlop; James's wife, Agnes, comes and says she would not believe Benjamin on oath and is fined 40 sh.

DECEMBER 3, 1751.

(236) Bumgardner vs. Christopher Francisco—dismissed acct. of death of Christopher.

(237) Francis McBride sumd. to settle accounts as guardian of his deceased brother's infants.

(239) Jane Denton—wife of Jonas Denton.

(239) Susannah Carson—relict of Henry Carson.

(239) Alexr. Fullerton—servant of Val. Sevier.

(240) Thos. Smith fails to provide for his children in a Christian-like manner and they are to be bound out.

Page

(240) John Smith convicted of larceny and whipped.
(Called Court.)

FEBRUARY 19, 1751/2.

(241) Court for proof of public claims and propositions and grievances.

(241) Certificates for wolves' heads amounting to 50,600 lbs. tobacco certified.

(241) Petition that the Episcopal Minister's salary be raised; certified to Genl. Assembly.

(241) Petition of John and Reubin Harrison for reward for killing 2 persons under Ute Perkins; certified to Genl. Assy.

(242) Petition to encourage making linen cloth; read and certified to Genl. Assy.

MAY 20, 1752.

(242) New commission to: James Patton, Thos. Lewis, Wm. Jameson,* James Lockhart,* Benj. Borden,* John Lewis,* Robt. Cunningham,* Andrew Lewis, Erwin Patterson, Richd. Woods, Peter Sholl, John Wilson, David Stewart, Ro. McClenachan,* John Mathews.* (Those marked (*) qualified.

(245) Mathew, Ludwick, Michael, Daniel, Catherine and Christian Rinehart, orphans of Michael Rinehart, decd., to be bound out by Ch. Wardens.

(246) Elizabeth Campbell relinquished dower in 514 acres, conveyed by her husband, Patrick Campbell, to Charles Campbell, in Orange.

(247) James Urrey, Steven Hans Burger, John Fought, Wm. Burk, Saml. Thornhill, John Fornice, Little Patrick, Jacob Miller and son, Adam Miller and son, Charles Cross, Henry Lung, Jacob Coger, George Warrell— to be added to Hans Magart's road hands on road from Shanando River to top Blue Ridge.

(247) Petition of inhabitants of Linvil's Creek. These persons to clear a road from Brock's Creek to Francis Hughes's, thence to the main road leading to Fredericksburg: Jonathan Duglass, Wm. Smith, John Miller, James Claypole, Wm. Claypole, Ro. Williams, Rees Thomas.

(247) Thos. and Jno. Paxton and John Berrisford, to value improvements of John Lowry on 2 tracts on No. Br. of James River.

(248) In calf-pasture—Wm. Smith to be overseer with the following persons, viz: Wm. Elliott, Ro. McCutcheon, William Smith, William Ramsey, John Marke, Robert Foyle, Wm. Guy, James Stevenson, Rob. Gay, John Guy, Samuel Looney, Saml. Guy, John Hanley, John Smith, John McGuiney. Road from Wm. Guy's to Ro. McCutcheon's mill, and thence to Robert Campbell's.

(248) John Dorrick exempted from public levy on acct. of great age and infirmity.

(248) John Mulholland—same.

(248) John Peter Frothingham—same.

(248) John Harger and others, to value John Mathew's 350 acres in Forks of James.

(248) Road ordered from Jenning's to Swift Run Gap. John Hare to mark it from No. River to said Gap, "the main road that leads to Swift Run Gap."

(249) Joseph Kenaday fined for abusing the Court.

(249) Elizabeth Perkins and her two sons, George and William Skillern, bound to peace towards James Carr.

(249) Road ordered from Widow Jackson's to Ueris Creek. Nap. Gregory to do it.

May 21, 1752.

(250) Thomas Paxton petitions that his son, Samuel, is listed as a tithable, but is under 16. Exempted.

(250) Elizabeth Bushon, an orphan, is to be bound to Ro. McClenachan.

(251) Peter Scholl qualified Justice.

(251) Child of James Boggs, likely to become a charge on the County, to be bound out.

(251) Road ordered from Robert Poage's to Picken's Mill, thence to Forks of the River near John Madison's, thence to Swift Run Gap.

(252) Andrew Lewis qualified Justice.

(252) John Davis petitions to be levy free by reason of great age—rejected.

(252) James Caldwell—overseer of road from Nutt's Mill Creek, near his meadow, to Co. Ho.

(253) Patrick Porterfield exempted from levy.

(254) James Miller appointed Constable in Staunton.

(254) Commission appointed to inspect the rum, wine, whiskey and beer sold and report any not sufficient.

(254) Rob. Bratton, guardian of Archibald Crockett, against Rob. Davis and Margaret Ramsey, for detaining part of orphan's estate—order to summon.

(256) John Grymes, Hugh Hicklin and Rob. Grymes to be summoned for detaining children of Thomas Smith.

(257) Jonathan Newcom proved his importation direct from Great Britain.

(257) Richard Simston—same.

(257) James Parman—same.

(257) Sheriff to give notice that at next August Court will be let the building of a Court House forty by twenty-six feet in the clear.

(258) James Rosebrough summoned for detaining freedom dues of Terrence Carraby.

May 27, 1752.

(258) Called Court on James Cachill. Not guilty of picking pocket, but was disorderly, and to receive ten lashes.

June 17, 1752.

(259) New commission as last month.

(259) Robert Graham ordered to deliver James Graham, an orphan bound to him, to John Graham.

(260) John Halteman to keep ordinary. Halph Hughs, secy.

(260) James Akry, convicted of speaking disrespectfully of the King, and fined and bound to the peace.

(261) John Shields appd. guardian *ad litem* for John Shields, orphan of James Shields.

(262) Jacob, Hannah, Rachel, Jonathan Hodge, orphans of Elizabeth Hodge, to be bound by Ch. Wardens.

(262) Abegail, relict of Jacob Goldman, summoned to qualify as admx. of her husband.

(262) Jacob Tommer's estate to be appraised.

(263) John Walker arrested on suspicion of assisting Thomas Davis, a horse thief who had lately committed some robberies of that kind, confessed that he was forced into Davis's service in Prince William County, who brought him into these parts, and with whom he continued about 2 weeks. During that time Davis told him he had stole from the Commissioners, now gone out on a treaty with the Indians, a horse, mare and six blankets, all of which he now has, and received from the said Davis. Davis promised him the mare stolen, but left him and he was taken up. Bailed, and the Attorney ordered to prosecute him for receiving stolen goods.

JUNE 18, 1752.

(265) Robert Cunningham qualified Justice.

(265) Saml. Wilson—allowed to keep ordinary.

(266) Attachment to be further served in hands of garnishees who had not appeared by reason of alteration of Court day.

(269) Alexr. Gibson qualifies Admr. of his deceased father, Daniel Gibson, Elizabeth, the relict having refused.

(270) William Baskins summoned to pay freedom dues to his late servant, Elizabeth Burnes.

(270) Benj. Borden qualifies Justice.

JUNE 19, 1752.

(278) Peter Scholl petitions that he is security for Jane Scone on her deceased husband's estate and that she has since intermarried with William Draper—prays counter security.

JUNE 20, 1752.

(290) Henry Morrow makes oath that he *was imported* immediately from Great Britain into this Colony.

(295) Asabel Hodge has removed out of this County.

(297) William Cunningham bound over for abusing the Sheriff.

(297) John Kingkade, a witness from Albemarle.

(297) Wm. Edmondson, a mason.

(302) Hugh McGarrock, a witness fromAlbemarle.

(304) James Cachill, servant of Andrew Lewis, formerly servant of Ro. Breckinridge.

(304) Borough Kingkade, a witness from Albemarle; Joseph Kingkade, a witness from Albemarle.

AUGUST 19, 1752.

(310) James Patton qualified Co. Lieutenant, Coroner and Justice.

(312) Charles Campbell, qualified Captain of a Co. of Foot; Ebenezer Westcourt, qualified Captain of a Co. of Foot; Daniel Harrison, qualified Captain of a Co. of Foot; Peter Scholl, qualified Captain of a Co. of Foot and Coroner; Wm. Jameson, qualified Coroner.

(312) John Lynn, an orphan boy complains that Ro. Edge had brought him from the lower parts of this Colony and indentured him to John Ramsey, and he to Henry Smith, and he to Silas Hart. Indenture declared void and Wardens ordered to bind him out.

(312) Proof of Robert McKay's will; Zechariah refuses to administer; James swears that Moses and Robert McKay are Quakers.

(313) James Campbell, qualified Captain of Foot; John Maxwell, qualified Captain of Troop of Horse; Robert Renix, qualified Cap. of Troop of Horse; John Poage, qualified Cap. of Troop of Horse; James Edmondson, qualified Cap. of Troop of Horse; John Hogshead, qualified Cap. of Troop of Horse; Mathew Edmondson, qualified Cornet; Adam Harmon, qualified Cap. of a Troop of Horse; George Anderson, qualified Cap. of Troop of Horse; Augustine Price, qualified Lieut. of a Troop of Horse; Jacob Harmon, qualified Cornet.

(314) Hugh Martin to be levy free on account of age and infirmity.

AUGUST 20, 1752.

(314) John Fleming complains that James Young and Sarah, his wife, detain him contrary to law, and they sumd.

(314) Huan Mathews to be levy free on acct. of age and infirmity.

(314) Wm. Dougherty appd. Constable in the Cow-Pasture.

(315) Elizabeth Thomas qualifies Admx. of her deceased husband, John Windlekite.

(315) Mary Goldman, widow of Jacob refuses to administer. John Bingman, Ro. Norris, James Cohoon, and James Miller appd. appraisers of Goldman.

(316) Patrick Martin and Alexr. Richey to be overseers of road from Young's Mill to Alexr. Richey's smith shop, thence to Buchanan's mills, with these hands: Adam Thompson, Geo. Peary, Ro. Young, James Peary, John Campbell, John Buchanan, James Moody, Andrew Cowan, James Callison, John Jameson, Walter Smiley, James McCorkle, Ro. McCorkle, Nathan Gilliland, Wm. McNabb.

(316) Robert Breckinridge's mark recorded—a cross and slit in the left and an underkut in the right ear.

(316) Hermanus Decker's—mark recorded.

(317) Moses McKay prays for counter security from Barbara Job (now Leath) and Ephriam Leath, Admrs. of Caleb Job.

(317) Benj. Hawes, orphan, to be bound.

(317) Road ordered from Wm. Cleghorn's to Waters of Purgatory.

(317) Elizabeth Harper complains of her husband, Hans Harper, and Michael Harper, who is bound to the peace. She says Hans has turned her out of doors and refused her the common necessaries, and prays separate maintenance.

(317) William Owler added to list of tithables.

(317) Ann Miller relinquished dower in 200 acres conveyed by her husband, John Miller, to Ro. McClenachan.

(317) John Brown, qualified Major of Horse; Alexr. Sayers, qualified Captain of Horse; Robert Sayers, qualified Ensign; John McCreary, qualified Captain of Foot; Alexr. Black, qualified Lieut. of Foot; William Smith, qualified Captain of Foot; Thomas Gilham, qualified Captain of Foot; Robert Armstrong, qualified cornet; Joseph Coulton, qualified Captain of Troop of Horse; Andrew Hays, qualified Lieutenant of Foot; Hugh Hicklin, qualified Cornet.

(319) Alexr. Walker, qualified Ensign; Wallace Estill, qualified Captain of Troop of Horse; Steven Wilson, qualified Lieut. Troop of Horse; John Miller, qualified Capn. Troop of Horse; Andrew Lewis, qualified Colonel Troop of Horse; David Stewart, qualified Colonel Troop of Horse; Robert Scot, qualified Captain of Compy. of Foot.

(319) Andrew Lewis, qualified Justice.

AUGUST 21, 1752.

(321) Peter Scholl, qualified Colonel of Foot; Low Todd, qualified Lieut. of Horse; John Dunbar, qualified Capn. of Horse; John Fitzwater, qualified Ensign; Francis McBride, qualified Cornet; Ro. McFarland, qualified Lieut.; Ro. Young, qualified Capn. of Horse.

(321) James Patton and Wm. Elliott ask counter security from Anne Dunlop, Admx. of her decd. husband. She has since married Ro. Bratton.

(322) Finishing of a Court House now let to Wm. Murray.

(326) On motion of Richard Woods, on behalf of himself and others, ordered that a Presbyterian Meeting House in Forks of James River, in this County, be and is hereby recorded a Public Place of Worship.

(326) Rev. Alexr. Craighead, a dissenting minister, took the oaths, subscribed the test, and the 39 articles, except what is exempted by the Act of Toleration, which is ordered to be certified.

(326) Robbert Bratton in open Court made oath to his deposition in favor of Margaret Woods, proving her to be the lawful wife of James Woods.

(328) Thomas Stewart, Isaac White, John McClure, Edward Hall, James Patton, John Black, James and Gabriel Alexander, and James Bell—clear and keep a road from Edward Hall's to Wm. Long's Mill.

(328) Charles Campbell, Wm. Long, Joseph Love, John Wilson, Wm. Wright, Anthony Black, James Robinson and Patrick Campbell—clear and keep a road from Wm. Long's mill to Charles Campbell's

(328) Alexr. Thompson qualified Cap. of Foot.

(328) Nicholas Smith, a free mulatto, has moved out of the County and left five small children—to be bound out.

AUGUST 22, 1752.

(329) Orphans Court.

Page

(347) James Mays } Deft. having informed the Court that the plt.
vs. } had employed both the attornies practising
Charles Whitaker } at this court, has Gabriel Jones assigned him.

(360) Daniel Richardson, Joel Hornback, John Cunningham, and Henry Carr—appraisers of George Sea.

November 15, 1752.

(361) Samuel Givins, Robert Patrick, to view, and Ro. Patrick, Wm. Hines, John Hawes, Joseph Bell, Wm. Bell, Wm. Finla, Archd. Stewart, Richd. Pilson, Wm. Johnston, Ro. Wilson, John Hind, Geo. Skilleron, Hugh Ross, Andr. Baskin, John Givins, Saml. Henderson, John Ramsey, Alexr. Henderson, Saml. Henderson, Nathl. Woodroof, David Logan and George Duglass, clear and keep in repair, a road from James Givin's Mill to the road over Wood's New Gap at foot of mountain.

(361) Mary Moffett, widow of John Moffett, has since intermarried with John Trimble.

(361) James Simpson and Michael Stump, overseers, with Jeremiah Osburn, Geo. Osburn, Mones Alkier, Heorndkis Corlock, John, Jacob and Wm. Westfall, Michael Stumph, Henry Harris, Henry Shipler, and Philip Moore —view and mark and keep in repair, on petition of inhabitants of the South Branch, a road from their wagon road up the So. Fork to Peter Reed's Mill.

(363) Neil Cassidy exempted from levy on account of great age and poverty.

(363) William Patterson petitions that in his way from the northward he camped in the woods in company of one Thomas Homes, who in the night time picked his pocket of eleven pieces of eight and one Caroline, for which he was apprehended and taken before B. Borden, but escaped, leaving behind him a mare and saddle, which are ordered to be advertised in the Va. Gazette, and sold.

(363) William Scholl, qualified Captain; James Simpson, qualified Captain; John Smith, qualified Major of Foot and Coroner; Humphrey Madison, qualified Under Sheriff.

November 16, 1752.

(365) John Walker, on So. Branch of Potomack, is exempted from levy on acct. of great age, infirmity and poverty.

(365) County Levy—116 wolf heads.

(365) Levied for finishing the new Co. Ho. 2317 tithables. (See this for list of names.)

(366) John McFarland, qualified Ensign; Joseph Crocket, qualified Captain Co. of Foot; Ro. McFarland, qualified Lieutenant.

(368) Valentine Sevier—leave to rebuild a mill.

(369) William Christian qualified Capn. Co. of Foot.

(369) Grand Jury Presentments: James Young, in Forks of James— taking toll twice.

November 17, 1752.

Page

(371) Motion of James Lockhart, Exr. Patrick Cook. Jane, relict of Patrick, has since intermarried with Andrew Steel, and is about to remove from the plantation and leave it waste.

(372) John Moore qualified Capn. of Co. of Foot.

(376) Humphrey Baker's removal.

November 18, 1752.

(377) John Fleming complains that James and Sarah, his wife, Young, detain his son, John Fleming—ordered to be given up.

(377) Certified that in a fight Saml. Newgally bit off part of one of John Bingaman's ears.

(377) John Buchanan quald. Col. of Horse and Foot and Coroner.

(378) John Patton quald. Capn. Co. of Foot.

(378) John Ramsey and Margaret, his wife, late Margaret Crockett.

November 18, 1752.

(379) James Cathey } Genl. Ct. sets aside the non suit and cause
vs. } certified to Genl. Court.
Thomas Storey }

(379) Alexr. and Wm. Sayers, Charles Sinclar and Humphrey Baker, to appraise Daniel Murphy's estate, on Reed Creek.

November 20, 1752.

(384) John Cunningham paid for mending the benches and bar of the Co. Ho.

(388) James Cohoun bound over towards James McCall.

(391) John Mathews qualified Justice.

(391) Patrick Martin qualified Capn. of a Troop of Horse.

(392) John Buchanan to build a mill on Forks of Reed Creek.

(403) Wm. Preston qualified Depy. Surveyor.

November 21, 1752.

(404) In suit of James Patton vs. James Cohoun, the jurors returned into Court unable to agree and asked to be discharged, having been four days in retirement, but the plaintiff's counsel objected, and they were ordered to consider further and if they could not agree, then to return next Court.

(406) £9, Penna. Cury.= £7, 2, 6, Va. Cury.

(410) Maurice O'Frield, John Trimble, Wm. McFeeters, Wm. Martain, James Young, Jacob Lockart, James Vance, Patrick Martin, Wm. McClintock, Rob. Young, Thos. Piery, John Campbell, James Peary, Robert Davis, James Philips, John Spear, John McMurry, Alexr. McMurry, David Stuard, Hugh Young, John Jameson, Rob. McClellon and John Brown—to work the road under Saml. Wallace from top of North Mountain to this Co. Ho.

(411) James Lockhart qualified Capn. of Foot; Saml. Stalnaker qualified Capn. of Foot.

Page

(411) Jonathan Douglas committed for trial for horsestealing.

JULY 22, 1752.

(412) Catharine McGinnis, alias Quin—acquitted.

SEPTEMBER 27, 1752.

(412) Thomas Walker qualified Deputy Surveyor.

MARCH 21, 1753.

(414) John Buchanan, James Clark, Jacob Lockhart, Thomas Kirkpatrick, John Berry, John Bartley, Wm. Martin, Josias Richards, William McFeeters, John Jameson, James Young, Hugh Young, Robert Young, William McClintock, Wm. Ledgerwood, John Trimble, Maurice O'Frield, Samuel Wallace, Robert Davis, Robert McClenon, James Moody, James Philips, Wm. Akry, Cornelius Donaho, George Peary, Adam Thompson, Thomas Peary, John Campbell, James Peary, Wm. McNab, Robert Scot, Thomas Reed, Abraham Masha, Thomas Dunn, Francis Dunn, Major Scot, John Bigham, John Black, Samuel Downing, Alexr. McFeeters, Andrew Cowan, James McCorkle, John Vance, James Gilmore and Patrick Martin— to keep road formerly laid off from James Young's Mill to said Buchanan's Mill.

(415) Joseph Long and James Young, overseers, with Robert Young, Joseph Long, Samuel Gibson, Solomon Whitley, John Collier, William Hall, Gilbert Crawford, George Gibson, John Ruckman, Thomas Burton, Wm. Wadington, Wm. Brown, James Moore, John Hanna, James Huston, Wm. Todd, James Bats, James Todd, James Young, Patrick Young, John Carr and James Campbell—keep the road from Joseph Long's Mill to James Young's Mill, thence to the Great Road on James Thompson's Plantation.

(415) Elizabeth and James Carlile, widow and son of James Carlile, Admrs. of James.

(416) Henry Knave, appraiser of Christian Strickly.

(416) Elizabeth and David Moore, widow and brother of Saml. Moore, Admrs. of Saml.

MARCH 22, 1753.

(419) Conrad Harness, qualified Lieut. of Foot; John Wilton, qualified Capn. Troop of Horse.

MARCH 22, 1753.

(419) David Robinson, qualified Lieut. of Foot; John Cunningham, qualified Lieut. of Foot; Henry Cartwright, qualified Ensign of Foot; Joseph Langdon, qualified Captain of Foot; James McKemy, qualified Ensign of Foot; Thomas Langdon, qualified Lieut. of Foot; Cornelius Ruddle, qualified Capn. of Horse and Foot.

(420) Robert Caldwell, qualified Lieut. of Foot; Archd. Ruddle, qualified Ensign of Foot; Henry Long, qualified Ensign of Foot; Wm. Bethell, qualified Lieut. of Foot; John Denton, qualified Capn. of Foot; Paul Lung, qualified Lieut. of Foot.

(420) Henry Lancisco, a German Protestant, having produced a certificate from a Protestant clergyman of his having taken the sacrament and made oath of his being an inhabitant of this Colony upwards of twelve years, and having taken the usual oaths to his Majesties' Person and Government, and made and subscribed the test. Certificate of Naturalization.

(420) James Patton | The jury impannelled and unable to agree at last
vs. | term being called and John Smith, one of them,
James Cohoun | not being present, is fined. Defendant's Att'y.
moved the Court to dismiss the jury and impanel a new one, but plaintiff, in person, objected, and Court was of opinion that the cause be continued and the same jury try the issue.

(421) Benj. Scot, eldest brother of James Scot, decd., qualified Admr.

(424) Michael Harness, son in law of Euric Westfall, decd., Admr. of Euric.

(424) Benjamin Scot, eldest son of Alexr. Scot, decd., Admr. of Alexr.

(426) John Robinson, qualified Capn. of Co. of Foot.

MARCH 23, 1753.

(427) John Black, greatest creditor of Michael Riley, qualified Admr.

(428) John Walker, qualified Capn. of Co. of Foot; John Hamilton, qualified Cornet; John Dickenson, qualified Captain of Horse.

(432)   Wm. Bethel | Attachment. Defendant cropped with James
vs. | McNeal and Zachary McCoy.
Torrance Carryl | MARCH 16, 1753.

(437) Barnaby Agan, qualified Ensign of Foot; Saml. Odell, qualified Capn. of Foot.

(439) Sheriff to sell estate of James Gwin, who lately died in the house of James Miles.

(441) Anne Rothgap, relict of John Jacob Rothgap, now the wife of George Hollyback.

MARCH 17, 1753.

(444) Lucretia Griffith, Admx. of her husband, but now married to James Burk.

(448) Robert Armstrong, qualified Capn. of Foot; James Armstrong, qualified Lieut. of Foot.

(449) Thomas Armstrong, qualified Ensign of Foot.

MARCH 18, 1753.

(453) Duncan McFarland and his son, William.

(453) Ephraim Vance, qualified Capn. of Horse.

(454) John Pickens | Dedimus to Anson Co. No. Co. to take deposition
vs. | of Henry Jones.
James Price |

(455) Robt. McClenachan claims a 21 yr. lease on lots 1 and 2 in Staunton on which the Co. Ho. stands, and a new Co. Ho. is about to be built on same lots. Court is of opinion that the order of Court and McClenachan's lease

in pursuance thereof were contrary to law, but the Court could not crush it. Comrs. appointed to confer with a lawyer practising in Genl. Court and have lots reconveyed.

MAY 19, 1753.

(457) Thomas Kilpatrick and son, Maurice Offriel, et als., to keep road from Brown's Bridge to Glebe Land.

(458) Robert Davis, an Exr. of Robert Crockett, is about to leave this Colony, and begs to be released. John Ramsey, who married Robert Crockett's widow summoned.

MAY 21, 1753.

(477) £4, 10, Penna. Cury.= £3, 7, 6, Va. Money.

MAY 22, 1753.

(490) Catharine Quin, having come from amongst the small-pox, so that it is feared she may spread the infection—ordered, that the Sheriff convey her out of town, and that in case she presume to return she be imprisoned during the sitting of this Court.

(498) Petition of Robert McCoy, an Exr. of his father, Robert.

(498) Relict of Abraham Job has married Thomas Bragg and required to give counter security.

(498) Ephraim Leith and Barbara Job, Admrs. of Caleb Job. Barbara Job has married Leith. Counter security.

(499) Patton vs. Colhoun } Jurors failing to appear—to be summoned to next Court.

AUGUSTA COUNTY COURT RECORDS.

ORDER BOOK NO. IV.

AUGUST 14, 1753.

Page

(1) New Commission.

(2) William Battersby qualifies Attorney.

(3) Ephraim Love to clear a road, his place to main road that leads from the South Branch over Swift Run Pass.

(6) Richard Dun, servant of Saml. Henderson.

(7) Charles Conner, servant of Wm. Robinson.

(7) John Denton, qualified Lieut. Co. of Foot; John Denton, Jr., qualified Ensign Co. of Foot; James Borsland, qualified Lieut. Co. of Foot.

AUGUST 15, 1753.

(8) Peter Hoult tried and acquitted of murdering Nicholas Trout who was killed by accident in a scuffle.

AUGUST 16, 1753.

Page

(9) Ludwick Francisco, qualified Captain; Edward McDaniel, qualified Cornet; Jeremiah Sciler, qualified Captain of Foot; Luke Collins, qualified Ensign of Foot.

(10) Walter Patterson receives a certificate of good character in order to practise law.

(10) Lewis Morgan, servant of Michael Kaufman.

(11) James Bell to be sumoned to show cause why he does not administer on his decd. brother's estate.

AUGUST 17, 1753.

(15) Sarah, wife of John Stevenson, relinquished dower in deed, John S.—to Archibald Husten.

(17) Saml. Cloyd added to tithables.

(22) Suit abates by John Rutledge's death { Underwood, &c., vs. Galespy and Rutledge.

(26) John Neilly, no inhabitant.

AUGUST 18, 1753.

(30) Robert Roy vs. George Neill and Momus Land } Abates by death of plaintiff.

(38) Wm. Burk vs. Edward McGinniss } Deft. lives in Frederick.

(60) James Huey removed out of this Colony.

(61) Pierce Costley removed out of this Colony.

(62) Mandamus from General Court to County Ct. requiring it to dismiss the jury in case of James Patton vs. James Cohoun—which is done and case continued.

NOVEMBER 21, 1753.

(66) Benj. Barnett, infant of Richard Barnett, decd., 16 yrs. old, chooses guardian.

(66) John Figare and Edward Figare, his son, bound to peace.

NOVEMBER 22, 1753.

(68) County levy—wolf heads.

(72) George Trout, brother of Nicholas Trout, qualifies on latter's estate—the widow refusing.

NOVEMBER 23, 1753.

(73) John Paxton to be overseer of road from Edmonston's Mill to Fork Meeting House, with these: James Trimble, Michael Finney, John Berrisford, Wm. Holdman, John Hardin, Hugh Means, Joseph Lapsley, Peter Wallace, Saml. McClure, Abram Brown, John Moore, Robert Moore, Stephen Arnold, Saml. Paxton, Jas. Edmondson.

Page
(75) John Mathews to be overseer of road from North Fork of James River, near John Mathew's, to Renix's Road, with these workers: Henry Brown, John Smiley, James Trimble, John Berriford, James Edmondson, Wm. Edmondson, Michael Finney, Wm. Holdman, Stephen Arnold, Hugh Means, John Harger, Wm. Scot, Edward Bishop, Alexr. McCorkall, Pat. McCorkall, Henry Fuller, Joseph Pain, Edwd. Baley, James Baley, John Peter Salling, Jas. Simpson, James Wolson, Alexr. Beggs, John Mathews, Joshua Mathews, John Maxwell, Jas. Frazier, John Hutcheson, Senr., John Hutcheson, Jr., George Salling, Richd. Beton, Wm. Boil, John Sprowl, John Smith, Saml. McClure, John Smiley, John McCuley, Richd. Mathews, Sampson Mathews, Daniel Sancion, Saml. Paxton, Wm. Paxton, John Oleston, Samuel Oleston, Saml. Walker.

NOVEMBER 24, 1753.

(76) Road ordered from Saml. Stalnaker's, on Holston River, to James Davis's—Saml. Stalnaker to be overseer, with these workers: James Davis and his sons, Frederick Corlock, David, George and Conrad Corlock, Frederick Starn, Jacob and Adam Stalnaker, Jacob and Henry Goldman, Isaiah Hamilton, Hamilton Shoemaker, Timothy Coe, Humphry Baker and son, George Stalnaker, Adam Andrews, Mathias Sarch, Michael Hook, Martin Counce, Jacob Mires.

(76) Road ordered—Wm. Bryan overseer—from Wm. Carravan's plantation to Wm. Bryans on Roan Oak. These workers: James Campbell, Joseph Love, Wm. Bryan, Jr., John Bryan, James Bane, Henry Brown, Jr., James Neilly, Henry Brown, Sr., Alexr. Ingram, Edward Patterson, Jacob Patton, John Wood, Erwin Patterson, Andrew Cox, Jasper Terry, Wm. Terry, John Woods, Edward Moore, Peter Craven, Aron Hart, Miles Hart, Wm. Graham, Neal McNeal, Malcom Campbell, Wm. Armstrong, Tasker Tosh, Thomas Tosh, Daniel Evans, Uriah Acres, Thos. Acres, John McAdoe, Wm. Akers.

(76) Road ordered—Wm. Carravan, overseer—from Charles Millicons to Wm. Carravan's, with these workers: Wm. Ralston and his sons, Charles Millicon, James, Joseph and Edward McDonald, Joseph and David Robinson, James Galliad, Archd, Graham, David Miller, Hugh Mills Richard Kerr, Wm. Miller, Wm. Graham, David and Joshua McCormick, Tobias Smith, Steven Rentfro.

NOVEMBER 26, 1753.

(77) James Mitchell complains that his master, Valentine Severe, abuses him—several of these complaints by several of Valentine's servants.

(78) Overseers appointed for the Indian Road from the North Fork to the Main Branch of the James River.

(105) Clerk ordered to send for a proper seal for this County.

(106) Ordered that no money be paid to the persons building the new Court House without consent of the Court.

MARCH 20, 1754.

(107) Momus Lawler, servant of John King.

Page
(109) Bridge to be built at the place called Brown's Bridge.
(109) Mary, wife of Alexr. Gibson, released dower in 26½ acres conveyed by Alexr. to James Reaburn.

MARCH 21, 1754.

(113) Susannah Patton qualified Admx. of her decd. father, Jacob Patton. (For military qualifications see *infra* under 15 May. These qualifications not indexed.)

(115) Isaac Schooley—appraisers appointed—also in Frederick Co.

(115) John Porton, infant, servant of James Miles and Thomas Hamilton, released from indenture.

(116) Richard Hadley and Wm. McDaniel, servants of Ephraim Vance.

(116) Causeway ordered to be built over the Marsh between the Co. Ho. and Tinkling Spring.

(117) John Buchanan, Weaver—special bail.

(118) Anthony Thompson, decd.—his goods to be delivered into Court.

(123) Gibson vs. Wm. Scot } Following attached—5 pewter basins, 20 plates, 6 dishes, 1 looking glass, 1 silver punch ladle, 6 porringers, 3 punch bowls, 4 blankets, 2 pillows.

(124) John and Agnes Mills, witnesses for Lunenburg.

MARCH 23, 1754.

(126) Liquors rated.

(126) Road ordered from Campbell's School House to Renix's Road—Saml. Walker, overseer—with these workers: William Bradshaw, John Maxwell, James Frazier, John McColley, John Peter and George Salley, Henry Fuller, Joseph Ryan, John Hutchings, John Hutchings, Jr., John Sprowl, Mathew Vance, Richard Benton, Wm. Burt, John Smith, Joseph Smith, John Allison, Wm. Byers, Richard Mathews, Sampson Mathews, Saml. Walker, Thos. Shaw, Stephen Arnold, John Peteet, Wm. Noble, Saml. Allison.

(126) Road ordered from North River to Campbell's School House. John Mathews, overseer, with Alexr. McCorkell, Edmund Crump, John Harger.

(129) Elizabeth McDonald—death abates suit.

(129) On motion of Cap. Andrew Lewis, Wm. Pere, Josias Baker, Terrence Sweney, John Shaw, John Smith, Joseph Baxter, Bartholamy Burns, Geo. McSwine, who were listed for his Majesty's service, took the oaths.

(130) George Bigham petitions for Admn. of estate of Robert Foil, decd., as being nearest of kin—rejected.

MARCH 25, 1754.

(142) Wm. Leopard, overseer from Bingaman's Ferry to Roan Oak, near Tobias Bright's, also from Widow Draper's to Jacob Brown's.

(142) Road to James Miller's on Reed Creek.

(142) Road from Alexr. Sayer's Mill to James Davison's, on Holdston's River, James Davis and James McCall, overseers.

Page

(142) Road from Jacob Brown's, on Roan Oak, to Isaac Taylor's—John Robinson, Sr., overseer.

(147) Road from Frederick Hartsaw's Mill, on Craig's Creek, up the Creek and across a mountain to James McAfee's. Henry Holdston, Jr., surveyor.

March 26, 1754.

(168) Joseph Bell—witness.

March 27, 1754.

(181) Benj. Scot, security for Judith Scot, Admx. of John Scot, decd., who has since married Joseph Carpenter, prays counter security.

April 3, 1754.

(186) Patrick Hair, convict servant of John Anderson, convicted of stealing out of the courtyard, nigh the house of Wm. Murray, sundry goods, property of Rev. Robert McMordie.

April 17, 1754.

(187) John Smith, servant of Archd. Carns.

May 15, 1754.

This date is deferred—here follow military qualifications including and since 21 March.

(118) George Robinson—Captain of Foot; Wm. Gray—Lieut. of Foot; Wm. Dyer—Lieut. of Foot.

Prior to March 21, in Vol. IV, military qualifications are not noted in this book and must be looked up—down to 15 May.

(193) Thomas Harrison qualified Lieutenant.

(194) Road ordered from Widow Sloans to end of Carravan's new road, and John McGown be overseer.

May 16, 1754.

(194) Robert McMahon qualifies Admr. of his son, Saml. McMahon.

(195) David Miller qualifies Admr. of his father's (Wm. Miller) estate.

(197) James Murphy, child of Catharine Quin.

(198) Thomas Rutledge Admr. of John Rutledge, decd., Thomas and John were brothers.

(200) Alexr. McKenny, servant of Wm. Murray.

May 17, 1754.

(205) John Clark entered last night Ro. McClenachan's house and demanded satisfaction for a decision rendered by Robert in a cause in Court—bound to peace.

(206) Many attachments vs. Wm. Murray, who was contractor for the new Court House; also vs. John Harmon.

Page

(210) John Wilson's death abates suit.

(214) Scire facias ordered on recognizance of Joseph Collet, charged by Henry Brown for robing him of his wife and sundry goods.

May 18, 1754.

(219) Anne Brown, wife of James Brown, came into Court and called Justice William Wilson a "rogue, and that on his coming off the Bench she would give it to him with the Devil," bound to good behovior.

(227) Jacob Miller
vs. } Elizabeth is an infant.
Elizabeth Thomas

May 20, 1754.

(247) Daniel Drody—juryman.

(251) James Patton
vs. } Submitted to arbitration. Patton was under obligation to deliver 2 patents to Calhoun, con-
James Calhoun } tracted when there was no fee to the Governor for signing the patents. Before patents were delivered, law was enacted giving Governor a fee. Patton charged this to Calhoun. Award is that each pay fee for one patent.

May 21, 1754.

(252) George Berry petitions that his father, James Berry, be relieved from levy—granted.

(252) James Murphy, Sarah and Rebecca McGinas, children of Catharine Quins to be bound out, Catharine being a charge on the County.

(252) Esther Smith, a child of Nicholas Smith, to be bound out, he being an idle person without visible means.

August 21, 1754.

(253) Christian Wilson, wife of William Wilson, informs the Court that her husband has left the Colony and left three small children, two of whom she cannot support, viz: Danl. and Elizabeth Wilson, who are ordered to be bound out.

(254) Isabella Moore, servant of Robert Poage.

(255) Saml. Pegg, servant of James Allen; Edwd. Hays, servant of Wm. Robertson; Robert Gaw, servant of Ro. Renix.

(256) Owen Callihan, servant of John Wilson.

(259) John Atkins and Henry Cristwell committed for fighting in the courtyard.

August 22, 1754.

(262) Wm. Russell
vs. } Certiorari from Genl. Court. Co. Ct. replies that issue is made up here and should be tried
Francisco, et als. } here unless there is a further order from Gen. Ct.

(263) Nicholas Mills qualified Lieut. of Foot.

(268) Thomas Weems, John Malcome—witnesses.

Page

(269) Abraham Smith qualified Captain of Foot.
(269) Low Todd—Special Bail.

AUGUST 23, 1754.

(273) Patrick McKendrick—a witness.
(275) Archd. Huston qualified Lieut. of Foot.

AUGUST 24, 1754.

(288) William White bound to David Hays.
(288) Patrick Crawford vs. Thomas Story } James Randolph, a witness, is about to leave the Colony. Ded. Potestm. de bene Esse.
(289) James Mitchell, qualified Capn. of Foot.; Wm. Engles, qualified Capn. of Foot; Israel Christian, qualified Capn. of Foot.
(289) Lettice Gleghorn to be examined for relinquishment of dower in land conveyed by her husband, Wm. Gleghorn, to Mary Chittman.
(289) John Stagg servant of John Harrison.
(290) Wm. Stagg, a bastard, 2 yrs. old, to be bound out on motion of John Harrison.
(290) Charles Stringam—a juryman.

AUGUST 26, 1754.

(302) DedimusPotestatem to Bedford Co. to examine the witnesses Agnes Mills, Eliz. Mills and Eliz. Mills, Jr.

OCTOBER 10, 1754.

(318) Court of Claims—grievances and propositions.
(318) David Stuart—allowed for patrolling; John Dickenson, allowed for patrolling.
(319) John Brown, allowed for patrolling; Danl. Harrison allowed for patrolling.

NOVEMBER 20, 1754.

(320) Henry Brown has only one, instead of two, tithables.
(321) Joseph White says his child was bound to David Hays when he was absent and he is capable of raising it—ordered to be returned to him.
(321) John and James McKee relieved of levy this year, not being inhabitants of this Co. on 10th June last.
(322) John Halefor allowed for 1 wolf head.
(322) Robert Hastings, for guarding the jail.
(323) Elizabeth Bendall, servant of John Ramsey; Francis Adams, servant of Wm. Lewis; Wm. Donley, servant of Andrew Lewis.

NOVEMBER 21, 1754.

(323) John Mitchell indented servant to John Hanna.
(325) James McDonald, indented Servt. to Wm. Bell.
(326) Comn. to Bedford Co. to examine Mary Ewing for relinquishment of dower in tract conveyed by her husband, Robert Ewing, to Benj. Sterrett.
(326) Comn. to No. Carolina to take deposition of Wm. Scot.

Page

(327) John Lockhart of No. Carolina—is paid a debt in Court.
(327) Comn. to take deposition of Patrick McKendrick and Sarah.

NOVEMBER 22, 1754.

(330) Maxwell McCormick, servant of James Campbell.
(330) John McCurry was lately drowned.
(331) Saml. Doak and John Mitchell, guardians of the orphans of John Greer—settled accounts.

NOVEMBER 23, 1754.

(336) Thomas Weems and David Ormont—jurors.
(338) James McCochran, servant of Wm. Armstrong.

NOVEMBER 25, 1754.

(343) Jacob Goldman—suit dismissed by his death.

JANUARY 23, 1755.

(375) Robert Hamilton to be tried by Genl. Ct. on suspicion of having killed James Kachell (Rachell?).

MARCH 19, 1755.

(376) Nicholas Scone appd. Appraiser.
(377) John Semple qualified Attorney.
(379) Pheby Moore—wife of Thomas Moore.

MARCH 20, 1755.

(382) New Commission of Justices.
(383) Denis McAnenis, servant of Joseph Mays; John McGaw, servant of John McGown.
(383) Wm. Bell says process in suit Saml. Hughes vs. Wm. Bell was served on Wm. Bell, his father—injunction granted.
(390) Robert Gray—not an inhabitant.

MARCH 21, 1755.

(394) Saml. Hughes—juror.

MARCH 22, 1755.

MARCH 24, 1755.

(411) Road ordered from Isaac Taylor's to Tarr's shop.
(412) Audley Paul qualified Lieutenant of Foot; Henry Murray, qualified Lieutenant of Foot.
(413) Thos. Reed says that on Friday, 21st inst., John Risk assaulted him and bit off part of his left ear.
(415) Francis Kerkley, a witness from Culpeper Co.

<h1 style="text-align:center">March 25, 1755.</h1>

Page

(419) Adam Thompson, qualified Lieutt. of Horse.

<h2 style="text-align:center">May 21, 1755.</h2>

(423) Abraham Brown appd. Constable below the Brusby Hills, in the Forks of James River.

(427) Road from James Beard's Ford to Chamberlain's Run, thence to the Stone Meeting House.

<h2 style="text-align:center">May 22, 1755.</h2>

(429) Joseph James, Saml. Herring—appraisers.

(432) David Stuart, security for John Miller, Admr. of James Jones, decd., who is not in this Colony, petitions for counter security.

(433) Jacob Frederick Courts petitions that he has lately come from the northward and purchased land on Stover's Mill Creek—has leave to erect a mill.

(433) Anne, wife of Robert Bratton.

<h2 style="text-align:center">May 23, 1755.</h2>

(436) John Warnock—a juror.

(437) James Mitchell, servant of Val. Seviar.

(438) Wm. Hinds—juror.

(439) Wm. Crawford—witness from Bedford.

(440) Agnes Edmondson released dower in 350 acres from her husband to Hugh McCleeve.

(440) Wm. Bishop, servant of Charles Campbell.

<h2 style="text-align:center">May 24, 1755.</h2>

(442) Andrew Viney—witness from Hampshire.

(442) Charles Stringam—juror.

(443) James Patton at the Assembly (?).

<h2 style="text-align:center">August 20, 1755.</h2>

(464) New Court House being finished. Comrs. appointed to view it.

(465) Mathew Pigg, a wagoner of John Davis's, produced an acct. for services done for the army under Braddock.

(465) James King, servant of George Rankins.

(465) John Hogshead, qualified Lieutt. of Foot.

(466) Valentine Eastin, servant of John Paxton.

<h2 style="text-align:center">August 21, 1755.</h2>

(467) Court House received.

(467) Alexr. and Jannet Allison, servants of John Stevenson.

(468) Audley Paul produced account for services done Braddock's army and for a horse lost on the expedition; Major Scot, a carrier employed by David Stuart, ditto; Wm. Scot, a carrier, ditto.

Page

(470) Joseph Carpenter committed on charge of having supplied Indians with ammunition.

(470) Daniel McCoy, orphan of Duncan McCoy—to be bound.

(471) Hanna Glen, a witness from Frederick.

OCTOBER 25, 1755.

(490) Propositions and grievances: John Hunter for services, wagoning; James Alexander, for patrolling; Wm. Wilson, Wm. Cunningham, Domnick Barrel, Mathew Thompson, John Atkins, Saml. Black, patrolling; John Brown for victualling men patrolling under Cap. David Lewis; Wm. Thompson for patrolling and going on an express; George Caldwell, for patrolling; Robert Poage, for waggoning; Israel Christian, patrolling; Israel Christian, claim of David Moore for provisions provided Cap. David Lewis's Co. of Rangers which provisions were received by Christian.

(491) Newman McGonagle, for patrolling; Wm. Williams, for patrolling; Wm. Christian, for patrolling; Alexr Thompson, for patrolling; John Simmons claim for guarding arms and ammunition sent for the use of this County; Wm. Duncan, for patrolling; Robert Thompson and John Galespy, patrolling; Charles Patrick, for patrolling; Joseph Martin and Wm. McFeeters, for patrolling; Wm. Lockhart, for patrolling; Barny Riley, going on express.

(492) Saml. and James McDowell, patrolling; Andrew Scot, horse impressed; Daniel Harrison, patrolling.

NOVEMBER 19, 1755.

(492) John O'Neal complains that he was assaulted by Edward McGarry and Danl. Sullivan, but they would not be arrested—Sheriff ordered to raise the force of the County and arrest them.

(494) Cornelius and Daniel Murley died intestate and estates committed to Sheriff.

(495) James Patton's Exrs. allowed for his Burgess wages 11,200 lbs. tobacco.

(496) Alice, wife of Joseph Bryon—Private Exn.

(496) James Annan, servant of John Stroud.

(497) Daniel Plumer, orphan of Robert Plumer—Edward Hall appointed guardian.

(497) Capn. Perry, a drover from Carolina—his cattle to be sold and money lie until further orders.

(497) Michael Coager, orphan of Nicholas Coager, Adam Miller appointed guardian.

NOVEMBER 20, 1755.

(499) James Lockridge qualified Lieutt. of Foot.

(499) Francis Earns, servant of Henry Kirkham.

(499) John Graham, qualified Lieutt. of Foot; George Wilson, qualified Capn. of Horse.

(501) Thomas Armstrong, qualified Capn. of Foot; Andrew Foster, qualified Ensign of Foot.

NOVEMBER, 21, 1755.

Page

(503) Wm. Ratchford, servant of Wm. Lusk.

(504) Danl. Harrison ⎱ Attacht. was levied before deft. removed out of
   vs. ⎰ the Co. and is dismissed.
   Joseph Bryan

(507) Wm. Akry has removed out of the Colony. James McMurdie witness from Bedford. Robert Means's will proved. Admr. moved for by Thos. Thompson, his nephew and heir-at-law, and also by John McClung, who married Jennet, niece of decd.—given to Thomas.

NOVEMBER 22, 1755.

(514) John Jameson qualified Ensign of Troop of Horse.

NOVEMBER 24, 1755.

(517) Alexr. Anderson, servant of John Lowry.

(Additional Notes from Order Book IV. from beginning of Book IV. to March 21, 1754.)

AUGUST 17, 1753.

(1) New Commission of Justices dated 16 June 1753: James Patton,* Peter Scholl,* David Stewart, Richard Woods,* Robert Breckinridge, James Simpson,* John Buchanan,* Silas Hart, James Lockhart,* John Mathews, William Wilson, George Robinson,* Andrew Lewis, Robert McClenachan,* Christopher Guest, William Bethell.* (Those marked (*) qualified.)

(2) James Grymes, orphan, to be bound to Peter Scholl.

(5) Alexr. McNutt chose John Brownlee his guardian. Esther Robinson qualifies Admx. of decd. husband, James Robinson. Appraisers are John Robinson, Ephraim Voss, Isaac Taylor, James Campbell.

(6) Robt. McClenachan bound to peace for abusing Benj. Thompson in Co. Ho.

(7) John Denton, qualified Lieutenant of Foot; John Denton, Jr., qualified Ensign.

AUGUST 16, 1753.

(9) Ludwick Francisco, qualified Captain; Edward McDaniel, qualified Cornet; Jeremiah Sciler, qualified Captain; Luke Collins, qualified Ensign.

(9) Wm. Leeper appointed Constable on New River, vice Adam Harman. John States and Alexr. Painter appointed overseers for a new road from North Mountain Gap, called Brock's Gap, near Thomas Mish, to the mouth of Lost River, leading to North Mountain.

AUGUST 17, 1753.

(15) James Urrey appointed Road Surveyor, vice Hance Magot.

Page

(24) Wm. Robinson, qualified Lieutenant of Horse.
(28) Saml. Wilson—ordinary license.

NOVEMBER 21, 1753.

(64) Ro. Breckinridge qualified Sheriff.

NOVEMBER 22, 1753.

(68) Wm. McCurry to be levy free on account of great age and infirmity.
(73) Ro. McClenachan—ordinary license.

NOVEMBER 23, 1753.

(75) John Lusk, Sr., relinquished right to land to Robert Moberry.
Mathew Patton, qualified Lieutenant of Foot.
(76) Humphrey Madison, qualified Under-Sheriff.

NOVEMBER 27, 1753.

(105) Clerk to provide a Seal for the County Court.

MARCH 20, 1754.

(107) Ephraim Love, qualified Captain of Foot; Ro. Ralston, qualified
Lieut. of Foot; John Hinton, qualified Ensign of Foot.
(110) Henry Fuller—common disturber of peace.

(O. B. IV.)

MARCH 21, 1754.

(118) George Robinson, qualified Captain of Foot; Wm. Gray, qualified
Lieutenant of Foot; Wm. Dyer, qualified Lieutenant of Foot.

MAY 15, 1754.

(200) James Patton, President of the Court.

AUGUSTA COUNTY COURT RECORDS.

ORDER BOOK No. V.

NOVEMBER 25, 1755.

(1) James Anglen has removed out of the Colony.
(2) Jane Bourland, late Jane Jackson.

Page

(10) George Parks
vs.   } John Perry removed out of the Colony.
John Perry

(14) Edward Patterson
vs.   } Andrew Gahagen removed out of County.
A. G.

(14) Jacob Goldman removed out of County.
(14) Josiah Cumings, servant of Ro. Sayers.
(16) Wm. Canthorn removed out of County.
(17) John Warnock removed out of County.
(19) Repentance Townsend removed out of County.
(20) John Culbertson removed out of County.
(23) Patrick McKendrick, removed out of County.
(26) Wm. Carlile—no inhabitant.

FEBRUARY 14, 1756.

(29) John O'Neal, tried for speaking treasonable words, acquitted, but committed for abusing the Government and cursing the Bible.

MARCH 17, 1756.

(30) Margaret Looney qualified Admx. of her deceased husband, Robert Looney, Jr.

(31) Jane Elliott, servant of Thomas Tate. James Hays, orphan of George Hays, decd., of the age of 18 years, chose guardian—William Edmondson.

(32) Ananias Dart, servant of Wm. Wright; same, Malcome Allen.

(32) Mary Whiteside prays separate maintenance from her husband, Wm. Whiteside.

(33) James King, servant of Hugh Ross.

(33) Elizabeth, wife of Adam Thompson, private examination. Thompson to Saml. Kingkade.

(33) John Burns, servant of James Greenlee.

(34) Valentine Utter and Mary, his wife, servants of John Paxton, set free by their master for £12.

MARCH 18, 1755.

(34) James McDowell, 18 years old, chose John Bowyer guardian. Michael March and John Brown, servants of Jacob Frederick Curts.

(35) James Hughs—license to keep ordinary. Israel Christian, surety.

(37) Robert McKetrick
vs.   } One fiddle attached.
John McGuire

(38) Margaret Campbell makes oath that the left ear of her son, James Beard, was bitten off by a horse.

(39) George Watts, servant of Thomas Watterson, petitions for freedom dues. John Woods, servant of Charles Dever.

(41) Robert Tedford, garnishee.

Page

(43) Jonas Newcum, servant of Ro. McClenachan, has a child likely to be a charge—to be bound out.

(43) Richard Sansile, servant of Ro. Breckinridge, was abused by Peter Galespy.

(43) Robert A'Dair convicted of threatening to favor the inroads of the enemy Indians.

(46) Arwalker Johnson—juror.

(47) Robert Scarbrough, a witness from Frederick Co.

(48) James Huey, removed out of the Colony.

MARCH 20, 1755.

(49) Robert Bratton, qualified Captain of Militia.

(50) James Huey
vs.   } Both removed out of the Colony.
Patrick Downing

(51) Archibald Bourland—a non-inhabitant.

MARCH 23, 1756.

(57) James Hughs, qualified Lieutenant of Militia.

(61) Valentine Henderson
vs.   } James Hughs—juror.
James Trimble

(62) Liquors rated.

(63) James Allen, qualified Captain of Foot.

(64) William Wilson does not provide for his son, Daniel Wilson, in a Christianlike manner—to be bound out.

MARCH 24, 1756.

(101) John Johnston
vs.   } Plaintiff having died, *scire facias* awarded.
Thos. Fitzpatrick.

(107) George Campbell, fined for absence from divine worship.

APRIL 29, 1756.

(108) Claims, propositions and grievances: James Beard, claim for ranging; John McClenachan, claim for going express; Robert Bratton, claim for ranging; George Wilson, claim for ranging and provisions for his Company; Abraham Smith, claim for ranging and provisions for his Company; Israel Christian, claim for ranging and provisions; Joseph Kenaday, claim for ranging; Patrick Lowrey, claim for ranging; George Campbell, claim for ranging; John Dickinson, claim for ranging and provisions for his Company; James Dunlop, claim for ranging and provisions for his Company; Archd. Stuart, claim for ranging; John Campbell, claim for ranging.

Page

(109) Robert Stevenson, claim for a bell impressed; Saml. Norwood, claim for ranging; Wm. Baskins, claim for ranging; Jeremiah Sealey, claim for ranging and provisions; George Robinson, claim for ranging; James See, claim for ranging; Henry Reaburn, claim for ranging; John Moore, claim for ranging.

May 19, 1756.

(110) Henry Harmon about to remove.

(113) Robert Moore, overseer for James Beard. Wm. and Peggy Henson, servants of David Wilson—their two children to be bound out.

May 20, 1756.

(117) Orphans of James Cumings, not being provided for in a Christian-like manner, to be bound out.

(119) Jane Elliott, servant of Thos. Tate.

May 21, 1756.

(125) Catherine Finn—servant of Patrick Martin.

(126) Walter Smiley, bound to peace. Catherine McGinnis, or Quin, released from jail on condition she depart from this County.

(128) Jacob Harmon—dead.

May 22, 1756.

(129) Catherine Utt, orphan of Casper Utt, to be bound out.

(133) Moses McCown's deposition to be taken—about to remove out of the Colony.

May 24, 1756.

(137) Thomas Merry, dead. William Beverly, dead.

(138) Jacob Harmon, dead.

(139) George Moffett, dead.

(159) John Meeley, servant of Patrick Wilson.

(159) William Preston—lately commander of a fort on the frontiers.

May 25, 1756.

(164) William Johnston, having departed this life since the last Court.

(178) John Bourland, a late servant of Robert Patterson, has served his time and is released.

July 15, 1756.

(186) George Wilson bound to good behavior for having spoken disrespectfully of the Government.

(188) Darby Sullivan, a suspected person, took all the oaths, but, being of ill behavior, is committed to jail.

(188) Alexander Herron qualified Lieutenant.

Page

(189) John Hegg, servant of Saml. Huston, has served his time by indenture faithfully and honestly and is released. James Bringenham, servant of Josiah Wilson, petitions for freedom dues. Mary Whiteside's complaint for separate maintenance vs. her husband, William, is groundless and dismissed; but it appearing that John Underwood and Mary, his wife, Richard Burton, Joseph Underwood and Elizabeth Underwood, relations of Mary, have stirred up differences between William and Mary and threatened the life of William—bound over.

(191) Andrew Heslep, added to tithables.

(193) Francis Kerkley, Jacob Shell, Jacob Lingle, Christian Bingaman, John Bingaman, Henry Bingaman, added to tithables.

AUGUST 20, 1756.

(198) William Goodens—witness.

(201) Henry Maury (Muray)—juror.

AUGUST 21, 1756.

(209) William Bishop—dead.

(219) Jonathan Whitley vs. Hanah Kirkham, widow of Robert Kirkham. Martha, Jane and Elizabeth Kirkham, infant daughters of Robert.

(223) Michael March and John Brown, servants of Jacob Frederick Curts, have served their time by indenture and are released.

(225) Esther Clendenning—dead.

(240) James Bower and Jane summoned to show cause why they have not paid Thos. Geiger, their servant, his freedom dues.

NOVEMBER 17, 1756.

(242) Robert Armstrong, with two other tithables, added to list of tithables. Hannah, widow of Robert Sayers, refuses to administer, and David Sayers qualifies.

(243) John Fleming, servant of John Paxton.

(244) County Levy.

NOVEMBER 18, 1756.

(245) Mary, widow of John O'Neal, refuses to admr. Thomas Moore, with one other, added to tithables.

(246) John Campbell, orphan of John Campbell, aged 16, chooses guardian. Jane and Maiy Sprout, admrs. of John Sprout, about to leave the Colony.

(247) Sampson Archer qualified Lieut. of Militia.

NOVEMBER 19, 1756.

(248) John Burns, servant of James Greenlee; John Woster, servant of Danl. Smith; Thomas Garland, servant of Joseph Kenaday.

Page
(251) Will of Robert Sayers produced and disputed by David Sayers because not signed, but ordered to record. Admr. granted to David Sayers as next of kin. Hannah, the widow, refused to admr.

NOVEMBER 22, 1756.

(256) Julian Mahanee, servant woman of John Ramsey.
(257) Richard Mihills, servant of Wm. Preston, agreed not to enlist in his Majesty's service, and Wm. acquits him of one year's service.

NOVEMBER 23, 1756.

(267) Thomas Storn—suit abates by his death.
(270) James Mays, Sr.—suit abates by his death.

NOVEMBER 24, 1756.

(278) John Bird—suit abates by his death.
(279) Alexr. Mathewson, suit abates by his death. John O'Neal, suit abates by his death.
(292) George Willson ⎫ Judgt. But this judgt. is not to bar the deft.
       vs. ⎬ from whatever money is now due to him from
  Robert Knox ⎭ the country as a patroller and which may come
into the hands of the plaintiff as his Captain.
(300) James Ward, servant of Patrick Wilson, prays freedom dues. Domnick Barrett, witness.

DECEMBER 3, 1756.

(302) Claims, propositions and grievances: Danl. Harrison, for ranging and provisions expended in his Company; Wm. McFeeters, for horse impressed; Danl. Deniston, for horse impressed; James Henderson, for horse impressed; Thomas Armstrong, for ranging and provisions for his Company.

MARCH 16, 1757.

(304) Wm. Cunningham, qualified Lieut. of Militia; James Henderson, qualified Lieut. of Militia; Jacob Sybert, qualified Captain of Militia.
(305) Opopheone, widow of Mark Miller, refuses to Admr.
(305) Thos. O'Neal, 16 years old, chose his guardian.

MARCH 17, 1757.

(310) James Hughes—ordinary license.
(311) Nathaniel Phipps, servant of Adam Looney.
(312) John Wood, servant of John Davis.

MARCH 18, 1757.

Page
(357) David Logan—suit abates by his death.
(360) William Lewis—took the oaths.
(360) Andrew Hays—took the oaths.

APRIL 16, 1757.

(364) Called Court.

JUNE 15, 1757.

(364) Adam Jordan appointed Constable in Bull Pasture.
(367) James Bruister appointed Constable.
(367) New Commission.
(368) Francis Kirkley, Jr., qualified Captain of Militia.

JUNE 17, 1757.

(371) John Smith's will presented. Exrs. refused to act. Abraham Smith, one of the Exrs. and heir-at-law, was summoned, but failed to appear; two of the witnesses are dead. Robert Renix, the remaining witness, proved it, and the Court, knowing the signatures of testator and witness, it is recorded.
(379) Thomas O'Neal, aged 16 years and 6 months, agrees to serve as apprentice to Henry Murray.

JUNE 20, 1757.

(382) John Smith—suit abates by death of.
(385) Patrick Cain—returned no inhabitant.
(385) Bryon McDonald—suit abates by death of.
(386) James Montgomerie—returned no inhabitant.
(391) Joseph Crockett—returned no inhabitant.

JUNE 21, 1757.

(414) John Cockrane vs. George Lewis   Geo. Lewis appeared and swore he was not the person indebted—alias summons awarded.
(417) Mathew Waters—suit abates by death of.
(426) Mortain Cornet—servant of Henry Smith.
(426) On motion of John Madison, security for David Stuart, admr. of John O'Neal, decd., setting forth that he was fearful from these troublesome times the said estate might be wasted—counter security.

AUGUST 17, 1757.

(428) Peter Horse—naturalized—received the sacrament of Rev. John Bernard.

Page

(435) Peter Bruner and Saml. Thornhill added to list of tithables.

(435) David Hughes, orphan child two years old, to be bound out.

(436) John Ramsey $\left\{\begin{array}{l}\text{Attacht. It appearing to the Court that deft.} \\ \text{had not absconded, but was in his Majesty's} \\ \text{service—dismissed.}\end{array}\right.$
vs.
Charles Stringham

(440) Ann Breckinridge, wife of George—private Exn.—returned.

AUGUSTA COUNTY COURT RECORDS.

ORDER BOOK No. VI.

AUGUST 19, 1757.

(1) Court—Patrick Martin, Richard Woods, Robert Breckinridge, Patrick Martin, John Bowyer, Daniel Smith, James Buchanan, John Archer.

(8) William Bell., Sr.—suit abates by death of.

(11) Edward Hughes vs. Joseph Paxton—*a capias.*

(14) John Walker removed out of the Colony.

(17) George Bee, servant of John Stuart.

AUGUST 20, 1757.

(20) Jacob Woodley and servantman, John Pinkerton, added to tithables.

(24) John Wicks—witness.

(25) Motion Joshua Mathews—Robert and John Poage to be summoned to say whether either will administer on estate of Robert Renix, decd., they being nearest of kin.

(30) John Denniston, exempted from levy. Isaac South, exempted from levy.

(32) John Vance—his death abates suit. William Williams—returned no inhabitant of County.

(34) John Brown, servant of John Anderson.

(34) George and William Hutcheson—added to tithables.

OCTOBER 3, 1757.

(35) Court Oyer and Terminer, on slave Hampton, charged with housebreaking and larceny. Convicted and sentenced to be hanged on Thursday, the 30th inst.

NOVEMBER 16, 1757.

(39) Jennett McDonald administers on estate of her deceased son, Randall McDonald. Esther Brown qualifies admx. of her decd. father, Henry Brown, Esther, the widow, having refused.

Page

(41) William Gay's estate to be settled and dower assigned to the widow, Margaret Hamilton.

NOVEMBER 17, 1757.

(41) Andrew Newman, orphan of 10 months, to be bound.
(41) John Dickinson qualified Justice.
(42) Christian Bumgardner—Lieut. of Foot—qualified.
(42) Conrad Yates exempted from levy—an object of charity.
(42) Ann Stewart, admx. her husband, James Stewart, decd.
(42) James Frame and son, Thomas, added to tithables. Thomas Lewis, with six others, added to tithables. Gabriel Jones, with five others, added to tithables.
(42) Michael Warren, qualified Captain of Foot.
(43) Last will of John Smith, Jr., proved—Abraham Smith, heir-at-law of John, came and relinquished all his right under the will.
(44) John Mathews took the usual oaths which is ordered to be certified.

NOVEMBER 18, 1757.

(45) Joseph Bell appointed Constable in Staunton, vice Alexr. Wright.
(46) James Graham exempted from levy—being an object of charity.
(46) Agnes, widow of John Wilson, renounces all claims under her husband's will and admn. granted her.
(51) James Lockhart qualified Justice.
(51) Abraham Smith, eldest son and heir-at-law of John Smith, now a prisoner in the French Dominions, refused to admr., whereupon Israel Christian, a creditor, qualifies during Smith's absence.

NOVEMBER 19, 1757.

(70) John King added to tithables. John Christian qualified Justice.

NOVEMBER 21, 1757.

(76) John Cunningham to provide candles, keep fires and clean the Co. Ho., and bring in his charge at next levy.
(84) On application of above, Ro. McClenachan refused to deliver up keys of Co. Ho., claiming a property right in the Co. Ho. and Jail, to which he offered to execute a lease to the County, which is referred to the General Court, and Sheriff is ordered to procure a lock and key, and Gabriel Jones to prosecute Robert in General Court.

DECEMBER 21, 1757.

(85) Margaret Anderson swears that she was well acquainted with Wm. Francis, of Chester Co., Township of East Nottingham, now decd., and that John Francis, of this County of Augusta, was the eldest male issue of the said William by Ann, his first wife, which, on motion of John, is certified.

Page
(86) James Keith qualified Attorney.

(87) Michael Stump, Leonard Knave, Peter Howe and Harman Shook—appraisers of Christian Tosher.

(87) Wm. McMurry petitions that John Madison, with a company of men, entered his house on their march to the Shawnees and took some rye—rejected.

(87) Andrew Muldrough—mark recorded.

(87) Martin Cornet—servant of Henry Smith.

(88) John Berry, orphan of James Berry, aged 15 years, chose McGill his guardian.

(88) Neal McCleaster—mark recorded.

March 16, 1758.

(89) Probate of will of John Black, decd. Saml. Black, heir-at-law, consents.

(91) John David Wilpert had married Anna Maria, relict of Henry Baughman, decd., and is appd. admr.

(92) Daniel Drady, a garnishee.

(92) Last will of Adam Breckinridge is proved by John McNulty, one of the witnesses, which is ordered to be certified.

(94) Robert Patterson, qualified Ensign of Militia.

March 18, 1758.

(107) James Alexander, qualified Lieut. of Militia.

March 20, 1758.

(114) James Lewis, removed out of the Colony.

(115) Catharine Hickey, removed out of the Colony.

(124) Robert Donald vs. Israel Christian, admr. John Smith. John Smith having returned from his captivity, it is ordered that the administration of his estate granted the defendant is revoked.

(126) William Lusk—mark recorded.

(139) Henry Churchill—Attorney.

(141) James Hughes, ordinary license. Joseph Bell, ordinary license.

(141) From the recommendation of Ro. McClenachan and David Stuart to be added to Justices, Wm. Preston and Patrick Martin dissented, because they had been turned out of the Commission.

(142) Ro. McClenachan agreed to release to the Co. his right in the lands on which the Co. Ho. is built. John Harvie appointed to prepare the deeds.

(142) Adjourned until tomorrow.

April 14, 1758.

(142) Called Court on Hugh McNamara, charged with being aiding and assisting the Shawnee Indians in alliance with the French Nation for and

endeavoring to mislead the Cherokee Indians, his Majesty's friends and allies—to be tried at Court of Oyer and Terminer in June next, to be carried to Williamsburg.

(143) Court of Claims—propositions and grievances: Saml. Norwood, claim for ranging and provisions expended in his Company. John Bowyer's claim for provisions delivered to John Woods, a Captain of a Company of Rangers. Andrew Hays, for ranging and provisions for his Company. Andrew Hays, for provisions to John Woods, as above. David Stuart, for ranging and provisions for his Company. Joseph Bell, for dieting soldiers. John Williams, for ranging.

(144) Robert Campbell, for dieting Capt. Wood's soldiers and for a horse impressed. William Christian, for ranging and provisions for his Company. John Brown, for guarding provisions to Dickenson's Fort when attacked by the enemy Indians and for provisions on their march. Saml. Wilson, for provisions delivered to John and William Woods, Captains of Rangers. James Bell, for going express to the Commanding Officer of Albemarle by order of Major John Brown of this County. Ephraim Love, for ranging and provisions expended in his Company. Abraham Smith, the same. James Clark, for provisions to John Wood, a Militia Captain. Domnick Barret, for ranging. Wm. Edmiston, for ranging. John Cunningham, for use of a horse impressed. James Hughes produced a claim for service done the country, to which he made oath and ordered to be certified. John Robinson, for provisions delivered to David Lewis, Captain of the Militia. George Robinson, for ranging and provisions expended in his Company. James Cull, for ranging. Elizabeth Preston, for horse impressed.

MAY 17, 1758.

(146) Edward Breedin, indentured servant of Wm. Anderson, agrees to serve William twelve months longer in consideration of William's supporting Edward's daughter, Mary Breedin. James Bell, aged 17, orphan of James Bell, decd., chose John Moore his guardian. Robert Frazier's mark recorded. Mary Ann Bell, aged 14, orphan of James Bell, chose Rachel Bell guardian.

(147) James Crockett, aged 17, orphan of Robert Crockett, chose Thomas Thompson guardian. Saml. Craig appointed guardian of Jane Bell, infant orphan of James Bell. Lettice Campbell, aged 14, orphan of Gilbert Campbell, chose George Campbell her guardian. Wm. McFeaters appointed guardian to Andrew Crockett, orphan of Robert Crockett.

MAY 18, 1758.

(148) Erwin Patterson, removed out of this County. James Hughes, special bail.

(149) Robert Gay, removed out of the Colony.

(151) Robert Gay and wife, removed out of the Colony.

(157) Robert Breckinridge took the usual oaths which is ordered to be certified.

(158) James Hughes, appraiser of John Hutcheson's estate. John McFeaters appointed guardian of Alexr. Crockett, infant orphan of Robert

Crockett. Eleanor Sharp, servant of George Anderson, petitions for freedom dues.

MAY 19, 1758.

(160) Ephraim Vanse, removed out of the Colony.

(162) Wm. Hutcheson, removed out of the Colony. Daniel Ramey, suit abates by death.

(168) Robert Hook, qualified Captain of Militia.

MAY 20, 1758.

(174) Thomas Davis, removed out of the Colony.

(175) Richard Dunn, removed out of the Colony.

(177) John Brown, servant of David Long. Matthew Patton appointed guardian of Hannah House, infant orphan of Henry House, decd.

AUGUST 16, 1758.

(179) Margaret Reaburn, widow and admx. of her decd. husband, has since married with Robert McMahon, and she is summoned to show cause why her children shall not be bound out. Conrod, aged 12, last June; Savina, aged 8; Katrina, aged 6, orphans of Conrod Kensley, to be bound. John and Elizabeth Price, orphans of Wm. Price, to be bound out. Philip Williams, orphan of Henry Williams, to be bound to Augustine Price. Wm. Wilson summoned for not providing for his daughter, Margaret, in a Christianlike manner, and she to be bound. Sarah Bird, orphan of John Bird, decd., aged fifteen, chose John Dean her guardian.

(180) Charles Tarrell, orphan of John Tarrell, to be bound out. Catharine Goodman qualifies admx. of her decd. husband, Michael ('Trise?). Jacob Harmon took the oaths and naturalized.

AUGUST 17, 1758.

(181) Barbara Wingard summoned to admr. on her decd. husband's estate.

(182) Catharine Brook, servant of Wm. Brown, complains of inhuman treatment by her master, which is found by the Court, and he bound to the peace.

(183) Joshua Canterall, servant of John McMahon.

AUGUST 18, 1758.

(184) John Earley and two negroes added to tithables. John White, with his son, and negro, added to tithables.

AUGUST 19, 1758.

(196) George Dair, removed out of the County.

Page

(198) John Ramsey intermarried with Margaret Crockett, mother of Alexr. and John Crockett. Caleb Harmon complains that he was bound by his guardian, Walter Davis, to Robert Reed, contrary to law; indenture set aside and Caleb chose John Bowyer his guardian. John Fitzwater, a witness from Culpeper.

(199) Ann, widow and admx. of James Montgomerie, has removed out of the County.

(200) William Erwin, suit abates by death of. Alexr. Crawford and one other, David Stuart, Wm. Hodge, Jacob Van Leers, John Henderson, with three others, added to tithables. Alexr. McKenny added to tithables.

(203) John Bowyer disturbed the Court while sitting by playing at fives. Fined 5 shillings.

(204) Patrick Hayes petitions for freedom dues against his late master, Thomas Paxton. And, on motion of Patrick Hayes, Robert Cunningham to be summoned to show cause why he has not paid his wife, Eleanor Hayes, her freedom dues.

AUGUST 21, 1758.

(205) John Fletcher—his death abates suit.

(206) Silas Hart—qualified Justice.

(207) Robert McClenachan refuses to pay over certain moneys due the County—ordered that he be prosecuted in General Court.

NOVEMBER 15, 1758.

(208) James Wilson qualifies admr. of Josiah Wilson, decd., as brother and heir-at-law.

NOVEMBER 16, 1758.

(211) Israel Christian qualifies admr. of Joseph Bell, Margaret, the widow, having refused. James Hughes, appraiser of Joseph Bell.

(211) Wolrick Conrad qualified admr. of Hance Conrad, being brother and heir-at-law.

(212) Dal. Smith qualifies admr. of Henry Lawrence, decd. (formerly granted to Jacob Sivers, now decd), it appearing to the Court that Windle Sivers, heir-at-law, refused to take burden of goods not administered. Rosanna Ralston and her husband, Wm. Ralston, being persons of ill-fame—bound to peace.

(213) Orphans of Joseph Love, decd., to be bound by Church Wardens.

NOVEMBER 17, 1758.

(213) Wm. Russell—his death abates suit.

(219) Appraisers appointed for the estate of Moses Moore, decd., in Green Brier. Jacob Halderman removed out of Colony.

(222) John Buchanan qualified Lieut. of the County.

(223) John Smith qualified Colonel of Militia. Wm. Preston qualified Major of Militia.

Page

(228) Joseph Bell—suit abates by his death.

(233) James Lockhart, Robert Breckinridge, Abraham Smith, and James Alexander, qualified Captains of Militia. Sampson Archer, qualified Lieut. of Militia.

NOVEMBER 22, 1758.

(234) Called Court for examination of John Thompson on suspicion of killing James McKee. Not guilty.

MARCH 21, 1759.

(235) Wm. McGee summoned to pay freedom dues to his late servant, Frederick Frits.

(236) Same as to Janet Frits, wife of Frederick. Andrew Loduskie and others to lay off a road.

(236) Margaret Cancill refuses to qualify as admx. of her husband, Conrad Cancill, which is so inconsiderable that the Sheriff is ordered to sell it.

(237) Abraham Bletcher—death abates suit.

(240) William Farrell, orphan of John Farrell, to be bound out.

(241) Andrew Muldrough's will to lie for further proof.

(241) Barbara Ferrell—same as 240, *supra*.

MARCH 22, 1759.

(242) Elizabeth Contz, late Elizabeth Armentrout, summoned to give counter security as admx. of her husband's estate.

(244) Andrew Muldrough—his death abates suit.

MARCH 23, 1759.

(247) John Hutcheson ⎫
       vs.   ⎬ Dismissed—having been served on a muster day
   Patton's Exrs. ⎭

(247) Michael Warren, Ephraim Love and Alexr. Thompson, qualified Captains of Militia. Abraham Bird, qualified Ensign of Militia.

APRIL 14, 1759.

(256) Called Court on Mary Elliott for larceny. James Hughes a witness.

MAY 16, 1759.

(257) Nathan McClure exempted from levy.

(258) Robert Finla appointed Constable, vice James Hughes.

(259) Orphans of George Buffenberry, decd., to be bound out.

(260) Adam Hider—a witness from Hampshire.

MAY 17, 1759.

(264) Wm. Campbell's will partially proved.

Page

(270) Caleb Harmon—his death abates suit.

(276) Joseph Bell's estate granted to Wm. Wilson, who informed the Court that he had bound to him Joseph Bell, a mulatto natural son of Joseph begot upon a white woman, and he had no other relations in this Colony.

(277) George Woolridge—a witness.

(278) James Hughes appraiser of John Cain's estate.

(278) Wm. Christian qualified Captain of Militia.

MAY 19, 1759.

(280) James Hughes—Ordinary license.

(286) Gilbert Christian, qualified Ensign. James Robinson, qualified Ensign.

AUGUST 15, 1759.

(287) Wm. Buchanan qualifies on estate of James Buchanan, the heir-at-law having refused. John Potts, appraiser of Robert Clark.

(289) Richard and Mary Sorrel, parents of Mary Sorrel, who is bound to Ro. Cunningham, complain of his treatment of her, and she is released from indenture. Thomas Drady, son of Daniel Drady and Elizabeth Drady, to be bound out; Daniel has left the Colony.

AUGUST 16, 1759.

(290) Saml. McDowell, qualified Captain of Militia. James McDowell, qualified Lieut. of Militia. John Lyle, qualified Ensign of Militia.

(290) Archibald Stuart, with his son; Robert Cunningham, Patrick Mc-Callom, with his son, and Daniel Kidd, added to tithables.

(290) John Poage and Saml. Henderson qualify admrs. of Elizabeth Robinson, decd., Mathew Robinson, the heir-at-law, refusing.

(291) Francis Kirkley, qualified Captain of Company of Foot.

(292) Martha Borden, aged fourteen, orphan of Benj. Borden, chose John Bowyer her guardian. John White, with three others, added to tithables. Saml. McMurty, aged fifteen, orphan of Alexr. McMurty, chose Mathew Lyle, guardian. George and Wm. Hutcheson added to tithables.

AUGUST 17, 1759.

(295) John Galespy, son of Thomas Galespy, added to tithables.

(297) Wm. Preston, qualified Lt. Col. of the County. Thos. Stewart, with two others, added to tithables. John Jacob Fough (?) added to tithables. Ducking stool ordered.

AUGUST 18, 1759.

(298) George Bigham removed out of the Colony.

(304) James Hutcheson and James Hughes, added to tithables.

(307) Daniel Smith, qualified Captain of Foot.

Page

(309) Hugh Ross, removed out of the Colony.

(312) Audley Hamilton and James Hughes, qualified Lieutenants.

OCTOBER 24, 1759.

(312) Called Court on William Williams for murder of Terrence Mc-Guire. Acquitted.

NOVEMBER 2, 1759.

(312) Court of Claims, &c.

(312) Lieutenant John Hopkins, for ranging. William Christian, for ranging and provisions for his Company. James Bell, for a horse impressed. John Henderson, for ranging. Saml. McDowell, for ranging.

(313) Daniel Higins, for going express by order of Col. Smith to Captain Lockhart.

NOVEMBER 21, 1759.

(314) Ro. McClenachan, with three others, added to tithables.

(315) Joseph Gray, orphan of John Gray, chose Saml. Gray his guardian.

(316) Henry Cay, mark recorded. Robert Conerley, exempted from levy. Wm. Preston, qualified Sheriff, Coroner and Escheator.

(318) Isabella Hall (now wife of Robert Hall), qualified admx. of her late husband, Robert Ramsey.

(318) Benj. Gray, orphan of John Gray, aged 14, chose William Gray his guardian.

(319) Sarah, relict of James Armstrong, summoned to show cause against James's nuncupative will. John Spear and Robert Stuart, added to tithables. David Moore and George Moffett, qualified Captains of Militia. Wm. Canady, qualified Lieut. of Militia. Thomas Gardner and James Cowder, qualified Ensigns of Militia.

NOVEMBER 22, 1759.

(319) Michael Hogshead took the oaths.

(320) Administration of John Gilmore was moved for by James Gilmore, eldest son, and also by Thomas Gilmore, the younger son—granted to Thomas. Jacob Clements, witness to will of Wm. Campbell, is dead. Jane Scott, aged 16, chose Danl. Smith guardian.

(321) John Lowry—suit abates by his death.

NOVEMBER 23, 1759.

(326) Mathew Peggs has removed out of the County.

(334) George Skillern and William Skillern, added to tithables.

(335) Abraham Smith, qualified Major of Militia. Wm. Craven, qualified Ensign. John Smith qualifies admr. of Benj. Davis, Decd. Elithorn Davis, his eldest brother, having refused to take the admn. John Smith took the usual oaths.

(336) Jesse Saunders, John Cobb and Edward James, witnesses in this County—their depositions to be taken. John Johnson, having proved by James Hughes that Robert Rogers bit a piece out of his ear in a difficulty—certified.

MARCH 19, 1760.

(346) Elizabeth Calwell acknowledges satisfaction of freedom dues from her master, John Steel. David Cloyd, appointed guardian of Mary, infant orphan of John Cloyd. James Henderson qualified Ensign. John Cloyd, orphan of John Cloyd, chose David Cloyd his guardian.

(347) John Bandy, servant of Sampson Mathews. William Moffett, orphan of John Moffett, chose George Moffett his guardian. Peter Hog, get certificate of good character for practicing law.

MAY 20, 1760.

(347) Peter Hog admitted to practice law.

(348) Mary Gay, widow of John Gay, renounces the will, and agrees to maintain and educate her child, Henry, without making charge for the same.

(351) William Speers, orphan, 12 years old, to be bound.

(355) Hugh Thompson has lost his reason, and Bryce Russell and Andrew Leeper are appointed to take care of his estate. John Maxwell, qualified Captain of Militia.

(356) —— Dillon (attacked by Stevenson, Beard, Gilbert, and Harrison) has run away.

MAY 22, 1760.

(361) George Puffenbier, orphan of George Puffenbier, to be bound out.

(362) Charles Stewart, very aged, freed from levy. James Rogers—death abates suit.

MAY 23, 1760.

(366) Thomas Thompson—his death abates suit.

MAY 24, 1760.

(377) Thomas Waters—his death abates suit.

(380) William Long—his death abates suit.

JUNE 11, 1760.

(389) Called Court on Wm. Smith—larceny—acquitted.

JUNE 19, 1760.

(389) Called Court on Andrew Little—larceny—acquitted.

AUGUST 19, 1760.

(390) James Hughes, appraiser of Saml. Wilson.

Page
(391) Christian Galley's will not allowed to go to record because of his insanity.

August 20, 1760.

(392) Henry Brown's wife, Alice, in Bedford, to be privately examined as to dower in land conveyed by Henry to Thos. Walker.

(392) Joseph Mays ⎤
       vs.   ⎬ Dedimus issue to Cumberland County, Pa., to
John Ramsey ⎦ take deposition of John Gregg.

(392) James Lockhart pleaded his advanced age and infirmities against qualifying Justice.

(393) William Drady, aged five, orphan of Daniel Drady, to be bound out. Barbara, aged three, daughted of Alvanus Bowyer, to be bound out—he is not able to support and educate her. Barbara Pence, aged twelve, orphan of Jacob Pence, to be bound out. John Pence, aged thirteen, same as above.

(394) Admn. of estate of George Mouse taken from Michael Mallard and granted to Fred. Mouse, brother and next of kin to George.

(395) John Patrick, qualified Lieut. of Militia.

August 21, 1760.

(396) Orphans of Patrick Fitzpatrick to be bound out.

(397) Commission to issue for private examination of Jean, wife of Thomas Lewis. Thomas to Andrew Lewis. Hugh Thompson, very aged and infirm, exempted from levy.

August 22, 1760.

(402) Patrick Barnard and wife give bond that their children do not become burdensome to the parish.

(406) Peter Vaneman, Paul Shaver, Philip Harper, and Honecle Huffman, added to tithables.

August 23, 1760.

(409) John King—his death abates suit.

(421) John Flood's admrs. summoned to render an account.

(423) George Welsh, very aged and infirm, exempted from levy.

(426) Robert Lusk—witness from Louisa.

November 19, 1760.

(429) John Hughes—six old wolves heads assigned him.

(431) Andrew Greer—Ordinary license, with James Hughes surety.

(432) John Bags, Thomas Bags, Jacob Trumbeau, Jacob Bear, Isaac Brackfield, Conrad Lamb, John Richards, Jacob Richards, Thomas West, Daniel Cain, Martin Whitsell, Uriah Humble with one, Martin Humble, and Jacob Caplinger, added to tithables.

(433) John Lankford, aged two, son of Thomas Lankford, who is unable to support him—be bound out.

Page

(434) Conrad Custard, aged eighteen, orphan of Arnold Custard, chose Abraham Bird guardian.

(434) Orphans of Patrick Fitzpatrick to be bound out.

(436) Elijah McClenachan, qualified Lieut. of Militia. Commission for privy examination of Elianer, wife of Erwin Patterson. Patterson to Israel Christian.

NOVEMBER 21, 1760.

(439) Andrew Bird, with two others, and William Logan, Teterick Counts and John Counts, added to tithables.

NOVEMBER 22, 1760.

(448) Daniel Looney—death abates suit.

(451) George Parker removed out of the County.

(454) Benjamin Morgan added to tithables.

(455) John Mathews acquits his servant man, Daniel Goodwin, of further service—for good service.

(456) Motion of Mary Gay, relict of John Gay. Henry Gay, executor of John, to be summoned to settle accounts.

NOVEMBER 24, 1760.

(458) Sheriff instructed to sell, and Israel Christian and Felix Gilbert to convey, lots unsold in the land conveyed by Beverley.

(458) Michael Harper and Patrick Barnet, very aged, exempted from levy. Israel Christian took the usual oaths and qualified Captain of Militia.

DECEMBER 11, 1760.

(461) Called Court on Daniel Montgomerie on suspicion of larceny—ten lashes. Same on Julian Mahoney for taking a gold ring from James Hughes—thirty-nine lashes.

FEBRUARY 17, 1761.

(462) Rebecca, wife of Abraham Hite—Commission for private examination. James Carr—hog and cow mark and horse brand recorded. Saml. McCune—same. Saml. Samples—same.

(463) Jane, wife of Wm. Sprowl—Commission for private examination. Catherine Murley, aged 16, orphan of Daniel Murley, chose Uriah Humble guardian.

(462) II. Zachariah Smith's mark recorded. Patrick Fitzpatrick's children not to be bound out, as formerly ordered, but to remain with their father-in-law, William Glasgow, he giving security to the Church Wardens.

FEBRUARY 18, 1761.

(463) II. Commission for private examination of Agnes, wife of John Ward.

Page

(472) Robert Shanklin, qualified Captain of Militia. John Davis, qualified Lieutenant of Militia. Thomas Gardner appointed guardian of Mary Gardner, orphan of Thomas Gardner. William Graham, decd., his son, David Graham, chose William Man his guardian.

(473) James Wilson, a witness. Dedimus to take his deposition in Lancaster County, Pa.

(475) Called Court on Michael Kelly for larceny—taking a horse without a press warrant—twenty-five lashes.

FEBRUARY 20, 1761.

(475) Surveyor to have a book to record his surveys in.

(479) James Looby—juryman.

FEBRUARY 21, 1761.

(480) John, James and John Fowler—jurymen.

(483) Silas Hart—his death abates suit.

FEBRUARY 23, 1761.

(489) Patrick Davis—removed out of this Country.

(490) Johnston Hill—his death abates suit.

(493) Two eldest daughters of Barbara Anderson be bound out—eldest to Agnes Preston, the other to Mary Preston.

(497) James Hughes—a witness.

APRIL 27, 1761.

(499) Called Court on Edward McGarry for forgery. He is sick and the Court adjourns until tomorrow to see if Edward cannot be brought.

AUGUSTA COUNTY COURT RECORDS.

ORDER BOOK No. VII.

MAY 19, 1761.

(1) New Commission of Justices.

(3) Mary McClune, widow of Nathaniel, qualifies admx. c. t. a.

(3) Agnes Buchanan qualifies admx. of her late husband, James McFarron, decd., now wife of Archibald Buchanan.

(4) Commission ordered to privily examine Martha Givens, wife of Saml. Givens, as to deed to Saml. Bell.

(5) James Hughes (with James Lockhart, security), ordinary license.

(5) Johnston Hill's will presented, but Court, being satisfied he was *non compos,* it is set aside.

(6) Mary Brown qualifies admx. of her decd. husband, William Brown. John Graham fined for calling Israel Christian a rogue, a cheat and a rascal. Josiah Davidson, orphan of Danl. Davidson, aged 16 years, chose John Harrison his guardian.

MAY 20, 1761.

(9) Lilley Bowen qualifies admx. of Moses Bowen. Maundling and Philipina Kinsley to be bound out. Rebecca Roberts, a mulatto, given her freedom.

(10) Wm. Hamilton, reason of great age and infirmity, exempted from County levy.

(10) Nathan Abbott and Andrew Knight, witnesses from Hanover.

(14) Hugh Green, reason great age and infirmity, exempted from levy.

(15) Benj. Harrison qualified admr. of Gideon Harrison.

(16) Saml. McDowell's mark recorded. Saml. McClure, witness from Louisa.

MAY 21, 1761.

(16) Saml. McDowell and Richd. Woods appointed guardians to Samuel, Arthur, Elizabeth, Esther and Charles, orphans of Charles Woods, decd.

(17) Commission ordered for privy examination of Elizabeth, wife of John Drapier.

(18) William Hobleman appointed Constable, Long's saw mill to Andrew Scot's.

(19) Gowen West, servant of George Moffett.

(20) James Pollock, witness. Absalam Bilbo, witness from Culpeper.

(21) John McDonald bound to the peace towards John Pickens.

MAY 22, 1761.

(30) Neomi Hill qualifies admx. of Johnston Hill.

(31) Widow of John Colley summoned to show why she does not provide for her children in a Christianlike manner.

(31) Commission ordered to take deposition of Sampson Archer, about to remove out of the Colony.

(31) Luke Bowyer, aged 16, orphan of Michael Bowyer, chose John Bowyer his guardian.

MAY 23, 1761.

(31) Neilly vs. Erwin Patterson—abates by death of defendant.

(33) Givens vs. Holt Richardson—defendant being removed out of County—dismissed.

(36) Erwin Patterson vs. Mathew Emack—plaintiff having died since last Court.

(47) John Cunningham to his son, Walter—deed acknowledged.

(47) Commission for privy examination of Agatha, wife of John Madison. Commission for privy examination of Alice, wife of Henry Brown, in deed to Thos. Walker—report recorded.

(48) Rating of liquors, diet and lodging.

Page

(49) Examination of Edward McGarry, on suspicion of felony. Principal begged the Court to consider his unhappy circumstances, and prayed the Court that he receive his punishment immediately without further trial. Given his choice of standing in the pillory for one-quarter hour or be removed to Williamsburg for trial—chose the former.

June 17, 1761.

(49) Called Court for examination of Robt. McGarry, on suspicion of his breaking the jail and setting at large Edward McGarry and other prisoners. Acquitted.

August 18, 1761.

(50) Robert Armstrong, reason great age and infirmity, exempted from County levy.

(51) James McClure's will proved. Wm. Beard and Wm. McClure, two of the witnesses, are dead, and John McClure, eldest son and heir of decd., appeared and said he had no objection to proving the will, it is recorded. Wm. McClure, one of the executors named, is also dead, and Wm. Givens, the other executor, lives in South Carolina. Admn. is granted to James McClure, son of decd.

(52) John McAdoe and Neill McNeill—appraisers. Samuel, son of Joseph Rutherford, exempted from County levy.

(53) Joseph White exempted from payment of County levy.

(52²) (Two pages, numbered 52 and 53.)

Thomas Meek appointed guardian of Wm. Meek, orphan of John Meek.

(53²) John McFarron qualified admr. of his son, John, Jr.

Frederick Easter appointed guardian of Daniel and Catherine Mouse (?)—Mouse (y)—infants of Daniel Mouse.

Archd. Buchanan appointed guardian to John McFarron, orphan of James McFarron. In consideration of this appointment Archd. agrees to educate, clothe and bring up at his own expense the orphan, and when of age pay him the estate with lawful interest.

Margaret Gray complains that her husband, James, abuses her, and James is summoned—also Geo. Malcom and Sara summoned as witnesses.

(54) Martha Givens, wife of Saml. Givens, relinquishes dower to Saml. Henderson.

(54) Jane Evans, late Jane Looney, prays for admn. on her husband's estate, heretofore granted to David Looney, and David summoned.

(54) Robert Adair appointed Constable in Staunton, vice Samuel Cloyd.

August 19, 1761.

(55) Thomas Paxton, reason of great age and infirmity, relieved of levy.

Page

(55) Mary Miller, now wife of John Miller, qualifies admx. of her former husband, John Ingles.

(56) Henry Smith and John Malcome, to view ground from Mr. Hart's to the Meeting House on Cook's Creek, for road.

(56) Thomas Walker relinquishes his right to a piece of land lying in Burk's Garden to Patton's executors.

(56) Commission for privy examination of Sarah, wife of James Trimble.

(57) Elizabeth Black qualifies admx. of her deceased husband, Anthony Black. John McAnulty declared bankrupt and discharged. Thomas Jones died possessed of a very small estate—Sheriff ordered to take possession.

(58) John Skean appointed guardian of Elianor Milsap.

(59) Among articles levied on by attachment is a horse running near the Town of Staunton.

(59) David Corlock, reason age and infirmity, to be levy free.

(60) Martha Jackson produced an account of her administration of her late husband, William Claypole's, estate. Ann Bryans, servant of Wm. Baskins.

(61) Gowin West, servant of Geo. Moffett. Robert Hill, orphan of Johnston Hill, 16 yrs. old, chose Danl. Smith guardian. Danl. Harrison appd. and quald. guardian to Jane Claypole, infant orphan of Wm. Claypole.

AUGUST 20, 1761.

(62) John Chambers exempted from County levy.

(62) Fulton vs. Edward McGarry } Rob. Shankland and Rob. McGarry produced bills of sale for horses levied on, which were declared fraudulent.

(62) Margaret Patterson, heir at law of Erwin Patterson.

(64) Mark Mallcome—a juror. Theobald Meigham, a witness from Amherst.

(66) Smith vs. Miller } Judgt. for 12 sh.—but being under £5, suit is dismissed with costs vs. pl.

AUGUST 21, 1761.

(68) John Furnis—witness.

AUGUST 22, 1761.

(71) Archibald Bryce, gent., represents that the store lately kept by him in the Town of Staunton is broken up and the company and partnership is dissolved; proved by oath the accounts on the store book; the store was the property of Coutts & Crosse.

(72) Charles Syms—a witness.

AUGUST 24, 1761.

(81) Edward McGarry returned no inhabitant.

Page

(81) See the many suits vs. Edward.

(84) Robert Harrison vs. McAnulty—abates by Robert's death.

(86) £113, 7, Pennsylvania money = £99, 3, 9, Virginia money.

(90) Adam Stevens returned no inhabitant.

(91) Mary Montgomerie, mother of Elizabeth Robinson, appointed guardian *ad litem* for Elizabeth.

(94) David Edwards vs. Thos. Jones—abates by death of plaintiff.

(96) Thomas Pointer returned no inhabitant. Saml. Gay returned no inhabitant.

(102) Order to summons John Grymes on complaint of Wm. Grymes, orphan of David Grymes, dismissed.

NOVEMBER 17, 1761.

(104) Commission for privy examination of Catherine, wife of John White—deed to Wm. Peoples.

(106) County Levy. To John Porter, wolf; Francis Graham, wolf; John McKamy, wolf; John Hughes, wolf; John Cunningham, jailer.

(106) Commission for privy examination of Mary, wife of Edward Beard.

(106) George Martin added to list of tithables.

(107) Daniel Love represents that he was security for Margaret Johnston, admx. of Arthur Johnston, but she has since married Wm. Gregg—prays counter security.

(107) William Hutcheson, George's son.

NOVEMBER 18, 1761.

(107) John Buchanan qualified Sheriff.

(108) Privy examination of Jane, wife of Wm. Sprowl. Felix Gilbert and Randal Lockhart qualified vestrymen. Thomas Smith, servant of John Graham. Elianer Roberts, servant of Wm. Holdman. Margaret, widow of Francis McCown, rejected the provision for her in his will.

(109) Joseph Wright does not provide for his children and Church Wardens ordered to bind them out.

(110) John and Saml. Moore bound to peace towards John Thompson. James Galespy exempted from levy; reason, age and infirmity.

NOVEMBER 19, 1761.

(111) Meeting House on Cook's Creek.

(112) John Files—attachments of all personal effects.

(115) Valentine Yoacum, witness from Bedford.

(115) Commission for examination of Jane, wife of James Beard.

(115) Thomas Gilmore ⎱
        vs.   ⎰
  George Wilson

Agreed case submitted, viz: During the late war the Indians came to the plantation where plaintiff lived, and after killing his father and mother, robbed them and plaintiff of almost everything they had, and amongst other things, the horse in dispute. Defendant and several

93

others pursued the Indians several days and retook great part of the things belonging to the plaintiff. The inhabitants of Car's Creek, the plaintiff not one of them, offered to any persons that would go after the Indians and redeem the prisoners they should have all plunder belonging to them.

(116) Joseph Jenkins—witness.

(118) Robert Poage qualified Captain of Militia.

NOVEMBER 20, 1761.

(118) James Holles, juryman. George Woolridge, juryman. Lazarus Inmace, juryman.

(119) Wm. Griffith exempted from County levy.

(124) Craven Taylor, an infant, to be bound to John Dickinson.

(125) Dated 20th, but probably 21st, as 20th is on page 118.

(129) Elizabeth Waters vs. James Littlepage—abates by plaintiff's marriage.

(133) John McMahon and Richd. Stockdon, bail for Rob. McMahon.

(140) James McKeachey vs. John Mason, eldest son and heir-at-law of John Mason—abates by death of defendant.

(141) Cornelius Cain returned no inhabitant.

(145) Jacob Peters admitted defendant in ejectment. Certificate of freedom of Edward Tarr.

(146) Sarah Newman, a servant woman of Sampson and George Mathews, came into Court and agreed to serve her masters three years after her present time by indenture is expired on their consenting to her marrying Hugh Conner, but it is further agreed that in case she should not have issue that her said masters are to pay her the sum of £5 per annum, deducting only her clothes.

(147) Jane Barren, a servant woman of Andrew Smith.

DECEMBER 12, 1761.

(150) Called Court for examination of Thomas Murray, charged with the felonious killing of James Boreland. Committed for trial at General Court.

FEBRUARY 16, 1752.

(151) Called Court for examination of Thomas Story, charged with receiving stolen goods, property of John Givens.

(152) Committed for trial at Williamsburg.

(153) Same as to Julian McMahon, for stealing—convicted of stealing some thread lace from Sarah Stewart; value, 10 pence, and given 39 lashes.

(153) Same as to Bridget Lee for stealing—acquitted.

FEBRUARY 17, 1762.

(154) Saml. *Mousey*, witness to a deed.

(155) Joseph Lion exempted from County levy.

(155) Catherine Brown to be bound to John Kerr.

Page

(156) Rob. Armstrong is appointed guardian of Lydia, James and Jane Armstrong, orphans of James Armstrong. William Wilson, orphan of John Wilson, chose Roger Keys his guardian. Church Wardens to bind out John and Christian Stiffey, Walter, James and Francis Dunn. Children of Philip Hoofman to be bound out. Commission for examination of Rachel, wife of Andrew Kerr. John Stuart, orphan of James Stuart, to be bound out.

(157) Ordered that Michael O'Hara, aged 12, September 11th last, be bound to Alexander Millroy. Jane Lettimore, servant of Alexr. Stewart. John Stuart, orphan of James Stuart, aged 14, chose Henry Murray his guardian. James Stuart, aged 18, orphan of James Stuart, chose John Hamilton his guardian. Ralph Stuart, aged 15, orphan of James Stuart, chose Robt. Stuart his guardian. Ordered that the following orphans be bound: William Meek to William Warwick, Mary Meek to Andrew Settleton, Martha Meek to James Walker, James Meek to William Wilson, Jane Meek to Moses Moore.

FEBRUARY 18, 1762.

(158) Commission for examination of Elizabeth, wife of Wm. Lusk.

(159) Moore vs. Geo. Anderson } John Anderson, a garnishee, declares he has one *clock* belonging to defendant.

(159) Orphans of Geo. Shillinger to be bound.

(161) Lawrence Huntsman, a garnishee.

(162) Solomon Turpin to view a road.

FEBRUARY 19, 1762.

(163) James Bane's negro *Coco* adjudged 11 years.

(164) John Lewis, gent., vs. Margaret Bell—abates by death of plaintiff.

(164) Will of Hugh Thompson proved by one witness—lies over for further proof.

(165) Eleanor Morgan, servant of John Bowen, arrived in this Colony 3d June last.

FEBRUARY 20, 1762.

(166) Philip Fagan, a witness.

(166) Thos. Lewis obtained certificate for 3,393 lbs. hemp.

(167) Joseph Maynard—a witness.

FEBRUARY 22, 1762.

(168) Called Court on Andrew Little, charged with stealing—guilty and 39 lashes.

(169) Francis Gernor, a juryman.

(170) Wm. Lapsley vs. Wm. Johnston—abates by death of plaintiff.

(170) Francis Gardner, juryman—see page 169, *supra*.

FEBRUARY 23, 1762.

(171) Minute says 1761, but must be 1762.

Page

(172) Suit abates by death of James Leister.

(172) David Frames vs. Joseph Hannah—Set for hearing on bill and answer, and parties allowed to examine witnesses on the trial.

(173) James Mitchell vs. James Lockhart and Sampson Mathews—Agreed case submitted, viz: Joseph Love made power of attorney to his wife Margaret, 22 Dec., 1752. Margaret executed mortgage to plaintiff, 1753, of a slave. The debt was paid, except £15, 10. Defendants seized the slave upon attachment, but he made his escape. Plaintiff had seized the slave to satisfy the £15, 10. Slave died in hands of James and Sampson.

(176) James Burnsides vs. James and John Jackson—John Jordan security.

(181) Wm. Lapsley vs. Wm. Johnston—Abates by death of defendant. See page 170, *supra*.

(183) Nicholas, etc. vs. Jacob and Adam Pence—Catherine Pence, mother of defendant, Adam, appointed guardian *ad litem*.

(187) Valentine Butcher—bail.

(188) Davis Colmer, removed out of the County.

(195) Wm. Hadden—a juryman.

(196) Wm. Robinson appointed guardian *ad litem* for Elizabeth Robinson, orphan of John Robinson, at suit of David Robinson.

FEBRUARY 24, 1762.

(198) Wm. Carr, assignee, vs. John Chambers—Defendant having made oath that he is not the person indebted—dismissed.

(204) Thos. Fulton vs. Robt. Buckley—Sheriff has attached 31 wigs, 6 razors, and beds, chairs, etc.

(204) Sampson Mathews declares that he saw Joseph Love bite off the left ear of John Noland—certified.

MARCH 18, 1762.

(204) Called Court, examination of John Bocock, for stealing £75. Committed for trial at General Court.

(205) Same of Ann Williams, for stealing £100. Guilty and same. Same of Edward Kelly—same judgment.

MARCH 19, 1762.

(206) James Carmickle and Adam McCormick, for stealing—acquitted.

(206) Thomas Brown, breaking the store house of Alexr. Boyd. Acquitted.

APRIL 5, 1762.

(207) James Carmickle and Adam McCormick, for stealing. Convicted and sent to General Court.

(207) Thomas Liddle, for stealing—acquitted.

(208) Charles Alsberry, for stealing—acquitted. John Nugent, for stealing—acquitted.

Page
(208) John Hicklin appointed Constable, vice Adam Jordan.
(210) Commission for examination of Hannah, wife of John Miller.
(211) John Herd—appraiser.
(211) Following received certificates for naturalization: Henry Stone, Sebastian Hover, Gabriel Kyle, Henry Peninger, Woolrick Coonrod, Mack Swadley, John Dunkle, Michael Mallow, Michael Props, George Hammer, Nicholas Havenor, Henry Pickle, Ludwick Havener, Frederick Easter.
(213) Peter Tresler. (See Index to Judgments.)
(214) Robt. Breckinridge appointed guardian to Peter Looney, an infant, to prosecute a suit in Chancery against his grandfather, Robert Looney.
(214) Margaret Gragg, late Margaret Johnston, has since married William Gragg.
(214) Saml. Scot, orphan of Saml. Scot—Wm. Pickens, guardian. Commission for Jane, wife of James Thompson.
(215) John Duncan to be bound to John Moore to learn trade of a joiner, and Moore qualifies guardian of Duncan, who is orphan of James Duncan.
(215) David Sayers qualifies guardian of Joseph, orphan of James Duncan. Janet Duncan, same as to James Duncan.
(215) Mary Folley (Tolley ?), servant of James Alexander.

May 19, 1762.

(215) John Hopkins and John Herdman, surveyors of highway, from Ephraim Love's to James Wait's.
(216) Fenix Shalpman appointed Surveyor.
(217) Peter, Elizabeth, Hannah, Barbara, Catherine, orphans of Jacob Rodcap, to be bound to Geo. Hollowback. Moses Maiden to be bound.
(217) Commission for examination of Zurubiah, wife of Gabriel Pickens.
(218) John Bush, a soldier under Capt. John Blagg, arrested for debt.
(218) Neomi Hill vs. Rob. McGarry—Abates by marriage of plaintiff.

May 20, 1762.

(223) Robert Fletcher—witness.
(224) Samuel Ferguson—prays and is allowed to sue *in forma pauperis*.
(224) Patrick Hara, Thos. Brannon, John Hays, soldiers, march into Court with their hats on and insult the Court. Committed to jail during pleasure.
(226) Isabella Lorrimer, a witness; John Lorrimer, a witness; Robt. Belshire, a witness; Robt. Duffell, a witness; Isabella Johnson, a witness.
(226) George Anderson declared insolvent. James Buntin—juror.
(227) Thos. Cooper, servant of Robt. Campbell.
(228) Robert Moseley, witness from Prince William, 140 miles.
(229) Robert Young, aged 18, orphan of Robert Young, chose James Young his guardian.
(229) Road to be viewed from Dove's to Capt. John Dickinson's.

Page

(231) William Smith, servant of Robt. Graham.

(232) John Stewart
vs. } Slander—judgment for plaintiff.
James Crawford

(233) Thomas Moore, Quaker, an arbitrator. £42, 3, 9, Penna. money =
£33, 15.

(234) Road ordered from Graham's Clearing to Catawbo.

(234) Thos. Tosh appointed Constable, vice Uriah Acres.

(234) Road from Jones's Ford to John Scots.

(236) Joseph Ray produced the books of James Leister and swore to the entries and charges which were made by himself.

MAY 24, 1762.

(237) Isaac McDonald, returned no inhabitant.

(238) Daniel Smith, Mathew Patton and Michael Mallow, surviving partners of Robt. Harrison, vs. Wm. Crow.

(241) Esther Brown vs. John Daily—Abates by death of Esther.

(245) John Robinson, Richard Tunstall and James Mills, executors of Wm. Beverley, vs. William and Andrew Hamilton.

(249) On motion of John Dickinson, gent., it is ordered to be certified that he is known and commonly reputed to be the only son and heir of Adam Dickinson, late of this county, deceased.

(251) Simon Robinson petitions that he has been at considerable expense in conveying from Roanoke three prisoners committed by Israel Christian—allowed £1, 10.

(253) Liquors rated. James Young, a juror impanneled, failed to answer when called; fined and suit continued. Alexr. McClenachan, Thos. Crow, Joseph Bell, George Francisco, disturbed the Court by playing at ball, and are fined.

(253) James Ewing qualified Captain of Militia.

MAY 25, 1762.

(255) Neomi Hill vs. Jonathan Douglas—Abates by marriage of plaintiff.

(270) Israel Christian petitions that he bought, in 1756, 6410 lbs. tobacco levied by the Country proportion in Lunenburg for use of this County, and sold it to Horden Burley, but it turned out there was only 3410 lbs. due and Burley lost £30, 4, 2, which Sheriff is ordered to pay.

(270) James Underwood exempted from County levy.

(270) Alexr. Hay returned no inhabitant.

AUGUST 16, 1762.

(281) Called Court on Elizabeth Smith for stealing—39 lashes.

AUGUST 17, 1762.

(282) Malcom Allen, with his son, Hugh, added to tithables.

Page

(282) Martha Givens, wife of Saml. Givens, relinquished dower in 151 acres conveyed to Saml. Henderson.

(283) Indenture of apprenticeship from John Edwards to Wm. Hide— recorded.

(284) Agnes Tosh qualifies admx. of Tasker Tosh, her husband, decd.

(284) Wm. Edmondson notifies the Court that Mary Drumer lately died at his house leaving a very small estate—ordered to be sold and William's debt paid.

AUGUST 18, 1762.

(285) Alexander Love, a garnishee.

(286) Margaret Craven filed account of her administration of estate of her late husband, Wm. Dyer. Robert Looney exempted from County levy.

(286) Andrew Smith's will proved by one witness and ordered to lie for further proof. Henry Peninger qualified administrator.

(287) James Coursay, orphan of Brush Coursay, ordered bound to George Francisco.

(288) Israel Christian
vs.   } George Salling, garnishee.
George Salling

(288) John Henderson complains of his father, George Henderson, setting forth that he uses him ill—George summoned.

(289) Edward Warner, witness to will of Mathew Erwin. William English exempted from County levy. Mary Gregory qualifies admx. of her deceased husband, Naphthalum Gregory. Samuel Steel, with two others, added to tithables. James, Steel, John Steel, John Findley, and John Findley, Jr., added to tithables.

AUGUST 19, 1762.

(291) Commission for examination of Mary, wife of William Johnston.

(291) Alexr. and John Collier, Saml. Lindsay, James Clemons—jurors.

(292) Israel Christian complains that John Bowyer, gent., interrupted and ill-used him in his efforts to suppress gaming—bound over to Grand Jury.

(293) James and Joseph Scot, orphans of John, chose David Scot their guardian. Philip Phagan, Saml. Tencher. Joseph Kenaday abused the Court while sitting and is fined.

(294) Skidmore Mousey, a juror.

(295) Elizabeth Chittam, a witness from Frederick. Will of John Lewis presented and witnesses ordered to be summoned.

AUGUST 20, 1762.

(297) Margaret Farrell, servant of Andrew Greer, complains of ill-usage by her master, but Court orders 25 lashes.

(298) Saml. Easlick, Daniel Mausume, jurors. John Seviar, witness from Frederick. James Deniston, servant of John Christian, gent.

(301) Mary Boughan, servant of George Wilson.

AUGUST 21, 1762.

Page

(302) Davys Colmer, Clerk, vs. Robt. McClenachan—judgment.

(302) Samuel Easlick, Daniel Maupin, James Means—jurors.

(305)   Nicholas Hedrick vs. Jacob and Adam Pence } Decree that Adam convey the land when he becomes 21 years.

(305) Israel Christian vs. Margaret Patterson, only daughter and heir-at-law of Erwin Patterson—Decree for conveyance by Margaret when she becomes 21, or three months after.

(306) Israel Christian released to George Wilson his interest in a bill of sale now on record to him from Robt. Adair.

AUGUST 23, 1762.

(308) Robert Graham returned no inhabitant.

(308)   John McMahon vs. George Anderson } Sheriff returns on the attachment that he could find no estate of defendant.

(310) Beverley's Executors vs. John Gay and Wm. Hamilton and Margaret, his wife, late Margaret Gay, Executor of Wm. Gay, decd.—Agreed.

(311) John Knox returned no inhabitant. Saml. Johnston returned no inhabitant.

(313) Samuel Hutton, security.

(314) James Milligan, returned no inhabitant.

(315) Thomas Lloyd, returned no inhabitant.

(317) Archd. Hopkins, special bail.

(324) Henry Maury, juror.

AUGUST 24, 1762.

(329) Napthalum Gregory vs. Stephen Wilson—Abates by death of plaintiff.

(335) Henry Chapman, returned no inhabitant.

(336) Joseph Donaldson, returned no inhabitant.

(337) On motion of Eleanor, widow of Hugh Thompson, it is ordered that Commissioners lay off and assign her her dower in the said land which James Thompson, the heir-at-law, hath conveyed to Saml. Henderson.

(339) John Stagg, a garnishee.

(340) John Laney returned no inhabitant.

AUGUST 25, 1762.

(341) Archd. Clendenning appointed Constable on the waters of the Greenbrier.

(343) Robert Campbell and James Taylor, returned no inhabitants.

(353) William and Samuel Tencher, witnesses.

Page

(355) Boslen Hover, grand juryman. James Moody, reason great age and infirmity, exempted from levy. John Brooks, deceased, Wm. Wilson qualified administrator.

(356) County levy. To Nathaniel Wiltshire, wolfhead; to Evick Thomas, wolfhead; to Patrick Duffey, guarding the jail.

(357) To George Dunkill, wolfhead; to Wm. Hide, building a jailor's house, £139, 15, or 33,540 lbs. tobacco.

(358) James Gatlive, decd., Robt. Montgomerie qualified administrator. Rebecca, wife of Abraham Hite, release dower in deed to John Wright. John Inzer, reason age and infirmity, exempted from County levy.

NOVEMBER 17, 1762.

(359) Jane, wife of James Thompson, releases dower in deed to Samuel Henderson. John Mason's orphans to be bound out. William Wallace added to tithables. James Wallace added to tithables.

(359) Michael Williams, aged 17, and George Williams, aged 15 years, to be bound to Augustine Price. Thomas Peerie's will produced and order to summon witnesses. Commission for private examination of James Simpson's wife, Jane, in deed to John Handley. John Hunter, with two others, added to tithables.

(361) James McGill, qualified Lieutenant of Militia. James Hook, qualified Ensign of Militia.

(362) Ezekiel Drady, an orphan, to be bound to Wm. Scot.

NOVEMBER 18, 1762.

(363) Egnier Verden, witness to will of John Wright.

(363) Benj. Harrison, Andrew Bird and Abraham Bird took the oaths as Captains of Militia.

(364) Daniel Smith appointed guardian *ad litem* for Mary Harrison, an infant, vs. Andrew Hamilton.

(364) Saml. Harrison vs. Alexr. Herron } Commission to take depositions of Jeremiah Harrison, Senior and Junior.

(364) John Carlile and Mary Carlile are appointed guardians for Ruth and Isabella Clemons, orphans of Jacob Clemons.

(364) John McKem, executor in will of James Gray, summoned to show cause why he has not proved the will.

(365) Margaret Woods vs. Thomas Loyd } Sheriff attached—One bottle rhubarb, 1 paper rhubarb, 14 boxes Lockyer's pills, 3 bottles Daffy's Elixir, some spirits of hartshorn, 2 papers senna, 1 paper black brimstone, 1 gally pot and vial.

(366) John Ramsey vs. John Hamilton } Sheriff attached a wagon.

(388) Michael Waring (Warren), juror.

(389) Michael Bowyer and James McDowell given permission to erect a house 18 feet in length on the lot belonging to the County fronting the street near William Crow's, they agreeing the said house shall belong to the County at the expiration of Rob. McClenachan's lease of the old Court House.

NOVEMBER 19, 1762.

(390) James Lawson, decd.—John Smith appointed administrator.

(390) Bingamon and wife to Thomas Staunton, Sr., deed. Bingamon and wife to Thomas Staunton, Jr., deed.

(391) John Weltshire, Alexr. Sayers and Jacob Castle, to view and report value of improvements by John Staunton on two tracts on New River. Jane, widow of John Erwin, renounced the will.

(392) Thomas Fitzpatrick refused in open Court to take the usual oaths to his Majesty's person and government when tendered to him. Joseph Herndon, decd.—Rob. Kinkade qualified administrator. Wm. McGill, Benj. Kinsey, jurors.

(394) John Goldsmith, Joseph Jenkins, jurors.

(395) James Deniston, servant of John Christian.

NOVEMBER 20, 1762.

(396) William Smith petitions that Rob. Graham, to whom he was bound, has not complied with the tenor of the indenture, and William is discharged from further servitude.

(398) John Carpenter returned no inhabitant.

(401) Richard Doggett and Rhoda, late Rhoda Evans, vs. Abraham Dunklebery—Abates by death of defendant.

(401) Corneliue Bogard returned no inhabitant.

(404) John Slaven—witness.

NOVEMBER 22, 1762.

(406) William Holton vs. John Burk } Abates by death of plaintiff.

(408) Frederick Goile returned no inhabitant.

(410) James Littlepage returned no inhabitant.

(418) Nicholas Mase—defendant.

(435) Thorp and Stumps vs. James Emacks and John Cocks.

(441) John Thompson, Henry Ferguson and Hugh Mills to view the nearest and best way from the Stone House to Bedford Line.

(442) Christian Evick vs. Andrew Full } Defendant returned no inhabitant.

NOVEMBER 23, 1762.

(448) John Poage, gent., took the usual oaths to his Majesty, &c., which were ordered to be certified.

FEBRUARY 15, 1763.

Page

(449) Commission for private examination of Elizabeth, wife of Andrew Fought.

(450) Alexr. Anderson, decd.—Saml. Huston qualified administrator as greatest creditor.

(450) Commission for examination of Christ, wife of Rob. Fletcher.

(450) James Gatliff, decd.—administration heretofore granted to Robt. Montgomerie is revoked and granted to the widow, Martha.

(451) Commission for examination of Jane, wife of Andrew Brown. Commission for examination of Barbara, wife of Adam Reed.

(451) James Warrington to be bound to John Cunningham.

(452) Fredk. Frits, a garnishee. Henry Heath, a garnishee.

(452) Motion William Mann, John Graham, late guardian of David Graham, summoned to account.

(452) James Lapsley, having been committed to jail as a vagrant and idle person, is discharged, no person appearing to make good the complaint.

(452) James David refuses to qualify executor of James Young.

FEBRUARY 16, 1763.

(453) Danl. Lawrence, decd.—John Lawrence qualifies administrator.

(453) Jeremiah Osborn and Charles Wolson prove the will of Anthony Bogard. Adam Rotherback, an appraiser.

(457) Samuel Vernold, appointed viewer. James Gatlive (Gatliff) 's appraisement.

(458) John Bingamon to Thos. Staunton, Jr. Ann Croxan, servant of Mary Greenlee.

(459) James Young's will proved by one witness and lies for further proof.

(460) David McCoumus, witness.

(461) Commission for examination of Agnes, wife of Wm. Wilson.

FEBRUARY 17, 1763.

(462) John Johnson, aged 18, orphan of Arthur Johnson, chose Daniel Smith his guardian.

(462) Margaret Van Pelt qualified admx. of her late decd. husband, Peter Bowman.

(462) John Anderson petitions that Rev. John Craig detains him as a slave, contrary to law. Rev. John is summoned and it is further requested that he allow Anderson to go to Brunswick County to summon his witnesses.

(468) Robert Knox, juror.

(468) Nicholas Hamner, witness from Albemarle.

FEBRUARY 18, 1763.

(477) Andrew Russell, with two tithables, William Palmer, William Martin, Alexr. McDonald, Wm. Thompson, Alexr. Thompson, John Thompson, George Caldwell and his two sons, Wm. Henderson and John Wallace, to work the road from Christian's Creek to Rockfeil Gap.

Page

(477) John Bowyer, gent., having been fined by justices for gaming in a public house, appealed to the Court when he appeared and confessed, and judgment for fine and costs.

(480) George and John Francisco committed for debt.

February 19, 1763.

(482) Sheriff ordered to purchase a pair of iron dogs for the Court House chimney and employ workmen to repair the hearth.

(482) John Bowyer offers 12 sh. 7 pnc. for what over tobacco is levied in the country proportion for this County.—Accepted.

(484) John Dickenson, gent., acknowledged a power of attorney to John Boller, which is ordered to be certified.

(486) Jacob Parsinger and Catharine, late Catharine Pence, vs. Miller, executor of Pence.

(486) Viewers for road from Stone House to James McAfee's, or James McCown's, on Catapo, viz: Edward Garwin and James McCune.

(487) Coutts and Crosse vs. Alexander Anderson } Abates by death of defendant.

See page 501 also.

(495) Thos. Patton appointed Constable. James Ward, goaler.

February 21, 1763.

(497) Archibald Cunningham returned no inhabitant.

(504) Malcomb Campbell vs. Joseph Cravens } Abates by death of defendant.

(504) Robert Lusk vs. James Greenlee } Abates by death of defendant.

AUGUSTA COUNTY COURT RECORDS.

ORDER BOOK No. VIII.

February 21, 1763.

(2) James Ewing vs. John Jones } Israel Christian, Gabriel Jones, Peter Hog, John Madison, John Bowyer and Daniel Smith—special bail.

(3) Thomas Nowell, defendant.

(17) Moses Hamilton's declared estate heretofore ordered to be sold by Sheriff.

(24) John Bowyer makes oath that he was whole and sole legatee under Caleb Harmon's will, but the will was lost—administration granted to John.

Page

(25) Alexr. Dunlop, aged 18, orphan of Alexr. Dunlop, decd., chose John Dunlop his guardian.

APRIL 20, 1763.

(26) Cornelius Ruddle, security for John Skeen, administrator of Ruben Allen, prays counter security—John summoned.

(27) John Ledford to Isaac Taylor—power attorney—James Farlie witness. Wm. Dean and Wm. Blantin—jurors. Commission for privy examination of Margaret, wife of Isaiah Curry. James Catchey (Carthrae).

(28) Rev. John Jones, clerk, witness to prove will of Rob. Armstrong.

(29) James Arbuckle and Thomas Thompson appointed Constables in the Pastures.

(30) James McCatchey—See page 27, *supra*.

(31) James Reaburn complains that William McMullen does not provide clothes nor teach a trade to his apprentice, Henry Reaburn.

(32) Ishmael Abbit—garnishee.

(33) Elizabeth, wife of Thomas Fulton. Thomas Story, garnishee, declares he has the following of Thos. Fulton's: One corner cupboard, one old bed rug and blanket, one pair iron dogs, two tubs and churn. Many attachments vs. Fulton.

APRIL 21, 1763.

(37) Wm. Minter, Adam Dean, Robert McCitrick.

(38) Lancelot Graham and John Clark misbehaved in Courtyard by acting in a riotous manner—bound to good behavior.

(39) Commission for private examination of Elizabeth, wife of Joseph McDonald.

(39) Following deeds partially proved and ordered certified: William Moore to Francis Smith, Thomas Hill to David Miller, Elijah Isaacs to Robt. McGee, Paul Garrison to John Donally.

(39) John Atkins misbehaved in a riotous manner in the Courtyard and bound to good behavior.

(40) John Newbanks—juror.

APRIL 22, 1763.

(41) James Hartgrove—juror.

(42) Private examination of Martha, wife of George Robinson, recorded.

(42) James Crow came into Court and made oath that he, with his wife, Eleanor, and his children, Thomas, Elizabeth and Fanny, came to dwell in this Colony in the year 1762, &c.—50 acres each.

(43) Isaac McDonald—juror.

(45) Teagle Trader appointed Constable, vice Felix Sheltman.

(45) Road ordered from Walker's Place to Warm Springs. Thomas Feemster, surveyor from Walker's to Charles Lewis's.

(45) Inhabitants on Back Creek, in the Calf Pasture, and inhabitants from Hance Harpers downwards in Bull Pasture.

(46) Jerman Backster, Adam Dean.

Page

(46) George Wilson not an inhabitant of this County and therefore released from fine for not serving as juror.

APRIL 23, 1763.

(51) William Grymes, James Neilly and William Robinson to be road overseers from Grymes Clearing to the head of the run above Madison's plantation; John Craig from thence to New River on the lands of John Buchanan, gent., and Alexr. and William Sayers from thence to Fort Chiswell; Wm. Preston is to apportion tithables as far as Fort Lewis, and Wm. Thompson from thence to Fort Chiswell.

APRIL 25, ·1763.

(53) Anderson Poulson, administrator of Remembrance Williams, decd., unadministered by Catherine Williams, decd., late administratrix, &c., vs. Peter Vaneman. Dismissed; agreed.

(54) James Littlepage, returned no inhabitant.

(58) Agnes Clark
   vs. } Abates by marriage of plaintiff.
James Trotter

(59) Oliver Wallace, returned no inhabitant.

(69) Wm. Dean and Mary, late Mary Cooke, only daughter and heiress of Patrick Cooke, vs. Hugh Young.

(82) Francis Liver—special bail.

(85) Francis Mousey—special bail.

(90) John Greenlee appointed guardian of Mary Greenlee, orphan of James Greenlee.

(91) John Sheldon, witness from Winchester.

(91) William Preston's mark recorded.

(91) Called Court on Wm. Jones for "buggery"—convicted and sent to Williamsburg for trial.

APRIL 26, 1763.

(101) William Preston appointed surveyor from Grymes Clearing to Catapo. Stephen Willis—Juror.

(105) Order that Sheriff pay Patrick Ryley for repairs to jail.

JUNE 21, 1763.

(106) Ann Vare acknowledged deed to Richard Shankland. Samuel Sproul exempted from levy—great age and infirmity. Low Todd, a witness from Bedford County.

(107) James Harmon exempted from levy—great age and infirmity.

(107) Martha Miller relinquished dower in land conveyed by her husband, John Miller, to David Stewart.

(107) William Armstrong, eldest son and heir of James Armstrong, decd., qualified administrator c. t. a.

(108) David McCawrins petitions that Silas Hart detains his daughter Margaret—Silas to be summoned.

Page
(108) Joseph Wilson, orphan of George Wilson, aged 12, to be bound to James Laird.

(108) George Bush took the oaths for naturalization.

(109) Margaret Leeper qualified administratrix of her deceased husband, James Leeper. William Beard, greatest creditor, qualifies administrator of John Sheldon.

(113) New Commission—John Chiswell, John Buchanan, John Wilson, Silas Hart, Andrew Lewis, James Lockhart, Richard Woods, Robert Breckinridge, Patrick Martin, Wm. Preston, Alexr. Sayers, John Bowyer, John Dickenson, John Christian, Francis Tyler, Daniel Smith, John Archer, James Buchanan, Archd. Alexander, Israel Christian, Mathew Patton, John Maxwell, John Poage, James Lockridge, Felix Gilbert, Abraham Smith, James Trimble, Charles Lewis, Samuel McDowell, George Moffett, Benj. Hawkins, Francis Kirtley, Andrew Bird—dated 16 April, 1763.

JUNE 22, 1763.

(114) George Helvick, orphan, aged three years and four months, to be bound to Wm. Fleming, gent.

(115) Viewers appointed for a road from South River above Joseph Hanah's over Coles's Ford to Mathew Thompson's.

(117) Will of Malcomb Campbell proved—the executors refuse to act, as also Isabella, the widow, and Elizabeth Campbell qualifies.

(118) Commission for examination of Ann, wife of Samuel Caldwell.

(120) Robt. Rowland, security for Margaret Rentfro, late Margaret Looney, admx. of her deceased husband, asks counter security.

(122) Petition of John Anderson vs. Rev. John Craig, for detaining him as a slave. Deposition of Joel Barker, taken in Brunswick County, shows that Anderson is son of a free white woman and was bound by the Church Wardens of the Parish of Saint Andrews, in Brunswick County, to serve till 21, and he is now of that age. Judgment of the Court that he be released.

JUNE 23, 1763.

(124) Commission for examination of Margaret, wife of James McCown.

(131) Thomas and Robert McCullough, witnesses from Albemarle.

(132) John Campbell committed for abusing Henry Fillbrick and disturbing the Court. Charles Campbell committed for abusing the Court.

(133) George Clark and George Hope—jurors.

JUNE 24, 1763.

(134) Benj. Bennett—juror.

(135) John Maury, James Horner.

(136) Thomas Paxton, millwright—juror.

(138) Richard Williams and Abby vs. Ezekiel Richardson and Mary.

(138) Robert Graham, admr. of Florence Graham, decd., vs. Joseph Vachub—abates by death of plaintiff.

(138) Alexr. Read—juror.

Page
(139) Liquors rated.
(139) John Caldwell ⎫
　　　　vs. 　　　⎬ Alexr. Reed, witness from Amherst.
James Kennedy ⎭
(142) Ephraim Hubbard—juror.

JUNE 25, 1763.

(162) John Crank returned no inhabitant.
(164) Joseph Waughub ⎫
　　　　vs. 　　　　⎬ Abates by death of defendant.
Robert Graham ⎭
(189) Robt. Graham, assignee Timothy Sullivan, vs. Thomas Mann—abates by death of plaintiff.
(211) Complaint of James Reaburn vs. Wm. McMollen, for ill-using his apprentice, Henry Reaburn, is dismissed as frivolous.
(212) Henry Reaburn, aged 16, orphan of Edward Reaburn, chose James Reaburn his guardian.

AUGUST 16, 1763.

(212) Andrew Lewis, qualified Lieut. of the County; Wm. Preston, qualified Colonel of the County; Walter Cunningham, qualified Captain of Militia; Alexr. McClenachan, qualified Captain of Militia; William Crow, qualified Captain of Militia; John McClenachan, Michael Bowyer and David Long, qualified Lieutenants of Militia; James Ward, qualified Ensign of Militia.
(213) John Bowyer, qualified Captain of Militia.
(213) Ann Clendenning qualified admx. of her husband, Archd. Clendenning.

SEPTEMBER 20, 1763.

(213) Called Court for examination of Hugh Beard, charged with feloniously biting the ear of Wm. Farris—not guilty.
(214) Same of Joseph Garrot, on suspicion of felony—not guilty of stealing, but of receiving stolen goods—35 lashes.
(214) Same of Priscilla Hughes for felony—guilty—Grand Jury.
(215) Ann Kinkead qualified admx. of her husband, Burrough Kinkead.
(216) Rebecca Dougherty qualified admx. of husband, Charles Dougherty.
(217) James Wordlaw, as greatest creditor, qualified admr. of Thomas Jones. James and John Gilmore qualify admrs. Thomas Gilmore. Wm. Gilmore qualified admr. of Wm. Culberts.
(217) Wm. McKee qualified Lieutenant of Militia.
(218) Henry Larkin bound to peace towards Andrew Brown. Jacob Cooper, an orphan, to be bound to Saml. Paxton. Power of attorney from Wm. Young to John Madison partially proved and to lie for further proof.

SEPTEMBER 21, 1763.

(219) Saml. McDowell qualifies admr. of John Woods. James McDowell

qualifies Captain of Militia.   Felix Gilbert qualifies admr. of John Murphy.
Felix Gilbert qualifies admr. of John Williams.

(220) Felix Gilbert qualifies admr. of Lawrence Huntsman.

(224) John Ray appointed Constable in lower end of County.   Patrick
Frazier qualified admr. of James Underwood.   George Teater, garnishee.

(227) Complaint of John Lynn, that Silas Hart detains him contrary to
law, continued.

(230) Agnes Bush, an orphan, to be bound out to John Montgomerie.

(230) Sarah Griffith, servant of John Hamilton.

(233) Robt. Curry qualified Ensign of Militia.

(235) Daniel Holdman, a witness from Frederick.   John Heren—a witness.

(237) John Strain, Adam Edgar, jurors.

(238) Saml. Davidson, a witness from Albemarle.

(239) Charles Marlow, an orphan of 11 years and 9 months, the 4th of
this inst., until 21, to Jesse Harrison, he teaching him to read and write according to the condition of a former indenture.

(239) John Greenlee qualified Lieutenant of Militia.

(240) Wm. Edmiston qualified Lieutenant of Militia.   Samuel Edmiston
qualified Ensign of Militia.

SEPTEMBER 23, 1763.

(248) Jane Pickett, a witness.

(249) James Gregory, orphan, aged 16, to be bound out to Saml. Varner.

SEPTEMBER 24, 1763.

(254) George Wilson vs. John Williams.—Abates by death of defendant.

(255) Joseph Kenaday returned no inhabitant.

(269) Nicholas Mildeborger—special bail.

(286) Chas. Julian vs. Alexr. McClenachan.—Abates by death of plaintiff.

(293) Thos. McGregor—juryman.

(296) John Trimble and two others and 597 acres added to tithables.
Walter Trimble and 159 acres added to tithables.

(303) James Kenady vs. Josiah Ridgway.—Deft. returned no inhabitant.

(304) Felix Gilbert vs. John Murphy.—Abates by death of defendant.

(305) Thos. Armstrong and Ann, his wife, late Ann Stewart, admx. of
James Stewart, summoned to render account.

(306) Bowyer and McDowell vs. James Jackson.—Abates by death of
defendant.

SEPTEMBER 26, 1763.

(320) Thomas Bowyer, with his man, John Domnark, added to tithables.

NOVEMBER 9 1763.

(324) Court of Oyer and Terminer for trial of Tom, slave, for murder
of John Harrison by shooting in back.   Confessed; judgt. guilty, and that he
be hanged by the neck on Saturday, 19th inst., and his head be severed

and affixed on a pole on the top of the hill that leads from this Court House to Edward Tarr's. Memo.—Tom valued at £50.

NOVEMBER 15, 1763.

(326) John Robinson exempted from County levy—no cause given.

(327) Robt. Scott, 3 tithables, and 820 acres, added to tithables. Six tithables of Stephen Willis added to tithables. Will of John Harrison, Jr., proved by John Hopkins and lies for further proof.

(327) County Levy. To John Bowyer, for executing negro Tom, £3, 4, 3.

(329) 390 acres of Geo. Hutcheson's land added to tithables.

NOVEMBER 16, 1763.

(329) John Harrison, Jr.'s will proved and recorded.

(330) George Watt added to tithables.

(331) Blakely Brush qualified admr. of his father, Richard Brush.

(332) 320 acres of Thos. Stevenson added to tithables.

(332) William Erwin, son of Jane Erwin, with 241 acres, added to tithables. 550 acres of Patrick Quin—same. 104 acres of John Jameson—same. 300 acres of John Kilpatrick—same. 400 acres of Thos. Kilpatrick—same.

(336) 500 acres of James Green—same. Charles Griffeths exempted from levy.

(337) James Findley qualified admr. of his deceased brother, Robert Findley. Will of John Jackson proved by two witnesses and ordered to be certified.

(342) John Robinson (near Coulton's) exempted from levy.

(342) John Smith, Wm. Grymes, James Nealey and Israel Christian to view the roads that lead from Vance's over the New River on the lands of John Buchanan and likewise by Ingles's Ferry to the lead mines.

(342) Adam Harmon to be bound to peace towards Wm. Thompson.

(342) 451 acres of John Kerr's land added to tithables. 190 acres of Wm. Kerr's land added to tithables. 375 acres of Saml. Hind's land added to tithables. 112 acres of Wm. Mather's land added to tithables.

NOVEMBER 18, 1763.

(353) John Sallow returned, not found in his bailiwick.

(355) John Scott vs. Wm. Wyatt.—Defendant arrested, but made escape.

(356) Philip Rinehart returned not found in his bailiwick.

(372) Thos. Sumpter committed to jail for want of special bail.

(374) 320 acres of John McCoy added to tithables. 200 acres of Moses Hall added to tithables.

(378) Jeremiah Seeley returned not found in my bailiwick.

(379) Margaret Risk qualifies admx. of husband, James Risk.

(380) Michael Woods, witness from Albemarle. Samuel Woods, witness from Albemarle.

(381) George Henderson exempted from levy.

November 19, 1763.

Page

(382) Robert McClenachan ordered to pay the rents in arrear for the old Court House to the Sheriff.

(382) Jeremiah Ponder relinquished dower in land conveyed by her husband, Daniel Ponder, to Joseph Rutherford.

(382) James Huston and Archd. Hamilton qualified Inspectors of Flour.

(383) Brown's Bridge—to be repaired.

December 20, 1763.

(384) Geo. Mathews qualified admr. of Joshua Mathews, Mary, wife of Joshua, having refused.

January 2, 1764.

(384) Called Court on Paul Armstrong, charged with murder of Thomas Hicks—acquitted.

(385) Oyer and Terminer for trial of Fanner, a negro slave of John Harrison, for aiding and abetting Tom in the murder of John—acquitted.

March 20, 1764.

(387) Many certificates of hemp.

(389) Jacob Scott, aged 16, orphan of John Scott, chose John Davis his guardian.

(389) Road petitioned for from John King's Mill, on Naked Creek, to John King's Mill, on Middle River.

(389) Comn. for examination of Rachel, wife of James Arbuckle. Comn. for examination of Martha, wife of James Gilmore.

(390) Saml. Hunter bound to peace towards Wm. Henderson. Wm. Kelly exempted from levy.

(390) Comn. for examination of Elizabeth, wife of Samuel Hays.

(391) Comn. for examination of Jane, wife of Daniel Love.

(391) Charles Campbell qualified Ensign.

(391) Jane Armstrong, widow of James Armstrong, renounced provisions of his will.

(391) Bridge to be built over run near Robt. Poage's.

(392) Christian Godfrey Milliron bound to appear on suspicion of murder of John Mathews—appeared and judgment that tho' the facts are not fully proved, yet the Court have some reasons for suspecting him—bound to next March Court.

March 21, 1764.

(395) Jennett McDonald, admx. of Randall McDonald, to be summoned to render account.

(395) Charles Lynch, as greatest creditor, qualified admr. of Valentine Yocum.

(396) William and John Candler, appraisers of Yocum. Frederick See, as greatest creditor, qualifies admr. of Frederick See. On motion of Henry Stone and Catherine, his wife, admx. of her late husband, Jacob Zorn—by a mistake the inventories of Jacob Zorn and of Henry Horse were drawn together as inventory of Jacob alone. Clerk ordered to alter the minute book and record.

(399) Margaret Rentfro, late Margaret Looney, required to give counter security to Robt. Rowland or deliver up the estate to him.

(399) Mathew Bracking, a Constable.

(400) Commission to value improvements of Geo. Givens on 400 acres on James River.

(400) Patrick Shirkey asks counter security from Elizabeth Campbell, admx. of her father, Malcolm Campbell.

(400) Sarah Wilson, servant woman of John Cockrane.

(400) John Griffeth qualifies admr. of his brother, Morris Griffeth. John Griffeth qualifies admr. of his brother, Benj. Griffeth.

(401) James Trimble appointed guardian for Ann and Lydia Berrisford, orphans of John Berrisford.

MARCH 22, 1764.

(402) Thomas Brannon—juror.

(403) John Dailey vs. Wm. Dinguid.—Abates by death of defendant.

(405) James Keith of County Frederick.

(406) Bryan McDaniel appointed road overseer from Fort William to the Market Road. James Neeley, ditto, from Fort Lewis to the Great Lick.

(408) Will of John Mathews proved—Sampson and George Mathews qualified executors, the other executor being dead.

(410) Commission for examination of Amey, wife of Henry Smith. John Bigham, security for Isabella Hall, admx. of her late husband, Robert Ramsey, prays counter security from Isabella and her husband, Robert Hall. James Wright, orphan of John Wright, decd., to be bound to John Fitzwaters. David Stuart et als., bail for Thos. Fulton in many suits offered to deliver him up, but the Court refused to allow it because there had not been judgment.

(411) Jesse May declared insolvent.

MARCH 23, 1764.

(412) James Lockhart complains that Wm. Foster has abused him in execution of his office.

(412) David Bryon and executors of Erwin Patterson ask counter security from Rhoda Evans, now Rhoda Doggett, admx. of her decd. husband, Daniel Evans. Rhoda and Richard Doggett, her husband, summoned.

(413) Liquors rated.

(417) Peter Scholl, witness from Frederick—45 miles.

(418) Lawrence Mills, convict servant of Jeremiah Ragen.

MARCH 24, 1764.

Page

(427) Thomas Fulton committed for debt.

MARCH 26, 1764.

(436) Wm. Stevenson returned not found in bailiwick.

(447) Andrew Johnston, returned no inhabitant. Wm. Winston, returned no inhabitant.

(456) Robert Jackson vs. Wm. Tutt.—Abates by death of plaintiff.

(466) Samuel McCord, returned no inhabitant.

(475) Conrad Yocum, returned no inhabitant.

(479) Joshua Mathews, &c., vs. James McBride.—Abates by death of plaintiff.

(489) *Cohonggorooto,* a negro slave of Peter Hog, adjudged seven years.

APRIL 24, 1764.

(491) Sarah Birdwell, convicted of receiving stolen good, and 30 lashes

MAY 15, 1764.

(492) Alexr. Painter qualified administrator of Catharine Painter.

JUNE 19, 1764.

(494) Rebecca Gardner qualified administrator of her husband, Thomas Gardner.

(495) Thos. McLamor bound to peace towards Edward Erwin.

(495) Bridge ordered over the Long Meadow where the road crosses it that leads from Francis Alexander's to William Tees's.

(496) John Ramsey chosen guardian by Mary McDonall, aged 16; John McDonall, aged 14, and the Court appoints him guardian for Francis, Hugh, Rebecca, William, Elizabeth and Saml. McDonall, all orphans of John McDonall.

(496) John McCastlin, greatest creditor, qualified administrator of William Fitzjarrell.

(496) Will of Adam Wall proved by one witness (James Calloway) and ordered to lie for further proof. No exr. being named, Apple Wall qualified administrator.

(497) Susanna Hall qualified admx. of husband, James Hall.

(498) John Cants, security for Susanna Armemtrout, late Susanna Power, for admn. of Christian Calley, decd., asks counter security.

(498) Augustine Price and Fredk. Armentrout qualify admrs. of John Calley, formerly granted to and unadministered by Stophel Armentrout.

(498) Alexr. Crawford, security for Thos. Gardner, now decd., for administration of estate of Thos. Gardner, decd., asks counter security, and Rebecca, administratrix of Thomas, summoned.

(499) Commission for examination of Grissell, wife of John Handley.

(499) Wm. Foster bound to peace towards James Lockhart.

(500) John Maxwell refused to swear in as Justice.

JUNE 20, 1764.

(500) Wm. Gray exempted from County levy.

(503) Dennis Getty vs. John Lowry.—Abates by death of defendant.

(503) John Wilson refused to qualify justice.

(506) Conrad Fudge, witness. Michael Earhart, witness from Culpeper. Mary Hinds, aged 3 years and 2 months, bound to Elizabeth Crow.

(507) Conrad Fulsh, juror.

JUNE 21, 1764.

(507) Saml. Thornhill exempted from County levy.

AUGUSTA COUNTY COURT RECORDS.

ORDER BOOK NO. IX.

JUNE 22, 1764.

(3) Thomas Stevenson, returned no inhabitant.

(4) John Burkin, special bail.

(6) Martha Gatlive, returned no inhabitant.

(7) Jacob Carsall, returned no inhabitant.

(7) Peachey R. Gillmore vs. Wm. Frazier.—Abates by death of defend't.

(15) Frederick Shivel, returned no inhabitant.

(24) Philemon Askins, returned no inhabitant. Robert Eastham, Jr., returned no inhabitant.

(27) William Givens vs. Wm. Fitzjerrald.—Abates by death of defendant.

(40) George Pearis, returned no inhabitant.

(43) Daniel McCoy, an orphan, to be bound to John McNeill, gent. Jane and Edward Thompson qualified admrs. of Thos. Thompson. Felix Gilbert qualified admr. of John Lorrimer.

(49) John Melly, returned no inhabitant.

(50) Moses Crofford, returned no inhabitant. John Low, returned no inhabitant.

(52) John Greedy, returned no inhabitant.

(53) John Little exempted from levy.

(54) Susanna Fitzpatrick to be bound to Thomas Poage.

(62) King vs. George Lewis, for driving his wagon on Sabbath day.

June 17, 1764.

Page

(65) John McNeill qualified Colonel of Militia.

(65) Thomas Fulton, declared bankrupt.

July 17, 1764.

(66) Called Court on Priscilla Ladd, for larceny. Prisoner craves corporal punishment and 39 lashes.

August 21, 1764.

(67) Elizabeth Fulton, aged 16, orphan of John Fulton, chose John Young guardian.

(67) Comn. for exn. of Mary, wife of Christopher Thompson.

(67) Elizabeth Wallace qualifies administratrix of husband, Samuel Wallace.

(68) Jacob *Slover's* estate—John Bowen, administrator.

(69) William and Hugh Young, orphans of Robert Young, choose James Young their guardian, and James is appointed guardian of Joseph Young, another of the orphans.

(69) Patrick Lacey, servant of John McClure.

August 22, 1764.

(70) Valentine Coil receives certificate of naturalization.

(70) George Gibson, one other, and 195 acres added to tithables; 196 acres of Isabella Gibson added to tithables.

(70) Commission for examination of Mary Adams, wife of William Adams, in deed William to George Jameson.

(74) James Frazier qualifies administrator of father, Wm. Frazier.

August 23, 1764.

(80) Michael Bowyer bound over for insulting Abraham Smith in execution of his office as Magistrate.

(80) James Baldwin, servant of John McNeill.

(84) Abraham Slover, orphan, to be bound to John Bowen.

(85) Viewers of road from North Branch of James River to Buffelow report in favor of turning it by one Abraham Brown's.

August 24, 1764.

(91) Joseph Lindon—witness. Sarah Bigham, servant of John McNeill. Sarah Cartwright, servant of John McNeill. Sarah Walkley, servant of John McNeill.

(94) Felix Kenon exempted from County levy.

(94) George Mathews appd. guardian of Thomas Renix, infant orphan of Robt. Renix.

(99) Deeds from James McDowell and Frances, and Commission for examination of Frances.

AUGUST 25, 1764.

(118) John Sallord, returned no inhabitant.

(120) One large English-bodied wagon attached.

(139) Nathaniel Lyon, returned not found in bailiwick.

(143) James Johnston, Henry Harmon and Mathew Lindsey, returned no inhabitants.

NOVEMBER 20, 1764.

(155) Dabney Carr qualified Attorney.

(156) Wm. Black qualified administrator of father, Alexr Black.

(157) John McCollom qualified administrator of Saml. Hunter. The King vs. Saml. Hunter, continued, the prosecutor being in his Majesty's service.

(158) Commission for examination of Mary Headley, wife of Thomas Headley, in deed to George Poage—directed to Cumberland Co. No. Co.

(159) County levy. John Raveling, wolfhead; Alrick Hurtsman, wolfhead; Wm. Delwood, wolfhead.

(160) Damis, wife of John Mann, relinquishment of dower.

NOVEMBER 21, 1764.

(161) Jacob Peterson naturalized.

(161) Mary McBride chose Joseph Lapsley guardian.

(162) John Davis and Judith, his wife, admrs. of John Scott—produced an account and recorded.

(162) Joseph Carpenter, guardian of Joseph, James and Jacob Scott, orphans of John Scott, summoned to account.

(162) Wm. Bowyer added to tithables.

(162) Israel Robinson, Peter Bowman and Thomas Beard, exempted from levy.

(163) Andrew Lewis, four tithables, and 1,420 acres added to tithables.

(163) Patrick Lacey, servant of William Snodon, complains that William does not provide him clothes nor employ him as a servant, and William summoned.

(163) Indenture by Church Wardens binding John Cole to James Campbell is assigned to Saml. McMurty.

NOVEMBER 22, 1764.

(169) Thomas Bowyer, added to tithables. Michael Bowyer, servant Tom, and 226 acres, added to tithables. Wm. Henderson, one other, and 765 acres, added to tithables. James Henderson and 450 acres, added to tithables. Nathan Gilliland and 332½ acres, added to tithables. John Buchanan, three others, and 489 acres, added to tithables. Wm. Crow, four others, added to tithables. Moses Williams, George Bigham, James Hugart, Francis Gardner, and John Askin, added to tithables.

Page

(171) Robert Reed ⎫ David Graham, garnishee, says defendant and
        vs. ⎬ he agreed to swap a horse for a watch; that
James Hamilton ⎭ defendant left the watch with him to examine
and appointed a day in Staunton to consummate the agreement, but ran
away before the appointed day came.

(172) Richardson Watson, servant of John Caldwell.

(172) Edward Tarr's old shop, on the road from North Branch of James.

(173) Ordered that the Church Wardens of Augusta Parish bind Michael
Eagin, of the age of nine years in September last, son of Patrick Eagin, to
John Patrick—the father of the said Michael having *run away according to
law.*

(173) George Skillern took the usual oaths to his Majesty's person and
Government subscribed the abjuration oath and test which is, on his motion,
ordered to be certified.

(175) John Andrew—juror.

NOVEMBER 23, 1764.

(202) John Rutherford, returned no inhabitant.

(203) Robert Neeley, returned no inhabitant.

(205) Michael Smith, special bail.

(209) Alexr. McAllister and Hugh Millikan, being some time ago committed to the jail of this County on suspicion of their favoring the design of
the enemy Indians, but nothing appearing against them, it is ordered that
they be discharged.

(209) Cormick McCarkrey, discharged from custody.

(209) Alexr. West, Andrew Fowler, and Charles Clendenning, exempted
from levy.

(210) George Madison took usual oaths, &c.—certified.

(210) Saml. Black and 120 acres, added to tithables. James Henderson
and 590 acres, added to tithables.

(212) Robert McClenachan qualified administrator of James Simpson,
formerly granted to George Wilson.

(213) Alexr. Sayers, gent., having insulted the Court by appearing before
it intoxicated and twice abusing the Court, committed to Sheriff.

NOVEMBER 24, 1764.

(213) Elijah McClenachan exempted from County levy.

(213) David Graham bound over for insulting John Christian in discharge
of his office as magistrate.

(214) Alexr. Sayers, having made proper concessions for abusing the
Court yesterday, released from his recognizance.

(215) Martha Hassell complains of master, Andrew Greer, and he is
summoned.

(215) James Randal, returned not found in bailiwick.

(222) Wm. Fleming took the oaths and test—certified.

(222) Hugh Donaho and one other and 380 acres, added to tithables.

(224) Patrick Ryley and Alice, his wife, late Alice English.

Page

(224) Alexr. Crawford vs. Mathew Harper.—Abates by death of plaintiff.

(227) £84, Penna. money = £84, Va. money.

(230) County levy = 3 shillings.

FEBRUARY 8, 1765.

(230) Called Court on Samuel Woodward and Mary, his wife, for larceny—discharged.

MARCH 19, 1765.

(233) James Cunningham's will proved—Moses Cunningham is the surviving executor.

(234) Esther Boyd, aged 15, orphan of Robert Boyd, chose Archibald Huston her guardian.

(234) John Frazier exempted from County levy.

(234) Francis Gardner appointed guardian to Robert Boyd, orphan of Robert Boyd.

(235) Peter Evans appointed road surveyor from Stone House to Fort Lewis.

(235) Zachariah Smith's son John exempted from levy.

MARCH 20, 1765.

(236) Road from the Duck Ponds to Alexr. Blair's.

(236) Patrick Lacey vs. Wm. Snodon, complaint dismissed.

(237) Michael Corn, a witness from Bedford—80 miles.

(237) Joseph King exempted from levy.

(238) Christopher Warren, servant of James Brinster.

(238) Charles Floyd vs. Henry Murray } Hugh Allen and Wm. Hyde report as to work done by defendant for John Trimble, Saml. Wallace, Hugh Young and John Brown, trustees for the congregation, for erecting a Meeting House near Brown's.

(239) Attachments vs. Wm. Dean—all his property.

(243) Elizabeth Bell complains of her master, James Crawford.

MARCH 21, 1765.

(247) Thos. Fulton acknowledged Power Atty. to John Jeremiah and ordered to be certified.

(247) John Frazier and Wm. Nailer to be summoned for not providing for their families.

(247) Elizabeth and Letitia Orum to be bound to Wm. Hyde. John Dunn, a servant of David Laird's, bound over for stabbing Hugh Donaho—39 lashes.

(248) John Craven appointed guardian of Roger and John Dyer, orphans of Wm. Dyer.

(248) John Elliott exempted from County levy.

(248) Geo. Weaver has in his possession Elizabeth Countzmann and does not provide for her—summoned.

Page

(249) Wm. Bowyer bound to peace towards Daniel Kidd. Patrick Duffy, garnishee. Danl. Kidd bound to peace towards John Andrews.

(251) Wm. Robinson, James Neeley and Wm. Bryans to view a road from Vanse's by Inglis's Ferry to Peak (Poak) Creek. Wm. Ward qualified deputy sheriff, to which James Trimble dissented. Nicholas Harplore, Paul Shaver and Jacob Wees, to view road on North Mill Creek from the Upper Tract to the County line below Jacob Peterson.

March 22, 1765.

(252) Examination Wm. Thompson for counterfeiting. Bound to General Court in £1,000—Wm. Inglis, Daniel Goodwin, Wm. Tutt *et als.*, witnesses.

(253) Esther Boyd to be bound to John McGill. James Dunlap to be bound to William Lockhart.

(254) Edward Sampson—a witness.

March 23, 1765.

(257) George Wilson, gent., witness from Hampshire—80 miles

(258) Mary Bence, servant of Thos. Bowyer, given 20 lashes for beating Elizabeth Taylor.

(265) Philip Eskin returned not found in bailiwick.

(266) Archer Mathews, special bail.

(268) James Hutchison returned not found in bailiwick.

(280) David Wilson returned no inhabitant.

(281) Wm. McKnight having been arrested and made his escape, suit is dismissed.

(283) James McGrawger vs. James Crawford.—Abates by death of plaintiff.

(284) Robert Campbell returned no inhabitant.

(299) James Colquhoon—defendant.

(306) Alexr. Wright } At time of serving out the writ, defendant
vs.
Andrew Johnston } was in his Majesty's service as a soldier.

(307) Sarah Cartright and James Burns, servant of John McClenachan, cured of venerial disease. (Many of same.).

(307) David Lang in debtor's prison.

(308) Commission for examination of Abigail, wife of Alexr. Herron.

(311) Elizabeth Bell, servant of Thomas Fulton.

(312) Tithables of Staunton to work the roads leading thereto.

March 26, 1765.

(318) George Shillenger vs. John McNeill, gent.—Abates by death of defendant.

(319) Daniel McCoy, orphan, heretofore ordered to be bound to John McNeill, gent., decd., be bound to Andrew Lewis. Complaint of Martha Hassell vs. Master Andrew Greer is continued.

(320) William Patton's servant, Jane Caruthers, the indenture was burnt in his house by the Indians.

(322) Hannah Robinson, servant of Thos. Bowyer.

APRIL 15, 1765.

(334) Court of Claims and Grievances. Robert Bratton, claim for provisions for militia. James Kenaday, sergeant, for self and others, ranging. John Dunlop, provisions. John Dicksin, provisions. James Ewing, provisions. Hugh Fulton, provisions. Saml. McCutcheon, provisions.

(335) Wm. Elliott, provisions. John Finley, provisions. Mary Trimble, relict of John Trimble, for horse of John's impressed and provisions. Wm. Armstrong, provisions. Henry Criswell, horse impressed. Samuel Wilson, provisions and horse impressed. John Miller, provisions. David Doage, provisions. Ralph Laverty, provisions. Thos. Beard, provisions. John Trimble, provisions. Nathan Gilliland, carriage of "flower." John McClary, provisions.

(336) James Mateer, provisions. John Risk, provisions. Wm. Beard, provisions. Charles Erwin, provisions. Joseph Waughub, provisions. Thos. and John Brown, provisions. John Bodkin, provisions and horse impressed. Robert Hartgrove, horse killed. John Young, pasturage, horse impressed. John McPheeters, provisions. Wm. McNabb, provisions. John McKarney, provisions. Thos. Feemster, provisions.

(337) James Bell, provisions. Wm. Bell, provisions. Wm. McCutcheon, provisions and horse impressed. John Rosemond, provisions. Andrew Cowan, enlisting men to garrison Fort Lewis. Walter Trimble, provisions. Thos. Alexander, provisions. John Francis, provisions. James Kirk, provisions. Rob. Armstrong, provisions. Wm. Christian, self *et als.*, ranging. Loftus Pullen, provisions. Rob. Christian, provisions. Danl. O'Freild, provisions. Thos. Poage, provisions. Charles Kilpatrick, provisions. George Moffett, for Wm. Mann *et als.* Benj. Estill, horse impressed. Andrew Hamilton, provisions. Wm. McClenachan, provisions. Wm. McKarney, self *et als., ranging.*

MAY 18, 1765.

(338) Examination Thomas Spencer, cont. servant of Rob. Elliott, larceny—convicted and 39 lashes.

(339) Examination Judith Neil, cont. servant, same—acquitted. Examination Ann Conner, cont. servant, same—15 lashes.

MAY 21, 1765.

(340) John McAdoo appointed Constable.

(340) Plycord Syler to Nicholas Welsh—partly proved.

(341) Elizabeth Mouse, aged 14, orphan of George Mouse, chose John Dunkle guardian.

(342) Mary Wilsby, servant of Wm. Goodwin. Alexr. White admitted to practice law. Catherine Thomas, servant of John McClure. Wm. McCutcheon, merchant, appointed road overseer.

Page

(343) Wm. Montgomery appointed constable on Reed Creek.

(343) Jane Erwin does not provide for children—summoned.

(344) James Montier appointed road surveyor.

MAY 22, 1765.

(344) Private examination Elizabeth Norwood, wife of Saml. Norwood, recorded.

(345) Power of attorney from Mary, Joseph and Rosanna McBride to Wm. McBride—certified.

(345) Hugh Conner, servant of Thomas Smith, to learn carpentering.

(345) Wm. Long, age and infirmity—exempted from levy.

(345) Saml. Flower's estate—Joseph Cloyd, administrator.

(347) John Gratton and Francis Green appointed highway surveyors from Edward Shanklin's to Widow Thomas's old place, near Brock's Gap.

(348) John Flinn, garnishee.

(348) James McGill qualified Captain of Militia.

(349) Rob. Steen, garnishee.

(350) Peggy Lewis, orphan, to be bound to Charles Lewis.

(351) Following attached: 1 pair stockings, 1 gray coat, 1 bell.

(352) Saml. Love and Dorkees—deed.

MAY 23, 1765.

(355) Elizabeth Moser qualifies administratrix of Elizabeth Moser.

(355) Private examination Sarah, wife of Thos. Harrison.

(356) Rob. Hartgroves—ordinary license.

(357) Joseph Ray vs. Wm. Chandler } Jury brought in verdict, but it appeared to Court that jurors had misbehaved themselves in bringing it in, and the verdict is declared idle and void, and Sheriff ordered to summon a new twelve.

(357) Dedimus to take deposition of John Sutton in Carolina.

(357) Wm. Fleming and Sampson Mathews, in Staunton; Alexr. McClenachan, near Staunton; George Skillern, ten miles from Staunton; Benj. Estill, in calf pasture, and Wm. Bowyer in Staunton, recommended as Justices. Wm. Mead, witness from Bedford—80 miles.

(358) Wm. Cunningham vs. Alexr. Sayers.—Abates by death of defendant.

(359) John Seewright and Saml. Henderson ask counter security from Margaret Leeper, administratrix—husband, James Leeper.

(360) Egenier Verden—witness. Robt. McGee, great age and infirmity, exempted from levy.

MAY 24, 1765.

(363) Peak Creek.

(365) Michael Carn, juror.

(367) Michael Carn, witness from Bedford—80 miles.

(367) George Henderson vs. James Pollock.—Suit being abated by death of plaintiff.

(368) Stephen Lay—naturalized.

(373) Sampson Mathews—Ordinary license.

(374) Jacob Morlen qualified administrator, father, Jacob Morlen.

(375) James Trimble's mark recorded. John Poage's mark recorded. Danl. Smith's mark recorded.

MAY 25, 1765.

(377) James Emacks, no inhabitant.

(409) Thomas Davis and Jane vs. Thos. Hicklin, Wm. Eddens and Abraham Haffenstall.—Abates by death of plaintiffs.

(414) Daniel Harrison vs. John Seviar and Arthur Trader.—One of the defendants returned no inhabitant.

(418) Frederick Uff vs. Peter Shamie.—Defendant no inhabitant.

(420) Margaret Freeland, orphan, to be bound out to Rob. Reed until such time as her parents or relations apply for her, or, in case they do not, until she comes to lawful age.

(420) Michael Bowyer has permission to build a kitchen, 20x16, on the lots belonging to this County on the North end of this Court House, near the lots of James Findley, to which James Trimble dissented.

(422) Philip Phegan returned no inhabitant.

(429) William Brown bound to peace on complaint of his wife, Isabella Brown.

(429) Thos. Bowyer allowed to build kitchen, 20x16, adjoining the old jail.

(431) Alexr. Sayers indicted for blasphemy.

(434) Order for summoning George Henderson on complaint of son, John Henderson, is abated by death of George. Order to summon Thomas and Ann Armstrong dismissed.

JUNE 18, 1765.

(434) Charles Fredk. Severt—adjudged bankrupt.

AUGUST 20, 1765.

(436) Commission for private examination of Elizabeth, wife of Thos. Feemster.

(437) Henry Aulford exempted from County levy. John Lapsley exempted from County levy. Gilbert Campbell exempted from County levy. Commission for private examination of Mary, wife of Hugh Hays.

(439) James Knox exempted from levy. Thos. Peerie, orphan of Thos. Peerie, aged 16, chose John Peerie his guardian. Dedimus to take deposition of John Edmondson, about to leave the Colony. John Kirkham, orphan of Henry Kirkham, aged 16, chose James McDowell guardian.

(440) New Commission. Francis Gardner and Thos. Bradshaw ask counter security of Rebecca Gardner, administratrix of husband, Thos. Gardner—summoned. Margaret Robinson qualified administratrix of husband, Wm. Robinson.

Page

(441) John McCreary exempted from working roads. Susanna Shaddon qualified administratrix of husband, Mathew Shaddon. Mary Magdalene Kimberland qualified administratrix of husband, Jacob Kimberland. Valentine Seviar, 1 other and 846 acres added to tithables. Mary Gardner, aged 16, orphan of Thos. Gardner, chose John Finley guardian. Jacob Nicholas naturalized.

(442) James Robinson qualified Captain of Militia.

(443) Ro. Bratton and Thos. Hughart appointed road surveyors from Widow Grays to Samuel Hodges's. David Martin witness from Amherst. Mathew Bray committed to jail on suspicion of being a lunatic, but is now restored and discharged.

(444) David and James Robinson to view the hill whereon Fort Lewis stands—for road.

August 21, 1765.

(444) David Nelson qualified administrator of son, John Nelson.

(445) David Nelson exempted from working on roads. Wm. Duncanson, age and infirmity, exempted from levy.

(448) Susanna Cockran qualified administratrix of husband, John Cockran.

(450) Joseph Donaldson—debtor's prison.

(451) John Gordon bound to peace on complaint of John Archer.

August 22, 1765.

(452) Samuel Howell vs. John Cockrane.—Abates by death of defendant.

(454) Dennis Getty vs. John Hamilton.—Agnes Hamilton, daughter of defendant.

(455) Pat. Martin appointed to make deeds to purchasers of County lots, vice Israel Christian, he having removed to a great distance.

August 23, 1765.

(465) Alexr. McClemun—juror.

(468) Dominick Hiland—juror.

August 24, 1765.

(484) John Reese returned no inhabitant.

(489) Thos. Branham returned no inhabitant.

(497) Robert Sayers, eldest son of Alexr. Sayers, returned no inhabitant.

(507) John Harmon and Mary returned no inhabitant.

(510) Robert Lusk returned run away.

(512) William Dean vs. Francis Jackson } Defendant pleads gambling consideration and cause dismissed.

(514) Richard Prior returned not found in bailiwick.

(525) John Smith and Mary, late Mary Stevenson.

(528) Wm. Ralston exempted from levy. George Wilson, witness from Hampshire—80 miles. Wm. Bryans exempted from County levy. Alexr. Campbell added to tithables.

Page

(529) Francis McGinnis examined for counterfeiting—acquitted.
(530) Francis McGinnis examined for counterfeiting—acquitted.

AUGUSTA COUNTY COURT RECORDS.

ORDER BOOK No. X.

OCTOBER 14, 1765.

(1) Examination of Judith Ryley for murder of her bastard child. Convicted and sent to General Court.

OCTOBER 15, 1765.

(2) Commission for examination of Rachel, wife of George Poage.
(2) Charles Campbell and Charles Campbell appraisers.
(2) Jane, wife of Moses McCown, decd., qualifies administratrix.
(4) Thos. Woddell and 545 acres added to tithables. John Buchanan and two others and 513 acres added to tithables. Alexander and John Walker and 359 acres added to tithables.
(5) John Eaken and 522 acres added to tithables.
(6) Thomas Lorimer qualifies administrator of his deceased brother, John Lorimer. James Sayers refused to qualify executor of Samuel Wallace.
(7) Mary, wife of Robert Buchanan, private examination commission.

OCTOBER 16, 1765.

(8) Catherine, wife of Jeremiah Harrison, priv. examination commission.
(8) Jacob Harper, Alexr. Painter, John Seller, Augustine Price, Jacob Parsenger, Henry Lung and Michael Neese—Naturalized. } The order says they qualified justices!
(8) Mary, wife of John Maxwell, private examination commission.
(8) Mary, wife of Nathaniel Evans, private examination commission.
(9) John McKnight, orphan, to be bound to James Campbell.
(9) Margaret, wife of Alexr. Hamilton, priv. examination commission.
(10) Action by David Sayers against Robert Sayers, an infant, son and devisee of Robert Sayers, deceased.
(10) ——— ———, the wife of Peter Cockran, priv. exn. commission.

(12) vs. Thomas Kelley Handley } Walter Cunningham, garnishee, states that if defendant's pay as a soldier comes into his hands he will have £8.

(12) 220 acres of Hugh Lusk added to tithables.

(14) Bowman vs. John Benson and Margaret } Dedimus to take deposition of Isaac Johnston, a witness, about to remove to Carolina.

Page

(15) George Skillern appointed guardian to John Wall, infant orphan of ———— Wall, deceased.

(15) Francis Gardner's motion to be appointed guardian of the orphans of Thomas Gardner rejected.

OCTOBER 17, 1765.

(16) William McCamey and one other and 190 acres added to tithables. Thomas Kilpatrick and one other and 300 acres added to tithables. John Maxwell and one other and 200 acres added to tithables. James Campbell added to tithables. Wm. McElhenny and 400 acres added to tithables. Henry Bowen and 323 acres added to tithables. Audley Paul and one other and 350 acres added to tithables. Benj. Watson and 170 acres added to tithables.

(17) Robert Lowrey and 208 acres added to tithables.

(18) Bondy Estill—juror.

(18) Cowdon vs. Robert Lynn.—Same order as page 12 above.

(19) John Allford added to tithables.

(21) John McClenachan and one other added to tithables.

(21) Mary, wife of Saml. McDowell, privy exn. commission.

(23) Thomas Barker convicted of larceny—39 lashes.

(24) Andrew Hays vs. John Moore } Dedimus to take deposition of Jane Hays, about to remove to Carolina.

(24) Margaret Looney, orphan of Daniel Looney—David Looney appd. guardian.

(29) Samuel Peggs—juror.

(32) Joel and John Crenshaw of Hanover—witnesses.

(32) David Crenshaw of King William—witness.

OCTOBER 19, 1765.

(34) John Cramey—juror.

(34) James Hill added to tithables. Wm. Bowyer and one other added to tithables. Andrew Johnston added to tithables.

(37) Wilson vs. John Hutchison, Jr.—John Hutchison, Sr., witness.

(40) John Greenlee appointed surveyor of highway from John Mathews, Jr., *deceased,* to Sinclair's Gap. Thomas McFarron appointed surveyor from Catawlo to Pedlar's Ford.

(44) Mary Clark vs. John Stewart and Thomas Fulton } Abates by marriage of plaintiff.

(45) George Poage appointed surveyor of highway from the Pedlar Ford, on James River, eight miles up. William Gallespy appointed surveyor from eight miles above Pedlar Ford to Capt. Dickinson's. John Potts appointed surveyor from mouth of Pott's Creek.

(46) The King vs. John Bowyer } On an indictment for beating and abusing Israel Christian, a magistrate in the execution of his office. The defendant waives his former plea because he will not contend with our Lord the King.—Convicted and fined.

Page
(47) John Henderson added to tithables.

OCTOBER 21, 1765.

(55) Moses Hurt returned no inhabitant. Moses Evans returned no inhabitant. Henry Hendrix returned no inhabitant.
(58) John Hays returned not found in bailiwick.
(69) Richard Doghead returned lives in Bedford bailiwick.
(72) William Wilson returned no inhabitant.
(77) Mathew Emacks returned lives in Bedford.
(78) Nicholas Seaborn, Jr.
      vs. } Abates by death of defendant.
    John Ray
(88) George Anderson returned not found in bailiwick.
(89) William and Thomas Crow and three others added to tithables.
(90) £60, 9, 4, Penna. money = Same in Va. money.
(94) Many suits versus Saml. Cowdon.—Did he fail?
(101) John Blagg, gent., imprisoned for debt.
(102) John Blagg—juror.

OCTOBER 22, 1765.

(104) Elizabeth Gray, servant of Rob. McClenachan.
(111) Levy Smith—Sheriff returned could not find.
(112) Wm. McNaught, returned not in this County.
(112)   Woods } "The Sheriff having returned that the second time it came to my hand, I tell as before, he is out of the County."
      vs.
    Andrew Cowan, Jr.
(113) Martha Hassell, servant of Andrew Greer.
(132) Findley vs. Moses Hamilton.—Abates by death of defendant.
(133) John Nash, returned not found in bailiwick.
(134) Findley vs. Jacob Dodson.—Sheriff returned he did not know the defendant.
(134) Same vs. Ann Kelly.—Same return.
(135) James Findley, admr. of Robert Findley, } John Stewart makes affidavit that the acct. is a true copy from plaintiff's books.
      vs.
    Shannon, admr. of Young.
(And the same in many suits.)
(135) Same vs. —— Carson.—Returned no inhabitant.
(136) Same vs. Sarah Robinson.—Could not find defendant.
(136) George Pearis, returned no inhabitant.
(142) John Harmon to be bound to John Armstrong.
(143) County levy. To Robert Campbell, for a screed for the use of the County, £3, 10, 0.
(145) John Blagg, witness from Westmoreland County, 150 miles.
(147) Road ordered changed around the hill at Fort Lewis.

JANUARY 28, 1766.

Page

(148) Daniel McAnare misbehaved by appearing in Court drunk and giving Gabriel Jones, gent., Deputy Attorney for the King, the lie, and likewise insulting the Court.

MAY 8, 1766.

(149) Called Court on John Thompson and Margaret, his wife, for larceny.—Convicted and sent to Grand Jury.

MAY 20, 1766.

(151) Margaret Clark qualified admx. of husband, Wm. Clark.

(152) Charles Campbell (Borden's land) appointed Constable.

(153) Stephen Arnold imprisoned for debt.

(154) James Cloyd appointed surveyor from lower end of John Bowyer's plantation of James River by Cedar Bridge to Mathew's Road, to work these tithables: Of Christopher Vineyard, John and Wm. Hall, John Logan, James Skidmore, Geo. Wilson, John Berry, John Jones, James McClure, Mathew Hair, John Bowyer, George Skillern and Conrad Wall.

(158) Erwin vs. John Henderson.—Abates by death of defendant.

(161) Margaret Thompson (see page 149 above), discharged.

MAY 21, 1766.

(162) Four wooden noggins attached, also one iron candlestick, one Dutch blanket, one hand towel.

(169) Wm. Winston, Jr., vs. Israel Christian, gent., admr. of Alexr. Sayers and Walter Buchanan.—Abates by death of defendant (Buchanan?).

(171) Andrew Erwin vs. John Burnsides.—Abates by death of plaintiff.

(177) Attached—2 iron crooks, 6 spoons, 3 candlesticks, 2 funnels, 1 washing tub, 1 cooler, 1 tin saucepan, 1 tea kettle.

(184) Samuel Caldwell returned no inhabitant.

(188) Christian, admr. Sayers, vs. Joseph Donaldson.—Abates by death of defendant.

(190) James Wiley and Martha, to Alexr. Noble, partially proved and certified.

(191) George Mathews qualified Captain of Militia.

(191) Michael Valentine and Henry Trout, orphan of Nicholas Trout, to be bound out.

(192) William Martin qualified admr. of father, Hugh Martin. Dawson Wade, appraiser.

(194) Virginia ale, bottled, to be sold at 6 pence per quart.

AUGUST 19, 1766.

(194) Patrick Henry, Jr., qualified Attorney.

(194) Mary Owler qualified admx. of husband, Wm. Owler. John Felts, Michael Cogar, Woolrick Horshman, and Jacob Shell, appraisers of Owler estate.

(196) Thomas Hicklin, Sr., exempted from levy by reason of great age and infirmity.

(197) Stephen Trigg and Wm. Simpson, greatest creditors, qualified administrators of Henry Fields. William and Edward Cowen, appraisers.

(200) David Harmon summoned for not bringing up his children in a Christianlike manner.

(200) Thomas Wright, servant of John Hanna.

AUGUST 20, 1766.

(204) Robert Kinkead and Anna Helena, his wife.

(204) Israel Christian and Andrew Miller qualified administrators of John Miller.

(205) David Wilson, son of William Wilson, formerly bound to Andrew Erwin, deceased, to be bound to Francis Erwin, Jr., heir-at-law and executor of said Andrew, he teaching him the trade of a shoemaker. Elizabeth Wilson, daughter of Wm. Wilson, to be bound to Francis Erwin, Jr.

(206) Saml. McClure, security for Mary McClure, admx. of husband, Nathaniel McClure, asks counter security.

(206) Rosanna Marlen complains that Maurice O'Friel and Robert Wallace detain her children, viz: James, Sarah and Margaret Ralston.

(207) Michael Riney exempted from levy—age and infirmity. Henry Hicks, same.

(209) Audley Paul }
       vs. } Judgment on a judgment obtained in Hampshire County.
  Saml. Stalnaker }

(213) Betty Smith, Nicholas Smith, Johnny Smith, John Yates and David Yates to be bound out.

(213) Samuel Glass and 236 acres added to tithables.

(214) Thomas Madison awarded certificate of probity, &c., for applying for license to practice law.

AUGUST 21, 1766.

(215) Andrew Hall, late of this County, deceased, possessed of a small estate, and Sheriff ordered to sell it.

(215) Edward Faires }
      vs. } A second James Bryans appeared and claimed the property, and it is adjudged his and not defendant's.
  James Bryans. }

(216) Christopher Best and Hugh Galbreath, witnesses.

(216) A paper endorsed by Alexr. Boyd, deceased, as a true copy of his will, and is adjudged by the Court not to be the original, and Andrew Boyd qualifies administrator.

(217) George Birdwell—juror.

(221) Andrew Kline committed to debtor's prison. Many suits against him. Was it customary for prisoners for debt to act as jurors? See *supra*.

(224) John Graham committed to the stocks for one-half hour for contempt and bound to peace towards James Lockhart.

(224) Joseph McBride, aged 19, orphan of Thomas McBride, chose Wm. McBride his guardian.

Page

(226) Ordered that Gabriel Jones prosecute John Graham on the recognizance this day entered into.

AUGUST 22, 1766.

(227) Above order (page 226) vacated.

(227) Michael Harper vs. Robt. Duffield.—Abates by death of plaintiff.

(228) Commission for deposition of Lovice Looney.

(230) Joseph Donaldson, deceased, possessed of very small estate. Sheriff ordered to sell.

(231) David Graham was arrested for contempt, but made his escape before judgment. Now rearrested and bound over.

(232) Jacob Campbell, one other and 317 acres, added to tithables.

(233) Davis Harrison appointed road surveyor.

(Adjourned until tomorrow, but no heading follows, but records continue.)

(234) Adam Dunlap, Ezekiel Evans—jurors.

(237)　　David Cloyd　⎫　Agreed case.　Indians rifled plaintiff's
　　　　　　　vs.　　　⎬ house.　Militia recovered property and
James Montgomery ⎭ divided it, &c.

(239) Viewers for a road from Edward Erwin's to the Market Road that leads to Swift Run.

(240) Michael Bornet, a mulatto, to be bound.

AUGUST 25, 1766.

(242) John Skelton vs. John Miller.—Abates by death of defendant.

(245) John Forish imprisoned for debt.

(249) Uriah Akers, returned could not find.

(249) Alexr. Boyd's death abates suit.

(275) James Campbell (Calf Pasture).

(284) James Walker vs. David Via.—Abates by death of defendant.

(290) Road to be viewed from North Branch of James, round the Poplar Hills to Buffalo Creek.

(291) Francis Gardner and Thomas Bradshaw, securities for Rebecca Gardner, admx. of husband, Thomas Gardner, since intermarried with Robert Brown, demand counter security.

(298) Nathaniel Dunlap, returned no inhabitant. John Leahe, returned "could not find."

(302) George Buff, returned no inhabitant.

AUGUST 26, 1766.

(309) Thomas Smith, a witness from Amherst.

(311) John Love, orphan of Joseph Love, decd., to be bound to Joseph Love, Fuller.

(316) Joseph Goodbon, witness from Amherst, 27 miles.

(328) Phebe Moore, wife of Thomas Moore, late wife of Daniel Davidson, assigned dower.

(328) Motion of Jacob Conrad and Hannah—John Westfall, admr. of Abraham Westfall, who was admr. of John Bogard, summoned.

(329) Called Court on James Johnston for larceny.—Sent to Genl. Court.

(330) Same on John Brown and Anthony Fewell for same. Being convict servants, they receive 39 lashes.

SEPTEMBER 16, 1766.

(331) John Fowler's still house, about a mile from Edward Shanklin's—David Nelson's—Jacob Nicholas's—road located.

(332) Andrew Kline—adjudged bankrupt.

NOVEMBER 3, 1766.

(332) Called Court on George Watt and Edward Peyton—horse stealing.—Sent to General Court.

NOVEMBER 18, 1766.

(334) Thomas Madison qualified to practice law and admitted. John Madison, Jr., qualified Deputy Clerk.

(336) Robert Brown appointed guardian to Francis and Samuel Gardner, orphans of Thomas Gardner.

(336) George Kepels, servant of James McDowel.

(337) These added to tithables—viz: Wm. Jordan, James Jordan, Anthony Johnston.

(338) John Boyd and 115 acres added to tithables. Thomas Boyd and 248 acres added to tithables. David Williams and 348 acres added to tithables.

(338) Wm. Robinson built by contract a causeway at Vanse's and died.—Money ordered paid to Margaret, his widow.

NOVEMBER 19, 1766.

(339) Road to be viewed from Wm. Elliott's to McCutcheon's Mill, thence thro' Buffalo Gap.

(340) Joseph Carpenter, Sr., and Wm. Whooley appointed road surveyors from Fort Defiance to Handley's Mill, with these workers and their tithables: Peter Wright, Solomon, Thomas, Nathaniel Carpenter, John Umphries, Thos. Carpenter, Zopher Carpenter, Ezekiel Johnston, Edward and John McMullin, James Williams, Joseph Leeper, John Fieler, William Christian and Peter Whooley, Wm. McMurry, Thos. Wright, Rob. Galesby, Pat. Corrigan and Joseph Carpenter, Jr.

(340) Wm. Herbert, gent., qualified administrator of Robert Andrew. George Forbes, appraiser.

(341) Hannah Hoffman, a witness about to remove out of Colony.

(342) Hook vs. John Ritchie.—Defendant delivered up to Sheriff.

(342) Martha Ryan summoned for not bringing up her children in a Christianlike manner.

(342) Abraham Goodpasture, orphan of Jacob Goodpasture, to be bound to Danl. Pierce, to be taught to be a carpenter.

(343) Danl. Pierce qualified administrator of Jacob Goodpasture.

(344) Wm. McCutcheon appointed guardian of John Duncan, orphan of James Duncan.

(345) David Moore, orphan of David Moore, aged 14 years, chose Henry Gay guardian.

November 20, 1766.

(348) One wig, two fiddles, one pottle noggin—attached.

(349) John Murray, Deputy Sheriff, returned list of prisoners in jail, to wit: Edward Peyton, George Wall and James Shaw. Edward Shaw, son of James Shaw, to be bound to James Hill.

(350) Deposition of John Smith, aged 65, and lives 60 miles from Court House.

(351) William Wood, a witness from Bedford.

(351) Wm. Chambers exempted from County levy.

(352) Saml. Hull, exempted from County levy.

(353) John Thompson, convicted of larceny—25 lashes.

(354) James Robinson, Saml. Robinson and Martha McCormick, late Martha Robinson, executors of George Robinson.

November 21, 1766.

(356) David Cloyd vs. James Montgomery.—Judgment upon case agreed for plaintiff.

(357) James Findley committed to jail for debt.

(358) Saml. Briggs, witness. Wm. Joy, witness. John Sleet, witness from Orange County, 78 miles.

(359) Richard Taylor, witness from Orange County, 70 miles.

November 22, 1766.

(364) Alexr. Moore vs. Wm. Fleming.—Abates by death of plaintiff.

(365) Thomas Rhoades—juror.

November 24, 1766.

(373) George Woolridge, returned not found in bailiwick.

(374) John Findley, son to William.

(382) Mathew Peartree, not an inhabitant. Wm. Vowter, not found in bailiwick.

(384) James Kenady, not found in bailiwick.

(417) Sheriff ordered to repair the pillory and underpin the stocks two feet from the ground and place a gate at each side of the bar.

(417) Ann O'Brien, servant of James Crow, agrees to serve him two years in consideration of his agreeing to her marrying Tiadey Flinn.

Page
(424) Thomas Smith, witness from Amherst. Thomas Landrum, witness from Orange.

NOVEMBER 25, 1766.

(429) James Clark, returned not an inhabitant.

(455) John Baskins, no inhabitant of this Colony.

(456) North River, commonly known as Swift Run.

(457) Alexander Kile, not an inhabitant of this Colony.

(460) Two delph plates attached, also 5 delph bowls, also half dozen knives and forks, 1 pair brass candlesticks.

(462) Judith Neal, servant of Wm. Walterson.

MARCH 17, 1767.

(463) Wm. McCutcheon (merchant) appointed road surveyor.

(464) Jane Davis and Saml. Davis qualify administrators of James Davis. James David qualifies administrator of John Cryton.

(465) Saml. Peffer, greatest creditor, qualifies administrator of James Carty.

(465) Commission for priv. examination of Margaret, wife of Robert Miller. Commission for priv. examination of Jane, wife of Robert Gwinn, Jr. Commission for priv. examination of Mary, wife of Malcom Allen.

(467) Margaret and Wm. Farris, orphans of James Farris, to be bound out.

MARCH 18, 1767.

(472) Robert Sayers, aged 15, orphan of Alexr. Sayers, chose Robert Breckinridge his guardian.

(472) Many certificates for hemp recorded and certified.

(474) John Jones, servant of Andrew Bird.

(475) Robert Doby, exempted from levy.

(475) Joseph Ray delivered up his security into custody of Sheriff.

(476) Andrew Hays, Jr., qualified Captain of Militia.

(477) On petition of Frederick Stern, Isaac Job, Thomas Grayson, John Bell, Henry Skaggs, Joseph Hix, John Draper, George Baker, Joseph Hord, Levy Smith, Erasmus Noble, Saml. Peffer, James Coudon, Edmund Vansell, Humphrey Baker, Anthony Bledsoe, James Newell and Alexr. Page, viewers appointed for a road from Vanse's, by Ingles's Ferry, to Peak Creek, on north side New River, viz: James Neeley, Philip Love, Wm. Christian, Wm. Bryans.

(477) Abraham Goodpath to be bound to John Sutton. Children of George Watts to be bound.

(478) James Cloyd qualified Captain of Militia. James Lapsley qualified Ensign.

MARCH 19, 1767.

(481) Joseph Blain exempted from levy—great age and infirmity.

(482) Samuel Woods, Thomas Goodson, John Richards, Wm. Ward, Hugh Crockett, Jacob Kent, Robert Crockett, Philip Love and Joseph

Crockett, petition for a road from Vanse's to Saml. Woods's.—Viewers appointed.

(484) Alexr. and John Dale—jurors.

(485) Road by William McBride's shop.

MARCH 20, 1767.

(493) Margaret Leeper, widow of James Leeper—dower assigned.

MARCH 21, 1767.

(495) The King
vs.
Joseph Bell
} Indictment for forging the banns of matrimony between Ann Wallace and Edward Sampson, a little deformed tailor.

(496) Wm. Grayson—witness from Albemarle.

(498) Francis Dunn, orphan, heretofore bound to Robert Young, now to be bound to John Miller, to be taught trade of wheelwright.

(500) Abraham Smith qualified Lieutenant Colonel of County.

MARCH 23, 1767.

(503) David Stewart's death abates suit.

(514) John Long, returned not found in bailiwick.

(516) James Kenady, returned moved out of the County. Wm. Means, returned not found in bailiwick.

(527) Samuel Gist vs. Thomas Reed and George Brackenridge.—Alexr. Breckenridge, security.

(530) David Bryan's death abates suit.

AUGUSTA COUNTY COURT RECORDS.

ORDER BOOK No. XI.

MARCH 23, 1767.

(20) Mathew Robottom, returned no inhabitant.

(33) William Brown, returned not found.

(35) Andrew Steel's death abates suit.

(40) David Long, returned not found.

MARCH 24, 1767.

(52) Thomas Porter, witness from Orange—70 miles. Thomas Landrum, witness from Orange—80 miles.

(58) Thomas Madison, qualified Captain of Militia.

(58) Euphemia Hughes—ordinary license.

(58) Certain articles belonging to James Hughes, decd., are declared to belong to his estate and not to his stepdaughter, Margaret Kenedy.

May 19, 1767.

Page

(59) Commission for private examination of Catherine, wife of Benj. Bennett.

(59) Elizabeth Edwards, aged 19, orphan of John Edwards, chose John McClenachan, guardian.

(61) Saml. Henderson, Andrew Taylor and many others—certificates for hemp.

(64) Margaret Scott, alias Bradley, to be bound out.

(64) Jacob Lockhart qualifies admr. of his brother, Charles Lockhart.

(65) Road ordered from Adam Reader's mines to Isaac Robinson's, thence to Thos. Harrison's.

(65) Joseph Bousart to be summoned to show why he detains William Viges, son of Francis Viges.

(65) Alexr. Maxwell, servant of John Henderson.

(66) Randal Lockhart commd. to debtor's prison.

May 20, 1767.

(69) Margaret Campbell, mother of Margaret Campbell, is appointed guardian to bring a suit versus James Cotton.

(71) Saml. Wallace qualified Lieutenant of Militia.

(73) Mathew Arbuckle qualified Lieutenant of Militia. James Robinson qualified Ensign of Militia.

(74) Cowdon vs. John Jones — Attached following: Two linen handkerchiefs, 1 snuff box, 2½ yds. ribbon, 3¼ yds. ribbon, 4 yds. ribbon, 7 yds. Chex., 2¼ yds. calico, 7 yds. thickset, 1¾ yds. scarlet, 2 yds. plush, ½ yd. velvet, 11 yds. hair, 9 yds. callimanco.

(75-76) Attachments versus George Pearis.

(76) Wm. Watterson bound to peace for abusing Abraham Smith in execution of his office.

(79) Hugh Crockett appointed Constable on Roanoke.

(81) The King vs. Joseph Bell — For forging banns of matrimony.—*Nol pros.*

(81) John Campbell relieved of County levy—age and infirmity.

May 21, 1767.

(82) Wm. Renix appointed overseer road, vice Rob. Bratton.

(82) Jonathan Smith qualified Captain of Militia.

(82) Geo. Baxter appointed surveyor of highway, vice John Thomas.

(83) Commission for examination of Martha, wife of John Dickinson.

(83) Hester Baker, servant of Wm. Fleming.

(85) John Buchanan appeals to General Court from establishment of a road from Vanse's to Peak Creek, by English's Ferry, on ground that it is on the lands of the Western Waters and it is contrary to his Majesty's proclamation to grant any order for clearing any road thereon.

(86) Thos. Bradshaw appointed highway surveyor, vice David Trimble. Chas. Donnerly appointed highway surveyor from Painter Gap to James Gay's.

Page

(87) John Robinson and John Henderson appointed highway surveyors from head of North Fork of Roanoke to Capt. John Robinson's Mill.

(87) Anthony Crockett, orphan, to be bound to Saml. Crockett.

(88) Abraham Goodbath and John Sutton to be bound.

(88) Isaac Robinson appointed road overseer, vice Mathias Rider.

(88) Wm. Dye, aged 14 years the 29th of April last, orphan of David Dye, to be bound to Saml. McKee.

(88) George Carpenter appointed surveyor of of highway, vice James Brinster.

MAY 22, 1767.

(91) George Eager bound over as an idle vagrant person. Dudley Boyl bound over as an idle vagrant person.

(92) Jacob Persinger appointed surveyor of highway, vice Ludk. Francisco.

(93) George McCown appointed surveyor of highway, vice Thos. Vance.

MAY 23, 1767.

(100) Dennis Kelly and John Crasey—jurors.

(102) John Cowarden, Saml. Maggott, John Castey—jurors.

(118) Robert Maxwell—witness from Hampshire—80 miles.

MAY 25, 1767.

(121) George Malcolm, returned no inhabitant.

(131) James Harris, returned no inhabitant.

(136) Hugh Hamilton vs. Felix Gilbert — It appears that defendant (?) is not an inhabitant of this County; suit to be dismissed unless defendant appear and give security for cost.

(138) John Davis (Hunter), security for John and Charles Allison.

(152) McCaul versus Phillip Barrier.

(154) James Shaw—no inhabitant.

(155) Grindstone—attached.

(165) Jacob Hite, gent., returned no inhabitant.

(169) John Graham (Christian's Creek), security.

(174) Wm. Brown and Robt. Rodgers, sureties.

(177) John Warwick and John Davis (Hunter), sureties.

(179) John Stewart vs. James Lockhart.—Plaintiff not an inhabitant of this Colony.

(197) Julius Webb, returned not found in bailiwick.

(202) John Etten, returned no inhabitant.

(207) Francis Beaty vs. John Cavin and David McCaveis — John Cavin not found.

(208) Elizabeth Bryan, executrix of David Bryan, demands counter security from Rhoda Doggett, late Rhoda Evans, admx. of late husband, Daniel Evans, and lately married to Richard Doggett.

Page

(210) Mary Renolds, aged 16, orphan of James Renolds, chose Nathaniel Evans guardian.

(211-212) The following produced certificates for hemp: Alexr. Gibson, Francis Brown, Thos. Paxton, Saml. Newberry, Saml. Henderson, Nichs. Sollace, Edward Sharp, Henry Larkin, Alexr. Walker, John White, John Black, James Trimble, Saml. Downey, Walter Cunningham, Moses Trimble, James McClung, John McClure, Halbert McClure, Joseph Long, David Campbell, James Walker, Joseph Lapsley, Israel Christian, Henry Lung, Jonan. Whitley, John McElwroth.

(213) The following produced certificates for hemp: Hugh Miller, James Craig, James Montgomery, Wm. Maze, James Lawrence, Thos. Wilson, John Hall, Pat. Miller, James Patterson, Robt. Frazier, Saml. Buckanon, John Hays, Jr.

(114) The following produced certificates for hemp: James Stewart, Saml. Cartmill.

(114) John Price, indented servant, imported from Great Britain, binds himself to Joseph Ray for 4 years, to be taught to be a carpenter and joiner.

(215) Ro. Allen appointed surveyor of highway, vice Isaac White. Ro. Gragg appointed surveyor of highway from Duck Ponds to Middle River. Wm. Patton appointed Constable, vice Wm. McCandless.

(215) Margaret, wife of John Buckanon, relinquishes dower to Saml. Bradford.

(216) Thos. Walker and Mildred to Andrew Lewis.—Comn. for Mildred.

(216) James Cloyd qualified administrator of John Cloyd, his brother.

(216) John Casaty to be summoned to show cause why he does not qualify on estate of father, Neil Casaty.

(216) James Casaty to be bound to Michael Kirkham. Patrick Casaty to be bound to Wm. McBride.

(216) Saml. Scott, aged 18 years, orphan of Saml. Scott, decd., chose Skidmore Mousey guardian.

(217) Jane Erwin, having been heretofore presented for keeping a disorderly house and having been tried and adjudged to pay a fine which has been collected, it appears she had no notice and she is recommended to Governor for pardon.

(217) Saml. Henderson appointed surveyor of highway from John Madison's to Givens's Mill.—Tithables from James Craig's up Middle River to James Givens and on South River from William Patterson's to Christian Clemons. John Madison appointed surveyor of highway from his house to Jones's Ford, tithables on Middle River from James Craig's downwards, and on South River from William Patterson's downwards, and as low as said Madison's. Andrew Fought appointed surveyor of highway, vice Archd. Huston.

(218) John Anderson and Wm. Ralston appointed surveyors of highway, vice Robert Geegg, from the Duck Ponds to Middle River.

(218) John Grenby bound to peace towards Susanna Cockrain.

(218) Priv. examination of Lettice Breckinridge, wife of Robt. Breckinridge, to land sold by Robert to Stephen Loy.

(219) John Robinson appointed surveyor of highway from his mill by the Den to the County Road leading to Warwick.

August 19, 1767.

(219) Deed from Richard Stanton and Cloraty, his wife, to Wm. Herbert, partly proved. John White (Borden's Land) exempted from levy—great age and infirmity.

(219) George Adams appd. Constable, vice Wm. Montgomery.

(220) Sarah Young, aged 16, and James Young, aged 15, orphans of Patrick Young, chose Saml. Todd guardian, and same was appointed guardian of Jennet and Elce Young, orphans of Patrick.

(220) John Beard and James Sayers, Jr., appointed surveyors of highway, vice Robert Armstrong.

(220) Deed John Adams and Elizabeth to Andrew Woods, partly proved.

(220) Hugh Allen appointed surveyor of highway from James Given's Mill, by his house, to Stone Meeting House, and the following to work the road: Saml. Hinds, Robt. Stevenson, Wm. Kerr, John Stewart, John Campbell, James Allen, John Anderson, Hugh Allen, William McClure, James Allen, Saml. Bell, Andrew Lockhart, John Burnside, Saml. McKee, James Searight, Thos. Storey.

(221) John Cartmill and John Cartmill, Jr.—appraisers.

(222) Following produced certificates for hemp: John Boller, Wm. Bondes and Sampn. Christian.

(224) Andrew Fitzpatrick ⎫
         vs. ⎬ Following articles attached: One old
   John Jones ⎭ saddle, 1 fine shirt and stock, 2 coarse shirts, 2 pr. old drawers, 7 fawn skins, 2 skirts of a Jackett.

(224) Robert Hall and Isabella, late Isabella Ramsey, ruled to give John Bigham counter security as surety for their administration of her husband's (Robert Ramsey's) estate.

(225) Aaron Hughes appointed surveyor of highway, vice John Phillips.

(225) Deed Daniel O'Hona to Rev. Alexr. Miller, Master of Arts.— Comn. for priv. examination of Elizabeth, wife of Daniel.

(225) John Skidmore qualified Captain of Militia.

(227) Many attachments versus John Pearis.

(229) John McElhenny, imprisoned for debt.

(230) Overseers of roads appointed: Thos. Hicklin, Jr., vice John Estill; John Dailey, from North to South River; Walter Smiley, vice Wm. Kennedy.

August 20, 1767.

(232) Joseph Love—certificate of hemp.

(233) Wm. Christian, John Handley, James McKain, John Archer, Zachh. Johnston and John Hunter—certificates of hemp.

(235) Anthony Fewell, run away servant of Wm. Campbell.

(236) Joseph Hyde's mark recorded—a swallow fork in the right and an underkill in the left.

Page

(236) John Ely, James Mitchell, George Weer, James McElhenny—jurors.

(237) Richd. Lawson, run away servant of James McKain. Richd. Bookin, Jr.,—witness.

AUGUST 21, 1767.

(238) Certificates for hemp: John Bowyer, John Nickel.

(239) Charles Campbell, Wm. Findley, Mathew Patton—certificates for hemp.

(239) Witnesses: John Murray, John Thompson.

(239) James Watson to be levy free, age and infirmity.

(239) Joseph McMurty and George McAfe to view a way from McMurty's Mill, through McAfee's Gap, to the Wagon Road.

(239) James McAfee, Sr., and Bryan McDonald appointed surveyors of highway from Fort Williams to head of Catawbo.

(239) Surveyors of highways appointed: Patrick Shirley and Wm. Watkins, from James Montgomery's at Catawbo to the side of Craig's Creek Mountain where John Potts quit clearing; James Cloyd, vice Wm. Preston, from Graham's Clearing to James Johnston's; Saml. McRoberts, from James Johnson's to Josiah Ramsey's cabin, vice William Preston.

(240) Michael Cloyd, from his house to the branch below James Moore, Sr.; Henry Dooley and John Thompson, to view road from the Welshman's Run to the Bedford Line; Israel Christian, from the Great Lick to Graham's Clearing, vice Wm. Graham.

(240) Anthony Bledsoe has leave to build a mill at Fort Chiswell.

(241) Road to be viewed (both old and a new one) from McClenachan's Mill to William Haldman's.

(241) Robert Thompson appointed surveyor of highway, vice Alexander Thompson. Henry Heffman (Keffman), same, vice Charles Willson.

(244) Mary Bredley, alias Scott, not to be bound by Church Wardens, but to remain in hands of James Laughlin, who is to be summoned.

(244) Witnesses: Patrick Frazier.

(245) John Frazier, Wm. Beard, Geo. Carpenter, Jr., Randall Lockhart, Catherine Shirley.

(245) Accounts of Wm. Simpson and Elizabeth, his wife, late Elizabeth Campbell, admx. of Malcolm Campbell.

AUGUST 22, 1767.

(247) Witnesses: Robert Armstrong, John Willson, Moses Collier.

(248) John Sproul.

(248) Certificates of hemp: Alexr. Telford, Wm. McFeeters, Jr.

(248) David Roberts to be bound out.

(248) Randall Lockhart in custody for debt.

(250) Witnesses: John Bunchanon, Dennis Getty.

(250) Jurors: John Seviar, William Foster, James Gilmore, John Weer, John Weer.

(250) Witnesses: Thomas Kennerley, David Bell, Adam Dean, Robert Allen.

Silas Hart, gent., late High Sheriff of Augusta,
vs.
Randal Lockhart, Sampson Mathews, John Brown, Felix Gilbert, Hugh Young, John Stewart, and Andrew Lewis and George Mathews, admrs. of David Stewart, decd.

Randal delivered up in custody of Sheriff.

(252) Jurors: Wm. Hinds, Jr., Robert Allen, Jr.

(252) Surveyors of highway appointed: Francis Erwin, Jr., from Charles Campbell's Run to John Davis's Mill, vice Michael Dickey.

(252) Witness: John Murray.

(257) Jurors: John Ray, Moses Williams, John Gray, Nicholas Seahorn.

(257) Wm. Mathews, Wm. Anderson and George Moffett, to value improvements of John Archer on 260 acres and 83 acres.

(258) Witnesses: George Ware, Wm. Lowrey.

(258) Mary and Eve Shaver to be bound to Hugh Hays.

(258) John McCandless bound to peace on complaint of Joseph Ware.

AUGUST 24, 1767.

(263) William Dean, returned no inhabitant..

(265) James Cowan, returned no inhabitant.

(267) James Bell (North Mountain), surety.

(277) Alexr. Miller (Clerk), vs. David Rice (Clerk).

(291) Gilbert Carr, returned no inhabitant.

(295) James Frame and Wm. Willis, special bail.

(301) George Jamison
vs.
James McDowell and John Cloyd

Abates by death of John Cloyd

(302) Joshua McCormick and Martha versus late Martha Robinson, Saml. and James Robinson, Exrs. of George Robinson.

(304) Thos. Rhoades committed to debtor's prison.

(309) Robt. Scott and Richd. Bodkin, Jr., special bail.

(312) Hemp certificates: Robt. Christian, John Christian, John McClure.

(313) Saml. Love, Wm. Crow, hemp certificates.

(313) Surveyors of highway: Wm. Bryans, from Fort Lewis to Peters Creek; Thos. Barnes, from Peters Creek to Tinker Creek; John McAdoo and John Thompson, from Tinker Creek to County line.

(313) Saml. Pepper appointed Constable.

(315) Witnesses: Thos. Alsberry, Wm. Meeks.

(316) Witnesses: Jacob Nicholas, Jacob Parsinger, John Murray.

(322) John Taylor versus Malcolm McCown (son to John). James Gilmore, witness.

(330) Andrew Lewis, Patrick Martin, John Dickenson, recommended for Sheriff.

In pursuance of the Act of Assembly for settling the titles and bounds of lands for preventing unlawful hunting and ranging thereon, Court orders the Vestry to divide so much of their parish as lies in Augusta into precincts for processioning, to appoint two intelligent, honest freeholders in each precinct processioners, and times to be between last day of September and last of March.

Page

(333) Thos. Fulton appointed Constable, vice Davis Harrison.

(334) James Lockhart committed for debtor's prison.

(334) Mary Nahan, servant of Ann Moore.

(335) Elizabeth Mathews, aged 14, orphan of Joshua Mathews, chose George Mathews her guardian.

(336) Samuel Kent, having been committed to jail on charge of being a runaway servant, and nothing appearing against him—discharged.

NOVEMBER 17, 1767.

(336) Wm. Johnson, two tithables and 100 acres, added to tithables. John Johnson, one tithable and 120 acres, added to tithables.

(337) Hemp certificates: John Dean, Christr. Vinyard, James Hogshead, John Trotter, Alexr. Walker, Saml. Davis, Andrew Russell, Saml. Gibson, John Davison.

(338) Hemp certificates: David Wallace, Thos. Hill, James Gilmore, Wm. Henderson, Robt. Hamilton.

(338) George Conrad qualifies administrator of Stephen Conrad.

(338) Hugh Donaho appointed surveyor of highway from Thos. Connelly's house to James Beard's ford, vice Alexr. Walker.

(339) Thomas McClure, aged 14, orphan of Nathaniel McClure, chose Halbert McClure guardian. John Cassaty, aged 16, orphan of Neil Cassaty, chose Saml. Davis his guardian. Samuel Davis qualifies administrator of Neil Cassaty.

(339) Jonas Friend appointed Constable, vice Peter Vaneman.

(339) John Montgomery qualifies administrator of Alexr. Buse (Bruce).

(340) James Anderson and wife, Elizabeth, bound to peace towards Wm. Robertson.

(340) 375 acres of Roger Kilpatrick added to tithables.

(340) George Bryans, having been committed to jail on suspicion of being a runaway servant, and it appearing that he was no servant—discharged.

(341) Saml. Cockrane exempted from levy—age and infirmity.

(341) Grand jurors: Nathanl. Evans, Joseph Raburn, Saml. McPheeters, Francis Erwin, Robt. Thompson, Henry Stone, James McCain, John Ramsey, Archibald Fisher, John White, Henry Campbell, Saml. Briggs, Richd. Renalds, Hugh Hays, Joseph Malcolm, David Laird, John Francis, John Black, James Leatherdale, John McClure, Hugh Donaho.

(341) Richard Murray and Catherine, his wife, late Catherine Highlands, summoned on complaint of John Chrisman for not bringing up the children of Henry Highlands in a Christianlike manner.

(341) Alexr. Dale appointed Constable, vice James Young. Joseph Bell appointed surveyor of highway from James Lessley's to fork of road leading to Staunton, vice Archd. Hamilton.

(342) John Young, servant of James McGarock.

(342) Abraham Brown, one tithable and 460 acres, added to tithables.

(342) Road established from Craig's Mill to the Mouth of South River, and from the Mills to the Great Road leading to Staunton.

(342) Hemp certificates: John Hall, David Cloyd, Charles Lewis.

Page
(343) Hemp certificates: Andrew Hamilton, Dawson Wade, James Burnsides, John Montgomery, Thos. Brown, Edwd. Erwin, Postle Hover, James Crow, John Henderson.

(343) Surveyor of highway appointed: James Davis, vice John Hanna.

(343) James Cloyd's mark recorded—a crop in the left ear and a slit in the right and a half penny on each side of the slit.

(344) John Hall and John White appointed surveyors of highway from George Campbell's to Wm. McClenachan's Mill.

(344) 120 acres of Henry Cartmill added to tithables. Added to tithables: Saml. Ferguson, John Peary and Hugh Allen.

November 18, 1767.

(345) James Simpson appointed surveyor of highway from Cow Pasture to Gilmer's Gap, and the workers from Wm. Dougherty's down to Captain Christian's.

(346) Hemp certificates: Christopher Williams, John Moffett, John Mills, Thos. Turk, Wm. Blanton, Wm. Robertson, Wm. Campbell, John Patrick, John Mitchell, Saml. Hamilton, Rob. Stuart, Wallas Estill.

(347) Hemp certificates: Margaret Robinson, James Ledderdale.

(347) Thos. Tosh, Danl. McNeill and Francis Grymes, to view a road from the Stone House to Evans's Mill. David Campbell and Samuel Downey appointed overseers of road from John McCreery's to James Moffett's, vice James Callison and David Cunningham.

(347) Danl. Smith, greatest creditor, qualifies administrator of Nicholas Null. Jacob Nicholas, John Coats and Augustine Price, appraisers of Nicholas Null.

(347) John Bowen appointed overseer of the road from the ferry on James River to the Warm Springs, opposite to John McClure's.

(348) Timothy Keith, runaway servant of Alexr. McPheeters.

(348) Walter Trimble appointed Constable, vice James McCreary.

(349) John Coalter appointed surveyor of highway from Benj. Stuart's Branch to the Court House Road.

(349) James Ledderdale asks counter security from Margaret Looney, admx. of Peter Looney, since intermarried with James McKain.

November 19, 1767.

(350) Thomas Rhodes, discharged in bankruptcy.

(350) Hemp certificates: Wm. Tees, Francis Stewart, Saml. Wilson.

(351) Hemp certificates: Gabriel Alexander, Nicholas Solles, Israel Christian, James Henderson, David Robinson, John Buckanon, Robt. Steel, Wm. Wordlow, John Brown.

(352) John Seewright appointed surveyor of highway from Stone Meeting House to Naked Creek. Gawin Leeper, same, from Gratton's Store to Naked Creek. Felix Gilbert and Joseph Dicktom, same, vice, John Cravens.

(354) John Robinson, M. R., garnishee.

(357) Thos. Carr, runaway servant of James McGill.

(358) Peter Vaneman qualified Lieutenant of Militia.

(358) Wm. McCutcheon appointed surveyor of highway, vice John Risk.

(359) Jurors: John Rusk, Jeremiah Ragen, Saml. Clark, John Brown, Wm. McKee, Joseph Kinkade, Francis Stewart, James Henderson, John Findley, Saml. Black, Wm. Long, John Caldwell.

(359) Wm. Tees vs. Michael O'Donald.—Abates by defendant's death.

(360) Joseph McMurty and George McAfee reported that there were not enough tithables convenient to make a wagon road from McMurty's Mill thro' McAfee's Gap to the wagon road, and it was only practicable to clear it for carrying loads on horseback until the country is better settled, which is ordered, and Joseph McMurty and James McAfee, Jr., to be surveyors and work with the tithables on Craig's Creek and its branches from Gatlive's up, and on Catabo from Alexander Smith's up.

(361) Jacob Pence appointed overseer of road, vice Jacob Parsinger. Michael Shirley appointed surveyor of highway, vice Nicholas Null. Zebulon Harrison, same, vice John Phillips.

(361) Jurors: James Hill, John Long, Pat. Christian, Saml. Caldwell, Joseph Gamwell, James Lawrence, David Moore, Hance Harper, Saml. Crockett, Wm. Cowdon, Jeremiah Telford, Saml. Lawrence.

(361) 1,916 acres of Mary Wood added to tithables.

(362) 600 acres of John Wood added to tithables.

(362) Wm. Black appointed surveyor of highway, vice John Black.

(362) Witnesses: James Callison, John Kirk, James Clark.

(363) John Bowen.

(365) George Weaver, bound to peace towards John Hill.

NOVEMBER 20, 1767.

(366) Hemp certificates: John Fulton, Saml. Lawrence, John Poage.

(366) George Francis, James and Adam Reaburn, to view improvements of John Archer on 345 acres and 75 acres.

(366) Road ordered from John Archer's Mill to Robert Fowler's; John Blair and John Young, surveyors.

(366) Witness: Samuel Crockett.

(367) Jurors: Samuel Buchanan, James Lawrence, Wm. Lawrence, John Craig, Benj. Keys, Wm. Kennedy, Joseph Gamwell, Thos. Picken, Jacob Woodley, Saml. Caldwell, John Fulton, Alexr. Reed.

(368) Jurors: Wm. Watterson, John Trotter, Pat. Buchanan, John Thompson, John Long, Wm. Huchison, Edward Thompson, John Bamier, Joseph McClung, Thomas Rhoades, Saml. Caldwell, James Armstrong.

(368) George Poage qualified Captain of Militia.

(369) Jurors: Wm. Christian, Andrew Greer, Wm. Baskins, James Fowler, Saml. Henderson, Wm. McKee, John Graham, John Fulton, James Buchanon, John Stuart, Joseph Gamwell, Adam Murray.

(369) Thos. Hughart, two tithables and 600 acres, added to tithables.

(369) Witnesses: Winifred and Robert Kinkead.

(369) Jurors: Patrick Evans, James and John Brown,, Wm. Willis.

(369) Witnesses: Thos. Kerr, Wm. Long, Saml. Wright.

Page
(370) Witnesses: Wm. Brown, Walter Davis, Wm. Black, John Caldwell, John Long, Wm. Christian, Wm. Wright, Alexr. Long, John Black Joseph Love.

(371) Thos. Bowyer authorized to repair the house he now lives in and be reimbursed by the County or out of the rents.

NOVEMBER 21, 1767.

(371) Robert Cunningham exempted from County levy—great age and infirmity.

(371) Saml. and James McDowell, John and Daniel Lyle, to view the old and new roads from Timber Ridge Meeting House to Isaac Taylor's.

(372) Jurors: Thos. Levasey, James Hill, John Francisco, John Clark, John Caldwell, Robt. Christian, Wm. Black, John Long, Robt. Clark, Alexr. Long, Thos. Black, Jonathan Douglas.

(372) Silas Hart qualified Justice.

(372) Witness: Walter Davis, John Stuart.

(373) Mary O'Donald qualified admx. of her deceased husband, Michael O'Donald. Appraisers, Isaac White, John McClure, Saml. and Wm. Black.

(374) Witnesses: John Murray, John Thompson, Mathew Reed.

(374) Hemp certificate: James Bell.

(377) George Skillern swore to list of delinquents. Francis Smith swore to list of delinquents.

NOVEMBER 23, 1767.

(378) Nicholas Null vs. John Craig.—Plaintiff's death abates suit.

(382) Mary McClure vs. John and Charles Allison.—Abates by plaintiff's death.

(384) Stephen Conrad vs. George Hoffmans.—Abates by plaintiff's death.

(384) Margaret Barrier vs. Isaac Burns.—Defendant returned no inhabitant.

(388) Alexr. Miller (Clerk) versus David Rice (Clerk).

(410) John Graham (Crooked), special bail.

(411) Wm. Bedford vs. John Steel.—Abates by defendant's death.

(421) Mathew Lindsay, returned no inhabitant.

(422) Special bail: John Cawley, Robert Hartgrove.

(426) Special bail: Henry Enoch.

(431) Special bail: John Murray.

(432) Andrew Greer appointed surveyor of highway from John Harrison's, at the Big Spring, to the County Line.

(433) John and Wm. Davis, Uriah Acres, James Roland—viewers.

(436) Jurors: Mathew Reed, John Francisco, John Clark, Archer Mathews, John Wallis, John Thompson, James Buchanan, Alexr. Thompson, John Bigham, Joseph Henderson, Thos. Rhoades, Michael Dickey.

(438) Witness: Francis Smith.

(441) Archd. Gilkeson appointed surveyor of highway, vice George Moffett.

(447) Juror: William West.

(449) Robert Hartgrove appointed Constable in Staunton.

Page

(450) Witnesses: Samuel Henderson, John Seewright, Gawin Leeper, Michael Dickey, Margaret Leeper.

(451) Mathew Lindsey, returned no inhabitant.

(453) Witnesses: Jacob Arckenbright, John Fudge, Samuel Maggott.

(455) Mathew Mullen, returned no inhabitant.

(456) Francis Burk, returned no inhabitant.

(459) Elizabeth Stuart's (late Elizabeth Wallace) account of administration of Samuel Wallace's estate.

NOVEMBER 24, 1767.

(468) Ordered that Thos. Lewis, Thos. Gorden and Abraham Smith lay off dower of Margaret Gregg, late widow of Arthur Johnston, deceased, in 237 acres of her late husband.

(469) Abraham Smith appointed guardian to Andrew Johnston, orphan of Arthur Johnston, to defend a suit brought by Bowyer.

(469) Euphemia Hughes appointed guardian *ad litem* of Euphemia, Jane and Mary Hughes, orphans and co-heirs of James Hughes.

(483) Order for summoning Wm. Thompson and John Buchanan continued. Order summoning Martha Bryan dismissed. Order summoning Joseph Bonsant, on complaint of Francis Viers, is dismissed. Order summoning Joseph Gamble continued. Order summoning John Cassaty dismissed. Order summoning Isabella and John Robinson continued. Order summoning Humphrey Baker discontinued.

(483) James Kennerley has leave to build a mill on his own land on South River.

NOVEMBER 25, 1767.

(484) County levy.

(485) John Murray Montague, creditor of the County.

MARCH 15, 1768.

(489) Hemp certificates: Peachy Ridgeway Gilmore, David Doak, John McKee, Jacob Anderson, Ro. Allison, Rob. Rodgers.

(490) Hemp certificates: John Patterson, John Moore, John Parks, Tim. Caul, Wm. McClellon, Wm. Bear, Wm. Campbell, Michael Coulter, Nathan Peoples, James McCrary, Rob. Whitley, James Hays.

(491) Hemp certificates: Jonathan Cunningham, James McCown, James Campbell, John Thompson, John Willey, Alexr. Deal, James Thompson, Thos. Kilpatrick, John Nickle.

(492) Hemp certificates: Moses Cunningham, David Robinson, William Robinson.

(492) James Hartgrove appointed Constable, vice Rob. Hartgrove.

(493) Lazarus Inman to work the road of which Robert Allen, Jr., is overseer.

(493) Hemp certificates: John Gilmer, John Walker, Peter Wallace, David McGee, John McClung, Andrew Larney.

(494) Hemp certificates: James McKee, Andrew Boyd, Alexr. Dunlap, John Campbell, James McCampbell, James McDowell, George Moffett, Andrew Mis Campbell, John Lyle.

(495) Hemp certificates: Joseph Alexander, Ro. Kenny, Wm. Alexander, John Failey, Saml. McDowell, Adam Reaburn.

(495) James Blair, Jr., and David Erwin appointed surveyors of highway.

(495) William Gay, orphan of Wm. Gay, deceased, to be bound to John Wahub.

(496) Wm. Alexander appointed surveyor of highway, vice Wm. Lowry. Robert Fowler appointed surveyor of highway, vice James McGill. James Crockett appointed surveyor of highway from Painter Gap to Samuel Hodges.

(496) Isaac Robinson qualified administrator of George Ghest.

(497) Halbert McClure appointed guardian to Margaret McClure, aged 11 years, and Moses McClure, aged 8 years, orphans of Nathaniel McClure, deceased.

(497) Thomas Connolly appointed surveyor of highway, vice Hugh Donaho.

(497) George Wilson, runaway servant of John Stewart.

(498) Samuel Todd has a writ *ad quod damnum* before building a water mill on his land on Whistle Creek.

MARCH 16, 1768.

(499) John Mann qualifies administrator of Caleb May.

(499) Halbert McClure bound to peace versus James McClure.

(500) Hemp certificates: Baptist McNabb, James Crockett, Thos. McCallock, Pat. Hays, Andrew Hall, Andrew Woods, Elizabeth Taylor, Andrew Lewis, Alexr. Evans, David Forbes, John Hopkins, Archd. Hopkins.

(501) Hemp certificates: Saml. Lyle, Robt. McAfee, John Hall, James McAfee, Wm. McAfee, John Lyle, Jr., Geo. McAfee, John Berry, James Lyle.

(502) Hemp certificates: Andrew Haling, John Stuart.

(502) Wm. McCutcheon bound to peace versus James Cooper.

(503) David Mitchell has leave to build water grist mill on his own land on Catawbo.

(503) Mary Green, servant to John Graham.

(503) Following orphans of Charles Whitman to be bound: Hurson Mathias Whitman, to James Gregory, to learn trade of a weaver. Catherine Whitman, to Andrew Sitlington. Jacob Whitman, to John Warwick, to learn trade of shoemaker.

(504) James McDowell bound to peace versus Samuel Henderson.

(504) Road to be viewed by Peter Wallace, Saml. Wallace, James McNabb and Halbert McClure, from William Hall's Mill to Wm. McKee's.

(504) Alexander Walker's mark recorded; also John Walker's.

(504) Thomas Dryden appointed guardian to Margaret McClure, infant orphan of Nathaniel McClure.

(505) Michael Kirkham, servant of John Skelton.

(505) Jame Trimble, aged 15, orphan of John Trimble, chose George Moffett guardian.

(505) Order of yesterday appointing Halbert McClure guardian of Moses and Margaret McClure is set aside, and Saml. McClure is appointed guardian to Moses.

(505) Ann Marshall, servant to Andrew Hall.

(505) Jacob Woodley appointed Constable.

(505) John Lyle appointed guardian to Mathew Eaken, aged 14, orphan of Walter Eaken.

(505) Andrew Lockridge qualified Captain of Militia. James Elliott qualified Lieut. of Militia.

(506) Thomas Stockton petitions to build mill on his land on Catawbo, and Court directs a jury.

(506) John Ward, Sr. (Jackson's River), exempted from levy.

(506) Henry Dooley to be surveyor of road from the Welshman's Run to Bedford Line—ordered to be established.

MARCH 17, 1768.

(507) Hemp certificates: James Laird, Wm. McBride.

(507) Thomas Gray, orphan of Walt Gray, to be bound to Wm. Poage. Jonathan Smith appointed guardian to Peter Looney, orphan of Peter Looney. John Jackson appointed guardian to Jane Claypole, orphan of William Claypole.

(507) Benj. Tuder (Tudson), apprentice of Andrew Miller.

(508) John Robinson (blacksmith), garnishee.

(508) John Bodkin appointed surveyor of highway, vice John Estill, from James Given's to head of Cow Pasture River.

(509) Commission for priv. examination of Annabella, wife of David Robinson, to deed to Francis Smith.

(512) Hemp certificates: Thomas Stuart, James Ewing, James Greenlee, Rob. Breckenridge.

(513) James Crawford vs. Saml. Patterson. } Following attached: Forty deer skins, 12 other skins, 1 fox skin.

(516) John Madison took the usual oaths to his Majesty's person and government, repeated and subscribed the adjuration oath and test, which is, on his motion, ordered to be certified.

(517) Jurors: Tully Davitt, Saml. McRoberts, John Ware, Danl. Ponder, John Gordon, George Poage, Wm. Poage, Jacob Woodley, Hugh Ware, Wm. Barefield, George Taylor, James Montgomery.

(517) Witness: James Stuart, Mathew Patterson.

(518) Walter Power informs the Court that Isabel and Alexander Angely, children of Peter Angely, were bound to him in March, 1765, the girl for four years and the boy for six years, but their indentures have been stolen.

(518) Witness: Paul Teter.

MARCH 18, 1768.

(519) Jurors: James Baits, Thomas George.

(520) Hemp certificates: Thomas Crow, Wm. Preston, Francis Smith, John Paxton, James Campbell, James Alexander.

Page

(521) Commission ordered to privily examine Elizabeth, wife of George Wilson, to deed to Charles Donnelly.

(521) Witness: Margaret Patton.

(522) Witness: Wm. Cowdon.

(522) Jurors: James Turk, James Callison, Saml. McClure, Saml. Lawrence, James Beats, Wm. McCutcheon, Francis Stuart, Wm. Moore, James McCain, Wm. Craddock, Wm. Christian, Jacob Lockhart, Nicholas Leahorn, Jr.

(522) Witnesses: James Montgomery, Hugh Ware.

(523) Witnesses: George Ware, John Ware, John Willson, Hugh Ware, Joseph Ware, Mathew Huston, and Moses Cober; Richard Campbell, from Frederick County, 60 miles; John Seviar, from Frederick County, 50 miles.

AUGUSTA COUNTY COURT RECORDS.

ORDER BOOK No. XII.

MARCH 19, 1768.

(2) Witnesses: Robert Clark, Hugh Johnston.

(5–6) Witnesses: Jacob, Jonathan and Uriah Woodley.

(6) William Crawford is appointed guardian to Mary Crawford, orphan of Alexr. Crawford.

(12) Jacob Woodley is appointed Constable.

MARCH 21, 1768.

(26) John Graham (Chris. Creek), special bail.

(65) Simon Powell, returned not found in bailiwick.

(70) Isaac Robinson vs. George Ghest.—Abates by defendant's death.

(71) Wm. Baskins, not found in bailiwick.

(92) Jacob Kent appointed Constable, vice Hugh Crockett.

(92) Overseer of the road from the Stone House to the Tinker Creek—make an alteration therein with assistance of Robert Breckinridge.

(94) Robt. Armstrong appointed surveyor of highway from Archer's Mill to the Dry Branch Gap.

MARCH 22, 1768.

(101) Called Court on Thomas Lynch, charged with larceny—acquitted.

(108) Robert Richards, returned no inhabitant.

(114) Samuel Pegs, returned no inhabitant.

(127) Thomas Barnett, son of Pat. Barnett, to be bound to Jacob Miller.

(130) Order summoning James McCain and Margaret (Looney, widow of Peter) dismissed.

(130) Order for summoning Rebecca Dougherty, to give counter security as admx. of husband, Charles Dougherty, not executed—continued.

(131) Order for summoning Richard Murray and Catherine, his wife, late Catherine Highlands, for not bringing up the orphans of Henry Highlands in a Christianlike manner—dismissed.

(131) Saml. Frazier appointed surveyor of highway from Long Meadow Bridge to Rockfish Gap Road, vice Francis Alexander.

MARCH 25, 1768.

(131) Wm. Morrice, examined for horse stealing, &c., convicted.

MAY 17, 1768.

(133) Oyer and Terminer on Tom, a slave of Robt. Bratton—housebreaking and horse-stealing.—Convicted—39 lashes and ear cropped.

MAY 19, 1768.

(137) See page 156.

(138) Hemp certificates: Henry Larkin, Abraham Brown.

(139) Hemp certificates: Henry Tamewood, John Tillery.

(140) Hemp certificate: George Clark.

(141) Surveyor of highway: James Phillips, vice Thomas Bradshaw.

(141) Rebecca Crawford, aged 16, orphan of Alexr. Crawford, chose William Crawford her guardian.

(142) Constables: Adam Pence, vice Peter Runkle; John Gordon, vice Thomas Fulton; John Douglas, vice James Seewright; John Johnson, vice James Laird; Joseph Bosart, vice Andrew Fought; Thomas Wilson, vice Thomas Wilson (Chestnut Hill).

(143) James Robinson, Hugh Crockett and Philip Love—to view a road from James Montgomery's to the Old County Line leading from Catawbo to New River.

MAY 18, 1768.

(144) John Murphy, a witness from Bedford.

(145) Constables: Geo. McAfee, vice David McGee; John Clemons, vice Wm. Patton; Robt. Fletcher, vice James Crockett.

(145) Deed: John Brown and wife to John Trimble, John Finley, Wm. McPheeters, Jr., George Berry and Hugh Young, representatives or commissioners appointed by the Congregation of the Meeting House, lately called by the name of Brown's (by the approbation and under the conduct or incumbency of the Rev. Chas. Cummins)—recorded.

(145) James Cloyd allowed to build a mill on Long's Entry Creek.

(146) Hemp certificate: Jane Muldrough.

(147) Hemp certificate: Christopher Williams.

(148) Hemp certificate: Wm. Palmer and Wm. Dalton.

(149) Witness: Wm. Ozburn. Constable: Jacob Anderson.

(150) Witness from Hanover: John Hughes.

(153) Alexr. Walker, Jr., appointed Constable, vice John McMahon.

Page

(156) See page 137.

(157) Constables: Mathias Yoakam, vice John Neelley; Thomas Patton, on New River.

(158) Constable: John Clark, vice William Hunter.

(160) Surveyor of highway: Francis Stuart, vice Alexr. Herron.

(163) Mathias Lair qualified admr. of Ferdinando Lair, and is appointed guardian of George, Ferdinando, Margaret, Catherine and Mathias, orphans of Ferdinando Lair.

(163) Robert Via, aged 6 years the 15th of this instant, son of David Via, deceased, to be bound out.

(164) Adam Dean, witness from Albemarle.

(165) James Murdock, bound over for insulting Sampson Mathews in his office.

MAY 20, 1768.

(167) Wm. Donald, a witness from Hanover.

(167) Surveyor of highway: Wm. Hutchinson, vice Geo. Mathews.

(168) Surveyor of highway: John Patterson, from John Anderson's Meadow to George Mathews.

(168) Sampson Mathews appointed guardian *ad litem* for Martha Mathews, orphan of Joshua Mathews.

MAY 21, 1768.

(174) Conrad Coger, exempted from levy.

(174) Constable on South Branch: James Dyer.

(174) Micajah Chiles, a witness from Albemarle. Samuel Woods, a witness from Amherst.

(175) Henry Cresswell—witness.

(175) Mathew Patton, qualified Captain of Militia.

(175) Constable: William Hall, vice Samuel Walker.

MAY 23, 1768.

(178) John Thompson vs. George Rodgers.—Abates by defendant's death.

(191) William Forkner, returned no inhabitant.

(231) Michael Reasner, returned no inhabitant.

(251) Hemp certificates: Andrew Huling, John Stuart, Borden's land.

(253) John Gambell vs. Sarah Sharp.—Abates by defendant's death.

(253) Wm. Watts, runaway servant of James Patterson.

(253) Mary Lawson, a servant of Thomas Black, was imported in the ship *Harriot,* Captain Thomas Herdman, and arrived 15 Sept., 1766. Her indenture was lost when Sampson and George Mathews's store was broken open September, 1767.

(266) John Pigman—witness.

(273) John Price, witness from Albemarle. Wm. Wood, witness from Albemarle.

Page

(274) Hemp certificates: Nicholas Zehorn, Jr., Alexr. McKenny.

(275) John Bowyer's mark recorded—a swallow fork in each ear and brand 63.

(287) John Welsh, servant to David Bell, agrees to serve David nine months in consideration of being taught the tailor's trade.

(290) John McFawle, returned no inhabitant.

(301) Silas Pearce, returned no inhabitant.

(303) Constable: John Gardner, vice James Stevenson.

(309) Thomas Bowyer qualifies administrator of James Jackson.

AUGUST 18, 1768.

(310) Luke Bowyer admitted to practice in this Court.

(310) Jacob Miller's nuncupative will partly proved and Catherine, widow of Jacob, qualifies admx.

(311) Nicholas Welsh, witness to deed, Staunton to Paulin, is dead.

(312) Hemp certificates: Paul Whitley, Wm. Lame, Moses Cavit.

(314) John Caton, runaway servant of Rob. Stevenson.

(314) Constable: James Hall, vice Charles Campbell.

(314) Overseers road: James Gamwell, vice John Anderson; Robert McMahon, from John Seewright's Mill to Thomas Connerley's.

(315) John Hannah has leave to build a mill on his own land on Collier's Creek.

(315) Constable: James Burnside, vice Edward Hynds.

(315) Mary Richardson, orphan of Joseph Richardson, to be bound to Mathew Robertson.

(315) Francis Smith qualifies administrator of David Miller.

(316) Constable: John Boyd, vice George Adams.

AUGUST 17, 1768.

(316) Robert Lusk qualified Ensign.

(317) Martha Allen, wife of Robert Allen, relinquishes dower in tract— 44 acres—conveyed to John McClenachan. Surveyor of road, Wm. McKee.

(318) Hemp certificates: John Mills, James Gilmore.

(319) Hemp certificates: Andrew Buckanon, Thomas McCollock and Andrew Smiley.

(319) Jonathan Whitley appointed guardian *ad litem* to Lilley Whitley. Margaret Clark appointed guardian *ad litem* to James Clark.

(320) "Lie Bill" by Elizabeth Inzer to Ephraim Love—ordered recorded.

(323) Wm. Watterson summoned for not providing for his servant, Elizabeth Wiley.

(326) Hugh Hays imprisoned for debt.

(327) Tithables in the bent of Jackson's River from Robert Galespy's to Fort Young—exempted from working on the Cow Pasture Road.

AUGUST 18, 1768.

(333) Hemp certificates: Sampson Christian, John Davis (Mossy Creek).

(334) On motion of John McElwrath, deeds Borden's executors to Robt. McElwrath be altered from Robert to the name of John McElwrath.

(335) Saml. Weer, Saml. Steel and Robert Steel (miller)—to view a road from Steel's Mill to James Telford's.

(335) Richard Moore granted leave to build a mill on his own land, near Fort Chiswell, at the mouth of Lick Run.

(335) Peter Cassaty, orphan of Neal Cassaty, to be bound to Saml. Wallace, to learn trade of carpenter.

(336) Richard Campbell, witness from Frederick. John Seviar, witness from Frederick.

(336) Patrick Martin, two tithables and 752 acres—added to tithables.

(337) Abraham Hempenstall—witness.

(338) Witnesses: Joseph, Elizabeth, Joseph, Jr., Thomas and Robert Rutherford.

(339) Witness: Valentine Seviar, Jr.

AUGUST 19, 1768.

(341) Robert Gragg, from Winchester—witness.

(343) Alexr. McWiller, being arrested as a servant, discharged, nothing appearing against him. Allden Willott, same. Alexander McGuillen, same (McWillen, *supra?*).

(343) William Morris, runaway servant of John Wilson.

(344) Mary Wilson qualifies admx. of decd. husband, James Wilson.

(344) John Ellis, runaway servant of Samuel Hind.

(345) Witnesses: James Harris, John McNutt.

(348) Witnesses: John Frogg, John Pigman.

(349) Juror: Robert Minnis.

AUGUST 20, 1768.

(352) Surveyor of highway: John Hogshead, vice James Sayers, Jr.

(352) Sarah Buckthorn, servant of William Lockhart.

(352) Jurors: Joseph Goore, Henry Goore.

(353) James Cowan, Jr., appointed Constable, vice John Hunter.

(354) Witness: Joseph McAdams.

(354) Walter Gray, runaway servant of William Poage.

(363) Thomas Moore's will produced and witnesses summoned.

AUGUST 22, 1768.

(369) John Campbell, Jr. (near Stone Meeting House), special bail.

(385) Two "Stone Plates" attached and sold for 5/6.

(391) Andrew Boyd vs. John Bryan. } One Tom Hawk attached and sold for 1ˢ/.

(415) Margaret Robertson, admx. of —— Robertson, versus Abraham Haines.—Abates by plaintiff's marriage.

(440) Constable: John Craig (Robert's son), vice John Frazier.

Page

(442) Elizabeth Wallace—no inhabitant.

(444) John Shanklin, Charles Callachan, John Hopkins—to view road from Thomas Gordon's to Aaron Oliver's.

August 23, 1768.

(450) Overseer road: John Black, vice Robert Reed.

(450) Sarah Walkly, runaway servant of George Berry.

(455) Witness: Edward Biggs.

(464) John Hughes, returned no inhabitant.

(466) Witness: Abraham Towson.

(466) Road surveyor: David Bell, vice John Anderson.

September 7, 1768.

(467) Called Court for examination of John Dunn—larceny—39 lashes.

September 20, 1768.

(467) Last August, Court having recommended Patrick Martin, John Christian and John Dickinson to appointment as Sheriff, Martin withdraws, and at his request and with consent of Christian, John Bowyer's name is placed in his stead.

November 15, 1768.

(469) Tithables added: Arthur McClure and one other, John Davis, Robert Allen and two others, Samuel Lindsey and two others.

(469) County levy.

(470) County levy: To John Bearling, wolf scalp; to Solomon Turpen, wolf scalp.

(471) John York, runaway servant of Robert Gilkison.

(472) Constables: Joseph Hicks, vice Saml. Pepper; Andrew Calvin, on Little River of New River; James Curry, vice John Clark.

(472) Road surveyor: Thomas Rowland, vice Samuel McRoberts.

(472) Constable: Thomas Brown, vice Walter Trimble.

(473) Admn. granted to Saml. McDowell and Pat. Martin on estate of Wm. Wilson, on motion of Ann Pollock, wife of James Pollock.

(473) Surveyors of highway: Cornelius Ruddle, from Reeder's Mines to Michael Warring's; John Crawford, vice George Poage, from Pedler Ford to Bullett's Springs.

(474) Constable: Thomas Patterson, vice John Dixon.

(474) John Mitchell (in Forks of James) exempted from levy. Charles Boyles, exempted from levy.

(474) John Nelson complains of being detained as a servant of James Cotton.

(474) James Anderson, Jr., (son of James Anderson, deaf) be summoned for not supporting his children in a Christianlike manner.

(474) Robert Reed, runaway servant of David Hogshead.

Page

(476) John Bowyer qualified Sheriff.

(476) Nicholas and Eleanor King, orphans of Joseph King, to be bound to Robert Clark.

(477) Constable: William McClalen, vice Andrew Neelly.

(482) John Davis appointed guardian of Mary, John, Daniel and Michael Higgins, orphans of Daniel Higgins.

NOVEMBER 17, 1768.

(490) Highway surveyor: Henry Erwin, vice Benjamin Harrison, from Linvell's Creek to Mole Hill.

(494) Robert Belsher, vice Samuel Mousey.

NOVEMBER 18, 1768.

(494) Road surveyor: Moses McElwain, vice William Renix.

(495) Constable: Samuel Blackwood in Cap. Christian's Co.

(495) John Summers, James Gilmore and Moses Colier, to view a road from George Gibson's at the House Mountain to John Hanna's Mill.

(495) One panther skin attached.

(497) James Robinson (South River) exempted from levy.

(499) Mary Sanders, servant of John Sharp Watkins.

(504) Lydia Lyon to be bound to Francis Smith.

NOVEMBER 19, 1768.

(507) Lilley Pratt, servant of James Kennerley.

(508) County levy—continued.

(508) Elizabeth Wiley, servant of William Watterson.

AUGUSTA COUNTY COURT RECORDS.

ORDER BOOK No. XIII.

NOVEMBER 21, 1768.

(1) Thos. McFarron vs. Wm. Moore.—Attachment on one tomahawk.

(11) Attachment on one cuttoe knife.

(31) Wm. Stewart vs. James Anderson.—Abates by plaintiff's death.

(32) Thomas Bullitt, returned no inhabitant.

(42) John Nelson to be bound to Wm. Hyde, to learn trade of carptnter.

(45) John McCreery appointed road surveyor. John Hamilton appointed road surveyor from Warm Springs Road to Cap. Dickenson's, and to work with the tithables on Jackson's River, from Wm. Mann's to Duncan McFarland's, and tithables on back Creek—vice John McClenachan.

Page

(47)   Andrew Greer   ⎫ Conveyance to be made as
               vs.   ⎬ soon as Euphemia, Jane and
James Hughes's admrs. and heirs ⎭ Mary Hughes come of age.

(48) Ephraim Wilson—witness from Pittsylvania.

(48) Margaret Crow, wife of William Crow, releases dower.

(49) John Sevior, witness from Frederick.

(50) Abraham Townsend, witness from Albemarle.

(52) Andrew Lewis qualified justice in Court of Chancery.

(61) Robert Brown and James Sawyer, Jr., to view the nearest and most convenient way thro' Buffalo Gap to the road leading to Staunton. Thomas Hughart and Andrew Hamilton to view the most convenient way from John Hodges' to the Buffalo Gap road

NOVEMBER 23, 1768.

(70) John Redpath, runaway servant of Samp. Mathews.

(70) County levy is 4 pence.

NOVEMBER 26, 1768.

(71) Called Court for examination of Robert McMahon, charged with the murder of Robert Reaburn.—Sent to Williamsburg for trial.

NOVEMBER 29, 1768.

(72) Oyer and Terminer on George and Poll, slaves of John Rice, of North Carolina, for housebreaking.—Guilty, but as they were under the influence of George Hendricks, ought not to suffer death, but receive 39 lashes and ears cropped.

MARCH 21, 1769.

(75) John Magill qualified attorney at law.

(77) Hemp certificates: Nicholas Sollas, Thomas Arnett.

(78) Jane Graham, widow of deceased, and Joseph Vohub, qualify admrs. of David Graham.

(78) Thomas Clofford, runaway servant of Robert Fowler. William Brewer, runaway servant of Hugh Campbell.

(79) Miss Susanna Evans, aged —, orphan of Daniel Evans, chose Wm. McClenachan her guardian.

(79) Hemp certificates: John Parks, James McCroorey.

(80) Hemp certificates: William Uly, Thomas Bland.

(81) Hemp certificates: James Templeton.

(82) Following to be bound out by Church Wardens, viz: Mildred Viers to John Campbell; Elizabeth Viers to Robert Campbell; Gideon Viers and David Viers to David Laird.

(83) Road surveyor: John Finley, vice Robert Allen.

(83) Abraham Christman proposes to build a mill on his own land on Crab Creek.

Page

(84) Road surveyor: Robert Hamilton, vice John Gilmore.

(84) Court appoints William McPheeters, Jr., guardian of Alexr. and Robert Crawford, orphans of Alexr. Crawford.

(84) Constable: John Summers, vice Alexr. Dale.

(84) Road surveyor: John Hays, vice Jacob Anderson.

MARCH 22, 1769.

(85) John Gilmore qualified administrator of Margaret Lynn.

(86) Adam Stroud naturalized.

(86) James McCrachy appointed Constable, vice Mathias Loacum.

(87) John Paxton appointed road surveyor, vice John Bowyer.

(88) John Lynn, orphan of Robert Lynn, to be bound to Archibald Reah.

(89) John Stewart, security for Susanna King, admx. of her deceased husband, John Cockrain (wife of Henry King), asks counter security. Henry and Susanna also summoned to show cause why they do not provide for their children.

(90) Mary, wife of David Frame, relinquishes dower.

(90) Viewers to report on a road from Dry Gap to John Archer's Mill.

(94) One sheperdee attached.

(96) Timothy Warren appointed Constable, vice William West.

(96) Following orphans of Francis McCown to be bound: Agnes, to John McCown; Francis, to Tully Deavitt; Catherine, to Robert Christian.

(99) Jacob Lorton appointed Constable, vice Samuel Pepper.

MARCH 23, 1769.

(102) One frizer and ring attached.

(103) Samuel Ekerling versus Valentine Zinn, son and heir-at-law of Garrett Zinn.—Chancery.

(104) John Sibert binds himself to Jacob Argenbright.

(104) Patrick Mooney exempted from County levy.

MARCH 24, 1769.

(109) Sheriff informed the Court that negroes George and Poll, belonging to George Rice, of North Carolina, had lain in jail three months, and asked directions.—Ordered that he provide iron collars, stamped with the letters A. G., and hire them out until their master comes and proves property.

(110) Following attached: Smothing iron, fire shovel.

(110) Following garnishees: William Thomas, Joseph Boshire, Nathan Rigland, John Rayreigh.

(111) Attached: One chaff bed.

(112) Witness: Henry Eyness.

(113) Felix Gilbert and Michael Shirley appointed surveyors of the road from Jacob Nicholas's to Hance Magots.

(116) John Murray and Elizabeth, one of the co-heirs of her uncle, John Mathews, deceased, plaintiffs, versus Martha Mathews.—Division of the estate.

(119) Witnesses: Jacob Moyer, Windlw Evert, Christiania Evert.

(119) Wm. Crane beat his master, Henry King.—Complaint dismissed because Henry was not hurt.

March 25, 1769.

(125) Charles Donnerly and John McCreery appointed surveyors of road from Capt. Charles Lewis's to the Fork of Dickinson's Road.

(139) Wm. Craig versus Robert Archer.—Dismissed; no inhabitant.

(141) Lilley Whitely versus John Thompson.—Abates by plaintiff's marriage.

(148) James Dever versus Robt. Henderson.—Dismissed; no inhabitant.

March 27, 1769.

(169) Wm. Christian granted certificate that he is of probity, honesty and good behavior.—Attorney's license.

(169) Henry Pauling, Joseph Murty and John Potts—to view a road from Joseph Murty's house down Craig's Creek and Patterson's Creek into the main road from John Crawford's to the Stone House.

(169) George Skillern qualified Justice.

April 18, 1769.

(196) Alexr. McClenachan qualified Deputy Sheriff.

April 19, 1769.

(196) Court of Claims and Grievances.

June 20, 1769.

(197) Hemp certificate: Archd. McCurdy.

(199) Overseers of road: Thomas Reed, vice Malcolm Allen; Mathew Kinney.

(199) Jacob Hornberrier—naturalized.

(200) Constables: Wm. Carren, vice Joseph Robinson; Wm. Rutledge, vice Alexr. Gibson; Wm. Lusk, vice John Carlile; Robt. Gamble, vice John Clark.

(200) Overseer road: John Buchanan, vice Samuel McCutcheon.

(202) Constable: Richard Mays, vice John Clendennin.

(203) James Lynch, runaway servant of Rob. Stephenson; Wm. Wooldridge, runaway servant of Michael Coulter; Joseph Webb, runaway servant of Joseph Moore.

(204) Constable: William Craig, vice Adam Pence.

(204) Road overseer: Henry Stone, vice Henry Pickle.

(204) William Beates, runaway servant of William Crawford.

Page

(205) Hemp certificate: Robert McAfee.

(206) Hemp certificates: James McAfee, Jr., Alexr. Airron.

(207) Constables: James Edmiston, vice John Gardner; Wm. McGee, vice George McAfee.

(208) William Christian committed to jail for debt.

(210) Constable: John Peoples, vice Daniel Lyle.

(211) Constable: John Herdman, Jr., vice John Gordon.

(212) Overseer of road: Thomas Moore, vice Andrew Greer, from County Line to Fork of Road by John Harrison's.

(212) Children of Daniel Clark and Christian Boyd to be bound.

(214) Complaint of Eleanor Dunn—James Stewart to be summoned to show cause why he does not teach his apprentice, Walter Dunn, his trade and cloathe and provide for him according to law.

(217) Juror: James Bambridge.

(218) Robert Armstrong, Henry Cresswell and James Bell—to view the most convenient way from Buffalo Gap to Staunton.

JUNE 22, 1769.

(220) Aaron Hughes, John Moore, Thomas Moore and Jacob Woodley— to view the road from Hughes's Lane by Mathew Harrison's Mill to County Line.

(222) Following recommended for appointment as Justices: Mathew Harrison, William Ingles, William Christian, George Mathews, John Mc-Clenachan, James Robertson, Stephen Trigg, William Horbert, Philip Love, Anthony Bledsoe, John Bowman, John Thomas, Robert Doage and John Montgomery. The following to be left off and reasons given to the Governor by the Clerk: John Chizwell, John Wilson, John Archer, Alexr. Boyd, David Robinson, Benj. Estill, John Maxwell, Charles Lewis, Andrew Bird, Richard Woods.

(224) Margaret Woods, late Margaret Robinson, widow of William Robinson.

(225) Aaron Hughes appointed Constable, vice Jacob Woodley.

(226) John Southerland, an orphan, to be bound to Thomas Lookey.

(227) Road surveyor: George Baxter, vice John Thomas.

JUNE 23, 1769.

(229) Witness: Nathan Ragland.

(234) Overseer of road: William Herren, vice Benj. Harrison.

(237) Witness: Samuel Irons.

(240) Witness: Sibera Trader.

JUNE 24, 1769.

(252) John Hill has leave to build a grist mill on his own land on Strumples Creek.

JUNE 26, 1769.

(260) Robert McMahon vs. John Jones.—Abates by plaintiff's death.

Page

(301) Blanton, Assignee, vs. Lorimer.—Abates by defendant's death.

(302) John Cockrain, son of John Cockrain, decd., to be bound to Hugh Allen, he teaching him the trade of a wheelwright and joiner.

(302) Following orphans of John Cockrain, decd., to be bound according to law, viz: Robert, James, Elizabeth and Mary.

(305) Wm. McCutcheon, security for Margaret Clark, admx. of her husband, since intermarried with John Smith, claims counter security.

(313) John Dean appointed road surveyor from Forks of Lewis and Dickenson Road to the Warm Springs, vice John Hamilton. Road to be surveyed from Davis's cabin to Warm Springs.

(316) John Black appointed overseer of road, vice Robert Reed.

AUGUST 15, 1769.

(316) Barbara Sivert, daughter of Charles Frederick Sivert, to be bound to Philip Horless.

AUGUST 16, 1769.

(319) Following children of Francis Siver to be bound out: Francis Peter Siver, to Peter Churn, to learn cooper; Margaret Siver, to Adam Haverstick; Mary Siver, to Simon Nicholas.

(319) James Caghey, Wm. Terry and Wm. Cox—to value improvements of John Mills on 550 acres on South Fork of Roanoke and 1,170 acres on the Wolf Creek, a branch of Roanoke, and 180 acres on Roanoke.

(320) Appraisers appointed on estate of George Darr.

(322) Appraisers appointed on estate of John Buchanon, viz: On James River, John and Jonathan Smith and George Skillern; at New River, John Blackmore, Samuel Pepper and Joseph How; at Reed Creek, John Montgomery, David Looney and Josiah Ramsey.

(323) Richard Moore has leave to build mill on South Fork of Reed Creek, about two miles above the wagon road.

(324) Following recommended as Justices, viz: Mat. Harrison, Wm. Ingles, Wm. Christian, George Mathews, John McClenachan, James Robertson, Stephen Trigg, Wm. Herbert, Philip Love, Anthony Bledsoe, John Bowman, John Thomas, Robert Doage, John Montgomery, Alexr. Thompson, James Craig, Walter Crockett, Andrew Lockridge, Walter Cunningham and James McGavock. The following to be left off, reasons to be given by the Clerk and former order discharged, viz: John Chiswell, John Buchanan, John Wilson, John Archer, John Maxwell, Charles Lewis, Alexr. Boyd.

AUGUST 17, 1769.

(325) "Massauntting" mentioned.

(328) Catharine Sawyers, orphan of Alexr. Sawyers, aged 15 last March, to be bound to Daniel McNare.

(329) Benj. Carr—witness from Culpeper.

(331) William Charlton appointed appraiser of John Melley's improvements.

ORDER BOOK No. XIV.

AUGUST 18, 1769.

Page

(2) John Buchanan vs. Robt. Sayers.—Death of plaintiff abates.

(11) Adam Broyle vs. John Buchanan.—Death of plaintiff (?) abates.

OCTOBER 17, 1769.

(20) James Troro's estate committed to Samuel Erwin, greatest creditor.

(21) James Young, aged 14, orphan of James Young, chose John Young guardian.

OCTOBER 18, 1769.

(22) John Neeley (son of James) appointed guardian of Catharine Evans, orphan of Daniel Evans.

(25) James Gamwell vs. Thos. Gillespie.—Abates by plaintiff's death.

OCTOBER 19, 1769.

(27) John Munks, being committed to jail as a runaway servant, is discharged, nothing appearing against him.

(27) Wm. Henry, executor of Wm. Jevon, vs. Francisco.—Judgment.

(29) Anna, wife of Francis Smith, priv. examination—deed Francis Smith to Robert Findley.

(32) George and William Mathews and John Maury appointed guardians of John, Moses, William, Ann and Elizabeth, orphans of John Bowen.

OCTOBER 20, 1769.

(43) Mathews vs. Mirian Cloyd.—Attached—one Dutch oven.

(56) John Bowyer, Sheriff, informs the Court that he is apprehensive that the County is about to be divided, when his house will be in the new County, having served but one year, prays that the Court will recommend his brother, William Bowyer, for Sheriff, which is done.

OCTOBER 21, 1769.

(59) James Frow vs. John Archer.—Abates by plaintiff's death.

(59) George Null, eldest son and heir of Nicholas Null, vs. John Craig. Decree in chancery for plaintiff for 400 acres.

NOVEMBER 13, 1769.

(59) Called Court on Jacob, a slave for felony.—Not guilty of housebreaking, but of shooting at the children of Alexr. Moore—39 lashes.

NOVEMBER 22, 1769.

(61) Called Court on James Denniston, for breaking into shop of John Abney and stealing silver coin—39 lashes.

Page
(61) Two stoves to be purchased for the jail.

DECEMBER 19, 1769.

(62) David Black's will contested by his widow, Elizabeth Black, on ground of insanity, but overruled and recorded.

(62) Dower to be laid off to Margaret McMahon in 300 acres conveyed by her husband to Hugh Donaho.

MARCH 20, 1770.

(64) John Stevenson appointed guardian to James Rusk, orphan of James Rusk.

(64) William Strother Madison qualified Deputy Sheriff.

(64) Elizabeth Rutherford qualifies admx. of Thomas Rutherford.

(65) John Kerr, eldest son of deceased, qualifies admr. of James Kerr.

(65) John May took the oath of an attorney.

MARCH 21, 1770.

(66) The surveyor ordered to run the dividing line between Augusta and Botetourt as far as the Western Waters.

(66) Alexr. McClenachan appointed guardian of John, Andrew, James, Elizabeth and David Black, orphans of David Black.

(66) Following recommended as Justices: Mathew Harrison, John Mc-Clenachan, George Mathews, Michael Bowyer, James McDowell, Alexr. Robertson, John Gratton, John Hays, Jr., Thomas Hugart, John Stewart, James Craig, Elijah McClenachan.

(68) Attached—a piece of Sagathy, one capuchin.

(69) Mildred Randal to be bound to Hugh Donaho. Rachel Randal to be bound to Samuel Hunter.

MARCH 28, 1770.

(80) Estate of Mary Creist, being very small, is committed to the Sheriff.

(80) Samuel Henderson and Jane ordered summoned to prove the will of John Stevenson.

(80) John Anderson vs. Christian Bingaman.—Defendant no inhabitant.

(100) William Fowler vs. James Stevenson.—Abates by death of plaintiff.

(100) Andrew Hays vs. Moses Cunningham.—Abates by death of deft.

MAY 15, 1770.

(102) Catharine Madison, aged 16, orphan of Humphrey Madison, chose John Madison her guardian.

(102) John Gratton, Alexr. McClenachan, John Poage, Saml. McDowell, George Moffet, Archibald Huston, John Hays, Wm. Bowyer, John Mc-Clenachan—qualified vestrymen.

JUNE 19, 1770.

(103) New Commission.

(104) John Caldwell has leave to build an *oil* mill on his land on South River.

June 20, 1770.

June 21, 1770.

August 21, 1770.

August 22, 1770.

August 25, 1770.

August 27, 1770.

August 28, 1770.

November 20, 1770.

(149) Elizabeth Campbell complains of her father, William Campbell, that he does not provide for her and his other children—to be summoned.

(149) George Mathews qualified Sheriff.

NOVEMBER 21, 1770.

(150) William Long, aged 15, orphan of Wm. Long, chose Thomas and Charles Lewis guardians.

NOVEMBER 26, 1770.

(156) Elizabeth Wilson, aged 16, orphan of Samuel Wilson, chose Alexr. McClenachan her guardian, and he is appointed guardian for Martha, her sister.

NOVEMBER 27, 1770.

(157) Charles Boddy fined for peddling without license.

NOVEMBER 28, 1770.

(162) William Hugart } Decree for plaintiff for sale of 160 acres on
vs. } Jackson's River, part of 782 acres patented to
Joseph Carpenter } Joseph June 1, 1750. Memo.—The land was sold by Edward McMullen, Jan'y., 1771, at public auction, and bought by plaintiff for £90.

(169) Henry Coffman's death abates suit.

NOVEMBER 29, 1770.

(177) It appearing that Archer Mathews is no longer capable of instructing his apprentice, Robert Shaw, as an apprentice, and that James Shaw, Robert's father, is incapable of bringing him up in a Christianlike manner—to be bound to John Frogg, to learn the same trade.

JANUARY 15, 1771.

(179) Estate of Arthur Frogg, decd., committed to his brother John Frogg.

MARCH 17, 1771.

(180A) The record says 1772—the leaf pages 181-182 have been torn out and the pages 180A-183A were once sealed together.
(See page 328, infra.)

(180A) Conrad Custard's nuncupative will proved, the widow consenting—estate committed to his son, Paul Custard.

MARCH 19, 1771.

(180) Mary Huffman, orphan of Nicholas Huffman, to be bound to David Magert.—He agrees to give her £8, 10, and a new spinning wheel when she comes of age and teach her to read and write. Elizabeth Huffman,

orphan as above, to Samuel Morgert.—He gives her £9, 16, a new spinning wheel and teaches her to read and write.

(180) Estate of William Christian committed to Wm. Bowyer, creditor.

MARCH 20, 1771.

(183) On complaint of Henry King and Susanna, Hugh Allen summoned to show cause why he illegally detains and does not teach his apprentice, John Cockrane, his trade and give him sufficient clothing.

MARCH 21, 1771.

(184) Elliott Rutherford appointed guardian of Robert, Joseph, Reuben and Mary Rutherford, orphans of Thomas Rutherford.

(188) Estate of Wm. Floyd, decd., committed to his eldest brother, Samuel Floyd.

MARCH 22, 1771.

(189) Alexr. Miller vs. John Brown.—Verdict of not guilty.

MARCH 23, 1771.

(190) Jacob Woodley, security for Elizabeth Rutherford, admx. of Thos. Rutherford, decd., her late husband (since intermarried with Evan Price), asks counter security.

(191) John Pairtree natrualized.

MARCH 27, 1771.

(196) Pat. McCorkle vs. Wm. Christian.—Defendant's death abates suit

MARCH 28, 1771.

(197) James Dunn to be bound to Thomas Smith, who is to teach him trade of carpenter and joiner.

(204) Henry Picket's death abates suit.

(208) Malcom McCown vs. William Christian, Jr.—Defendant's death abates suit.

(208) William Kennedy, returned no inhabitant.

(214) Liquors rated.

MARCH 21, 1771.

(215) Called Court on Mathew Thorpe, for horse stealing from Joseph Pearce of Westmoreland.—Committed for trial.

(215) John Todd, Jr., qualified attorney.

(217) Elizabeth, wife of James Anderson, relinquished dower in 100 acres—deed to Joseph Reaburn.

MARCH 22 1771.

(218) John McClenachan qualified Captain of Militia.

(218) William Glaves appointed guardian *ad litem* for Esther Glaves, orphan of Mathew Glaves, deceased.

(218) Wm. Watterson, confined in jail for debt, applies for release as a bankrupt.

MARCH 23, 1771.

(222) Nancy Childs, daughter of Elizabeth Carroll, to be bound to Elizabeth Cunningham.

MARCH 24, 1771.

(224) Gabriel Jones, Felix Gilbert and Daniel Smith inform the Court that smallpox in the natural way is come in their neighborhood within two or three miles of their plantations.—Leave is given to Dr. John McDonald and every other doctor to inoculate the said families or any other in any or what part of the County any person that chooses to be inoculated.

MARCH 27, 1771.

(231) David Beard vs. John Stuart.—Abates by defendant's death.

MARCH 28, 1771.

(231) John Stuart vs. Sampson Mathews.—Abates by plaintiff's death.
(242) Archer Mathews—no inhabitant.
(246) Robert Armstrong—no inhabitant.
(250) Mary Dice qualifies admx. of husband, George Dice.
(251) William Strother Madison qualified Deputy Sheriff.

AUGUST 21, 1771.

(254) Samuel Craig is appointed guardian of John Black, orphan of Anthony Black.
(255) Isabella Scott proves the importation of herself and children, viz: Nathaniel, Mathew, John, William, Jean, Francis and Isabella.
(255) Frances McNutt, the same—her children, viz: James, John, Frances, Agnes and Isabella.
(255) James Scott, same, for himself and wife, Rachel.
(255) Robert Cowardin, same, for himself and wife, Mary.

AUGUST 23, 1771.

(256) John Edmenston's death abates suit.
(258) Court requests that Andrew Bird be left out of the commission of the peace because he was guilty of wilful and corrupt perjury in the suit, Bird vs. Thomas Moore, for slander.

MARCH 29, 1771.

(273) James Gregory vs. James Cochrane.—Abates by plaintiff's death.
(278) Joseph Long—no inhabitant.
(279) William Slaughter—no inhabitant.

November 19, 1771.

Page

(288) Ann, wife of John Trimble, released dower in 200 acres—deed to James Elliot.

November 20, 1771.

(288) Called Court on Jane Dove for murdering her child—not guilty because insane.

(289) Agness Dean, admx. of husband, John Wilson.

(290) Mary Kelly, orphan of John Kelly, to be bound to John Malcolm.

November 21, 1771.

(291) Administration of estate of James McDowell, decd., granted his widow, Elizabeth, and his brother, Samuel.

(295) William and Michael Bowyer, John and Alexr. McClenachan, Daniel Smith, Samuel McDowell, Archibald Huston and Alexr. Thomson qualified Vestrymen.

November 22, 1771.

(296) The orphans of Thomas Hackett, decd., in the possession of their stepfather, Thomas Hackett, (?) to be bound out.

November 26, 1771.

(301) Benjamin Lindon, son of Joseph Lindon, to be bound to William Boone.—He agrees to give him when free a horse and saddle, value £10; a suit of clothes, value £8, and two years' schooling.

November 27, 1771.

(303) County levy.

(303) To Thomas Trimble, son of David.

(304) Euphemia Bowers (Bowen?) to be bound to Thomas Smith.

(306) The old Court House in which Alexr. St. Clair now lives, to be leased for 5 years.

November 28, 1771.

(307) William Christian, security for Elizabeth Bryan (widow and admx. of her husband, David Bryan, but since intermarried with John Bowman), asks counter security.

(307) County levy is 2/6.

(307) William Christian, security for Margaret Robinson (widow and admx. of husband, Wm. Robinson, but since intermarried with Saml. Wood).

(318) John Dailey—no inhabitant.

(319) James Moore—death abates suit.

(323) Andrew Buntin and John Smiley—no inhabitants.

January 2, 1772.

(324) Court of Claims and Propositions and Grievances.

Page

(324) A certificate of Saml. McDowell to Wm. Gilmer for provisions for the Militia of Augusta and Botetourt ordered certified.—Same to John Thompson and Moses Cunningham.

(324) A certificate from Charles Lewis and John McClenachan to Wm. Shorp and Thomas Drinnen for services done by them—ordered certified.

(324) Claim of Charles Lewis and sundry other persons for services—certified.

(324) Petition for appointment of new trustees for town of Staunton ordered certified.

FEBRUARY 18, 1772.

(326) Ann Heatherly, daughter of Thomas Heatherly, to be bound to Alexr. St. Clair—her father being unable to provide for her.

MARCH 17, 1772.

(326) See page 180[A] above.—Same orders in both places.

(329) Hugh McGlaughlin, orphan of Hugh McGlaughlin, aged 14, to be bound to John Hogshead, he teaching him the trade of a currier, farmer and shoemaker.

(329) Admn. of estate of Samuel McDonald granted his brother, Henry McDonald.

MARCH 18, 1772.

(331) Robert McNight to be bound to James Hogshead, Jr.

(331) Patrick Boyd to be bound to John Crawford to learn trade of blacksmith.

(331) Ann Cafferty to be bound to John Askins.

MARCH 19, 1772.

(335) John Gratton qualified Vestryman.

(335) Margaret and James Ramsey to be bound out.

(335) Wm. Given's estate committed to John Carlile.

MARCH 20, 1772.

(337) John Lewis and John Lyle qualified Vestrymen.

(338) William Campbell, security for Mary Donald (admx. of husband, Michael O'Donald, since intermarried with John Adair), counter security.—Division between the orphans of Michael ordered.

(339) Rating of liquors.

MARCH 23, 1772.

(341) Letter from Wiat Coleman authorizing the binding out of his son, Samuel Coleman, ordered recorded.

Page
(346) Samuel Clark—no inhabitant.
(350) John Kerr's death abates suit.
(354) William McNabb—no inhabitant.
(354) Andrew Fitzpatrick—no inhabitant.
(361) William Gwinn's death abates suit.
(361) Mary Kettle to be bound.
(361) Sheriff to advertise repairing of jail and making a ducking stool.

APRIL 11, 1772.

(362) Oyer and Terminer on 2 slaves for murdering Thomas Marmeon—guilty—to be hanged on 13th of present month between 12 and 2—heads to be severed—one to be affixed on a pole below the town near the road at the rocks and the other near the road leading from Wm. Mitchell's to Staunton.

(364) James McCaumus and George Wallace to be bound out.

(365) Lewis Wamanstaff, aged 4 years, to be bound to Ludwick Wagoner.—The father has run away.

(366) Charlotte Rea to be bound out to David Robertson.

(366) Hannah McNeiley bound out.

MAY 20, 1772.

(368) James McGlaughlin, son of Hugh McGlaughlin, to be bound to James McVey, to learn trade of carpenter.

MAY 22, 1772.

(376) Following to be paid as patrollers, viz: Valentine Cloninger, John Redpath, James Culbertson, Thos. Smith, John Cawley, Thos. Rhoads, John Andrew, Alexr. St. Clair, Christopher Graham.

MAY 23, 1772.

(380) Alexr. Wright's death abates suit.
(389) James McDonald's death abates suit.
(390) William Hamilton—no inhabitant.
(394) Joseph Currans—no inhabitant.
(396) New jail ordered to be built.
(397) Daniel Henderson's death abates suit.

AUGUST 18, 1772.

(400) Barnard Moore qualified attorney.
(400) Admn. of estate of James Stuart committed to widow, Isabella.
(401) Admn. of Paul Shaver granted to widow, Elizabeth.
(402) Archibald Alexander qualified coroner.
(402) Admn. of Sebastian Neigley granted to John Shull.
(403) Admn. of Mark Swadley granted to Sebastian Hover.

AUGUST 19, 1772.

Page

(403) Michael and George Kentner naturalized.

(403) John Karr to be bound to Isaac Morrison.

(404) Jane Claypole, aged 18, orphan of William Claypole, chose John Gratton guardian.

(404) Admn. of Jacob Gillespy granted son, Jacob.

(404) John Gilmore, aged 14, orphan of Thomas Gilmore, chose John Gilmore and John Thompson guardians.

(408) John Lickings and Dorothy, late Dorothy Caplinger, widow of Samuel Caplinger.

(408) William Woolridge to be bound to William Reah.

(408) Admn. of Daniel Henderson granted to John Henderson.

AUGUST 20, 1772.

(409) Charles Lewis qualified Lieutenant Colonel of County.

(409) Robert Lyle bound over towards Moses Trimble to keep the peace, and his name stricken from the list of recommendations as Sheriff.

(409) George Moffett qualified Vestryman.

(410) Thomas Lorrimer's estate to be appraised.

(411) Charles O'Donald, aged 17, orphan of Michael O'Donald, chose Thomas Stuart guardian.

AUGUST 22, 1772.

(424) Stephen Loy—no inhabitant.

(432) John Frogg to be paid for repairing the jail and building the ducking stool.

(432) Martha Mathews, orphan of Joshua Mathews, chose Sampson Mathews her guardian.

SEPTEMBER 1, 1772.

(435) Called Court on Frederick Speer, charged with horse stealing—bound over to grand jury.

SEPTEMBER 21, 1772.

(436) Called Court on William Mosely for larceny—sent to Williamsburg for trial.

NOVEMBER 19, 1772.

(438) Admn. of Robert Hook, Jr., granted to his widow, Jane Hook, *et al.*

(438) Timothy Ryan being runaway, his children, viz: Mary, aged 8; Martha, aged 5, and Jeremiah, aged 2, to be bound out.

(438) Daniel Smith qualified Sheriff.

(438) Admn. of Wm. Sutlington granted to Andrew Sutlington.

(439) Admn. of Jacob Roleman granted to Christian Roleman.

(439) Mary McCoy to be bound to William Wallace.

NOVEMBER 18, 1772.

(443) Lettice Kilpatrick to be bound to Thomas Kilpatrick.

(443) Francis Gardner appointed guardian to Francis and Samuel Gardner, orphans of Thomas Gardner.

NOVEMBER 19, 1772.

(446) County levy.

NOVEMBER 20, 1772.

(448) Mathias Lair vs. John Gratton.—Order for leave to add Aaron Hughes and John Hughes as parties—
(449) Robert Jordaine vs. James Cunningham.—Debt—judgment.

NOVEMBER 21, 1772.

(450) Rachel Gibson vs. William Briscoe.—Abates by plaintiff's marriage.
(453) John Dunlap vs. William Sutlington.—Abates by defendant's death.
(453) Michael Mallo vs. Valentine Maleer.—Abates by plaintiff's death.
(461) Michael Doyle—no inhabitant.
(468) County levy—2/4.

FEBRUARY 18, 1773.

(470) Called Court on William Place—larceny—guilty.
(470) *Finis. Coronat. Opus. Opus triginta dierum.*

W. URQUHORT, *Scripsit.*

AUGUSTA COUNTY COURT RECORDS.

ORDER BOOK No. XV.

MARCH 16, 1773.

(1) New commission—Justices, viz: Silas Hart, John Dickinson, Daniel Smith, John Poage,* Abraham Smith,* George Moffett, Alexr. McClenachan,* Mathew Harrison, George Mathews,* Alexr. Robertson,* John Hays, James Craig,* John Frogg,* William Tees, James Lockhart, John Christian, Archibald Alexander,* Felix Gilbert, Samuel McDowell, Sampson Mathews, William Bowyer,* John McClenachan,* Michael Bowyer,* John Gratton, Thos. Hugart,* Elijah McClenachan,* Josiah Davidson, John Skidmore.— Dated November 6, 1772.
(Those with (*) qualified.)
(1) Michael Bowyer qualified coroner.
(2) Hemp certificates: Ludwick Shadow, Jacob Doran.
(3-4) Hemp certificates: John Tedford, Alexr. Tedford, Jr.
(5) Hemp certificates: Jeremiah Tedford, Adam Reed.
(5) Nicholas Butcher qualified admr. of father, Valentine Butcher.
(6) Constable: John Lingle, vice Hieronimes Tack.
(6) Charles Rush qualifies admr. of Henry Strutsenocker.

(6) Robert Davis qualifies admr. of brother, William Davis.

(6) Mary, widow of Michael Mallow, refuses to administer, and Adam Mallow and Fredk. Keister appointed.

(7) Constable: Thomas Hill, vice Joseph Weer.

(7) Hemp certificate: Richard Renolds.

(8) Hemp certificates: James Weer, David Tedford, Thos. Cooper.

(10) Thomas Blizard and Archibald Dickson qualified Constables.

(10) Highway surveyor: John Hall, vice Robert Wiley.

(11) John Wilson's estate committed to son, Mathew Wilson.

(11) Highway surveyor: James Gay, vice Thomas Kinkead.

(11) John Ramsey bound to peace for beating Elizabeth Fleming, wife of William Fleming. She has been laid up for 13 weeks and her life is still despaired of.

MARCH 17, 1773.

(13-14) Many hemp certificates.

(16) Felix Gilbert, George Moffett, John Gratton, William Tees, qualified justices.

(17) Samuel Crawford, aged 14, orphan of Alexr. Crawford, chose Saml. McPheeters guardian.

(19) Joseph Poindexter, road surveyor, vice John Black.

(19) John Frazier vs. James Thompson } Attacht. Judgt.—Should Mary Thompson or her heirs ever appear in this Colony to demand a legacy given to her by her father.

(20) Road surveyor: James Gallespie, vice John Patrick.

(20) Cornelius Fitzjarel, runaway servant of William Dover.

(21) Samuel, Ruth, Sarah and Margaret Henderson, orphans of Daniel Henderson to be bound.

(21) John Crawford qualified Constable.

MARCH 18, 1773.

(22) Silas Hart qualified justice.

(22) Rebecca Brownlee, late Rebecca Gardner, admx. of Thos. Gardner.

(22) Hemp certificate: Peter Angely.

(23) Hemp certificate: Alexander Dale.

(25) Liquors rated.

(25) William McElhenny—witness from Botetourt.

(25) Henry Bowen—witness from Botetourt.

(31) Constable: Johnston Nelson, vice John Blake.

MARCH 19, 1773.

(32) William and Catherine Dillen to be bound out.

(32) Hugh McGlauchlin having run away, his children, Jane and William, to be bound out.

(32) Abraham Smith qualified Colonel of Militia.

(32) Zachariah Murphy, child of Mark Murphy, who is unable to support him, to be bound out.

Page

(32) Jacob Miller (near George Weaver's), to be summoned for not providing for his children.

(35) Witnesses: William, James and John Elliott, Robert McKettrick.

(36) Thomas Smith agrees to set free Thomas Day on condition of certain furniture be made by Day.

March 20, 1773.

(39) Hemp certificate: William Bell—South River.

(40) Samuel McDowell qualified justice.

(40) John Dickinson qualified justice.

(47) Ann Hix, servant of Doctor John Sharp Watkins.

March 22, 1773.

(49) Valentine Cloninger qualified Constable.

(49) Walter Cunningham qualifies (with consent of the widow, Sarah,) admr. of his father, John Cunningham.

March 23, 1773.

(56) Samuel Kerr—no inhabitant.

(56) Mathias Keissinger—no inhabitant.

(70) Peter Alemback—no inhabitant.

(81) Highway surveyor: Seth Rodgers, vice William Hutchison.

(92) John Buchanon—no inhabitant.

(94) Thomas Mathews and Mary and Wm. Saulsbury convicted of being disorderly persons and keeping a disorderly house, entertaining servants, &c.

May 18, 1773.

(95) John Skidmore qualified justice.

(95) Hemp certificate: Samuel Henry.

(96) Hemp certificate: Abraham Dick.

(96) Appraiser appointed for estate of Wm. Stalp (Halp).

(97) Constable: John McCutcheon, vice Robert Clarke.

(97) Frederick Woolfat and John Stalp took the oaths, which is to be certified (?).

(97) Appraiser appointed for estate of Adam Reader, deceased.

(97) Appraiser appointed for estate of Thomas Wilson, deceased.

(97) Constables: Alexr. Shack, vice Alexr. Fitzpatrick; Norton Gumm, vice Isaac Lincoln.

(98) Road surveyors: James Magill; Frederick Keister and Michael Welfong, vice Mark Swadley; Robert Campbell, vice Arthur Connelly.

(98) Viewers to report on a road by Trimbles Mill, from Staunton to Buffalo Gap.

(98) Appraisers appointed of estate of Rev. Thomas Jackson.

(99) Appraisers appointed of estate of Rev. George Caplinger.

Inter *alias* Aaron Vanscoy.

(99) Elizabeth, daughter of Thomas Kelly, to be bound to William Magill, son of James.

(99) Nathan Gilliland is about to remove out of County.

(99) Overseer of road: James Trimble (son of David), vice James Bell.

(100) Henry Stalp, aged 14, orphan of Wm. Stalp, decd., chose Archibald Huston his guardian.

(101) George McCown, heir at law of Francis McCown.

MAY 19, 1773.

(102) John Gabriel Jones intends to practice law, and gets certificate of good behavior.

(103) Robert Wardlaw appointed road surveyor, vice William Berry.

(103) Constable: Peter Harmon, vice Peter Lingle.

(103) James Thompson's estate to be appraised.

(103) Priscilla Long informs Court that her husband, Charles Long, has gone beyond seas, leaving her destitute.—There is a small sum in hands of the Sheriff belonging to Charles.—Ordered in hands of trustees for benefit of Priscilla and her child.

(104) Road established from Staunton to Love's Ford on Henderson's Creek.—Walter Davis to be surveyor.

(104) Alexander Thompson qualified Lieutenant Colonel of the County.

(104) Robert Thompson qualified Captain of Militia.

(106) Margaret Sollas petitions that her husband, Nicholas Sollas, bound out their son, James Sollas, aged 13 years, to Henry Hall and ran away.— James could be better educated if bound to Adam Wall (a son of Margaret by another husband) with whom Margaret now lives—ordered.

(109) Sarah Campbell, aged 13, orphan of Robert Campbell—Elijah McClenachan appointed guardian.

MAY 23, 1773.

(116) Hemp certificates: John Mackey, Martin Nalle, Moses Binnell.

(120) Road surveyor: Robert Russell, vice Alexander Gibson.

(120) William Nalle and Francis Kirtley qualified Captains.

(120) Constable: Adam Bratton, vice Thomas Kinkead.

(120) Henry Mace, servant of David Laird.

(121) John Maxwell—a witness from Botetourt.

(121) Robert Jameson—a witness from Botetourt.

(121) William Kerr—a witness from Botetourt.

(122) Christian Cameron—a witness.

(122) John Wowman—witness from Botetourt.

(122) William McElhenny—witness from Botetourt.

(122) Jame Cameron—witness.

MAY 21, 1773.

(123) This ought to be (24th).

(123) Elinor O'Neal—witness from Dunmore.

MAY 22, 1773.

MAY 24, 1773.

AUGUST 17, 1773.

Page

(152) Mathew Lattimore agrees to give up his freedom dues in consideration that his master acquit him of the remainder of his time of servitude.

(152) John Kerr, orphan, formerly bound to Isaac Morris, to be bound out.

(152) Gabriel Powell exempted from County levy.

(152) Following to be bound: Barbara Painter, to John Painter; Mathias Painter, to Christian Painter; Margaret Painter, to Nicholas Kern; Mary Painter, to Jacob Mayer.

(152-3) Many hemp certificates.

(153) Seriah Stratton—arbitrator.

(153) Road surveyor—Edward Rutledge.

(154) Thomas Fulton and Ephraim Love—road overseers.

(155) John Price—witness from Amherst.

(155) Adam Dean—witness from Albemarle.

(155) James Turk—witness from Albemarle.

(155) Richard Pilson—witness from Albemarle.

(155) John Murphy—runaway servant of Thomas Tate.

(155) Alexander Stuart qualified Captain of Militia.

(156) Alexander Koch qualified Constable.

(156) Thomas Hetsell—runaway servant of William Johnston.

(157) Robert Dowling—runaway servant of Hugh Dever.

(157) Sarah Pritchard—servant of Thomas Smith.

(158) Anthony Johnston, vice William Stewart—road surveyor.

(159) John Britt's estate to be appraised.

(160) Archibald Armstrong—road surveyor from Painter Gap to Widow Elliott's.

AUGUST 19, 1773.

(164) Robert Graves—runaway servant of James Callison.

(164) Thomas Acton—runaway servant of Sampson Sawyers.

(164) John Gay, vice John Lewis—road surveyor from Cow Pasture River to Liard Bell's.

(164) Constable on Walker's Creek—Michael Coulter.

(165) Thos. Brown and Wm. Crawford—road surveyors on new road from Staunton to Buffalo Gap, via Trimble's Mill.

(167) Jacob Moore—witness from Albemarle.

(167) Benjamin Calvard—witness from Albemarle.

(173) James Huston—witness from Botetourt.

AUGUST 20, 1773.

(174) William Craig (son of Robert)—witness.

(174) William Craig (son of James)—witness.

(177) John Lilley—witness from Dunmore.

(178) Witnesses: Margaret Bryan, Joseph Goore, Margaret Benson, Joannah Sevior.

(178) John Peyton—witness from Prince William.

Page

(179) William Mann—witness from Botetourt.

(179) William Miller—runaway servant of Martha Downey.

(181) Robert Crowly—runaway servant of John Gratton.

(185) Ray }
vs. } Defendant moved for a *dedimus* to take deposition of William Watterson, a witness residing in
Dickinson } Amherst, alleging that he broke jail in Augusta and would be arrested if he came back—granted.

AUGUST 23, 1773.

(196) Thomas Johnston, Jr., security for Frances, widow, and admx. of David Via, now married to John Edie, asks counter security.

(197) Charles and David Beard, sons of Edward Beard, who fails to bring them up in a Christianlike manner, to be bound to James Allen, Jr., to learn trades of carpenter and wheelwright.

(197) Hemp certificate: Edmund Stevens.

(198) John Collins—runaway servant of Thomas Smith.

(199) Joseph Bell appointed guardian of Jennett Patterson, daughter of John Patterson, decd. (she is an idiot.). John Patterson appointed guardian of Mary Patterson, daughter of John Patterson, decd. (she is deaf and dumb).

AUGUST 24, 1773.

(204) Thomas Ray—witness from Albemarle.

(207) John Cumpton—overseer of road from Brock's Gap to Hampshire County line.

AUGUST 25, 1773.

(219) John Thrifft—runaway servant of Robert McClenachan.

(219) Thomas Wallace, servant of Sampson and George Mathews.

(220) Called Court on John Dunn for larceny—39 lashes.

NOVEMBER 16, 1773.

(220) Charles Simms qualified attorney.

(222) County levy.

(222) To Thomas Lewis, son of Thomas. To Samuel Dunn, for wolf head.

(222) Jacob Van Law agrees to remit time of his servant, Mary Lane, on condition she acquit him of freedom dues.

(222) John Painter's estate to be appraised by Mathias Reader, John Moore, David Robertson and Aaron Hughes.

(223) Henry Peninger, Constable, vice Thomas Wilmoth.

(223) Edward Rabint, runaway servant of James Lessley, Jr.

(223) Norton Gunn qualified Constable.

(223) Daniel Givin qualified Constable.

(223) John Smith qualified Deputy Sheriff.

(223) William Mateer, vice Wm. Kinkead, road overseer. John Caruthers, vice Moses Whitesides, road overseer.

Page

(224) John McCutchan qualified Constable.

(224) George Nicholas appointed road overseer.

(224) James Graham, witness in Botetourt.

(224) Adam Painter's estate to be appraised.

NOVEMBER 17, 1773.

(225) Mary Handlin, servant of James Langsby's.

(225) John Hodge, vice Thomas Hughart, road surveyor.

(225) Joab Fletcher, hemp certificate.

(226) Garrett Green, hemp certificate.

(228) John Needham and John Harrison, vice Wm. Hinton—road overseers.

(230) Thomas Mathews, confined on a *capias pro fine* for selling liquor without license—prays corporal punishment and release—20 lashes.

(231) Francis Dunn, son of Elinor Dunn, to be bound to Andrew Russell, Jr., to have trade of a weaver, and to read, write and cypher as far as the rule of three.

(231) Hugh Kelso, vice Michael Coulter—Constable.

(233) Joshua Russell, vice Saml. Pilson—Road Surveyor.

(234) Alexr. Long, qualified Captain; Francis Long, qualified Lieutenant; William Bell, Ensign.

(235) Wm. Bell, witness from Orange.

(235) Cornelius Fitzpatrick, runaway servant of Hugh Diver, Sr.

NOVEMBER 18, 1773.

(239) Wm. Gragg, vice John Crawford—Constable.

(239) Chas. Callaghen, vice John Gurn—Road Overseer.

(239) Road established from Buddy House to David Bell's, in Cow Pasture—Saml. Wilson surveyor. Tithables on Black Thorn and from head of Bull Pasture to Joseph Malcom's to work it.

(240) Michael Aberman and Andrew Johnson, to view road from Lanticur, at mouth of North Fork, at Joseph Bennett's.

NOVEMBER 19, 1773.

(244) George Cutlip, witness from Botetourt.

(244) Joseph Haynes qualified Under Sheriff.

(244) John Lewis qualified Captain of Militia.

(247) Doctor George Parker, servant of Saml. McChesney, buys his freedom.

(249) James Abbott, witness from Fincastle.

(249) Alexander McDonnald, witness from Botetourt.

(250) Edward Bandsgrove, runaway servant of Edmond Stephens.

NOVEMBER 20, 1773.

(250) James Blair, returned no inhabitant.

(269) John Craig, Jr., returned no inhabitant.

(298) County levy brought forward.

Page

(302) New Commission of Justices, viz: Silas Hart, John Dickison, Danl. Smith, John Poage, Abram Smith, George Moffett,* James Lockhart, John Christian, Archibald Alexander, Felix Gilbert, Samuel McDowel,* Sampn. Mathews, Alexr. McClenachan,* Mathew Harrison, George Mathews,* Alexr. Robertson,* John Hays, James Craig, John Frogg,* William Tees, George Croghan, John Connelly,* Thos. Smallman, Wm. Bowyer,* John McClenachan,* Michael Bowyer, John Gratton,* Thos. Huggart, Elijah Mc-Clenachan, Josiah Davidson, John Skidmore, John Campbell, Edward Ward, Dawsey Penticost, John Gibson. (Those marked (*) qualified.)

(303) Wm. Gragg qualified Constable. Constables appointed: Jacob Van Matre, Dinnis Springer, John Harden, Jr., John Connor, Hennery Taylor, Thomas Bay, Francis McGuire, Andrew Ramsey, Jonathan Coborne, Jr., Thomas Douglas and Philip Ryley.

(303) Constable—James Montgomery, vice Thomas Keit.

(304) Christopher Kisling's (deceased) estate committed to widow, Christiana.

(304) David Caldwell and Andrew Alexander, to view a road from James Breeding's house, on head of Middle Branch of Back Creek, to the foarding between Robert Gray's and Patrick Keenan's.

(305) John Randals—hemp certificate.

(306) Robert Haislip—hemp certificate.

(307) John Ramsey, vice John Gillespy—road overseer.

(308) John Connelly qualified Captain Commandant of the Militia of Pittsburg and its dependencies.

(308) Mathew Wilson—road surveyor.

(309) William Dunlap's will partly proved.

(309) John Poage, Archibald Alexander and Michael Bowyer, qualified Justices.

(310) John Lambert and Jane, to be summoned for not bringing up their child properly.

(310) John Findley, Middle River.

(310B) Wm. Alexander, vice Joseph Alexander—Constable. John Thompson, vice Samuel Lyle—Constable.

(310B) Called Court on Wm. Givans, for murder of his servant, James Brown.—Justifiable homicide.

MARCH 16, 1774.

(312) Adam Hoverstick, naturalized.

(312) Andrew Moore—certificate for examination as lawyer.

(313-14) Hemp certificates.

(317) Wm. Thompson, vice Hugh Kelso—Constable.

(317) John Bigham's estate committed to John Bigham.

(317) Following qualified Justices, &c., viz: Felix Gilbert, Abraham Smith, John Hays, Elijah McClenachan.

(318) Road objected to because of steep grade, no water and no range for horses.

Page

(319) Saml. Smallbridge, convict servant of John Gum, adjudged eleven years old.

(319) Adam Bratton, vice Robert Bratton—surveyor of road.

(319) George Gibson qualified Lieut. in Capt. Robert Thompson's Company. William Findley, same, as Ensign in same.

(320) Robert O'Neal, witness from Dunmore. Michael Roahk, witness from Dunmore.

(321) John Christian qualified Justice, &c.

(322) George Moffett appointed guardian of Robert Reaburn, orphan of Robert Reaburn, deceased.

(323) Thos. Hughart qualified Justice, &c.

MARCH 17, 1774.

(323A) Hemp certificate: James Walker—Walker's Creek.

(325) William and Thomas Lowry, orphans of Thomas Lowry, to be bound out.

(325) Thomas Smith, vice Valentine Cloninger—surveyor of streets of Staunton.

(326) Road from Jacob Aberman's Mill to the North Fork, at mouth of Seneca Creek—to be viewed by Jonathan Smith, Wm. Smith, Jacob Stalnaker and John White.

(327) Road from Joseph Gregory's to William Hamilton's, on Monongahela River, to be viewed by Jacob Warrick, John Warrick, Richard Eliot and Ralph Stuart.

(327) Constables: Joel Westfall and Daniel Hazel.

(327) Road overseer: Leonard Bell, from Mathew's store in the Calf Pasture to his house, to work with tithables from Wm. Black's to Jos. May's on Calf Pasture.

(329) Charles Patrick, witness from Albemarle.

(330) Adam Painter's death abates suit.

(331) John Seborn, witness from Dunmore. Nicholas Seborn, witness from Dunmore.

MARCH 18, 1774.

(332) Samuel McClure, witness from Botetourt.

(339) Samuel McDowell appointed guardian of James McDowell, orphan of James McDowell, deceased.

(340) Thomas Wallace died possessed of very small estate.—Sheriff to sell and report.

MARCH 19, 1774.

(343) Francis McClain is about to leave the Colony.

MARCH 21, 1774.

(355) Ordinary rates.

(384) Edward Gill, no inhabitant of County.

MARCH 22, 1774.

(425) Henry Howard's death abates suit.

(425) William Alford, no inhabitant.

(425) Charles Parsons, no inhabitant.

(433) William McFarland, no inhabitant.

(435) Sariah Stratton, Wm. Brisco, Joseph Henderson and Wm. Mitchell to inspect the jail built by Joseph Kinkead, and if according to contract, to be received.

(437) John Hunter's death abates suit.

(439) Benjamin Coffey, no inhabitant.

(441) Christopher Graham, storekeeper for William Bowyer, being about to remove to foreign parts, has leave to prove the several accounts and balances due said William.

(442) Workmen to be employed to build the jail chimney ten feet higher.

APRIL 19, 1774.

(442) Wm. Crawford qualified deputy surveyor under Thomas Lewis.

MAY 17, 1774.

(443) Sampson Mathews qualified Justice, &c.

(443) Hemp certificates: Mathew Kenny, James Pollock, John Dean.

(445) Hemp certificates: George Taylor, Andrew Taylor.

(445–446) Hemp certificate: Elizabeth Taylor.

(446) Hemp certificates: Richard Randal, Hugh Holse.

(447) Hemp certificate: Andrew Anderson.

(447) Grand Jury: Peter Vineman.

(448) Rev. John Craig's estate committed to George Moffett and James Allen, Jr., the widow refusing.

(449) John Lock, runaway servant of Archibald Hopkins. Solomon Lein, runaway servant of James Pollick.

(450) Mary Moore, servant of Pat. Hays.

(450) Philip Harper and Jacob Aberman—naturalized.

(450) Constables: James Montgomery, John Thompson and Henry Penninger.

(451) John Skidmore, vice Jacob Conrad—road surveyor.

(451) Daniel Nelson exempted from County levy.

(452) Hemp certificate: Alexander Hindman.

(453) Martin Nalle and Owen O'Neal—hemp certificates.

(455) Robert Edmondson, witness from Amherst.

(455) Samuel Vance qualified Lieutenant of Militia.

(455) Frederick Haynes, vice John Coutts—road surveyor.

(455) John Redman exempted from County levy.

(456) Following to be bound: Israel Freidley to Capt. Rush; Barbara Freidley to John Armentrout.

(456) Robert Mitchell, vice Samuel McCutchon—road surveyor—from John Tate's Mill to Bradley's Run.

(456) Samuel Craig committed for debt.

Page

(457) Road established from Tiger's Valley to mouth of Seneca.

(457) Jacob Stalnacker, Sr., and Jesse Hamilton, to be overseers from Tiger's Valley to top of Allegany Mountain, with tithables from Francis Deer's to Joseph Baker's.

(457) Paul Teeter, overseer from top of Allegany to mouth of Sinacor, with tithables on the North Fork from Michael Aberman's to Joseph Heau's.

(457) John Paul, vice Robert Feoris—road surveyor.

(457) Elizabeth Haywood, late Elizabeth Branch, complains of her master, John Lyle, for her freedom.

(459) James Risk's estate committed to his mother, Jane Risk, and John Alexander.

MAY 18, 1774.

(459) David Beard to be bound to Samuel Caruthers.

(459) Charles Beard to be bound to John Caruthers, to learn trade of breechers makers and skin dressers.

(462) Hemp certificate: Martin Leo.

(463) Hemp certificates: David, Robert and Alexr. Tedford and Anthony Lewis.

(464) Rev. John Craig, hemp certificate.

(465) David James.

(468) Ephraim Richardson and Wm. Martin—road surveyors from Francis Wier's, on Monongahela River, to Thorny Creek, on waters of Greenbrier. John Warwick, Richard Elliott and Ralph Stewart are exempted from working on above road until it is built. William Hadden is ordered to clear from Thorny Creek to Nap's Creek, with tithables living below him on Nap's Creek, and from Alexr. Dunlap's to William Sharp's on Greenbrier. Jacob Warwick, road overseer, from William Warwick's to Back Creek, with tithables from Thomas Cartmell's up Greenbrier to the head and down Nap's Creek to Moses Moore's.

(471) Samuel Black, vice James Bell—road overseer.

(471) On petition of John Hopkins, Samuel Moral, Peter Vaminon, Michael Wolf, John Gordon and Nicholas Harpole—to view a road from the widow Moses's to Gabriel Cock's.

(471) John Whitton—naturalized.

(474) Jane Smith, wife of Daniel Smith, relinquished dower in land conveyed by Daniel to Jasper and Henry Laurence.

(475) Darby Toran—hemp certificate.

(475) James Dobbin, vice Archibald Dickson—Constable.

(476) John Davis and Robert Minnis—special bail.

MAY 19, 1774.

(479) Robert Caruthers, vice Wm. Alexander—Constable.

(483) Ann Grigsby, witness from Dunsmore. John Payton, witness from Prince William.

(483) John Payton and Tucker Woodson—Jurors.

MAY 20, 1774.

(486) John Dickinson, qualified Justice, &c.

MAY 21, 1774.

Page

(489) Hugh Donaho vs. Wm. McClenachan.—Suit dismissed by defendant's death.

(509) Henry Pickle and Caleb Russell—no inhabitants.

(510) Mathew Scott—no inhabitant.

(511) Peter Mickle—no inhabitant.

(521) William Dean—no inhabitant.

(522) James McNutt, returned inhabitant of Botetourt.

(526) James Burnsides—no inhabitant.

(530) Alexander Moore—witness from Botetourt.

(531) Thomas Fulton—qualified Captain.

AUGUST 16, 1774.

(532) Isaac Robinson, deceased—estate to be appraised.

(532) Martin Humble, deceased—estate commd. to Conrad Humble.

(543) To be bound out, viz: Noah Custard to Paul Custard; Arnold Custard to Conrad Custard.

(535) Neal McNeil, deceased—estate commd. to Daniel Kidd.

(535) Elizabeth Coats, orphan of Joshua Coats, to be bound to William Carruthers.

The last Court held under authority of the King was May 1, 1776.

The first Court held under authority of the Commonwealth, July 16, 1776.

AUGUSTA COUNTY COURT RECORDS.

ORDER BOOK No. XVI.

AUGUST 16, 1774.

(2) Wm. Gilmore and Alex. Brownlee qualified Constables. Robert Curry qualified Captain of Militia.

(3) David Jennings, servant of Thomas Smith, declared free.

(6) John Hunter exempted from County levy.

(7) Joseph Barkley, being committed on complaint of Randal Slack—discharged.

AUGUST 17, 1774.

(9) Hemp certificate: John Bing.

(9) Joseph Haynes qualified Captain of Militia.

(10) Conrad Humble qualified Captain of Militia.

(10) William and John Gilmore to be surveyors of road from head of Carr's Creek to North River—new road established.

(11) Silas Hart qualified Justice, &c.

(11) Joseph Campbell, vice John Maxwell—road overseer.

(11) John Givens, vice Edward Rutledge—road overseer.

(12) Catherine, wife of Jacob Pasenger, relinquished dower deed, Jacob, to Anthony Aler.

(13) Ludwick Lehdown's estate.

(13) John Leeper, vice John McMahon—road overseer.

August 22, 1774.

(14) Called Court on John Hunter for murder of Jacob Peoples.—Acquitted.

October 18, 1774.

(16) John Campbell, Thomas Smallman and Dawsey Penticost—qualified Justices.

October 19, 1774.

(16) Meet and adjourned.

November 15, 1774.

(17) Robert Carruthers and Wm. Thompson qualified Constables.

(17) James Campbell, vice John Hall—road overseer.

(18) Archibald and Rebecca (his wife) Houston, witnesses to will of Conrad Blaze, are dead—at proving of same.

(18) Andrew Moore qualified attorney.

(19) Michael Props exempted from levy.

(19) Thomas Dunbarr's estate to be appraised, and administration to be granted to Thomas Smith.

(19) Dennis Donnerley, runaway servant of Michael Coger.

(19) Francis Smith, son of Wm. Smith, aged eleven years 1st June last, to be bound to Henry Tamewood.

(21) William Marshall, vice Joseph Love—Constable.

(21) Elizabeth Shirtley, wife of Francis Shirtley, deceased, renounced her claims under Francis's will.

(21) Saml. Hemphill, vice John Herdman, road overseer, from Martin Argenbright's to Nehemiah Harrison's.

(21) John Hopkins qualified Captain.

November 16, 1774.

(22) Ann, wife of John McClenachan, deceased, renounced her right under her husband's will.

(22) Administration of estate of Doctor William McClenachan granted to his father, Robert McClenachan.

(23) Joseph Rutherford, Sr., road overseer of new road from Daniel Smith's to Felix Gilbert's.

(24) Mathew Todd, runaway servant of James Bruster.

(24) Administration of John Aberman's estate is granted to his widow, Mary, and his brother, Michael.

(25) Henry and Nicholas Maze—naturalized.

Page
(26) County levy.
(27) Agatha Frogg refuses to administer on estate of her husband, John Frogg—proved by Thomas Jones.

NOVEMBER 17, 1774.

(28) Administration of estate of John Dunwoody granted to his brother, James Dunwoody.

JANUARY 9, 1775.

(29) Timothy Brannon, convicted of larceny—39 lashes.

JANUARY 17, 1775.

(30) New Commission from Dunmore, viz: Silas Hart, John Dickinson, James Lockhart, John Christian, Daniel Smith,* John Poage, Abraham Smith,* George Moffett,* Alexr. McClenachan,* Mathew Harrison, Michael Bowyer,* John Gratton, Thomas Hughes, Elijah McClenachan,* Josiah Davidson, John Skidmore, John Campbell, Thos. Smallman, John Gibson, John Stephenson, John Cannon, Silas Hedge, William Gee (McGee?), Archd. Alexander, Felix Gilbert,* Samuel McDowell,* Sampson Mathews,* William Bowyer,* George Mathews,* Alexr. Robertson,* John Hayes,* James Craig, John Frogg, Wm. Teas,* George Croghan, Edward Ward, Dawsey Pentecost, Wm. Crawford, John McCullough, Geo. Vallendegham and David Shepherd. (Those marked (*) qualified.)
(31) John Christian qualified Sheriff.
(32) Thomas Trent and Ralph Stewart, qualified Captains of Militia.
(32) William Stewart qualified Lieutenant of Militia.
(33) Administration of estate of John Williams, deceased, granted to John Wilson.
(33) Alexander McClenachan and Alexander Sinclair are, on their motion, appointed guardians of John McClenachan, orphan of John McClenachan.
(34) Court of Claims: Of Andrew Hamilton, for diets for Militia; of Robert McClintock; of John Finley; of James Kirk, claims of the Militia.
(35) Of Hugh Allen, deceased, for a horse proved by brother, James Allen; of John Ladlers, for driving pack horses; of sundry persons for work on the expedition under James Allen and Hugh Allen—certified by Andrew Lewis; of Wm. Kinkead, for sundries for Militia; of Ralph Stewart, for provisions for his Company of Militia.

JANUARY 18, 1775.

(36) Of John Hays, for diets of Militia; of Thos. Harrison, for diets of Militia; of Elizabeth Harrison, for diets of Militia.
(38) Of Francis McAndrew, for an axe.
(42) Of John David, Michael Rush and David White, spies; of William Long, commissary.
(44) Of Capt. Joseph Haynes, pay-rolls for himself and others.
(45) Of Capt. John Dickinson, pay-rolls for himself and others.

Page

(46) Claims continued.

(47) Capt. Wm. Scotborn, pay-roll for himself and Company; of Daniel Warner and Andrew Dawson, spies.

(48) Of Wm. Naull, pay-roll for himself and others; of John Hays, for attendance to settle accounts as pack-horse masters; of Sampson Mathews, sundry claims at the Calf Pasture; of Wm. Robertson, for provisions found themselves; of James Thompson, for sundry horses, their hire, and drivers in the service; of Geo. Mathews, two pay-rolls for self and others; of Wm. Hamilton, for riding express; of Wm. McCune, cow herd; of Thomas Posey, for sundry horses, their service.

(49) Majesty's writ of adjournment read and ordered that the Court meet at Fort Dunmore on 3d Tuesday in next month.

MARCH 20, 1775.

(51) Called Court—Robert Crawford.
(52) Called Court.
(53) Called Court—William Campbell.
(55) Called Court.

MARCH 25, 1775.

(55) Adjourned by his Majesty's writ from Fort Dunmore.

(55) Administration of estate of Hugh Allen, decd., granted to widow Jane and brother James. (Was Hugh killed on the expedition of 1774? See Court of Claims, *supra*.)

(57) Alexr. Walker's will proved and administration granted to Elizabeth, the widow, and Robert Walker, the son.

(58) Administration of estate of David White granted to Jacob Aberman, the widow, Catherine, having refused.

(58) Thomas Patton, orphan of Thomas Patton, to be bound to Walter Moffett till he comes of age, to be taught the weaver's trade.

(59) Elizabeth Lamb complains she is held by George Taylor as a servant illegally—summons.

(60) Robert Minnis appointed Constable.

(60) Elias Barker qualified Lieut. of Militia.

(60) Edward Sparks, runaway servant of Martin Naule. Dennis Connerley, runaway servant of Michael Coager.

(61) Bethuell Herring, vice Daniel Guinn—Constable.

(61) Administration of estate of James King granted to Morris Ofreel.

(62) Robert Minnis qualified Constable.

(62) Administration of estate of Thomas Hog granted to his brother, Peter Hog.

(62) John Poage qualified Justice, &c.

(63) Thomas Smith, vice Valentine Cloneger—Constable.

(63) John McCoy, vice Samuel Wilson—overseer road.

(64) Administration of estate of Michael Bush granted to John Lewis, widow Catherine refusing. Appraisers, viz: Sam. Pringle, Charles Fallingash, Paul Buster, Edward Tanner.

Page
(64) Admn. of estate of Wm. Magert granted to widow Catherine.
(64) William Bush, vice Peter Hashman—Constable.
(65) John Henderson, vice William Gragg—Constable. Jacob Woodley—Constable.

MARCH 26, 1775.

(67) Robert Lockridge, vice Archd. Armstrong—road overseer from Painter's Gap to Joseph Wacheb's.

(67) Margaret Ann McClenachan, widow of John McClenachan, petitions the Court to set aside the former order appointing guardians of her infant son, John, then two months old, alleges that the guardians are those to whom the reversion would go—granted.

(68) Ordinary rates.

(70) Adjourned by writ to 3d Tuesday in May next at Fort Dunmore.

JUNE 3, 1775.

(71) Called Court on Henry Mansening.
(72) Called Court on John Brown.

JUNE 5, 1775.

(72) Called Court on James Duffy.

JUNE 20, 1775.

(73) Adjourned from Fort Dunmore.

(74) John Cawley's will proved—Margaret, the widow, refuses to accept the provisions.

(74) Administration of estate of John Collins granted to Wm. Langsdale.

(74) Andrew Lockridge, security for Elizabeth, widow of Robert Graham (now married to Samuel Guinn), prays counter security.

(75) Elizabeth Law's complaint versus her husband, Robert Law is dismissed—no prosecution.

(75) Administration of estate of John Galespy granted to Saml. Lyle.

(76) William Mateer, vice Adam Bratton—Constable.

(76) Samuel Hunter, vice Alexander Brownlee—Constable.

(76) John Kennerley, vice James Lessley—Constable.

(76) Thomas Galespy, orphan of Jacob Galespy, aged 14, to be bound to John Rissner.

(76) Alexr. Gibson petitions that William McFarland, his son-in-law, has moved out of the Colony, and his children are not properly provided for, viz: Isabella, Alexander, James, Mary, Daniel, Eleanor and John.—They are to be bound to said Alexander, their grandfather.

(76) Thomas Hughart qualified Justice.

(78) Andrew Lockridge appointed guardian of Sarah and Jane Graham, orphans of Robert Graham.

(78) Elizabeth and Lanty Grimes, executors of John Grymes, to be summoned to show cause why they have not rendered an account.

(78) Tully Davitt, vice James Bodkin—Constable.

Page

(79) Called Court on William Gripping.

AUGUST 15, 1775.

(81) Administration of estate of **Abigail Gartham** granted to Francis Gartham.

(82) Mathew Robertson, vice Robert Caruthers—Constable.

(82) William Leescomb, runaway servant of Robert North.

(82) Mary Ann Estill relinquishes dower in tract of land conveyed by her husband, Wallace Estill, to John Peoples.

(83) Administration of estate of John Watson granted to Mary Allen.

(84) John McCoy, overseer of road from head of Bull Pasture to Peoples's and from Samuel Wilson's (deceased) to Bell's place, Cow Pasture.

(84) Bartholomew Archbold complains of his master, Roger North.

(84) Thomas Allen, servant of John Peoples.

(84) Admn. of estate of John Poller granted to Robert McKetrick.

(85) Barbara Wilson, runaway servant of Andrew Scott.

(86) Adjourned to 3d Tuesday in next month at Fort Dunmore.

AUGUST 22, 1775.

(86) Called Court on John Reed, servant of Jacob Peck.

AUGUST 31, 1775.

(87) Called Court on John Askins.

NOVEMBER 21, 1775.

(88) Adjourned from Fort Dunmore.

NOVEMBER 22, 1775.

(89) County levy continued.

(94) John Hanna added to tithables (2); John Mitchell added to tithables (1).

(94) Dower to be laid off to Elizabeth, widow of Francis Kirkley.

(94) Robert Dunlap, vice David Martin—Constable.

(95A) Mary Gragg, orphan, to be bound to Wm. Gragg.

NOVEMBER 23, 1775.

(95B) Sampson Wilson, orphan of Saml. Wilson, chose Thomas Hughart guardian.

(96) County levy continued.

(97) John Christian qualified Sheriff.

JANUARY 4, 1776.

(97) Called Court on Bartholomy Archbald—horse stealing.

Page

(98) Called Court on John Jones—horse stealing.

FEBRUARY 20, 1776.

(99) Administration of estate of Thomas Anderson granted to Samuel Anderson and William Anderson—the father, Samuel Anderson, having refused. Isaac Cannon, one of the appraisers.

(99) Admn. of estate of Henry Laughten granted to Neel Hughes.

MARCH 19, 1776.

(99) Richard Madison qualified Deputy Clerk.

(100) Deed, John Kennerly and Mary to ——, was proved by Joseph Strother, who came with them from Carolina into this Colony in order to prove the same.

(101) Nicholas Harpole and Adam Lock, securities for Barbara Oldham, widow and administratrix of George Fultz, but now wife of John Oldham, demand counter security.

(101) Administration of estate of George Cameron granted to Charles Cameron.

(101) Administration of estate of Francis Miller granted to John Miller.

(101) Administration of estate of Mark Banister—to Benj. Harrison.

(102) Robert and Alexander McClenachan are appointed guardians for John McClenachan and Robert McClenachan, orphans of Robert McClenachan, deceased.

(102) William Parris exempted from County levy.

(103) Administration of William Church granted to Joseph Hays.

(103) John Guffee, runaway servant of John Trotter.

(103) Administration of John Jameson granted to Thomas James.

(103) Daniel Kidd—overseer of streets of Staunton.

(105) John Kerr, orphan, to be bound to John Henton.

(105) John McKenny exempted from levy.

MARCH 20, 1776.

(105) Alexander Sinclair qualified vestryman.

(105) Roger North, vice Valentine Cloninger—Constable.

(108) John O'Dair to be summoned on complaint of Randal McDaniel for detaining him without warrant.

(108) Abell Griffith, vice John Anderson—road overseer.

(108), Capt. Thomas Hewit—garnishee.

(109) Adjourned by writ to 3d Tuesday next month at Fort Dunmore.

MAY 1, 1776.

(109) Called Court on Sylvester Cofer—horse stealing.

Page

(110) First Court by authority of the Commonwealth.

(110) Samuel McDowell and Sampson Mathews administered oaths to Archibald Alexander, who administered to Samuel and Sampson and Michael Bower.

(110) John Christian qualified Sheriff. Richard Madison qualified Deputy Clerk. Wm. Bowyer qualified Justice.

AUGUST 20, 1776.

(110) John Madison qualified Clerk. Gabriel Jones and Peter Hog qualified Attorneys. John and Wm. Christian qualified Deputy Sheriffs.

(111) Thomas Hughart, Daniel Smith and John Poage qualified Justices.

(112) Thomas Hughart is appointed guardian of Ruth Wilson, daughter of Samuel Wilson.

(112) James Robertson's will partly proved.

(112) Alexr. Robertson, James Kerr and Robert Kenney are appointed guardians of Sarah, Elizabeth, Rachel, Mary and Agnes Lessley, orphans of James Lessley, Jr.

(112) William Wright's will partly proved.

(113) George Moffett, Elijah McClenachan, Felix Gilbert and Alexr. ——, qualified Justices.

(113) Administration of estate of Mary Thompson granted to William Thompson.

(113) Mathew Kinkead's will partly proved.

(113) *Ad quod damnum* awarded on petition of John Lollor to build a mill on his own land on Leeken Creek.

(114) John Gum to be summoned to show cause why he has not paid freedom dues to Sarah Dowman, late Sarah Redman.

(114) Alexander McClenachan qualified Justice, &c.

(114) Administration of estate of George Robinson granted to Jane Robinson.

(115) David Stewart, on account of age, exempted from levy.

(115) Christopher Warwick, servant of Joseph Bell, punished for raising a riot in the Court Yard.

(118) Following recommendations: Zachariah Johnston, Captain; Christopher Graham, Lieutenant.

OCTOBER 3, 1776.

(121) Called Court on William Brannon for horse stealing.

NOVEMBER 19, 1776.

(124) County levy.

(126) John Bratton, eldest son and heir to James Bratton. John Mc-Castle and John McRoberts—appraisers.

(127) John Risk's will partly proved.

(128) New Commission, viz: Silas Han, John Christian, Archibald Alexander, Felix Gilbert, Samuel McDowell, Sampson Mathews, Alexr.

Robinson, John Hays, James Craig, John Lewis, Charles Campbell,* John Dickinson, Daniel Smith,* John Poage,* Abraham Smith, George Moffat,* Michael Bowyer, John Gratton, Thos. Huggart,* Elijah McClenachan, Alexander St. Clair,* John Kinkead, James Tate.* (Those marked (*) qualified.)

(128) Alexander McClenachan and Wm. Bowyer administered the oaths.

(129) Admn. of estate of Ernest Harmon granted to George Huffman.

(129) Stophel and Ernest Harmon chose George Harmon guardian.

(129) Archibald Alexander qualified Sheriff.

NOVEMBER 20, 1776.

(131) William Alexander qualified Deputy Sheriff.

(131) Stephen Conrad, vice Frederick Haynes—road overseer.

(132) Elenore Askins complains of Walter Cunningham for not using her child well.

(132) John Abney appointed Constable.

(133) Peter Angleman appointed road surveyor.

(133) Samuel Givins = Samuel Gibbens.

(134) Elijah McClenachan and Alexr. Robertson qualified Justices, &c.

(134) Patrick Boyd complains of abuse by his master, John Crawford.

(135) Witness: George Burley.

(135) William Black and others to view a road from William Wilson's leading to the road that goes down to the Bull Pasture.

DECEMBER 17, 1776.

(136) John Christian qualified Justice, &c.

(136) John Abner allowed his account as Captain of the Patrollers of Staunton.

(136) Alexander McClenachan qualified Justice, &c.

(138) 137 missing.

(138) County levy: To John Abner, as above, and then to the following (no doubt Abner's men), viz: John Parell, Henry Hall, William Smith, John Griffin, John Crosswhite, Alexr McKensey, James Dunn, Thomas Bell, William Evans, Israel Crisby, John Meredith, Robert Shall, Jacob Peck, Robert Gamble, John McDonough, Francis Hall, James Brush, Owen Owens, James Thomas.

DECEMBER 18, 1776.

(139) Benjamin Forsythe qualified Deputy Sheriff.

(139) Admn. of estate of David Hastings granted to Richard Madison.

(139) Abraham Smith qualified Justice, &c.

(140) County levy: To Thomas Rhoads, jailor. Sheriff forbidden to pay salary to Gabriel Jones, Deputy Attorney, until he gives his reason for not attending this Court and declares whether he intends to serve in that capacity or not.

(141) Called Court on Mary Wolfinger—felony—guilty and asked corporal punishment; her husband appeared and said he was the principal offender and asked that he receive the punishment—20 lashes—which was adjudged, "we do desire that the Sheriff put the same in immediate execution as we think that the most guilty ought to suffer."

Page

(142) Called Court on John Smith, larceny.—Guilty and sent to General Court.

(144) Same on Margaret Masters—larceny.

(There is nothing but the title; then follow the records of a regular term.)

(144) Francis Davis, orphan, to be bound to Rob. Wilson.

(145) Sampson Mathews and Samuel McDowell qualified Justices.

(146) Administration of estate of John Douglas granted to Charles Campbell. Mary Murphy, next friend to deceased, appeared and relinquished her right.

(147) Admn. of estate of Roger North committed to his widow, Catherine North.

FEBRUARY 14, 1777.

(148) Called Court on Mary Smith—larceny.—Guilty.

MARCH 5, 1777.

(149) Court called to consider advisability of inoculation—allowed to any person or physician, but not to be done farther than three miles from any place where the smallpox makes its appearance. Everybody forbidden to have intercourse with persons having smallpox, and vice versa, and Sheriff ordered to give public notice.

MARCH 18, 1777.

(150) John Lewis qualified Justice.

(152) Administration of estate of Samuel Black, deceased, granted to Rebecca Black and James Henderson. Same of Thomas Wilson granted to Martha, his widow.

(155) Admn. c. t. a. of estate of David Williamson granted to widow Peneripy.

(156) James Alderman, aged three years, son of Richard Alderman, to be bound out.

(156) Admn. of estate of Peter Buzzard granted to Nicholas Michael.

(157) James Lowrey, orphan of John Lowrey, chose Robert Lowrey guardian.

(157) John Herdman, Sr. and Jr., to appraise estate of Wm. Church, decd.

(158) John, William, James and Mary, children of James Brown, to be bound out.

(160) Thomas Huett—special bail.

(160) William Reah and John Campbell appointed guardians to William, Hugh and John Reah, orphans of Archibald Reah, Jr., deceased.

(161) Charles Williamson, orphan of Roger Williamson, to be bound to Richard Williamson.

(161) Felix Gilbert qualified Justice, &c.

(162) William Teas refused to qualify Justice.

(162) Admn. of estate of Joseph Blair, decd., granted to Elenore, the widow, and James Blair.

Page

(163) Account of estate of Jacob Cammerlon recorded.

(163) Liberty to inoculate against smallpox granted the citizens of Staunton and three miles around.

(165) These recommended for Justices, viz: George Boswell, John Thomas, Wm. McPheeters, James Steel, James Dyer, Thomas Huett, Wm. Nalle, Samuel Lyle, Robert Davis, John McCreary and Henry Ewing.

(165) John Kinkead, gent., qualified Justice.

(166) Called Court on Hester Brown, wife of James Brown.—Guilty and ten lashes.

MARCH 19, 1777.

(170) Ordinary rates.

(171) Catherine Gratton, daughter of John Gratton.

(174) Every Captain required to appoint a Constable in his Company.

(174) Commission for priv. examination of Phiany, wife of Michael Bowyer.

(175) Michael Bowyer qualified Justice, &c.

APRIL 1, 1777.

(176) Called Court on William Jones—larceny.—Guilty and sent to General Court.

APRIL 8, 1777.

(177) Called Court on John Carr.—Acquitted.

APRIL 16, 1777.

(178) William Reese—Called Court—guilty—larceny.

MAY 20, 1777.

(179) Admn. of estate of Thomas Brown granted to William Brown.

(184) William McBride and Mary Burke to be bound to Thomas Huit.

(184) Commission to Cumberland County, Pennsylvania, for privy examination of Janet, wife of William Hays—deed to James Mitchell.

(186) Admn. of estate of John Needham granted to George Henton.

(186) Commission for priv. examination of Sarah, wife of James Patten.

(186) Siner Needham, orphan of John Needham, chose George Hinton guardian.

(186) Mary Price, orphan of Calem Price, to be bound out.

(188) John Wilmoth, likely to become a charge on the Parish, to be bound out. Barbara Mallow, to be bound to Jacob Havener. Michael Mallow, to be bound to John Bright. John Newby, to be bound to James Magill.

(190) Jacob Keslinger, orphan of Christian Keslinger, to be bound to Philip Lingle.

(190) Mathew Wilson, recomd. Captain; John Boyd, recomd. Lieutenant; Samuel Weir, recomd. Ensign; Michael Coger, recomd. Captain, vice Capt. William Nalle, resigned; Samuel Vance, recomd. Captain; Jacob Warwick, recomd. Lieutenant; John Boyd, recomd. Ensign.

(191) John Cunningham, recomd. Captain; Robert Clark, recomd. Lieutenant; John Wilson, recomd. Ensign, Capt. James Ewing having resigned.

MAY 21, 1777.

(191) Josiah Davidson qualified Justice, &c.

(191) Sarah, wife of Abraham Smith—commission for priv. examination. Deed to Smith Tandy.

(192) James Ramsey qualified Constable.

(192) Viewers to report on a road from William Robertson's saw mill to William Teas's.

(193) Alexr. Gibson, Sr., road surveyor, vice James Ramsey.

(193) Jacob Fridley, orphan of Ludowick Fridley, to be bound to John Argenbright, to teach him to read, write and understand figures as far as the rule of three, to pay him £10 in lieu of a suit of clothes and freedom dues, to teach or cause him to be taught trade of blacksmith.

(194) William Robson, runaway servant of Jacob Peck.

(196) Andrew, Margaret and Robert Russell—witnesses.

(196) Christopher Graham qualified Lieutenant.

(196) Elizabeth McMahon, orphan of Abraham McMahon, to be bound to Joseph Bell, to give her a cow and calf, a spinning wheel, cloth to make a bed and two sheets over and above her freedom dues.

JULY 14, 1777.

(198) Called Court on Wm. Hartley (Heathley)—larceny of three silver dollars, six pistoles, &c.—Guilty and sent to Williamsburg for trial.

AUGUST 19, 1777.

(201) Judith, wife of George Boswell—commission for her priv. examination. Deed to John Carthrae.

(201) William Ellis, aged three years, to be bound to Wm. Wright.

(201) Indenture from the Sachems of the Six Nations of Indians to George Croughan, formerly partly proved in the Court of West Augusta, now proved by Thomas Walker, Jr., and recorded.

(203) Abraham Hintle, Thomas Miller and John Bennet—to view the road from Hampshire to the mouth of Dry Run, on the North Fork of the South Branch of the Potomac.

(204) George Bucher, aged 15 on the 29th of last January, to be bound to Henry Shuck, to learn trade of a blacksmith, reading, writing and arithmetic to rule of three and to give him £7 as freedom dues.

(204) Edward Callahan, runaway servant of Benjamin Brown.

(205) William Trotter, orphan of John Trotter, to be bound.

(206) Mary Black, widow of John Black, deceased, qualifies admx.

(206) Following took the oath of allegiance, viz: Daniel Smith, William Bowyer, Elijah McClenachan, James Tate, Sampson Mathews, Thomas Hugart, Charles Campbell, John McCleerey, Alexr. Robertson—Justices.

(206) Nat, an Indian bound boy in the custody of Mary Greenlee, who detains him as a slave, complains of being held unlawfully. Commission awarded to take depositions in Carolina or elsewhere.

(207) Thomas Blizard, vice Mathew Dice—Constable.

(211) William McMahon, aged 15, orphan of Abraham McMahon, to be bound to John Carruthers.

(211) Jacob Mack's will proved and widow Margaret qualifies admx.

(213) Following recommendations: John Givens as Captain, vice Capt. Laird; Robert Campbell, as First Lieutenant; James Crawford, as Second Lieutenant; Felty Shirley, as Ensign.

(214) Catherine Price, orphan of Calem Price, to be bound.

(215) Following recommendations: Anthony Reader, as Captain, vice Adam Reader; Thomas Boggs, as Captain, vice Martin Humble; William Lowderson (West Fork), as Captain; Benj. Wilson (Tygers Valley), as Captain; Robert Shaw, as Second Lieutenant, and Richard Madison, as Ensign, in Capt. Thomas Smith's Company.

(216) Samuel McCutchon, as Captain; Robert Harris, as First Lieutenant; John Smith, as Ensign.

(217) John Cunningham qualified Captain of Militia, Robert Clark as Lieutenant, and John Wilson as Ensign, in Capt. John Cunningham's Company.

(218) Isaac Newly and Rachel Newly, orphans of Wm. Newly, to be bound to Hybert Brig.

AUGUST 20, 1777.

(219) Silas Hart and John Dickinson qualified Justices. John Dever qualified Constable.

(220) Commission for priv. examination of Marsa, wife of John Bailey. Deed to Joseph Lemmon.

(220) Recommended to Governor, viz: William Robertson (West Fork), as Captain; John Hamilton (Tygers Valley), as Captain.

(220) Sarah Patterson, wife of James Patterson, relinquished dower in land conveyed to Robert Walker.

(221) Zachariah Johnston qualified Captain.

(221) Tithables to be taken in following Companies: Capt. John Gilmore's, Capt. John Lyle's, and Capt. David Gray's, and oath of allegiance to be administered to all.

(222) Tithables to be taken in following Companies: Capt. Charles Campbell's, Capt. Alex. Stewart's, Capt. Matthew Wilson's, Capt. Andrew Moore's, Capt. James Tate's, Capt. John Cunningham's, Capt. Samuel McCutchan's, Capt. Patrick Buchanan's, Capt. Francis Long's, Capt. John Young's, Capt. Robert Thompson's, Capt. Zachariah Johnson's, Capt. Thomas Smith's, Capt. George Moffett's, Capt. Wm. Anderson's, Capt. Wm. Henderson's, Capt. Alex. Robertson's, Capt. David Bell's, Capt. John Given's, Capt. John Hopkins', Capt. John Stephenson's, Capt. Robert Craven's, Capt. George Pence's, Capt. James Frazier's, Capt. Wm. Nall's, Capt. Thomas Hewit's, Capt. Daniel Smith's, Capt. Reuben Harrison's, Capt. Thomas Bogg's, Capt. Abraham Lincoln's, Capt. Anthony Rider, Capt. Ralph Stewart's, Capt. Benj. Wilson's, Capt. Wm. Robertson's, Capt. Samuel Pringle's, Capt. Robert McCreery's,

Capt. Samuel Vance's, Capt. John McCoy's, Capt. John People's, Capt. Andrew Lockridges', Capt. John Skidmore's, Capt. Paul Teeter's and Capt. Robert Davis'.

(224) Following recommended to be added to Commission of Peace, viz: Joshua Humphries, Joseph Bell, William McDowell, Peter Hanger, Anthony Rider, John Fitzwaters, William Westfall, Benj. Wilson, William Lowther, Isaac Hinkle, Jonas Friend.

(224) William Lowther, West Fort, recommended as Captain.

SEPTEMBER 16, 1777.

(226) Commission to take priv. examination of Sarah Hartgrove, in South Carolina, wife of Francis Hartgrove. Deed to David Griner.

(226) John Campbell and Thomas Connerly appointed guardians of Elizabeth Walker, orphan of Alexander Walker, Jr., deceased. Elizabeth Walker, wife of Alexander Walker, relinquished dower in land conveyed to *Alexander Walker*. Martha Grimes, late Martha Walker, widow of Alexander Walker, Jr., relinquished dower in land possessed by her late husband to her two children, Jane and Elizabeth Walker.

(227) James Shoemaker is about to remove out of the County.

(227) Commonwealth vs. John Archer. } For disaffection to the Commonwealth. He took the oath in Court, but was bound to his good behavior for one year.

(229) Philip Sciler, vice John Buchanan—road surveyor.

SEPTEMBER 17, 1777.

(230) Jacob Peck, vice John Abney—Constable.

(230) Mary Greenlee to be summoned on the complaint of Nat, an Indian or Mustee boy.—Court finds that Mary uses the boy inhumanly and orders him to be hired out by the Sheriff.

(231) Commonwealth vs. Alexr. Miller, M. A.—Guilty—£100 and two years' imprisonment.

(232) Samuel McCutchon qualified Captain, and in his Company qualified, viz: John McKenny, First Lieutenant; Robert Harris, Second Lieutenant, and John Smith, Ensign.

(233) Martin Cryder found guilty, as Alexr. Miller—£50 and 3 years.

SEPTEMBER 18, 1777.

(236) John Cryder, tried on same charge as Alexr. Miller, above, and convicted—£2 and two years' imprisonment.

(237) William Hinton, same—£400 and four years' imprisonment.

(238) Following were witnesses against the same, viz: Thomas Alderson, David Harned, Joseph Burgess, John Bright, John Owens, Samuel Felps, Joseph Smith and Elizabeth Scothorn.

(239) Sheriff ordered to make the jail secure.

OCTOBER 23, 1777.

(239) Called Court.

NOVEMBER 18, 1777.

Page

(243) Ann Hynes, wife of Thomas Hynes, a soldier in the Continental Service, allowed £15 for herself and two small children.

(243) Complaint of Nat, Indian boy, against Mary Greenlee, continued in order to allow Mary's son to take depositions in Carolina.

(243) Mathew Wilson qualified Captain.

(244) John Boyd qualified Lieutenant.

(244) Francis Allen complains of his master, John Paul, for bad usage.

(244) Barbara, widow of David Bosang, qualifies admx. c. t. a.

(245) Admn. of estate of Robert Shaw granted to James Hill, greatest creditor.

(245) Old Court House to be rented to the highest bidder.

DECEMBER 1, 1777.

(246) Called Court on John Pence, for stealing Robert Hook's steer.— Evidence not sufficient to take his life, and sent on to next Grand Jury.

DECEMBER 9, 1777.

(249) Called Court on James Brown and Josiah Blankenship, for breaking house of Woolrick Waggoner and larceny.—Guilty and sent to Williamsburg for trial.

(250) Called Court on Richard Harris, for housebreaking and larceny.— Not guilty.

DECEMBER 16, 1777.

(252) County levy: To Thomas Rhoades, jailor.

(253) Elizabeth Forris agrees to serve her master, Owen Owens, for one year for purchasing her from her former master.

(253) William Purris exempted from County levy.

(253) Alexr. Scott as Second Lieutenant, Wm. McClenachan as Ensign in Capt. Patrick Buchanan's Company—recommended.

(253) Robert Kenny as Second Lieutenant, and Alexr. Robertson as Ensign, in Capt. Alexr. Robertson's Company—recommended.

(253) Walter Cowden to be bound to John McDonough according to an agreement made with Walter's mother.

(254) Admn. of estate of John Counts is granted to his widow, Elizabeth Counts.

(254) John Hix, servant of Joshua Humphreys, gives up his freedom dues in consideration of being set free.

(255) Samuel Thomas, committed as a deserter, was examined and recommitted to jail, and the jailor ordered to advertise him.

(255) Mary Warr, wife of James Warr, and their four children, allowed £25. James enlisted for three years.

(255) Mary Linden, wife of James Linden, and their two children, allowed £15. James enlisted for three years.

(256) Ann Hynes, wife of Thomas Hynes (enlisted for three years), and two children, allowed £15.

Page

(257) John Givens qualified Captain.

(258) Joseph Blair recommended as Ensign in Capt. John Cunningham's Company.

(260) Admn. of estate of John Hays granted to his widow, Elizabeth.

(261) Ordered to be certified to the Governor that the following Justices are recommended for appointments as Justices will fall in the new Counties, viz: In Rockingham—Silas Hart, Daniel Smith, Felix Gilbert, Abraham Smith, John Gratton, Josiah Davidson, John Skidmore, George Boswell, Thomas Hewett, John Thomas, William Nall, Robert Davis, James Dyer, Henry Ewing, William McDowell, Anthony Rider, John Fitzwater, and Isaac Hinckle. In Rockbridge—Archibald Alexander, Samuel McDowell, John Hays, Charles Campbell, and Samuel Lyle. In Augusta—John Dickenson, John Christian, John Poage, George Moffet, Sampson Mathews, Alexr. McClenachan, William Bowyer, George Mathews, Michael Bowyer, Alexr. Robertson, Thomas Huggart, Elijah McClenachan, John Lewis, Alexr. St. Clair, John Kinkead, James Tate, William McPheeters, James Steel, John McCreery, Joshua Humphreys, Joseph Bell, Peter Hanger, James Craig— the two last to be left out for refusing to take the oath of allegiance.

(263) Samuel Vance and John Wilson, of Jackson's River, recommended to appd. on Commission of the Peace.

(263) Sarah McGraw, wife of Charles McGraw, a soldier in public service, and one small child, allowed £20.

(264) Sampson Mathews recommended as County Lieutenant.

(264) George Moffett recommended as Major.

MARCH 17, 1778.

(264) Christian Fudge, wife of John Fudge, relinquished dower in deed to Jeremiah Beesley.

(267) Robert Campbell qualified Lieutenant.

(268) John Poage qualified Sheriff.

(269) Admn. of estate of William Anderson granted to Margaret, his widow.

(270) Admn. of estate of John Stuart granted to William Hamilton.

(271) Admn. of estate of James O'Neal granted to Robert Gum.

(271) John Fowler, runaway servant of John Cowarden.

(272) Benj. Wilson, Samuel Vance and Thomas Hicklin qualified Captains.

(272) Will of William Teas partly proven.

(273) Mary McKnight, Mary O'Bryan and Mary Raddon, soldiers' wives with small children, allowed each £10.

(275) Admn. of estate of Darby Connerly granted Benjamin Wilson.

(275) George Moffet, William Bowyer, Alexander St. Clair—appointed Commissioners for the Tax. Ordinary rates.

MARCH 18, 1778.

(277) John Cowarden, executor of Peter Burns, to be summoned to settle accounts.

(277) Joseph Skidmore's will partly proved.
(278) George Moffet qualified Major.
(278) John Poage qualified Surveyor.
(278) Admn. of estate of James Bowyer granted Wm. Bowyer.
(279) Jacob Peck qualified Constable.

April 14, 1778.

(280) Called Court on Andrew Wilson for murdering his wife Jane.—Guilty, and sent to Williamsburg for trial. Nicholas and Mary Elsey witnesses.

April 20, 1778.

(281) New Commission of the Peace, viz: Thomas Adams, John Poage, Sampson Mathews, Wm. Bowyer,* Michael Bowyer, Thos. Huggart, John Lewis, John Kinkead, Wm. McPheeters, John McCreerey, Joseph Bell,* Samuel Vance, John Dickenson, George Moffet,* Alexr. McClenachan,* George Mathews, Alexr. Robertson,* Elijah McClenachan,* Alexr. St. Clair, James Tate,* James Steele, Joshua Humphreys,* Peter Hanger, John Wilson.* (Those checked (*) qualified.)

(283) Will of Morris O'Friel partly proved.

(284) Barbara Gross, late Barbara Bosand, disclaimed the provisions of the will of her husband, David Bosand, and claimed her dower.

(285) Dower to be laid off to Ann Storey, widow of Thomas Storey.

(285) Joseph Gum, Lieutenant, and Abraham Hempenstall, Ensign, qualified.

(286) Elenor Cochran and Elizabeth Wilson, soldiers' wives and having young children, allowed £15 each.

May 19, 1778.

(286) Sampson Mathews, Samuel Vance, James McCreery, James Steel—qualified Justices.

(287) Sampson Mathews qualified Lieutenant Colonel of the County.

(289) Admn. of estate of John Watkins granted Stephen Loy.

(290) Will of John Logan partly proved.

(291) John Masey's children to be bound out.

(291) Susannah Taler and Elenor Eskins, soldiers' wives with young children, allowed, to first, £25, and to second, £5.

(291) Robert and James Wilson, children of Andrew Wilson, to be bound out.

(291) Jonathan Smith, George Westfall and George Jackson—appointed Constables.

(292) William Beard, vice William Thompson—Constable. John Clemmons, vice William Allison—Constable.

(294) John Lambert to be sworn to show cause why he does not provide for his children.

(294) Several defendants petition that the only two attending attorneys at this time are employed by the plaintiff—ordered that Capt. Peter Hog, one of the two attorneys, appear for the defendant.

(294) David Henderson, vice Samuel Love, appointed road surveyor from Richard Payne's to the Tinkling Spring.

(295) John Hawkins, runaway servant of James Patterson.

(299) Inhabitants on the West Fork of Monongahela and the River Buchanan, and in Tyger's Valley, petition that there is no Justice attending in that district to tender the oath of allegiance—petitioners are ready to take the oath—which is ordered to be certified to the Assembly, being out of the jurisdiction of the Court.

(300) George Moffet, James Tate, Alexr. St. Clair, David Henderson, James Steele, Wm. Bowyer, Patrick Buchanan, Joshua ——, John McKenny—qualified Vestrymen.

(300) Colonel Alexander Thompson, Colonel of the County, being called on to act, refused, and George Moffet is recommended in his place.

(300) William Bowyer recommended Major, Richard Madison as Second Lieutenant, and James Thomas as Ensign; James Mitchell as Second Lieutenant, and Alexander Brownlee as Ensign.

(300) David Henderson, James Tremble, James Trotter, Jr., Thomas Rankin, Benjamin Wilson and Jonas Friend—recommended on Commission of the Peace.

MAY 20, 1778.

(302) Petition of Nat, a mullato or Indian boy, against Mary Greenlee for freedom. The facts appear, viz: Sherwood Harris, of Granville County, No. Co., conveyed by bill of sale for £10 the boy to someone, and by several assignments he was made over to James Greenlee, deceased, late husband of Mary.—Decided Nat is a free man and not a slave. John Stewart, of Walker's Creek, makes oath he is not the defendant, and suit is dismissed.

(303) Robert Estrop bound to peace on complaint of Judy Price.

(305) Elizabeth Vernon to be summoned for not providing for her children.

(305) Jacob Aberman, witness from Rockingham.

MAY 21, 1778.

(306) George Benson's death abates suit.

(307) Robert Hartgrove's death abates suit.

(308) George Wilson's death abates suit.

(308) William Crow, no inhabitant.

(308) Patrick Coutts's death abates suit.

(309) John McClenachan's death abates suit.

(309) Jones Clerk's death abates suit.

(310) Sarah McDowell, infant, by next friend, Samuel McDowell, vs. James Stewart.—Abates by death of plaintiff.

(310) Thomas Hog's death abates suit.

(310) John Kennerley's death abates suit.

(311) William Wilson's death abates suit.

(311) John Gabriel Jones's death abates suit.

(312) James Bratton's death abates suit.

(312) Peter Neil, returned no inhabitant.

Page
(312) John Jones's death abates suit.
(313) Nancy Fling's death abates suit.
(313) James Bowyer's death abates suit.
(314) George Taylor, returned lives in Amherst.
(314) Mathew Reed's death abates suit.
(315) John Counts's death abates suit.
(316) Andrew Hurling's death abates suit.
(325) John McCutchen's death abates suit.
(326) David Roberts's death abates suit.
(326) William Gilmore, returned no inhabitant.
(327) Robert Scott, returned no inhabitant.
(328) Joseph Skidmore's death abates suit.
(329) Thomas Dooley, Charles Campbell, Timothy Warren and Jacob Custard—defendants.—Suits against them to be transferred to Rockingham.
(329) Moses Thomson's death abates suit.
(329) Jacob Aberman, Jacob Linderbach.—Suits against them to be transferred to Rockingham.
(330) Elliot Rutherford, Peter Runkle, John Christler, William and Mary Elliott, Adam Wise.—Suits transferred to Rockingham.
(331) John Davidson, vice Thomas Rankin (recommended yesterday, as John lives more convenient to the people.) Smith Tandy and Wm. Lowther recommended as Justices.
(332) County levy continued.
(332) Conveyance of Andrew Wilson, a madman, to jail.
(333) Jacob Warwick as First Lieutenant, David Gwinn as Second Lieutenant, Jonathan Humphreys as Ensign—recommended for appointment in Capt. Samuel Vance's Company.

JUNE 16, 1778.

(334) George Moffet qualified Colonel of the County, and William Bowyer, Major. John McMahon qualified Second Lieutenant in Capt. Wm. Anderson's Company.
(334) Jane Tees, orphan of William Tees, chose David Henderson her guardian.
(335) Richard Madison qualified Second Lieutenant.
(336) John Patrick appointed road surveyor. Thomas Frame, vice John Erwin, appointed Constable.
(337) John Wilson to take tithables in Tyger's Valley, Buchon and the West Fork of Monongahela.
(337) Samuel Vance in Captains Vance's and Lockridge's Companies. John McCreary, on South Branch of Potomac, in Captains McCreary's, Hicklin's and McCoy's Companies. Col. Moffet, in Captains Henderson's and Young's Companies. Capt. Alexr. Robertson, in his own, Capt. Givens's, and Capt. Wm. Anderson's Companies. Joseph Bell, in Captains David Bell's and Johnson's Companies. James Steel in Captains Long's and Thomson's Companies. James Tate in his own and Capt. McCutchon's Company. Elijah McClenachan in Capt. Buchanan's and Capt. Cunningham's Company. Wm. Bowyer in Capt. John Young's Company, N. M. (?) Alexr. St. Clair in Capt. Thomas Smith's Company.

(338) Robert Poage qualified assistant surveyor to John Poage.

AUGUST 18, 1778.

(340) Commission for priv. examination of Cecilia, wife of Archibald Smithers, as to land conveyed to Alexr. Hamilton.

(342) Margaret, widow of John Logan, qualified admx.

(342) George Jackson qualified Constable.

(344) John Kelly, an orphan, to be bound.

(346) Viewers to locate a road between North Mountain and North River, beginning at John Percey's, thence the nearest way leading from Brock's Gap to Staunton.

(346) Thomas Frame qualified Constable.

(346) James Phillips, an aged and infirm witness.

(347) Court is informed that Mathew Reed has been dead about two years and no person has qualified administrator, his brother and heir having refused. Sheriff ordered to take charge until further order.

(347) Valentine Shirly and Jacob Barrier, vice James Kennerly, appointed road surveyor.

(348) Margaret, wife of Samuel McPheeters, to be privily examined. Deed to John McDougall.

AUGUST 19, 1778.

(349) William McClenachan qualified Ensign in Capt. Patrick Buchanan's Company. James Thomas qualified Ensign in Capt. Thomas Smith's Company.

(349) George Taylor, a child of Thomas Taylor's, to be bound out to John Findley, the father not being able to bring him up in a Christianlike manner.

(350) Joseph Long as Second Lieutenant, and Robert Christian as Ensign—recommended in Capt. Francis Long's Company.

(350) Witnesses to be summoned to prove the will of Gasper Eaker.

(350) James Trimble recommended as Captain of the Company formerly commanded by Col. George Moffet. John Garner as Second Lieutenant, and James Hogshead, Jr., as Ensign in the same Company.

(351) Joseph Ray, Deputy Sheriff under John Christian, having collected taxes from several supernumeraries since expiration of his term, John is to be summoned to account with the County. Archibald Alexander, late Sheriff, same.

(351) Abraham Taylor, child of Thomas Taylor, to be bound to Owen Owens.—See page 349, *supra.*

(351) Susannah Leeper, wife of John Leeper, relinquishes dower in land sold to Anthony Ailor.

(352) William Bowyer recommended Lieutenant Colonel of the First Battalion of the Militia. Alexander Robertson recommended Major of the First Battalion of the Militia.

(353) Thomas Adams recommended Colonel of Second Battalion; John Dickinson as Lieutenant of same, and Andrew Lockridge as Major of same.

(363) William Kinkead as Captain, vice Andrew Lockridge; James Bratton as First Lieutenant; John Vachob as Second Lieutenant, and Andrew Hamilton, Jr., as Ensign—recommended.

(53) Robert Keny as Captain, vice Major Alexr. Robertson; John McCune as First Lieutenant, Alexander Robertson as Second Lieutenant, Gasper Clemmonds as Ensign—recommended.

(353) Following recommended on Commission of Peace: David Henderson, James Trimble, James Trotter, Jr., Benj. Wilson, Jonas Friend, John Davidson, Smith Tandy, Wm. Lowther and Andrew Davidson. John Christian to be left out as he refuses to serve longer.

(353) Michael Carpenter recommended as First Lieutenant, Henry Fleisher recommended as Second Lieutenant, and Thomas Metter as Ensign.

(354) All in Capt. William Lowther's Company.

(354) William Lowther qualified Captain.

(354) David Frame appointed road surveyor from his house to William Black's, also from Widow Lewis's to Col. Mathews' plantation in Calf Pasture. John Peebles appointed road surveyor from his house to John Redman's, with tithables from James Montgomery's to Lofty Pullin's. Joseph Gwinn from John Redman's to top of the Calf Pasture Mountain. William Lockridge from top of the Calf Pasture Mountain to the road leading from Staunton to Warm Springs.

September 15, 1778.

(355) It appears to the Court that Nicholas Ellzee and Mary, his daughter, recognized to appear before General Court in the prosecution against Andrew Wilson, as too poor and in too bad health to travel to Williamsburg.—Sheriff ordered to convey them and bear expense out of the County levy.

(356) James Gay appointed road surveyor from Jenning's Gap to John Hodge's house. Adam Bratton appointed road surveyor from the place above Andrew Hamilton's where William Matear leaves off to Col. Mathews's storehouse. Charles Donnelly appointed road surveyor from Col. Mathews's store to Leonard Bell's former bounds. Andrew Anderson appointed road surveyor from the Middle River to William Poage's, with tithables from William Wallace's down.

(357) Thomas Smith appointed road surveyor from Thomas Poage's to Staunton, with George Craig's tithables.

(357) William Kinkead and James Trimble qualified Captains. Robert Christian, Jr., and Andrew Hamilton, Jr., qualified Ensigns. Andrew Lockridge qualified Major.

(358) John Kelly, orphan of Joseph Kelly, to be bound to William Mann, to learn trade of a weaver.

(358) James Allen, Jr., appointed road surveyor from Middle River to John McMahon's.

(358) Catherine Kelly, orphan of James Kelly, to be bound to Dennis Callahan.

(359) James Bratton qualified First Lieutenant.

Page

(361) New Commission of the Peace, viz: Thomas Adams, John Christian, George Moffet,* Alexr. McClenachan, Michael Bowyer, Thos. Hugart, John Lewis, John Kinkead,* Wm. McPheeters, John McCreary,* Joseph Bell, Samuel Vance, David Henderson,* James Trotter, Jr.,* Jonas Friend, Smith Tandy, John Dickenson, John Poage, Sampson Mathews,* William Bowyer, Alexr. Robertson,* Elijah McClenachan, Alexr. St. Clair, James Tate,* James Steele,* Joseph Humphreys, Pat. Hanger, John Wilson, James Tremble, Benj. Wilson, John Davidson, Wm. Lowther, Andrew Davidson. (Those marked (*) qualified.)

(362) Samuel Black qualified Second Lieutenant in Capt. Robert McCreary's Company, and James Steel as Ensign in Capt. Robert Thompson's Company. Charles Baskins qualified as First Lieutenant, James Gibson as Second Lieutenant and James Graham as Ensign. James Frazier qualified Second Lieutenant in Capt. Robert Thompson's Company.

OCTOBER 21, 1778.

(363) Samuel Vance qualified Justice.

(363) Samuel Neal, orphan of James Neal, to be bound to Lanty Graham; James Neal to Robert Gwinn.

(364) Alexr. Robertson qualified Major of First Battalion; Robert Kenny qualified Captain.

(365) James Young recommended as Second Lieutenant in Capt. John Young's Company. Richard Mathews recommended as Ensign, vice James Hogshead, who refuses to serve in Capt. James Tremble's Company. John McCune qualified First Lieutenant.

OCTOBER 22, 1778.

(366) David Wilson recommended as Ensign in Capt. James Tate's Company, vice Alexr. Brownlee, Jr., who refuses to serve. George Anderson recommended as Ensign, vice Casper Clemmons, who refuses to serve, in Capt. Robert Kenny's Company.

(367) William Buchanan recommended as Ensign in Capt. Samuel McCutchon's Company. Nicholas Seyvert recommended as First Lieutenant in Capt. John McCoy's Company, vice Nicholas Harper; and Henry Fleisher as a Second Lieutenant.

NOVEMBER 17, 1778.

(368) Joseph Bell, Elijah McClenachan and Jonas Friend qualified Justices.

(369) John Madison, Clerk of the Court, resigned on account of age and infirmities, and Richard Madison was unanimously chosen in his place.

(370) Mary Thompson, a soldier's wife, with small children, allowed £15. Mary Waugh, a soldier's wife, with small children, allowed £25.

(370) Admn. of estate of Jacob Springstone granted his widow ——.

(372) Admn. of estate of Joel Westfall granted to William and Jacob Westfall.

Page

(373) Aaron Richeson to be summoned to produce the will of his brother, Ephraim Richeson.

(373) Edward McGlaughlin exempted from levy.

(373) Elenore, wife of Robert Thompson, relinquished dower in deed to John Carruthers.

(373) Sarah Windon, widow (wife of James Windon, who is in the Continental Service), allowed £15.

(374) Samuel Gardner, orphan of Thomas Gardner, chose John Poage his guardian.

(376) John O'Dare bound to peace on complaint of his wife, Mary O'Dare.

(378) John Bing appointed road surveyor. Walter Davis appointed road surveyor.

NOVEMBER 18, 1778.

(379) Alexander Simpson recommended Captain, vice Capt. John Young, who hereby resigns.

(379) Admn. of estate of Israel Christian is granted to John Christian.

(380) Alexr. McClenachan, Smith Tandy and John Davidson qualified Justices. Alexr. Simpson qualified Captain.

(381) Alexr. and Elijah McClenachan and Alexr. St. Clair to inspect the old Court House and report in what condition it is and whether it was left in tenantable repair.

(381) Moses Henshaw ordered confined as a deserter until he can be delivered to some Continental officer.

(382) Martha Warner, orphan of Edward Warner, to be bound, preference being given to James Patterson.

NOVEMBER 23, 1778.

(382) Called Court on Samuel Malcom, for larceny from the house of Loves Usher.—Guilty and 30 lashes.

DECEMBER 4, 1778.

(383) Called Court on James Smith, for stealing leather from the tanyard of Herman Lovingood.—Guilty and sent to Williamsburg.

DECEMBER 15, 1778.

(385) Thomas Hughart and James Trimble qualified Justices.

(386) Admn. of estate of Lanty Elliot granted to his mother, Jane Elliot.

(387) County levy: 2,000 tithables at 2 shillings.

(388) Church Wardens to bind Agnes McGray to James Sawyer, who agrees to give her when free one cow and one good calf and such a suit of clothes as £3, 10 would have bought when she was first bound by consent of her mother in 1773.

JANUARY 6, 1779.

(388) Called Court on Chrismass Meecans, of Cumberland County, Va.—larceny. (Richard Madison, Clerk, being absent on his lawful business, Peter Hog appointed Clerk *pro tem.*).—Guilty and sent to Williamsburg.

Page

(391) Richard Madison, being absent, as page 388, Court appoints James Thomas, Clerk *pro tem*.

(391) William Bowyer, Alexr. St. Clair and Benjamin Wilson qualified Justices.

(393) Michael Bowyer qualified Justice.

(393) Wm. Cleaver, Daniel Westfall, Francis Wire and John Warrick— to locate a road from Jonas Friend's to Darby Connolly's (deceased) plantation, in Tyger's Valley.

JANUARY 20, 1779.

(394) James Lachey appointed road surveyor of the road located by John Warrick and Ralph Stewart, from plantation of Darby Connolly, deceased, to Lewis's quarter on Nap's Creek.

JANUARY 22, 1779.

(395) Called Court on Rosannah Ramsey, for horse stealing.—Not guilty.

FEBRUARY 16, 1779.

(396) Elenore Askins, mother of a child bound to Walter Cunningham, complains of Walter for not using her child well.—Summoned. Witnesses: Rosana Steel, David Steel, and Mary, his wife, Hanna and Mary Lessley.

(397) William Bowyer qualified Lieutenant Colonel. David Gwinn qualified Lieutenant.

MARCH 16, 1779.

(400) Garrat Wheeler exempted from levy.

(400) Commission for examination of Jane, wife of Robert Buchanan. Deed to Philip Sciler.

(402) Elizabeth, wife of James Thorpe, soldier in the Continental Army, with small children, allowed £25.

(402) Joseph Crouch recommended as Captain, Alexr. Maxwell as Lieutenant, and Patrick Hamilton as Ensign.

(403) John Lewis, Wm. Lowther and Andrew Davidson qualified Justices.

(404) William Robertson, Captain, and Nicholas Sybert, as First Lieutenant—qualified.

(406) Commission for priv. examination of Mille, wife of Charles Cummins, as to deed to Robert Cummins.

(406) Joseph Crouch as Captain, Jacob Warwick and Alexr. Maxwell as First Lieutenants—qualified.

(407) Elizabeth Wilson, soldier's wife, with small children, allowed £20.

(407) Admn. of estate of William Wallace granted widow Jane.

(408) Court appoints John Graham guardian of Joseph Graham, orphan of David Graham.

(409) John Gum appointed road surveyor from Peter Hob's Mill to the road over the mountain to Burdy House.

Page
(410) Joshua Humphreys and John Wilson qualified Justices.
(410) Anthony Sedusky appointed road surveyor in Tyger's Valley.
Daniel McLain appointed road surveyor in Tyger's Valley.
(413) Thomas Watterson's death abates suit.
(416) John Nickle exempted from County levy.

MARCH 18, 1779.

(433) Samuel Pritchard's death abates suit.
(437) David Griver, vice Jacob Peck, appointed Constable.
(439) Michael Bowyer qualified Attorney.

MARCH 19, 1779.

(439) Ordinary rates.

APRIL 20, 1779.

(441) Richard Madison, Clerk of this Court, being in the service of the State as Lieutenant of Militia, Peter Hog appointed Clerk *pro tem.*
(441) Executors of Francis Weir (Daniel Westfall and Benjamin Wilson) petition that appraisers be appointed for Francis's estate, as the times in that part of the country are so troublesome from the incursions of the Indians and the stock of the testator are exposed.
(442) John White qualified Lieutenant.

MAY 18, 1779.

(444) Joseph Patterson recommended Captain, vice Captain William Anderson; John Campbell as Lieutenant, and David Gibson as Ensign.
(445) Randall Slack and Sarah, his wife, failing to appear as witnesses to the will of Casper Ekert, are fined unless they appear, &c.
(447) Joseph Patterson qualified Captain; also John Campbell as Lieutenant, and David Gibson as Ensign.
(447) David Griner qualified Constable.
(448) Patrick Savage to be summoned to show cause why his children should not be bound out, it appearing that he is not capable of bringing them up in a Christianlike manner.
(449) Thomas Rankin recommended Captain, vice Robert Kenny; Gasper Clemmons as First Lieutenant, George Anderson as Second Lieutenant, and James Rankin as Ensign.
(450) Commission granted to take deposition of Sarah, wife of John Caldwell. Deed to Jacob Gabbert.
(450) Thomas Rankin qualified Captain.
(451) Michael Simms indicted for rescuing his horse, impressed in country's service. Stuffe How, for opposing and resisting an officer empowered to press a horse for said service, by Geo. Nicholas, Jacob and Martin Coyle.
(452) Rebecca, widow of Andrew Lewell, qualifies executrix.
(453) James Hughes, witness—18 miles.

Page

(454) Ann Wells, wife of Thomas Wells, soldier in the service of the Republic.

(456) John Middleton, child of Elizabeth Bradshaw, to be bound to George McNutt.

(456) Robert Thompson recommended as Ensign.

MAY 19, 1779.

(457) William Watson's death abates suit.

(458) Joseph Peace's death abates suit.

(463) Admn. of estate of John McClintock, deceased, is granted to Wm. McClintock, whose security is William McClintock, Sr.

(464) Elenore Cockrain, widow of Samuel Cockrain, who died in Continental Service, allowed £40. Elenore Forehand, widow of Darby Forehand, allowed £20.

(465) Charles Hyde, aged 15, orphan of John Hyde, to be bound to John McDonough.

(466) Commission granted to take priv. examination of Mary, wife of Martin Sherman, who resides in Albemarle. Deed to Wm. Richards.

(467) Robert Thompson qualified Ensign.

(471) Alexr. Robertson qualified Vestryman.

(474) Abraham Kerkendoll's death abates suit.

(475) Brian Breeding's death abates suit.

MAY 20, 1779.

(479) Benjamin Hawkins's death abates suit.

(483) William Mann's death abates suit.

(484) Joseph Hinkle's death abates suit.

(489) John Hawkins's death abates suit.

(506) William Head, returned no inhabitant.

(510) Alexander McCoy, returned no inhabitant.

(547) William Hays, returned no inhabitant.

(568) John Cowley's death abates suit.

(577) John Hutchinson and John Henderson, returned no inhabitants.

(577) John Frogg's death abates suit.

(585) James Ewing, returned no inhabitant.

(591) Archer Mathews, returned no inhabitant.

(594) Mary Wilson's marriage abates suit.

(613) Jacob Hart, no inhabitant.

(613) John Stevenson's death abates suit.

(614) George Peoples, returned "Lives in Rockbridge."

(623) On petition of Patrick McDavid, Commissioners to lay off dower to Martha Cowden, widow of Samuel Wilson, deceased, in half the lot in Staunton and the outlot belonging.

(624) Hugh Campbell, orphan of Robert Campbell, chose Elijah McClenachan his guardian.

MAY 21, 1779.

(625) Persons to take tithables in the following Captains Companies.

James Tate, in Tate and Long's Companies; Elijah McClenachan, in Buchanan's and Simpson's; George Moffett, in Trimble's and Henderson's; John Davidson, in Rankin's and Givens's; Alexr. Robertson, in Johnston's and Thompson's; James Trotter, Jr., in McCutchon's and Cunningham's.

(626) Joseph Bell, in Patterson's and Bell's; Joshua Humphreys, in Smith's; Thomas Huggart, in Capt. Kinkead's, Hicklin's and McCreary's; John Wilson, in McCoy's and Vance's; Benj. Wilson, in Tyger's Valley; Andrew Davidson, on West Fork and Buchanan's.

(630) William Hutchinson, returned no inhabitant.

AUGUSTA COUNTY COURT RECORDS.

ORDER BOOK No. XVII.

MAY 21, 1779.

(6) John Burnsides, no inhabitant.
(13) Wm. Bowyer vs. Robt. Denniston.—Transferred to Rockingham.
(24) Wm. Bowyer vs. John Eaken.—Transferred to Rockingham.
(26) Wm. Bowyer vs. John Steel.—Abates by death of defendant.
(37) —— vs. Godfrey Bumgardner.—Transferred to Rockingham.

MAY 22, 1779.

(39) George Moffet, Alexr. St. Clair and James Tate are appointed to examine the money in Augusta County, agreeable to an Act of Assembly passed in October, 1778.

JUNE 15, 1779.

(40) Constables appointed, viz: James Kirkpatrick in Capt. John Cunningham's Company; Manoah Singleton in Capt. Long's Company.
(40) Road surveyor: John Patrick, vice Joseph Poindexter.

JULY 20, 1779.

(41) Samuel Vance qualified Justice.
(41) Michael Bowyer appointed Escheator.
(41) John Cowden, by consent of his mother, Martha Cowden, his father having been many years absent from the State and it appearing to the Court that his education is much neglected, to be bound to John Griffin.

AUGUST 17, 1779.

(42) James Kirkpatrick qualified Constable.
(42) William Cyer to be bound to George Benson, to be taught to read, write, cypher as far as the rule of three, and when free to be given two suits of clothes which would have been of the value of £32, 10, six years ago, and one set of cooper's tools.

(44) Zachary Norton exempted from County levy.

(45) Arthur Connoly, vice Thomas Frame, appointed Constable.

(46) Adam Murray exempted from County levy.

(46) Adam Staunton exempted from County levy.

August 18, 1779.

(52) Jacob Stalnaker and Ralph Stewart appointed Constables.

(54a) Nicholas Harper appointed road overseer from Peter Flesher's to Conrad Woolry's Mill.

August 19, 1779.

(54b) Sheriff to employ workmen to repair the old prison house, also to repair the underpinning in the Court House and windows, so that business may be done therein; also to rent out the old Court House in which Thomas Rhoades now lives to the highest bidder for one year.

(66) Thomas Rennix's death abates suit.

(66) William Fleming's death abates suit.

August 20, 1779.

(93) Thomas Bradshaw's death abates suit.

(124) Elizabeth Miller, wife of Daniel Miller, relinquished dower in lot in Staunton and woodland lot. Sold to George Spotts.

August 21, 1779.

(125) Deputy Attorney to prosecute the several assessors appointed by the Commissioners of Augusta County who refuse to serve.

(134) Joseph Bell and John McCreery appointed Coroners.

August 24, 1779.

(135) Called Court on Henry Lawrence—larceny.—Guilty and sent to Williamsburg. William Murray, of Amherst County, a witness.

September 21, 1779.

(136) Philip Phogle, orphan of Anthony Phogle, to be bound to Samuel Runkle.

(137) Admn. of estate of Catharine Friel granted to her son, Danl. Friel

(138) Wm. Gillespy, vice John Ramsey, Jr., appointed road overseer.

October 19, 1779.

(139) John Berry proved his services as a soldier in America in the war between Great Britain and France under Major General Jeffrey Amherst.— Granted certificate for 50 acres agreeable to the King's Proclamation, 1763. John Askins, in First Virginia Regiment, commanded by C. W. Byrd, same.

(139) William Bowyer and Joseph Bell appointed Tax Commissioners according to the Act passed May, 1779.

Page

(139) Called Court on Ann Corbett, charged with larceny from William Gilham—15 lashes.

NOVEMBER 16, 1779.

(143) Grand Jury presentments for retailing liquors without license, viz: Col. Sampson Mathews, Daniel Kidd, Wm. Thomas, David Griner, Patrick McDavid, George Smith, Valentine Cloninger, Thomas Colony, Edward Brookbank, Thomas Price, John Alexander, John Anderson, John Blair, William Burk, John Burk, James Hill, Robert Reed, Alex. Kilpatrick, Euphemia Hughes, Anthony Mustae, Jacob Grass, Elizabeth Hartgrove, Arthur Conoly, William Blair, John Hind, William Kyle, Abel Griffith, Enos Jones, Valentine Shirley, Peter Caphart, Andrew Scott, James Langsby, Robert Gregg, Thomas Poage, Jane Wallis, John McClenachan, John Black, Mary Tees, Thomas Smith, David Bell, Henry Swink, John Ramsey and William Foster.

(144) James Bell, John Beard and Alexander Kirk made proof by Alexr. McClenachan of their services as soldiers in an Independent Corps on the expedition under Colonel Boquet in 1764.

(144) George Moffet qualified Sheriff.

(144) Mary, wife of Sampson Mathews, and Ann, wife of George Mathews, relinquished dower in land sold to James Hill.

NOVEMBER 17, 1779.

(146) John Elliot appointed road overseer from Buffalo Gap to the end of the Brown Hill next to his house.

(146) Mary Thompson, soldier's wife, with small children, allowed £30.

(147) Mary Waugh, same, £60. Mary Linden, same, £45.

(147) Joseph Ray proves that he entered into the Virginia Regiment as a Cadet, and as such marched up to Fort Ligonier, where he was appointed by General Stanwix as Superintendent of a Company of Artificers, received Captain's pay and rations, and continued in the same station during the campaign in the year 1759, until the army retired into winter quarters, and has never received any allowance of land for said service.

(147.) Walter Cunningham, who served as a Lieutenant in the First Virginia Regiment, commanded by Colonel Wm. Byrd, heretofore obtained a warrant for 2,000 acres, agreeable to Proclamation of 1763, now makes further proof of having served as a Captain of Independents in the expedition commanded by Colonel Boquet against the Indians in 1764, and is now allowed 1,000 acres additional.

(148) John Moffet qualifies executor of Rebecca Carruthers.

(148) Robert Fearis proves service in a ranging company under command of Capt. Peter Hog; that he was enlisted in the company on their march to Bedford County, and continued therein until it was discharged, which was within three months of the time of his enlistment.

(149) On motion of Richard Madison, Clerk of the Court, four large books ordered for the use of the County.

(149) It appearing that Thomas Taylor cannot bring up in a Christian-like manner his child, John Taylor, John is to be bound to Joseph Blair.

(149) Thomas Scott proves his service in a ranging company commanded by Capt. Lewis—allowed 50 acres.

(149) James Sawyers and John Clark, Sergeants, proved their services in a ranging company under Colonel Boquet and allowed land.

(149) Charles Lewis, deceased, having served as a Lieutenant in Capt. William Preston's Company of Rangers, and obtained a warrant for 2,000 acres under the Proclamation of 1763, it is now proved that he served as Captain of a Company of Independents in the Expedition commanded by Colonel Boquet in 1764.—Certificate for 1,000 acres additional granted.

(150) Sheriff ordered to take possession of the old Court until the jail house is properly prepared.

NOVEMBER 18, 1779.

(150) Proof is made that John Smith, deceased, who served as a Sergeant in Capt. Wm. Preston's Company of Rangers, never received any land therefor. Certificate is granted to Thomas Smith, the heir-at-law, for 200 acres.

(150) Certificate for 2,000 acres granted to Alexr. St. Clair and Alexr. McClenachan, guardians of John McClenachan, orphan and heir-at-law of John McClenachan, deceased, who served as Lieutenant in Capt. Charles Lewis's Company of Independents on the expedition commanded by Colonel Boquet, 1764.

(151) Certificate for 50 acres granted to Thomas McGregor for services as a soldier in Capt. Preston's Company of Rangers. Certificate of 50 acres each granted to John McMahon and Thomas Kibbeath.

(151) Thomas Rhoades, being summoned to show cause why he would not deliver possession of the old Court House to the present Sheriff, was desired to deliver up the same immediately.

(152) Admn. of estate of George Weldon granted John Sawyers.

NOVEMBER 19, 1779.

(164) Thomas Ralph, an enlisted soldier, given 15 lashes for using James Thomas's horse illegally.

(165) John Poage qualified Justice.

(171) Elizabeth Hill, widow of James Hill, relinquished dower in deed to Wm. Fleming.

(173) Certificate for 50 acres granted to William Henderson, a soldier in Capt. McClenachan's Company of Independents under Colonel Boquet.

(173) Guardians of John and Robert McClenachan, sons and heirs of Robert McClenachan, prove that deceased served as a soldier in Capt. Alexr. McClenachan's Company in the expedition under Colonel Boquet.

(174) Thomas Adams, John Dickinson, Michael Bowyer, William Mc-Pheeters and Peter Hanger to be summoned to the next March Court to show cause why they will not swear into the Commission of the Peace.

(174) John Lewis, John Kinkead, James Steel, John Wilson, David Henderson, James Trimble, to be summoned to the next March Court to show cause why they will not attend the Court to do business.

(174) John Christian being dead; Jonas Friend, as being incapable of his duty and not attending, and John Davidson, Smith Tandy, Wm. Lowther and Andrew Davidson, because of non-residence in the County, recommended to be left out of Commission.

DECEMBER 20, 1779.

(175) Called Court on Chrismass McKings, alias Samuel Allen, alias William Jones, alias Samuel Thomas, for stealing the horse of Colonel Minger of the Convention Troops. Guilty and sent to Richmond for trial. Witnesses—James Bell of Amherst and Colonel Minger of the Convention Troops—James McGraw of Halifax.

DECEMBER 21, 1779.

(176-177) John McLain appointed Commissioner in Tyger's Valley.

(177) Mrs. Elizabeth Murray, widow and heir of John Murray, deceased, proved service of her husband as Ensign in Capt. McClenachan's Company in Boquet's expedition, 1764.—Certificate for 2,000 acres.

(178) James Brown and Adam Guthery granted certificates as nephews and heirs at-law of James Dunlap, deceased, who served as Lieutenant in Capt. Hog's Company of Rangers and was destroyed by the enemy at the fort in the upper tract on the South Branch of Potomac in 1758, and James and Adam are the only legal heirs now in this State.

(178) Proved that Joseph Hawkins served as a soldier in Capt. McNeel's Company in 1st Virginia Regiment until he was duly discharged by Colonel Adams Stevens in 1762.—His certificate was assigned by Joseph before a justice in Culpeper County to Thomas Stuart.

(179) Proved—Nicholas Sallis served as a soldier in the 1st Virginia Regiment, and has received a certificate which was assigned to Sampson Mathews.

(179) David Hogshead, son to James, is appointed Constable in Capt. Trimble's Company.

JANUARY 18, 1780.

(180) William Kinkead allowed certificate for 50 acres for services in Capt. Charles Lewis's Company in Boquet's expedition. John Carlile allowed certificate for 50 acres for services in Capt. Preston's Company in 1758.

(180) Colonel Wm. Bowyer appointed Commissioner of Tax, vice Colonel George Moffett, now Sheriff.

(181) John Dickey recommended Captain, vice William Henderson, who has removed to Kentucky; Joseph Waddle as Lieutenant, and John Bell as Ensign in said Company.

(181) Alexr. Kilpatrick qualified Deputy Sheriff.

FEBRUARY 15, 1780.

(182) David Hogshead qualified Constable.

(182) Sarah Windon, soldier's wife with small children, allowed £50.

(183) John Kinkead allowed certificate for 50 acres for services as a soldier in Capt. Wm. Preston's Company of Rangers. Major Andrew Lockridge, guardian of orphan of Robert Graham, deceased, is allowed certificate for land for Graham's services as a soldier in Capt. Preston's Company, 1758.

(183) Following allowed certificates for land for military services: John Kinkead, Thomas Hicklin, Robert Gwin, Lofftus Pullin, William Black, Patrick Miller, William Jackson, in Capt. Wm. Preston's Company of Rangers, 1758. Wm. Kinkead, Thomas Kinkead, John Montgomery, of Capt. Lewis's Company, Boquet's Expedition, 1764.

(183) Thomas Smith, eldest son and heir-at-law of Thos. Smith, who served as a soldier in Capt. Dunlop's Company of Rangers, 1758, and also as proper heir-at-law of Wm. Elliot, who served also, granted certificates for land.

(184) William McPheeters qualified Justice.

(184) Thomas Jones, runaway servant of Moses Hays.

(184) Margaret Erwin, late Margaret Lewell, one of the executors of Andrew Lewell, deceased, summoned to give counter security.

(184) Andrew McCaslin, James Gay, Anthony Johnston, appointed Constables.

(184) ———— Gay to be summoned to show cause why he doth not use his apprentice, John Harris, according to law.

(185) Catherine Fogle, not being able to bring up in a Christianlike manner her son, John Fogle, ordered that John be bound out.

FEBRUARY 18, 1780.

(185) Called Court on Francis Hughes, for larceny.—Sent to Richmond for trial. Witnesses: Hugh Brown, and Rebecca, his wife.

(186) Called Court on Violet, a negro slave of Sampson Sawyers, for feloniously burning her master's dwelling house on the night of the 4th inst. Guilty—to be hanged by the neck, &c., on 4th of March next at or near town of Staunton at 12 o'clock at noon, and after she is cut down, that her head be severed from her body by the neck and stuck upon a pole in the public place near Staunton. Adjudged value, £1,800.

MARCH 21, 1780.

(187) Andrew McCaslin qualified Constable. Thomas Adams qualified Justice.

(187) Charles Smith allowed 200 acres for services as Sergeant in Capt. Wm. Preston's Company of Rangers in the late war between Great Britain and France.

(188) Joseph Bell, Alexr. Robertson and John Moffet are appointed Commissioners of Tax.

(188) Thomas Davis allowed land for services as Sergeant in First Virginia Regiment in 1756.

(188) Admn. of estate of Joseph Gamble granted his widow, Isabella, and William Patton.

(188) On motion of Ann Pebbles, late Ann Hinds, widow and executrix of Edward Hinds, deceased, who served as a Corporal in Capt. Preston's Company of Rangers, in 1758, certificate for land granted to Edward Hinds, orphan of said Edward, deceased.

(190) David Greiner allowed 50 acres for services as a soldier in late war between Great Britain and France. Robert Ross, of same Regiment, allowed 50 acres for services.

(190) Following allowed for military services: Robert Hall, in Capt. Preston's Company of Rangers in 1758; also John Vahab, Wm. Stuart, John Bodkin and Hugh Bodkin; John Graham, grandson of John Graham, who served in Capt. Preston's Company of Rangers, 1758; James Bodkin, in Capt. Preston's Company of Rangers, 1758—50 acres each.

(190) Elizabeth Wilson, Ann Miles and Mary Johnston, soldiers' wives, allowed three bushels of grain each, valued at £45.

(190) Alexander Gillespy allowed land for services as armourer and blacksmith in First Virginia Regiment, commanded by Colonel Byrd.

(191) Jeremiah Edwards, John Buster, James Bridgells, John Welsh, John Fulton (of Capt. Dickenson's Company of Rangers in 1759), John Shields and William Shields—50 acres.

(190) John Plunkett allowed 50 acres for services in Capt. John Dickenson's Company of Rangers, 1759.

(191) John Nanby, orphan of John Nanby, to be bound out.

(191) George Anderson recommended Ensign in Capt. Thomas Rankin's Company, and William Finley as Captain, vice Robert Thompson, resigned.

(191) Mary Night, soldier's wife, allowed £30.

(193) Samuel McCutcheon allowed 50 acres for services as soldier in Capt. Lewis's Company of Rangers in 1758. Alexr. Gallispy, allowed 50 acres. Andrew Fowler exempted from poll tax.

MARCH 22, 1780.

(193) John Frogg proves that in 1755 he went out on the frontiers of this State with a body of men under his command as a Colonel or Major and served on the frontiers for some considerable time, but whether as a ranging battalion or volunteers, or what other capacity, does not appear.

(195) Jacob Doran, executor and only heir-at-law of Ludwick Shadow, deceased, produced a certificate under the hand and seal of Col. Henry Boquet's, dated 15 November, 1762, of said Shaw's service as a Sergeant on Boquet's expedition.—Allowed a certificate.

(195) Ordinary rates.

(196) Joseph Bell qualified Coroner.

(196) John McMahon, Sr., granted license to keep an ordinary—on motion of John McMahon, Jr., his son.

(198) Ellis Wright qualified Deputy Surveyor.

(199) Commissioners reported following persons as refusing to swear to their taxable property: George Nicholas, John Flesher, Wolrick Conrad, Jr., John Snider, Nicholas Simmon, Peter Smith, Barten Smith, Jonathan Buffington, Benj. Abett, Charles Fomelson, Wm. Hamilton, James Lackey, Joseph Fonelson and John Lacky—all to be prosecuted.

Page

(201) Francis Stewart—witness from Rockingham. Agnes Rodgers—witness from Washington—230 miles and 3 ferriages.

MARCH 24, 1780.

(206) David Bell ads. Commonwealth.—Abates by death of David.

(212) James Beard, returned no inhabitant.

(216) James Cumptain's death abates suit.

(217) Thomas Smith qualified Vestryman.

(217) Thomas Bowyer proves that in 1760 he was appointed Lieutenant of a Company of Regulars raised in the Virginia Regiment, at that time commanded by Colonel Byrd, since deceased; that he served in said office until said regiment was disbanded, and that on the said regiment's being disbanded he entered into the Virginia Regiment then raised, commanded by Colonel Hopkins, in 1762, as a subaltern in said regiment.

MARCH 25, 1780.

(221) Account of Thomas Rhoades, late jailor, allowed. Account of Alexr. Kilpatrick, present jailor, allowed.

(222) County levy—13/.

MARCH 29, 1780.

(223) Called Court on Sarah Constable for larceny—39 lashes.

(223) Called Court on Mary and Elizabeth Woods, receiving stolen goods—discharged.

(223) Called Court on John and William Woods for breaking John Beard's mill and stealing grain—discharged.

APRIL 18, 1780.

(225) Andrew Ramsey appointed Constable—225 qualified.

(225) Elizabeth, wife of Anthony Gholston, relinquished dower in deed to Stephen Beck.

(225) Admn. of estate of Jane Elliott granted to James Elliott.

(225) Samuel McCune, Sr., appointed road surveyor. Gabriel Alexander appointed Constable.

(226) William Jordan, Thomas Gifford and Charles Floyd exempted from levy.

MAY 18, 1780.

(226) Wm. Fleming, vice David Greever, appointed Constable.

(227) Thomas Frazier, orphan of John Frazier, to be bound to John Hunter.

(227) Admn. of estate of James Ralston granted to widow Jane.

(228) Elizabeth Sun, soldier's wife, allowed six bushels of corn, valued at £60.

(229) Frances Dunbarr, soldier's wife, allowed ten bushels of corn, valued at £100.

(229) John Warwick allowed 50 acres for services as soldier in Boquet's expedition in 1764. Samuel Erwin, of Capt. Hog's Company, 1757, allowed 50 acres. Robert Stuart, of Capt. Dickenson's Company, 1758, allowed 50 acres. John Blair, of Capt. Hog's Company, 1758, allowed 50 acres.

(230) Road ordered (bridle way) from James Bratton's to Little River Meeting House, over the Calf Pasture Mountain, to be worked by tithables from Widow Grimes, living on Big River of Calf Pasture, to John Wilson's; then from John Meeks's, on the Little River, to Jones Henderson's; thence to the Rockbridge Line.

(230) John Wilson qualified deputy surveyor.

(230) George Bratton appointed road surveyor from Robert Wiley's to Jonathan Humphrey's, with tithables from James Kilpatrick's to John Alfall's. Wm. Anderson, vice John Findley, appointed road surveyor.

(231) John Kinkead appointed road surveyor from Wm. Black's to Joseph Givin's.

(231) Thomas Hughart appointed Colonel of Second Battalion, and John McCleery, Lieutenant Colonel.

(232) George Jameson appointed road surveyor from County Line to William Murphy's plantation, and Thomas Nelson from William Murphy's to James Mitchell's.

(234) Moore Fauntleroy, vice James Gay, appointed road surveyor— tithables from Tully Davit's to William Wateers.

(235) Robert Christian recommended Second Lieutenant in Capt. Francis Long's Company, and Joseph Bell as Ensign in the same Company.

(235) William Fleming qualified Constable.

(236) Henry and Andrew Honeyman—witnesses.

MAY 19, 1780.

(241) Margaret Blair, wife of James Blair, relinquished dower in 330 acres sold to Mathias Link.

(141) Joseph Bell recommended Captain, vice Capt. David Bell, decd.; Andrew Anderson as Lieutenant; James Poage as Ensign.

MAY 20, 1780.

(242) Thomas Dryden's death abates suit.

(244) Jennet Duncan vs. John Wilson.—Abates by plaintiff's marriage.

(244) William Kyle's death abates suit. William Coil's death abates suit.

(259) John Flesher's death abates suit.

JUNE 8, 1780.

(263) Called Court on James Denniston for stealing from Charles Hunt $400 Continental Currency—39 lashes.

JUNE 20, 1780.

(264) Peter Wilson (lately discharged from the Continental Army) allowed 50 acres for services as soldier in Capt. Stephen's Company, 1761.

(264) Ann Ord, soldier's wife, allowed 5 bushels of corn, valued at £75.

(264) Tithables to be taken in Companies, as follows: David Henderson, n Tate's, Long's and Thompson's; Alexr. St. Clair, in Buchanan's, Smith's ind Johnston's; James Trotter, in McCutchon's, Cunningham's and James Bell's; James Trimble, in Patterson's, Dickey's and Trimble's; Joseph Bell, in his own, Rankin's and Givens's; Benj. Wilson, in Tyger's Valley; Thos. Hughart, in Kinkead's; John McCreery, in McKay's, Hicklin's and Mc-Creery's; Samuel Vance, in his own.

AUGUST 15, 1780.

(265a) John McCoy, James Woods, George Puffenberry—to view road from Capt. McCoy's, in Bull Pasture, to Michael Wilfong's, thence over the mountain to the Gap of the North River.

(265a) James and Joseph Bell qualified Captains. John McCreery qualified Lieutenant Colonel of Militia.

(265a) Commission for priv. examination of Elizabeth, wife of Joseph Nickle, of Greenbrier County. Deed, Nickle to Andrew Nickle.

(265b) Robert Givin to be summoned to show cause why he detains James O'Neal, orphan of James O'Neal, contrary to law.

(265b) Andrew Anderson qualified Lieutenant. James Poage qualified Ensign. John Dickey qualified Captain; Joseph Waddle, Lieutenant, and Joseph Bell, Ensign.

(266) Herman Lovingood, vice Peter Angleman, appointed road surveyor.

(266) David Wilson qualified Ensign.

(266) Alexander Maxwell qualified Deputy Sheriff.

(266) Mary Ann Wright, orphan of John Wright, to be bound.

(266) William Findley qualified Captain.

(266) Hugh Nelson bound to peace on complaint of Henry Peachman.

(267) Robert Christian qualified Lieutenant.

(267) Henry Miller is incapable of bringing up his children in a Christianlike manner—son, Peter Miller, to be bound.

(267) Ordinary rates.

AUGUST 16, 1780.

(268) Called Court on Mary Woods for being concerned in stealing scythes from Jacob Neighdebour—acquitted.

(268) George Bratton appointed Constable.

(269) John Elliot appointed guardian of Margaret and Sarah Elliot, orphans of William Elliot.

(272) John Gullet—witness from Greenbrier.

(272) William Gullet—witness from Greenbrier.

AUGUST 17, 1780.

(273) Admn. of estate of Susannah Jenkins granted Rebecca and Elizabeth Bouch.

AUGUST 18, 1780.

(280) Joseph Blair appointed road surveyor from James Campbell's field to James Trotter's. John Campbell, vice John Bigham, appointed road surveyor.

August 19, 1780.

Page

(281) Thomas Reeves, returned no inhabitant.

(281) Robert Kirpatrick, returned no inhabitant.

(297) Mary Woods to be summoned to show cause why her children should not be bound out.

(297) James Lessley's will proved by witnesses to handwriting and comparison of papers by the Court, the witnesses John and William Stuart being dead. Sarah, the widow, qualified executrix.

(299) Thomas Hughes appointed Surveyor of Streets of Staunton.

(299) John Price, to whom William Hunter, orphan boy, was bound, petitions that he is about to move out of this State, and that William be bound to Francis Moore, to be taught leather breeches making, which is ordered.

(300) Called Court for examination of John Woods, charged with stealing two scythes from Jacob Neighdebour.—Guilty—sent to Richmond.

September 9, 1780.

(300) Called Court for examination of Samuel Thomas, alias Chrisman McCann, for burglary.—Guilty and sent to Richmond.

September 19, 1780.

(301) John Waughub qualified Second Lieutenant.

(301) James Lackey, Jr., and Christopher Troby appointed Constables.

(301) Thomas Huggart qualified Colonel; Jacob Westfall, Jr., as First Lieutenant, and Conrad Bogert as Ensign, in Capt. Wilson's Company—recommended.

(302) John Graham appointed guardian of Rebecca Graham, daughter of Lanty Graham.

(302) At request of Col. Sampson Mathews, to disqualify him from serving as Senator at the end of the next session of Assembly, recommended Coroner.

(302) Admn. of estate of Jacob Sigerfoos granted to Wm. Rusk—Christiana, the widow, having refused to administer.

October 17, 1780.

(303) Sampson Mathews recommended Coroner.

(303) Elijah McClenachan and James Trotter, Jr., appointed Commissioners of Specific Tax.

(303) Hugh Hicklin appointed road surveyor from the County Line to the School House in the Indian Draft; Charles Donnerly, thence to Leonard Bell's. James McChesney appointed road surveyor from where Thomas Mines now lives. Samuel McCutchon appointed road surveyor from Mines's to Rusk's Mill.

October 18, 1780.

(304) Contract to fill up the gully in the courtyard to be let to the highest bidder.

Page

(304) John Cartmill, as Captain, and Robert Thompson, as Lieutenant, in the Company formerly commanded by Robert McCreery—recommended.

(304) John Oliver recommended Captain, vice Samuel Vance, who has resigned.

(304) John Poage, Robert Kenny, John Christian, Sr., William Mc-Pheeters and James Trimble are appointed overseers of the poor.

(305) John Cartmill, as Captain; Robert Thompson, as Lieutenant, and Jonathan Humphreys, as Lieutenant—qualified.

(305) Commission for priv. examination of Elizabeth, wife of John Gillespy. Deed to Christopher Graham.

(306) Mary Price, wife of John Price, a soldier in Continental Service, is allowed subsistence for herself.

(307) James O'Neal, orphan of James O'Neal, to be bound to Robert Givin.

(307) Jacob Cole appointed Constable in Capt. Cunningham's Company.

NOVEMBER 22, 1780.

(308) Alexr. Crawford recommended and qualified Ensign in Capt. Cartmill's Company.

(308) George Moffet qualified Sheriff.

(308) County levy.

(308) Joseph Long qualified Lieutenant.

(308) Joseph Mathews qualified Deputy Sheriff.

NOVEMBER 23, 1780.

(310) County levy.

NOVEMBER 24, 1780.

(318) James Langsby, returned no inhabitant.

(320) Alexr. Kilpatrick, jailor, allowed account for keeping Tories and deserters.

DECEMBER 4, 1780.

(321) Called Court on John Wilfong for the murder of Sebastian Hover, Jr., who was killed 27 April last.—Guilty and sent to Richmond for trial.

DECEMBER 19, 1780.

(322) County levy: To William Gillespy, for his wagon and team, one day, working on the public road.

(322) These to work on the road from Staunton to Christian's Creek, with their tithables, viz: William Lewis, Henry Moura, John Brooks, Peter Moura John Bird, James Graham, Nicholas Sprigg, Robert Russell, Mr. Hunt, Andrew Scott, Jacob Sciler, Peter Grass, John Graham, Christopher Graham, Joshua Russell, James Coursey, Thomas Scott, Wm. Burk, Robert McClenachan, Samuel Fraizer and James Hill.

(323) Ann Harrington, wife of Charles Harrington, a soldier now in the Continental Army, allowed two barrels of corn, valued at £70; 100 lbs. pork, valued at £120—for herself and child.

Page

(323) Amos Butt, Thomas Staunton and William Ross exempted from payment of levies.

(323) County levy, 60/.

(324) William Buchanan qualified Ensign.

FEBRUARY 20, 1781.

(324) Richard Madison, Clerk, being absent on public service, Thomas Hughes to act as Clerk *pro tem.*

(324) John Oliver qualified Captain.

(324) Admn. of estate of Thomas Nelson granted to Elizabeth and Thomas Nelson.

(325) Michael Coulter qualified Lieutenant. George Anderson qualified Ensign. George Barry, William McPheeters and John Campbell qualified overseers of the poor.

MARCH 20, 1781.

(325) Admn. of estate of Hugh McEvoy, a soldier killed in the service, granted Thomas Beard.

(325) John Wilson recommended Major of Second Battalion.

(325) Dedimus to take deposition of William Longsdale, who is about to remove to Pennsylvania.

(326) Robert Baggs produced a certificate signed by the Clerk, and Wm. Fleming, Esq., Commissioner of Kentucky, of having a primitive right, which, he swears, he delivered to Col. Daniel Boon, of which he understands he was robbed.

(327) A motion continued because of absence of witness, Sampson Mathews, who is in the service of his country.

(327) Sheriff ordered to collect 12 per cent on all property in this County and pay to Samuel Hunter, who is appointed to purchase a wagon and team, &c., for public service, agreeable to Act of Assembly.

(327) Mary Price, soldier's wife, and child, to receive £300 in lieu of two barrels corn and 100 lbs. pork.

(327) John Wilson qualified Major.

(327) Elijah McClenachan, Thomas Hughart and James Trotter, returned duly elected Commissioners of the Tax. Thomas and James qualify; Elijah urged his infirmities, and is excused, and Joseph Bell is appointed in his room—and qualified.

MAY 15, 1781.

(328) Ordered that Daniel Gillespy be prosecuted for speaking disaffected words towards the State.

(328) Admn. of estate of Archd. Loughlin, decd., granted to Dr. John Jackson.

(328) John Archer's will proved—widow Rebecca renounces its provisions and claims dower.

(329) Elizabeth Son, wife of Michael Son, a soldier in the Continental Army, to be allowed £600 for her and her children.

Page

(329) John Black allowed an account £1,883, 8/, for expense in boarding a wounded soldier.

(330) Mary Porter, wife of William Porter, a soldier in the Continental Army, allowed £360 for her and her children.

(330) Charles Cameron, as Captain; William McCreery, as Lieutenant, and Patrick Young, as Ensign—recommended for appointment in Second Battalion. Cameron and Young qualified.

(330) John Brown is recommended and qualifies in room of Capt. Cartmill.

(330) Henry Miller, aged 18 months, to be bound out.

(330) Sarah Wiger, wife of David Wiger, soldier in Continental Army, allowed £360 for herself and child.

(330) Alexander Robertson allowed account of £1,634 for his service as a Commissioner of the provision law.

(330) Samuel Rucker recommended and qualifies as Lieutenant in Capt. Oliver's Company.

MAY 16, 1781.

(330) George Roots qualified Attorney.

(332) John Moffet allowed an account of £1,485 for services as a Commissioner of the provision law.

(334) John McKinney qualified Deputy Sheriff.

MAY 17, 1781.

(340) William Scott's death abates suit.

(346) Tithables to be taken in Companies, as follows, viz: Daniel Henderson, in Tate's, Long's and Finley's; Alexander St. Clair, in Buchanan's, Smith's and Johnston's; Wm. McPheeters, in McCutchon's, Cunningham's and Bell's; Alexander Robertson, in Rankin's, Bell's and Givens's; James Trimble, in Patterson's, Dickey's and Trimble's; Thomas Hughart, in Kinkead's; John McCreery, in McCoy's, Hicklin's and McCreery's; Samuel Vance, in Oliver's.

(346) The Sheriff to rent out the old Court House for one year to the highest bidder in hard money, or the value thereof in paper money, when it comes due.

(346) John Young appointed road overseer, vice James Allen, Jr.

JUNE 19, 1781.

(346) Richard Madison, Clerk, being absent on militia duty, the Court appoints John McComney *pro tem.* Henry King, vice Samuel Hunter, is appointed to purchase the wagon and team heretofore ordered.

JUNE 20, 1781.

(347) George Poage, David Givin and Peter Hole recommended to the Governor to be appointed Captains for the 2d Battalion; George Poage for part of the Company formerly commanded by Capt. Oliver; David Givin for the other part of the said Company; Peter Hole for the Company formerly under Capt. McCoy.

(347) Charles Hamilton is appointed Lieutenant under Capt. Givin, and Wm. McCreary, Lieutenant under Capt. Cameron—appointed.

(347) David Givin, Peter Hole and George Poage qualified Captains.

(347) Charles Hamilton and Wm. McCreery qualified Lieutenants.

(347) Henry Fleisher qualified Ensign.

(347) Andrew Foster allowed account for services in receiving 320 lbs. public hemp.

June 14, 1781.

(347) Called Court on James Hays for biting Capt. Thomas Marlin's (Martin?) thumb, by reason of which it is likely the said Marlin will lose his thumb at least, or perhaps his arm or life.—Guilty and recognized to appear at General Court.

(348) Called Court on William Ward and Lewis Baker on suspicion of treason against the Commonwealth. Guilty of levying war against the Commonwealth, and held for further trial. Henry Swadley, John Snyder, Christian Stone and Capt. Robert Davis bound as witnesses for Commonwealth, to appear at such time and place as the Governor shall direct by proclamation for the trial.

August 21, 1781.

(348) Barnette Lance appointed road surveyor, vice John Gum.

(348) John Hogshead appointed road surveyor, vice John Kirk.

(349) Admn. of estate of James Wallace granted Jane Wallace.

(349) Admn. of estate of John Hogshead granted to Ann Hogshead.

(349) William Tate qualified Captain.

(349) Charles Cameron recommended Colonel of 2d Battalion, vice Colonel Hughart, resigned.

(349) Samuel Vance recommended Colonel, vice John McCreery, who has resigned.

(349) William Jordain exempted from levies.

(350) Thomas Hicklin recommended Captain of the Company he formerly commanded; James Bratton in room of Capt. Kinkead, resigned; Joseph Gwin as First Lieutenant in Capt. Hicklin's Company; Joseph Day as Ensign in Capt. Poage's Company.

(350) John McKittrick is appointed Ensign in the room of Ensign Gardner of Capt. Trimble's Company—resigned.

(350) Thomas Bratton and James Hicklin qualified Captains.

August 22, 1781.

(350) On account of several escapes from jail, through negligence of Alexr. Kilpatrick, jailor, it is recommended to Sheriff, George Moffett, to dismiss Alexr.

(350) Wm. Carrol, aged 14 years, to be bound to John Paris.

(350) Wm. Bell is appointed to buy one wagon and team in the place of Samuel Hunter.

Page
(351) Called Court on William Ashley for larceny from John Griffin.—Guilty and bound over to the Grand Jury.

SEPTEMBER 18, 1781.

(352) Hugh Jinkins having rendered himself incapable of taking care of Ann Jinkins, an orphan child, ordered that said *Johnston* be summoned.

(352) David Buchanan recommended Lieutenant in P. Buchanan's Company, vice Alexr. Scott, resigned. Andrew Anderson recommended Captain, vice Joseph Bell, who has resigned. James Poage recommended Lieutenant, and John Poage, Jr., recommended as Ensign in Capt. Anderson's Company.

OCTOBER 8, 1781.

(352) Called Court on John Richey, Jr., and George Savage for passing counterfeit hard dollars.—George, 39 lashes.—John, bound to Grand Jury.

OCTOBER 16, 1781.

(353) Thomas Hughart allowed an account for services in receiving and storing the specific tax.

(353) Called Court on Edmund White for larceny.—Guilty and bound to Grand Jury.

OCTOBER 23, 1781.

(354) Called Court on James Richardson for passing counterfeit money and having large quantity in his possession. Guilty and sent to Genl. Court.

NOVEMBER 20, 1781.

(355) Admn. of estate of Henry Brandes granted to Andrew Sumesalt.

(355) Admn. of estate of Thos. Shields granted to Margaret, his widow.

(356) Thomas Cartmill recommended and qualified Ensign in Capt. Poage's Company.

(356) Admn. of estate of Robt. Brawford granted to Rebecca, his widow.

(356) John and William Jordane exempted from levies.

(356) Thomas Hughes qualified Justice.

(357) William Blair, vice Wm. Fleming appointed Constable.

(358) George Moffett, Sheriff, allowed the use of the old Court House free of rent, as the old jailor's house is not tenantable.

(358) John Reglar, aged 7, formerly bound by his mother to Samuel Burnsides, deceased, to be bound to Francis Moore until 21.—To be taught trade of a breeches maker.

(358) Robert Clark, vice James McCleery appointed road surveyor.

DECEMBER 19, 1781.

(358) Admn. of estate of James Fulton granted Mary Fulton and John Ward.

Page

(358) William Blair qualified Constable.

(359) Sarah Wiger, wife of David Wiger, soldier in the service of the Commonwealth, and child, allowed, in addition to former allowance of £350, 1 bbl. of corn, 100 lbs. pork, 124 lbs. beef. Mary Porter, wife of Daniel Porter, and 2 children, the same. Patsy Cole, wife of Richd. Cole, the same.

(359) Alexr. McClenachan qualified Sheriff.

(359) James Davis qualified Deputy Sheriff.

(359) Wm. McPheeters and Mathew Kenny are appointed Commissioners of the specific tax.

(359) John Dickinson, who refuses to act; John Christian, deceased; Michael Bowyer, Attorney at Law; James Tate, deceased; Joshua Humphreys, removed out of the County; Peter Hanger, who refuses to act; Benj. Wilson, Jonas Friend, Wm. Lowther, John Davidson and Andrew Davidson, out of the County—recommended to be left out of the Commission of the peace.

(360) James Miller to be summoned to show cause why he doth not take proper care of his children.—Overseers of poor to inspect his family, and if they find them suffering, are to take them in charge until next Court.

(360) Old Court House continued to new Sheriff until the jailor's house can be repaired.

JANUARY 15, 1782.

(360) Admn. of estate of Jacob Fulwider granted to Mary, his widow.

(360) Zachary Johnston refused to qualify Justice on the ground that he ought to study the law one year or two first.

(362) Ordinary rates fixed.

FEBRUARY 13, 1782.

(363) Alexr. St. Clair and Thos. Hughes appointed to purchase and equip one wagon and team according to Act for Supplying the Army, and produce same at next Court.

FEBRUARY 19, 1782.

(364) Charles Cameron qualified Colonel.

(364) Joseph Bell, Elijah McClenachan and John Poage appointed to assess land in First Battalion. Thomas Hughart, James Kinkead and James Bratton in the Second Battalion.

(364) Charles Baskins recommended Captain, vice Capt. Zachary Johnson, resigned; James Johnson, as Lieutenant, and Wm. Calbraith, Ensign.

(364) Admn. of estate of James Richey granted Wm. Wilson.

(364) Commissioners to lay of the thirds of the lands whereof Robert Cochran is possessed, as heirs-at-law of John Cochran, deceased.

(364) Margaret Edmonds, orphan of George Edmonds, to be bound to John Dalhouse.

(364) Rebecca Estill is appointed guardian of Priscilla Estill.

(365) The Clerk appointed to draw the lists of the different districts for supplying clothing, &c., to the Army, required to furnish the different districts with a copy of the late proceedings.

Page

(366) Admn. of estate of Alexr. Cunningham granted John Cunningham.

(366) John Brown and Archibald Stuart produced licenses and took oath of attorney.

(366) Pat. Bohannon qualified deputy surveyor.

(366) George Poage qualified Justice.

(366) Martin Whitsell exempted from levy.

(366) Tithables to be taken as follows, in Companies: By James Trimble, in Patterson's and Dickey's, vice John Poage; Capt. John Lewis, in Hicklin's and Hole's, vice John Wilson; George Poage, in his own and Givens's Company, vice Samuel Vance.

(367) Mary Price, wife of John Price, soldier, is allowed 3 bbls. corn and 100 lbs. pork.

(367) Wm. Logan appointed Ensign in Capt. Samuel McCutchon's Company.

(367) Admn. of estate of John Hinds granted to Wm. Hinds.

MARCH 20, 1782.

(369) Agnes Jenkins to be bound.

(369) Admn. c. t. a. of estate of John Estill granted Rebecca Estill, Wm. Hutchison having refused, and the other executor, Benj. Estill, having for some time past been of insane mind.

(369) James Poage as Lieutenant and John Poage and Wm. Logan as Ensigns—qualified.

(370) Rev. James Waddle's negro wenches, Isabella and Maud, exempted from levy.

(370) Ann Burk, widow of William Burk, deceased, intestate, certifies she will not administer—granted to William Burk.

(370) Court allowed public claims which are recorded in the Claim Book.

MARCH 22, 1782.

(371) Assignment of dower by Catherine Carpenter, relict of Nicholas Carpenter, to Michael Bowyer—ordered recorded.

(371) James Johnson as Lieutenant and William Calbraith as Ensign—qualified.

(371) See Claim Book for proceedings of any Court not here inserted.

MARCH 25, 1782.

(372) Sheriff ordered to proclaim that the Court of Claims will be held on third Tuesday in April next.

APRIL 16, 1782.

(372) George Muler presented license and took oath of attorney.

Page

(372) John McKittrick recommended Captain, vice James Trimble, resigned; John qualified, and William Anderson as Lieutenant and Robert Anderson as Ensign; Robert qualified; John Campbell qualified Captain, vice Joseph Patterson, and William Allen qualified as Lieutenant and Arthur Connerley as Ensign.

(373) James Hamilton exempted from levy.

(373) On petition of the Company formerly commanded by Francis Long, he is recommended to be reinstated.

(373) Jane, relict of Isaac White, refused to administer.

APRIL 19, 1782.

(373) Wm. Steel qualified Deputy Clerk.

APRIL 22, 1782.

(374) George Moffet qualified Justice.

APRIL 26, 1782.

(375) County levy—2,000 tithables at 5/4.

(375) Thomas Tate and Andrew Anderson are appointed Commissioners of the Specific Tax—1st Battalion. John McCreery, same, in 2d Battalion.

(375) Admn. of estate of Wm. Fleming granted widow, Margaret.

(376) Called Court on William Furr for stealing a fur hat.—Guilty.

MAY 21, 1782.

(377) John Vance's will partly proved.

(378) John McCown exempted from levy.

(379) Admn. of estate of Joseph Wright granted widow, Elizabeth.

(379) Adam Stevenson appointed road overseer from Miller's Iron Works to Skidmore's Camps, thence to top of North Mountain.

(380) Road ordered from Bethel Meeting House to Peter Hanger's mill.

(380) William Wilson, Archibald Scott, Benj. Erwin and James Waddle, Presbyterian Ministers, are licensed to celebrate matrimony.

MAY 22, 1782.

(380) George Nicholas produced license and took oath of attorney.

(381) Edward Parks's death abates suit.

(382) Joshua Perry recommended and qualified Ensign in Capt. Francis Smith's Company.

(383) Robert Carlile's death abates suit.

(384) Thomas Lowrey, 8 years old, to be bound to James Fleming.

(385) George Bratton qualified Lieutenant.

(385) Thomas Hughart allowed £30 for services as land assessor, and John Kinkead £20 for same.

Page

(385) Levi Moore, George Hole and John Deniston to mark a road from Levi Moore's on Naps Creek to Back Creek, from William Green's to Crab Bottom on head of South Branch of Potomac.

(385) John Hind's and John Archer's deaths abate suits.

(390) William McPheeters appointed land assessor, vice John Poage.

MAY 24, 1782.

(390) Lazarus Inman's death abates suit.

(390) Peter Hog's death abates suit.

(391) William Burk's death abates suit.

(399) Deaths of James Wallace and Josiah Greenwood abate suits.

(410) Reuben McClenachan returned, no inhabitant.

(411) Ordinary rates.

(412) Claims allowed and recorded in the Book of Claims.

MAY 25, 1782.

(412) Ann Helena Attwaters relinquished dower in a lot and house in Staunton and lot of woodland in deed by her husband to Wm. Crawford, Moses Estey and John Beech.

MAY 27, 1782.

(412) William Tate qualified Justice.

JUNE 18, 1782.

(412) Joseph Long recommended and qualified Captain, vice Francis Long.

(412) Martha, widow of John Vance, qualifies admx. c. t. a.

(414) Charles Hamilton qualified Captain, vice David Green.

(414) Ulrick Fulwider is appointed guardian to Margaret Fulwider, orphan of Jacob Fulwider, deceased.

(414) Tithables to be taken as follows in Companies: William Tate, in Capt. Tate's Company; James Trotter, in Cunningham's and McCutcheon's; Wm. McPheeters, in Capt. Bell's; James Tremble, in McKittrick's and Dickey's; Alexr. Robertson, in Campbell's and Givens's; David Henderson, in Capt. Long's; Joseph Bell, in Capt. Anderson's; John Poage, in Capt. Rankin's; James Steel, in Baskin's and Finley's; Thomas Hughes, in Smith's; George Poage, in Poage's and Hamilton's; John Kinkead, in Hole's and Hicklin's; John McCreary, in Brown's and Bratton's; Elijah McClenachan, in Buchanan's.

(415) Richard Graves exempted from levy.

JULY 18, 1782.

(416) Elizabeth Gilham, wife of William Gilham, relinquished dower in a house and lot in Staunton purchased by Enos Atwater.

Page

(416) Isaac Campbell petitions that the County Court of Lincoln would not grant him lands in that County because he could not make proof that he was in public service of the country when the Commissioners sat for the District of Kentucky—in consequence of a certificate from the Court of said County of Lincoln, it is certified that proper proof was made that the said Campbell was in the aforesaid service when the said Commissioners sat for the said District.

AUGUST 20, 1782.

(419) Archibald Dixon is appointed guardian to Thomas Story, orphan of Thomas Story, deceased.

AUGUST 21, 1782.

(420) Deed from Robert Caldwell to Robert Black ordered recorded, and Elizabeth, widow of Samuel Caldwell, relinquished dower.

(421) Joseph Bell allowed £47 for services as land assessor.

AUGUST 22, 1782.

(422) Arthur Connerly bound to peace towards his wife.

AUGUST 23, 1782.

(425) Catharine Kelly, orphan, to be bound to Robert Burns, vice Dennis Callachan.

(425) Wm. McDowell vs. Alexr. St. Clair.—This ejectment involves Lot No. 3, in Staunton.

SEPTEMBER 17, 1782.

(430) Tully Davit appointed road surveyor, vice Moore Fauntleroy.

SEPTEMBER 18, 1782.

(431) Alexr. Kilpatrick, late jailor, allowed account for keeping Tories.

SEPTEMBER 26, 1782.

(431) Called Court on Benjamin Patterson, for stealing from William Howlam.—Sent to Richmond for trial.

OCTOBER 15, 1782.

(434) William Sloven appointed and qualified Ensign, vice Jonathan Humphreys.

(435) Hugh Oliver vs. James Link.—Dedimus to take deposition of Archibald Blackburn, who lives in Nolechukey.

(435) Mary Rock, wife of John Rock, a Continental soldier, allowed provision for herself and children.

NOVEMBER 19, 1782.

(435) County levy.

(435) William Blair, captain of patrollers, 4 nights (26 June to 29 July, 1782), 40 lbs. tobacco; Francis Mora, captain of patrollers, 4 nights, same; Anthony Mustoe, captain of patrollers, 4 nights, same; Dennis Callaghan, captain of patrollers, 3 nights, 30 lbs. tobacco; Valentine White, captain of patrollers, 3 nights, 30 lbs. tobacco; Wm. Blair, Francis Mora, Anthony Mustoe, captains of patrollers, 5 nights each, 50 lbs. tobacco; David Griener, captain of patrollers, 3 nights, 30 lbs. tobacco; Dennis Callaghen, captain of patrollers, 1 night, 10 lbs. tobacco; Dennis Callaghen, captain of patrollers (20 April to 24 May).

(437) John Gamble recommended in Capt. John Camble's Company.

(438) Samuel Vance qualified Lieutenant Colonel of Militia.

NOVEMBER 21, 1782.

(440) James Trotter recommended and qualified Captain, vice John Cunningham.

(441) Abraham Smith's death abates suit.

(441) Jane Seawright's marriage abates suit.

NOVEMBER 22, 1782.

(454) Thomas Hamilton's death abates suit.

(464) John Berry's death abates suit.

NOVEMBER 23, 1782.

(468) Ordinary rates.

NOVEMBER 25, 1782.

(469) County levy: 2,283 tithables at 1/.

(470) Thomas Rhoades, jailor, allowed account for keeping criminals and deserters.

DECEMBER 17, 1782.

(470) Isaac Price, orphan, to be bound.

(471) Mathew Smith recommended Captain, vice Charles Baskins, resigned.

AUGUSTA COUNTY COURT RECORDS.

ORDER BOOK No. XVIII.

JANUARY 21, 1783.

(1) Commission for priv. examination of Susanna, wife of Andrew Kinneer. Deed to John Brown.

(1) Inquisition on body of Garet Phelan recorded.

(2) Alexander Gibson, Jr., appointed guardian of Daniel Gibson, orphan of Daniel Gibson.

(2) Will of John Christian presented and ordered that witnesses be summoned to prove it.

(4) Andrew Foster allowed account for receiving public hemp.

MARCH 18, 1783.

(5) Called Court on Philip, a negro slave of Henry Garrett, and formerly property of Major Thomas Johnston, of Louisa County, charged with murdering Alexander Hunter, of Augusta County, and wounding the wife of Samuel Henry.—Guilty and to be hanged on 16th April next at 10 o'clock a. m. His value is fixed at £65.

(7) Inquisition on body of John Mitchell recorded.

(7) Ann and Esther Coleman to be bound to Ralph Laverty.

(7) Margaret Edmunds (formerly ordered to be bound to John Dalhouse) to be bound out.

(8) Joseph Gwinn qualified Lieutenant.

(9) Commission for priv. examination of Margaret, wife of John Brown. Deed to George Gall.

(9) Robert Anderson qualified Captain, vice John McKittrick, resigned.

(9) On motion of George Moffett, Colonel of County, judgment granted versus following Collectors of Districts: John McKemy, Richard Madison, George Sholtz, Seth Rodgers and Richard Buchanon.

(9) Andrew Lewell, orphan of Andrew Lewell, to be bound to William Gibson.

(9) Robert Curry appointed road overseer from Skidmore's Camp up the North River to the first main Fork above the Great Lick.

(10) George Buffenberry, from said Fork to the South Fork of South Branch of Potomac.

MARCH 20, 1783.

(22) Francis Riffle's death abates suit. John Mitchell's death abates suit.

(36) Robert Estrop appointed Constable.

(36) "Attorney for the Commonwealth" first mentioned.

(40) Tithables to be taken as follows, viz: By James Trotter, in Capts. Tate's and Trotter's Companies; Wm. McPheeters, in Capts. McCutcheon's and Bell's Companies; James Trimble, in Capts. McKittrick's and Dickey's Companies; Alexr. Robertson, in Capts. Givens's and Rankin's Companies; John Poage, in Capts. Campbell's and Anderson's Companies; David Henderson, in Capt. Long's Company; James Steel, in Capts. M. Smith's and Finley's Companies; Thos. Hughes, in Capts. Buchanan's and Smith's Companies; John McCreery, in Capts. Bratton's and Brown's Companies; John Kinkead, in Capts. Hicklin's and Hole's Companies; George Poage, in Capts. Poage's and Hamilton's Companies.

(41) Census to be taken by above, distinguishing blacks from whites.

(41) Alexr. Buchanan and Wm. Allen (Middle River) appointed Commissioners of Specific Tax in First Battalion. John Peoples, same, in Second Battalion.

Page

(41) Called Court on Hannah Holland for larceny.—Guilty and 39 lashes.

APRIL 15, 1783.

(43) Commission to take deposition of James Hall, who is about to remove to Ireland.

(43) Admn. c. t. a. of estate of John Russell granted Andw. Russell.

(44) Admn. of estate of Jonathan Dunbarr granted Valentine Cloninger.

(44) David Trotter, vice Joseph Blair, resigned—recommended Lieut.

(44) Admn. of estate of James Potter granted Wm. Steele. Dedimus ordered to take depositions of Jacob van Lear and Israel Christian, witnesses to will of John Christian, who are too aged and infirm to attend Court.

(45) William Wilson, vice Patrick Buchanan, resigned—recomd. Captain.

(45) Edward Hart McDonough to be bound to John McDonough.

(45) It appears to the Court that James Cunningham and John McKemey are unable to support themselves through inability occasioned by wounds received in the service—ordered to be certified to the Assembly.

MAY 20, 1783.

(50) John Christian's will produced with the dedimus and deposition of one of the witnesses, another being dead and the third not appearing—the will being made twenty-five years ago and the testator having had five children since—not allowed to be recorded—the widow refuses to administer and administration granted to Gilbert Christian, son of deceased.

(51) William McClung granted certificate to be examined for license to practice law.

(51) Robert Nolly, an orphan, to be bound.

(51) Elizabeth Flowers, an orphan, to be bound.

(51) John Yeager, a soldier in the 7th Virginia Regiment, who lost his arm at the Battle of Stillwater, allowed a pension.

(51) William Francis, a soldier in the 16th Regiment, Virginia, disabled in the service, recommended for further pension.

(51) Admn. of estate of Ambrose Powell granted.

(51) John Dickenson recommended for further pension.

(52) Pension of Joseph Mays, wounded at Point Pleasant, 1774, to be continued.

(53) Benj. Blackburn proved that he was disabled in the service at the Battle of Point Pleasant by losing the use of two of the fingers of his left hand.

MAY 21, 1782.

(54) Samuel Henderson and Alexander Barnett, who married two of the daughters of William Long, Sr., deceased, petition that the testator left 400 acres of land to be divided between their wives, and William Long, grandson of deceased, pray that a guardian be appointed for said William Long, an infant, and persons be appointed to make the division.—Samuel Long, uncle of said William, is appointed guardian and Commissioners appointed to make division.

Page

(55) William Rodgers exempted from payment of poll tax.

(58) Mathew Smith qualified Captain.

(59) Sarah Buchanan, wife of James Buchanan, a soldier killed in the service, allowed 75 lbs. bacon and 10 bushels wheat for herself and two children.

MAY 22, 1782.

(71) Dedimus to take deposition of James Graham, about to remove to Kentucky.

(71) Joseph Bell and John Wilson took oath of equalizers of land in the County.

(72) John Brown allowed claim for attendance in Staunton as Deputy Quartermaster for examining and taking in claims, 17 days.

(72) Thomas Rhoades allowed claim for keeping soldiers (Continental) in jail.

JUNE 6, 1782.

(73) Called Court on Henry Pousman for larceny—discharged.

JUNE 12, 1782.

(73) Called Court on Samuel Reeves for counterfeiting—discharged.

JUNE 17, 1782.

(75) Thomas Poage proves that he obtained pre-emption warrant for 1,000 acres to be located in Kentucky, which warrant he delivered to Claugh Overton, and he is convinced that Claugh Overton has been killed by the Indians and warrant lost—ordered to be certified.

(75) Wm. Wilson as Captain, and David Trotter as Lieutenant—qualified.

(77) Tithables ordered to be taken as before.

JULY 10, 1782.

(78) Called Court on Daniel Joseph and David Garwin, charged with passing one-half Joe—Court appoints James Buchanan, Clerk, in absence of Clerk.—Discharged.

JULY 15, 1782.

(78) James Kenny, oldest brother of Joseph Kenny, who died in Continental Service, has it certified in order to obtain land.

(79) Peter Wilson exempted from levies.

(79) Admn. of estate of Joseph Kenny granted heir-at-law, James Kenny.

AUGUST 19, 1782.

(80) Admn. of estate of Robert Gibson granted widow, Mary.

(80) Sarah Cunningham, orphan of Charles Cunningham, to be bound to Charles Berry—and Ruth Cunningham to James Harris.

(81) Certified to the Auditors that John Mitchell, deceased, was killed at Ninety Six, and William Mitchell is his heir-at-law.

(81) John Hatfield chose John Campbell guardian.

(82) Mathew Latimore's will proved and the executors named being dead, administration granted to Sarah Tate and John Tate, and it is certified that Mathew was a soldier of the Virginia line and killed in the service, in order that the administrators may obtain the land due and willed to James Tate, deceased.

(84) David Buchanon recommended Ensign in Captain McCutcheon's Company.

AUGUST 20, 1783.

(85) Philip North, orphan of Roger North, chose Sampson Mathews his guardian.

(88) John Kirk, vice Robert Anderson, resigned, is appointed Captain, and David Finley, vice John Young, and William Edmonston, Ensigns.

AUGUST 21, 1783.

(90) Thomas Hughes, issuing Commissary at Staunton, having returned in his account, "a scale man," it is certified that the scale man is Peter Hane.

AUGUST 22, 1783.

(99) William Hamilton, returned no inhabitant.

(113) Nancy Reily, orphan of John Reily, to be bound to John Stuart.

(113) Dedimus to take deposition of Robert Palmer, who is about to remove to North Carolina.

(113) Ordinary rates fixed.

(113) Court of Claims proclaimed for September Court.

(114) On page 113 (22d August, 1783,) Court was adjourned until tomorrow morning. On page 114 there is no heading—no date given.

(114) James McGonegal and Margaret, his wife, late Margaret Fleming, admx. of William Fleming, vs. Griffith Evans.—Petition—judgment.

(117) Isaac Carson's will proved—executors refuse to execute the trust and Rebecca, the widow, qualified administratrix, c. t. a.

SEPTEMBER 16, 1783.

(124) Dedimus for deposition of W. Cunningham, who is about to remove to Kentucky.

(128) Dedimus for deposition of Samuel Bell, who is about to remove to Kentucky.

(128) David Findley recommended and qualified Lieutenant in Captain Kirk's Company.

(129) Elizabeth Thorpe, wife of James Thorpe, a soldier in the Continental Army, allowed provisions.

(129) David Buchan recommended and qualified Ensign in Captain Mucheon's (McCutcheon's?) Company.

(129) Walter Cook, an orphan child, to be bound to John Gregory for 8 years, to learn art and mystery of a tailor.

Page
(130) John Steel, Lieutenant of the 1st Virginia Regiment, made oath that Robert Bower, a soldier in the Continental Army, died in Charlestown in August, 1780, and it is certified that Euphemia Mitchell, wife of James Mitchell, and Elizabeth Barnes, wife of George Barnes, are the only heirs.

SEPTEMBER 17, 1783.

(130) John Lewis and Wm. Banks granted license to keep ordinary at Warm Springs.

OCTOBER 21, 1783.

(131) Mary Jasper, wife of John Jasper, relinquished dower in 256 acres conveyed by John to Manoah Singleton.

(132) James Moore, son of Moses Moore, exempted from County levies, being unable to support himself by labor.

(132) James Cunningham ordered to be continued as a pensioner.

(133) Walter Cook, orphan of William Cook, deceased, to be bound to John Gregory, he being now 10 years and 5 months, until he is 19 years old.

(133) Mary Price, widow of John Price, a Continental soldier, proved that John departed this life June 9, 1782; it is further certified that he was enlisted September 30, 1780, and that Isaac Price is the eldest son and heir-at-law of John.

OCTOBER 22, 1783.

(135) Samuel Swearingham—witness from Maryland.

NOVEMBER 18, 1783.

(137) County levy.

(141) William Bowyer being commissioned Sheriff—informs the Court that he cannot find security.

(141) William Crawford is appointed guardian to Thomas Sawyers, orphan of James Sawyers.

(141) William Patterson, a dumb man, is exempted from payment of the County levy.

(141) William Ramsey is appointed guardian to John Ramsey, orphan of James Ramsey.

(147) William Tate, Justice, has removed.

(148) George Moffett recommended as Lieutenant of Augusta County, vice Sampson Mathews, removed. William Bowyer recommended as Colonel, vice George Moffet. Alexr. Robertson recommended as Lieutenant Colonel, vice Wm. Bowyer. Thomas Smith recommended as Major, vice Alexr. Robertson. Richard Madison recommended as Captain, vice Thomas Smith. Joshua Perry recommended as Lieutenant, vice Richard Madison.

NOVEMBER 20, 1783.

(152) John Madison, admr. of John Frogg, returned no inhabitant.

(163) Edward Erwin and John Dixon returned no inhabitant.

(166) William Young appointed guardian *ad litem* of Abraham Carson, son and heir-at-law of Isaac Carson.

Page

(167) John Steel is appointed guardian of Isaac Price, orphan of John Price.

(167) Admn. of estate of George Searight granted Jane, the widow.

(169) James Shields recommended Captain, vice William Tate, removed. 170, qualified.

(169) William Bowyer qualified Sheriff.

(170) James Curry is appointed to examine John Poage, Jr., as a surveyor and make report tomorrow.

DECEMBER 17, 1783.

(171) County levy, 2/6.

(171) Charles Cameron appointed inspector of hemp, deer skins, &c., &c , at Staunton.

(171) Sheriff ordered to employ some persons to glaze the Court House windows, mend the doors, windows, shutters, and mend the holes in the weather boarding.

FEBRUARY 17, 1784.

(172) Admn. of estate of Edward Ladd granted Edward Barker.

(172) Sheriff ordered to apply to Hannah Sawyers, widow of James Sawyers, deceased, for sundry articles taken from Benjamin Crow and Patrick Ferren.

MARCH 16, 1784.

(173) Admn. of estate of James Hook, deceased, granted George Hook, William Hook, the eldest brother having relinquished his right.

(174) Sarah Welch, widow of John Welch, deceased, proved that John, her late husband, had obtained a certificate under the proclamation of Governor Dinwiddie for 200 acres for services as a Sergeant in the Virginia Regiment commanded by William Byrd, which is since mislaid, and it is certified that Sarah is the only relation and heir of said John in these United States.

(175) Charles Cameron qualified Justice.

(175) Alexander Martin, wounded at Guilford, is allowed as a pensioner.

MARCH 17, 1784.

(177) Richard Madison makes oath that he had obtained a warrant from the Register's office for 1,875 acres, which he delivered to William Madison, now deceased, and it is lost—ordered certified.

(180) James McClure vs. John Frazure.—John McClure, son of Hugh McClure, security for costs.

MARCH 19, 1784.

(191) William Shanks, no inhabitant.

(196) William McDowell, no inhabitant.

(198) Owen Owens, returned no inhabitant.

(204) Mary Simms to be bound to Andrew Thompson.

Page

(205) John Bosler and Wm. Murphy returned no inhabitants.

(212) Henry King to be summoned to show cause why alimony shall not be decreed to his wife Susanna pending suit for divorce.

APRIL 20, 1784.

(217) William McDowell granted certificate of good character for obtaining license to practice law.

(217) Farrow ⎱ Dedimus to take depositions of James Woods, vs. ⎰ Isaac Shields, Richard Woods, Gilbert Searight, Alexr. Searight William Searight, William Stuart, William and John Moore, residents of Pennsylvania.

MAY 18, 1784.

(220) James Shekelford indicted for swearing.

(220) Nimrod Crane, aged 6, to be bound to James McGonegal; Mary Crane, aged 10, to be bound to Wm. Anderson; Kezia Crane, aged 9, to be bound to George Anderson.

(222) Thomas Smith qualified Major. Alexander Anderson qualified Ensign.

(223) John O'Neal, a Continental soldier, entered pensioner.

(223) Leonard Foolwiller swears he has lost a certificate granted him by Patrick Buchanan for service in the Militia at the time of the battle in Cowpens.

(223) Anthony Mustoe, Captain of the Patrollers in Captain Thomas Smith's Company, made several returns, which are ordered to be certified.

MAY 20, 1784.

(234) Robert Gaines and Benjamin Fleck, returned no inhabitants.

MAY 21, 1784.

(242) Robt. and John McMahon's death abates suits—see page 248, *infra*.

(245) Hugh Gwin exempted from pole tax and levies on account of age and infirmities.

(246) Joshua Perry appointed Captain, vice Richard Madison; William Burk as Lieutenant and David Perry as Ensign.

(248) James Henderson's death abates suit.

(248) William Bowyer qualified Colonel.

(248) Ordered to be certified that Timothy McNamara entered into the service in the beginning of the year 1777 and continued therein until the end of the war, and received several wounds therein, particularly at the Waxaws, where he received four wounds in his head, one in his shoulder, and one in the leg by which means he is incapacitated to procure subsistence.

Page

(251) Called Court on Stephen Meechant for larceny—39 lashes.

June 15, 1784.

(253) Dedimus for priv. examination of Jane, wife of John Bigham. Deed to Thomas Scott.

(253) James McNutt to be repaid taxes paid by him, he being formerly exempted.

(254) Alexander Robertson qualified Lieutenant Colonel.

(254) Hannah Sawyers, widow of James Sawyers, exempted from taxes for Harry, a negro.

(254) Thomas Hall qualified Attorney.

(255) John Gamble, William Young, James Searight, Anthony Ailor and Edward Erwin to locate a road from Staunton to Herodsburg.

(256) William Crane to be bound.

(256) John Tate qualified Justice.

July 20, 1784.

(257) Mr. Madison being absent, James Curry was admitted and sworn Deputy Clerk *pro tem.*

(258) Thomas Baker, aged 6 years, son of Elizabeth Baker, to be bound to the Rev. Mr. Wilson.

(258) David Trotter recommended Captain, vice Capt. James Trotter, who is about to remove to Kentucky.

(259) John Wilson recommended Lieutenant, vice David Trotter, and John McCutcheon as an Ensign.

(260) Horse, saddle, bridle and other articles attached to be advertised in the Virginia Gazette, and if no one appears to claim them, then they are to be sold and the proceeds applied to paying the judgments of Alexander Cummings and others against William Brooks. (These goods were supposed to have been stolen by Brooks.)

(261) Thomas Turk, Jr., is ordered to deliver the books of said Brooks to the Sheriff.

August 17, 1784.

(263) David Trotter as Captain, and John Wilson as Lieutenant, qualified.

(263) Admn. of estate of William Smith granted his widow, Jane Smith.

(264) John Gilham is appointed guardian of James Wright.

(264) George Ramsey is appointed guardian of Alexander Ramsey.

(264) Thomas Dean, 8 months old, to be bound to Jarret Erwin.

(265) David and Joseph Pinkerton, being charged with taxes for 1783, previous to their being in the County, to be exempted therefrom.

August 18, 1784.

(265) James McClure's death abates suit.

(269) Joseph Bell is appointed guardian of David Bell.

Page
(270) Joshua Perry qualified Captain—also William Burke as Lieutenant and David Perry as Ensign.

(271) Admn. of estate of Charles Floyd granted William McKemy.

AUGUST 19, 1784.

(284) David Martin ordered to appear at next Court to show cause why Jane Allison Martin, a child under 3 years, shall not be bound out.

(283) Richard Collins ordered to show cause why his children shall not be bound out.

(283) Sheriff to be allowed for John Shonts's tax, he not being of age.

AUGUST 20, 1784.

(297) Kezia Crane, aged 9 years, to be bound to Valentine White.

(308) Sheriff ordered to have made doors for the jury room and gates at the barr.

SEPTEMBER 21, 1784.

(309) Dedimus to take deposition of John Richey, who is about to remove to Georgia.

(310) John Moreman, runaway servant of Sampson Mathews.

(310) Admn. of estate of Mathew Kenny granted George Hook.

(310) Commission to issue to take priv. examination of Sarah, wife of John Caldwell, of Lincoln County, Kentucky, touching her dower in land sold by John to Robert Black.

(310) Will of John McMahon proved by Rev. Mr. Wilson, and certified for further proof.

(311) James Searight and John King are appointed guardians of John and Margaret Searight, orphans of George Searight.

(311) Thomas Williams and Sarah Kyler to be bound out, it appearing to the Court that they have not hitherto been brought up in a Christianlike manner, unless security be given to the overseers of the poor by Richard Collins and Ann Collins for their proper education and maintenance.

SEPTEMBER 30, 1784.

(311) Called Court on James O'Neal and James Murry for larceny—39 lashes.

OCTOBER 19, 1784.

(313) Admn. of estate of Sarah Scott granted Robt. Scott. (This should be Sarah Hutcheson instead of Sarah Scott.—See page 131, O. B. XIX.)

(313) Admn. of estate of Thomas Peircy (Percy) granted Sarah Peircy (Percy) and Thomas Waddell.

(313) William Black appointed road surveyor from James Bell's to John Coulter's, vice Samuel Black, deceased, and to work with tithables on South side of the road including James Bell's and James Best's to James Brent's on Back Creek.

Page

(323) Court adjourned until tomorrow morning.

(324) No heading to this Court.

NOVEMBER 16, 1784.

(341) Joseph Simpson exempted from levy.

(343) County levy.

DECEMBER 25, 1784.

(344) Andrew McKnight, aged 2 years, to be bound to James Hessent.

(345) Mary Campbell, alias Hackett, admx. of Robert Campbell, to be summoned to give counter security.

(346) Adam Burback's will partly proved.

(346) John Poage allowed claim for running the line between Augusta and Greenbrier Counties.

JANUARY 18, 1785.

(347) Mary Scott, orphan, aged 9 years, to be bound out.

(347) George Lewis exempted from payment of levies.

(347) Lewis Spearman, aged 14 years, to be bound to Peter Grass.

(348) David Henderson proved himself nearest heir-at-law of John Henderson, deceased, who was a soldier in Colonel Grayson's Regiment.

JANUARY 19, 1785.

(348) Robert Donaldson exempted from payment of levies.

(348) Justices, in accordance with the Act of May, 1784, ordered to take a list from each person in his precinct, containing the number of person in each family and the number of buildings, distinguishing dwelling houses from other buildings.

(349) Persons appointed to examine the Clerk's Office and see how many of the late Sheriffs have not settled their accounts with the Court.

(350) County levy: To Thomas Rhoades, jailor, 2,000 tithables at 3/.

FEBRUARY 15, 1785.

(351) It is proved that James Elliot is nearest heir to Archibald Elliot, a soldier in Capt. Hays's Company, who was killed in the action at Germantown.

AUGUSTA COUNTY COURT RECORDS.

ORDER BOOK No. XIX.

MARCH 15, 1785.

(1) Alexander McClenachan appointed Clerk of the Court, vice Richard Madison, deceased, and James Lyle, Jr., qualified Deputy.

March 16, 1785.

Page

(2) William Bowyer insisted that the appointment of Clerk was illegal, but the Court refused to reverse it.

(3) John Fairies exempted from levies.

(4) County levy: To John Awfull, for one old wolf.

(6) Mary Hacket, late Mary Campbell, admx. of George Campbell, decd., to be summoned to give counter security.

(7) Agatha Madison, mother and next friend of Richard Madison, decd., to be summoned to appear here to contest the said decedent's non-cupative will if she see cause.

(8) Adam Blakemore appointed road surveyor of new road from Back Creek to Jackson's River.

(8) James Hill exempted from working on the highway.

(8) Children of widow Dabage to be bound.

(9) John Poage refuses to act as Justice on account of age, &c.

(9) David Henderson refuses to act as Justice on account of want of books. John McCreery, Samuel Vance, John Kinkade and George Poage refuse to act as Justices on account of distance from Court House.

(10) William Bowyer ordered to deliver to the present Clerk all the records of this County and all things belonging to the said office which he took into his possession on the death of the late Clerk.

March 17, 1785.

(10) Nicholas Simmons to be exempted from payment of County levy and poll tax.

(11) Valentine White qualifies Deputy Sheriff under William Bowyer, Sheriff.

(11) County levy: To Henry Casebolt, one wolf.

(11) William Bowyer qualified Sheriff.

(12) Tithables ordered to be taken.

April 15, 1785.

(13) Called Court on James Parks for horse stealing.—Not guilty, but is of bad fame and bound to good behavior.

April 19, 1785.

(14) On motion of Ellenor Askins, Robert Thompson ordered to be summoned to show cause why he detains her child in his service.

(15) Cornelius Alexander naturalized.

(15) Nathan Reaglen's will partly proved.

(16) Henry King allowed for 7,230 lbs. flour furnished for public use.

(16) Report of Inspectors of Clerk's office.

(16) Proceedings of Court not recorded from 21 March, 1774.

(16) Deeds since 21 January, 1783, to present are not recorded.

(16) Wills, inventories, bonds, powers of attorney since 16th March, 1784, are not recorded.

Page

(16) Vouchers of taxable property returned are in great disorder. Papers in suits ended are not filed alphabetically. Dated 15 April, 1785.

(17) Jacob Lawrence is allowed 12 days' service as a wagon master at 7/6 per day. Thomas Forster is allowed for 66 days' service as a purchasing commissary at 4/ per day and 40/ for a house rented for a public store.

(17) Sampson Mathews is allowed for 14 months' rent of a house rented in February, 1784, for storing the hemp received in payment of public taxes. Samuel Anderson (the lesser) appointed road surveyor from Miller's Iron Works to Middle River, and Enos Jones from thence to Staunton.

(17) James Pinkerton, by David Pinkerton, his father and next friend.

MAY 17, 1785.

(18) New Commission, viz: Thomas Adams, William Bowyer, Thomas Hughart,* Alexr. St. Clair, Charles Cameron, William McPheeters,* Joseph Bell, Samuel Vance, John Givens, David Stephenson, Richard Mathews, Robert Porterfield, Jacob Warrick, George Moffet, Alexr. Robertson, Elijah McClenachan,* Thomas Hughes,* George Poage, James Steel, John Wilson, Samuel Lewis, John Taite,* Robert Gamble, James Crawford, Jr., James Davis, Alexr. Crawford, John McKemey. (Those marked (*) qualified.)

(19) Samuel McConkey qualified Deputy Sheriff.

(21) Robert Thompson (see page 14, *supra*) proves that the daughter of Ellenor Askins was bound to him by her father.

(21) Sarah Hatfield, daughter of Hannah Hatfield, to be bound to John Harper.

(23) Will of William McClintock partly proved.

(23) James Davis and John McKeemy qualified Justices.

(24) Alexander Reid appointed guardian of John Walker, orphan of Alexr. Walker.

(24) Hugh Donaho is appointed guardian of Barbara Walker, orphan daughter of Alexander Walker.

(25) Philip Bowman naturalized.

MAY 18, 1785.

(27) Robert Gaines returned no inhabitant.

(36) Thomas Hewett's death abates suit.

(38) John Allison, Jr., returned no inhabitant.

(46) Mary Moody, daughter of Elizabeth Moody, to be bound to William Blair.

(47) Doctor Valentine Hamm produced an account against the United States, date July, 1778, scale specie £2, 3, 7; also an account of £32, scale October, 1780, versus State of Virginia, specie, 9/.

(49) George Moffett, Joseph Bell, Alexr. St. Clair and Richard Mathews qualified Justices.

(49) Ally Peery, aged 2 years last March, daughter of Jane Peery, to be bound.

MAY 19, 1785.

(54) Joseph Niscor, security for James Neill.

Page

(56) Charles Donally and George Clendenning returned no inhabitants.

(59) Archibald Strange, Peter Hindricks, John Henderson, Abraham Kelly, John Campbell, Sr., Daniel Harvie, John McKenny—returned no inhabitants.

(62) Margaret Gay's death abates suit.

(69) John Lewis vs. William Wiatt.—Ordered removed to General Court.

(79) Capt. John Oliver's claim of £4, 10/, for beef furnished the Militia on duty, is allowed.

(81) Robert Gamble and Robert Porterfield qualified Justices.

MAY 20, 1785.

(83) Azariah Randolph, returned no inhabitant.

(83) William Smith's death abates suit.

(95) Henry Leese's death abates suit.

(97) James Hays, returned no inhabitant.

(102) Valentine Cloninger's death abates suit.

(108) James Old, witness—40 miles. Dudley Jones, witness—40 miles. James Ignew, witness.

MAY 21, 1785.

(117) James Blair and William Hinds, returned no inhabitants.

(121) Admn. c. t. a. of Richard Madison granted Wm. Bowyer, on motion of Priscilla, the relict.

(121) Peter Hane is allowed 45/ per month for 8½ months' service as scalesman at Staunton.

(126) Sarah Hutcheson's death abates suit.

(126) Petition versus Charles Tease.—Dismissed, "the defendant being removed," &c.

(131) On motion of William Henderson, ordered that James Henderson, Esq., of Greenbrier, be summoned to administer on estate of Susannah Henderson, deceased, if he sees fit.

(131) Administration of estate of "Sarah Scott" granted Robert Scott in October last should be "Sarah Hutcheson"—*Vid* O. B. XVIII., page 313.

JUNE 21, 1785.

(132) Moses Moore allowed for one beef furnished for public use.

(132) John Wilson qualified Justice.

(136) John Nimick—special bail.

(136) William Bowyer qualified County Lieutenant.

(136) Alexander Robertson qualified Lieutenant Colonel.

(136) John Givens and John Wilson qualified Majors.

(137) Deed from John Kinkade and Sarah, and Agnes Dean, wife of John Dean, to Brownlee—recorded.

(137) Admn. of estate of Jacob Grass granted Elizabeth Grass.

(137) On motion of Peter Weaver, ordered that Christiana Weaver be summoned to produce the last will of George Weaver, deceased.

(138) On petition of Honor Cook, ordered that John Gregory be summoned to answer complaint of said Ellinor touching his treatment of her son Walter, bound apprentice to John.

JULY 19, 1785.

(138) Samuel McCune and Bozwell Hackett, returned no inhabitants.

(139) William Gay, John Parker, William Wood, William Long, returned no inhabitants. James Rankin, returned no inhabitant. Wm. Thompson, returned no inhabitant.

(141) David Stephenson qualified Justice.

(142) David Laird presented claims for wagons and horses impressed and arresting a deserter, which are allowed. Henry King allowed claims, viz: For services as forage master, 360 days; for beef, flour and bacon furnished.

(143) William Craig, for horse hire and articles furnished, which are allowed.

AUGUST 16, 1785.

(144) On motion of John Dinwoody, ordered that a *scire facias* issue against Peter Cumings and ——, his wife, late —— Busheers, admx. of William Busheers, deceased, to revive a judgment versus Wm. Busheers.

(148) Henry Hatwell, aged 10 years and 6 months, orphan of Mansfield Hatwell, deceased, to be bound out.

AUGUST 17, 1785.

(152) Charles Cameron qualifies Justice.

(159) Robert Hall vs. Richard Buchanan.—All the attorneys being retained by defendant, the Court assigns George Nicholas for plaintiff.

(160) Rev. Archibold Scott, Presbyterian, authorized to solemnize matrimony.

(160) Alexr. McClenachan and James Brookes appointed guardians of Edward and Diana McDonagh, orphans of John McDonagh, deceased.

AUGUST 19, 1785.

(193) David Hanna, returned no inhabitant.

(194) Jacob Still, returned no inhabitant.

AUGUST 20, 1785.

(231) Thomas Kinkade, returned no inhabitant.

(233) On motion of Zachary F. Estill, who intermarried with Rebecca Estill, admx. of John Estill, deceased, accounts to be audited.

(237) Joseph Irving vs. Philip North.—Deft. being infant, can only appear by his guardian *ad litem.*

(243) Called Court on James Stephens, charged with larceny.—Guilty and sent to General Court.

(246) John McKinney, who has received a pension in consideration of wounds and injuries received in the public service, by losing one arm and being otherwise disabled, is not able to procure sustenance by labor, and is allowed £5 per annum additional.

(249) James Hamilton, having been heretofore allowed a pension of £12 per annum for wounds in the public service, his pension continued.

(250) Catharine Reid, aged 3 years 22d July last, daughter of Barbara Reid, to be bound.

(250) Lots in town of Staunton purchased by James Hughes to be conveyed to his co-heiresses.

SEPTEMBER 21, 1785.

(252) Ten acres to be laid off for prison bounds.

OCTOBER 1, 1785.

(253) Called Court on Peter Flack, charged with horse stealing from William Jordan, Sr.—Guilty and sent to General Court.

(254) Reuben Moore, Quaker, of Shanando, to be summoned a witness in above cause.

OCTOBER 18, 1785.

(255) Alexr. Robertson qualified Justice.

(256) Charles Donally qualified admr. of Andrew Donally.

(257) Ordinary rates fixed.

(257) Alexr. Martin allowed a pension of £18, being incapacitated from labor by wounds and injuries received in the public service.

NOVEMBER 4, 1785.

(258) Called Court on Thomas Griffin, charged with being accessory to William McCafferty in larceny of a negro slave.—Discharged.

NOVEMBER 15, 1785.

(259) County levy.

(260) Thomas Frame qualified overseer of poor.

(261) Rev. William Wilson, Presbyterian, qualified to perform marriage ceremony.

(263) James Steele qualified Justice.

NOVEMBER 16, 1785.

(265) County levy: 2,090 tithables at 2/9.

(267) William McPheeters, John Taite, John Christian and William Young, having refused to act as overseers of the poor, the Court appoints Joseph Bell, Robert Kenny, John Wilson and Joshua Parry. John Wilson qualified.

(267) Called Court on William Harper for forgery.—Guilty and sent to General Court.

DECEMBER 20, 1785.

Page

(269) James Hunter, son of Catherine Hunter, to be bound to John Dalhouse.

(271) Abraham Laywell to be bound.

(271) Henry Cease, aged 6 years and 3 months, to be bound to Francis Huff. Peter Reed, aged 7 years 20th April last, to be bound to Jacob Grove.

(271) Joshua Parry qualified overseer of the poor.

(273) Rev. Samuel Shannon, Presbyterian, authorized to solemnize matrimony.

JANUARY 2, 1786.

(273) Called Court on Thomas Torst and Sophia Torst, his wife, charged with murdering William McCutchen.—Discharged.

JANUARY 17, 1786.

(277) John Campbell appointed guardian of Joseph Conkin, orphan of George Conkin.

(277) John Taite qualified overseer of poor.

FEBRUARY 21, 1786.

(270) (280) Alexr. Robertson informed the Court he could not find security as Sheriff and his commission is returned to the Governor.

(270) (280) Leave granted Alexr. St. Clair and other citizens of Staunton to build a market house on the County land.

(273) (283) Stephen Howe and Catherine, his wife, Catherine Howe, Jr., Henry Howe, Philip Seyvert and —— Howe presented for interfering with Alexr. Gibson in collection of taxes.

MARCH 21, 1786.

(274) (284) Thomas McGregor exempted from payment of poll tax.

(274) (284) John Breckinridge, having obtained a license to practice as an attorney at law, took the usual oaths of qualification, as also did Charles Magill and Robert White.

(274) (284) John King, orphan of Joseph King, aged 18 years the 7th of May next, to George Smith.

(275) (285) Joseph and Mathew Wamsley, orphans of John Wamsley, deceased, chose William Wamsley guardian.

(278) (288) Samuel Vance and Alexr. Crawford qualified Justices.

(283) John Wilson is to examine John Poage, Jr., as a deputy surveyor.

(283) Alexr. Gibson's claim as assignee of John Chesnutt, for 22 days driving cattle from Augusta to Williamsburg—allowed.

(284) Admn. of estate of Alexr. Gardner granted his son, John Gardner.

(284) James Hamilton, a pensioner, proved that he received his wounds in the service of this Commonwealth in Capt. Patrick Buchanan's Company of Militia from Augusta County, in the action at Hotwater, June 26, 1781. He is aged 30 years and resides in this County.

(284) Alexander Martin, a pensioner, proved that he received his wounds at the battle of Guilford, in North Carolina, 15 March, 1781, in Capt. Joseph Alexander's Company of Militia from Rockbridge County. Is aged 27 and resides in this County.

(285) James Dobson's claim of £7, 10, the balance of said Dobson's pay as a sadler under the direction of Capt. Isaac Homes; also another claim for £27, 7, 3, for the same service under direction of Capt. Thomas Hamilton.

March 22, 1786.

(286) Thomas Hughart qualified Sheriff.

(288) Robert Mills's death abates suit.

(288) John Poage, Jr., qualified deputy surveyor.

(290) Admn. of estate of William Baxter granted John Baxter.

(291) John Stunkard exempted from County levies.

March 23, 1786.

(295) Thomas Brown's death abates suit.

(306) Thomas Neill, returned no inhabitant.

(306) Peter Wallace's death abates suit.

(314) William McCutchen's death abates suit.

(322) James Davis appointed guardian of *Abraham Millor, deceased*, he being under 14 years.

(324) William Bell, eldest son and heir-at-law of David Bell, deceased, and Florence and Joseph Bell, executors of said David, versus John Francis. Bill dismissed.

(329) William Hughes, John Caldwell, James Porterfield, Joseph Ray— returned no inhabitants. Robert Ferrill—returned no inhabitant.

(335) John Patterson vs. Florence Elliott, late Florence Bell, executrix of David Bell and George Elliott, who intermarried with said Florence.

(337) John Smith, Wm. Dinwoodie, John Richey, Gasper Fought—returned no inhabitants.

(354) David Cole exempted from payment of poll tax by reason of being blind.

(354) Tithables ordered to be taken.

(355) Joseph Bell and John Wilson appointed Comrs. of Land Tax.

(356) Rev. Samuel Carrick, Presbyterian, authorized to solemnize matrimony.

(356) Thomas Hughes, one of the Justices, is removed out of the County.

April 18, 1786.

(357) James Forster exempted from County levies.

April 19, 1786.

(358) William Francis, a pensioner, proved that he received his wounds in the service of the United States in the additional Regiment commanded by Colonel Grison, in 1788. Is aged 40 and resident in this County. He also produced a certificate of inability from John Griffin, a surgeon.

(360) William Casteel, son of Jinny Jewell, to be bound to John Doak.

ORDER BOOK No. XX.

MAY 20, 1786.

Page

(55) Zachariah Ricketts, returned "no inhabitant."

(70) Called Court on James Ross for larceny—39 lashes.

JUNE 20, 1786.

(71) James Lyle, Jr., qualified Deputy Clerk.

(72) Admn. of estate of Thomas Brown granted the widow Elizabeth.

(73) Admn. of estate of Robert Hogshead granted to James Hogshead and John Ewing. Ann, the widow, appeared and refused to administer.

(74) Admn. of estate of Thomas Scott granted Alexr. Scott.

(74) Jacob Sweet, formerly bound to Bernard Lance, now deceased, to be bound.

(76) John Yeager, a pensioner, proved that he lost his left arm in the service of the United States at the battle of Stillwater, 19 September, 1777, in the Seventh Virginia Regiment, on Continental establishment. Is aged 36 years and resides in Augusta.

(77) Admn. of estate of Terisa Bowyer granted William Bowyer.

(77) David Jones to come of age 22 July, 1790, to be bound to William Gilkison, to learn trade of blacksmith.

JULY 18, 1786.

(80) Peter Wilson, orphan of Peter Wilson, to be bound to Ro. Gamble.

(80) Elijah McClenachan allowed £3 for boarding William Porter, a Continental soldier, when in the smallpox.

(80) William Burk's estate allowed for wagon hire.

(80) George Crawford allowed for a gun lost in the service.

(82) Present Clerk ordered to examine the claims which have been allowed by the Court before his appointment, and certify to the Auditor such as have been neglected.

(83) Admn. of estate of Barnabas McGraw granted to Mary McGraw.

(83) Following recommended as Captains, viz: Thomas Turk, Jr., James Crawford and James Bell, Jr. As Lieutenants, viz: John Stuart, James Rankin and John Trimble. As Ensigns: David Henderson, James Kerr, Michael Kellar.

AUGUST 15, 1786.

(84) James O'Nail presented by Grand Jury for breach of the Sabbath in carrying home meal from the mill.

(85) Wm. Connell and John Gillaspie to be summoned to produce the will of John Guy, deceased.

(89) Additional Justices appointed: James P. Cocke, Zachariah Johnston, Alexander Gibson, James Ramsey, James Stephenson, Moses Hinkle. James Ramsey qualified.

Page

(93) Alexr. Gibson and Moses Hinkle qualified Justices.

AUGUST 17, 1786.

(100) William Bowyer qualified Justice.

AUGUST 19, 1786.

(121) Anthony Bleameat returned no inhabitant.
(125) David Frame allowed for 72 days wagon hire.

AUGUST 22, 1786.

(137)   William Kyle   ⎱ Special verdict finds that at the
            vs.   ⎰ time of issuing the writ Susannah
James Call and Susannah Call ⎰ had intermarried with John Chapman, a prisoner of war, but was residing here as a prisoner of war; but
with the permission of the British officers, subject to be recalled at their
pleasure.

(160) Wm. Bowyer, late Sheriff, informs the Court that malicious persons
have reported to the Governor that he has mis-applied taxes for years 1783,
1784. He is allowed to prove his collections, which is certified to the
Governor.

SEPTEMBER 19, 1786.

(167) Admn. of estate of Susannah Henderson is granted William Henderson; James Henderson, heir-at-law, having resigned his right.

(169) Following officers of militia recommended: Robert Gamble, as
Lieutenant Colonel; William Hinds, as Captain; John Hogshead and David
Parry, as Lieutenants; Jacob Perey and Samuel Cargo, as Ensigns; and for
a light company to the First Regiment—Alexander Gibson, as Captain; John
Poage, Jr., as Lieutenant; James Steel, as Ensign; for a light company to
the Second Regiment—John Lewis, as Captain; Charles Donally, as Lieutenant, John McCreery, Jr., Ensign.

SEPTEMBER 20, 1786.

(170) Rachel, wife of John Alexander, relinquished dower in land conveyed by her husband, John and James Alexander, to John Long.

(171) Officers recommended—William Sharp, Captain; Thomas Cartmill, Lieutenant; David Moore, Ensign.

OCTOBER 17, 1786.

(175) Timothy McLamore, inhabitant of this County, proved that he received wounds in the service of the United States at Buford's defeat in 1780,
a soldier in Capt. Stoakes' Company, and is allowed pension of £10.

(176) Admn. of estate of Philip Woolwine granted Elizabeth Woolwine.

DECEMBER 19, 1786.

(185) County levy.

(186) To William Christian, for his services as Adjutant of the Militia, allowed by the Court Martial £20. 1,860 tithables at 3/.

(187) Claim of Joseph Thompson for one gun, appraised at £800, reduced by scale to £3, 4/ specie—allowed. Claim of Robert Stuart for 1 beef. Claim of John Sutlington for 3 bushels wheat. Claim of John McClung for 422 lbs. beef. Claim of James Hughart for 787 lbs. beef. John Dickinson for beef. Ralph Lafferty for beef. Wm. Rhea for beef. James Young for 3 days driving cattle. Alexr. Kirk for 2 days driving cattle. Isham Berry for one certificate for militia service under Capt. Wm. Grissem of Albemarle for £4, 13, 4, dated 9 July, 1783. Isham Berry for one certificate for militia service under Capt. Henry Burke, dated June 4, 1783.

(189) John Heager to be naturalized.

(189) Charles Albright to be bound to Patrick Butler.

JANUARY 16, 1787.

(191) Sarah Ross's sons to be bound—John Ross to John Blair, and David Ross to James Blair.

(191) Alexander Wilson, son of Elizabeth Wilson, to be bound to George Craig.

FEBRUARY 20, 1787.

(195) Deed of Elisha Estes and Gabriel Long to Thos. Kirtley, formerly partly proved at November Court, 1774, is now fully proved by Francis Kirtley, Jr., but the Court refuses to have it recorded because said Kirtley refuses to pay the tax of 3 pp hundred acres.

(199) Peter Boon, 12 years old, to be bound; also Joseph Linden, 11 years old.

(200) Hance Patton, William Shields, Sr., James Botkin and William Lockhart are exempted from levies.

(200) Jacob Peck has a writ *ad quod damnum* for proceedings to erect a merchant mill on his lands on Christian's Creek.

FEBRUARY 21, 1787.

(201) Called Court on Charles McKee for attempting to murder Charles Wall—not guilty of the charge, but has committed an assault amounting to an attempt to take his life.

MARCH 21, 1787.

(218) Militia officers recommended—James Frazier, Captain, vice Wm. Findley, removed; Alexr. Hall, Lieutenant; Andrew Fulton, Ensign.

(245) Robert Campbell's death abates suit.

MARCH 24, 1787.

(248) Robert Douthat, Robert McCullough, Robert Stuart, Hugh McDowell, Wm. McDowell, Robert McDowell, Robert Aistrop, Charles Markle, John McKibbon and Robert Gamble, merchants, granted licenses for retailing goods agreeable to the Act of Assembly "Imposing New Taxes."

Page

(248) Anthony Mustoe qualified land searcher for the District of Staunton.

APRIL 17, 1787.

(249) Elizabeth Miller, relict of Abraham Miller, appears and relinquishes right to administer.

(251) William Workman is exempted from County levies.

APRIL 18, 1787.

(252) Following exempted from County levies: David McCloskey, Wm. Patterson, Sr., Wm. Villelly, John Joice, Daniel Anderson, William Ingleman.

(254) Militia officers recommended: Captains, William Shields, Robert Doak; Lieutenants, Wm. Bell, John Gamble, James Mitchell; Ensigns, Wm. Bell, Jr., Alexr. Reed, James McCune, David Williams, Wm. Brownlee, Wm. Henderson.

(255) John Dickinson, pensioner, proved that he received his wounds at the Battle of Point Pleasant on the 10th of October, 1774, in the service as a Captain of the Militia of this County, ordered on the Shawney expedition by Lord Dunmore, then Governor.—He is aged 56 years and resides in this County.

APRIL 26, 1787.

(257) Called Court on William Armstrong for grand larceny.—Guilty and sent to Richmond.

MAY 15, 1787.

(258) Indictment vs. Isaac Hanna, for unlawfully marrying his *uncol's* wife, Rebecca Carson, within 12 months.

(267) Joseph Trotter granted license for retailing goods.

MAY 17, 1787.

(278) Wm. Kyle vs. James and Susannah Call (Cale).—Judgment for plaintiff—see special verdict, page 137 *supra*.

(283) John McCutchen recommended Captain, vice David Trotter, who is romoved—and John Ewing, Ensign.

MAY 18, 1787.

(291) George Snodden—witness from Rockingham.

(293) George Mallow—witness from Rockingham.

MAY 19, 1787.

(330) Called Court on John McKee, charged with highway robbery.—Guilty and sent to Richmond for trial.

Page

(334) Following to be bound out: Polly Woland, to Charles Markle; Samuel Blakemore, to Abraham Rust; Peter Reed, to John Moore; William Breasline, 4 years old, to Thomas Mitchell; Henry Hatfield (formerly bound to John Francis, deceased), to Wm. Farris; John Reglan, to Jacob Peck; Sarah Blakemore, to Adam Bickle.

(334) George Cordell appointed Constable, vice Anthony Mustoe.

(335) Following exempted from levies: Stephen Biche, Robert Fairbern, Henry Butt, Garrett Dolson, Richard Erwin, James Erwin, Thomas Nelson, Daniel McGuines.

(335) Admn. of estate of John Galloway granted Thomas Frame. Admn. of estate of John Bourland granted relict, Elizabeth Bourland.

(336) Rev. Adolph Spindle, Dutch Lutheran, authorized to marry.

(337) Admn. of estate of John O'Nail granted Mary and John O'Nail.

(340) Abraham Carson, orphan of Isaac Carson, aged 16 years, chose John Gardner his guardian.

(340) William Hay qualifies admr. of Mathew Mathewson.

(341) William Bell qualified Lieutenant, and William Bell Ensign.

JULY 17, 1787.

(343) Alberdina Cole, relict of David Cole, produced his will, which is partly proved.

(345) Following reported as refusing to give in their taxes to Commissioner: Archibald Armstrong, Rebecca Black, John Black, Ephraim Bates, Daniel Callison, Christopher Crummett, Frederick Crummett, John Cowgar, Owley Conrad, Sr. and Jr., Samuel Carlile, Wm. Guy, Joanes Henderson, Henry Hufman, Robert Hutcheson, John Hinsher, John Lambert, Jr., Nathan Man, John McCutchen, John McLaughlin, William Joseph Newton, William Sexton, Henry Smith, Leonard Simmons, George and John Simmons, Jacob Snider, Peter Sickafoss, Leonard Simmons, Jr., Henry, Mark and Michael Simmons, Edward Thompson, Francis Tackett, Michael Woolfong, Elihab Wilson, Christian Waggoner.

(347) Claims of David Laird allowed:

(347) Pay advanced to Levi Thomas, a soldier, for beef for use of troops at Albemarle Barracks, with credits September and October, 1780.

(347) Following reported as refusing to give in list of taxes: Samuel Henry, David Clarkson, Jacob Daggy, Archibald Hamilton, Jr., Joseph Hamilton, Patrick Lacey.

(348) Robert Gay exempted from poll tax.

AUGUST 21, 1787.

(350) Commonwealth vs. Samuel Henry (vid, page 347).—Dismissed.

SEPTEMBER 18, 1787.

(397) Elizabeth Yeager, relict of Andrew Yeager, refused to administer, and administration granted to George Yeager.

(398) Isabella, wife of George Givens, relinquished dower in lands—deed to John Givens.

(398) Admn. of estate of Thos. Rankin granted Mary and John Rankin.

(399) Betsy Kinder to be bound to Levi Abraham.

(400) James, David and Mary Allen, all over 14, orphans of David Allen, chose Robert Allen their guardian. George Anderson, aged 15 years, chose John Christian guardian.

(402) Admn. of Andrew Alexander granted Martha Alexander and Samuel Hunter.

(403) Rev. James Chambers, Presbyterian, authorized to marry.

(404) Thomas Cook to be bound to Frederick Hanger, and Peter Laywell to Peter Hanger, Jr.

(404) John Burton, a pensioner, proved that he received his wounds in 1760, in the old Virginia Regiment—is aged 46 and resides in this County.

(404) Nicholas Powlas exempted from poll tax.

OCTOBER 16, 1787.

(406) Ordinary rates established.

(407) Admn. of John Miller granted his son, Patrick Miller.

(408) James Fraizer and John Erwin, Captains; Alexr. Hall, Lieutenant; Hugh Fulton, Ensign; qualified.

(408) Will of John Faris partly proved.

(409) Thomas Poage swears that he has advertised three several Court days his intention of applying for an act to vest in him the property of the lot No. 6 in Staunton.

OCTOBER 17, 1787.

(410) Called Court on Wm. Freehold for larceny—39 lashes.

NOVEMBER 3, 1787.

(411) Called Court on Isham Berry for larceny—discharged.

NOVEMBER 10, 1787.

(412) Called Court on Oliver Livingston for larceny—discharged.

NOVEMBER 20, 1787.

(416) Elijah McClenachan produced his commission as Sheriff, but informed the Court that he could not find securities.—His commission is returned to the Governor.

NOVEMBER 21, 1787.

(431) Robert Reid, a foreigner, took oath of allegiance to Virginia.

DECEMBER 18, 1787.

(438) Charles Cameron resigned as Commissioner of tax, and Samuel Vance appointed.

(439) County levy—To Joseph Bell, Coroner, for holding inquests on bodies of Samuel Swadley and Patrick Breezley.

(439) To John Tate for an inquest on body of John Shields.

(439) Thomas Rhoads, jailor.

(439) 2,858 tithables at 3/9.

(440) Margaret Reed, relict of Robert Reed, deceased, qualified admx. of his estate.

(442) James Bogs, 5 years old November 15, last, to Samuel Steele, blacksmith.

(442) Officers recommended: Robert Douthat, Captain; Wm. Chambers, Lieutenant; Robert McCullough, Ensign.

DECEMBER 26, 1787.

(444) Called Court on James Riely for larceny—guilty—25 lashes.

(444) Called Court on a slave for barn burning—discharged.

JANUARY 3, 1788.

(445) Called Court on Wm. Covern, horse stealing—guilty and sent to Richmond.

JANUARY 15, 1788.

(448) John Ryan, a pensioner, to receive £12 per annum.

(449) John Dickinson, a pensioner, to receive £50 per annum.

(449) William McPheeters qualified Sheriff.

(451) Abraham Laywell, orphan of Andrew Laywell, deceased, aged 14 years, chose Samuel Runkle his guardian.

(451) Philip Ingleman is appointed guardian of Samuel Laywell and Peter Laywell, orphans of Andrew Laywell deceased.

FEBRUARY 19, 1788.

(452-454) Alexr. Martin, pensioner, to receive £30.

(454) John Burton, a pensioner, to receive £10.

(454) Elizabeth Wilson to be bound to John Wallace.

(455) Estate of Margaret Crawford, deceased, comd. to John Crawford.

(455) George Anderson, orphan of George Anderson, chose John Wallace guardian.

(456) Estate of Wm. Blair, deceased, granted his relict, Elizabeth Blair.

(457) Militia officers recommended: John McKemy, Captain; David Buchanan, Lieutenant; Alexr. Sprowl, Ensign; in the First Regiment. John McCutchen, Lieutenant in Second Regiment. Samuel Steele, Jr., Lieutenant, and Wm. Davis, Ensign, of the Light Company belonging to the First Regiment.

(457) David Cunningham appointed Constable, vice Jacob Cole, removed.

MARCH 19, 1788.

(464) John Graham, returned no inhabitant.

Page
(473) David Greiner's death abates suit.

MARCH 22, 1788.

(497) James Hamilton, a pensioner, to receive £10 for 1786 and £10 for 1787.

(497) Militia officers recommended: Augustine Argenbright, Captain; Samuel McClintock, Lieutenant, and George Kellor, Ensign, of the new company in First Regiment.

(497) Leave is granted to Dr. Alexr. Humphreys to build an elaboratory on the prison lot, on such part thereof as may be designated by Commissioners.

(497) Sampson Mathews, Alexr. St. Clair, Michael Bowyer, Robert Gamble, James P. Cocke, William Bowyer and Alexander Nelson are appointed Commissioners to draw a plan of a new Court House, to be built on the Court House ground, and to fix the place whereon the same shall be set, and advertise the building thereof to be let to the lowest bidder, on such terms and conditions as the Court may direct at April next.

APRIL 16, 1788.

(501-502) John McCutchen qualified Captain in First Regiment.

(502) Joseph Maze proved that he received his wounds at Point Pleasant on October, 1774, under command of Colonel Andrew Lewis.

(503) Samuel Wallace, age over 14, orphan of Wm. Wallace, chose Samuel Hunter guardian.

(504) Archibald Hamilton exempted from levy.

(504) William Holliday, formerly bound to Andrew Alexander, deceased, to be bound to Mathew Alexander.

(504) William Francis, pensioner, to receive £8 for 1787.

(504) William McCutchen and Jane, late Jane Duncan, admx. of Andrew Duncan, to be summoned to render account of the estate.

(506) Robert Douthat, Captain; Wm. Chambers, Lieutenant, and Robert McCullough, Ensign, of the First Regiment qualified.

(506) Plan of new Court House returned and same Commissioners as before (except Nelson) ordered to let the building.

MAY 10, 1788.

(508) Called Court on James Cole for larceny—bound to grand jury.

(509) Called Court on Geo. Rymer for larceny—bound to good behavior.

MAY 20, 1788.

(510-511) John Nicholas qualified Attorney to practice in this Court.

(512) James Leviston and John Lambert, Jr., returned no inhabitants.

(514) Conrad Missinger and Thomas Armstrong, returned no inhabitants.

(518) John Campbell, Sr., fined for misbehaving in presence of the Court.

(518) George Wilson fined for misbehaving in the presence of the Court.

Page
(537-538) Timothy McNamara, pensioner, to receive £10 for 1787.
(537-538) John Campbell's fine (page 518) remitted.

MAY 28, 1788.

(540) Called Court on George Rymer for housebreaking—discharged.

JUNE 17, 1788.

(541-545) Andrew McComb's will proved; Jane, the widow, refuses to execute it.

(546) George Wilson's fine (page 518) remitted.

(546) Augustine Argenbright, Captain, and Samuel McClintock, Lieutenant, in First Regiment, qualified.

(546) Mary Miller's son, Daniel Miller, to be bound to Andrew Peck.

(547) Zachariah Taliaferro, Tax Commissioner.

(548) Alexr. McFarland proved that he received his wounds at Point Pleasant October 10, 1774, under command of Colonel Andrew Lewis—is aged 38 and lives in Augusta.

(548) Nuncupative will of Jane Wallace rejected on the objection of Samuel Brawford that it is not sufficiently proved.

JULY 3, 1788.

(549) Called Court on Lucy (slave) for barn burning—39 lashes.
(550) Called Court on Pleasant (slave) for barn burning—39 lashes.

JULY 15, 1788.

(551) Joseph Mays, pensioner, to receive £8 for 1786, and £8 for 1787.

(555) David Laird exempted from County levy.

(555) John McKinney to receive £15 pension for 1786 and same for 1787.

(556) Lewis Spearman, orphan to be bound.

(557) Thomas Waddle recommended Ensign in First Regiment.

(557) James Campbell, Sr., exempted from levy.

AUGUST 20, 1788.

(567-569) Nicholas Pace, since dead.

AUGUST 22, 1788.

(584-590) John McCutchen qualified Lieutenant of Second Regiment.

SEPTEMBER 16, 1788.

(601–603) John Edde appointed road surveyor from his own house to Scotch Town, vice Leonard Bell.

(604) Sophia Chestnutt qual. admx. of deceased husband, Wm. Chestnutt.

(604) John Tate, aged 14, orphan of James Tate, chose Robert Tate his guardian, and James is also appointed guardian of Isaac Tate.

(606) Zachariah Green, no inhabitant.

(608) Anthony Mustoe to be paid £6 out of County levy for removing the Court House.

(608) Andrew Anderson recommended Major of the First Regiment.

(608) Hugh Campbell to be summoned to qualify admr. of Robert Campbell if he sees fit.

October 21, 1788.

(609) Hugh Campbell qualifies as above.

(612) Following to be bound out: James and John Foster to Elijah McClenachan; Cornelius Brown to John McAdams; Joseph Nutty to Wm. Armstrong, and the orphans of George Edmunds, deceased.

(612) Depositions to be taken of John Campbell and James Agnew, about to remove.

(613) Peter River granted ordinary license.

(613) James Davis and Moses Hinkle, Justices, having removed.

October 22, 1788.

(614) William Forbes recommended Ensign in First Regiment. Andrew Cutler recommended as Ensign in the Light Company belonging to First Regiment.

(615) Court appoints James McChesney guardian of his son George, infant under 14 years, who is a legatee of Patrick Crawford.

November 18, 1788.

(616) Andrew Anderson qualified Major of First Regiment.

November 20, 1788.

(634) James Sprowl vs. William Hunter.—Defendant lost his senses.

(638) Deposition to be taken of Isaac and Alice Mynes in North Carolina.

November 22, 1788.

(654) William Bell recommended Captain of First Regiment. John Crawford recommended Lieutenant of First Regiment.

(658) William Stuart and Margaret, his wife, and their sons, Edward Stuart and William Stuart, Jr., infant—3 suits vs. Beith for slander.

December 16, 1788.

(660-662) County levy.

(663) To balance for building new Court House, £799.

(664) James Johnston to be bound to Moses Thorp.

(664) Absalom and Charles Johnston to be bound.

DECEMBER 17, 1788.

(666) On account of the inclemency of the weather and the Court House being in bad repair, Court is adjourned to the house of Mr. Peter Heiskell.

(666) County levy, 2,766 tithables at 10/.

(669) James, Andrew, Polly, Nancy, Betsey, John, Samuel and William Burk, children of John Burk, to be bound out, John having neglected to provide for them and to bring them up in a Christianlike manner.

JANUARY 20, 1789.

(670) Robert Carlile (son of John) appointed Commissioner to value property taken in execution.

(671) James Searight qualified Justice.

(671) Admn. of estate of George McChesney granted to his father, James McChesney.

(672) William Blackmore to be bound to James Searight; William Foster to William Moffett; Thomas Williams to Gabriel Pindle.

(673) Admn. of estate of James Shaw granted his brother, George Shaw.

(673) John Elliott, removed.

(674) Archibald Stuart appointed Deputy Attorney, vice Gabriel Jones.

(674) William McPheeters qualified Sheriff.

(674) John Burton to be paid his pension of £5 for 1788.

JANUARY 21, 1789.

(676-678) David Steel proved that he is disabled by wounds received in the service of the United States at Guilford, March 15, 1781.—He belonged to the Militia of this County—resides in this county and is aged 30.

(679) William Bowyer ordered to receive a deed from the County for lot No. 20 in Staunton.

FEBRUARY 17, 1789.

(680) James Moffett recommended as Captain for the First Regiment; Samuel Bell for Lieutenant; Robert Renick and Robert Fulton for Ensigns.

(681) Alexr. McFarland to receive £10 for pension for 1788. Joseph Maze to receive £10 for pension for 1788. John Dickinson to receive £50 for pension for 1788. Wm. Francis to receive £8 for pension for 1788.

(681) William Brown, orphan of James Brown, aged 9 years 1st of May next, to be bound to Daniel Donovan.

(681) John Gibson exempted from levy.

(682) George Smith to be bound.

AUGUSTA COUNTY COURT RECORDS.

ORDER BOOK No. XXI.

MARCH 17, 1789.

(1-4) Philip Enoch qualified Attorney-at-Law.

(6) James Poage qualified Justice.

Page
(8-13) Death of John Poage abates suit.

(21) Thomas Waddle qualified Ensign in the First Regiment.

(35-40) Thomas Rodgers—no inhabitant of this State.
(40) William Wilson and Luke Barret allowed to sue *in forma pauperis*.

(44-45) James Hamilton to receive £10 for pension for 1788.
(45) William McCormack to be bound to John Hunter, and William Porter, orphan, aged 14 last January, and Henry Blackmore to be bound.
(45) Merchants licensed, viz: Robert Stuart, Robert McDowell, Robert McCullough, Robert Aistrop, Robert Gamble, William McDowell, Hugh McDowell.

(47-48) Timothy McNamara to be paid £10, his pension for 1788.
(48) John Poage qualified surveyor.
(50) James Brown, formerly bound to Samuel Armstrong, now deceased, to be bound to Andrew Cutler, by consent of Wm. Armstrong, executor of Samuel Brown—is to have six months' schooling, freedom dues, and learn the art, trade and mystery of a saddler.
(51) Alexander Martin to be paid £15, his pension for 1788.
(52) Robert Kirk recommended Captain of a troop of Cavalry in First Regiment; William Forbes as Lieutenant, and John McDowell as Cornet; Oliver McCoy, as Captain of troop of Cavalry in Second Regiment, and John Berry as Lieutenant.
(52) Tax on William Bowyer's house and lot in Staunton is fixed for 1787 at the yearly rate of £25, and for 1788, £20.
(53) Richard Burns exempted from levy for his son Richard, who is subject to the Falling Sickness.
(53) Tax on Michael Bowyer's house and lot in Staunton fixed as for William above at £14 and £11, respectively. Same of Alex. St. Clair, for 1787, £30.
(53) Continued until 3d Tuesday in May next.

(54) Thomas and John Wells.

(81) John Yeager to be paid his pension for 1788— £15.

Page

(88) Called Court on Thomas York, of Botetourt, for larceny—15 lashes.
(89) Called Court on William Eyers for receiving stolen goods—30 lashes.

JUNE 16, 1789.

(93) William Young, Sr., exempted from levy.
(93) Robert McClenachan, orphan of Robert McClenachan, chose Alexander McClenachan his guardian.
(95) Isabella Abney, executrix of John Abney, deceased, who was one of the executors of John McDonagh, deceased.
(97) James Brown, orphan of Thomas Brown, deceased, aged 14 years or upwards, chose Alex. St. Clair his guardian.
(97) John Murphy appointed guardian of John and Nancy Murphy, orphans of William Murphy.
(98) Elizabeth Jones, aged 4 in March last, and John Ruffhead, son of Margaret Ruffhead, to be bound out.
(98) Sheriff to sell the old Court House, the purchaser to remove the house, fill up the cellar and clear the street.

JULY 21, 1789.

(99) Jacob Grass's will partly proved.
(101) Robert Gray, an orphan, to be bound to George Harding.
(101) Jane McCommus, aged 11 years, to be bound out.
(103) Alexander St. Clair appointed to keep the standard of weights and measures. Robert McClenachan, the former Seal Master, to deliver to him.

AUGUST 18, 1789.

(104) George Moffet, *et als.*, took oath required by Congress, pursuant to Article VI, Constitution, United States.

AUGUST 19, 1789.

(112) Alexander McClenachan, *et als.*, took oath required by Congress, pursuant to Article VI, Constitution, United States.

AUGUST 20, 1789.

(116-118) James Poage reported an efficient engineer.

AUGUST 22, 1789.

(127) James Williamson is about to remove.

SEPTEMBER 15, 1789.

(133-137) Mary Hempenstall, late Mary Wilson, executrix of Samuel Wilson.

Page
(137) Andrew Erwin qualified Lieutenant.
(137) Samuel Blackmore, orphan, to be bound.
(138) Elizabeth Ross, orphan, aged 14 years and 3 weeks the 3d instant, to be bound to Robert Craig.
(138) It is certified that Mr. John Hall has resided in this County from his infancy and is a person of honesty, probity and good demeanor. John Hall qualified Deputy Clerk.

OCTOBER 1, 1789.

(140) Called Court on Patrick Finley, charged with larceny—39 lashes.

OCTOBER 20, 1789.

(141–142) Viewers to examine the new Court House and report whether it is to be accepted.
(142) Elizabeth Holland, an orphan to be bound.
(142) Estate of Jacob Syler c. t. a. granted—the widow Dorothy refusing.
(142) David Greiner, orphan of David Greiner, chose Anthony Mustoe guardian.
(142) John Slaven to be exempted from County levy.
(144) James Peary is granted a commission to take the privy examination of Nancy, the wife of John Kelly, as to dower.
(145) Rachel, wife of John Christian, relinquishes dower in deed to James Moffet.

NOVEMBER 17, 1789.

(147) Robert Jouet and Theodosius Hansford qualified to practice attorneys.
(149) Henry Hall's death abates suit.

NOVEMBER 18, 1789.

(152–153) Presentment vs. Samuel Carlyle abates by his death.
(154) *Thomas Nail, Thomas Nail,* and David Nail—witnesses.

NOVEMBER 19, 1789.

(156–164) Stophel Owe, witness—45 miles.

NOVEMBER 21, 1789.

(167–168) Henry Hall's death abates suit.
(168) Adam Stephenson's death abates suit.
(176) Sheriff ordered to sell the old Court House and an old house on the prison lot, near the jailor's house, the purchaser being required to remove them as soon as possible—the ground around the new Court House to be leveled, and posted with locust posts or chains in such manner as the Commissioners shall direct. Robert Gamble, James P. Cocke, Robt. Douthat and Michael Bowyer appointed Commissioners.

(177) William Hind, administrator of John Hind, lives in Kentucky.

DECEMBER 15, 1789.

(177–178) Thomas Gillaspie's will presented and witnesses summoned to prove it.

(178) Cornelius Brown, an orphan, to be bound out.

(178) John Brownlee, Sr., summoned to show cause why the order to bind Elizabeth Holland, alias Hallingsworth, shall not be rescinded on the motion of Margaret Hallingsworth.

(180) County levy—181—to William Bowyer, Anthony Mustoe and Wm. Chambers, for alterations and additions in building the Court House, the Commissioners appointed having reported that the said building is completely finished—£45.

(181) David Finley is appointed guardian of John Trimble, orphan of Joseph Trimble.

DECEMBER 16, 1789.

(182–184) Michael Bowyer is appointed guardian of Henry Hall, orphan of Henry Hall, deceased, for the express purpose of binding said Henry to George Harding, to learn hatter's trade.

(185) Francis Mahan, son of John Mahan, aged 3 years and 2 months, to be bound.

(185) County levy continued.

(186) Credit by an old Court House, sold to Anthony Mustoe for £3, 17/2. 2,742 tithables at 2 shillings.

JANUARY 12, 1790.

(187) Called Court on Thos. Clifford (Clifton), larceny.—Not guilty.

JANUARY 19, 1790.

(188–189) Admn. c. t. a. of John George Weaver granted the relict, Christiana Weaver, and John Weaver.

(191) James Steel qualified Sheriff.

(193) Admn. *de bonis non* of Andrew Duncan granted James Brownlee.

FEBRUARY 16, 1790.

(197) A compact of 61 inhabitants of Staunton, forming a fire company, is ordered recorded.

(197) Edward Day exempted from County levy.

(198) William Dinwoody and John Berry recommended Captains of the 2d Regiment; Leonard Wade and Robert Givens, for Lieutenants; William Stevens and Mathias Benson, for Ensigns.

(199) Thomas and Nancy Smith to be bound.

Page

(203–204) William Hunter, apprentice of John Price.

MARCH 16, 1790.

(206) Hugh Holmes admitted to practice in this Court.

MARCH 20, 1790.

(231) Benijah Thompson, James McKibben, John Keys, Thomas McCullock and John Redpath—no inhabitants.

(233) Commission for deposition of Robert McClenachan, aged and infirm witness.

APRIL 20, 1790.

(235) Since 20th October, 1789 (page 141, *supra*), the instruments "Indentures" and "Deeds" have been recorded.

(237) Walter Kenady, an orphan, to be bound.

(239) Order to bind Wm. Foster to Wm. Moffett rescinded.

(241) John Clements, as Lieutenant, and Benj. Kennedey, as Ensign—recommended in 1st Regiment.

(241) Andrew Hamilton, William Lockridge and John Carlile exempted from working on roads on account of great age.

(242) Robert Hall and Samuel Shannon, witnesses to the will of Joseph Maze, are residents of Kentucky, and their depositions to be taken.

(243) William Hutcheson exempted from payment of County levy on account of age and infirmity.

(243) Peter Heiskell appointed seal master, vice Alexr. St. Clair, who refuses.

MAY 18, 1790.

(244) Thomas Smith's death abates suit.

(245) James Divier's death abates suit.

(245) Robert Garland, James Allen, and James Brooks qualified to practice as attorneys.

MAY 20, 1790.

(255) Robert Cockran resides in Kentucky, and deposition to be taken.

(258) John and Jeremiah Warder, no inhabitants.

MAY 21, 1790.

(261) Death of John Abney and Thomas Smith, executors of John McDonagh abates suit.

(262) Alexr. McNutt, no inhabitant.

(268) John Rankin's death abates suit.

JUNE 15, 1790.

(276–277) Francis Huff's will partly proved.

(280) Road established from the Great Road from Swift Run Gap at the Dry Spring Run up Lewis Creek to Staunton—and the public *to find rails for a fence* to be made through Joseph Bell's lands.

(282) Admn. of estate of Samuel Craig granted Alexr. Craig.

(282) Inquest on body of John Peck to be recorded.

(284) Mary Teas, executrix of Wm. Teas, required to give counter security on motion of William Bell, heir-at-law of David Bell, security for Mary.

JULY 20, 1790.

(285-286) Robert Williams and Henry Gabhart, returned no inhabitants.

(288) John Wade, Sr. (Back Creek), exempted from levy.

(289) John Dailey continued road surveyor from Jacob Cain's to William Wilson's, thence to the Bull Pasture Road over the mountain to the Sitting Hill—tithables from Coonrad Isacks's to Jacob Cain's.

AUGUST 17, 1790.

(290) Robert White takes oath as attorney.

(292) William Hibler, no inhabitant.

AUGUST 18, 1790.

(297-301) Commission for depositions of William Hook and Robert Campbell, who are about to remove to Kentucky.

(302) Robert Jouett—bail.

AUGUST 20, 1790.

(306-310) James Johnston recommended as Captain in 1st Regiment, Thomas Calbreath as Lieutenant, and Zacharian Johnston, Jr., Ensign.

AUGUST 21, 1790.

(311) Andrew Huffman about to remove to Pennsylvania.

SEPTEMBER 16, 1790.

(316) Called Court on Patrick Curry for burglary.—Sent to Genl. Court.

(318-323) Agatha Stuart (late Agatha Frog), witness to will of John Lewis.

(325) Benj. Hinkle, German Lutheran, qualifies to solemnize matrimony.

(327) Henry King, witness, about to remove to Kentucky.

(328) Alexander Hall appointed guardian of Elizabeth Tate, orphan of James Tate.

(330) David Greinor, apprentice to Adam Bickle.

OCTOBER 19, 1790.

(331) Ordinary rates.

(332) John Clements qualified Lieutenant of 1st Regiment, and Benj. Kennerly, Ensign; Edward Rutledge recommended Captain of 1st Regiment; Jonathan Brooks, Lieutenant, and James Henderson, Ensign.

(332) James Hicklin recommended Captain of the 2d Regiment; Edward Stuart, as Lieutenant; Samuel Pullen, as Ensign.

(333) Mary and Catherine Breezley to be bound to William Rodgers, who has maintained them for some time.

(333) Elizabeth Ross, 14 years old 17th December last, to be bound, with consent of her mother, to John Burke.

(334) James Steele, Sheriff.

(336) Admn. of estate of Mathew Reed granted Archibald Stuart.

NOVEMBER 16, 1790.

(341) Cuthbert Harrison admitted attorney.

NOVEMBER 17, 1790.

(346-349) Benoni Cosho, witness—22 miles.
(350) Robert, Isabella and Ann Duffield—witnesses.

NOVEMBER 19, 1790.

(355-358) John Givens's death abates suit.

DECEMBER 22, 1790.

(368-371) Certified that John Coalter has resided in this County for one year last past, and that he is a man of honesty, probity and good demeanor.

(372) County levy.

(373) County levy: To Wm. Moffet Jordan, one old wolf; to John Tate, for inquest on body of Thomas Stephenson.

JANUARY 18, 1791.

(375-376) Admn. of estate of Wm. Buchanan granted to John Buchanan.

(377) Admn. of estate of Thomas Rodgers granted Alex. Nelson, Jr.

(377) Samuel Neal to be bound to John Bell until he is 21 years, which will be 7th February, 1792, to learn trade of wagon maker.

(378) Walter Davis and Robert Scott are appointed guardians of William, Joseph and Rebecca Blackwood, orphans of William Blackwood.

(378) Admn. of estate of Eleanor Johnston granted Reuben Shackelford.

(378) William Moffet and John Kirk are appointed guardians of James and George Kirk, orphans of James Kirk.

(379) James Steele qualified Sheriff.

(379) Report of viewers of road being returned (from Cornelius Ruddles's to Fenton's mill), *it is ordered that the landowners be summoned.*

(380) Anthony Mustoe to be paid £64, 18/10, deducting the price of *an old Court House* bought by him.

Page
(381) Called Court on Anthony Kyle for receiving stolen goods.—Sent to *next District Court* at Staunton.

FEBRUARY 15, 1791.

(383) Joseph Maze to be paid £8, his pension for 1790; John Dickinson to be paid £50, his pension for 1790; John Burton to be paid £5, his pension for 1790; John McKinney to be paid £15 per annum for 1788, 1789, 1790.

(383) Andrew Coulter, orphan, to be bound to Smith Thompson.

(387) Andrew Anderson, vice Lieut.-Col. Robert Gamble, removed, recommended as Lieut-Col. of 1st Regiment; and John Campbell for Major.

(392) John Fogle to be bound to Jane Rutledge—formerly bound to Thos. Rutledge, now deceased.

(393) John Lowne, aged about 12 years, to be bound to Jacob Peck.

MARCH 15, 1791.

(394–397) Death of Lawrence Smith abates suit.
(391) John Coalter qualified Sheriff.
(399) Death of Andrew Lockridge abates suit.

MARCH 16, 1791.

(401–407) Isaac Ong, arbitrator.

MARCH 17, 1791.

(408–414) John Green exempted from levy.

MARCH 21, 1791.

(432) Mathews vs. Isabella Burns, executrix of Robert Burns, James Curry, and Mary, his wife, Asher Waterman, and Sarah, his wife, and Margaret Cunningham Burns, infant—Chancery.

(435) It is certified that Jacob Kinney has resided in this County for one year, and is of honesty, probity and good demeanor.

APRIL 19, 1791.

(436–437) Admn. of estate of Thos. Stephenson granted Jacob Swallow.
(438) Jane, David, Isaac, James and Gordon White, to Steele—deed.
(439) Thomas Calbreath qualified Lieutenant of the First Regiment.

MAY 4, 1791.

(439) Called Court on Robert Morton, shoemaker, for larceny—20 lashes.

Page

(447) Alexr. McNutt ⎫ Involves a lot in Staunton, with depositions
        vs. ⎬ giving some account of Staunton, 1761–1785.
William Bowyer. ⎭ Alexr. McClenachan testifies that Israel Christian was put in possession of the lot about 1762–1763 under a precept from the General Court. Alexander lived contiguous to the place, and understood defendant claimed under Christian. Thomas Rhoads testifies that in 1776, or 1777, he rented a stable of John Madison, deceased, on said lot, and the following year he rented the lot of defendant at public auction, at the rate of £5, 0, 7, per annum. Christopher Graham testifies. John Gordon deposes that he rented a house which he used as a smith shop on the lot aforesaid of the defendant at the rate £4, 10/ per annum, in 1785, but before the rent became due Thomas Smith, deceased, claimed the lot and received the rent. Michal Seyford also rented a house on said lot at same time as Gordon.

MAY 19, 1791.

(453–460) Deposition of Thomas Brown to be taken in Kentucky.

(463) Alexr. McFarlin to be paid £10, pension for 1789, and same for 1790.

MAY 21, 1791.

(464) Rebecca Gardner, relict and administratrix of Thomas Gardner, Francis and Samuel Gardner, orphans of said Thomas, versus John Brown, Rebecca Brown, widow of Hugh Brown, deceased, Sally and Margaret Brown, orphans of Hugh Brown. Sally and Margaret are infants.

JUNE 21, 1791.

(469–470) John Gay and Sarah and *James Gay, his brother,* to Henry Hicklin.

(471) Will of Joseph Maze, Sr., partly proved.

(471) Margaret, wife of Alexander Wiley, relinquishes dower in deed to Andrew McCartney.

(472) James Kirk, orphan of James Kirk, aged 18 years, appears and consents to serve William Abney as an apprentice until seven months after he is of age.

(477) Andrew Anderson qualified Lieutenant Colonel, and John Campbell, Major, qualified.

(477) Henry Shown, orphan of Leonard Shown, aged 15, chose Nicholas Spring his guardian.

(477) Estate of Laurence Smith, deceased, committed to Sheriff.

(477) Mary, wife of Hugh Richey, releases dower. Deed of trust to Abel Geoffey.

(478) Joseph Bell, son of Samuel, appointed Constable.

(479) Pillory and stocks ordered to be built.

(480) Motion of Michael Garber that Alex. Humphrey's shop, built on the public ground by order of Court, be removed as a nuisance—is dismissed.

Page

(481–486) Admn. of estate of Daniel McNair granted David McNair.

(487) Henry Hall, orphan of Henry Hall, aged 14 years the 14th September last, to be bound to John Gun, to learn trade of a hatter.

(489) Alex. Humphries, M. D., has leave to lease for eight years to come the house and inclosure he now occupies on the prison lot, for the purpose of indemnifying him for erecting the said building, &c., at the expiration of which term all the improvements are to be the property of the County.

(489) Commissioners to view a road passing thro' the lands of Joseph Bell, now in the possession of his son, William.

AUGUST 5, 1791.

(490) Called Court on free negro, Beverly Legan, for stealing a fiddle and other things from the slaves of Alexr. McClenachan—39 lashes.

(490) Called Court on Peter Masterson for passing a counterfeit guinea, valued at 27 sh. 6 d.—Discharged.

AUGUST 16, 1791.

(492-494) Depositions to be taken of William Guy and Joseph Wahub, about to remove to Kentucky.

AUGUST 20, 1791.

(512-514) Moses Easty and John Beach, no inhabitants of this Country.

(515) Rebecca Brown, no inhabitant of this Country.

(521) Deposition to be taken of Christopher Graham, removing to Kentucky.

(521) Daniel Miller's death abates suit.

———

AUGUSTA COUNTY COURT RECORDS.

ORDER BOOK No. XXII.

SEPTEMBER 17, 1791.

(1) Called Court on John Bullitt for horse stealing—sent to District Court.

SEPTEMBER 20, 1791.

(3) Timothy McNamara to be paid for pension at rate of £10 per annum.

(3) To be bound: Sarah Curtain, orphan, aged 2 years June last; Thos. Duncan (Duncum), son of John Duncan (Duncum); John Burns 7 years old 15 June last; Isaac Burns, 5 years old 15 inst.

Page

(4) Isabella, wife of Christopher Graham, releases dower in deed to James Alexander, dated 7th March, 1782.

(6) It is suggested that Henry Daily Shields, Sarah Bryan and Hannah Barret are insane, and Commissioners to examine them.

(9) Certified that Alex. Stuart has resided in this County for one year and is a man of honesty, probity and good demeanor. Same as to John Bowyer.

OCTOBER 18, 1791.

(11-12) Andrew Coulter, orphan, to be bound to Abraham Grove, to learn the art and mystery of a saddler.

(13) John and Mary Rankin being dead, admn. *de bonis non* of Thomas Rankin, deceased, is granted James Rankin and Robert Crawford.

(13) William Moffet, &c., to superintend the proportion alloted by the will of William McClintock, deceased, to his widow and relict, Martha McClintock.

(13) Mathew Gambill qualified Deputy Clerk.

NOVEMBER 15, 1791.

(14) Archibald Magill qualified attorney.

(19) This page is as follows: "Orders of the County Court of Augusta commencing 18th October, 1791, in the 16th year of the Commonwealth, under the care and direction of Mathew Gambill, Deputy Clerk for said County."

OCTOBER 18, 1791.

(21) Mathew Gambill qualified Deputy Clerk.

NOVEMBER 16, 1791.

(29-30) William Walton qualified Deputy Sheriff.

NOVEMBER 17, 1791.

(36) Augustian Kyar—a witness.

(42) Rachel Regular requested that James Johnston be appointed her guardian, but Court is of the opinion it cannot be done at Quarterly Court.

DECEMBER 20, 1791.

(54) John Oliver's will produced and proved, but contested by Sarah, the relict, and contest continued to next Court.

(57) John Bowyer qualified Attorney.

DECEMBER 21, 1791.

(60) James McCullough choses Robert McCullough his guardian.

(61) Charles Page chose John Gordon his guardian.

(61) Joshua Parry appointed seal master.

(61) County levy—2,524 tithables at 2/6.

(63) Albneazer Thornton, aged 14 years the last of this month, son of
————, to be bound to Peter Hiskell.

JANUARY 14, 1792.

(64) Called Court on Mary Hall, of Staunton, for stealing from William
Walton sundry pieces of silver—11 lashes.

JANUARY 17, 1792.

(65) George Taylor, formerly bound to John Finley, to be bound to David
Finley.

(66) Admn. of estate of John Bosang granted Elizabeth Bosang and
Edward Burk.

(67) Joseph Bell qualified Sheriff.

FEBRUARY 21, 1792.

(68-69) On motion of Lewis Myers, Commission to settle accounts of
Mary Myers, late Mary Lamon, executrix of Jacob Lamon (Lamor), decd.

(68-69) Jacob Speakard, 16 years old 11th April next, to be bound to
Thomas Tombelason (?).

(70) George and William Edmondson to be bound to James Burgess
Mary Curtin to be bound to Wm. Henderson.

(70) Alexr. Stuart qualified Attorney.

FEBRUARY 22, 1792.

(72) John McKenny to be paid pension of £15 for 1791. John Dickenson to be paid pension of £50 for 1791. Alex. McFarland to be paid pension of £10 for 1791.

(75) Joseph Moore's death abates suit.

APRIL 18, 1792.

(97–98) James Lyle, Jr., appointed, vice Robert Gamble, who has removed, to convey the County lots to purchasers.

(99) Isham Burk, orphan, to be bound to Philip Dyer, to learn trade of
baker.

(100) James Thornton, formerly bound to James Perry, to be bound to
James Henderson.

(101) John Risk exempted from levy on account of being lame.

(101) Certified that James Lyle has resided in this County for seven
years and is a man of honesty, probity and good demeanor.

(101) Henry West, orphan, about 12 years of age, to be bound to Dr.
Alex. Humphreys, to learn apothecaries' business.

MAY 15, 1792.

(103-110) William Robertson qualified Justice.

MAY 19, 1792.

Page

(126-127) Rebecca Gardner, &c., vs. John Brown, &c.—Robert Brown and Rebecca, his wife, formerly relict and widow of Thomas Gardner, decd., are added as plaintiffs.

MAY 21, 1792.

(135) See page 115, following. These records are recopied and new paging.

JUNE 19, 1792.

(146-148) Admn. of estate of Robert Burgess, deceased, granted the widow, Elizabeth Burgess, and James Burgess.

(152) James Hart, aged 5 years the 8th July next to be bound out.

JUNE 20, 1792.

(155-156) Stone bridge to be built across the run that passes through the town above Joseph Mathews'.

JULY 17, 1792.

(159–160) James Lyle resigned as Justice and qualified attorney.

(167) William McDavitt, witness to will of Robert Armstrong—residence, South Carolina.

JULY 18, 1792.

(168–169) Ordinary rates fixed.

NOVEMBER 16, 1791.

(171 or 19) William Walton qualified Deputy Sheriff.

JANUARY 14, 1892.

(44) Called Court on Mary Walton.

JANUARY 17, 1792.

(44) Robert Wilson, named as executor in will of John Oliver, qualified as administrator of said will.

(150) (Down to here, from page 171, old paging, or page 19, new paging, the records are recopied. The records from page 19, old paging, were all by Mathew Gambill, and are very badly done; with the new paging, a new scribe begins, and the records are excellently kept.)

AUGUST 1, 1792.

(150) Called Court on Sarah Sorrels for larceny.—Sent to District Court.

AUGUST 4, 1792.

(151) Called Court on slave of James Lamb.—Not guilty.

Page

(152–155) Alex. McClenachan sued by overseers of the poor.

(156) Alex. McClenachan, Clerk, resigns on condition that Jacob Kinney be appointed, which terms are accepted by the Court, and Jacob qualifies. This proceeding is objected to by several Justices, because they conceive that the acceptance of a conditional resignation is contrary to the Constitution of the Government.

AUGUST 22, 1792.

(156–158) Certified that James Stuart has resided in this County for one year, and is of honesty, probity and good demeanor.

AUGUST 25, 1792.

(175) Called Court on George Kinkead, late of Greenbrier, for horse stealing.—Bound to good behavior.

(177) Deposition to be taken of John Craig, who resides in N. Carolina.

SEPTEMBER 18, 1792.

(181) Admn. of estate of John McKenny granted to James, William and Eleanor McKenny.

(182) John Wiley's will partly proved.

(183) Thomas Riddle, a witness, is about to remove from the State.

(184) Peter Genewine, a landowner, summoned on a road petition.

(185) On the motion of John Williams, and Catherine, his wife, late Catherine Burk, it is ordered that Philip Dyer deliver up an apprentice boy named Isem Burk, bound to him by said Williams and wife, to learn the art and mystery of a miller.

OCTOBER 16, 1792.

(187–189) Ignatius Turkey (Turley)—a witness.

(189) Admn. of estate of George Peerson granted James Anderson.

(190) Witnesses to be summoned to prove the will of Sarah Lessley.

NOVEMBER 20, 1792.

(193) James Stuart qualified attorney.

(196) Thomas Shankling, apprentice of Robert Torbett—motion to be discharged.

NOVEMBER 23, 1792.

(202–204) Death of Lawrence Crown abates suit.

NOVEMBER 24, 1792.

(207–209) Florence Elliott, late Florence Bell, executrix of David Bell, deceased, and George Elliott, who intermarried with Florence, and William Bell, heir-at-law of said David.

(210) On motion of Elizabeth Brown, adminixtratrix, &c., of Thomas Brown, Margaret Brown, executrix of John Brown, deceased, is required to give security to save the estate of Thomas Harmless by reason of his being security for Margaret, and John Brown becomes security.

DECEMBER 12, 1792.

(211) Called Court on Mary Holmes for larceny—discharged.

DECEMBER 18, 1792.

(212-213) Rachel, widow of William Crawford, deceased, releases dower in land conveyed by William's partners to Robert McCullock.

(214) John Strain, orphan of James Strain, deceased, chose Andrew Keith his guardian.

(215) George Curtis, aged 11 in May next, and John Curtis, aged about 8, to be bound.

(215) Isham Burk, orphan of Isham Burk, deceased, supposed to be over 14, to be bound.

(215) Isaac Waugh, witness to will of Richard Rankin, is dead.

DECEMBER 19, 1792.

(216) County levy: 160 lbs. tobacco is equivalent to £1.

(217) Stephen Unemerman, orphan of Isaac Unemerman, deceased, aged 16 years the 22d of this month, chose Jacob Kinney his guardian.

JANUARY 8, 1793.

(221) Called Court on James Essex, charged with burglary—he and wife, Christiana, being persons of ill-fame, are bound to peace.

JANUARY 15, 1793.

(223) Following to be bound out: Jane Ross, 6 years old March 6th next; Daniel Caphart, 4 years old 13th of May next; Dinah Hunter (daughter of Elizabeth Hunter), 3 years old 3d of this month.

(224) Joseph Bell qualified Sheriff.

(224) John McNeal, orphan of Thomas McNeal, chose James Johnston his guardian.

JANUARY 16, 1793.

(226) County levy: 2,566 tithes @ 18 lbs. tobacco = 2 shillings.

(227) Stophel Mantle and James Allen, agent for John Allen, land-owners, to be summoned on a road petition.

(228) Notation dollars and cents first noticed.

JANUARY 19, 1793.

(229-231) Joseph Mays to be paid £8, pension for 1791, and same for 1792.

Page

(233) John Wheeler to be paid £8, pension for 1792.

MARCH 19, 1793.

(235–237) Samuel Anderson, road surveyor, no inhabitant.

MARCH 25, 1793.

(258) Andrew Anderson recommended as County Lieutenant, John Campbell as Major of 1st Battalion, William Wilson as Major of 2d Battalion.

(258) Thomas Turk, Jr., James Frazer, James Crawford, John Erwin and William Bell as Captains in 1st Battalion—recommended.

(258) James Bratton, William Shields, Robert Doak, John McCutchen, and Augustine Argenbright as Captains in 2d Battalion—recommended.

• (258) John Clements, Alex. Hall, James Rankin, Andrew Erwin and John Crawford as Lieutenants in 1st Battalion—recommended.

(258) John McCutchen, Robert Christian, James Mitchell, John Wilson, David Buchanan, Lieutenants in 2d Battalion—recommended.

(258) Benj. Kennerly, Andrew Fulton, David Henderson, Thos. Waddle, Wm. Bell, Jr., Ensigns in 1st Battalion—recommended.

(258) Wm. Armstrong, Joseph Bell, Robert Fulton Ewing, David Williams, Ensigns in 2d Battalion—recommended.

(258) William Chambers as a Captain of Infantry in 1st Battalion—recommended.

(258) Samuel Steele, recommended as Captain of Infantry in 2d Battalion.

MARCH 25, 1793.

(259) James Allen as Lieutenant of Company of Infantry in 1st Battalion—recommended. Robert Rennick as Lieutenant of Company of Infantry in 2d Battalion—recommended. Alex. Anderson as Ensign of a Company of Infantry in 1st Battalion—recommended. Alex. Crawford as Ensign of a Company of Infantry in 2d Battalion; Robert Gratton as Captain of a Company of Cavalry to be raised in Staunton—recommended. David Parry as First Lieutenant of said Company; William Abney as Second Lieutenant of said Company; Jacob Geiger as Cornet of said Company.

APRIL 16, 1793.

(259–261) Selina Devine, aged 14 the 7th of this March, to be bound to William Armstrong.

(261) Sarah Devine, aged 10 the 9th of this November, 1792, to be bound to Thomas Shanklin. William Rice to be bound to Isaac Ong. James Wilson, aged 13 the 2d January last, to be bound to John Price. Lucy Wilson, aged 8 the 29th December last, to be bound to John Price.

(263) Rachel Poage, late Rachel Crawford, executrix of John Crawford, deceased, to settle her accounts.

(263) John Dickenson to be paid £50, pension for 1792.

(264) William Wheeler, aged 11 years 27th February last, to be bound to Lawrence Trimper.

MAY 21, 1793.

(265) Thos. Stevens and George Martin, apprentices of Gideon Morgan, to be summoned to show cause why they have absented themselves without leave.

(265) The Grand Jury present an act entitled, "An Act to regulate the Militia of the Commonwealth of Virginia, passed in Richmond, 22 December, 1792, as being partial, offensive, partly unintelligible, and contrary to the principles of a Republican Government."

MAY 24, 1793.

(276-277) Isabella Walker, orphan of Alex. Walker, deceased, has intermarried with Robert Reed, and suit abates as to her.

MAY 25, 1793.

(279) Robert Bailey, and Elizabeth, his wife, late Elizabeth Bosang, administratrix of John Bosang, deceased.

(284) James Gillespie, a witness, who resides in the Southwest Territory.

MAY 30, 1793.

(287) Called Court on George Allen, laborer, late of Rockbridge, for larceny—30 lashes.

JUNE 18, 1793.

(288-289) Martin Witzell exempted from levies on account of age and infirmity.

(290) Thomas Cooper, aged 16, chose James McKenny guardian, orphan of James Cooper, deceased.

(290) Joseph Hanna, witness to will of Catherine Clements, deceased, is since dead.

(291) Benj. McCorkle, aged 12 years the 23d August next, son of Mary McCorkle, to be bound to Robert Mays.

(292) John Diddle, 16 years old in August next, to be bound to Andrew Cutler to learn art and mystery of a saddler.

(294) The persons recommended on pages 258 and 259, *supra*, as military officers, qualified as follows: Andrew Anderson, John Campbell, Thomas Turk, Jr., Robert Gratton.

(294) John Burton to be paid £5, pension for 1791, and same for 1792.

JUNE 19, 1793.

(295) On motion of Charles Cameron, guardian to James Vance, orphan of John Vance, deceased, John McCarty and Martha, late Martha Vance, widow of John, to be required to settle accounts.

(296) Philip Ingleman is appointed guardian to Hannah Laywell, orphan of Andrew Laywell, deceased.

(300) Jacob Geiger qualified Cornet, as see page 259, *supra*.

(300) John Coalter qualified Clerk of District Court.

JULY 16, 1793.

(301) John McKinney to be paid £15, pension for 1792.

(301) James Fox, aged about 14 years, to be bound.

(302) Robert Doak and James Frazer qualified, see pages 258-9.

(303) William Bell qualified deputy surveyor. John Crawford qualified Lieutenant, see pages 258-9; Wm. Bell, Jr., qualified Ensign, see pages 258-9.

(307) Certified that Patrick Ready lost part of his right in a fight with Dennis Maloney.

AUGUST 24, 1793.

(324-332) William Henderson, no inhabitant.

(336) William McGowen, a witness about to leave the State.

AUGUST 26, 1793.

(337) Called Court on John Bullett for horse stealing.—Sent to District Court.

SEPTEMBER 7, 1793.

(339-341) John Brown, Sr., is exempted from County levy on account of old age and infirmity.

(341) Samuel Kirkland, witness, is about to remove from the State.

SEPTEMBER 17, 1793.

(342) Gabriel Alexander appointed guardian for Francis Alexander, orphan of Francis Alexander, deceased.

(342) Mary Ann Ham, orphan of —— Ham, chose Bridget Campbell guardian.

(342) Andrew Erwin qualified Lieutenant in 1st Battalion.

(342) Admn. of estate of Wm. Vasteen granted Joseph Mathews.

(342) Admn. of estate of Dominick Barret granted James Mitchell.

(343) Nathaniel, aged 10, and Sarah Devine, aged 11, to be bound to Jacob Deary (Peary).

(343) John Devine, aged 7, to be bound to Michael Garber.

(343) Margaret Mooney, aged 3, to be bound to Jacob Barrier.

OCTOBER 15, 1793.

(343-344) Moses Jackson appointed guardian for Catherine Walter.

(344) Charles Bruce, orphan of James Bruce, chose Alexander Reed his guardian. Robert Bailey is appointed guardian for William and Mary Bosang, orphans of John Bosang.

Page

(345) William Ham chose John McGlammery guardian.

(345) Clerk is directed to purchase a bell and have it hung in the Court House.

(346) Sheriff to erect a gallows within 30 feet of the road leading from Staunton to Peter Hanger's, opposite to the Slaughter House, the East side.

(347) Moses and Joshua Russell, orphans of Joshua Russell, chose Robt. Thompson their guardian.

October 16, 1793.

(350) Ordered that the fork of the roads leading from Staunton to Miller's Iron Works, and to Peter Hanger's be considered as the place of execution of all condemned persons in future which may by law be executed by the Sheriff of Augusta.

AUGUSTA COUNTY COURT RECORDS.

ORDER BOOK No. XXIII.

November 23, 1793.

(17-24) Mary Holmes, infant, by John Holmes, her father and next friend.—Her marriage abates suit.

December 17, 1793.

(32-33) Isem Burk, aged 14 in February last, heretofore bound to Adam Bickle, now to be bound to Andrew Cutler, to learn art and mystery of a saddler.

(33) John Surface exempted from further payment of County levy.

(34) William Chambers qualified Captain of the Light Infantry in the 1st Battalion, 32d Regiment, and Alex. Anderson, Ensign, the same.

(35) Mary Dick, orphan, chose Samuel Wilson guardian.

(35) Charles Hendrick, aged 18 years, to be bound to James Cochran to learn art and mystery of a saddler—Adam Bickle, his former master, consenting.

(35) Dower to be laid off for Agnes, widow of Thomas Meek, deceased.

December 18, 1793.

(39) County levy.

January 21, 1794.

(41-42) Walter Kennedy chose George Hook his guardian.

(42) Alexander Hall qualified Lieutenant in 1st Battalion, 32d Regiment.

(44) John Tate qualified Sheriff.

(44) John McClintock, orphan of John McClintock, chose Philip Ingleman guardian.

(44) William Wilson qualified Major of 2d Battalion, 32d Regiment.

JANUARY 22, 1794.

Page

(45) County levy continued—2,896 tithables @ 25.

(46) The Clerk has liberty to keep the records in the Court House until further order.

FEBRUARY 18, 1794.

(50) Edward Broback exempted from County levy on account of age and infirmity.

(51) Judith Miller and her children allowed £10, her pension for 1793.

(52) Joseph Mays to receive £8, his pension for 1793.

(53) William Wilson and Francis Bell qualified deputy surveyors.

(53) John Alexander appointed guardian of Ruth Ross.

(54) Rev. Charles O'Neill, Episcopalian, authorized to celebrate matrimony.

(54) Michael Iseerhower, apprentice of Jacob Leas.

FEBRUARY 19, 1794.

(54–57) Alex. McFarlin to be paid £10, pension for 1792, same for 1793.

(57) John McKinney to be paid £15, pension for 1793. John Wheeler to be paid £8, pension for 1793. John Burton to be paid £5, pension for 1793.

MARCH 18, 1794.

(58) David Holmes took oath of qualification as Attorney.

MARCH 20, 1794.

(66) Stevenson vs. Rebecca Stephenson, relict of Adam Stephenson, deceased, James Waddle and Ann; John Hair and Sarah; William, James and Rebecca Stephenson, heirs of Adam Stephenson.

MARCH 22, 1794.

(73–76) Certified that Gilbert Christian has resided in this County for 12 months and is a man of honesty, probity and good demeanor.

APRIL 16, 1794.

(78–79) William Abney qualified Second Lieutenant of a troop of Cavalry in Staunton, and in 3d Division.

(80) Col. John Dickinson to be paid £50, pension for 1793.

(80) John McCutchen qualified Captain in 2d Battalion, 32d Regiment.

(80) Cornelius Brown, son of Mary Hart, aged 13 years 13 June next, to be bound to John Cline to learn art, trade and mystery of saddle tree maker. ———— Keith, aged 10 years May next, to be bound to John Rapp.

(81) Court certifies that Captain James Bratton is entitled to the rank of Major in 2d Battalion, vice William Wilson, who was recommended by mistake and has qualified.

(81) James Guy recommended as Captain in 2d Battalion, 32d Regiment. James Berry recommended as Captain in 2d Battalion, 32d Regiment.

(81) Henry Hall, heretofore bound to John Gunn, to be bound to Philip Hopkins.

MAY 20, 1794.

(82) Augustus Elias Brevost Woodward, attorney, admitted to this Court.

JUNE 17, 1794.

(119) Sarah Armstrong, aged 9 years last May, to be bound to John Hawke. Margaret Fulwider, orphan of Jacob Fulwider, aged 14, chose Michael Ott guardian. Emmanuel Law to be bound to Samuel Wallace, to learn the trade of saddler.

(124) Robert Anderson recommended Captain in 1st Battalion, 32d Regiment, it appearing there are men enough to form a new Company. Alex. Anderson, Lieutenant, and Thomas Hogshead, Ensign, same.

(126) Eleanor Rutledge releases dower in deed by her husband, James Rutledge, to George Rutledge.

(126) Admn. of estate of Sarah McClenachan granted Alex. St. Clair and Alex. McClenachan.

JULY 15, 1794.

(135) Gilbert Christian admitted to practice law.

(135) Jacob Swope qualified Justice.

(136) Allan McClean Gwinn Curry to be bound to Smith Thompson, to learn trade of a weaver.

(137) Tavern rates established.

(138) Depositions to be taken in contested election for Senator between David Stephenson and John Oliver.

SEPTEMBER 16, 1794.

(156) John Kennedy, orphan of Mathew Kennedy, above 14, chose John Campbell guardian.

(156) Admn. of estate of Agnes Meek granted to Daniel Meek.

(157) William Jones, aged 17, to be bound to Lawrence Simmerman, to learn trade of weaver.

(158) Sarah McDowell, widow of Hugh McDowell, refuses to accept her husband's will.

(158) Levi Strickling, aged 12 years, to be bound to Jacob Deary, to learn trade of shoemaker.

(159) Joseph Bell, Jr., recommended Captain, 2d Battalion, 32d Regiment, vice Capt. Shields, resigned. James Brand recommended Lieutenant, vice Robert Christian, resigned. Wm. Thompson recommended Ensign, vice Joseph Bell, Jr. Edward Rutledge recommended Captain of a new Company taken off Capt. Shield's Company. Jonathan Brooks recommended Lieutenant. James Henderson recommended Ensign. David Buchanan recommended Captain of a new Company taken off Capts. Shield's and

Argenbright's. David Williams recommended Lieutenant. Charles Hudson recommended Ensign. James Berry recommended Captain, vice James Bratton, resigned. Wm. Armstrong recommended Lieutenant, vice John McCutchen, resigned. Samuel Lockridge, Ensign, recommended Lieutenant. Samuel Bell recommended Captain of a new Company taken off Captain Argenbright's Company. Francis Bell recommended Lieutenant. James Bell recommended Ensign. Frederick Hanger recommended Lieutenant, vice David Buchanan, recommended Captain. Peter Jenewine recommended Ensign, vice David Williams, recommended Lieutenant.

(160) John Gamble recommended Captain in 1st Battalion, 32d Regiment, of a new Company taken off Capt. Erwin's Company. William Young recommended Lieutenant. James Allen recommended Ensign. David Parry recommended Captain of a new Company taken off Capt. Bell's Company. Andrew Cutler recommended Lieutenant. Michael Garber, Jr., recommended Ensign. Mathew Robertson recommended Ensign, vice Benjamin Kennerly, who has removed. Alex. Watson recommended Ensign of Infantry, vice Alex. Anderson, resigned.

(165) Wm. Alexander, Archibald Stuart, Alex. Nelson, Alex. Humphreys, and Robert Douthat are appointed commissioners to report a plan to the next Court for a jail.

OCTOBER 21, 1794.

(166) James Noble, above 14, chose Samuel Sommerville his guardian.

(166) Joseph Bell, Jr., and Samuel Bell qualified Captains in 2d Battalion, 32d Regiment. Wm. Thompson qualified Ensign.

(167) Admn. of estate of John Lowry granted Mary and John Lowry.

(169) James Berry qualified Captain 2d Battalion, 32d Regiment. James Brand qualified Lieutenant. Wm. Armstrong qualified Lieutenant. John Gamble qualified Captain.

NOVEMBER 18, 1794.

(175–176) Mathew Robertson qualified Ensign, 1st Battalion.

NOVEMBER 21, 1794.

(180–182) James Rankin qualified Lieutenant, 1st Battalion.

DECEMBER 16, 1794.

(194) Barnet Shields chose Wm. Shields guardian.

(196) Alex. Hall recommended Captain in 1st Battalion, vice James Frazer, resigned. Andrew Fulton recommended Lieutenant, vice Alex. Hall. Andrew Steele, Jr., recommended Ensign, vice Andrew Fulton. Thomas Caldbreath recommended Captain of a new Company taken off Capt. Frazier's Company. Robert Graham recommended Lieutenant. Petterson Thompson recommended Ensign. David Buchanan, Sr., recommended as Captain of new Company in 2d Battalion taken off Capt. McCutcheon's Company. Alex. Sprowl recommended as Lieutenant. James Clarke recommended as Ensign. Jonathan Brooks recommended as Captain, vice Edward

Rutledge, who has removed. James Henderson recommended as Lieutenant, vice Jonathan Brooks. Alex. Henderson recommended as Ensign, vice James Henderson. Charles Hudson recommended as Lieutenant, vice David Williams, resigned. Thomas Caldwell recommended as Ensign, vice Charles Hudson..

(198) Frederick Hanger qualified Lieutenant, 2d Battalion. Peter Jenewine qualified Ensign. James Bell qualified Ensign. Francis Bell qualified Lieutenant. Samuel Lockridge qualified Ensign. William Young qualified Lieutenant, 1st Battalion. James Allen qualified Ensign.

(199) Frederick Steele exempted from levy by reason of age, &c.

(199) John Keith, aged 5 18th January next, to be bound to Colonel Alex. Robertson, to learn art and mystery of a farmer. Joseph Hook, aged 4 years 2d June 1794, to be bound to John Read, to learn art and mystery of a weaver. Peter Kendell, aged 14 next March, to be bound to Wm. Throckmorton, to learn art and mystery of a printer. Philip Overshine, aged 9 last fall, to be bound to John Tees to learn blacksmith.

(200) Jail commissioners reported and ordered to advertise for bidders.

JANUARY 3, 1795.

(208) Called Court on Edward Swards, laborer, for stealing an axe—sent to District Court for trial.

JANUARY 20, 1795.

(209) John Tate qualified Sheriff.

(210. Viewers appointed for road from Adam Miller's, near North Mountain, to the Dutch Meeting House.

(212) John Dickinson to be paid £50, pension for 1794. He is unable to travel to Court, but was alive on 17th inst.

(212) Certified that John Allen has resided 12 months, and is of good demeanor, &c.

(213) James Simpson, orphan, to be bound to Michael Poffenbarger, to learn art and mystery of a potter.

JANUARY 21, 1795.

(213-214) County levy.

JANUARY 22, 1795.

(220) County levy—2,953 tithables @ 72c.—Increase for purpose of building a jail.

FEBRUARY 17, 1795.

(221) Joseph Mays to be paid £8, pension for 1794. Alex. McFarlin to be paid £10, pension for 1794. John Burton to be paid £5, pension for 1794.

(222) Alex. Stuart to be paid £8, pension for 1794.

(222) Margaret Hamel (Hansel?) refuses to administer on estate of husband, George Hamel, deceased.

(223) George Hood's estate committed to Sheriff.

(225) Nancy McCames chose Jacob Nebergall guardian.

(225) Wm. McCorkle, aged 16 4th of this month, to be bound to Henry Moiser, to learn blacksmith.

February 18, 1795.

(227–228) Jail contract let to Jacob Kinney for £1,150.

(230) Patience Ritchey, aged 14 in April next, to be bound to John Poage, Jr., who agrees to pay her £6 as freedom dues.—She was formerly bound to John Burnsides, now deceased, and Frances Stuart, the only child of said Burnsides, is willing to deliver her up.

(233) Chesley Kinney qualifies Deputy Clerk.

March 17, 1795.

(235) John Allen qualified upon license as Attorney.

April 16, 1795.

(262) Called Court on James Ogle for horse stealing—sent to District Court.

April 22, 1795.

(263–264) Alex. Campbell exempted from levy on account of his infirmity.

(264) William Hart exempted from levy—old age and infirmity.

(264) Patience Ritchie to be bound to Alex. Sanders until 18.

(269) Richard Mathews proved that on 13th March, 1782, he delivered to Clough Overton Treasury warrants for 60,000 acres.—Overton was soon after killed by the Indians and the warrants were lost.

(270) Certified to Register of Land Office—John Cooper is heir-at-law of James Cooper, deceased, and he is above 21 years.

April 29, 1795.

(271) Called Court on Paul Ekerly for larceny—guilty.

June 16, 1795.

(312) Robert Fulton recommended Lieutenant in 2d Battalion, vice James Mitchell, resigned. Thomas Mitchell recommended Ensign in 2d Battalion, vice Robert Fulton.

(313) Elizabeth Armstrong to be bound to Jacob Worley. Nancy Hall to be bound to David Greiner.

(314) Samuel Craig, orphan, chose James Berry guardian. Margaret Corner, orphan, chose Samuel Long guardian.

(314) Jacob Puff, George Pickle, William Caldwell, Robert Caldwell, Nicholas Echers, exempted from levy and poll tax.

(315) John Shark recommended Ensign in 2d Battalion, vice John Ewing, dead.

(319) Robert O. Kelly to be bound to James Cummins to learn farming.

(319) Alex. Gibson's will proved.—Mary, widow, refuses to qualify, whereupon son, Alex. Gibson, qualifies.

JULY 16, 1795.

Page

(321) Called Court on John Kean for counterfeiting—guilty.

JULY 21, 1795.

(322–323) James Young appointed guardian to orphans of George Hood.

(323) Rebecca Stephenson, orphan of Adam Stephenson, deceased, chose William Stephenson guardian.

(323) John Nolly, aged 18, formerly bound to Robt. Brawford, deceased, to be bound.

(323) Elizabeth Armstrong's will proved by Susanna Breeze, late Susanna Brand.

JULY 22, 1795.

(328–329) George Puff, Jacob Pickle and Peter Wiseman exempted from levy.

(337) James Hall, orphan of Henry Hall, aged about 12, to be bound to Michael Garber, Jr., to learn art, trade and mystery of coppersmith.

JULY 30, 1795.

(337) Called Court on William Bratton for larceny—discharged.

AUGUST 18, 1795.

(338–340) Andrew Steel qualified Justice.

(340) County divided into 18 precincts for processioning, and processioners appointed. Each Company by names of Captains composes a district.

AUGUST 19, 1795.

(342) Alexander Dodd has ordinary license.

SEPTEMBER 15, 1795.

(359–362) Charles Hogshead to be examined whether fit to serve as deputy surveyor.

(363) John Ott, Sr., is exempted from paying poll tax, &c., on account of old age, &c.

(363) Michael Ott is about to remove out of the State and will be unable to attend to the duties of guardianship of Margaret Fulwider, who chose John Ott her guardian.

SEPTEMBER 19, 1795.

(365) Called Court for examination of Abraham Martin and Jacob Shore for larceny—discharged.

OCTOBER 13, 1795.

(365) Called Court for examination of John Lilley for counterfeiting—guilty.

OCTOBER 20, 1795.

Page

(366) Robert Porterfield Wallace, aged 8 years 24th August last, to be bound out.

(366) Andrew Davidson Wallace, aged 6 years 8th February last, to be bound out.

(366) Charles Hogshead qualified Deputy Sheriff.

(366) Mary Gold, aged about 15 months, to be bound to Thomas Myers.

(369) John and Ann Shields, orphans of Thomas Shields, chose William Wilson their guardian.

(370) William Douthat's will presented and witnesses summoned.

OCTOBER 21, 1795.

(373–374) Mary Elliott vs. John Caruthers.—Abates by marriage of parties.

(380) Certified that Alex. Stuart has acted as Deputy Attorney for the Commonwealth from January, 1789, to the present date, during which time there have been twenty Courts for examination of criminals and trial of slaves.

(381) Petition for bridle way rejected because the law does not authorize the expenditure of money for bridle ways.

NOVEMBER 21, 1795.

(390–393) There being a dispute about the boundary line between Rockingham and Augusta, commissioners are appointed to meet those from Rockingham and determine same.

DECEMBER 15, 1795.

(395) Susanna Barrier, orphan of Jacob Barrier, aged 14 years, chose Jacob Barrier as her guardian. Mary Roler, orphan, chose Adam Louks as her guardian. Mary Hunter, orphan, chose William Patterson as her guardian.

(396) Admn. of estate of Elias Woolman granted the widow, Esther Woolman.

(397) Admn. of estate of William Mitchell granted James Mitchell, Sr.

(397) John Foster, formerly bound to Alex. McClenachan, aged 4 years the 27th of July, 1788, to be bound to James Pinkerton.

(399) County levy.

(399) Patience Ritchey to remain with her mother, Catherine Campbell, and not be bound out.

DECEMBER 16, 1795.

(399) George Woolwine, aged 10 years the 23d April next, to be bound to Michael Harmon, to learn art and mystery of a hatter.

(401) Rockingham County Court having failed to appoint commissioners to run the County line, ordered that unless they do so in the next month the Augusta commissioners are to run it alone.

Page
(401) Commission to build a new jail report that the building may be received upon the contractors agreeing to make certain improvements, which report is adopted.

JANUARY 19, 1795.

(402-403) Alex. St. Clair qualified Sheriff.

(404) Commissioners appointed to report plan of a new Clerk's office.

(404) John Summers, aged about 20 years, son of John Summers, appeared with his father and agreed to apprentice himself to Jacob Leas for two years and a half to learn the art and mystery of a tanner.

(405) Nancy Keith, apprentice of John Robb.

(405) James Keith, aged 8 years the 18th of next month, to be bound to William Abney to learn mystery of a hatter.

(405) Ebenezer Thornton, formerly bound to Peter Heiskell, to be bound out.

JANUARY 20, 1796.

(406) Jacob Kinney appointed guardian of John McDowell, orphan of Hugh McDowell.

(406) County levy continued—3,000 tithables @ 75c.

FEBRUARY 16, 1796.

(407-409) James Boggs, aged 12 years last November, to be bound to Wm. Steel.

(409) Robert Strean, orphan of James Strean, chose John Gardner his guardian.

(410) Meredith Lively, aged 13 the 6th of last June, to be bound to Benj. Eagle to learn art and mystery of a blacksmith.

(410) Sheriff of Bath to pay John Dickinson £50, pension for 1795.

(411) Sheriff of Bath to pay Joseph Maze £8, pension for 1795.

(411) Admn. of estate of Edward Parks granted Sampson Mathews.

(411) Time for running line between Augusta and Rockingham extended to April.

FEBRUARY 17, 1796.

(411-414) Depositions to be taken of Robert and Elizabeth Wilson of Bath County.

MARCH 18, 1796.

(426-430) William Mitchell's death abates suit.

MARCH 21, 1796.

(450-451) John Bowyer recommended Captain of a Company of Artillery; John McDowell, First Lieutenant, and Robert McClenachan, Second Lieutenant.

APRIL 20, 1796.

(454) John Conrad Wright exempted from levy.

(455) George G. McIntosh took the oath of allegiance.

(456) John Hammel, aged 17 in January last, to be bound.

(457) Alex. Stuart to be paid £8, pension for 1795.

(458) Commission to run line between Augusta and Rockingham returned report and recorded.

(459) On motion of Elizabeth Woolwine, William Woolwine, aged 13 years 28 May last, to be bound to Michael Harmon, to learn trade of hatter.

APRIL 28, 1796.

(459) Examination of Joseph Byers for larceny—guilty.

MAY 21, 1796.

(480) Robert McDowell took the oath of fidelity.

AUGUSTA COUNTY COURT RECORDS.

ORDER BOOK No. XXIV.

JUNE 21, 1796.

(1) Andrew Laywell (son of Abram Laywell) aged 5 years the 12th November next, to John Coiner, to learn art of a farmer.

(1) Following to be bound: Polly Hutcheson, aged 4 years in October last, to Elizzabeth Mateer. James Brown, aged 12 years in November last. Mary Barnes, aged 14 years 14th September next. Margaret Barnes, aged 8 years 29th July next. Ann Barnes, aged 6 years 7th May next. William Barnes, aged 3 years this month.

(2) Abram Laywell (son of Abram), aged 2 years 29th January last, to Andrew Silling, to learn mystery of a weaver.

(2) Admn. of estate of James Hughes granted David Steele.

(3) Henry Welsh, heretofore bound to Alex. Humphreys, now to be bound to Mathew Patton, to learn mystery of a saddler. John Palmer, orphan of Cornelius Palmer, aged 17 years on 23d December, 1795, chose Robert Gratton his guardian for the purpose of binding him an apprentice to Peter Bratton, to learn the art and mystery of a blacksmith.

(7) Jane Brown, widow and administratrix of James Brown, deceased.

(8) Samuel Simpson exempted from levy on account age and infirmity.

(8) Certified that Mathew Kenny has resided in this County for many years and is a man of honesty, probity and good demeanor.

(8) Admn. of Patrick O'Brian's estate committed to Moses Hays.

(8) Admn. of James McCann's estate committed to Agnes McCann.

JUNE 22, 1796.

(12) Jacob Kinney to be paid £24, 41/—the price of a bell he purchased for the County.

(15) Robert Gratton qualified Major of a Battalion in a Regiment of Cavalry annexed to the 3d Division of Militia. John Bowyer qualified a Captain and John McDowell a Lieutenant, of a Company of Artillery in the 3d Regiment and 3d Division.

June 23, 1796.

(17–25) Commissioners appointed to place the bell in the end of the Court House if they find it can be done without injuring the Court House, otherwise to report the most convenient place.

(26) Robert McClenachan qualified Lieutenant of a Company of Artillery in the 3d Regiment and 3d Division.

July 26, 1796.

(26) Sarah Wilson, aged 7 years in May last, to be bound to Mary Hamilton. Phebe Martin, aged 2 years in June last, to be bound to David Straen.

(27) Benjamin Boyer, aged 14 years, to be bound to Henry Wachtel, to learn wagon making. John and William Bailey, about 8 years old, and Charlotte Bailey, about 10 years old, children of Barnabas Bailey, to be bound.

August 15, 1796.

(31) Called Court on Jacob Link for larceny—held to Grand Jury.

September 20, 1796.

(61–63) Collin Campbell choses guardian by Patience Richey, orphan.

(63) Sarah, widow of Moses Hays, refuses to administer.

(63) Admn. of estate of John Erwin granted William and Francis Erwin.

(65) Thomas Waddall recommended Lieutenant in 1st Battalion, 32d Regiment, vice Andrew Erwin, who has removed.

(66) John Michael recommended Ensign in 1st Battalion, 32d Regiment. George Berry, as Captain in 2d Battalion, vice John McCutcheon, resigned. John Scott, as Lieutenant, vice John Wilson, resigned. James Ewing, as Lieutenant, vice John Sharp, resigned.

(67) Adam Hawpe, as Lieutenant in a Company of Infantry in 2d Battalion, 32d Regiment, vice Robert Rennick, who refuses. Samuel Finley, as Ensign, vice Alex. Crawford, resigned.

September 26, 1796.

(68) Called Court on Benjamin Roberts for passing counterfeit bills—discharged.

October 18, 1796.

(69–70) Elizabeth, widow of William Armstrong qualifies admx. c. t. a.

(72) William Rafferty, aged 12 years 7th April last, to be bound to Wm. Martin, to learn trade of breeches maker.

(73) Charles Berry recommended Captain in 2d Battalion, 32d Regiment, vice David Buchanan, resigned.

Page

(74) James Wilson exempted from levy for his two sons, John and James Wilson.

(74) Samuel Miller recommended Captain in Staunton Cavalry, vice Robert Gratton, promoted.

OCTOBER 27, 1796.

(79) Called Court on Nathaniel Jefferies for larceny—forfeited recognizance.

NOVEMBER 11, 1796.

(80) Called Court on Adam Clarke, larceny—discharged.

NOVEMBER 15, 1796.

(81) Samuel Blackburn qualified to practice law.

NOVEMBER 19, 1796.

(88-91) A fight took place in Court between John Coulter and Alex. Gibson, Esquires—bound to peace.

DECEMBER 20, 1796.

(91–92) Michael Coiners' will proved, but not admitted to record on motion of Christian Balsley, who wishes to contest it.

(92) George Wright chose John Brown guardian.

(93) Christian Scyler, aged 12 months last September, daughter of Margaret Scyler, to be bound to Jacob Palmer.

(93) James Allen recommended Lieutenant in 1st Battalion, 32d Regiment, vice William Young, resigned.

(94) John Mead recommended in Allen's place.

DECEMBER 21, 1796.

(94-95) County levy.

(96) County levy.

JANUARY 17, 1797.

(97) Charles Berry qualified Captain in 2d Battalion, 32d Regiment. George Berry qualified Captain in 2d Battalion, 32d Regiment.

(98) John Dickinson to be paid £50 pension.

(98) Probate of Michael Coiner's will continued to next Court and witnesses to be summoned.

JANUARY 18, 1797.

(99–102) Alex. St. Clair qualified Sheriff.

(102) County levy: 3,000 tithables @ 54c. each.

FEBRUARY 21, 1797.

(109) Sarah Price, orphan of Samuel Price, deceased, of Henrico County, chose Robert Douthat guardian.

Page

(112) Called Court on Sebastian Wolfe for horse stealing.—Sent to District Court.

APRIL 18, 1797.

(134) Jacob Aker, aged 13 years, to be bound to John Weorly.

(134) Alex. Stuart to be paid £8 pension.

(135) Henry Wilson, orphan of Thomas Wilson, deceased, 5 years old in July last, to be bound to William Mitchell.

APRIL 19, 1797.

(136) George Eker, aged 18 years, chose John Weorly guardian.

(136) George Lemon, orphan, aged 8 years 22d January last, to be bound to Henry Mace.

(138) Lettitia W. McClenachan chose William Chambers guardian.

(138) Michael Garber, Jr., recommended Captain in 1st Battalion of 32d Regiment, vice David Parry, resigned.

(138) John McClenachan as Lieutenant, and Luther Morgan, Ensign—recommended.

(138) John McKenny, son of James, appointed Constable.

(139) Robert McClenachan resigned as Lieutenant in Staunton Artillery and is recommended as Captain of a Company of Infantry, vice William Chambers, who has resigned. William Bowyer is recommended in McClenachan's place in Staunton Artillery.

APRIL 20, 1797.

(139) Called Court on Enos McCaleb for larceny—5 lashes.

MAY 18, 1797.

(149–159) John Guthrey, for a scurrilous libel to the Court and acknowl·edged by him, is to be put in the pillory from 11 to 12 o'clock tomorrow.

MAY 31, 1797.

(164) Called Court on Eleanor Ryan, larceny.—Sent to District Court.

JUNE 20, 1797.

(165–166) James Ross exempted from levy by reason of being disabled in one of his hands.

(166) Admn. of estate of Elizabeth Caldwell granted to Catherine Caldwell, widow of John Caldwell, who was nominated executor in will of Elizabeth.

(169) The former order for binding George Lemon to Henry Mace is rescinded, they being no inhabitants.

(169) Following to be bound: Elizabeth Israel, aged 8 years 5th February last, to George Barnhart; John Bush, aged 4 years 20th December last, to George Barnhart; Jacob Meisner, orphan, aged 2 years 3d February last, to Jacob Lessley, to learn trade of weaver.

(169) John Tate allowed £50 for inquisitions on bodies of Absalom Greer, and the other on body of Jacob Steeley.

(169) Michael Coiner's will admitted to probate, but Christian Balsley appeals to District Court.

(169) John Stephenson exempted from levy until his infirmity is removed.

JUNE 21, 1797.

(171–177) Lieutenant James Allen remonstrated to the Governor versus the recommendation to supply the vacancy occasioned by resignation of William Chambers. The recommendation was made by the Court under the impression that Allen would not accept, and they now apologize and recommend Allen instead of Robert McClenachan.

JULY 15, 1797.

(177) Called Court on William Boyle for passing counterfeit notes.— Discharged. Called Court on Beeden Beard for passing counterfeit notes.— Discharged.

OCTOBER 18, 1797.

(232) Margaret McKenny chose Robert Harris as her guardian, who qualified, with Eleanor McKenny and William Corbee, securities.

(232) William C. Bowyer removed.

(233) County levy.

(233) Alice Rhodes, widow and relict of Thomas Rhodes, deceased, late jailor, presented his account versus the Commonwealth.

NOVEMBER 7, 1797.

(234) Called Court on John Maloney for murder of —— Staley.—Guilty and sent to District Court.

NOVEMBER 21, 1797.

(234) For several days not a sufficient number of Justices, and Court adjourned.

JANUARY 16, 1798.

(241) Rev. Christian F. Sleavey authorized to celebrate marriages.

(242) County levy continued.

(242) John Dickinson to be paid £50, pension 1797.

(244) County levy: 2,957 tithables @ 33⅓ cents.

(246) Susannah Brien, widow of Edward Brien, refuses to administer, and Hugh Paul and John Fackler qualify.

(247) Elizabeth, William and James Hogshead chose Nancy Hogshead guardian. They are the orphans of Robert Hogshead.

(248) Vincent Tapp was a Sergeant-Major, and Smith Thompson a soldier in the Continental Service.

(249) Polly Stuart, orphan of John Stuart, chose George Crawford as her guardian.

(251) Elizabeth, widow of Joseph Wilson, qualifies administratrix.

(252) George Wilson is appointed guardian of John, Margaret, Mary Lessley, Oliver, Betsey, Jenny and Joseph Wilson, infants and orphans of Joseph Wilson, deceased.

FEBRUARY 21, 1798.

(254) Isham Burke, stepson to John Williams, who is apprentice to Andrew Cutler.

MARCH 14, 1798.

(265) Called Court on Daniel, a slave, for taking out of the house of Robert Hansberger, on the night of the 6th inst., a negro man slave, named Stephen, with all his clothes and the chains with which he was bound.— Discharged.

MARCH 21, 1798.

(272) Francis Haywood, stepfather of Wm. Wheeler, apprentice of Lawrence Torniper.

MAY 16, 1798.

(303) David Parry is appointed to purchase thirteen pair of leather buckets of the usual size for the use of the water engine for Staunton, in addition to the number specified in an order of March Court last.

JUNE 19, 1798.

(316) Admn. of estate of James Bell granted John Bell.

(316) John Cummins exempted from levy on account of old age and infirmity.

(317) John Holmes exempted from levy on account of old age and infirmity.

(317) Elizabeth Slater, aged 10 years 19th May last, to be bound.

(317) Christopher Basseman, son of Christopher Basseman, exempted from levy on account of infirmity.

(317) George Hutcheson appointed guardian of Eleanor McClure, an insane person.

AUGUST 21, 1798.

(339-341) John Doake qualified Major of 2d Battalion, 32d Regiment, 7th Brigade.

AUGUST 22, 1798.

(345) Third Division of the Militia.

AUGUST 23, 1798.

(347) John Woodward receives certificate that he is 21 years old, and is of honest demeanor.

AUGUST 25, 1798.

(350-352) Jacob Kinney has a like certificate.

(359) Depositions to be taken of George House and Lewis Blowin in Stokes County, North Carolina.

(359) Dedimus to be directed to Peter House, Henry House and John Conrad. Also of Mitford Stokes, of Salisbury, in said State, dedimus to Spence McAuley, Evan Alexander and John Newman. Also of Mr. Franklin, formerly a Commissioner of Army Accounts, now an inhabitant of Surry County, North Carolina. All in suit of John Johnston vs. John Miller.

SEPTEMBER 18, 1798.

(360-363) William Scott petitions for a change of road from Staunton to Brownsburg so as to pass through the streets of a town laid off by him on his own land.

SEPTEMBER 24, 1798.

(365) Called Court on Samuel Haythorn, charged with receiving stolen goods.—Guilty and sent to District Court.

OCTOBER 16, 1798.

(366) John Wayt, James Cochran, James McNutt, Jr., David Parry, James Flack, John Fackler and William Steel—qualified Justices.

(366) Edw. McFadden, orphan, chose Christian Lukenbill his guardian.

(371) James Draper, orphan of Abraham Draper, chose David Buchanan guardian. Catherine Harmon, orphan of Peter Harmon, chose John Towell her guardian.

(371) John McCutchen granted hawker's and peddler's license.

(371) Nancy O'Neal, aged 12 years last March, to be bound to John Berry.

OCTOBER 17, 1798.

(372) John Painter, orphan of John Painter, chose Michael Garber guardian.

(376) James Edwardson accepts in full satisfaction from the County £80 for deficiency in the lot sold by the County to James Hughes.

OCTOBER 18, 1798.

(379-387) William Forbes, jailor.

(387) County levy.

(387) Thomas Jones, aged 15 years in November next, to be bound to Martin Lonshbough to learn trade of cabinetmaker.

OCTOBER 22, 1798.

(388) Called Court on George Miles for horse stealing—.Guilty and sent to District Court.

NOVEMBER 22, 1798.

(400-419) Rev. Wm. King, of Episcopal Methodist Society, authorized to celebrate matrimony.

NOVEMBER 23, 1798.

Page
(420–422) Sampson Darrel, not an inhabitant.

NOVEMBER 24, 1798.

(425–430) James Holmes and Jane, his wife, late Jane Astrop, executrix of Robert Astrop, to be summoned to give counter security.

DECEMBER 18, 1798.

(436–438) Middleton Keith, heretofore bound to John Robb, to be bound to Sampson Eagan to learn trade of wagonmaker.
(438) Admn. of estate of Adam Bickle granted Mary Bickle.
(443) Margaret Hogshead, orphan of John Hogshead, over 14, chose John Hogshead her guardian.
(443) Jacob Hempt, heretofore bound to Lewis Wiseman, to be bound to Jacob Miller to learn the trade of a wagonmaker.

DECEMBER 19, 1798.

(443) County levy: 3.084 tithables @ 50 cents.
(444) List of subscribers to a fire company in Staunton recorded.
(444) Admn. of estate of William Spence granted Thomas Hogg.
(448) William Blair, tanner, a witness, and his son, William Blair.

DECEMBER 20, 1798.

(448-454) Ann Chambers, wife of William Chambers, acknowledged deed of William to Robert McDowell.

JANUARY 15, 1799.

(457) James Kennerley is appointed guardian for John Goshen.
(458) John Burk, heretofore bound to Hugh Alexander, to be bound to William Preston, of Botetourt, to learn trade of a nailer instead of a weaver.
(458) John Goshen, orphan of —— Goshen, to be bound to James Kennerley, to learn the trade of a millwright—aged 17 years in August next.
(459) John Dickinson to be paid his pension of £50 for 1798.

FEBRUARY 1, 1799.

(462) Called Court on Bob, a slave, for larceny—39 lashes.

FEBRUARY 7, 1799.

(463) Called Court on Dicey, a negro woman (the property of Hugh Campbell, of the County of Amherst, and late in the possession of Sarah McDowell, of Staunton) for murdering her child.—Discharged.

FEBRUARY 19, 1799.

(464) John Hogshead's will proved, and widow Rebecca refuses to administer. William Hogshead, the eldest son, is not an inhabitant of this State. Son, John Hogshead, qualified.

Page

(468) David Stephenson qualified Sheriff the second time.

(469) John Jackson, orphan of John Jackson, chose Alex. Reed his guardian.

(470) Charlotte Bailey, aged 10 years 24th May last, to be bound to Daniel Garber.

(470) George Crawford exempted from levy on account of age and infirmity.

FEBRUARY 20, 1799.

(470–472) Allen P*iercey* (orphan of George *Pearcy*, deceased), aged about 15 years, to be bound to David Bell, to learn trade of wheelwright. Also John *Piercey*, orphan of same, about 13 years of age, to be bound to Jacob Hanger, to learn trade of a tanner.

(472) Certified that William Sterrett has resided over one year in the County, and is a man of honesty, probity and good demeanor. Same certificate as to Thomas McClelland.

(474) Robert Douthat accepts £23, full satisfaction for deficiency in a lot sold by the County to James Huston, and by Huston's heirs to Robert.

MARCH 14, 1799.

(482) Called Court on Philip Goysel, a soldier of the United States, for stealing a hat.—Guilty and sent to District Court.

COUNTY COURT JUDGMENTS.

AUGUSTA COUNTY.

These notes are to the files of papers in the County Court marked "Judgments." These are the original papers in suits and causes that were instituted or adjudicated in this Court. They are filed in bundles, wrapped, and labeled with the term at which final judgment was entered. The references are to the bundle first and then to the style of the suit where the paper noted may be found. The letters used in designating the bundle are private marking and not a part of the official label.

Following the County Court Judgments, there are some pages of notes to the original petitions and miscellaneous papers which are filed with the original wills, settlements, &c. It is not possible to fix the date of these papers in many instances more definitely than that they were presented to the Court within the period set out on the label of the package.

COUNTY COURT JUDGMENTS.

FEBRUARY, 1745, TO MARCH, 1746.

Thomas McCune vs. Samuel Gay and Robert Turk.—Plaintiff of Salisbury Township, Lancaster County, Pa. Defendants of Augusta County. Bond dated 4th December, 1744.

John Smith vs. George Breckenridge.—Contract, 1742, by George to make 3,000 rails for John, which George did not perform.

John Coate and William King, administrators of Ann Doughaty, who died intestate and who was administratrix of Jacob Doughaty, vs. Adam Dickinson.—I, Adam Dickinson, of Hanover, in the County of Huntingdon, in New Jersey. Jacob was from Bethlehem, N. J. Bond dated 29th August, 1733. Suit brought 22d September, 1746.

James Patton vs. George Campbell.—George Campbell, blacksmith, now of Augusta County. Bond to James Patton, dated 15th August, 1746.

Rinkens vs. Cotner.—James Givens is about to leave the Colony—21st February, 1746.

APRIL AND JUNE, 1746.

Benjamin Borden vs. Samuel Davies and Edward Boyle.—Defendants of James River, Orange County. Bond 28th November, 1744.

John Trimble vs. Wm. Hartgrove.—Bond 3d February, 1738-9. Note.—Lives at ye forks of (   ) and married to ye Widow Barnet.

John Peter Sally vs. Benj. Borden and Magdalene, his wife, admx. of all and singular the goods of John McDowell, deceased.—Writ 12th February, 1745.

Jean McDowell vs. Henry Cresswell.—Petition filed February, 1745-6. Bond dated 8th November, 1744.

James Davis vs. Andrew McClure and James McClure.—Bond dated 25th August, 1743. Andrew was from Bucks County. James McClure from Augusta. James Davis of Augusta. Writ dated 25th January, 1744.

John Lewis, gent., vs. Joseph McCleland and Jane, his wife, admx. of Randall McDowell, deceased.

George Brackenridge vs. John Smith.—Petition on bond dated 10th December, 1745. Writ dated 14th February, 1745.

William Wright vs. Thomas Linville.—Writ 11th March, 1745. Thomas Linville told Robert Patterson that he had paid to William Wright a certain sum of money which was due to said Wright's father. Order by William Wright's, 10th December, 1744, to Robert Patterson to collect the account.

Young vs. Bordin.—Chancery. Writ dated 14th February, 1745-6. Robt. Young, orator. Robert Crockett purchased a tract of land from Benjamin Bordin, Sr., between James Young and Robert Young (orator) on 8th October, 1742. Orator bought Crockett's right and sues for a deed from Benjamin Bordin, Jr.

Jane Gibbons, admx. of James Gibbons, vs. David Davis.—Debt on bond dated 22d October, 1733.

John Anderson vs. Moses Thomson.—Debt on note, defendant to James Rutledge, dated 21st September, 1744.

Thomas Harrison vs. Edward McGill.—Debt. Writ dated 14th February, 1745-6.

Daniel Haldman vs. Samuel Rusk.—John Quin for plaintiff.

Burdin vs. Salley.—Petition of Benj. Borden and Magdalene, his wife, admx. of John McDowell. Writ dated 22d February, 1745-6.

Samuel Jordon vs. James Armstrong.—Samuel was merchant in Goochland 12th September, 1744.

John Carson vs. Richard Wood.—Richard Wood of Paxton. Debt on bond dated 10th November, 1738.

Caspar Wister, of Philadelphia, vs. John Mayfis, of County of Salem.—"Not found."

Andrew Reed, of Trenton, County of Hunterdon, Province of New Jersey, vs. Thomas Moffett, of Winsor, in the County of Middlesex and Province of New Jersey.—Bond dated 9th April, 1742. Writ dated 17th August, 1746.

Layman vs. Daives.—Note of Samuel Daives, dated Lancaster County, Pennsylvania, dated 10th January, 1743–4.

AUGUST, 1746.

Patrick Hays vs. Samuel Doak.—Defendant brother of John Doak. 17th April, 1746.

James Davis vs. David Morgan.—Attachment 17th July, 1746. George Breckenridge, surety.

Jacob Dye vs. Sigismund Hanley.—Attachment. Defendant from Lancaster County, Pennsylvania. Bond dated 25th April, 1745. (Hanley was a German.)

John Moffett vs. John Graham.—I, John Graham, of Nantmill, in County of Chester, Pennsylvania. Bond dated 22d September, 1743. Writ dated 11th February, 1745–6.

SEPTEMBER, 1746.

George Brackenridge vs. Robert Rennick.—Petition August, 1746.

John Hite vs. James Gill and George Forbush.—Defendants and plaintiff of Orange County. 18th August, 1743.

George Shoemaker vs. John Lewis, gent.—Plaintiff of Lower Dublin Township, Pennsylvania. February, 1745–6.

Calvert Anderson vs. Samuel O'dale (Odell).—Debt. 23d June, 1746. Writ dated 12th February, 1745–6. Letter dated 16th May, 1744, from defendant to plaintiff.

William Lewis vs. James Brackenridge.—Attachment. 19th June, 1746. Defendant absconded. Attachment levied in hands of Robert McClenachan and George Brackenridge. Note of James Breckenridge to Wm. Lewis, £3, 2, 8. Dated 23d December, 1744.

Elias Colting vs. John Meneers.—I, John Meneers, contranser (?) in Salem County, Province West New Jersey. Bond dated 3d November, 1743. "Not found." Lives at the head of the narrow passage at the North Mtn.

Cornelius Tebout vs. Jacob Dye.—Debt on note dated 30th October, 1734, in New York. Witnessed by Raphael Goelet and Richard Green.

George Brackenridge vs. John Preston.—Debt on note. Dated 7th August, 1744.

Leonard Lutses, of Lancaster County, Pa., vs. John Martin Levinstone, of Lancaster County, Pa.—Debt-Bond. Dated 20th January, 1743–4.

Casper Wister vs. John Mayfis.—Plaintiff from Philadelphia. Defendant from County of Salem. Wheelwright. Defendant lives North River Gap.

Jost Hite vs. Thomas Linville.—Breach contract. Agreement for rental of a mill by plaintiff to defendant. Dated 23d March, 1742–3.

Edward Herndon vs. John Pickens.—"Major" John Pickens's note. Dated 27th July, 1744. George Taylor, witness.

NOVEMBER, 1746.

Beverley vs. McCorkle.—John Robinson, of King and Queen. Ejectment. Copy of patent for 118,491 acres on Shenando River to William Beverley, gent.; Sir John Randolph, knight, and John Robinson, gent. Sir John Randolph, of City of Williamsburg; Richard Randolph, of Henrico. Recorded in General Court 15th October, 1736. Dated 6th September, 1736. Quit claim to Beverley 17th September, 1736. Letter from Wm. Beverley to Capt. Wm. Russell, dated "Octonia, Sept. 18, 1746," empowering Russell, his attorney, to appeal in all cases.

Tunis Hood, Defendant, vs. Adam Dickinson, Plaintiff.—Plaintiff from Prince George County, Maryland. Blacksmith. Defendant of Orange County. Bond dated 7th August, 1742.

Capt. Thomas Cresap vs. John Johnston, Sr.—Defendant from Prince George County, Maryland. Bond dated 14th January, 1743–4.

Benjamin Borden vs. John Smith.—Benjamin and Magdalene, his wife, executrix of John McDowell. Writ dated 26th July, 1746.

JUNE, 1747.

James McClelhill vs. Andrew McClure.—James and Jane, his wife, admrs. of Randal McDonnald. Writ dated 25th February, 1745.

Charles Clendenning vs. Thomas Anderson.—Attachment dated 14th February, 1745, levied in hands of John Maxwell—40 sh., paper money, due defendant from estate of James Brackenridge, late of this County, and I am informed of a certain tract of land joining the plantation of Alexr. Brackenridge, deceased, belonging to said James Brackenridge.

Pendleton vs. Linville.—Thomas Linville not to be found in my bailiwick. March, 1746.

Benjamin Borden vs. John Bombgardner.—Benjamin and Magdalene, his wife, late Magdalene McDowell, against J. B., on bond dated 6th August, 1743, to Magdalene while she was sole and unmarried.

Michael Lawler vs. James Armstrong and Thomas Letch.—Michael and Mary, his wife, lately called Mary Bloodworth. Debt on bond dated 22d March, 1743, to Mary while she was sole and unmarried. Writ issued 1746, 26th November. Receipt signed Mary Bloodworth, July 29, 1744. Receipt signed Michael Lawler, 23d May, 1745.

AUGUST, 1747 (A).

Thomas Gardner vs. William Anderson.—Chancery. *Supra,* 10th January, 1745–6.

Dickinson vs. Hunt.—Debt. Writ dated 22d February, 1746. Agreement, 22d April, 1743, between Thomas Lindley, of Pennsylvania, and Adam Dickenson, of Province of Maryland: Plaintiff agrees to secure a patent for 1,000 acres in Clover Creek, otherwise ye Cow Pasture, and settle two tenants thereon, and then convey to Lindley. Bond of Adam Dickinson, of Pennsylvania, and County of Lancaster, blacksmith, to Thomas Lindley, of same place, dated 1st January, 1741-2. This bond assigned, 19th February, 1745-6, by Hannah Lindley to Roger Hunt, of the County of Chester. Hannah was sole administrator of Thomas Lindley, deceased.

August, 1747 (B).

John Pickens vs. John Graham.—In June, 1747, and several years before, John Pickens was a trader and cattle dealer. Slander. Defendant said plaintiff ran away from Paxton Township, Pennsylvania (where plaintiff formerly lived), for debt.

Capt. Thomas Cresap vs. Johannis Cox.—Debt. Writ 23d ——, 1747. "He lives on Smith's Creek, near Lohe's (?) plantation. Ask Val. Sevior, he is his brother-in-law." "Not found in my bailiwick; he is run away. By me, John Edwards."

Brown vs. Smith.—Capt. James Montgomery, gent., living at the Cutappa prior to 15th July, 1747.

Philip Jones vs. Benj. Hardin.—Debt. Writ 22d June, 1747. "He lives at South Branch." "Not found in my bailiwick. He lives on James River." By me, John Edwards.

September, 1747.

Valentine Sevier vs. Thomas Linwell.—Attachment, 6th March, 1746-7.

Robert McMahon complains that Jean Robinson, of the Province of Pennsylvania, is indebted to him 15s. August, 1747.

George Sellers, of Frederick County, vs. Abraham Miller and Christian Miller, of Frederick County. Bond dated 8th October, 1745. "The defendants live near the narrow passage, by Falkenborgh's old place."

David Stewart vs. William Harrison.—Attachment, 2d September, 1747. Defendant "is privately removing his effects out of the County."

Ralph Laverty vs. James Waddell and John Lewis.—Chancery writ, 15th July, 1747. James Waddell, late of Augusta. Laverty became surety for Waddell to James Scott, but shortly afterwards Waddell ran away to some part of Pennsylvania and has never returned, being gone above —— years. In 1743 Waddell bought 224 acres from John Lewis.

David Hays vs. John McMaster. Bond of defendant to William Ree, 9th March, 1742. "And if not liking and recovering the tract of land in the Irish Settlement in Virginia the above note is void." Writ dated 24th August, 1747.

Jacob Dyer vs. Sigismund Henley.—Debt. Writ dated 22d May, 1746. Defendant of Lancaster County, Pennsylvania. Bond dated 25th April, 1745. Bail bond signed John Sigismund Henley.

William Henderson vs. Andrew McCord.—Andrew McCord, of Beverley Manor, County of Orange. Bond dated 1st June, 1742.

John Carmichael vs. John Wilson.—Debt on bond by defendant to Mary Anne Campbell, dated 25th March, 1746. Witnesses, John Hays and Wm. Adair. Assigned to plaintiff last day of March, 1747. Morgan Camell.

Alexander Gibboney vs. Thomas Carson.—Debt on bond dated 28th September, 1744. Defendant of Borough of Lancaster, County of Lancaster, Province Pennsylvania. Writ dated 24th August, 1747.

Andrew McCoole vs. James Steward.—Attachment 22d August, 1747. "Defendant is going to remove his effects out of the County." "Andrew McCoole, Priest of the World." Defendant has no effects in County.

Robert Davis *et als.* vs. John Finla and Alex. Stewart.—Order to summon dated 19th August, 1747.

John Harrison vs. James Lidderdale.—Debt. Writ 23d June, 1747. Defendant lives on James River.

NOVEMBER, 1747 (A).

James Patton, John Finley, John Christian, James Alexander and William Wright vs. Robert Turk.—Debt for years 1741, 1742, 1743, 1744, 1745, 1746. Asst. to pay plaintiffs as collectors for Mr. Craig's salary at £1 per year. A copy of the mutual obligations between the Congregation and their Commissioners:

Know all men by these presents yt we ye undernamed subscribers do nominate, appoint, and constitute our trusty and well beloved friends, James Patton, John Finley, George Hutcheson, John Christian, Alexander Breckenridge, to manage our public affairs, to choose and purchase a piece of ground and to build our meeting house upon it, to collect our minister's salary, and to pay off all charges relating to said affair, to get pay of the people in proportion for this end, to place seats in said meeting house, which we do hereby promise to reimburse them, they always giving us a month': warning by an advertisement on the meeting house door. A majority of the above five person, providing all be apprised of their meeting, their acting shall stand, and these persons above named shall be accountable to the minister and session twice every year for all their proceeds relating to the whole affair, to which we subscribe our names in the presence of the Rev. Mr. John Craig, 14th August, 1741.

We, whose names are hereunto subscribed, being appointed Commissioners to choose and buy a plot of ground to build a meeting house upon it and to place seats and collect the minister's salary and to levy the charges from the sundry persons in said Congregation: We do hereby promise and oblige ourselves to pay our proportion of said charges and to lay before the minister and session a true state of all our accounts, debtor and creditor, as also of all our transactions anyway relating to the above premises, twice every year, and to give the Congregation public notice one month before any demand be made on them for their proportion, appointing them time and place, where and when and to whom of said Commissioners they shall pay the money whose receipts shall be their sufficient discharge, as witness our hands before ye Rev. Mr. John Craig, 14th August, 1741.

This instrument by consent to be lodged in the hands of our minister. *Copia vera.* For the use of Capt. James Patton, Commissioner.

Rebecca Edgill, administratrix of Simon Edgill, deceased, vs. John Moffett and Robert Christian.—Note dated 22d July, 1735. Writ dated 19th February, 1747.

Mary Yates, administratrix of Abraham Yates (Frederick County), who died intestate, vs. John Smith.—Bond dated 23d June, 1743.

Robert McCoy, Jost Hite, Robert Green, Robert Green, being executor of William Duff, deceased, vs. William Linwell, Thomas Linwell and Morgan Bryan.—Debt on bond dated 18th June, 1746. Writ dated 24th August, 1747. Returned not found as to W. and T. Linwell.

FEBRUARY AND MARCH, 1748.

Rebecca Edgill vs. James Alexander, Samuel Crafford and William Crafford.—Debt on bond dated 20th December, 1733. Writ dated 19th September, 1747. Defendants of Octorarah, Drummore Township, in Lancaster County, Pennsylvania. Administration of estate of Simon Edgill granted to plaintiff, in —— County, Pennsylvania.

Zebbulon Harrison vs. John Dobbiken.—Debt. Writ 24th August, 1747. Account dated 1746.

David Evans vs. George Jourdan.—Attachment 18th June, 1746. George has removed. On November 20, 1747, ordered to be served in hands of Fred Carlock, on South Branch.

George Brackenridge vs. John Preston.—Debt. Writ 24th August, 1747. March, 1748, abates by death of plaintiff.

Robert Bratton and Ann, his wife, late Ann Dunlap, vs. James McDowell and Francis McCowing.—Debt on bond to Ann Dunlap, 18th June, 1745, while she was single. Ann Dunlap, of the Calf Pasture. Writ dated 23d June, 1747.

Thomas Harrison vs. Andrew Mitchell.—Case. Writ dated 18th August, 1748.

Campbell vs. Campbell.—Bond of Patrick Campbell to Maryan (Marion) Campbell, widow and relict of William Campbell, dated 1745. Assignment on back to John Campbell, dated 1747, and signed Maryan Buchanan.

MAY, 1748.

Joseph Walker vs. Abraham Clements.—Attachment, 8th April, 1748. Defendant about to remove.

William Caldwell vs. Francis Beatey.—Debt on note dated July, 1737. Affidavit by John Allison, in Lancaster County, Pennsylvania, dated 14th April, 1742.

Charles Milliken vs. John Mills.—Debt. Writ 20th February, 1747. Defendant lives on Roanoke.

Philip Jones vs. Benjamin Hardin.—Petition 20th February, 1747. Defendant has removed to South Carolina.

Robert Brown vs. Eastham Franklin.—Attachment 16th March, 1747.

I, the subscribere, is intendes to go to North Crittan (?), and I desires all persons that are indebted to me for goods to come and pay of their accounts to Margaret Fraser, in this County of Augusta, or to me at my dwelling house in Albemarle County, where I dwell, or they must expect to be troubled, &c. This is the first time.   JOHN BRUCE.
6th July, 1747.

Richard Morley vs. Johannes Bender.—Pet. His right name is Painter.

John Patterson vs. Benjamin Borden.—Chancery. When Benjamin came to Augusta he lodged at plaintiff's house and used it as a place to see persons wanting land. John was also his agent.

Robert Cunningham vs. John Beety.—Trespass A (S) and B. Writ. 1747. Eleanor Rutledge not summoned as a witness because she was where the smallpox was.

Benjamin Borden vs. John Shields.—Debt. Writ 1747. Bond 25th December, 1745. Defendant of Chester County, Pennsylvania. Returned "not found."

Benjamin Borden vs. Bryan McDonnell.—Debt on bond date 27th February, 1744-5. Writ 1747. Defendant of New Castle County, Pennsylvania.

Abraham Drake, administrator of Abraham Drake, Jr., deceased, vs. Zachary McCoy.

Cornelius Murley vs. James Boggs and Eliza, his wife, and Henry Boggs, his son.—As. and Bat.

MAY AND AUGUST, 1748.

Samuel Monsey vs. Joseph Harrison.—Writ 19th February, 1747.

John Preston vs. William Miller.—Attachment, 20th November, 1747.

Zachary McCoy vs. Abraham Drake, administrator of Abraham Drake, Jr.—Attachment, 14th September, 1747.

Gabriel Jones vs. David Evans.—Recites statute against removing without notice, enacted at Williamsburg, 1661. David Evans transported Richard Crunk from his plantation in Frederick County to Craig's Creek in Augusta on the road to Carolina, where the said Richard Cronk is since gone.

George Robinson and Simon Akers vs. Joseph Love, of Roanoke, in ye County of Orange, otherwise called Augusta.—Bond dated 13th December, 1744.

William Chapman vs. Terrence McMullin.—Debt. Writ 19th February, 1747. "He lives on South Branch." "He is gone to Carolina."

John McCreery, assignee of Alexander Lewis, vs. Thomas McCullogh.—Bond to Alexander Lewis, 22d November, 1745. Witnesses, John Lewis and Andrew Lewis.

Patrick Hays vs. Charles Milliken.—Debt on bond dated 4th June, 1745. Writ 19th February, 1747. Defendant of Township of Deny, County of Lancaster, Pennsylvania.

George Bigham vs. James Stewart.—Debt on Acct., 1747. Executed.

John Patterson vs. William Hunter and Benjamin Borden.—In 1740 plaintiff bought and settled on land from William Hunter in Borden's Survey, but got no deed. He expected to settle on the land a son-in-law whom he was expecting from Pennsylvania. Sues for a deed. May, 1748, abates by death of plaintiff.

William Mark vs. Abraham Potter.—Account for one saddle. Writ 21st April, 1748. Defendant lived near mouth of Linvill's Creek. Mark's wife was sister of Samuel Stuart (?).

Abraham Oldhouse vs. Jacob Miller.—Bond by plaintiff and defendant to John Miller, 4th February, 1746. Both of Township of Canistoga, Lancaster County, Pennsylvania.

Renich vs. Holmes.—James Murray recovered vs. Thomas Renich in the Common Pleas at Lancaster, Pennsylvania, in 1744. Judgment on a note by Thomas Renick, John Holmes and others, to James Murray, dated 31st December, 1741.

FEBRUARY, 1749 (A).

Mary Dyer vs. Hugh Douglas.—Chancery. Write dated 26th August, 1749. Mary, administratrix of her husband, Peter Dyer, oratrix. In 1746 Peter agreed to buy a plantation from defendant on Stinson's Mill Creek. Peter died intestate, leaving no child.

John Paul Vought, orator, vs. David Logan, defendant.—Chancery. Writ dated 22d August, 1748. In 1744 orator purchased 400 acres of David Logan on North River near John Bumgardner. The land was afterwards surveyed for Andrew Fought.

Francis Gardiner vs. Alexander Gibson.—Slander. Daniel McAnare was a miller.

Nicholas Gibbon vs. John Scull.—Debt for £30 "proclamation money" on bond dated 1st May, 1746. I, John Scull, of County of Gloucester and Province of New Jersey, to Nicholas Gibbon, of County Salem, New Jersey. "Defendant is a young man from Salem in ye Jersey." Writ dated 18th December, 1747.

Adam Andres, of Philadelphia, vs. Jost Dubs.—Debt on bond dated 9th March, 1746. Jost Dubs, of Frederick County, Virginia, trader.

Andrew Campbell vs. John Walker.—Being four of same name, I knew not which to execute process on, Robert Breckinridge.

Charles Dalhouse vs. Joseph Tees.—Slander. Verdict for defendant.

Edward Innes vs. David Stevenson.—A and B. 28th July, 1748.

James Armstrong vs. Robert Young and Agnes, his wife.—A and B by Agnes on Catherine Coleman, a servant of plaintiff. Verdict for defendant.

John Hind vs. John Kerr.—In consideration of marriage by plaintiff of Jane, daughter of defendant, defendant promised plaintiff land. Married 1749. Writ dated 4th December, 1749. Defendant refused to make conveyance and suit.

James Patton vs. Alexander Douglass (stone mason).—Contract to build a house for plaintiff with dimensions and plans. 25th October, 1746.

John Stephen vs. Robert Gamble.—Debt on bond dated 20th November, 1746. "I, Robert Gamble, of County of Bucks, in Pennsylvania." Robert (mark x) Gamble. Witnesses, James Coulter, James Halliday.

Hugh Donally vs. William Price.—Debt on bond dated 22d September, 1746. William Price, of Peneader Hundred, County of New Castle, Pennsylvania, weaver, to Hugh Donally, of same place, cordwainer.

FEBRUARY, 1749 (B).

Moses McClure vs. John Wilson, the distiller.—Bond dated 4th February, 1748-9.

Charles Millikin vs. Peter Kinder.—February, 1749. Abates by death of defendant.

Scott vs. Repentance Townsend and Mary, his wife.—May, 1749.

Robert Patterson vs. John Downey.—Petition 26th August, 1749. Defendant lives on New River.

James Porteus vs. George K (?) Gibbin.—Petition 26th August, 1749. Defendant lives on South Branch with Rutledge.

Order to summon Justices to qualify, 2d December, 1749. Thomas Steward summoned.

Russell vs. Porteus.—Dr. Hawson. 1749.

John Keney vs. James Rutledge.—Debt. Writ 26th August, 1749. Defendant lives at South Branch.

FEBRUARY AND MAY, 1747.

Adam Breckenridge vs. Robert McClenachan.—As. and Bat. in 1747. Writ dated 18th January, 1747-8, not executed by order of plaintiff.

John Tillory vs. James Anderson and Elizabeth, his wife, late Elizabeth Skillern.—Debt on note given by Elizabeth when single. Writ dated 28th January, 1747. Note dated 27th November, 1747.

Edward Franklyne vs. Robert Turk.—Debt on account. Set off account vs. Eastham Franklyne to feeding Rubin Franklyn's horse one month on account of Eastham Franklyn. Account dated May 17, 1746. To my son's work for you (carpentering). (Signed) Edward Franklin. Agreement for work dated 17th December, 1745-6.

George Brackenridge vs. John Holmes.—Debt. Writ 18th June, 1746. Bond dated 17th April, 1746.

Thomson vs. James Fowler.—Attachment, 24th February, 1746-7. Martha Thomson, wife of Mathew Thomson.

MAY, 1749.

James Given vs. John Stewart, taylor, of Staunton, and Thomas Fulton.— February, 1763. Bill filed. Writ 4th January, 1763. Attachment for answer 18th March, 1763. In December, last past, Stewart followed orator into the store of Felix Gilbert and importuned him to stay in town that day, and plied him with liquor until he was very drunk, when Stewart persuaded him to sell him a slave. Suit to set aside the sale.

Baird vs. John Thomas and John Dills.—Defendant lives on Roanoke, 1748.

Jacob Marlin vs. Samuel Finley.—Defendant lives at Jackson's, on River James. 20th February, 1748.

Hugh Young vs. Erwaker Johnston.—Defendant lives on Jackson's River. April, 1749.

Robinson vs. Hugh Mathards, tanner.—Petition on account. Dated, 1732, from Sussex County, on Delaware.

Samuel Hill and Ann, his wife, vs. Samuel Harrison.—T. C. Writ dated 20th March, 1748. Executed.

Philip Jones vs. Benjamin Hardin.—On account. Dated 1743. Defendant lives in Cowpasture.

AUGUST, 1749 (A).

John Graham vs. Henry Hardin.—Petition. Defendant lives in lower end of County. 2d May, 1748. "Not in my bailiwick."

John Harrison vs. James Louderdale (Smith).—Debt on bond dated 2d February, 1744-45. Writ dated 1747, 20th February.

John McPharrin vs. Benjamin Borden.—Chancery. Writ dated 17th April, 1746. In 1740, orator purchased 31 acres of Borden through John Patterson, Borden's agent, which Borden afterwards affirmed.

James Patton, *qui tam,* vs. Rev. John Hindman.—In 1747 defendant married James Anderson (alias Ute Perkins) and Elizabeth Skeleron, widow and relict of William Skeleron, late of Augusta, without license.

William Armstrong vs. William Lusk.—Debt. Bond dated 24th November, 1744. "I, William Lusk, of Lancaster County, Pennsylvania, Paxton Township."

John Hill, by William Hill, father and next friend, vs. William Case.—Slander.

Same vs. Thomas Haldman.—Defendant lives in a branch of Haldman's Creek.

AUGUST, 1749 (B).

The King vs. Henry Murray.—Assault and battery on Joseph McClenen. Errors assigned ———. Presentment for beating Joseph in the meeting house yard, whereas no yard is enclosed, and several public roads are adjacent thereto, so that the assaulting might be in a public road. That the presentment is for assaulting and beating at the time of the burial service, whereas the burial service amongst Presbyterian Dissenters is no act of religious worship. Was indicted by name of Henry Morrow, whereas his name was Murray.

NOVEMBER, 1749.

David Moore vs. Benjamin Borden.—Bill filed September, 1757, by David to compel conveyance by Benjamin, Jr., of land bought by David of his father, Benjamin, Sr.

William Hughs vs. William Miller.—Abates by death of plaintiff, 1749.

MAY, 1750 (A).

Brownlee vs. Smith.—Bond of John Smith, of Orange County, Virginia, to Alexander Brownlee, of Donigall, in the County of Lancaster, in Pennsylvania, dated 9th June, 1739. Conditioned that Smith shall make a title to Brownlee for 400 acres lying at head of the great Poplar Bottom, on the North River, at the lower end of the Great Stony Lick, before 1st July, 1740. Suit brought 25th February, 1746, by Alexander Brownlee, of Donigall, &c.

Daniel Harrison bid on the building of the Court House and says his was the lowest, but the Commissioners refused to give the contract to him, and he petitions the Court to know the reasons why.

James McDowell vs. Benjamin Borden.—Slander. Writ 25th August, 1747. James charges that Benjamin said on 17th August, 1747: "Thou art a rogue and a murdering villain, and I can prove it." And also: "He is a murderer, and brought the Indians upon the settlement (innuendo—the people settled in this County, a great number whereof being his Majesty's liege subjects were slain by the Indians in a difference that happened between his Majesty's subjects inhabiting the said County and the said Indians, some time in the year 1742)." Verdict for defendant.

Robert Foyle vs. John Erwin.—Slander. Charged that plaintiff had spoken treasonable words. Robert and Elizabeth, his wife, had resided in New Castle County, Pennsylvania, 8 years before 27th May, 1745. One of the Justices certifies that they were good citizens. Many of the citizens certify that they were a common disturber of the peace, both amongst Clergy and Commonwealth. Verdict for plaintiff. 1 penny.

MAY, 1750 (B).

Thomas Nevitt vs. Edmiston and wife.—Petition. George Heas (Hays) made note to plaintiff 12th June, 1745, and died, leaving widow, Sarah, who married James Edmiston. Writ dated 25th May, 1749. Thomas Nevitt was a Quaker from Lancaster County, Pennsylvania.

James Greenlee and Mary, his wife, vs. John Stevenson and Mary, his wife.—Slander.

George Brackenridge vs. Fergus Ray.—Debt on account, 1744. Defendant, long before 1744 and since, has lived in Goochland, and plaintiff sued defendant in Albemarle and recovered.

Isaac Anderson vs. Benjamin Borden.—Chancery. Writ dated 25th August, 1746. In 1741, orator bought land of Benjamin Borden, Sr., and now sues for title.

FEBRUARY, 1750.

Andrew Moor vs. Benjamin Borden.—Chancery. Writ dated 22d August, 1748. In 1738, after several conferences with John McDowell, gent., late of this County, deceased, John sold orator 700 acres in Borden's tract, but Benjamin Borden afterwards surveyed it to William Evans and George Henderson. John McDowell died 1742 intestate and Magdalene McDowell, his widow, became administratrix, and sometime afterwards intermarried with Benjamin Borden, Jr. John McDowell was agent for Benjamin Borden, Sr. Answer states that John McDowell bought 1,000 acres of Benjamin Borden and died intestate, leaving heirs.

James Bayard vs. Alexander Glaspy.—Alexander from Cecil County, Maryland. 2d January, 1741–2.

Thomas Campbell vs. Joseph Love.—Thomas was living in Philadelphia. 24th October, 1749.

Capt. Thomas Cresap vs. Humberstone Lyon.—Defendant from Prince George County, Maryland. 1st April, 1743.

Stephen Ruddle vs. Daniel Bulgier.—Daniel married Sarah James.

Agnes Reid vs. John Trimble.—John Scott, aged above 40 years, and Robert Reed, aged about 50 years. September 25, 1748.

NOVEMBER, 1750 (A).

John Theobald End vs. Jacob Miller.—I, Jacob Miller, of Conastogoe Township, Lancaster County, Pennsylvania, 6th December, 1745. Writ dated 5th September, 1750.

NOVEMBER, 1750 (B).

Edward Hall vs. Jacob Patton.—Petition on account. Writ dated September, 1750.

Peter Wallace, now in Virginia, vs. John Kyle.—Petition on account dated 1738. From Lancaster County, Pennsylvania. Writ dated 5th September, 1750.

Andrew Campbell vs. John Walker.—Debt. Writ dated 6th March, 1749. On judgment obtained in Frederick County, in 1743, on a note dated 1738.

John Foutch vs. John and Daniel Maggit.—Chancery. Writ dated 9th February, 1749. In 1745 or 6, plaintiff bought 300 acres on South side Shenando from defendants, and now sues for title deed.

Thomas Harrison vs. John Craig.—Debt on note dated 12th September, 1749.

AUGUST, 1750 (A).

William Mach vs. Samuel Stuart.—(Did William marry Stuart's sister? See *Supra*.)

AUGUST, 1750 (B).

Walter Denning vs. John Walker, Sr.—Debt. Writ 26th August, 1749. Defendant lives at South Branch.

AUGUST, 1750 (C).

Lawrence Stevens vs. James Gordon.—I, James Gordon, of Township of Gwyneed, County of Philadelphia, Pennsylvania. Debt on bond dated 20th April, 1748. Writ dated 6th March, 1749. Bail bond dated August, 1750

James Rutledge vs. John Storey (Thos. Storey, administrator of John).— Debt on account dated 1740. To 7 large steers sold John Storey in Carolina. Writ dated 20th April, 1747.

Thomas Stuart vs. John Oliphant.—Writ 22d March, 1748.

Joseph Culton vs. Robert Orr.—Writ dated 6th March, 1749. "Robert Orr in Borden's Land and in Augusta County, Virginia, Cooper." Bond 28th August, 1747.

John McKown vs. Philip Chittim and Samuel Chew.—Contract to build house for plaintiff with dimensions and descriptions. 18th May, 1748.

Samuel Smith vs. Beaty.—Mr. Michael Woods, formerly of Paxtunk, Pennsylvania. Account dated 1733. Thomas Renich, on 1st September, 1750, deposed: About 8 years ago, at his own house, he saw and spoke with said Smith and Robert Buchanan, the then Sheriff of Lancaster County. He heard Smith (then merchant at Connoy) say, &c., several accounts: Smith vs. James Cathey, 1737; Smith vs. Adam Thomson, 1736-7-8; Smith vs. William Robinson, 1739; Smith vs. Richard Woods, 1738; Smith vs. Mrs. Margaret McDowell, 1737; Smith vs. Mrs. Mary McDowell, 1737; Smith vs. Michael Woods, 1738-9; Smith vs. John Maxwell; Smith vs. Samuel Woods, 1734-5-8; Smith vs. Francis Beaty, 1735-6; Smith vs. John Christian, 1737; Smith vs. Robert Christian, 1733-4-5-6; Smith vs. Randell McDaniel; Smith vs. William Hutchinson; Smith vs. George Hutchinson. All sworn to by Samuel Smith, late of County of Lancaster, before a Justice, in Philadelphia, 13th October, 1743.

FEBRUARY, 1750 (B).

John Mathews, Jr., vs. James Huston.—Bond dated 30th May, 1749. Witness, John Mathews, Sr.

304

John Saller vs. Charles Hays.—Saller lives on Roanoke. 1749, August.

Loden vs. John Pickens.—May Court, 1750. Sheriff having returned, John not found.

Joseph Carroll, assignee of William Tuft, vs. James Bredin and David Dunbar.—Both defendants from Prince William County. Debt on bond dated 8th June, 1741. Writ dated 3d September, 1750. Returned, "Dunbar gone to Carolina, Bredin dead."

John Wallace vs. John Craig and Isabella Helena, his wife.—Slander. John was unmarried 8th March, 1750.

John Loden (Logan?) vs. George Blane.

Edward Hall vs. Jacob Patton.—Writ 3d December, 1750.

John Downing vs. Benjamin Borden.—Chancery. Writ 17 March, 1747. In 1743, plaintiff purchased of Benjamin Borden, Sr., through John Patterson, his agent, 300 acres on South side Galway's Creek, joining Galway and George Moffett. Suit for title.

NOVEMBER, 1751.

Willson vs. Patterson's administrator.—Deed and letter.

Glisterpipe vs. Glisterpipe, alias, Irish Doctor William Lynn of Fredericksburg, vs. Irish Doctor John Lynn, of Augusta.—Now here is Potts ye peddlars. Irish upon Irish.

JUDGMENTS AT RULES.

1751.

Bell vs. Borden's executor.—James Bell (one entry for himself and one for John Mulholland, his servant) prior to 1738, and on February 21, 1738, Alex. Breckinridge, George, James, Robert and Adam Breckenridge, John Moore, Quantin Moore, George Henderson, Thomas Armstrong, John Bell, John Walters, William McCanless, Robert Poage, Seth Poage, Daniel McAnaire and John Grove entered each 100 acres with Benjamin Borden, but got no deed. Suit by James Bell to get deed. Benjamin Borden, Jr., charges in answer that James Bell caused a servant wench of his to be dressed in man's clothes and made an entry in her name as a man, and also caused another woman, the wife of William McKenless, to appear in her proper person on a different part of land as the wife of another settler and thereby obtained another entry.

Edmon vs. Borden.—James Robison (Robinson), aged 68 years, July 3d, 1750. Jennet Robison (Robinson), aged 38 years July 3d, 1750.

Cravens vs. Fowler.—In 1750, Elisha Fowler was living in Carolina.

AUGUST, 1752.

Paul vs. Borden.—John McDowell died intestate, leaving Samuel McDowell, his eldest son and heir, and then Magdalen married Benjamin Borden, Jr.

Harrison vs. O'Neal.—Robert Harrison, infant, by Daniel Harrison, his father and next friend.

JUDGMENTS.

AUGUST, 1751.

Downs vs. Crawford.—Patrick Crawford was a horse trader.

COUNTY COURT JUDGMENTS.

AUGUST, 1751.

Heede vs. Phillips.—Stephen Phillips, Jr., came from New Brunswick, County Middlesex, Province East New Jersey.

Westfall vs. Richardson.—In 1750, Daniel Richardson piloted and transported Adam Breckenridge out of this Colony to Carolina, where Adam now is against statute. Adam was indebted to plaintiff..

West vs. Walling.—William Wallen had moved from Augusta to Carolina in 1751.

JUNE, 1752.

Montgomery vs. Cochran.—Peter Cochran (Coughan), late of Lancaster County, Pennsylvania, but now (1751) residing in Colony of Virginia.

NOVEMBER, 1752.

Bell vs. Callison.—James Bell vs. James Callison (otherwise lately called James Callison in the settlement Albemarle County, Virginia).

AUGUST, 1752.

Purvaiance vs. Strother, administrator of Rutledge.—William Purvaiance, of the Township of Paxton, County of Lancaster, Province of Pennsylvania. Bond to him by James Rutledge.

Dickinson vs. Lewis.—George Lewis, of Township of Cennery, and County of Lancaster, Pennsylvania. Yeoman bond to Nicholas Roberts, of Township of Coventry, and County Chester, Pennsylvania, 1742.

Breckenridge vs. Trimble.—Robert Breckenridge and Mary, his wife, late Mary Poake.

Dunning vs. Strother, administrator of Rutledge.—James Rutledge, of Lancaster, Pennsylvania, and Robert Dunning, of Ponsborough, in Lancaster County, Pennsylvania. Bond to Samuel Blanton, 1741.

Grub vs. Parker, administrator of Rutledge.—Benjamin Grub and Hannah, his wife (late Hannah Humphreys).

AUGUST AND PART NOVEMBER, 1752.

Moore *et ux.* vs. Mitchell *et ux.*—David Moore and Mary, his wife, vs. William Mitchell and Margaret, his wife. Slander. Filed December, 1749.

Draper vs. Connolly and Breckinridge.—Eleanor Draper complains of John Collony, otherwise John Connolly, and George Breckinridge, administrator of James Connolly (or Collony). Bond dated 1749.

Wright vs. Linn.—Dr. John Linn had left the County, 1752.

Ritchie vs. McClure.—Andrew McClure, obliger, to John Patton, obligee. 4th July, 1752.

JUNE, 1752.

Allen vs. Denham.—Daniel Allen, late of County of Bucks, Pennsylvania, was brought to the County by Joseph Denham as an apprentice on the plantation.

Westfall vs. Richardson.—John Story and John Rutledge, of the County of Chester, Pennsylvania, traders, obligors, to William Blyth, of Lancaster County, Pennsylvania, obligees, dated 1742. John Patton a witness. Rutledge "not found" in 1750.

Woodley vs. Lebo (Leyborn?) (Leborn?).—John Leebow, of County of Philadelphia, Pennsylvania. Yeoman. Bill of sale to Jacob Woodley, of Augusta County, dated 1747.

Devitt vs. Murley.—Charles Devitt married Jane Evans, grand-daughter of Cornelius Morley, in July, 1752, according to the ecclesiastical rights of Episcopal Church.

Griffiths vs. Job.—John Griffiths brings suit against Elisha Job, charging that Job assaulted John's son, Edward Griffiths, an infant, in 1750.

Fulton vs. Pickens.—John Pickens, of Augusta County, obligor to James Fulton. Dated 1746.

NOVEMBER, 1752.

Campbell vs. Campbell.—Moses Campbell, of Augusta County, obligor to Daniel and Alexander Campbell (of King George?), gone to Carolina in 1752 (he lived on South River). Not found in 1751 and 1750.

MARCH AND PART OF MAY, 1753.

Robinson vs. Patton.—John Patton's estate attached, September, 1752.

Robinson vs. Hugart.—Hugart's bond to John Robinson, Esq., of King and Queen, and John Lewis, dated 1750. Several suits, probably for land, against many different people.

MAY, 1753.

Bell's executor vs. Benjamin Borden.—Copy of bond of Benjamin Borden to Alexander Breckinridge, George, James, Robert and Adam Breckinridge, John Moore, Quantin Moore, George Henderson, James Bell, Thomas Armstrong, John Mulholan, John Bell, John Walters, William McCanless, Robert Poage, Seth Poage, Daniel McAneer, John Gwinn. *Condition*, that if Benjamin Borden will give each 100 acres where they have already chosen and entered with John McDowell, and shall build and improve on said 100 acres by 1st April next. Witnessed by John McDowell. Dated 21st February, 1738-9.

Michael and Augustine Price vs. Lorton and Patton.—In July, 1748, the Prices agreed with Israel Lorton to purchase from Lorton, land on New River. Lorton had bought 3 tracts from James Patton, 1, containing 400 acres, at mouth of Jones (Toms) Creek, where Lorton had entered and improved, called Lorton's First Improvement; 2d, 400 acres at Horse Shoe Bottom, called Lorton's Second Improvement; 3d, 400 acres at Beaver

Dam. Prices bought 1st and 2d. Bill filed, 1751. Tract No. 1 is in possession of Michael Price and Philip Horloes; No. 2 is in possession of Augustine Price and his brothers, Daniel and Henry Price. Amended bill filed, but Israel Lorton died, and bill for revivor. Jacob Lorton and Jacob Harman were Lorton's administrators.

Robert Robinson vs. James and John Shields.—In 1746, James Shields sold to William Snodon a tract of land in Borden's Grant, and Snodon sold to Robert Robinson, but no deed made (1748). In April, 1749, James Shields died intestate, leaving his son and heir-at-law, John Shields, an infant. Answer by John Shields, guardian of John Shields, infant. Sheriff returns (1752) that John Shields, infant, lives in Albemarle.

Joseph Mays vs. John Lewis.—In 1746, Mays bought 500 acres of Lewis in Cowpasture, and on Jackson's River, latter adjoining William Wilson, surveyor, was James Trimble, alias Turnbull.

Square and Compass vs. Pill and Bolus.—(Really Edward Beard against John Flood.)

Francis Sybert vs. Donnally and Garrison.—In 1749, Sybert bought of John Donnolly 300 acres on headwaters of Roanoke River in Colonel Patton's Grant of 5,000 acres, but John transferred his right to Paul Garrison.

Andrew Campbell vs. Thomas Gray.—Andrew Campbell, of Frederick County, obligee, from Thomas Gray, of same County. Bond dated 1747.

Call vs. Miller.—John Call, "alias Scull," vs. David Miller.

Peter Ruffner vs. William Miller.—Defendant had gone to Carolina in 1752.

John Harman vs. Benjamin Hardin.—John Harman sues Benjamin Hardin because Benjamin said John was a convict, meaning that the plaintiff was convicted in Great Britain, or Ireland, of some felonious crime and transported to his Majesty's plantation in America for the same.

The Seven Wise Masons, or St. George for England, with his Prime Minister of State, vs. William Richey.—Peter Scholl vs. William Richey, of Frederick County. Returned "living on Reed Creek, 1752."

Boyd vs. Scott.—Andrew Scott's bond to Adam Boyd, of Chester County, Pennsylvania, dated 1752.

JUNE, 1753.

William Davis vs. John Lightfoot and George Brown.—Bond of John Lightfoot and George Brown, both of Frederick County, to Davis, 1748. No return as to Lightfoot.

MAY, 1753.

Bourland vs. Whitaker and wife.—James Bourland complains that defendant said "William Gregg can prove James Bourland a dog thief in Pennsylvania (meaning that one William Gregg informed the defendant that the plaintiff in Pennsylvania had stole dogs) and that William Gregg could prove it."

Carpenter vs. Moses Thompson and John Patton.—Defendants live on South Branch.

James Montgomery vs. Brian Gauhagan.—Defendant in Carolina, 1753.

Rogers and Sutton vs. Vanderpool.—Not executed by reason Abraham Vanderpool lives on Greenbryer.

Cohoon vs. Miller.—Contract for building a dwelling with dimensions and descriptions.

John Paul Vaught (?) and Catherine, (?) Caspar Paul Vought and Elizabeth, his wife, vs. Robert Hooks.—24th March, 1750.

Ramsey vs. Elliott and Smith.—John Ramsey married Margaret Crockett.

Abraham Potter vs. Robert Craven.—In 1744, bought of James Fisher 350 acres. Fisher executed a bond and Potter agreed to make payment by last of August, 1745, at request of Robert Craven and Fisher, because Fisher was then going out of the Country, and Craven undertook to give Potter a good title. Land was on Cook's Creek. Fisher went to Carolina. Abraham Potter, otherwise called "Abraham Potter of Sussex upon Delaware." Bond by him to Robert Craven, dated 1745.

AUGUST, 1753.

Linsay vs. John Kelly.—John Linday of township of Gilford, County of Cumberland, Pennsylvania, obligee, in bond dated 1752.

Evans vs. Fleming.—James Evans vs. William Fleming, otherwise lately called William Fleming of Notingham Township, County of Chester, Pennsylvania.

Caldwell vs. Drening.—Walter Drening gone to Greenbryer.

Ross executors vs. Noland.—James Ross's executors vs. Andrew Noland. Returned "This defendant is run to Carolina with the Widow Rutledge, so not executed by me, John Lewis."

John Harland vs. Bourland.—John Bourland and Jane, his wife, late Jane Jackson, administratrix of William Jackson, deceased.

Underwood vs. Gillaspy and Rutledge.—John Rutledge dead. May, 1753.

Huey vs. Neigley.—John Nigley gone to Carolina.

Martin vs. Donohoe.—Executed on Donohoe, and his body put into prison, but he has broke and made his escape. 1753.

NOVEMBER, 1753.

Robert Ramsey vs. George Lewis.—George Lewis of Augusta County, 1749.

John Mulhollan vs. Thomas Williams.—Attachment in 1753.

Daniel Harrison vs. Samuel Wilkins.—Attachment. Daniel Harrison's account vs. Wilkins, dated 1746.

Israel Christian vs. Joseph Baxter.—Obligation of Joseph for £20 in ginseng.

AUGUST, 1753 (B).

Robert Hook and Robert Scot, executors of Samuel Scot, vs. William Picken and Ann, his wife.—Ann, his wife, late Ann Scot. Bond dated 1752.

Stuart assignee vs. Humblestone Lyon.—David Bell of Chesterfield County, 1752.

MARCH, 1754 (A).

John Smith vs. John Pickens.—Motion. To judgment obtained in Orange County, 1743.

John Chiswell vs. Henry White.—Henry White, of Goochland County. Colonel John Chiswell, of Hanover County, not executed by reason of his swift running.

Kinkead vs. Lockridge.—William Kinkead, an infant under the age of 21 years, son and heir-at-law of Thomas Kinkead, late of County of Augusta, by James Lockhart, his next friend. Bill filed May, 1753. Thomas Kinkead, in 1747, removed from the Province of Pennsylvania with orator and Thomas's family. On 19th November, 1747, Thomas bought 263 acres joining John Preston, Robert Lockridge, Robert Gwin, in Augusta County. Thomas died in 1750 intestate, leaving a widow and ——— children, of whom orator is eldest. Bond of James Lockridge, of Augusta County, with Thomas Kinkead of Lancaster County, Pennsylvania, dated 19th November, 1747.

Neill vs. Dougherty.—Michael Dougherty, of the township of New Londonderry, Chester County, Pennsylvania, storekeeper; William Neale and Thomas Provence of same County, &c. Bond to Simon Hadley of Miler (?) Creek Hundred in County of New Castle on Delaware. 5th January, 1737-8. Witness, James Jordan.

Davis vs. Whitaker.—Charles Whitaker "removed out of the Colony." 1753.

Jacob Gunn vs. Robert Craven.—Robert Craven had bought land of Joseph Hite on Linville Creek; Jacob Gunn came from Pennsylvania and bought the land from Craven, 1743. Bill filed March, 1746.

Scull vs. Drening.—Walter Drenning was living in Greenbrier, 1752.

Cochran vs. Durham.—John Durham, of Orange County, planter. Bond to Andrew Cochran & Co., merchants, in Glasgow, 1752. Witness, John Stewart.

Elizabeth McConnell vs. Robert Young.—"Not executed by reason of death of plaintiff," 1753.

Johnson vs. Neally.—Dr. John Neely in Augusta County.

MAY, 1754 (A).

Finny vs. Caldwell.—John Caldwell, of Ballibogan, in the Parish of Lifford and County of Donegall, Chapman, to be paid to William Hogg, of the City of Londonderry, merchant, dated 1st August, 1747. Process executed 1753.

Bourland vs. Pullin.—Archibald Bourland and Jane, his wife, late Jane Jackson.

James Patton vs. James Cohoon.—Slander. Cohoon said in 1750 Patton had made over all his estate to his children to defraud his creditors, and Patton had no title to the lands he offered for sale on Roanoke and New Rivers. Mandamus issued requiring Court to dismiss the jury from rendering a verdict.

AUGUST, 1754 (B).

Jackson vs. Mays.—Benjamin Murray, aged 50 years or thereabouts. Ann Murray's deposition.

Mary Elizabeth Sally, an infant by John Peter Sally, her father and next friend, vs. Abraham Dungleberry.—Action for breach of promise of marriage. Marriage was to have been performed 15th August, 1753. Decl. filed November, 1753.

NOVEMBER, 1754.

Purkins vs. Baskins.—Elizabeth Purkins sues Baskins for an assault on her son and servant, one ———— Skillern, and infant 18 years old.

John Hood, assignee of Andrew Barclay, vs. William McKinlay and Alexander McKinlay.

NOVEMBER, 1754 (B).

Magdalene Bowyer, late Magdalene Borden and *als,* vs. John Craig.—Craig's bond to Benjamin Borden. Dated 1752. Suit by Benjamin's executors.

AUGUST, 1754. (C).

George Lewis vs. Carmichael (John).—James Allison went to Carolina.

Hall vs. Hamilton.—James Hamilton, of Princeton, Somers County, New Jersey, cordwinder, bond to Francis Hall, of same place, shopkeeper, dated 24th October, 1750. Affidavit of Hall in Frederick County, Virginia, June, 1753. Affidavit in Somerset, New Jersey, May, 1753. Return, "Two of same name, and know not which is the man."

Alexander and Daniel Campbell vs. Thomas Dove.—Alexander and Daniel of King George County, 1750. Affidavit by Daniel in Frederick County, 1752.

Risk vs. Bell.—"I, Robert Bell, of Cecil County, Maryland." Bond dated 1750. Process executed 1754, February.

AUGUST, 1755 (A).

Quarles vs. Thompson.—Captain John Quarles, of King William County. Bond dated 1754.

Love vs. Steelman.—Deposition of John Donily, aged 78 years, 26th May, 1755.

NOVEMBER, 1755.

Bohannon vs. Breckinridge.—Robert Breckinridge, debtor to James Bohannon. To my wages, 72 days on the Shawnees expedition which you promised to pay me, sergeant's pay at ¼ per day. £4, 10, 2.

Adam Jordan vs. Docherty.—Account 1756.

NOVEMBER, 1755 (B).

David Bell vs. William Cawthon.—Wm. Cawthon, of Albemarle County. Bond dated 1751.

Rev. Robert McMurdo vs. William Murray and David Stewart.—Bond witnessed by Alexander Miller, A. M.

MAY, 1755 (C).

Thomas Moore and Phebe, his wife, vs. Abraham Smith and Gabriel Pickens.—Phebe, late Phebe Davison. "Phebe Davison, spinster." Bond dated 1751.

Andrew Lewis vs. John Pickens.—John Pickens had removed himself out of the County, 1754, 21st November.

George Parks vs. Samuel Harrison.—Attachment. Samuel Harrison is removing himself from the County. 14th March, 1755.

MARCH, 1755.

Russell vs. Francisco.—There was a patent (5,000 acres) in 15th December, 1733, to Jacob Stover, on Shenando, and this land descended to Jacob, Jr., son and heir of Jacob, Sr., but Jacob, Jr., failed to pay rents, and in 1746 William Russell got an order from the General Court forfeiting same.

MARCH, 1755 (B).

John Trimble vs. George Moffett.—John Trimble sues George because George charged that John had beat and murdered his wife, Mary.

Grand Jury presentments. 1752. Prison and Court House sufficient.

MAY, 1755.

Lewis vs. McMarry.—Benjamin Hardin gone to Carolina, 1754.

Bowyer and wife vs. McKendrick.—John Bowyer and Magdalene, his wife, who was Magdalene Bordin.

Jacob Miller vs. Jacob Thomas.—Miller bought land in December, 1740, from Nicholas Null, who had bought from Jacob Thomas, who died January, 1752, leaving his only daughter Elizabeth, an infant, his heir-at-law.

Samuel Patton vs. Nathan McClure.—Bond dated 1753.

Many suits by John Pleasants, Jr., of Henrico.

Many suits by William Thompson, of Hanover.

NOVEMBER, 1755.

John Green vs. Green.—John Green, of Orange, gent., orator, complains: Some time in 1746, orator's late father, Robert Green, of Orange, purchased of Robert McCoy, late of Augusta, land on Linville's Creek which Robert intended for John and his two brothers, James and Moses Green (they as well as orator, infants). In 1746—February (1747)—McCoy conveyed the land to John, James and Moses. Robert also owned other tracts jointly with Jost Hite and Robert McCoy. Orator has long since come of age, and is in want of part of the lands, but James and Moses are not of age. Bill for partition filed, 1754. Answer of James and Moses by Eleanor Green, their guardian.

MARCH, 1756.

Robert Harrison vs. Mathew Black.—Plaintiff must have been of age in 1754.

King vs. O'Neal.—Petition as follows: "To the Worshipful Court of Augusta County. The petition of sundry inhabitants of this County by this North Mountain, in Captain Harrison's and Captain Love's Companies, humbly sheweth:

That your petitioners are daily troubled by John O'Neal, a person of evil fame, who, being ill natured, evil, designing, citigious, wicked man, he often takes occasion to come to the houses of some of your petitioners and then designedly raises and foments disputes with them in which he makes use of the most opprobrious and abuseful words he can invent, and as he is bound to the peace, dares any one to strike him, therefore, should any of us strike or beat him we know not what might be the consequences as we are unacquainted with the law and his usual manner threatens to shoot us if he sees any of us out of our own plantations, that he will do us all the damage he can by killing our horses, cattle, &c., and when reproved of his misbehavior he tells us that if he does any action, be it ever so bad, that he will be cleared by this Court for two pieces of eight. His behavior is such that your petitioners are afraid to leave their families to go about their lawful affairs, not knowing but he may fulfill his threats before our return by killing our wives or children, burning our houses, or doing some other irreparable damage, and, as doubtless your Worships is well acquainted with the behavior of this malicious man, we hope you will take our case into consideration and fall upon some method to hinder him from being guilty of such outrages and irregularities for the future. That we, being subjects to his Majesty and the laws of the Dominion, may be no longer abused by such a person in the above manner, and your petitioners, as in duty bound, shall ever pray.—Daniel Harrison, James Magill, Daniel Smith, John McGarry, Robert Harrison, Gawin Black, John Lonkill, Patrick Cain, Aaron Oliver, (erased), Robert Gray, Henry Smith, Benjamin Kinley, John Smith, John McClewer, Gabriel Pickens, John Hinton and Robert Patterson.

Scire facias on recognizance, November 8th, 1754. Patrick Cain and Robert Patterson denied signatures. Gawin Black says he has nothing to say vs. John O'Neal, but was over-persuaded by some of the petitioners. O'Neal found guilty.

Smith vs. McMachen.—Samuel Lockhart declares, 24th September, 1755, that he expects to leave this Colony before next Court. Alexander Sutherland does the same.

Turk vs. Walker.—Thomas Turk and Margaret, his wife, vs. Moses Walker and Agnes, his wife.

MARCH, 1756 (B).

Gibbons vs. Brown.—Nicholas Gibbons (bens), Esq., assignee of Ann Grant, complains of Henry Brown, otherwise lately cai..'d I Henry Brown, of Mannington, in the County of Salem, in the Western Division of the Province of New Jersey, Yeoman. Bond to Ann Grant, dated 1729, 5th June. Process issued 3d November, 1753, and returned executed, and Henry Brown, Jr., and Isaac Taylor, bail.

Duglass vs. Harrison.—Letter of Robert McClenachan: "Sir, as his honor the Governor has appointed Colonel Stewart and I to find provisions for your Company and Captain Smith's, or any other Rangers in this Country, and 150 Cherokees when they come in, I would desire you would let me know where would be the most convenient place for you to send provisions to and allow a hand to receive the same and give receipt. And what quantity you now stand in need of, for I have sent for what salt will be necessary for salting of the winter provisions.

Captain Dickinson and his Company met with 9 Indians, and had a small scrimmage, when 1 white man was killed and 1 Indian and 2 small Indian boys belonging to the Cherokees, being captives, were released by our people and are now at Fort Dinwiddie, and Colonel Stewart and I have wrote down this morning to honor the Governor to see what will be done with them. If the 5 Cherokees are not yet gone, that you would x x them of it, perhaps it might exasperate them against our enemies. Your mother and sisters are in good health at present. I wish you good success, and may heaven protect you in all your undertakings, which is the sincere desire of your friend and humble servant.—Robert McClenachan. September 23d, 1755.

N. B.—Pray fail not in sending an answer immediately.

(Written on the reverse of a deposition in above mentioned cause.)

Kirkham vs. John Galbreath.—John Galbreath had left the County in January, 1756.

Mills, assignee, vs. Robinson.—William Mills complains of George Robinson of Augusta County: On May 22d, 1737, George made his bond to James Cunningham of Lancaster County Pennsylvania. Carpenter conditioned to sell land on Mill Creek to Mills. Bond assigned 12th August, 1745, by James Cunningham of Amilow County.

Rose's executors vs. Donnolly.—Anne Rose, Alexander Rose, Thomas Fitzhugh and John Rose, executors of Robert Rose, Clerk, complain of John Donnolly. Deposition of Philip Davis says that he was overseer for Robert Rose at a plantation of his on Tye river in Albemarle County, in 1743.

John Buchanon vs. John and James Allison.—We, John Allison and James Allison, late from the Province of Pennsylvania. Return "not found."

Charles Julian vs. John Cameron.—John Cameron of Orange County, 1755.

NOVEMBER, 1756 (A).

Patrick Davis, assignee of John McCapen, vs. Ralph Laverty.—Assignee of John McCapen and Elizabeth, his wife, late Elizabeth Watson. Bond by James Mais, Cooper, and Ralph Laverty, to Elizabeth Watson, dated 7th September, 1747.

Mills vs. Hamilton.—We, William Hamilton and Robert Hamilton, both late of Pennsylvania, yeomen. Bond dated 29th August, 1754.

MAY, 1755 (A).

Montgomery vs. Hamilton.—John Hamilton, of Mills Creek Hundred, in the County of New Castle on Delaware. Taylor and Moses Hamilton of same place. Carpenter and Alexander Montgomery of same place. Mason bond to Benjamin Swett of New Castle, affirmed tanner, dated 1748. John and Moses returned executors.

Ramsey vs. Jamesons and Gay.—John Ramsey, assignee of Charles Donnelly, who was assignee of John Handly, complains of John Jameson and Robert Gay, and Sarah, his wife, late Sarah Jameson. Bond dated 1754. Signed, Sarah Jameson.

Colberson vs. Fulton.—John Fulton and John Handly of Augusta. Bond to Robert Colberson of County Chester, Pennsylvania, 22d March, 1755.

Simpson vs. Campbell.—March 12, 1756. To the Worshipful bench of Augusta, we humbly request that you will take particular notice of Margaret Campbell (Cambal), for it is plainly known to all the inhabitants of the lower end of the Cowpasture that she is a common liar and troublesome to all them that she is in neighborhood with, and furthermore it is known that she will swear anything that comes into her mind, which the subscribers by report will make appear.—Hugh Morton, James Montgomery, Wm. Mortain, Wm. Memory, Edward Edwards, Agnes Memory, Wm. Gillespy, Mary Gillespy, Patrick Carrigan, James Beard, James Scot, Samuel McMorry, Margaret Cohiren, James Arbuckle, Thomas Simson, Robt. Gillespy, Margaret Arbuckle, Anne Montgomery, Thomas Fitzpatrick. This was an attachment vs. James Campbell by James Simpson, 17th March, 1756 (five days after above petition.)

AUGUST, 1756 (B).

Pullin vs. Lewis.—Loftus Pullin complains of John Lewis. One Thomas Hunt and one George Lewis (father of defendant) was indebted to one John Shaw and gave him their note dated 6th April, 1754.

Thompson vs. Henderson.—James Millor testifies that he was witness to a bond given by Michael Henderson to Samuel McElvenay for cattle, which said Henderson and Jeremiah Thompson drove from the Waxhows Creek in Carolany, about 1st of June, 1755.

Hugh Speere vs. Robert Young.—Robert Young, of Orange County, Virginia. Bond to Hugh Speere of same County, dated August, 1740.

Whitley vs. Kirkham.—Robert Kirkham, living on James River, died, leaving issue 3 daughters, infants, Martha, Jane and Elizabeth, and wife, Hanna Kirkham, guardian.

Pleasants vs. Skillem.—Thomas Pleasants complains of Eliza Skillem (August, 1752), otherwise called Eliza Perkins, otherwise called Eliza Anderson. Plea: Plaintiff ought not to recover, because at time of making bond and at time of issuing process in this suit she was married to one John Anderson, alias Ute Perkins. Bond dated 1750. Replication states she was known as Eliza Skillem and denied being married.

AUGUST, 1756 (A).

Pleasants vs. Lewis.—George (his x mark) Lewis of Augusta. Bond to John Pleasants and son, of Henrico, dated 13th October, 1753. Endorsed: "Received of John Pleasants and son, per order of my father, George Lewis, Benjamin Morrow's note of hand. Signed John (x) Lewis, 1754, October 15th.

NOVEMBER, 1756 (A).

James Lidderdale vs. John Harrison, Jr.—In March, 1744-5, James purchased land of John on South Branch of James River.

Mary Johnston vs. William Smith, Sr.—Mary, an infant (August, 1755), by John Johnston, her next friend and father. Slander.

August, 1756 (A).

Morlin vs. Borland.—Jacob Morlin complains of Archibald Bourland and Jane, his wife, late Jane Jackson, administrator of Wm. Jackson, deceased.

Null vs. Crossum.—Philip Charles Crossum, of Township of Tulpehocan, Lancaster County, Pennsylvania. Bond to Nicholas Deack, of same place, 16th May, 1742.

Robinson and Lewis vs. Thomas Wilson.—Thomas gone to Pennsylvania in 1754.

Johnson vs. Mills (Milles).—Richard Mills, of Nearlocke Township, County of Lancaster, Pennsylvania, husbandman, farmer. Bond to James Johnston, of Township of Drumore, County of Lancaster, Pennsylvania, farmer. Dated 4th July, 1748. Returned, not found.

Wilkie, assignee, vs. Sterling.—Bond by Frederick Sterling to George Smith, 1745, and assignment to Peter Wilkey. Returned 1755, "not executed by reason of the murder done on New River by the Indians."

Morris vs. Vanderpool.—Abraham Vanderpool, of Wallpack, of Morris County. Bond to William Morris, of Trenton, in County Hunterdon, dated 16th May, 1740. Assigned by William to his son, William Morris, 15th day of 10th month, 1749 (called December) 1755. Returned, "Lives on South Branch."

November, 1756 (B).

Trimble vs. Gardner.—John Trimble and Mary, his wife, complain of Alexander Gardner and Benjamin Copland. Bond dated 12th September, 1749. Made to Mary Moffett, who married Trimble. Suit begun 1755, 30th November.

Pickens vs. Bigham.—Bond to Robert Gregg (Grage, Gragg), 3d April, 1753.

Wallace vs. Dunlops.—James Wallace of Philadelphia (letter to Governor Jones, 27th September, 1754), complains of James and Charles Dunlop, otherwise lately called We, James and Charles Dunlop, of Cumberland County, Pennsylvania. Bond dated 19th October, 1751. James and Charles were brothers, and came to Augusta shortly before 27th September, 1754.

May, 1756 (B).

Stuart vs. Givens.—John Stuart, of Augusta, Taylor, and Sarah, his wife, late Sarah Givens, one of the daughters of Samuel Givens, late of said County, deceased, orator and oratrix. Samuel died, leaving Sarah, an infant, leaving will dated 22d October, 1740, and made his wife, Sarah (mother of oratrix, now wife of Robert Allen of County of Frederick), and oratrix's brothers, John and Samuel Givens, executors, which will was proved in Orange in 1741, John and Samuel qualifying as executors. Bill filed March, 1755.

MAY, 1756 (B).

Abercombie vs. Guy and wife.—Sarah Jameson, wife to William Jameson, deceased, in the Cowpasture. Bond dated 5th September, 1754. Sarah married Robert Guy. Suit brought March, 1756.

Hall vs. Fleming.—Deposition of John Collyer. William Hall was Collyer's brother-in-law. William Hall's wife said that she took in John Fleming, the defendant's (William Fleming) son for charity at the time he had the smallpox.

Mathew Campbell vs. William Thompson.—Thompson was guardian in socage of orator, who earned by teaching school during his infancy a considerable sum.

NOVEMBER, 1757 (A).

Maxwell vs. Allen.—John Maxwell was Captain of a Company in 1756 and called out Allen, one of his Company, to go against the Indians, but Allen refused and Maxwell sues *qui tam Malcomb* Allen. Maxwell denies he ever made out the writ.

Culberson vs. Gay.—John Fulton and John Gay. Bond to Robert Culberson, of Pennsylvania, dated 22d March, 1755.

Allen vs. Mathers.—James Allen, Captain, 1756, complains *qui tam* that William Mathers, a common soldier, refused to turn out when called. Process not served, because defendant is on duty in a fort.

AUGUST, 1757 (A).

Same, William Christian, Captain, vs. James Bell, Jr., 1756.
Same, William Christian, Captain, vs. Francis Alexander.
Same, William Christian, Captain, vs. Alexander Long.

MARCH, 1757 (A).

Green vs. O'Neal.—Eleanor Green, executrix, William Green and Robert Green, executors of Robert Green, deceased.

JUNE, 1757 (A).

Davis vs. Arbuckle.—Bond to be separated and returned.

Benson and wife vs. McKee.—John Benson and Margaret, his wife, November, 1756, late Margaret Calwell, administratrix of Robert Calwell, deceased.

Harper vs. that son of a Bishop, James Trimble.

Hopkins vs. Love.—John Hopkins vs. Joseph Love, on a note dated Philadelphia, 30th May, 1745.

George Wilson vs. Thomas Fimster.—Fimester charged that Capt. Wilson, while out with his men on the frontier, wronged the Country of its provisions, for he gave the provisions which belonged to the soldiers to women and children who had no right to it, and Captain Wilson's character will in a little time be as well known here as it is in Pennsylvania. (Notes by counsel of evidence. Defendant refused to muster and bred a meeting of which Fimster was spokesman). Verdict for plaintiff.

Davies vs. Gregg.—William Gregg of Albermarle is removing part of his estate out of this County, 9th August, 1757.

Dellinger vs. Bombgardner.—J. Godfrey Baumgartner, of Frederick County, in Virginia, shoemaker. Bond, 1755.

Ramsey vs. Gregg.—John Gregg had removed, 17th November, 1756.

Corry vs. Handly.—Thomas Jordan in 1744 and 1757 lived in New Castle County, Pennsylvania. John Handlin and William Handlin, late of Ireland, and now in Mill Creek Hundred, in New Castle County, upon Delaware, are bound to Samuel Corry of same place. Bond, 18th April, 1740.

Allen vs. Rooke.—James Allen, Captain, complains *qui tam,* because John Rook refused to answer call to go out vs. French and Indians, 1756.

Allen Stevenson.—Same vs. Thomas Stevenson, Jr., 1756.

Christian vs. Thomas Shields.—Same as above, 1756.

MARCH, 1757 (B).

Wilpert vs. Seeley.—John David Wilpert, Recruiting Sergeant, complains of Jeremiah Seeley, the said plaintiff, by virtue of his orders and instructions from his commanding officer, Captain Peter Hog, had enlisted several persons in the Virginia Regiment for his Majesty's service in the defense of this Colony, and among others a certain James Plucket, to whom the said plaintiff gave a pistole and a dollar in consideration of such enlisting, &c.

Henderson vs. Calvin.—James Calvin, James Trimble, William Trimble, David Trimble, all of New Castle, Province of Pennsylvania. Bond to Valentine Henderson of Belfast, County of Antrim. Dated 27th September, 1740. Henderson died during the progress of the suit.

Cook vs. Patton.—Bill of sale by Mary Cook to Henry Patton, dated 6th October, 1755. Witnesses, James McDowell and John Bowyer.

MARCH, 1758 (A).

McAnally vs. David Moor.—Bond by David Moor, Captain, to pay to Charles McAnally the wages of David Founton, an enlisted man in Moor's Company. 30th January, 1756.

NOVEMBER, 1758 (A).

Wm. Russell vs. Borden.—Benj. Borden's will dated 1742. He left his lands in New Jersey and lands in Bullshire, Smith's Creek, North Shenandore and James River, except 5,000 acres, which he devised to his daughters, Abigail Worthington, Rebecca Bronson, Debora, Lydia and Eliza Borden; other legacies and devises to sons, Benjamin, John and Joseph, and his wife, Zeruiah, and daughter, May Fearnley, wife of William Fearnley. Benjamin and Zeruiah qualified as executors. Fearnley refused. Afterwards (1746) Zeruiah, on account of bodily infirmities, resigned, and Benjamin took the whole estate. In April, 1753, Benjamin, Jr., died. John and Joseph, in 1753, conveyed their interests to William Russell. Benjamin Borden, Jr., had a daughter, Martha, an infant in 1754.

Buchanan vs. Martin.—List of men in Captain Martin's Company, 1756.

Finley vs. Christian.—John Finley, George Hutchinson and John Christian, surviving commissioners for collecting the Rev. Mr. John Craig's yearly salary, complain of Robert Christian, &c. For that whereas the 14th day of August, 1741, at the County aforesaid, a certain discourse was had and moved by and between the said plaintiffs, together with James Patton and Alexander Brackenridge, now deceased, and the said defendant of and concerning the Rev. Mr. John Craig's becoming their stated and fixed minister, and upon that discourse the said defendant, in consideration that the Rev. Mr. John Craig would come from the Province of Pennsylvania to Augusta County, in the Colony of Virginia, and there live as a fixed and settled minister amongst the inhabitants of the lower part of the Shenandore in the County aforesaid, and do and perform all the ministerial offices of a dissenting clergyman, he, the said defendant, the day and year aforesaid, at the County aforesaid, assumed upon himself and to the said plaintiffs, then and there faithfully promised that he, the said defendant, would well and truly pay yearly and every year to the said plaintiffs for the said Mr. Craig's use, 15 shillings, current money, towards his support and maintenance. And the said plaintiffs in fact say that in pursuance of the agreement aforesaid, the said Mr. John Craig did come immediately from the Province of Pennsylvania and settle and live, and still does continue a fixed and settled minister in the County of Augusta aforesaid, doing and performing all the necessary duties becoming a good and christianlike minister and preacher of the word of God. (Robert failed to pay for 16 years last past.)

Finley vs. Black.—Same as above against Thomas Black for yearly sum of 20 shillings for 14 years.

Stevenson vs. Shirkey.—On 25th February, 1743-4, John Stevenson and Patrick Shirkey became surety on a bond for James Rutledge. Rutledge died insolvent, and Stevenson sues Shirkey for one-half what he had to pay.

Young vs. Elliott (Aylet).—Lease by Robert Young, of Augusta County, to John Allet, lately came from Pennsylvania, 10th February, 1744.

NOVEMBER, 1758 (B).

Brown vs. John Stewart.—Suit as follows: "Mr. Jones, Sir: Please order a writ against John Stewart, Benden's land, and oblige

"Your humble servant,

"Deb. 10, 7, 6, ster.   ROB. BROWN."

Due p. p. acct. his passage to Pennsylvania.

NOTE.—"Speak to Brown whether his family's passage is included; if so, alter decl. Decl. says deft. is indebted for passage on board a ship from ——, in Ireland, to Pennsylvania. No date. Suit brought Nov., 1757."

Samuel Davis vs. James Tod.—Samuel Davis married Hannah Tod, daughter of James Tod, in 1758.

Patton's executor vs. Edmondson.—The widow Sara Hays married James Edmondson between 1748 (date of bond), and 1757 (bringing of suit).

Castleberry vs. McGeery.—David Castleberry, an infant (1757, August), by William Castleberry, his father and next friend.

Fletcher vs. Stevenson.—John Fletcher and Eleanor, his wife, who was sister of John Hyndman, clerk and only sister and heir of her brother, complain of John Stevenson, administrator of Hyndman, for an account. Account filed of effects and general charges of Rev. John Hindman.

AUGUST, 1758.

Paxton vs. Thompson.—John Fleming was indented servant of John Paxton.

Samuel Ferguson vs. Adam and Sarah Jordan.—Slander. Adam Jordan and Sarah, his wife. Process executed by Samuel Mathews. Richard Botkin, bail. Part of the charge was that Ferguson was a runaway from Pennsylvania and from Ireland.

Breckenridge vs. John Early.—John Early and Jeremiah Early were brothers. John Early, late of Augusta County, 1757.

Means vs. Thompson.—Edward Thompson of Augusta County and Hugh Means of Red Clay Creek Hundred, merchants, and held and firmly bound unto the Rev. Mr. Charles Tennent, of Mill Creek Hundred, County of New Castle. Bond dated 27th November, 1753. Assigned by Tennent, 13th September, 1757.

Thomas Thompson vs. John and William Handly.—John Handly and William Handly of West Nantmill Township, and County of Chester, weavers. Bond to Charles Tennent as above. Minister of the gospel, dated March 14, 1746–7, assigned by Tennent in January, 1748–9 to Robert Boggs of same County. Assigned by Boggs to Thomas Armor, August 28, 1749. By Armor, October 14, 1749, to Thomas Thompson of Augusta. William Handly, returned not in County, 1754.

Breckinridge vs. John Pickins.—John Pickens was gone January, 1758.

MAY AND NOVEMBER, 1759 (A).

John Stewart vs. John Blakely.—Deposition of James Martin, a soldier, that he, with some other soldiers, were in the room where John Stewart, tailor, works.

Finla vs. Wm. Bell.—Process not executed because defendant is a soldier in Captain Hog's fort. May, 1757.

Samuel Willson vs. Wm. McFeaters.—McFeaters was a tanner.

Orders of Court, 1756: Margaret Reaburn, widow, married Robert McMahan. Elizabeth Counts, late Elizabeth Armentrout, wife of John Counts.

MAY AND NOVEMBER, 1759 (A).

Armstrong vs. Galbraith.—Robert Armstrong died 12th November, 1754.

Peter Hog vs. Abraham Bird.—Peter Hog commanded at Brock's Gap. Abraham Bird tried to get Hog's soldiers to sign a petition for Hog's removal and tried to supplant him.

MAY, 1760 (A).

Thomas Waters vs. James Littlepage.—James Littlepage was an officer in the Virginia Regiment, 1757.

Hetrick vs. Counts and Wife.—Adam Hetrick, in 1742, then living in Pennsylvania, married his daughter, Elizabeth, to John Harmantrout, deceased, in 1759. In 1752 Adam came to Virginia and purchased land of Jacob Pence. John died in 1753, leaving a widow and two children. Elizabeth intermarried with John Counts.

Part August and Part November, 1761.

John Stewart vs. Smith.—Account dated 1741. (I think this ought to be 1761.)

Howell vs. McAnulty.—I, John McAnulty, of West Colon Township, Chester County, in Pennsylvania. Chapman. Bond dated 1st September, 1758.

May, 1761 (A.)

William Gregg and wife vs. Edward McGeery.—William Gregg and Margaret, his wife, late Margaret Johnson, administratrix of Arthur Johnson, deceased.

James Abbot vs. Littlepage.—Holt Richardson, Lieutenant, and James Littlepage, Ensign, were indebted to Abbot for board of fifteen soldiers from 21st May to 11th June, in 1759. Sworn to by Abbot in Hanover County.

Kennedy vs. Robinson.—Joseph Kennedy and John Madison against Elizabeth Robinson, an infant, as only daughter and heir-at-law of John Robinson, deceased, by Mary Montgomery, her mother and guardian, 1761. John Robinson lived in South Branch of Waters of Roanoke, and was surprised and murdered by the Indians about September, 1755.

John Bowyer vs. John Brown and wife Margaret.—Martha Borden was stepdaughter of John Bowyer and a "young gentlewoman." Defendants said, 10th August, 1759, that if Martha chose Bowyer as her guardian she would be a fool, as her estate would be wasted. Judgment for defendants.

February, 1761.

Scot vs. Scot.—Jane Scot, an infant, by Daniel Smith, her guardian, daughter of Samuel Scot, of Augusta, deceased, in 1749. Jane had a sister and brother. The widow Scot intermarried with William Pickins. Jane's oldest sister was Mary.

Martin vs. Smiley.—William Martin and James Martin were brothers.

August, 1761 (B).

Stewart vs. Given.—Samuel Stewart, an infant, by John Stewart, his father and next friend.

More vs. McClenachan (The White Horse).—Rob. McClenachan (The White Horse) was convicted of selling liquor without license.

Hugart vs. Wilson.—Josiah Wilson was a ranger in the Indian wars under Capt. James Dunlop, and went to Pennsylvania and never came back.

James Stevenson vs. Holt Richardson.—Abraham Boho, 25 years old (1761), deposes that in the fall of 1759 the plaintiff, in company with Wm. Givens, came as peddlers to Fort Ligonier, where defendant was commanding officer.

Kerr vs. Kennedy.—John Kerr, of Carlisle, and County Cumberland, Pennsylvania.

MAY, 1758.

John Boswell vs. Wm. Murray.—Account October 12, 1753. To, paid your brother, James Murray. Sworn to 12th July, 1757.

David Hays vs. John Shields.—Attachment 28th April, 1758. John has removed.

Robert Breckinridge vs. John Pickens.—Attachment 18th January, 1758. John has removed.

Mathew Campbell vs. Robert Renich, deceased (Joshua Mathews, administrator).—Account March, 1756, to schooling.

MARCH, 1758 (A).

Cochran & Donald vs. Laverty & Steward & Co.—Bond 1752. Ralph Laverty, Jones Steward, James McKoy and John Stevenson. Test., Alexr. Bain, Thomas Buchanan, Alexr. Boyd.

James Eaken vs. Thomas Paxton.—Trespass for taking and conveying away Elizabeth, daughter of James.

William Martin vs. Samuel Wallace and Jane.—Slander. Conrad Yates living in Sam's neighborhood.

Henry Murray vs. John Lewis.—October, 1748. To building a house 31 x 21, two dormer windows. To building house on the glebe.

MARCH, 1758 (B).

Repentance Townsend and Mary summoned May Court, 1755, on charge of not bringing up their children in a Christianlike manner.

Thomas Wats, John Blackly and Robert Dixon—summoned to Court on charge of not bringing up their children in a Christianlike manner.

Francis McCown, guardian of James McCord.

William Scot and Elizabeth summoned.

November Court, 1755.—Cornelius and Daniel Murley had died intestate. Elsa Green, wife of John Green.

Bratton vs. Montgomery.—Depositions Edward Thompson, 1758, and John Montgomery.

Henry Guy and Martha vs. John Ramsey.—Slander.

John Brown vs. John Stewart.—Passage for Ireland.

Patton's Executors vs. Nathaniel.—Bond of Nathaniel to James Patton, of Augusta, and Zachary Lewis, of Spottsylvania.

Adair vs. Connor.—Witnesses, 1757, Robert Anderson and Mary Watterson.

Stephenson vs. Fulton.—Witnesses, 1756, Samuel Cowdon and John Flieman.

John Woodfin vs. Joseph How and David Stewart.—Judgment, 1750, 22d May, *Sci. fa.*

Borden's Executors vs. Mitchell.—Note of David Mitchell to Benjamin Borden, dated 1751, to pay quit rent on 400 acres on South River for years 1741-2-3-4-5.

Alexr. Wright vs. Andrew Kerr.—June 14, 1754. To Rutherford, on faith. Henry, on sacrament.

Rachel Burnsides vs. Wm. Dougherty and Elizabeth, his wife.—Petition. Thomas Fitzpatrick and Alexander McElroy, arbitrators.

AUGUST, 1760.

Patrick Martin vs. John Smith and Margaret.

Pearis vs. Crow.—Richard Pearis's signature, 1769.

Gabriel Penn vs. Israel Christian.—Signature of defendant.

Sill vs. Stewart.—Signatures of Samuel Boyd, John Hardin and Lewis Stephens.

Stewart vs. Gibson.—Bond. George Wilson, of Augusta, to William Darlington, of West Nantmill, Chester County, Pennsylvania.

Frances Bowyer vs. Patrick McDonald and Mary.—Slander.

Vestry vs. John Lewis.—Contract by Lewis to build Glebe mansion and kitchen, 22d August, 1748, with dimensions. Adverse report of viewers, John Henderson and William Wilson, March, 1759.

Boggs vs. McGee.—Signatures, Cornelius and Isaac Ruddle.

MARCH, 1758 (C).

Grieder vs. Cloninger.—Deposition Madlena Bruback, 1758.

Quarles vs. Wilson.—Signatures George and Samuel Wilson and Hugh Hicklin.

Cochran vs. James Gay and John Montgomery, of Albermarle. Test: Robert Donald and Thomas Buchanan.

Borden's Executors vs. Samuel McClure.—Signature William Lusk and Samuel Gray, Robert Carlile and Esther.

Love vs. West.—Signatures of John Dunbar, Uriah Humble, James Johnson, Benjamin Kinley, Good Mowgainey.

John Ramsey vs. Robert Gay.—Defendant gone out of County.

Samuel Davis vs. James Todd.—Suit for dower of Hannah, wife of Samuel and daughter of James.

Gay vs. Gay.—Defendant (Robert Gay) lived on Calf Pasture and is gone.

Long vs. Hutchison.—Signatures of Wm. Long, Wm. Hutchison and John Lewis.

Risk vs. John Buchanan and James McCown.—Bond by defendants. Test: Samuel and John McCutchan. Signature: James Rosebrough.

McCaul vs. Vance.—Test: James Maccrow, Anthony Christian.

Borden's Executors vs. James Edmonson and Sarah, late Sarah Hays.—Was unmarried 17th May, 1748. James Hays, son of Sarah. Signature of Patrick Hays.

Lewis vs. Beard.—Contract for building chimney.

Samuel Hamilton vs. James Jackson and Mary.

William McGee vs. Francis McBride.—Signature: James Simpson.

John Stewart vs. John Blackley.—Plaintiff charges that in 1758 defendant set fire to plaintiff's dwelling house, and thereby some of his goods were damaged. James Martin's deposition before Francis Tyler.

Margaret Reaburn, widow, married Robert McMahon. August Ct., 1758.

Margaret Cancill, relict of Conrad Cancill, refuses to administer, and Court orders Sheriff to sell personality at public auction. March Ct., 1759.

William Ralston does not provide for his family and required to give bond. November Court, 1758.

John McFeeters, guardian of Andrew and Alexander Crocket, complains that their mother, Margaret, who married John Ramsey. August Ct., 1758.

Steel vs. Jones.—Signatures: Edward Beard and Samuel Givens.

Beard vs. Graves.—Signatures of James Craig, Archibald Huston, Samuel Henderson and Robert Shanklin.

Fitzpatrick vs. Peggs.—Signatures of William and John Lapslie.

David Campbell vs. Robert Cunningham.—Account, 1759, for keeping Robert's wife, Martha, whom Robert had turned out of doors, and burial expenses, &c.

McMachan vs. Sampson Mathews.—*Qui tam* for not voting for Burgesses, 1758.

Williams vs. Christell.—Signature: Robert Carithers.

McNeill vs. Lawrence.—Signature: Jeremiah Abbot.

AUGUST, 1759.

McAnore vs. Vestry.—Signature: John Ramsey.

Skidmore vs. Veneman.—Signatures: Thomas Caton, Joseph Skidmore.

Dr. John Sutherland vs. Thomas Gardner.—Signature.

Michael Mallon vs. Francis Kirkley.—Signature.

Arthur (Army Trader) (Arthur Trader) vs. Ralston.—Signatures: Thos. Moore and John Harrison, Robert Ralston and Ephraim Love, Howel Jones and Abigail Sempil.

Benj. Kendley vs. Capt. Daniel Harrison.—1754. To 20 days' service as Lieutenant of the Militia under your command at 25 lbs. tobacco per day. (Signed) Benj. Kendley.

John Hanna vs. Malcolm Allen.—1758. Not executed because the man lives out of the County.

Thomas Bowyer vs. William Cabeen.—Defendant did, on 10th September, 1757, assault, beat, challenge and provoke to fight the said plaintiff on account of money won by betting—gaming.

Richards, &c., vs. Sevier.—Signatures: Valentine Sevier, James Duncanson, Jahn Semple, Robert Phillips, George Frazer, Henry Willis, Daniel Fitzhugh, Thomas Chew, Rob. Duncanson, James Hunter, Fielding Lewis, James Esten. Proved in General Court, 22d October, 1754. Ben Waller, Clerk.

John McMachan vs. John Moore.—On July, 1758, election for Burgesses, and defendant did not vote.

AUGUST, 1758.

Thompson vs. Hendley.—Signature: Charles Tennent.

Means, Assignee, vs. Thompson.—Signature: Charles Tennent.

Samuel Ferguson vs. Adam Jordan and Sarah.—Sarah said Samuel was a thief and a wizard (meaning he had a secret, sinful, wicked and unlawful communication and correspondence with the devil.

August Court, 1755.—Copy of order accepting the Court House.

August 19, 1758.—Commissioners report that the Court House is completed except a door, which the Indians broke. (Signed—original) John Buchanan, Wm. Preston, John Christian, Francis Tyler, John Archer.

Fletcher vs. Stephenson.—Bill for settlement of estate of Rev. John Hindman shows costs of wake for deceased.

Hite vs. McDonald.—Signatures: N. Strother, John Jones, Frances Bend.

Greenfield vs. Beverley.—Attachment executed in hands of Lunsford Lomax, Lieutenant at Fort Young, when Major Lewis commands.

Quarles vs. Price and Howell.—Not executed, because defendant was in Majesty's service.

The Grand Jurors present Wm. Long, John Smith, William Fitzgerald— that they on 18th October, 1756, did with force and arms, in a riotous manner, enter the close and house of Alexr. Wright, in Town of Staunton, and then and there did beat, strike and abuse one Mary McDonnell, then in said house, and likewise break doors and windows.

MAY, 1760 (A).

William Scot and Elizabeth vs. Hughes.

Thomas Waters vs. James Littlepage.—Defendant an officer in the Virginia Regiment.

Abraham Farrow, of King William, to William Spiller, of said County. Bond 1756. Test: James and Ann Russell. James Graves.

APRIL, 1763.

Jordan vs. Jackson.—John Jackson, at Connoway.

McCord vs. Johnson.—William Johnson and his brother, John Johnson.

Dogget vs. Wm. Whiteside.—The following articles due by Anne Thompson, widow, now (1761) your (Whiteside's) wife. Rhode Dogget, late Rhode Evans, swears in Bedford County (wife of Richard Dogget).

Ephraim Hubbard complains that Israel Christian is indebted to him £5 for teaching two children to dance.

Fox vs. Robert Forbise, a schoolmaster.

Bratton vs. Cloyd.—Signature: Wm. Cabeen.

Jacob Miller and Adam Yeager vs. Godfrey Bumgardner.—Defendant is gone to settle on New River, 1762.

John Robinson, of Bedford County, 1762.

SEPTEMBER, 1763 (A).

Wm. Candler vs. Joseph Ray.—Affidavit by plaintiff in Bedford.

John Stewart vs. Archibald Hendley.—Plaintiff and defendant were partners in a team to follow the Army in the campaign made to the Southwest in the year 1760.

Pearis vs. Kennedy.—Richard Pearis and his brother, Robert Pearis.

Lynch vs. Ferguson.—Charles and Robert Lynch.

FEBRUARY, 1763.

Gilbert vs. Painter.—Rebecca Lovegrove, now Peartree.

Cowden and Executor vs. Fitzgerald.—James Cowden and Elizabeth, late Elizabeth Wilson, executrix of Samuel Wilson.

Samuel McCutchen vs. John Risk.—To one cow sold you in 1740 for which you was to pay me 22 years afterwards 29 yards of O hundred linen, &c.

Jacob Pence's will, 1750. Jacob's wife, Catherine, married Jacob Passenger. See Passenger vs. Miller.

Peter Steenberger vs. Nicholas Harbold.—Defendant on South Branch, not in this County.

APRIL, 1763 (A).

George Warfell of Strasburg Township, Lancaster County, Pennsylvania, vs. James Frame of Laycock Township, Lancaster County, Pennsylvania.—1750–1751.

Cresap vs. Drenning.—Walter Drenning, of Prince George's County, Maryland, trader, to Hugh Parker of Lancaster County, Pennsylvania, 1740.

SEPTEMBER, 1763.

Gilbert vs. Murphy.—John Murphy, living at Connalloges, near 41.

Robert Harrison's estate, debtor to administrators, vs. Thomas Rutherford.—George Anderson's deposition, 1763. Robert died between 1761 and 1763.

Martin vs. Carlile.—Signature, Robert Anderson.

McKittrick vs. Armstrong.—Thomas Armstrong, to Robert McKittrick and Jane McKittrick. To cash lent by my wife while sole.

Hughes vs. Stevenson.—Andrew Greer's signature.

MAY, 1763 (B).

Thomas Burk vs. Robert Ralston.—William Burk, deceased, brother of Thomas Burk, 23d October, 1763.

Thompson vs. Cunningham.—John McCullogh, Hampshire County. Deposition and signature.

Bowyer vs. McClenachan.—Borlinghan (Beringham) Franklyn's deed of affidavit. Brief to John Bowyer, 1762. Lately a soldier in the Virginia Regiment, in Captain Buckner's Company.

Hubbard vs. Reed.—Mathew Reed, to Ephraim Hubbard. To teaching Miss Cunningham to dance; 6 months @ 25/ per quarter. January 5th, 1763.

Peter Wright vs. Joseph Carpenter.—Thomas Carpenter, son of Joseph, 1763. John Davis and Joseph Carpenter. Thomas's deposition and signature. Joseph Carpenter, Jr.

FEBRUARY, 1763 (A).

Thorp and Stamps vs. Henry Ferguson.—Debt due plaintiff, on their books at the store formerly kept at the Peaks of Otter, 1762.

JUNE, 1763 (B).

Bell vs. Stewart.—John Stewart, peddlar, 1760. Caleb Wordly, juryman, June 23, 1763.

Cowdon & Co. (Stewart & Co.) vs. George Bruce.—Stewart & Company seem to have been successors to Cowdon & Company.

Margaret Rentfroe, late Margaret Looney, vs. John Crank.—Steven Rentfroe, 18th January, 1763.

OFFICE JUDGMENTS.

MARCH AND MAY, 1801.

John Bibee, infant, by Thomas Bibee, father, vs. Robert Brunton.—Writ, 8th December, 1800. Defendant about to remove out of the State.

COUNTY COURT JUDGMENTS.

AUGUST, 1801 (M to Z).

Rebecca Ray vs. John Shields.—Br. promise marriage, 179.

MAY, 1762 (B).

Coutts and Cross vs. Littlepage.—Bond, Henry Hinton to James Littlepage, 14th July, 1760. Hinton lives in Bedford and keeps a peddling store for Captain Sawyers. Writ, 4th April, 1761. Bond, James Littlepage to Archibald Bryce, 7th October, 1760.

Robert Breckinridge vs. John Milton.—Defendant, in 1761, became waggoner for that summer, a year's campaign. William Crawford deposes, in Frederick, 8th April, 1762: "As he returned from the Dunkar Bottom to Augusta he saw Captain Breckinridge's waggoner, &c."

William Crow and Charles Lewis vs. Adam Hoops.—Trover. Writ, 7th July, 1761.

Alexander McClenachan vs. Samuel Wilson.—In 1761, plaintiff was possessed of a silver hilted sword valued at £8, and casually lost it.

Andrew Suthington vs. John Davison.—Bond by defendant to plaintiff, 21st May, 1760.

Moses Collier vs. John David Wilpert.—Certificate giving information of Moses Collier, 22d May, 1762.

AUGUST, 1762 (B).

Gay vs. Cowan.—Henry Gay, guardian of Henry Gay, the younger son of John Gay, deceased.

Howell vs. John Givan.—Bond, John Givan. Chapman to Samuel Howell, 21st December, 1758.

Woods vs. Miller.—A duce harp.

Anthony Nisle vs. James Crawford.—To a house sold you in Miller's Town, alias Woodstock, September, 1761.

John David Wilpert, administrator Henry Baughman, vs. Mathew Lindsay.—Invoice of Henry Buchman's estate left in Greenbrier when drove off by the enemy. Witnesses are John Gay, John Warrick, Hugh Young and wife, John Meak (in which house saw same articles, Lawrence Hencemen. Witnesses when they killed the man, Felthe Yoken, Mathes Yoken, Nap. Gregory, Robert Allin, William Elliott.

John Harrison vs. Jacob Peters.—Ejected.

McClenachan vs. Augusta Vestry.—

Davis (Davy's) Colmer, Clerk, vs. Robert McClenachan.—Case writ 22d October, 1761. The plaintiff in September, 1761, was possessed of one sword mounted with silver, sword knot, one belt of the value of £8, two pairs of silk stockings @ £3, two shirts, value 5 shillings, one hat @ 40 shillings, one pair double channel shoes @ 15 shillings, and casually lost.

FEBRUARY, 1762.

John Gratton vs. David Carlock, of Brock's Gap.—Account 26th November, 1761.

Samuel Bell vs. James Kerr, of Cumberland County, Pennsylvania; John Hind, and Edward Rutledge.—Bond by defendants, 26th April, 1760.

James Stuart and Mary, late Mary Walker, vs. John Cunningham.—Bond by defendant to plaintiff, Mary Walker, June 7, 1757. Mary Stuart, late Mary Walker, admx. of William Walker, deceased.

William Lapsley vs. William Johnston.—In 1760 plaintiff built a smith shop on land of defendant on Christian's Creek.

MAY, 1762 (A).

Parsons vs. Trimble.—Thomas Parsons and Felix Seymore, of Hampshire County. 1761.

Wm. Kennedy vs. Joseph Kennedy and Borden's Executors.—In 1741 Ro. Galloway bought land of Borden, but Borden died before making deed—430 acres, Moffett's Creek. Galloway lived upon and improved the land until 12 or 13 years ago, when he sold to orator's father, Joseph Kennedy. Joseph lived on the land until 1760, when Joseph sold to William in consideration that William will pay so much, and also educate and bring up his four infant sisters. William entered, took care of his sisters, repaired the fulling mill, to do which he had to sell his own place. Writ: Feb. 25, 1759 (8?). Bill for deed from Borden.

William Bell vs. George Willson.—Plaintiff ran a saw mill.

AUGUST, 1762 (A).

David Robinson vs. Elizabeth Robinson.—James Robinson, cousin of orator, in 1746, entered 800 acres on South Fork Roanoke, intending it for his oldest son, John, and Thomas, and allotted the same to each. Patent taken in name of John, who was to convey his part to Thomas. John died 1756 intestate, leaving Elizabeth, his only child, about 8 years old. Thomas sold his 100 acres to orator in 1761.

Adam Thompson and Naome, admx. of Johnston Hill, vs. William Lawrence.

McNeil vs. Long.—Signature: Weldon.

NOVEMBER, 1762.

John Kenney vs. John Smith.—1760. To my wages, four months under your command, £4, 0, 0.

Steenberger vs. Bayard.—*Spa* 1761. For Abraham Kuykendall, Hampshire County.

Samuel Cowden & Co. vs. Wm. Grant, late of the Virginia Regiment.—1761. Account.

Wm. Stamps, of Bedford, vs. James Maze and John Lewis.—Bond 14th July, 1762.

Alexr. Sayers vs. William Baskins.—February 18, 1762. To your pay as soldier in my Company at Fort Ligonier, from 1st December to 1st March—90 days—£4, 10—paid you twice. (Signed) Alexr. Sayers.

NOVEMBER, 1762 (A).

Thomas Gilmore vs. James Gilmore, eldest son and heir of John Gilmore. Chg. writ. 1760.

MARCH, 1764 (B).

Frazer and Wright vs. Ralston.—Roger Dixon, in Spottsylvania.

Isaac Hest, of Spottsylvania, vs. Samuel Moore.—Account.

John Heren vs. William McGee.—William McGee's son, Philip.

David Edwards vs. George Lewis.—To 7 yards cloth delivered by my wife, Elizabeth Edwards; made oath to account 18th August, 1762.

AUGUST, 1762.

Hook vs. Munsey.—Daniel Smith deposes August 23, 1762, that being chosen guardian for Jean Scot, sister to Skidmore Munsey's wife.

Peter Elphinstone vs. Alexr. Gillaspy.—1761. To sundries at Reed Creek, Stalnahee and Long Island.

James Crawford vs. Widow Hanna Sawyers.—1761.

James Letsler vs. Doctor Thomas Lloyd.—1759.

NOVEMBER, 1763 (C).

Mathew Harper vs. John Handerson.—John is a shoemaker.

Madison vs. Kennedy.—William Robinson deposes 10th September, 1763, that in 1753 or 1754 his late brother, John Robinson, where deponent lives.

Price vs. Alderson.—Deposition of Patrick Henry, Jr.

Sallard vs. McDonald.—Lieut. John Sallard to Alexr. McDonald. Bond 23d March, 1762. Witnesses: Alexr. Stewart and Robert Fillson.

NOVEMBER, 1764 (A).

Allison vs. Hays.—Hugh Hays to Charles Allison. Bond 31st December, 1763. Witness: Alexander Greer.

Smith vs. Bowyer.—Mortgage, Col. John Smith to William Bowyer, 1762. Recorded. Witness: Wilton Walton.

More vs. Galloway.—Deposition of James Walker.

McFeeters vs. Patrick Ryley and wife, Alice, late Alice (Else) English.—Account dated November 10, 1762.

David Cloyd vs. Joshua McCormick.—To gold of mine received by you that was retaken from the Indians, 1764.

Same vs. Robert Miller.—Same.

Same vs. John Fowler.—Same.

Same vs. Andrew Miller.—Same

Same vs. Samuel McNabb.—Same.

Same vs. William Robinson—Same.

Shannon vs. Henry Smith.—1764. Before Henry went to Carolina.

JUNE, 1764 (A).

Gabriel Pence, of Amherst, vs. John Dailey.—Bond dated 9th Sept., 1763. Writ, 17th May, 1764. Caleb Wordly, bail.

Benjamin Estill vs. William and Thomas Whitesides.—Bond dated 19th December, 1763. Writ 29th March, 1764. Defendants live on or about Roanoke; one is out of County and the other is a soldier. Writ 17th May, 1764, executed.

William Fitzgerald (Fitzgerrell) vs. William Givin.—Bond by W. F. to W. G., 21st September, 1763. Writ 17th May, 1764. "The defendant is killed by the Indians."

William Crow vs. Robt. Eastham, Jr.—Writ 17th May, 1764. Defendant lives over the Ridge.

William Crow vs. Philemon Askins.—Writ 17th May, 1764. Defendant gone out of the Colony.

Adam Dean vs. Archibald Armstrong, Cord-winder.—Bond 18th November, 1762. Witnesses: John Ward and William Dean.

James Campbell vs. Samuel McClure and Mary.—Cov't.

Grand Jury presentment, 1761: John Moore, Benden's Land, for absenting himself from public worship; information of James Lockhart. George Lewis, for driving his wagon on Sabbath.

Mary McDaniel (McDanniell) vs. Daniel McCormick and Thomas Ramsey.—Bond 8th October, 1760.

Stephen Ruddell, of Hampshire, vs. John *McDonald* and Isaac *McDaniel.* Bond 12th May, 1763.

Felix Gilbert vs. James Emacks.—Case writ, 24th February, 1763, not found; writ 28th April, 1763, defendant soldier; writ 17th May, 1764, defendant soldier.

George Cox and Elizabeth, his wife, vs. Mary Berrisford.—Slander. Writ 22d February, 1764. Mary said in 1763 Betty Cox did poison John Berrisford (late husband of Mary) because John would not run away with her, whereas at time of speaking John had been dead some time.

John Madison vs. John Craig.—Trespass writ, 22d November, 1764. Defendant lives on New River.

Black vs. David Wilson—David moved to Bedford.

JUNE, 1764 (C).

Richard Daggett and Rhoda, late Rhoda Evans, vs. John Greedy.—Summoned 29th March, 1764. Note dated August 10, 1760.

330

George Skillem vs. Moses Crofford.—Petition 17th May, 1764. Defendant is gone to Carolina.

John Cusham vs. John Gray, Weaver.—Account, 1759–61.

Richard Read, Waggoner, vs. David Bryant, Farmer.—Note, 3d March, 1756.

Alexander Boyd vs. William Hutcheson.—Petition, 27th February, 1764. Defendant lately came from Frederick and lives not far from town.

Benjamin Estill vs. John Thomson.—Bond, 1st January, 1763. Writ, 29th March, 1764. Executed. Defendant lives on Glade Creek.

Alexander McClelan, Blacksmith, of York County, Pennsylvania, vs. John Ward, of Calfpasture.—Bond, October 26th, 1758.

Samuel Endsworth vs. Patrick McCallom.—Account dated Lancaster County, Pennsylvania, 1745.

MARCH, 1765 (B).

Samuel Moor vs. Philip Eskens.—Defendant lives near Thomas *Job* shop.

Johnston Carrick & Co. vs. Alexander McClenachan, Jr.—Writ, 17th May, 1764. Defendant is a soldier and in actual service.

Robert Campbell, Cutler, vs. Robert Campbell, son of John.—Writ, 28th November, 1765. Gone to Carolina.

Henry Smith vs. John Craig.—*Qui Tam.* Writ, 28th June, 1763. Roanoke (or Hance's) Meadow, near New River.

Bowyer & McDowell vs. James Hutcheson.—Debt. Writ, 29th March, 1764. Defendant is a soldier. Writ, 28th November, 1765. The defendant's uncle told me he was gone to Pennsylvania, and he had no home.

James Bell, of Amherst, vs. John Tillery, of Amherst.—Bond, 1762. Executed 28th November, 1765.

Benjamin Estill vs. William Carvin.—Writ, 29th March, 1764. Defendant lives in Roanoke and is a soldier.

William Givin vs. Alexander Crockett.—Writ, 29th March, 1764. Defendant, soldier.

MARCH, 1764 (C).

William Stamps vs. William Beard.—Writ, 28th April, 1763. Defendant lives on Roanoke or New River.

John Mann vs. Jeremiah Seely.—Ejected, 25th May, 1763. Fort Young.

Williams vs. Ambrose Stodghill.—Defendant, of St. Thomas' Parish, Orange County, to Shackelford. Bond, 6th July, 1761. Writ, 3d December, 1764.

Harrison vs. Heron.—Papers taken out. Only the answer.

John Madison vs. Samuel Henderson.—Writ, 18th September, 1763. Defendant a merchant in Borden's land.

Alexander McDonald vs. Thomas Sumter.—Bond, 27th November, 1761. Defendant, Sergeant in the Virginia Regiment. Witness, John Cameron, Lieutenant in same. Writ, 19th September, 1763 (third year of reign).

Felix Gilbert vs. James McElhenny.—Writ, 28th April, 1763. Greenbrier. Fort Young or somewhere else.

Felix Gilbert vs. John Young.—Writ, 28th November, 1764. Is a soldier. Writ, 25th February, 1763. Falling Spring.

AUGUST, 1764 (B).

Cresap vs. Walker.—Papers taken out.

Daniel Stringer, late of Chester County, Pennsylvania, vs. Morrow.—Chancery, 1761. Papers taken out.

MARCH, 1765 (A).

Doggett vs. Mathias Yoakum.—Writ 29th March (fourth year George III reign). Is a soldier.

McGranger vs. James Crawford, of Augusta, Storekeeper.—Bond, 27th April, 1762.

Jacob Peters vs. Ezekiel Johnston.—Writ, 25th June, 1764. Defendant lives at Fort Young, 28th August, 1764. Defendant a soldier.

Micajah Norman, of Amherst, vs. Charles Lockhart.—Note, 23d September, 1763.

Cowdon vs. Dean.—1761. Sergeant William Dean. Sundries by Captain Blagg's Order. Papers withdrawn.

Augustine Seaton vs. John Robertson.—Defendant is a blacksmith, 28th August, 1764.

Graham, Assignee, vs. Clark.—Bond. Defendant to Richard Pryer. 13th October, 1763.

MARCH, 1764 (A).

English vs. Abraham Haines.—Defendant a *stiller* in Forks of James.

Floyd vs. Morrow (Murray?).—Covering Brown's Meeting House. Papers withdrawn.

MAY, 1765 (A).

William English & Co. vs. Henry Dowley.—Writ, 28th November, 1765. Defendant lives in Bedford.

Benjamin Estill vs. Robert McGee.—Writ, 29th March, 1764. Defendant lives at Roanoke, and is a soldier.

Crawford vs. Alexander Sawyers (Sayers?).—Writ, 28th March, 1765. Defendant drowned. Writ, 25th June, 1764. Kept off by force of arms.

Captain William English vs. James Emacks.—Account, 1760. Sundrys at Fort Frederick. Writ, 28th March, 1765. Defendant lives in Bedford.

Grand Jury presentments.—Mathias and George Lewis, for driving wagon on Sabbath. John Henderson complains that his father, George, abuses him. Isabella Hall, late Isabella Ramsey, administratrix of Robert Ramsey. Susannah Armentrout, late Susannah Power, administratrix Christian Colley—Susannah lives in Hampshire. Elizabeth Campbell, administratrix of her father, Malcolm Campbell, 1764. William Beard lives in Bedford. June Court, 1764.

John Robinson vs. John Hamilton.—Writ, 28th August, 1764. A soldier.

Carpenter vs. Clark and Hays.—John is gone out of the Colony, 14th November, 1764.

Alexander Boyd vs. Alexander Sayers.—Writ, 28th March, 1765.

Samuel Davis vs. James McBride.—Writ, 17th May, 1764. Defendant, a soldier.

Daniel Ponder vs. William Cabeen.—Account, 1759, for wintering 9 pack horses for his Majesty's service, per your orders. This account withdrawn.

June Court, 1763.—Margaret Rentfro, late Margaret Looney.

Stamps vs. Bess.—1763. Defendant lives about J. Miller's mill. Roanoke or Catabe.

Stuart vs. Samuel Davis, Joiner.—July 1, 1762.

Alexander Wright vs. Robert Young.—Defendant lives in Forks of James River, 17th January, 1764.

Alexander Wright vs. Joseph Rea.—Account, 1759. Withdrawn. Writ executed.

Andrew Lewis vs. Patrick McCollam.—*Qui Tam* for stealing plaintiff's hog. Agnes Smith is about to remove for some time from the County, 21st August, 1762.

Letsler, Administrator, vs. Charles Lewis and Sarah.—Account vs. Miss Sally Murray, from 22d March, 1759, to November 24th, 1761. Writ, 28th June, 1763 (third year of George I).

JUNE, 1764 (B).

Henry Fillbrick vs. Thomas Bullitt.—Plaintiff was enlisted 17th May, 1762, in defendant's Company in Virginia Regiment. See papers withdrawn.

OCTOBER, 1765 (A).

William Woods vs. Andrew Crow, Jr.—Writ, 28th May, 1765. Removed from County.

Fulton vs. Crawford.—Robert Fulton, a schoolmaster.

Robert Finley's Estate vs. James Young.—Account, dated October 3, 1759. Petition, 28th August, 1765. Returned: "Dead, did live in Augusta."

Robert Patton vs. Richard Williams.—1765. Patton lives in Pennsylvania.

AUGUST, 1765.

Mathews vs. Henry Murray, Joiner.

Felix Gilbert vs. Richard Prior.—Writ, 28th March, 1765. Lives on Roanoke. "Not found."

John Smith and Mary, late Mary Stevenson, vs. James Hughart.—Writ, 28 May, 1765. Account *to my wife's freedom dues.*

John McDowell vs. Robert Lusk.—Writ, 29th March, 1764. Defendant is a soldier.

Wagner vs. Bush.—Writ, 28th August, 1764. Letter of Thomas Rhoads, a soldier, withdrawn.

OCTOBER, 1765 (B.)

Cowden vs. William Cabeen.—Account, 1761. Withdrawn.

Sitlington vs. Fleming.—Account, John Fleming to Charles Lewis. Credit by your pay as a soldier.

James McGavock vs. Marwood Timberlake.—Attachment, 12th September, 1765. Discharge of defendant, December 29, 1764, withdrawn.

Isabella Brown vs. William Brown.—Bill for divorce.

Benezet vs. Stewart.—Account withdrawn.

MARCH, 1765 (B).

George Scott vs. Robert Ralston.—28th November, 1765. Margaret Pickens gone to Carolina.

Wilson vs. Potts.—Bond 27th July, 1743. John Potts, of Amity, and County of Philadelphia, yeoman, to Owin Richards, of the same place.

McGill vs. Daniel Harrison.—Bond by Daniel Harrison, Jr., dated January 17, 1764.

Carpenter vs. Stevenson.—Andrew Hall is about to remove out of this Colony—27th August, 1764.

AUGUST, 1765 (A).

Cunningham vs. Craven.—John Harvy lived in Frederick, but disappeared from there.

Mathias Lair and Catharine vs. John Harrison and Mary.—28th May, 1765. Defendants had left the Colony before service could be made.

Bowyer vs. Reed.—Account Robert Reed, debtor to estate of Caleb Harmon, deceased. To cash you received of Cald. Preston, being the pay of said Harmon while a soldier under his command, £18, 14—(withdrawn). Account Caleb Harmon to Robert Reed, 1756-57—withdrawn. To cash paid David Long for washing when at the fort. To cash paid Capt. McNeill for you. Account Robert Reed to Wm. Preston, 1757-60—withdrawn. By Caleb Harmon's pay as a soldier, &c.

MAY, 1765 (B).

Wm. Crow vs. Patrick Lynch and John Gray.—Chancery. Patrick was debtor of plaintiff and gave plaintiff a note with John as security, but before note fell due Patrick moved to North Carolina, about 1755-6. Wm. sent the note to North Carolina by Andrew Dunbar, who made affidavit that he could not find Patrick and did not receive the money, but lost the note. Gray replies that after Patrick left Virginia a friend of John's named John Lawrence, from New Jersey, passed on his way to North Carolina and offered to collect the debt from Patrick. Lawrence returned and said he had seen Patrick, who declared he had paid the money to Dunbar. Notice 30th October, 1764, that deposition of Andrew Dunbar will be taken near Peach Bottom, Lancaster County, Pennsylvania.

FEBRUARY, 1763 (A).

Israel Christian vs. John Dickinson.—Defendant in February, 1762, at house of Francis Tyler, in Staunton, was present when many persons were playing hazard, and pass and no pass, and refused to issue his warrant and became liable therefor under the act against unlawful gaming.

John Low vs. Robert Bratton, admr. of James Dunlop.—John Lewis's affidavit, 11th November, 1758, that he served as a soldier under Capt. James Dunlop 22 days in the month of June, 1756, and never received any satis-faction for it.

Givens vs. Frame.—Signatures: James Anderson and Jesse Jackson, David Frame and John Botkin.

William Crow vs. Mordecai Howard.—Signatures: Alexr. Sayers, John Blagg, Wm. Preston, Samuel McDowell.

James Stevenson vs. George Wooldridge and John Ritchie.—Signatures.

Peterson vs. Hamilton.—Deposition Joseph Greer, as garnishee, February, 1763.

Felix Gilbert vs. George Anderson.—Attachment, 1762.

Tunis van Pelt vs. Samuel Hutton.—Defendant lives with his brother, James Hutton, in the Forks.

SEPTEMBER, 1763 (B).

Elizabeth Crawford vs. Stephen Loy.—Attachment, 17th April, 1763. Stephen Loy, of Frederick Town, in Maryland, to Thomas Fulton. Bond 25th March, 1762.

Walter and Samuel Cowdon vs. Rev. Davis Calmer, late of Virginia Regiment.—Attachment, 23d March, 1762. Alexander Boyd, paymaster, summoned as garnishee.

AUGUST, 1764 (A).

Henry Heth vs. Cowdon.—Henry and William Heth.

Moses McElvane vs. Mathew Linsey.—Defendant is an old man—horse jockey.

Dr. Sergt. Wm. Bell to Samuel Cowdon & Co.—1761, April, May, July, August—Liquors and furnishings.

Andrew Greer vs. Henry Harman.—Defendant in Carolina, July, 1764.

Ester Stevens vs. Bowman.—Deposition of James Urie, aged 60 years, 22d June, 1764. Defendant lives at the Great Lick.

Shippen & Co. vs. Francis Co.—Signature: Matthew Jordan.

Walker vs. Bowman and Abraham McClelan.—Many petitions by Walker, treasurer, on bonds.

George Skillem vs. John Frazier and Thomas Smith.—Defendant lives in the forest.

Matthews vs. McBride.—(Address) To Mr. Saml. Crawford, at George Gibson's, near Collierstown.

Andrew Smithers vs. Thomas Bates.—Defendant is a soldier, 20th June, 1764.

John Robinson, Treasurer, vs. John Robinson and Mathias Yoacum.—Yoacum a soldier, 25th June, 1764.

Benjamin Estill vs. Miss Elizabeth Campbell.—(Great Lick.) Signature: 10th April, 1763.

AUUGST, 1762 (A).

Robinson vs. Robinson.—David Robinson complains: In 1746 James Robinson, cousin of orator, now (1762) deceased, took up 800 acres on

South Fork of Roanoke, intending the same for his two sons, John, the eldest, and Thomas. In 1756 John died intestate, leaving Elizabeth Robinson his only child and heir-at-law an infant about 8 years old.

Adam Thompson vs. Lawrence.—Adam Thompson and Neome, his wife, administratrix of Johnston Hill, complain of James and William Lawrence.

Beverly vs. Gay.—William Hamilton and Margaret, his wife, late Margaret Gay, executrix of William Gay, deceased.

McMahon vs. Anderson.—George Anderson attached November, 1761, and returned no estate.

FEBRUARY, 1762.

Stewart vs. Cunningham.—James Stewart and Mary, his wife, late Mary Walker, administratrix of William Walker, deceased. James and Mary were from Cumberland County, Pennsylvania.

James Kerr vs. Bell.—James Kerr, in Cumberland County, Pa., 1760.

AUGUST, 1762 (B).

Gay vs. Cowan.—Henry Gay, guardian of Henry Gay, the younger, an infant, son of John Gay, deceased. Henry, the guardian, was grandfather of Henry, Jr.

Nicholas and Hetrick vs. Pence and Pence.—Jacob Nicholas and Adam Hetrick, in 1747, came to Augusta from Pennsylvania. Jacob Pence left a son, Jacob, his eldest, and heir-at-law. Jacob, Sr., and Valentine Pence were brothers. Valentine left Adam, his eldest son and heir, an infant 14 years old (in 1762). Jacob also had a son, George.

Graham vs. Armstrong.—Robert Graham and Jane, his wife, vs. Robert Armstrong and Mary, his wife.

Purviance vs. Given.—Samuel Purviance, of Philadelphia, 1761.

MAY, 1762 (A).

James Litsler vs. Robert Murphy.—Elizabeth Moore married Robert Murphy between 1761–62.

Kennedy vs. Kennedy.—In 1740 Robert Galloway, of Augusta, bought land from Borden, which Galloway sold to Joseph Kennedy in 1748–9, but Galloway had received no deed. In 1760 William Kennedy, son of Joseph, had four infant sisters, the oldest being 12 years old.

Arbuckle vs. Sayers.—This certifies that James Arbuckle and two sons have served as soldiers in my Company of Militia four months and sixteen days exclusive of what time they have received pay for. April 21, 1759. (Signed) Alexr. Sayers. Arbuckle sues for himself and two sons, who were his servants.

MAY, 1762 (B).

Goodman vs. Armentrout.—Catherine, wife of Jacob Goodman, was daughter of John Colly.

Robt. Breckinridge vs. John Milton.—In July, 1761, John hired himself as waggoner to Robert for the summer campaign to the southward, or wherever else his Majesty's service required.

Archibald Armstrong and Margaret, his wife, vs. Robert Grimes and Jane, his wife.—Slander.

Frame vs. Hannah.—David Frame, eldest son and heir of John Frame, deceased, vs. Joseph Hanna. Bill filed November, 1760. In 1748 John and Joseph bought land jointly on Naked Creek, and there was great intimacy between the families. John's wife was Margaret. The land was bought of Jennet Stark, alias McDonald.

NOVEMBER, 1762 (A).

John Craven and Margaret, his wife, late Margaret Dyer, administratrix of William Dyer, deceased.

SEPTEMBER, 1763 (A).

P. Henry, Jr., vs. J. Oliver.—Account of P. Henry, Jr., vs. Oliver. Affidavit of P. Henry, Jr., in Hanover, before John Henry.

FEBRUARY, 1763.

Gilbert vs. George Anderson.—In 1762 George Anderson was gone from Virginia.

Low vs. Bratton's Administrator.—John Low served in Capt. James Dunlop's Company twenty-two days, in June, 1756. He also served 231 days, from 1st March, 1757.

Israel Christian vs. George Wilson.—Israel Christian was Burgess prior to 1761, and was re-elected that year.

Hugart vs. Bratton's Administrator.—Josias Wilson was a soldier in Capt James Dunlop's Company.

APRIL, 1763 (A).

Cresap vs. Drenning.—Walter Drinen's note to William Griffiths, 1742. Walter Drenning, of Prince George's County, Maryland, trader. Bond to Hugh Parker, of Lancaster County, Pennsylvania, dated 18th December, 1740.

Stewart vs. Patterson.—Alexander Stewart married Mary, daughter of Robert Patterson, and sues Patterson because he did not get as much of Patterson's estate as the two other children.

Warfell vs. Frame.—James Frame, of Laycock Township, in Lancaster County, Pennsylvania, farmer. Bond to George Warfell, of Strasburg Township, same County, dated 16th March, 1750-51.

FEBRUARY, 1763 (A).

Philip Benezet, of Philadelphia, vs. Cunningham.—Archibald Cunningham, of Township of Drunmore, County of Lancaster, Pennsylvania, peddler. Bond dated 1st August, 1759.

Catherine Passinger, an infant, by Jacob Passinger, her father, vs. Jacob Pence.—Agreed to marry, 1762, but Pence broke his promise and suit brought.

June, 1763 (B).

May Court, 1762.—Margaret Gregg, late Margaret Johnson, wife of Wm. Gregg, and administratrix of her late husband, Arthur Johnson.

Stewart vs. Cloyd.—Alexander, Thomas and Benjamin Stewart.

Thompson vs. Davidson.—Adam Thompson and Neome, his wife, late Neome Hill.

Luney vs. Haines.—Margaret Luney, relict of Peter Luney, 1761.

May, 1763 (B).

Wright vs. Carpenter.—The spring before the Rangers were sent to Halifax County: Thomas Carpenter, son of Joseph Carpenter.

Callyson vs. Curry.—(On a scrap of paper): "This indenture made the —— day of April, 1763, between John Anderson, of the Township of West Easton, Province of——"

Bowyer vs. McClenachan.—Barlingham Franklin, of Augusta County, lately a soldier in the Virginia Regiment, in Capt. Bucknor's Company, binds himself for three years as a servant to John Bowyer. He was a tailor.

September, 1763 (B).

McClenachan vs. Calmer.—Rev. Mr. Davis Calmer was chaplain of the Virginia Regiment. Attachment issued against him 23d March, 1762. Alexander Boyd was a Commissioner to settle accounts with the soldiers and was ordered not to pay Calmer.

Ward vs. Howell.—Samuel Purviance and James (Samuel?) Howell were partners in Philadelphia, 1762.

November, 1763 (C).

Price vs. Allison.—Deposition of Patrick Henry, Jr., 27 years old. Deposition taken 22d October, 1763. He kept store in Hanover in 1758.

Madison vs. Robinson.—William Robinson was brother of John Robinson, who was murdered by the Indians. John Robinson sold land to Joseph Kennedy, who sold to McGavock, who sold to Madison. Land on Roanoke.

November, 1764 (A).

Brown vs. Daley.—Wm. Carlton and Esther, his wife, late Esther Brown.

Potts vs. Boff.—Conrad Boff, of East Nantmill Township, County of Chester, Pennsylvania, bound to John Potts, of Calebrook Dale, County of Philadelphia, Pennsylvania, 2d February, 1749. (Note.—Mary Boff, widow and executrix of Conrad, lives (at time of suit) on South Fork of South Branch.)

Man vs. Galloway.—James Walker deposes: That in fall of 1759, being stationed at Fort Young as a Lieutenant of a Company in the Frontier Battalion, the defendant, Man, acted under him as a Sergeant. (This was Wm. Man. His brother, Thomas, was also a soldier. Fort Young was on a river.)

Ruddle vs. McDaniel.—Stephen Ruddell, of Hampshire County, in 1763.

June, 1764 (B).

Fillbrick vs. Bullitt.—Henry Fillbrick was a soldier in Virginia Regiment under Capt. Thomas Bullitt in 1762.

McPheeters vs. Anderson.—"George Anderson is a soldier." 1763.

Fowler vs. Long.—William Fowler was a soldier under Capt. Long. 1762.

August, 1764 (B).

Stringer vs. Morrow.—In 1748-9 Daniel Stringer, of Fallowfield Township, Chester County, Pennsylvania, purchased an improvement near Buckley's Mill, *in said County*, of one James Orton, which Orton had bought of one William Morrow. This land, Stringer, intending to come to Virginia, sold to Robert Turner. John Taylor was Surveyor of Chester County.

Kerr vs. Bell & Hamilton.—James Kerr, of Cumberland County, Pennsylvania. Bond, 1760, conditioned to sell land on Christian's Creek by Bell & Hamilton to Kerr.

Upp vs. Stone.—Frederick Upp was a school teacher in 1760. Agreement by the Congregation on the Fork in Augusta County with Upp.

Looney vs. Looney.—In 1759 Peter Looney and David Looney bought land from their father, Robert Looney. Peter Looney is dead (1763), leaving Peter Looney, an infant, his son and heir, but Robert made a deed to the land to John Bowyer. Robert answers that at time of making the contract he was drunk.

Col. Thomas Cresap vs. Dr. Thomas Walker.—Van Swearingen's deposition taken in Frederick County, Maryland, 1764. He pastured horses in 1755 for Dr. Walker, who, he understood, was the King's Commissary. Cresap was from "Old Town." This suit was to recover costs and expenses in Braddock's expedition. Advertisement by Robert Leahe, Commissary, 13th February, 1756, that the Commissioners to settle accounts (Edward Shippen, Samuel Morris, Alexander Stedman and Samuel McCall) would attend at Lancaster, Pennsylvania, to settle accounts. Letter from Cresap to Walker and from Walker to Cresap. Walker's letter dated Castle Hill.

March, 1764 (B).

Rowland vs. Walker.—William Walker, of Augusta, also of Bedford Co.

Leister's Administrator vs. Charles Lewis and wife.—Charles Lewis and Sarah, his wife (was Miss Sally Murray).

Bowman vs. Bird.—Cornelius Bowman, father of George and Peter Bowman. Peter Bowman's widow, Margaret, married Van Pelt.

Daily vs. Dugind.—John Daily, late of Co. of Goochland, was there in 1747.

March, 1764 (C).

Seely vs. Carpenter.—Jeremiah Seely married the daughter of Joseph Carpenter, lately of the Province of New York. Joseph, in 1746, and after above marriage, moved to Jackson's River, where he and most of his children, then unmarried, settled. Jeremiah came in 1748.

Harrison vs. Herron.—Only the answer in the papers, but that shows that the complainant, Samuel Harrison, came to Augusta from the Colony of ——. Defendant, Alexander Herron, came from the same place. Harrison came first and settled on Linville's Creek. About time of Braddock's defeat Harrison went to Carolina. Robert Harrison was nephew of Samuel.

MARCH, 1765 (B).

Campbell vs. Campbell.—Robert Campbell, son of John Campbell, gone to Carolina, 1764.

MARCH, 1765 (A).

McPheeters vs. Lewis.—George Luice, of Augusta County. 1762.

Lang vs. Huston.—Capt. John Blagg deposes that in 1761 (4?), after Col. Byrd discharged James Huston, armorer, instructions came to proceed to Great Island, and Huston remained in the service eight days longer.

Crow vs. Cudy.—Attachment, and Robert Anderson summoned as garnishee, 10th January, 1765.

AUGUST, 1765 (A).

Walker vs. McCormick and Welch.—Daniel McCormick, a soldier, 1764. Thomas Welch, a soldier, 1764.

Love vs. Lusk.—Robert Lusk, a soldier, 1764.

Buchanan vs. Sayers.—Robert Sayers, eldest son and heir-at-law of Alexr. Sayers, deceased. May, 1765. Returned: "The boy is in Bedford at school."

Howell vs. Steel and Cochran.—John Steel and John Cochran, Chapmen, 1757.

MAY, 1765 (A).

Beard vs. Sayers.—Alexander Sayers, gent. "Not executed, the defendant being drowned." 1764-5.

Estill vs. McGee.—Robert McGee, a soldier, 1765.

Walker vs. Hamilton and Adams.—John Hamilton, a soldier, 1765.

Dunbar vs. Emacks.—James Emacks, a soldier in 1765, lives in Bedford.

John Daley vs. William Anderson.—William lived at Hart's Bottom, on North Branch of James, 1760.

Walker vs. McIlhenny and Ballor.—James McElhenny and John Ballor, both soldiers, 1765.

Davis vs. McBride.—James McBride, a soldier, 1765.

Deane and wife vs. Young.—William Deane and Mary, his wife. Deane's wife was only child of Patrick Cooke. Her guardian was Hugh Young, her uncle. Deane and wife were married 1763. Plaintiff says Deane and wife were never married, because the wife is under age. Replication says they were married by Rev. Ichabod Camp, minister of Church of England, on 14th June, 1762, in Amherst County.

MARCH, 1765 (B).

Scot vs. Ralstone.—Margaret Pickens gone to Carolina.

McGill vs. Harrison.—Daniel Harrison, Jr., of Augusta. Bond to James Magill, January 17, 1764.

McClung vs. Berrisford.—John Berrisford owned land on North Branch James River, adjoining William Halman, John Harper and James Edmondson. He sold in 1761 to James McClung, but before deed was made Berrisford died, leaving no sons, but seven daughters—Mary, Catherine, Margaret, Agnes, Frances, Lydia and Jennet. Most were infants.

Patrick Calhoun vs. Parris and Adams.—John Parris and George Adams. Bond to James Calhoun, of Augusta, 9th September, 1754. Adams pleads that he was 20 years and 9 months old when bond was given. Agnes Adams, mother of George, testifies that he was 30 years old Christmas, 1763. She sent him from Pennsylvania to Virginia and wrote letters to her friends at Red Creek.

Corrigan vs. Bratton, administrator of James Dunlop.—James Gill was a soldier under Dunlop.

William Crow vs. Patrick Lynch.—Patrick Lynch, then inhabitant of Augusta, in 1755, gave his bond to William Crow, but soon after moved to North Carolina.

October, 1765 (C).

Johnston vs. William Christian.—Defendant a soldier in actual service, 1764.

Crow vs. Bell.—Elizabeth Hog deposes 18th October, 1765: At time when *first fair* was held in Staunton, about three years ago, she and Miss Priscilla Christian, now dead, went to Crow's store and got "a fairing," which was a present of ribbon by the clerk.

Fowler *et als.* vs. John Stewart.—John Fowler and Margaret, his wife; William Patterson and Mary, his wife; Patrick Quin and Jane, his wife; James Skidmore and Sarah, his wife, sue John Stewart for a slave which Stewart bought of Jennet McDonald (McDonell), administratrix of Randolph McDonell. (Are these women daughters of Randolph?)

October, 1765 (B).

Brown vs. Brown.—Isabella Brown sues for separate maintenance from her husband, William Brown.

Boyd vs. Galespie.—Alexander Galespie is a soldier, 1764.

May, 1765 (C).

Looney vs. Looney.—Margaret Looney, an infant (only child), daughter and heiress of Daniel Looney (or David?), deceased. Bill filed September, 1763. Daniel was son of Robert Looney. Robert also had a son, Absalom.

October, 1765 (D).

Hamilton vs. Smith.—Col. John Smith, debtor to John Hamilton, for goods for his soldiers at the Dunkard Bottom, and himself, September, 1760: Col. John Smith, Lieut. Hansley, John Smith Boman, John Lukis, John Hamilton, Stamp Evins, Richard Dodd, Richard Newport, Thomas Deigs and John Cotril.

Moore vs. Fleming.—William Fleming, late of Pennsylvania, debtor, 1761, to sundries diets and lodgings, £1, 4, 4; to sunderie clubs for drinking, £0, 14, 4; to freight for saddles from Wilmington, £0, 6, 0; to passage for yourself and rum for seven days, £0, 12, 0; to one mare lent, which you killed by riding, £14, 0, 0; cash lent, £0, 6, 8. Affidavit to above account by Alexander Moor, in Bladen County, North Carolina, 6th May, 1765. (N. B.—Sd. Fleming is son to Samuel Fleming, of New London, and assisted in building a house for William Mogomnery in Salisbury. Process executed July, 1765.)

Long vs. Hutchison.—John Hutchison, debtor, 1766, to schooling your children, £1, 12, 9. (Signed) John Long.

Grymes vs. James Buchanan.—Defendant lives on Walker's Creek, 1766.

Smith vs. Hutchison.—William Hutchison, debtor, to Hugh Smith Account June, 1766. Sworn to by Smith in Orange County, North Carolina, June, 1766.

Wright vs. Lewis.—George Lewis, of Cow Pasture, debtor, 1764, to Alexr. Wright. Cash to B. Lewis, 2/6.

Summers vs. Campbell.—John Summers and Isabella, his wife, late Isabella Young, complain of James Campbell and Richard Woods. Bond dated 23d June, 1761.

Carpenter et als. vs. Fotch.—George Carpenter and Ann, his wife; Stephen Huntsberger and Ursilla, his wife; Mathew Heorce and Frances, his wife, daughters and co-heirs of John Shitly, deceased. John was a German, and died in Germany, leaving the above daughters, all infants, and —— ——, his widow. The widow came to America with the children and married John Fotch before coming. She died at Plymouth on the passage over. John Shitly left no estate, but his father, Malchior Shitly, left estate. The Shitlys went from Switzerland to Holland, where they took ship. They landed in Maryland, intending to settle at Tulpahocken, in Pennsylvania. Fotch left Germany in 1744. Mathew or Martin Heorse (called both).

AUGUST, 1766 (A).

Seegar vs. Kline.—Andrew Kline, of Borough of Lancaster, County of Lancaster, Pennsylvania, innkeeper. Bond to Frederick Seegar, of Lancaster Township, County of Lancaster, 6th April, 1765.

Clendenning vs. Cunningham.—9th July, 1764. This day Samuel Crockett came before me and made oath that he (Samuel) served as Sergeant at Capt. John Dickinson's, on Cow Pasture River, under the command of Capt. Walter Cunningham, and that John Clendennin served as a soldier from the 27th of November, 1763, to the 20th March, 1764, in said Company.

Bowman vs. Benson and wife.—George Bowman complains of John Benson and Margaret, his wife, late Margaret Calvie, 1765. Margaret Calwell, widow of Robert Calwell; Isaac Johnson and Isaac Robinson were brothers-in-law. Isaac Johnson is about to move to Carolina.

Doggett vs. Henry Dooley.—Richard Doggett and Rhoda, his wife, late Rhoda Evans. Defendant is a soldier and lives in Bedford, Glade Creek, Roanoke.

Anderson vs. Russell.—James Anderson and Elizabeth, his wife. 1766.

John Skelton vs. John Miller.—Defendant is dead—23d May, 1766.

Ro. Breckinridge vs. Stephen Loy.—Defendant's bond, dated 21st May, 1762, from Manochissie.

NOVEMBER, 1766 (B).

Patrick vs. Kinkead.—I. John Kinkead, of Albemarle County. Bond dated April, 1764.

Bowyer vs. Alexander.—William Alexander, son to Robert. 1765.

Thompson vs. Alexander and Andrew Campbell, *of Augusta.* 1764.

William Givins vs. Robert Stewart.—James Stewart, bail.

Evans vs. Chambers.—I, Robert Evans, of Cecil County, Maryland, power of attorney to his trusty friend and uncle, James Moore, to sue William Chambers for a debt, 29th October, 1765. William Chambers, of Millford Hundred, Cecil County. Bond to Thomas Montgomery, merchants at Cristona Bridge, dated 21st December, 1758.

Wetherall vs. O'Neal.—George Wetherall, of Culpeper, 1764, vs. William O'Neal. Attached in Culpeper, 1764. O'Neal married Elizabeth Stover, by whose means he has recovered a judgment in the General Court against Col. Patton's estate.

Ray vs. Chandler.—Capt. John Blagg commanded a Company of the Virginia Regiment in 1760. William Chandler, of Bedford County; Joseph Ray, of same County. William contracted to deliver goods for Joseph at Dunkard Bottom, on New River. This was when Blagg was with Col. John Smith, at Fort Lewis, August, 1760, during the campaign under Col. Byrd vs. the Cherokees.

Glassford vs. Willfunk.—I, George Willfunk, of Fairfax County, 20th July, 1761.

Harrison vs. Trader.—Reuben Harrison must have been of age. 1765.

MAY, 1766 (C).

Sayers vs. McMurray.—Samuel McMurray is a soldier. 1764.

MARCH, 1767 (A).

Ewing vs. Knight.—Argument between Charles Knight, schoolmaster, and subscribers. (1) He is to teach one year and have every other Saturday, or half of every Saturday, off. If any alarm of the Indians comes, they are to provide shelter and food and drink. Subscribers to raise £18. (Signed) Thos. Meek, Archibald Armstrong, Joseph Vachub, Robert McCutchen, Jos. Graham, John Vachub. Dated 3d May, 1765.

McClung vs. Fleming.—John *Flimon* was a soldier in Capt. Lewis's Co.

Faris vs. Harrison.—In 1759 John Faris bought a horse from George Anderson. Shortly afterwards George left the Colony. Edward McGarry shortly after George left forged an endorsement on the bond to Daniel Harrison, and then absconded. Robert Harrison was a son of Daniel, and then, after George's departure, lay on his death bed. Note dated 12th May, 1759, payable 1st August next. (Signed) John Pheris.

Stewart vs. Davis.—Thomas Stewart. 1765.

Patterson Executors vs. Carlton.—William Carlton and Esther, his wife, late Esther Brown, administratrix of Henry Brown.

David Cloyd vs. James Montgomery.—Account as follows: 1764—Mr. James Montgomery, debtor, March 24—to cash of mine retaken from the Indians and delivered to you by Lieut. (Francis) Smith, £137, 18, 0. Credit, 1764—April 21. By cash received from John Neilly, Michael Cloyd, Andrew Neely and Francis Smith, £19, 0, 0; B. G. Samuel McFerrin, Philip Watkins, Benj. Hawkins, James Montgomery, Jr., Wm. Montgomery, Jr., John Crockett, John McRoberts, Wm. McMullin, Wm. Robinson, John Fowler, Samuel Robinson, Joshua McCormack, John Clark, John Artus, Saml. McNabb, Saml. Gatliff, Jeremiah Puckett and Lanty Armstrong, each £4, 18, 6. Balance due, £31, 18, 0. Sworn to by David Cloyd, 24th April, 1765. Case agreed by attorneys as follows: "We agree that a party of Indians made an eruption into the Colony, attacked the plaintiff's house, rifled it and bore off upwards of £200 in gold and silver, several household goods and negroes. We agree that a party of the Militia pursued the enemy and overtook them on John's Creek, a branch of James River, at the distance of 30 or 35 miles, and attacked and killed one of the number. We agree that upon searching the Indians's budget a quantity of gold, some dollars and pieces of small silver, were found, which, upon being weighed, amounted to the sum of £137, 18, 0. We agree that the money found in the budget of the Indians consisted of the same coin which the plaintiff was known to have in his house when plundered by the Indians. We agree that after the money was recoverd from the Indians a dispute arose among the Militia to whom of right the money belonged whether it should be delivered to the plaintiff, who was deemed to have been the owner of it before it fell into the hands of the Indians, or whether the Militia were entitled to it in having recovered it from them, upon which dispute that sum of money was lodged in the hands of the defendant, to be by him kept till that point should be settled. We agree that the plaintiff made an offer of 30 shillings to each of the men who has assisted in the pursuit of the enemy. We agree that a part of the Company of Militia made an offer to the plaintiff of delivering up his negroes and household goods if he would allow them the money. We agree that the defendant paid the sum of money out of his hands to the Militia, and that several of them returned their dividends to the plaintiff amounting to £106, 17, 2. We agree that the plaintiff paid to several of the captors who returned him their dividends the sum of 30/, the premium by him before offered for their service. We agree that if the law, &c. (Signed) Gabrill Jones, for plaintiff; Peter Hog, for defendant." Hung jury and case agreed. Submitted August, 1766.

Harper vs. Christian.—Account by Matt Harper, administrator of Michael Harper, against Capt. Wm. Christian. To his bounty as a soldier, £2, 0, 0. To his pay as a soldier, 19, 0.

Rev. John Kingkade vs. Knox and Hamilton.—21st October, 1766.

MAY, 1767 (B).

Patterson vs. Looney.—John Harrison's order on Looney dated June 20, 1745.

NOVEMBER, 1767 (C).

Catherine Whitly vs. Jonathan Whitly.—Divorce.

Fitzpatrick vs. Jones.—John Jones. Bond, 27th August, 1766. Attachment against him, 1767.

AUGUST, 1767 (C).

Christian *qui tam.* vs. Bell.—Only paper. Williamsburg, October 21, 1763. On consideration of the information of David Stewart, late Colonel, September, 1762, and the deposition of John McCown, John Black and Capt. William Christian, relating to James Bell, Jr., within decreed to pay £20— one half to his Majesty. I do hereby remit the King's part of said fine and discharge the said James Bell and his security from the payment of said £10, or any part thereof, and order the Sheriff and all concerned to behave conformably. (Signed) John Blair, P. (Judgment was rendered August 19, 1757.)

Fisher and wife vs. Armstrong.—Archibald Fisher and Susanna, his wife, late Susanna Shaddon (1766), administratrix of Mathew Shaddon, November, 1765.

Johnson vs. Skidmore.—Thomas Johnson made a bond in Augusta, January, 1744–5.

MAY, 1767 (C).

Bowyer vs. Kinkead.—I, David Kinkead, of Albemarle County, 1755.

Lewis vs. Forkner.—Wm. Terrell Lewis vs. Wm. Forkner. Defendant lived at Fort Lewis, but went to Carolina.

AUGUST, 1767 (D).

Cawley vs. Thomas Patterson.—John Cawley and Margaret, his wife, late Margaret Woods.

MAY, 1767 (D).

Cabell vs. Bowen.—Malcolm Allen deposts, 13th March, 1767, that Dr. William Cabell said that as Moses Bowen's wound had been received in defense of his Country, the Country would pay him for curing Moses.

Martin vs. Lindsay.—George Chowning, aged about 32 years, 14th August, 1765, deposes: Rene Laforce, aged 42, August 8th, 1765. Agnes Laforce, his wife, aged 40, August 8, 1765. Robert Cawthon, aged 29 years, 8th August, 1765.

Thompson vs. Watterson.—Hanover, September 19, 1764. Ann Lyon, a convict servant from London, was imported in the Beverly, Captain Allan, and arrived in Rappahannock River, in Virginia, some time in the latter end of October, 1763. The original convictions and general goal delivery are to be seen in the hands of James Miller, merchant, in Port Royal, but there being only one made out for every separate goal, renders it impossible to send it along with each servant. (Signed) Robert Hart.

In pursuance and by virtue of Act of Parliament, made and appointed for the more effectual transportation of felons and convicts out of Great Britain into his Majesty's Plantation in America, I do hereby assign unto Cochran & Heart, their heirs or assigns, convict named Agnes Lyons within the said Statutes to serve for the term of 7 years from the 3d day of October, 1763, being the day of arrival in Virginia. (Signed) Captain Thomas Allong.

NOVEMBER, 1767 (E).

Smith vs. Alexander McClenachan.—Nicholas Smith vs. Alexander Mc-Clenachan. Account, 30th December, 1762. Sworn to by Smith before John Stewart in Spottsylvania County. Account runs December 23-30, 1762, for cash, meals, drink, meals for Ned Yeats, supper for Mr. Herse and Mr. Cock. Cash lent. Boarding Fanny from December 31, to July 26, 1763, @ 30 shillings per month.

Stantown, August 24, 1763.

Sir:—I understand, by Mr. Lewis, that Fanny has left your house, and was afraid you would stop her clothes for her board. But I hope you will not use her so bad, as you may depend as soon as I can get so much time I will be down and pay you all she owes you. I beg you would not let her want for anything till I come, which shall be as soon as ye Indians will give me leave to leave my fort, which is all, from your humble servant

ALEXANDER McCLENACHAN.

To Mr. Michael Smith in Frederick. (Suit brought 1766.)

Woodrow vs. McClenachan.—I, Alexander McClenachan, Ensign in the Virginia Regiment. Bond, 4th July, 1761. Account running June, July, August, September, November, 1759. Credits made by Lieutenant Mordecai Buckner, Ensign Philip Love.

Gist vs. George Breckinridge and Reed.—Alexander Breckinridge. Special bail, 1766.

Edwards vs. McCutchan and Wife.—Contract between Andrew Duncan of Augusta and David Edwards, late of said County, dated 1760.

NOVEMBER, 1768 (A).

Greer vs. Hughes.—In 1759 Andrew Greer and William Kinkead purchased land of James Hughes of Staunton, which Hughes had bought of James Paxton, but Hughes died before deed was made, leaving Euphemia, Jane and Mary, infants, and widow, Euphemia.

Martin vs. Dickinson.—John Dickinson's bond to David Martin, of Amherst County, 21st August, 1765. Martin bought two tracts of land in Mecklinburg County, North Carolina, from Dickinson—one on Sandy River, the other on Bullock's Creek.

Alexander Miller vs. David Rice.—Alexander Miller had preached 20 years. 1766. Elizabeth Miles, wife of Abraham Miles.

Francis vs. Anderson.—John Anderson, late of this County. 6th October, 1768.

AUGUST, 1768 (A).

Anderson vs. Watterson.—James Anderson, blacksmith, 1765.
Crow vs. John Stewart.—17th May, 1767. Attachment vs. John Stewart, who had removed.
Brown vs. Carpenter.—John and James Brown, his son, made affidavit, 1768.

MAY, 1768 (A).

Purviance vs. Timothy Terrell.—William Purviance, of Augusta County, December 28, 1767.
. Alexander Herron vs. Quin, Ejectment.—Daniel Harrison, 66 or 67 years old, deposes, 16th December, 1767: He was present when Colonel James Woods, then surveyor of the County of Orange (now Augusta) ran the lines in dispute. John Craven, aged 45, says same. William Gregg, aged 30, says same. John Harris was dead at time of taking this deposition.

MARCH, 1768 (D).

Archer vs. John Stewart and Elizabeth, his wife.—Exd., 1767.
Ewing vs. Mann.—Lawrence Miller, Michael Robinson, Edward Upton, James Brady, James Brown, George Cummins, Mary Griffiths, Mary Warrington, Mary Welsh. The above 9 convicts were sold unto Mr. William Crow, in Augusta, by McDonall, Cochran & Co., December 17, 1763.

MAY, 1768 (B).

Gist vs. Barnett.—Samuel Gist vs. Joseph Barnett (Barnet) of Amherst. Bond dated 1st November, 1763.

MARCH, 1768 (E).

Foster vs. Patton's executors.—William Foster bought, in 1750-55, land in the Forks of Cripple Creek, from Colonel James Patton. Colonel Patton was killed some time in 1755. Colonel Patton was prevented from taking out patents to his land on New River by a dispute ensuing between the Assembly and the Governor concerning a fee on a pistole for signing the patents. In 1763, when Colonel Buchan applied for patents, he was informed by the Governor and Council that his Majesty's proclamation forbidding his subjects to settle on and to withdraw from the waters of the Mississippi prevented any patent from issuing, but as soon as his Majesty should withdraw the proclamation and suffer his people to settle there, then Colonel Buchanan should have the patents. Deposition of Samuel Montgomery, aged 47 years. Deposition of William Sawyers, aged 40 year.
Laverty vs. Elliott.—Ralph Laverty and Jane, his wife, late Jane Grymes, administratrix of Robert Grymes, deceased, 1766.
William Simpson and Elizabeth, his wife, late Elizabeth Campbell, administratrix of Malcomb, vs. Joseph Craven.

Swink vs. Cowarden.—I, John Cowardin, Satler, in the *Coundi* of Bearckley, Saluda and John Swink, in Charleston, all bound to John Schutterle. Bond dated 7th May, 1763. Payable in South Carolina money.

Mathew Harrison vs. Reuben Rutherford.—Contract dated 1763.

McClure vs. McClure.—Ejectment. James McClure and Nathaniel McClure, sons and devisees of Nathaniel McClure, vs. Halbert McClure.

Footman vs. Mathew Harrison.—Mathew Harrison, of Frederick County. Bond dated 1765.

Paxton vs. Ward.—Thomas, Elizabeth and John Paxton depose. Elizabeth had a son, Samuel, 28th February, 1766.

MARCH, 1769 (A).

Philip Barrier vs. Isaac Burns.—Attachment, 15th February, 1769. Thos. Rodgers surety on bond.

David Bell vs. John Smallwood.—Attachment, February, 1769.

Matthews vs. William Christian, son to Sampson.

James Ewing vs. John Thompson.—Attachment. John Thompson, heir to Anthony and Robert Thompson, late of Pennsylvania. Captain John Willson, surety. Account as follows: "John Thompson, Dr. To your promise to pay me for your brother Robert."

William Robertson vs. William Teas.—Attachment, 15th November, 1768. Archibald Hamilton, surety.

Halbert McClure vs. James McClure.—James McClure not found, November, 1768.

Arthur McClure vs. Joseph Love.—Dr. Thomas Loyd, a witness, 1768.

Patrick Denny vs. George Gibson.—Trespass, 1767. James Young, Thos. McAllister, John McAllister, James Dillen, Richard McGee—witnesses.

Thompson vs. Bigham.—Attachment, 19th August, 1768. John Thompson (Robert Thompson, surety) vs. George Bigham, removed out of the County. Served in hands of John Bigham.

AUGUST, 1766 (A).

Israel Christian vs. John King.—Account 1757 to 1764. Credits—By patrolling under Colonel Stuart. By allowed for going to Sivers's Fort.

William Blackwood vs. James Callison.—Note by defendant and Richard Morris, 16th September, 1762, to plaintiff. Witnesses: Ro. Cunningham and Samuel Cloyd.

Audley Paul vs. Stalnaher (from Hampshire).—Bond showing signature of Audley Paul and David Cloyd.

Agnes Young, late the wife of Robert Young, vs. John Brown.—Writ of dower, 28th May, 1765.

MAY, 1765 (C).

Looney vs. Looney.

Greer vs. Boyd.—Note of Blagg and Grant.

OCTOBER, 1765 (D).

Robert Finley vs. Sergeant John Nash.—1757 account.

Cotton vs. Christian.—Account of Cotton as schoolmaster.

David Via vs. Thomas Johnson, Jr.—Account.

Church Wardens vs. Ward and Preston.—Suit on contract to build a glebe house.

Is. Christian vs. Dr. Robt. Hamilton.—Account 1759. "Your trial in Williamsburg."

Davis vs. John Young.—Writ 28th August, 1764. Defendant is a soldier.

John Hamilton vs. Capt. John Smith.—Lieut. Hansley. Various accounts vs. Smith, for bills of his soldiers at Dunkard Bottom, in 1760, assumed by him.

Henry Smith vs. Samuel Cowdon.—Henry on 15th September, 1758, becomes security for Thomas Fulton on a bond to Margaret Dyer—payable on or before 16th September next ensuing date. After same was payable and before it was paid it was assigned by John Cravens, who married Margaret, to Robert Cravens.

John Hope vs. Daniel Harrison.—Hope was Deputy Sheriff, and fearing his account would be short, went to Carolina, &c.

OCTOBER, 1765 (C).

Crow vs. Bell.—Elizabeth Hog deposes about the "fairing."

Evick vs. Gabriel Coile.—Wm. Green deposes, 3d October, 1765, aged 40 years. Michael Reager deposes 3d October, 1765, aged 30 years and upwards. Michael says four or five years ago he lived at John Lemley's, in Winchester, together with plaintiff Evick. The name is also spelled Guile.

McClenachan vs. Crawford.—Account Robert McClenachan, 1760–61, to wages as storekeeper of James Crawford.

Devit vs. Francisco.—Nathaniel Lyon was Robert Armstrong's brother-in-law, 26th December, 1764.

NOVEMBER, 1766 (A).

John Long vs. John Hutcheson.—1766. To schooling your children.

Hugh Smith vs. William Hutchison.—Sworn to by Hugh, Orange County, North Carolina, 23d June, 1766.

Patterson vs. Harrison.—Arbitrators: Daniel and Abraham Smith.

Burnsides vs. Joseph Edwards.—Joseph Edwards, a soldier. Orders by him on Charles Lewis for his pay, dated 27th August, 1764.

John Clendenning vs. Capt. Walter Cunningham.—To pay as a soldier.

Henry Heth vs. Philip Love.—1761. "To your club in mess an ye campaign" with Col. Andrew Lewis, Capt. Fleming et als., settled by the two former.

AUGUST, 1766 (A).

Johnston vs. Samples.—William English signature (Inglish).

Heneberger vs. Kline.—Andrew Kline, of Borough of Lancaster, County of Lancaster, Pennsylvania. Bond, 1765.

Briggs vs. Inglish.—Bond of Joseph Inglish, 1765.

Breckinridge vs. Loy.—Bond of Steven Loy, of Manockissie, 1762.

Cock vs. Ingless.—Bond of W. English (signed W. Ingles), 1764.

MAY, 1766 (C).

Marrow vs. Williams.—Sigs.: Archibald Huston and Joshua Boucher.

MARCH, 1767 (A).

McClung vs. Fleming.—Certificate that Fleming is a soldier.

John Pharis vs. Daniel Harrison.—George Anderson and William Cravens are going out of the Colony, 29th September, 1764.

Benjamin Hawkins vs. John Nealey.—Was John Nealey a physician? 1765.

NOVEMBER, 1766 (B).

Patrick vs. John Kinkead, of Albemarle.—Bond, defendant to John Shields, of Amherst, 1764.

Malcolm Allen vs. Martin Kersey and Caleb Worley.—Debt. Writ, 1766, 28th August. Only the summonses. Copy left.

Ray vs. Chandler.—Case: Writ, October, 1763. Deposition of Capt. John Blagg, of his service, withdrawn. Deposition of Col. John Smith withdrawn

Calloway vs. John Robinson.—Writ, October, 1763. Defendant is a mill wright by trade and lives near the Stone House on Roanoke.

Christian vs. John Henderson, shoemaker.—1765.

AUGUST, 1766 (C).

Alexander Wright vs. Capt. Christian Benjeman, in Hampshire.—1766–1764.

Givens vs. Cartmill.—James Cartmill, brother to John Cartmill, 1766.

Finley vs. John Crank.—Defendant of New River, 1759–60.

Gilbert vs. Campbell.—Wm. Campbell and Robert Campbell, brothers, 1764.

AUGUST, 1766 (D).

Thomas Huggart vs. Israel Christian.—To the reward offered by defendant for taking up Dinnes McAny, a deserter from the pack-horse drivers, in 1760.

James Greenlee vs. George Buff.—Petition, 24th October, 1765. Gone to Carolina.

William Fleming, carpenter, vs. Edward Sharpe.—Affidavit of William before Wm. Fleming, gent., 4th June, 1765.

Crow vs. Graham.—Dr. Joseph (James?) Donaldson, 12th May, 1764

Edward Long vs. James Ward.—1765. To making a suit of clothes for yourself and a coat for your son William.

MARCH, 1767.

Samuel Gist, of Hanover, vs. Andrew Steel.—Writ, 28th November, 1767. Defendant dead August, 1766—not found.

Robert Carlyle vs. George Francisco.—1766. To 10 bushels wheat @ 3/ per bushel.

John Campbell vs. Rev. John Kinkead.—1st March, 1766. Account showing cost of corn, coffy, labor, &c.

John Craig vs. William Beard.—24th October, 1765. Defendant is a son-in-law of John Mills.

Brown vs. Thomas Dun.—Defendant living at John Draper's, on headwaters of Peck Creek.

NOVEMBER, 1767 (B).

Mat. Harper, administrator Michael Harper, vs. Capt. William Christian. To Michael's bounty and pay as a soldier.

Cabell vs. Boyd's Administrator.—Account with signature Sam. Jordan.

Kinkead vs. Knox.—Deposition of Mrs. Kinkead.

Trigg vs. Clark.—Stephen Trigg's account.

Stephen Trigg vs. James Leatherdale.—1766. Assumpt. by James for his son James.

William Cabell vs. Mathew Mullen.—Defendant was formerly overseer for William Tees, but now lives about six miles from Tees's.

Robert Prit vs. Honorius Powell.—Agt. of rental and building a house.

Rady vs. Robert Crafford.—Defendant lives near Steele's Mill and is a shoemaker.

Mary McDonald, administratrix Edward McDonald, vs. William Simpson and Betty, administrators Malcolm Campbell.—Late Elizabeth Campbell, executrix Malcom Campbell.

NOVEMBER, 1766 (D).

Hinds vs. William Bell.—Writ, 25th October, 1765. Defendant lives at Col. Chiswell's mines—not executed—the defendant is at the mines. Wm. McC.

Thomas Barker vs. William Robinson.—Defendant is a shoemaker.

MARCH, 1767 (C).

McCaul vs. Robottom.—Writ, 10th Jan., 1767. Moved out of the County.

Dore vs. McIlhenny.—Order by McIlhenny to be paid out of his pay.

AUGUST, 1767 (D).

John Brent vs. Archibald Fisher and Susanna, his wife, late Susanna Shaddon, administratrix Mathew Shaddon, deceased.—Writ, 28th May, 1767. Mathew Shaddon's bond dated 20th March, 1762.

John Cawley and Margaret, his wife, late Margaret Woods, vs. Thomas Patterson.—Writ, 13th July, 1767.

Rutherford vs. Henry Tamewood.—Writ, 28th May, 1767. Defendant lives this side of Hance Maggot's, upon Mr. Thomas Lewis's land. He is commonly called *Temster*. (He is a German) from Frederick County.

John Taylor vs. Malcum McCown.—Defendant is widow's son.

MAY, 1767 (C).

Viers vs. Thomas Smith and Barbara.

Catherine Whitley, by Blakeley Brush, her next friend, vs. Jonathan Whitley, her next friend.—Bill for divorce for cruelty. Writ, 28th August, 1767.

AUGUST, 1767 (C).

Israel Christian vs. John Hutcheson, Jr., son to John, Christian's Creek.—Bond dated 20th August, 1765.

Samuel Pritchard vs. Dr. John Wood.—Account.

Hugh Murphy vs. Joseph How.—Defendant at New River. Petition, 28th May, 1767, not found. Account, 1766: "To your promise to pay me for my right of my wife's dower in the tract of land sold you by Mathew French."

Thomas Johnson vs. Joseph Skidmore.—Bond, 1744–5, payable in Virginia currency.

MAY, 1768 (A).

Reed vs. Evans.—Ezekiel Evans, living on Goose Creek, 18th November, 1766.

Christian vs. Mann.—Wm. Mann and Israel Christian. Contract by Israel to employ William as hunter or Indian trader.

John Stevinson vs. William Waterson.—Attachment, 6th April, 1768. On the back of paper is a fragment, as follows: "the said Robert Trimble is to have immediate possession of ye plantation of James Trimble, son of John Trimble, deceased."

Herron vs. Gwinn.—Papers withdrawn. Deposition of Daniel Harrison et als.

AUGUST, 1768 (A).

Wm. Hays vs. George Parris.—Account and paid. Att. by Hays to Israel Christian to collect withdrawn. George Paris now of Carolina, 6th June, 1768.

Gove vs. Phillips.—Plaintiff a school teacher—account.

Gore vs. Andrew Hueling.—Account and contract with the patrons withdrawn.

Arch. Mathews vs. John Ward.—To one man's saddle, per son John.

NOVEMBER, 1767 (E).

Robert Hall vs. Robert Armstrong.—Bond, 26th September, 1764, by defendant to plaintiff, of Orange County, Province of North Carolina.

Israel Christian vs. Isam O'Neal, son of Edmond O'Neal.—Acct. 1766.

Edwards vs. McCutchean and wife.—Contract to build and operate a fulling mill.

MAY, 1767 (D).

Rex vs. Joseph Bell.—Indictment for forgery—true bill—for forging order to Parson Jones to publish banns of Anne Wallace, daughter of Wm. Wallace, and Edward Sampson (March 9th, 1765), a deformed little tailor.

Crow vs. Buchanan.—Account, 1759. To £1, Carolina money, to be changed to Virginia money, is 13 shillings and 9 pence.

Thompson vs. Watterson.—Demurrer by Patrick Henry.

November, 1768 (A).

Kent vs. Love.—Deposition of Hugh Crockett. "Before Love went to live at Vanse's."

May, 1768 (A).

Israel Christian vs. William Curry.—Defendant near Staunton. Account.
Same vs. William McClintock.—Account.
Archibald Fisher and Susanna, his wife, administratrix of Matt Shaddon, vs. James Robinson.—9th August, 1766. Susanna Shaddon (alias Fisher), administratrix of Mathew Shaddon swears that her late husband stated the account vs. James Robinson. The money was due from George Robinson, deceased, and was never paid.
Mathew Glaspy vs. Robert Raburn.—Mathew is from Granville County, South Carolina. Account and affidavit.
James Logan vs. James Cowdon.—1767. Witness, Jane Steel, wife of Robert Steel.
Boyd vs. Levy Smith.—Defendant lives at New River.
Same vs. Wm. Dougherty.—Defendant lives at New River.
Same vs. Alexander Neelly.—Defendant is a tailor, and lives at Fort Chiswell.
Israel Christian vs. John Stophelmine and Jacob Mire.—Jacob Mire lives on Massanuteen, on South River, about 2 miles below one Millar's and Jacob Bear's.

August, 1768 (D).

Scott vs. Davis.—William Davies, living in the forks. 1766.
Scott vs. Mary Ann Young.—Defendant is daughter-in-law to William Young.
William Hutchison vs. Robert Galloway.—Account dated 1740. To wheat, rye and Indian corn. To cash lent at Rocky Ridge.
John Biggs vs. Robert Hamilton.—Defendant is a doctor.

November, 1768 (C).

McGinty vs. Skidmore.—Dr. Wm. Ginits vs. Joseph Skidmore. Account for schooling, dated Hampshire, 1766. Affidavit before Jonathan Heath.
Andrew Elliott vs. James Loyd.—Affidavit by plaintiff in Craven County, South Carolina, April 11, 1764, before James Wyley.
John Thompson vs. Perdue Courtney.—Account, 1763.

August, 1768 (C).

Reed vs. Allsup.—Bond by Robert Allsup of County Amherst, to John Reid of same County, 3d August, 1762.
Peter Grieder (Krieder) vs. James Neely.—Bond by defendant to plaintiff, of Northampton County, Pennsylvania, 8th May, 1766. Conditioned to make deed to plaintiff for land on Peters Creek.

Estate of Alexander Boyd vs. Joshua McCormack, North Fork.
Same vs. Elliott.
McDowell vs. Stuart.
Price vs. Allsup.
Robert Hall vs. Major Robert Breckenridge.—1759.—to my pay as a soldier. 44 days @ 1/ = £2, 4, 0. Hall's discharge dated 22d February, 1759. Summons dated 28th November, 1768.

Anderson & Co. vs. Alexander Boyd.—Defendant was of New London, in Colony of Virginia.

Fulton vs. Mann.—Order dated Fort Defiance, August 28, 1764.

William Allason vs. William Fleming (son-in-law of James Ryburn).— Account, 1763. Affidavit in King George, 1767.

MARCH, 1768 (D 2).

William Simpson and Elizabeth, late Elizabeth Campbell, vs. Michael Woods and William Holly, of Bedford.—Writ, 28th August, 1767. Bond to Elizabeth Campbell, dated 29th November, 1763.

Ewing vs. Man and McCutchan.—*Suit about* slaves. Showing transactions.

James Crawford vs. Samuel Patterson.—Attachment. Defendant is of Halifax County. Bond by him, 8th September, 1766.

Anderson & Co. vs. James Hynd.—Bond by defendant of Albemarle County, 19th November, 1764.

Crocket vs. Long.—Bond by Henry Long of Mechlenburg County, North Carolina, dated 15th August, 1766.

NOVEMBER, 1768.

Whitzell vs. McDonald.—June 11, 1755. Then received unto the Secretary's office John McDaniel's survey for 80 acres of land with 2 rights and 10/6, the patent fee, assigned to Martin Witsell, in whose names the patents will issue. (Signed) James Davenport.

MARCH, 1768 (E).

Dr. Robert Brown of Henrico vs. Alexander Boyd.—Account for medicines and attendance, 1764-5.

Clark vs. Thomas Carpenter.—Thomas commonly called Jacke.

Alexander Boyd Estate vs. Jacob Brown, No. Fork Roanoke.—Account.

Same vs. David McGee, North Fork.—Account.

Same vs. Thomas Goodson, South Fork.

Hutchins, Assignee, vs. John Thomson.—Bond by defendant to Robert Orr, dated 3d March, 1762. Assigned by Orr, 10th August, 1766. Witnesses, Henry Halstin and John Stephens.

Gabriel Jones vs. Mr. William Hughes, Adjutant, &c.—Account. Letter, Alexander Love to Lieutenant William Hughes, Winchester, Va.

MAY, 1768.

Alexander Boyd Estate vs. Wm. Moor, Craig's Creek.—1766, June 7. To 6 bushels hemp seed, £3, 0, 0.

Mathew Harrison vs. William McGee.—1767, April. By bringing 2 servants in your wagon from Winchester to the *Plains*.

James Clark, infant, by mother, Margaret Clark, vs. John Trotter.—Trespass on land. A. C., 28th August, 1768.

Andrew Crockett vs. James Scott.—Deposition, Peter Wylie, 17th June, 1769: "When Peter Cochran was on his journey to Halston River" he stopped at deponent's house.

Crow vs. Captain William Cunningham.—Account.

Samuel Cowdon vs. William Wallace.—John Murray swears, 17th August, 1769, that he assisted Samuel Cowdon in his store in 1762.

John Drake vs. Lanty Armstrong.—1761. Account.

Henry Begley vs. James Kelly.—From Hampshire County. Attachment, 12th March, 1765. Samuel Dew, Deputy Sheriff. Henry swears, 15th June, 1769, before Jonathan Heath, that James is removed out of the Colony.

James Bush of Amherst vs. Thomas Francis.

Mathews vs. William Christian.—Willian, son to Samson.

James Ewings vs. John Thompson.—To your promise to pay me for your Brother Robert..

Carter Henry.

C. H. Harrison vs. Dr. William Fleming.—Order, 18th October, 1766, by plaintiff on defendant. Cash lent you at Benj. Mosby's, while I served in the Virginia Regiment. (Endorsed) Accepted, May 28, 1767, Bedford Court House. Wm. Fleming. To Dr. Fleming in Staunton.

Moses Moore vs. Samuel Cloyd.—Samuel Cloid be pleased for to pay unto John Risk, my father-in-law, that money you owe me, for I have empowered him to act for me in my absence, &c. Dated 5th February, 1766. (Signed) *Moses Moore.*

Gay vs. John Dailey.—Bond by John Dailey to Caleb Wordley(?), 18th October, 1764. Assigned by Caleb, 14th February, 1765. Witnessed by Jesse Atkinson and Rebekah (her x mark) Wordley(?).

Thomas Yuille vs. George Parish.—Affidavit by Thomas before Wade Netherland, Cumberland County, 22d February, 1762.

Samuel Pepper vs. George Pearis.—July 5, 1763.

Boyd's Estate vs. Same.—At Bedford Store, 1764, March 27th. John Henderson swears, 10th March, 1767, he bought 2 tracts land of George Pearis on *North Fork Roanoke, alias Goose Creek.*

William Bowyer vs. George Pacer.—On 30th July, 1768, good hemp sold at 35 shillings for 112 lbs.

Andrew Greer vs. Peter Grub.—The paintiff being out in Carolina with a store of goods had purchased for the sale of those goods a house and lot.

Paxton vs. Ward.—One run of liquor made of Thos. Paxton's own grape.

James Ray vs. Hog.—William Chandler of Bedford County.

Smiley vs. Thompson.—John Smiley, Chapman, 1767.

John Street vs. John Collier's Executor.—John Collier's wife had a son, James Gault. Order on Mrs. Gault, jailer at Williamsburg. 15th November, 1765.

McAfee vs. Cochraine.—Original deed, Peter C. to James M. Original contract, 2d October, 1765. Recorded 16th October, 1765. Peter C. and Margaret. 11th March, 1765.

August, 1769 (A).

James Huston vs. John Henderson.—Hampshire County. 5th March, 1768. James Huston makes affidavit.

James McCorkle vs. John Skilton, Tailor.

Mathews vs. Robert Knox.—Robert Knox, shoemaker. Bond, 25th November, 1766.

Pepper vs. Johnson.—Signature, Anthony Bledsoe.

Smith vs. Berry.—William McKemey's signature.

Samuel Woods and Margaret, late Margaret Robinson, Administratrix William Robinson, deceased, vs. William Simpson and James Robertson.— Note by defendants to Margaret Robinson, 27th September, 1765. Writ, 29th June, 1769.

March, 1769 (A).

John Hanna vs. George Hendrix.—Attachment, 13th December, 1768. John Hanna, Jr. (John Hanna, Sr., surety.)

Robert and Mathew Reed, Administrators of George Rodgers, vs. William Watterson.—Attachment, 7th June 1768. Plaintiffs "have reason to be-lieve that defendant is about to leave the County or so absconds." Walter Cunningham, surety.

Mathew Reed and Hugh Johnson vs. James and William Jones.—Attachment, 24th January, 1769. Defendants about to leave the County. Suit on bond dated 16th September, 1768. Witnessed by John Verner and Margaret Reed.

John Dinwiddie (Dunwoodie) vs. William Busheers (Bearshears).—Attachment, 5th December, 1768. Robert Dunwody, surety.

Hugh Donaho vs. Joseph Dickinson.—Attachment, 19th March, 1769. Defendant about to remove. Property sold.

Joseph Paxton vs. Daniel Davis.—Attachment, 1st February, 1769.

Fowler vs. Skidmore.—Bill in Chancery, filed 1764–5. John Fowler and Margaret, his wife, William Patterson and Mary, his wife, Patrick Quinn and Jane, his wife, which said Margaret, Mary and Jane, together with Sarah, since intermarried with James Skidmore, were sisters and co-heirs of Randolph McDonald of Augusta County, deceased, against James Skidmore and Sarah, his wife. Randolph died intestate unmarried and without children. Randolph's mother was Janet McDonald. Randolph was 26 years old when he died.

Mathew Reid and Johnston vs. Wm. Fleming.—Attachment, 5th August, 1768. Defendant has removed. Bond by Mathew Read and Arthur Campbell. Witnessed by *Jest* Breckenridge.

Murray vs. M. Mathews.—Bill in Chancery, filed 1768, August. John Murray and Elizabeth, his wife, late Elizabeth Matthews, one of the daughters of Joshua Matthews, deceased, also niece and co-heir of her uncle, John Matthews, deceased. John Matthews made his will(?), 27th November, 1761, and devised land to his son Edward, his son John, his son George, and his three daughters, Lettice, Jane and Ann Matthews, all said children being then infants. Soon after making said will, John Matthews, his wife and six children all died, suffered to be murdered. Joshua Matthews was elder brother of John and was dead when John died, leaving daughter Elizabeth and her sister Martha, now an infant. Suit against Martha Matthews for a division. Answer by Sampson Matthews, defendant's guardian, says that John and his family were murdered and burnt in and with their house. Division decreed and set out in the papers. Will probated 22d March, 1764. John was brother of Sampson and George Matthews.

Palzer Smelzer vs. Frederick Stem.—Frederick Stem of New River, 1761. "Kept off by force of arms."

William Findley vs. William Teas.—Attachment, 3d September, 1768. Surety, John Stewart. William Teas, late of Albemarle County.

Akerling vs. Linn (Zinn?).—Bill filed 1767. Samuel Akerling (Ekerling), late of County of Augusta, in year 1750, owned land on Dunker Bottom, on New River, sold it to Garret Zinn. Bonds were put in hands of orator's brother, —— Akerling, who lived on Gawgawganie, where he was taken prisoner, his house and effects burned by Indians. Garrett Zinn, in order not to be murdered by the Indians, moved to Carolina, where he died intestate, leaving Valentine Zinn (defendant) his eldest son and heir, who sold the land to Israel Christian (defendant).

Moses More vs. Samuel Cloyd.—John Risk was father-in-law of Moses More, 5th February, 1766. Samuel Cloyd had removed, 1767.

McClenachan vs. Bromley.—Mary, wife of Captain David Moore.

Daniel Harrison vs. Jonathan Douglas.—Bill for foreclosure of mortgage filed 1768. Mortgage, 1763, of 300 acres, part of 2 tracks containing 400 acres each, whereof Nicholas and Henry Mace and Patrick Quin possessed the other part, the one tract granted to Douglas by Thomas Beal of Frederick County, Maryland, by deed 2d July, 1755, the other patented to Douglas, 11th July, 1761, on head of Broad Run, a branch of North River of Shenandore, where Douglas now lives.

JUNE, 1769 (A).

Israel Christian vs. Donald (Daniel) Campbell and James Bell.—Attachment, 28th November, 1768. Defendants removed from County.

James Bell vs. William Phillips.—Attachment, 30th January, 1769, in hands of Rev. George Cummins.

Esther Cobb (Easter Cob?) vs. Gabriel Powell.—Attachment, 13th November, 1768. Defendant about to remove. Jeremiah Harrison, surety.

S. and G. Mathews vs. John Stuart.—Attachment, 23d May, 1767. "John Stewart, late of Augusta County."

John Bowman vs. James Bryan.—Attachment, 27th January, 1768. On 19th February, 1768, Mrs. Elizabeth Bryan, Wm. Simpson and John Simpson declare that James Bryant, when he went to Pennsylvania, was indebted to Elizabeth.

William Spiller vs. Joseph Colven, alias Corbin.—Petition, 1768. Memo: The above Joseph Colven, at the time he contracted the debt, lived with one Wm. Loggins in King William County, and enlisted himself in the Regiment in 1760–61, but am informed is since married to widow, by whom he has several children, about 6 miles below Staunton, in Augusta, about ½ mile from Stone Meeting House. (Signed) Wm. Spiller. Spiller was from King William, 1760.

Harrison vs. Kinley.—Daniel Harrison, Sr., vs. Benj. Kinley. May, 1769.

James McKinney vs. John Thompson.—Joseph Steel deposes, 16th June, 1769. John Thompson's wife was Susanna, and he had a son, Billy.

AUGUST, 1769 (A).

David Looney vs. Wm. Crow, John Stewart, James Cowden, Hugh Hays and James Huston.—Stewart arrested, August, 1767.

Walter Stewart vs. Colonel John Buchanan.—Covenant, 29th June, 1769. "Not executed, the man is dead."

Alexander Stewart vs. Hugh Means.—Bond dated 1766. Witness, Benjamin Stewart.

John Stewart vs. Samuel Cowden.—Trespass Case, 1767. Account, 1762–1767. 16th January, 1762, breeches for your brother, Walter. July, 1767, to 1 pair breeches in Carolina.

Samuel Woods and Margaret, his wife, vs. William Simpson and James Robertson.—Margaret, late Margaret Robinson. administratrix of William Robinson, deceased.

AUGUST, 1769 (B).

Samuel Kirkham vs. Robert Stewart.—Case, 1767, June.

MARCH, 1769 (B).

Buchanan's Administrator vs. Sayers.—Bill filed 14th January, 1767. Archibald Buchanan, administrator of Walter Buchanan, late of County of Chesterfield, merchant, orator. In 1764 Alexander Sayers, now deceased, owned land in Dunkar's Bottom, on New River, and on Red Creek, at Fort Chiswell, and mortgaged the same to Walter Buchanan on 21st January, 1764. Alexander died 1765 intestate, leaving son Robert, eldest son and heir. Walter Buchanan died 1766. Archibald is brother of Archibald. Robert Breckinridge was guardian of Robert Sayers, May 1767. The mortgage was proved before the General Court, 28th April, 1764, by John Skelton, Robert Donald and Marty Handly, witnesses. John Fleming and Joseph Maynard were also witnesses.

Joseph Watson vs. Joseph How.—Joseph How, of Hampshire County. Bond to Joseph Watson of Fairfax County, dated 4th April, 1765, for making title to land in Hampshire.

Mathews vs. Hughes, Administrator.—Chancery. Suit begun 23d July, 1767. Sampson and George Mathews, orators. James Hughes, deceased, made will leaving his wife executrix and 3 small children, to wit: Euphemia Hughes, Jane Hughes and Mary Hughes, but wife refused to prove the will and administration was granted to Sampson Mathews. Jas. Hughes owned lots in Staunton, sold him by Wm. Preston, by order of County Court, being property of the County. Wife was Euphemia Hughes. Answer of children by mother.

Sampson Mathews vs. John Archer.—Commission, 1768, to North Carolina, to take deposition of Ephraine Wilson.

Rex vs. James Anderson.—James Anderson, indicted 1768, for poisoning Wm. Robertson's hogs, &c. On October, 1768, James Meeks was about to leave the Colony.

JUNE, 1769 (C).

Deed of apprentice by Michael Kirkham, son of Henry Kirkham, of himself, to John Skelton, to learn hatter's trade. 1763.

JUNE, 1769 (D).

Turk vs. Tees.—Letter of Thomas Turk to Gabriel Jones, 25th July, 1768, says Wm. Creag, son to Alexander Creag, deceased, used to drive a wagon for Samson Mathews.

Thos. Turk vs. James Greenlee and James McDowell.—James McDowell was a friend and relative of James Greenlee.

JUNE, 1769 (E).

James Dever and Elizabeth, his wife, vs. Daniel Henderson and Elizabeth, his wife.—Hugh Dever, brother of James.

Wm. Crow vs. Geo. Carpenter.—Slander. George was born in Germany.

OCTOBER, 1769 (A).

William Stewart's Executor vs. Wm. Christeele and John Archer.—John Stewart, executor of William. 29th June, 1769.

Stewart vs. Ray.—James Stewart, November 9, 1763.

JUNE, 1769 (F).

McCain vs. Breckinridge.—Margaret Cain, formerly Margaret Looney, wife of Peter Looney, deceased. January 22, 1768.

AUGUST, 1769 (D).

John Stewart vs. James Ward.—1768. James Ward makes oath that he never settled for 2 hides coined by his son William and delivered at the Dutch tanner's, which hides were property of John Stewart.

Cowden vs. McCroskey.—Daniel Smith, aged about 39, 25th March, 1769.
McKannie vs. Scatian.—Francis McKannie, living in Frederick in 1769.
Thomas Miller vs. James Anderson, son of Deaf James.

OCTOBER, 1769 (B).

Nicholas Null vs. John Craig.—Chancery. Bill filed, 1767. Revived, 1768, November. Nicholas Null, orator. Revived by George Null, eldest son and heir. Nicholas Null, late of Pennsylvania, but now of this Colony, came to Virginia, 1750. Applied to William Burk for a piece of land which Burk had bought of James Wood of Frederick. John Craig had a claim on the land. Null was a German. Valentine Pence was brother-in-law of Nicholas Null.

William Lamb and Margaret, his wife, late Margaret Reed, vs. Samuel Kirkham.—Bond to Margaret Reed, 30th March, 1766.

Lud Francisco vs. George Francisco.—Bond of George and John Francisco to Ludwick Francisco, dated 10th January, 1762.

Samuel Woods and Margaret, his wife, late Margaret Robinson, administratrix of William Robinson, deceased, vs. James Robinson.—Bond dated 27th September, 1765. Suit brought 29th June, 1769.

MARCH, 1770 (B).

Peter How vs. Grant.—Chancery. Bill filed 1767. Peter How, Esq., late of town of White Haven, in Great Britain, orator. In 1764, John Grant, of King George, mortgaged slaves to How for a debt. Deposition of Wingfield Wright, brother of John Wright, in King George, 1764-5, certified before John Stewart, in Spottsylvania County, 14th October, 1767. Each of the Wrights married a sister of Grant's. Letter of William Templeman, of Fredericksburg. Mortgage was executed by Colonel John Champe, agent of How, witnessed by Joseph Herndon, William Templeman, David Briggs and Charles Yates, and recorded in General Court, 29th October, 1764. William Templeman's deposition: After death of Col. John Champe, with whom he had lived as a clerk, he was employyed by Charles Yates of Fredericksburg, merchant, to collect the debts due to the store kept by the said Col. Champe for Peter How of Whitehaven.

Hetrick vs. Hetrick.—Chancery. Filed 28th August, 1768. In 1752-53, John Hetrick, defendant, brother of Caspar Hetrick, orator, went from Pennsylvania to the back part of this Colony and purchased land from John Bombgardner and then returned to Pennsylvania, where orator then lived. Land was cheap and the range for cattle good and fresh. Orator and defendant came to Virginia and settled on the land bought by John. William Frazer had entered a piece of land near which he gave to orator, but John sold it to Peter Tresser. This caused trouble between the brothers and orator built his own house on first piece of land. Orator heard defendant would not give him the land and removed his family to the house of Adam Hetrick and sent his neighbors, Valentine Pence and Frederick Harmentrout, to defendant, to know his intentions. Orator moved back on the land and had been living there 14 years in 1768. Bill to compel John to convey to him.

William Fulton vs. George Breckinridge.—Summons on petition, 23d October, 1769, on account for schoolkeeping. "Not executed by reason of high waters—John Bowyer."

MARCH, 1770 (B?)

James Stewart vs. Thomas Carpenter.—Petition. Summons, 22d August, 1769. Account dated 1766, for making a suit of clothes.

Robert and Mathew Read, administrators of George Rogers, vs. Dr. John Watkins.—Bond dated 1st June, 1768.

NOVEMBER, 1770 (A).

Thomas, Assignee, vs. Lange.—Chancery, bill filed 25th June 1770. Bond of Charles Lange, Reformed Minister, to James Johnson, for £45, dated 21st October, 1768. Bond assigned to John Thomas, who sues Chas. Lange. Charles failed to pay and departed from this Colony to parts unknown, leaving land which is decreed to be sold.

John Walmsley vs. Andrew Johnston.—Matthew Patton, gent., mentioned in 1765.

William Robertson vs. James Anderson, of Long Meadow.

Thomas Stewart vs. Thomas Black.—Petition on account dated 1766.

John Smith vs. Patton's Executors.—Bill filed May, 1767. In 1741, John Smith, orator, being joint partner with Zachariah Lewis, William Waller, Benjamin Waller, Robert Green, James Patton, in an order of Council for 100,000 acres on James River and Roanoke. The whole direction of the affair was committed to James Patton, by whom orator was appointed to see the land surveyed, in which service orator was employed until 1751, and was entitled to a large sum of money therefor. Patton purchased the parts of the other partners and got the whole grant in his hands, except orator's and the part of Zachariah Lewis. (James was a member of General Assembly, 1763-4.) Orator was also engaged in protection of frontiers, and was captured by the French and Indians in 1756 and remained a prisoner until 1758.

AUGUST, 1770 (A).

Zebulon Harrison vs. Daniel Prentice.—On a bond dated 1764, 31st October, payable to Zebulon Harrison.

Reuben Harrison vs. Joseph Reaburn.—1770, 2d April.

Eleanor Dunn's Petition.—Her son was bound to James Stewart, about 8 years ago, to learn trade of a tailor.

MARCH, 1770 (D).

John Anderson, Assignee of Robert Anderson and George Anderson, vs. Christian Bingaman.—Debt. Writ issued August, 1766. Bond dated 8th July, 1764. Assigned by George 10th July, 1765. Assigned by Robert 19th April, 1766.

William Anderson vs. John Dailey.—Writ 22d August, 1769.

James Anderson vs. Andrew and James Hays.—Debt. Writ 26th January, 1769.

Beard vs. Craig.—Bond. Thomas Beard, Schoolmaster, bound unto John Craig, £8. Dated 4th November, 1766.

Buchanan vs. Crow & Co.—Debt. 1769. Bond by James and John Calhoon and William Crow of Augusta to James Buchanan, merchant of Henrico, dated 23d October, 1765.

Alexander Baine vs. Alexander Boyd's administrator.—Writ issued 19th August, 1767. In 1764 Alexander Boyd mortgaged land and slaves to Alexander Baine, orator. Alexander Boyd died intestate and administration was granted to Andrew Boyd, his brother and heir-at-law. Land lay on branch of Roanoke River called Staunton River.

Crockett vs. Robertson.—Spa, dated 28th May, 1768. Agreement between Samuel Robinson of Cumberland County, Pennsylvania, and Saml. Crockett, of Augusta, dated 24th October, 1767. Robinson sold tract of land to Crockett on South Branch of Roanoke adjoining William Robinson and James Robinson, deceased, on main road to New River, it appearing that the right to the land is in an orphan of John Robinson, deceased. Bill re·cites: That one James Robinson, deceased, then living in Pennsylvania, with a pretty numerous family, sent his eldest son John Robinson (now deceased) to Roanoke, who bought land on his father's account from George Robinson. James came with his family and divided his land between his children. John had a brother William, also Samuel. The title to the land was taken in John's name, and he never conveyed his dividend to Samuel. John died, leaving his daughter, Elizabeth, his only child. The family was broken up by the Indians and French, and Samuel moved to South side of Blue Ridge and became very poor, and sold his land to Samuel Crockett. Elizabeth was an infant, and prayer for conveyance. Jacob Brown and Ann, his wife, depose, 17th Feb., 1768, to above facts. Ann was daughter of James Robinson.

MARCH, 1770 (E).

Cowan vs. Cowan.—Letter of Andrew Cowan to David Cowan, living in Albemarle, dated January 13, 1766. Loving Brother: This comes to let you know that we are all in good health at present, blessed be God for his mercies. Hoping that these few lines will find you in the same, I desire that you will go to James Cowan's and ask him for a note of mine that lies in my little trunk—a note of 2 pounds and five shillings, which William Teas(?) is due me against March 25, and get the money, for I am going to Carolina. I have nothing material to write you, but desire to be remembered to you all.

AUGUST, 1770 (B).

John Elliott vs. Elizabeth Stewart, executor of John Stewart.—Writ dated 23d October, 1769.

NOVEMBER, 1770 (B).

Walter Crow vs. John Stewart (Middle River).—Writ, 28th November, 1767. Charles Crow is about to remove to South Carolina, 21st October, 1766. Daniel Smith had a brother John Smith, deceased, 21st October, 1766.

Blair vs. Blair.—James Blair of City of Williamsburg, plaintiff. Defendant "Not found."

William Kennady vs. James Poage and Ann, his wife, administratrix of William Willson, deceased.—25th June, 1770.

Samuel Woods and Margaret, his wife, late Margaret Robinson, administratrix of William Robinson, deceased, vs. Anthony Bledsoe and Stephen Trigg.—29th June, 1769.

MARCH, 1771 (A).

Samuel Cowdon vs. John Stewart, Tailor of Staunton.—Chancery.—Writ, 8th February, 1770.

Blair vs. Patterson.—Nathan Page (Poage) is about to remove from the Colony, 28th January, 1771.

MARCH, 1771 (B).

Rev. Alexander Miller, Clerk, vs. Rev. John Brown, Clerk. Slander. Case damage, £100. Writ dated 9th November, 1769. Plaintiff was a Presbyterian. Defendant was a member of the Presbytery. Judgment deposing Mr. Miller. Depositions taken, North Carolina, Orange County, Upper Hyco, 6th February, 1771, at house of Rev. Hugh McAden: Mrs. Elizabeth Miles; Mrs. Sally McCoy (formerly Tolbert), sister of Elizabeth Miles; Abraham Miles; John Lea, aged 45 years; Thomas Barnet and Alexander Moore, Elders of Lower Hyco, and Hugh Barnet, Vestryman.

Litsler's Administrator vs. Hughes' Administrator.—Chancery. Writ dated. In 1765 James Hughes, of Staunton, Innholder, died intestate, leaving Euphemia, Jane and Mary Hughes. David Stewart died, 1757. Bill for title to a lot in Staunton bought by Litsler from James Hughes.

Henry Lang vs. James Young.—Chancery. Writ dated 28th August, 1768. Joseph Lang, father of Henry, many years ago purchased a tract of land from George Robinson, who was to take out patent in Joseph's name, but it was actually issued in name of Samuel Lang, deceased, brother of Henry, for half the tract. Samuel was of very poor intellect and quite an idiot. Joseph died and left will dated 11th September, 1757, wherein he gave a part of his land "The Welch Cabin" unto Samuel. James Young persuaded Samuel to convey his land to him, in consideration that James paid him in victuals, &c. Bill to set aside conveyance.

John Stewart was a tailor in Staunton in 1754.

MARCH, 1771 (C).

Richard Woods vs. William Kennedy.—Writ, 3d December, 1771. Defendant lives in Botetourt.

Richard Woods vs. John Stewart.—Writ, 1st September, 1770.

Robert Reed vs. John Stuart.—Writ dated 15th January, 1770. Bond dated 1765.

William Robertson vs. James Anderson (Long Meadow).—Trespass. James killed Robertson's fowls and hogs with ratsbane in 1767. James Meek's deposition, November 1, 1768. He was at James Anderson's house on Long Meadow. James wife was Elizabeth, and they had a daughter Jean. William Robertson's wife was Lettice. Elizabeth was sister of William Skillem and George Skillem(?). Verdict for plaintiff.

John Stewart vs. James Lockhart.—Writ 6th May, 1767. May Court dismissed unless security for costs.

John Stuart vs. David Stuart's Executors.—On account, 1762 to 1768, tailoring.

MAY, 1771. (A).

Sarah and Benjamin Harrison, Executors of Daniel Harrison, deceased, vs. James Blair, John Graham, Jr. and Sr., Lanty Graham and John Vaub ("Graham" is spelled "Grimes").—Defendant. Writ, 1st September, 1770.

Bryan Kenny vs. John Stewart (of Middle River).—Case. Writ, 20th March, 1770.

William Davis vs. Joseph Scott.—Writ, 23d November, 1771. "Scott is now in Carolina, but expected in. Captain Ewing is his uncle, where he resides when in Virginia."

MAY, 1771 (B).

Alexander Stewart vs. John Smith and Margaret, his wife, late Margaret Clark.—Debt. Writ, 15th January, 1770. Bond dated 20th January, 1769.

Halbert McClure vs. Nathaniel McClure and James McClure.—Bill filed March 1769. Nathaniel McClure, father of orator, left by will plantation to James and Nathaniel McClure, his sons. Halbert was also a son(?). Widow was Mary. James McClure went to Georgia(?). Nathaniel McClure's Sr., effects were set up at auction, at which time Nathaniel, Jr., was under age and James was of age.

John Stewart vs. Sampson Mathews.—Chancery. Sampson Mathews is brother-in-law to Randal Lockhart.

AUGUST, 1771 (A).

William Christell vs. John Archer.—Defendant affirms, 27th February, 1771, that John Stewart is very ill and he is likely to lose John's testimony.

Margaret Brown, executrix of John Brown, vs. John Stewart.—Debt. Writ dated September, 1770.

Edmondson and Kennedy vs. Borden's Executors.—Chancery. John Hart was an agent for Benjamin Borden.

NOVEMBER, 1771 (B).

Stevenson vs. McClung.—John Stewart, Borden's land, 21st June, 1771.

Henry King and Susanna, his wife, late Susanna Cochran, administratrix of John Cochran, deceased, vs. John Smiley.—Defendant, in 1771, lives in Botetourt.

Boone vs. Campbell et als.—Brice Hanna failed and ran away. Charles Campbell, Alexander Moore, William Walker and James Walker were commissioners to have work done at New Providence Church in 1766. Brice Hanna was contractor.

MARCH, 1772 (A).

Turk vs. Raferty.—Chancery. Writ 22d May, 1771. Thomas Turk and Margaret (Mary), his wife, William Grove, Elizabeth Grove, Michael Grove, Easter Grove and Matthew Grove, infants, by Wm. Grove, their guardian, complain. In 1760, father of oratrixes, Matthew Grove, died intestate, leaving widow, Esther (since intermarried with Thomas Laferty), defendants. Widow possessed herself of whole estate. Mary Turk and William Groves were of age. Suit for account.

Stamps and Seaton vs. Israel Christian.—*Sci ifa.* Defendant lives in Botetourt, 1771.

James McGill vs. John McClure.—Slander. Writ, 1770. "Would hang as high as Gilderoy." John declares that Archibald Campbell, of Caroline County, is a material witness, and that as he is a single person and, from his father's declaration, he cannot get the benefit of his evidence in the usual way. Prays a commission. 10th March, 1772.

John Stewart (Taylor)—vs. George Mathews.—Debt. 1772. On account, 1760 ——, with David Stewart's estate. Bonds and other papers signed by John.

MARCH, 1772 (B).

Edward Erwin vs. Benjamin Erwin.—Chancery. Writ, 1st April, 1771. Plaintiff very aged and infirm, and defendant made him drunk and induced him to sign a deed. Suit to annul.

Rebeccah Archer vs. John Archer.—Chancery. Writ 23d November, 1772. Plaintiff and defendant have been married upwards of 30 years, and has suffered most cruel usage from her husband. Prayer for separate maintenance. Answer admits all drunkenness. "Whereas John Archer has abused Rebekah, his wife, and denies his marriage to her, we, the under named persons, do certify that we were eye and ear witnesses to ye above persons being lawfully married in ye County Tiroon. Given under our hands, this 16th day of November, 1771. (Signed) James Sayers, Rebekah Sayers, Hannah Sayers, Sarah Renick, Sampson Archer, Elizabeth (her x mark) Stuart." Decree for separate maintenance, according to contract between the parties, dated 7th March, 1772.

MARCH, 1772 (B).

Bowyer vs. Andrew Fitzpatrick.—Debt. Writ, 12th December, 1772. "No inhabitant—gone to Carolina."

Robert Brown (of Henrico) vs. Dr. Wm. McClenachan.—Debt. On account for drugs, 1760–1770. Writ, 20th March, 1771.

Elizabeth Crawford, an infant, by George Crawford, her next friend, vs. John Archer.—Debt. Writ, 12th December, 1772.

William Clark vs. William McNabb. Debt. Writ, January, 1772. Defendant lives in Botetourt.

Robert Lamme vs. William Hook.—Debt. 1769. Robert, son to Robert Lamb.

AUGUST, 1772 (A ?).

James Scott vs. Mathew (alias) Tees Kuykendall.—Petition. Defendant on South Branch, not found. Gone to Hampshire, 1770.

William Steel vs. Andrew Greer.—Case, 1770. Suit by John Ellis vs. William Steele, late of County of Rowan (North Carolina), 1766 (Salisbury District Court).

John Stewart vs. Jacob Lockhart's Executors.—Petition, 1769. Account for tailoring in 1765.

Woods vs. Daniel O'Hara and Andrew Kinkead.—Debt. On bond dated 1762, 4th August. Andrew of Albemarle County.

AUGUST, 1772 (B).

Joseph Pearse (Peace) deposition, 8th April, 1771: Edward Sampson kept school in the neighborhood of Captain Andrew Bird's and boarded with Bird, and Thomas Moore's children went to him. He and Bird frequently got drunk together, and had frequent frolics, when Bird became violent and threatened to kill everybody. Joseph Reece was Bird's step-son.

Nevins and Wanock vs. Dr. John Watkins and Stephen Loy, Tanner.— Bond to plaintiff (apothecaries), dated 1768. Writ dated 6th July, 1770.

Patterson vs. Gamwell.—John Patterson, son of John Patterson, Middle River, 14th June, 1770.

AUGUST, 1772 (C).

Edward Rutledge and Sarah, his wife, late Sarah Armstrong, vs. John Archer.—Debt. Writ, 2d September, 1771. Bond dated 2d January, 1768.

NOVEMBER, 1772.

Turk vs. Turk.—James and Thomas Turk were brothers, April 3, 1772. Debt on account during 1764–65 to 1771. James Turk's wife was Mary, and they had a daughter, Elizabeth. Robert Turk deposes, 15th April, 1772. James Turk paid out £10 for Elizabeth Finley's education in Carolina. Thomas paid Henry Foster, husband of Elizabeth Finley, £40 out of his father's estate.

MARCH, 1773 (B).

Jas. McClure vs. John Adair and Mary, his wife, late Mary O'Donnell.— Trespass. Writ 24th August, 1772. For trespass by Mary on 10th February, 1771.

Thos. Matthews vs. Wm. Greg.—Debt petition. Writ, 24th August, 1772.

MARCH, 1773 (C).

John Madison vs. Robinson.—Chancery. Writ dated 26th March, 1767. Defendants are James Montgomery and Mary, his wife, late Mary Robinson, widow of John Robinson, deceased. Elizabeth Robinson, an infant and only daughter of said John Robinson, deceased, and Mary Montgomery. James Robinson empowered his son John to buy 800 acres on Roanoke from George Robinson, and patent taken out in John's name, but John to convey a share to each of his brothers, according to James's' appointment. James died and John made a conveyance to his brother, William, but never conveyed to his brother Thomas. John died intestate in 1756, leaving a wife, Mary, and one daughter, Elizabeth, an infant and widow, who has married James Montgomery. Thomas sold his right to Samuel Crockett and Crockett to Madison. Answer of Elizabeth, an infant, sworn to 6th August, 1771.

James Gamble vs. James Ewing, Sr.—Petition. Writ, 28th May, 1772. Defendant is son-in-law to Colonel Wilson.

MARCH, 1773 (D).

S. and G. Mathews vs. John Campbell.—Petition. Debt. Writ, 25th May, 1773. Defendant is son to Charles Campbell.

Elizabeth Wilson vs. John Francis and Mary, his wife.—Slander. Elizabeth had a brother John. Elizabeth, daughter of Wm. Wilson(?).

Charles Tees vs. Wm. (father) and James (son) Whitesides.—Chancery. 1772. Charles was in debt to Wm., who left the Colony and empowered James, his son, to collect. Charles paid James, but Wm. and James afterwards got judgment.

John Risk, Jr., vs. James Risk,—Chancery. Writ, 1st April, 1771. In 1763, John Risk bought land on Calfpasture from James Risk, and afterwards gave it to his son, John, orator here. James died without making title, leaving his son and heir, James, defendant here, an infant. Prayer for deed.

David Sayers, Jr., vs. Robert Sayers, son and administrator of Robert Sayers, deceased.—Debt on bond dated December, 1752. Writ dated 17th June, 1765.

MAY, 1773 (A).

Col. John Smith vs. McCaul & Co.—Chancery, 1771. In 1765 orator was in prison for debt, when William Crow agreed to pay the debt and satisfy all claims between them if orator would convey to Crow his tract of land, which orator agreed to do, and executed bond to Crow to that effect, but on account of his old age and infirmities Crow took advantage of him and assigned bond to McCaul & Co., who got judgment. Bill to annul the judgment and bond for fraud. George Smith testifies that in 1765 witness and Jonathan Smith were in Crow's store, and each bought a suit of clothes, which Col. John Smith told Crow to charge to his account. John Madison, of Botetourt, 1773. Luke Bowyer, of Botetourt, 1773. Notice to take depositions given by Crow April 30, 1773, to Col. John Smith and his son, James. Deposition of Abraham Smith; that his father, John Smith.

MAY, 1773 (B).

John Anderson vs. S. Mathews, Mathew and James Lockhart.—Chancery writ, 29th June, 1769. James Lockhart was Sampson Mathews's father-in-law, in 1765. Orator became joint security with Mathews on bond of James Lockhart and Randall Lockhart for collection of public levy in 1765; sometime after securities asked G. Jones and P. Hog to liquidate the account of the Lockharts, when a considerable defalcation was found. Patrick Lockhart was son to James. James Allen was son-in-law of John Anderson. Robert Bratton, aged 60 years, 20th May, 1772. Silas Hart, aged 50 years and upwards, 20th May, 1772. Randall Lockhart was son to James. William Crow, aged 30 years and upwards, 22d August, 1772. James Allen's deposition taken in Botetourt, 1771. Hugh Allen was James's brother.

MAY, 1773 (C).

Andrew Johnston vs. Alexander Wright.—Chancery writ, 20th August, 1766. In 174— orator and Charles Dick, of Fredericksburg, and Alexander Wright entered into partnership to conduct a store at Augusta County Court House. The business was continued until 1751, when it was dissolved. Orator carried on the business, but became involved, and in order to avoid prison he went to Carolina, leaving his books in defendant's possession. Wright cheated him and by indulgence of his creditors he returned to Virginia.

Thomas Meek vs. Michael Reiny.—Debt. Mary Sharp was daughter of John Meek and sister of plaintiff. Her deposition taken 1772; also Wm. Meek was plaintiff's brother.

AUGUST, 1773 (A).

Scathorn vs. Harrison Rutherford.—Capt. Mathew Harrison was in Winchester in 1769, and requested Joseph Scathorn to go with him to the Plains, where he would give Joseph land.

Arthur Johnston lived on Roanoke of Cook's Creek, which he desires to be divided between his two sons, John and Andrew. Capt. Dan Smith was chosen guardian of John, who married before he arrived at full age, when his guardian and stepfather gave him his moiety, which was where his stepfather Greeg lived, who moved off in consequence, and then John sold part to William Bowyer.

Daniel Smith vs. Wm. Bowyer.—Chancery writ, 19th December, 1772. Bond of Wm. Bowyer to Wm. Gregg, to convey to him land on headsprings of Hunter's Gully (Cook's Creek), which he bought of John Johnson; dated 1767. Assigned by Gregg to Robert Hill, 1768. Assigned by Hill to Wm. Bowyer, 1772. In 1759 Arthur Johnston died, with will proved in Augusta, devising lands to his sons, John and Andrew, adjoining the late Daniel Harrison, deceased. Arthur's widow, Margaret, married Wm. Gregg.

Thomas Turk vs. James Turk.—Case writ, 22d August, 1772. Deed by Thomas Turk, 7th April, 1758, apprenticing his daughter, Elizabeth Turk, to James Turk. Elizabeth is aged 5 years and 2 months.

Samuel Woods vs. David Claxton and Sarah, his wife, formerly Sarah Campbell.—Debt. Writ dated 25th May, 1773. Account vs. Sarah dated 1770, August 16.

Andrew Wilson vs. James Alexander.—Case writ, 18th February, 1773. Defendant a reedmaker, and gone to Greenbryer.

November, 1773 (A).

Ralph Laverty vs. John Estill.—Debt. Writ dated 1770. Contract of rental between plaintiff and defendant, dated 1765. Ralph rented to John land belonging to Ralph's step-daughter, which belonged to Robert Graham, deceased. Ralph married Robert's widow(?).

Mathews vs. Henry Pickle.—Debt. Writ, 15th June, 1773. Defendant gone to Carolina.

Mills vs. Neely.—Bond by Dr. John Neilly and Robt. Anderson to Sheriff of Botetourt, dated 9th April, 1773. Witness, Lettice Breckenridge.

Woods vs. Dr. Wm. McClenachan.—Writ, 1772. Officer was kept off by force of arms for several years.

November, 1773 (B).

Joseph Bell vs. William Hanna.—Answer of Hanna to bill of injunction. The defendant had no title to the slave, because the slave had promised Hanna in Ireland not to demand or receive any freedom dues.

Blair vs. Blair.—John Blair, Jr., Esq., administrator of James Blair (late of City of Williamsburg), who died intestate, complains of James Blair of Augusta County. Filed December, 1771. "Not found."

August, 1773 (B).

Briggs vs. Robinson.—Debt on bond dated 31st August, 1767, by Isaac Robinson, of Augusta, to David Briggs, of King George County. Writ dated 25th May, 1773. Returned, "The defendant is dead." (Signed) Danl. Smith.

Wm. Bowyer vs. Wm. Henderson (son of Wm., deceased).—Assignment. Writ, 25th May, 1773. Defendant lives in Greenbrier. Account running 1765—1773.

Wm. Bowyer vs. Wm. Fowler (son to Robert).—Debt on bond, 17th May, 1773. Writ dated 25th May, 1773.

David Briggs vs. Joel Robinson.—Debt. Writ dated 25th May, 1773. He (defendant) lives in Hampshire County.

Beard vs. Dickinson.—Debt. Writ dated 14th September, 1767. John Dickinson, only son and heir-at-law of Adam Dickinson, deceased.

Wm. Bowyer vs. *Lame* James Givens.—Debt. Writ dated 25th May, 1773.

Wm. Bowyer vs. John Montgomerie (Brock's Gap).—Case writ, 15th June, 1773. Defendant gone to Carolina.

John Gratton vs. Benjamin Scott.—Debt. Writ, 15th June, 1773. Defendant lives in Hampshire.

Reuben Harrison vs. Robert Williams and John Phillips.—Debt. Writ dated 28th June, 1773. Note to Reuben dated 31st October, 1764, for £13.

Samuel Woods vs. Ignatius Howard.—Debt. Writ, 19th April, 1773. Defendant gone to Greenbrier.

March, 1774 (A).

Bowyer vs. Stroud.—"Peter Stroud is dead." 28th August, 1773.

William Bowyer vs. Charles Parsons.—Debt. Writ, 28th August, 1773. "Defendant is gone to the New County."

George Wilson vs. John Davis.—A and B writ, 25th November, 1773. "Defendant lives at Monongahela," (?) &c.

MARCH, 1774 (C).

Rev. John Jones vs. Rev. Adam Smith.—Petition. Writ executed June 19, 1773. Account is as follows: 1773, Rev. Adam Smith, debtor, to the Rev. John Jones: To my fee for the marriage of Wm. Elliott, within the Parish whereof I am rector, which you received, £0, 7, 6; the same of Wm. Young, £0, 7, 6; the same of Daniel Taylor, £1, 0, 0; the same of James Patton, £0, 7, 6. William Elliott married a daughter of Joseph Wahub (Wachub), in February, 1773, at Alexander Hamilton's.

Wm. Edmonson, heir-at-law of John Edmonson, deceased, and Wm. Kennedy, heir-at-law of Joseph Kennedy, deceased, vs. Silas Hart, heir-at-law of John Hart and executor of Benjamin Borden.—Chancery writ, 24th August, 1772. John Hart was agent of Benjamin, Jr., and Benjamin sold land to John Hart, who sold to John E. and Joseph K. Bill for title.

Thomas Madison vs. Henry Reaburn.—Petition. Writ dated 22d September, 1773. Defendant is son-in-law to Wm. Christal, and lives in Botetourt.

MAY, 1774 (A).

Brown vs. Brown.—Chancery writ dated 1st April, 1771. Robert Brown and Rebecca Brown, late Rebecca Gardner, formerly the wife of Thomas Gardner, deceased, and Francis Gardner, eldest son and heir-at-law of said Thomas Gardner, orators. In 1763, Thomas Gardner and John Brown purchased a tract of land from John Coulter, in Beverly Manor. Deeds were made in September, 1763. Shortly after, Thomas Gardner died intestate, leaving above widow and son and heir. John Brown entered and took possession by survivorship and died, devising the land to his sons John and Hugh, with provision that his son James should make a deed to his brothers. It is charged that John Brown and Thomas Gardner agreed there should be no survivorship. Prayer for division. John, Jr., was younger brother of Hugh Brown. Hugh was infant at his father's death. John was not 15 years old at his father's death.

Beard vs. Abraham Lincoln.—Note dated June, 1772. Defendant of Linville's Creek.

John Frazier vs. David Frazier.—Case writ, 26th February, 1773. Defendant is gone to New River.

Brown vs. Pattison.—Chancery writ, 29th March, 1769. James Brown and Jane, his wife, late Jane Crawford, daughter of James Crawford, deceased, oratrix's father, died, 1751, possessed of considerable estate, intestate, leaving widow and two children, to wit, oratrix and her brother, James. Widow Elizabeth, Robert Patterson and George Anderson qualified administrators. Orator and oratrix married in July, 1769. Prayer for settlement. Patrick Crawford was brother of James, deceased. Elizabeth (widow) was Elizabeth Robertson, sister of William Robertson.

Samuel Ewing vs. Robert Sayers, eldest son and heir of Alexander Sayers, deceased, vs. James Buchanan.—Chancery writ, 28th August, 1767. Defendant bought land in 1755 on New River, where Humberstone Lyon was then living.

Wm. Bowyer vs. Henry Pickle, Jr.—Case writ, 18th June, 1773. Defendant gone to Carolina.

Richard Harvie vs. Wm. McClenachan.—Writ, 22d March, 1774. "Defendant is dead." Writ dated 25th September, 1773 and 19th February, 1774. "Kept off by force of arms."

Burr Harrison vs. Valentine Sevier.—Debt. Writ 25th November, 1773. "Not found."

AUGUST, 1774.

Ramsey vs. McClure.—Chancery writ, 25th May, 1773. In 1769, John Ramsey, Jr. and Hugh McClure bought land in Beverly Manor and heard that James Hunter of King George had bought the remainder of the Manor not sold and had employed James Kennerley to look out for purchasers. James Ramsey and John Ramsey were brothers and sons of John Ramsey. James Black and John Black were brothers.

Harris vs. Harris.—James Harris, alias Harrison.

MARCH, 1776.

William Bowyer vs. Thomas Morrow.—Petition, 18th June, 1773. Defendant is gone to Greenbrier.

Wm. Bowyer vs. Joseph Campbell, son to Charles.—25th May, 1773.

Wm. Bowyer vs. Mathew (Martin) Cockendale.—18th June, 1773. Defendant gone to Tyger's Valley.

Wm. Allison vs. Breeding.—Bond dated 20th April, 1771, by John Bryan and John Braiding to Wm. Allison. John Brading (son of Bryan) and his sons, Bryan Brading, Jr. and John Brading, Jr. Memo: Bryan Brading, Jr. and John Brading, Jr., are sons of John Brading.

MAY, 1778 (A).

David Boson vs. Abraham Haines.—21st August, 1777. Defendant is a soldier at Fort Randolph.

Carlyle vs. George Benston.—Bond by George of Summerset County, Maryland, to Robert Carlyle of Greenbrier and Botetourt County, Virginia, 25th May, 1772. Defendant is in the service.

MAY, 1778 (B).

Benjamin Harrison vs. Michael Law.—*Qui tam.*, 19th August, 1774.

MAY, 1778 (C).

Stewart vs. George Taylor.—21st August, 1777. Defendant lives in Amherst.

Wilson vs. McCreery's Executors.—May, 1772, George Willson's wife was Elizabeth, daughter of John McCreery.

McDowell vs. James Stewart.—James Stewart married a daughter of Hugh Montgomery.

MAY, 1779 (M).

Thomas Turk vs. Joseph Poindexter.—Trespass. A. and B. by defendant on Thomas Turk, son of plaintiff, on 1st December, 1773.

William Bell vs. Samuel Craig (son of James).—Debt. Writ, June, 1773.

Andrew Bourland, son and heir of James Bourland, deceased, vs. Robert Hall, Archibald Bourland and William Jackson, son and heir of William Jackson, deceased.—Spa. Chancery, dated 28th August, 1773. Not executed.

MARCH, 1779 (B).

Beanaman vs. Andrew Hays.—Bond by defendant of Augusta County in 1754.

Mathew Edminston vs. George Anderson.—Allat., 16th April, 1776. Defendant "some time ago of this County." Levied in hands of Wm. Anderson, son to John.

AUGUST, 1779 (A).

S. and G. Mathews vs. Wm. Young.—Case writ, 25th May, 1773. Defendant nephew to Hugh. Writ, 26th September, 1774. Defendant is in the service. Writ, 25th September, 1773. Not executed because he was gone to Ohio.

Miller vs. Archer.—John Archer, Jr., no inhabitant. 1773.

Mathews vs. James Anderdell and George Elliott.—Writ, 24th August, 1774. Elliott in the service.

MAY, 1779 (K).

James Anderson vs. John Erwin.—Petition. Writ, 24th August, 1774. "The defendant is gone out on the expedition."

MAY, 1779 (L).

Margaret Stokes vs. William Hutcheson.—Writ, 21st April, 1778. Defendant gone to Carolina. Writ, 16th March, 1778, returned: "Refused to be taken."

Alexander Stuart vs. John Frogg.—Writ, 20th September, 1774. Not executed. Defendant is in the service.

James Hettly vs. William Young, Sr.—Writ, 25th February, 1775. Defendant is oldest of the name of Young and lives near Long Glade.

Bond by William Young, of Cecil County, Province of Maryland, to James Hettly, of Lancaster County, Pennsylvania, dated 29th April, 1756, assigned to James Young, 28th February, 1775.

Wm. Bowyer vs. John Steel (Providence).—Writ, 27th July, 1774. Defendant is dead.

Thomas Posey vs. James Gray.—Indenture of apprenticeship by James Gray, late of Augusta County, aged 22 years, to Thomas Posey, of Botetourt, saddler, to be taught the art and mystery of a saddler. Dated 9th December, 1773.

Burr Harrison, of County Dunmore, vs. Josiah Davison.—Bond, 11th March, 1773.

William Morris vs. Alexander McCoy.—Debt. Writ, 28th March, 1774. Defendant is a schoolmaster and lives in Hampshire (?) County.

Isaac Zane vs. Wm. Frame.—Petition on account, 1767 to 1774. Writ, 28th March, 1774. Defendant is Widow Frame's son and lives near Stone Meeting House.

Henry Selzer vs. James Phillips.—Petition. Writ, 29th March, 1774. James is son of John.

Thomas Crow vs. Wm. McCutchon.—Petition. Writ, 6th July, 1774. Defendant son of Samuel.

David Edmonston vs. James Frazer and Samuel Paxton.—Writ, 6th July, 1774. Frazer lives in Amherst.

William Moore vs. John Peoples.—Writ, 28th April, 1778. Defendant lives in Rockbridge.

Thomas Mines and Wm. Sprowle vs. John Lockyer.—Writ, 18th March, 1779. "Listed for a soldier and marched."

James Wright vs. John Boreland.—Writ, 19th March, 1778. Defendant lives in Botetourt.

Darkis Hamilton vs. Alexr. McClain.—Writ, 21st April, 1778. Defendant lives in Tygart's Valley and not executed because "I could not ride for fear of the Indians."

Benj. Morgason vs. Wm. Anderson (son of John).—Writ, 28th March, 1774.

Wm. Bowyer vs. James Hill (Coffee Smith).—Writ, 27th July, 1774. Not executed. Defendant listed in the service.

Wm. Bowyer vs. Wm. Anderson (Adams's Overseer).—Writ, 30th May, 1774.

Wm. Bowyer vs. John Chisum.—Writ, 22d August, 1774. "Defendant is in the service. The defendant was going out on the expedition."

Wm. Bowyer vs. John Cowarden.—Writ, 26th September, 1774. Defendant is in the service.

John Clark vs. James Ewing.—Writ, 18th September, 1777. Defendant lives in Botetourt.

John Robinson vs. John Campbell.—29th July, 1774. Defendant lives in Fincastle.

MAY, 1779 (G).

John Anderson vs. George Bigham.—Writ, 22d March, 1779. Defendant deceased.

John Archer vs. John Burnsides, Jr.—Writ, 5th September, 1778. Defendant lives in Greenbrier.

Joseph Bennett vs. John Lambert and Mathias Lambert.—Writ, February, 1775. Defendant lives on North Fork, South Branch, Potomac.

Wm. Bowyer vs. Thomas Smith.—Writ, 22d August, 1774. Defendant was going out on the expedition.

David Kerr vs. William Russell.—Writ, 15th April, 1778. Defendant lives in Rockbridge.

Mathews vs. Wm. Allen.—Writ, 20th September, 1774. Defendant is in the service.

AUGUST, 1779 (A).

George Ruttledge vs. Wm. Armstrong.—Spa. Cha., 28th August, 1768. George was son of Thomas Rutledge. Most of Wm. Armstrong's debtors were in Carolina.

AUGUST, 1779 (C).

Wm. Crow vs. James Ewing. Writ, 19th April, 1773. Not executed by reason of the defendant's being gone to Holestone.

John Dickenson vs. William Crow.—Long before 22d August, 1769, Wm. Crow kept a common inn or ordinary in Staunton.

Jacob Grass and Barbara, his wife, administratrix with will annexed of David Bosong, deceased, vs. Philip Grover and Margaret, his wife.—Chancery Spa., 1st May, 1779.

William Hamilton vs. David McNeelley, Jr. (North River).—Writ, 24th August, 1774. Not executed, because defendant is in his Majesty's service.

AUGUST, 1779 (D).

William Bowyer vs. Tiddy McNaught.—Writ, 26th September, 1774. The defendant is in the service.

Bowyer vs. McCown.—Ejectment, 1st February, 1773. John Bowyer and Magdalene, his wife, late Magdalene Borden, widow and relict of Benjamin Borden, the younger, and Benjamin Hawkins and Martha, his wife, late Martha Borden, only surviving child and heiress of the said Benjamin Borden.

AUGUST, 1779 (E).

Archibald Smithers vs. John Bodkin and Thomas Nealle.—Writ, 19th March, 1778. Botkin draughted to the fort.

NOVEMBER, 1779.

Edward Parks and Catherine, his wife, late Catherine North, administratrix of Roger North, deceased, vs. James Campbell.—Writ, 22d Nov., 1779.

Wm. Blair vs. John Graham (Grymes).—Deposition of Christopher Grymes, of lawful age, says that some years ago his father, John Grymes, and William Blair, dated 19th August, 1778.

MARCH, 1780 (A).

Benston vs. Benston and Gwinn.—Deposition of Mathias Benston, 26th January, 1777. Mathias had a son George.

Wm. Blair and Mary, his wife, vs. Monsey.—Deposition of Abraham Lincoln, 16th November, 1779, and signature.

Commonwealth vs. Robert Craig, Sr.—10th September, 1779. Deposition of James Anderson, at the funeral of Widow Crawford, on first Tuesday or Wednesday in August last. Defendant said that the King was perjured for establishing the Catholic Church in Canada, when Craig said defendant was perjured for swearing allegiance to the State of Virginia. Craig was a violent Tory, as shown by the depositions.

MARCH, 1780 (B).

Andrew Johnston vs. Sebina Stewart.—Writ, 1st April, 1771. In 1749 Andrew Johnston purchased land of John Ramsey. Sebina Stuart was daughter of David Stewart. Deposition of Agatha Madison, 24th November, 1775, says Sabina married George Wilson. Andrew went to Carolina and made a mortgage to pay David Stewart £26 if he ever came back from Carolina.

Wm. Morrow and Jane, his wife, vs. Samuel Anderson, eldest son and heir of James Anderson, deceased.—Chancery. Writ, 20th February, 1780.

MAY, 1780 (A).

Peter Hog vs. Bryan Kenny.—19th February, 1774. Terence O'Bryan is about to depart the Colony and deposes 19th February, 1774: In January, 1772, some time before the great snow, Bryan Kenny had a son James. The great snow began on Sunday and lasted over Tuesday. Hog lost several hogs on account of the snow and the roads were impassable.

Bennett vs. McNabb.—Chancery. Writ, 3d December, 1771. Benjamin Bennett (orator), eldest son and heir of Richard Bennett. Richard died intestate, 1743, leaving orator an infant. Shortly before his death he bought 300 acres in Beverley's Manor, but died before getting a deed. Richard's widow, Martha, married William McNabb. William McNabb put two of his sons, James and Samuel, in possession of the land. Bill for title and accounting of personal estate. Richard had other children besides Benjamin. William Thompson, aged 62 (deposes 16th May, 1773), was brother-in-law of Martha Bennett McNabb.

Valentine Sevier vs. Thomas Reeves.—Chancery. John Sevier was son to Valentine. Thomas was brother to Brewer Reeves. Jonathan Douglas was 57 years old on 3d October, 1772.

MAY, 1780 (B).

Commonwealth vs. John Flasher.—19th November, 1780. Defendant is dead.

Hugh Campbell, eldest son and heir of Robert Campbell, deceased, who was oldest brother and heir of James Campbell, deceased, vs. John Campbell.—Chancery. Writ, 19th November, 1778.

McClure vs. McClure.—Chancery. Writ, 30th June, 1773. Oratrix Margaret McClure, an infant, by Thomas Dryden, her guardian, daughter of Mary McClure, deceased, with will dated 10th September, 1767. Oratrix had brothers and sisters. Halbert McClure qualified as administrator and died and his widow, Mary, qualified. Suit for accounting.

AUGUST, 1780 (A).

Thomas Kinkade vs. Sarah Cocke.—Slander. Elizabeth Adams, wife of Thomas Adams and mother of Sally Cocke, deposes, 29th April, 1780, that her daughter was baptized by the name of Sally and not Sarah.

Rebecca Archer vs. John Archer.—Petition for separate maintenance pending suit for divorce on ground of drunkneess and cruelty. 22d November, 1771.

John Simmons, executor, and Hugh Allen and Jane, his wife, executrix, &c., of Paul Whitley, deceased, vs. Mary Tees and Robert Love, executors of Wm. Tees, deceased, and Joseph Love.—Writ, 10th September, 1778.

AUGUST, 1780 (B).

Commonwealth vs. Hugh Ritchie.—22d January, 1779. For speaking disrespectful words of the Congress and other words tending to excite the people to tumult and disorder. He drank the British King's health and confusion to the Congress, and said he could raise 500 men in Greenbrier to fight for the British King.

NOVEMBER, 1780 (A).

John Herndon, of Spottsylvania, vs. Thomas Reeves (lately of Spottsylvania).—Chancery writ, 1st September, 1770. In July, 1768, defendant mortgaged negroes to plaintiff and then brought the slaves to Augusta and sold one to Robert Reid and one to James Crawford, also defendant's bill to enforce mortgage. Answers says the negroes were sold under execution in Rockingham and bought by defendants, Reid and Crawford. No service on Reid.

NOVEMBER, 1780 (A).

Francis Montgomery vs. Alexander McClenachan.—Petition. Writ, 20th March, 1776. Samuel Coleman (shortly to leave the County, 20th March, 1776) deposes, 21st March, 1776. He wrote a note, in August, 1774, for Thomas Jemison to Francis Montgomerie and endorsed on it that Captain McClenachan was to pay it out of Jamison's pay as a soldier in the expedition against the Shawnees.

NOVEMBER, 1780(A-B ?).

North's administratrix vs. Andrew Campbell, son to John.—Petition, 1779.

November, 1780 (B).

Commonwealth vs. Woobeck Conrad, Jr.—19th April, 1780. Not executed for fear of the Tories.

Commonwealth vs. Mary Whitzell (now the wife of Michael McClure).—On 10th October, 1774, Mary Whitzell received stolen goods. Summons, 24th May, 1778.

Henry Davis vs. John Trotter.—Writ, 30th May, 1774. Defendant is in the service.

May, 1781.

Daniel, Joseph and John Campbell vs. James Henderson.—Case writ, 27th March, 1780. Plaintiffs sold in 1779 to defendant a negro slave. Of the purchase money of £42, 16 shillings. Question—What rate in Virginia currency the same was to be paid. Arbitrators declared at the rate of 100 pieces in the present paper money, amounting to £4,280.

Many suits against the assessors for collection of public revenue. There was difficulty in collecting, some people refused to pay and some officers refused to act.

March, August and September, 1782.

Robert Kirk vs. Robert McKetrick.—Slander. Plaintiff was promised an Ensigncy in Continental Army if he raised a sufficient number of men, which he did, but defendant tried to prevent him and said he was a coward and a liar in 177—.

John McMahon vs. William Anderson (son to James).—Case writ, 16th March, 1782.

Crawford vs. John Logan of New Jersey.—Attachment on an account dated November 15, 1779. Attachment dated 1782.

May, 1782.

Thomas Price vs. John Dixon.—13th September, 1780. Wm. Kerr is about to move to other parts, "Blood and Battery."

Hugh Richey vs. Margaret Willson, alias Margaret O'Neal.—Writ, 26th November, 1781.

Commonwealth vs. James Anderson (Schoolmaster).—Summons, 26th November, 1780, for drinking confusion to the Congress.

James Bodkin and Diana, his wife, vs. Joseph Gwinn.—Slander. Writ, 15th August, 1774. On 9th February, 1779, Mathias Benston and his wife, Margaret, are about to remove.

Boyd vs. Gardner.—Chancery writ, 4th September, 1777. Robert Boyd, only son and heir of Robert Boyd, late of this County, who died intestate in 1752, possessed of land on Middle River. Widow Eleanor (mother of orator) qualified administratrix. Orator and his sister were the only surviving children of Robert, Sr., and both infants. When orator became 14 years old he chose Francis Gardner (defendant) as his guardian, who qualified in 1761. Bill for accounting.

November, 1782 (A).

McDowell vs. Sinclair.—Ejectment. Lot in Staunton, corner Augusta and Beverly streets, owned by John Stuart and Sarah, his wife.

Deposition of James McKeachey, 1782: Wm. Eaken lived on Little River, in Botetourt in 1752-3. 27th September, 1782, Wm. Akers, of Campbell County, bill of sale to James Mason of Botetourt.

Muddy Creek was in Greenbrier.

John Marshall summoned, 1780, to show cause why grant shall not issue to Thomas Kinkead for land in Greenbrier claimed by settlement.

Samuel Vance's commission (in place of Archibald Stuart) as commissioner for the purpose of adjusting titles in the District of Augusta, Botetourt and Greenbrier, 2d April, 1782. Commissions, 1st March, 1782, to Wm. McKee, Robert Davis, Thomas Adams and Archibald Stuart.

Contract by John Napper of Augusta, with Joseph Childers of Amherst to convey to Childers his right to a certain tract or parcel of land lying on the Great Kanawa, 9 miles below the falls in County of Botetourt, 14th August, 1776.

Suit of Frogg vs. Miller, for land in Greenbrier, with depositions.

(Above is a batch of odd papers principally relating to land disputes in Greenbrier.)

NOVEMBER, 1782 (C).

Robert Hale vs. John Offel.—Contract of lease by plaintiff to defendant, 4th November, 1778, of the plantation whereon Richard Eliott and Wm. Ramsey lived and known by the name of Fort Dinwiddie. "The tenant was not to meddle with the fort which plaintiff and his neighbors had erected for their mutual safety. Has burnt and destroyed it." Writ, 22d May, 1780.

Thomas Jervis and Elizabeth, his wife, vs. Levy Moore and Susanna, his wife.—Case writ, 19th July, 1781.

Bryan Kenny and Sarah, his wife, vs. Thomas Green and Ann, his wife, and Samuel Moses (Moris?) (Morra?) and Marcella, his wife.—Case writ, 25th October, 1782.

David Beard vs. Wm. McCune.—Writ, 27th September, 1774. Defendant in the service.

Robert Carlile and Elizabeth, his wife, vs. Robert Carlile and Agnes, his wife.—Case writ, 9th December, 1780.

John Carlyle and Elizabeth, his wife, vs. Robert Carlyle and Nancy, his wife.—Case writ, 20th August, 1782.

Charles Donnelly and Euphemia, his wife, vs. David Henderson.—Case writ, 12th January, 1782.

Mary Dunwoddy, an infant, by James (Charles?) Dunwoddy, her brother and next friend, vs. Peter Hale.—Case writ, 18th August, 1779. Peter was brother to George Hale.

Margaret Elliott and Sarah Eliott, children and orphans of Wm. Elliott, deceased, and now infants by John Elliott, their guardian and brother, vs. James Elliott, eldest brother of Margaret and Sarah.—Chancery writ, 21st November, 1780. Wm. Elliott died, 1771, leaving widow, Margaret, who died, 11th January, 1780. Margaret had a brother John. Jas. administered on the mother's estate and bill for accounting. (Was the widow's name Jane?)

Leonard Tuetwiller vs. Peter Kephart and Elizabeth, his wife.—Petition, 7th October 1782. No inhabitant.

John Gossom vs. James Owens.—A and B, 29th December, 1781. Gone to the Army.

MARCH, 1783 (A?).

Thomas Hamilton, A. D. Q. M. (Quarter Master) vs. Jacob Peck.—Writ, 28th December, 1781. Account horses and supplies purchased by the Government. On back of letter is part of receipt, "Greeable to directions received from Major Richard Claiborne, Deputy Quartermaster for the State of Virginia." (Here it ends.) Staunton, 29th November, 1781. Sir—Mr. William Coursey informs me that he had purchased of you public horses to the value of £25, 10 shillings, which he promises to pay for in 14 days with merchantable hemp at such price as Mr. Alexander St. Clair will give at that time, or when delivered for the performance of which I will hold myself bound. I am, sir, your humble servant, (Signed) Jacob Peck. To Thomas Hamilton,, A. D. Q. M.

Catherine Parks and Edward Parks, administrator of Roger North, vs. Joseph Bennett.—Writ, 21st June, 1780.—Defendant at Nolachucky.

MARCH, 1783 (A).

Catherine Parke, late North, vs. John Redmon.—Writ, 22d October, 1782. Was Edward Parks dead?

James Page vs. John Armstrong and Phebe, his wife.—Writ, 21st November, 1778.

John Scott and Jane, his wife, vs. Elizabeth Carroll.—Writ, 17th June, 1778.

MAY, 1783 (B).

John Abney vs. John Campbell and John Henderson.—Petition, 29th July, 1783. Henderson dead.

William Downing, infant, by Charles Campbell, next friend, vs. James Gilmore and Ann, his wife.—Case, 25th May, 1779.

James McGonegal and Margaret, his wife, late Margaret Fleming, administratrix of Wm. Fleming, deceased, vs. Griffith Evans.—Petition, 24th July, 1783.

Neil Hughes vs. Jacob Snowden.—Case, 18th October, 1780. Snowden on his march, ordered on a tour of duty on Rotation, agreeable to his division.

AUGUST AND SEPTEMBER, 1783.

Patrick Lockhart, one of the Commissaries of the United States of America, vs. William Reah.—Writ, 27th March, 1780.

Ann Seawright, infant, by George Seawright, her brother and next friend, vs. William Blair.—Case, 22d April, 1780. Ann had a sister, Jane.

Mary Stephenson vs. James Waugh and Mary, his wife.—Slander. Writ, 27th March, 1780. Elizabeth Wilson deposes, 30th August, 1780, Margaret, wife of James Blair, asked her for the loan of a bag to send grain to her mother, Margaret, and her sister, Mary. Wm. Anderson, owner of Anderson's mill. James Blair deposes, 29th May, 1780.

Parris vs. Bryans.—Petition, 28th September, 1783. "I, Christopher Bryans, of Greenbrier County, promise," &c., 7th March, 1782.

MARCH, 1784 (A).

John Carlile and Elizabeth, his wife, vs. Thomas Hicklin.—A and B writ, 14th September, 1780.

Samuel Currie vs. Abraham Carson, infant, eldest son and heir of Isaac Carson, deceased.—Chancery writ, October, 1783. Isaac sold land to Samuel in 1765, but made no deed.

William Elliott vs. John Hamilton.—Case writ, 19th August, 1780. Defendant sold plaintiff land on Tygart's Valley, known as Nicholas Nutt's Improvement, 1772. Breach of warranty.

Richard Harvie & Co. vs. Whaley Newby.—Whaley Newby's bond (Amherst County), 28th December, 1769. Writ, 20th September, 1774.

William Johnstone and Mary Johnstone, his wife, vs. Arthur Connely and Leon (Jean) his wife.—Case writ, 16th July, 1782.

MARCH, 1783 (B).

Bowyer vs. John Ecken.—Writ, 24th August, 1774. Lives in Greenbrier, in Botetourt.

Mathias Dice vs. John Miller.—Writ, 3d September, 1774. Defendant, the Parsons's son (Alexander Miller?).

William Downing, infant, by Charles Campbell, next friend, vs. James Perry.—Slander. Writ 24th August, 1779.

Martha Gray, infant, by Robert Gray, her next friend, vs. Alexander McKee.—Slander, spoken 17th May, 1779. Case writ, 16th December, 1782.

Mary Lessley vs. John Miller, of Bull Pasture.—Case writ, 29th April, 1779. John Montgomery in the service. Christopher Grahams in the service.

MARCH, 1784 (B).

Alexander McClenachan vs. Francis Tate, Assistant Commissary of Purchases for the Continent.—Bail bond (Richard Claiborne, D. Q. M., S. V., surety) dated 9th May, 1781. (Endorsed on bail bond) "Should the enemy take possession of this place or approach so near that a Court cannot with safety be held, the said Tate shall not be obliged to appear until some future Court and shall not be subject to the within penalty for non-appearance then." (Signed) Francis Tate, State Assistant Commissary General of Purchases.

John Linkorn vs. Jacob Peck.—A and B writ, 19th December, 1783.

MAY AND JUNE, 1784.

Robert Allen vs. Samuel Gay—Defendant a schoolmaster, May, 1780.

Samuel McChesney vs. Archibald Armstrong.—Writ, 26th March, 1783. "I certify that Samuel McChesney hath purchased three horses branded

U. S., the property of the United States (and other cattle) purchased from me this 19th day of November, 1778." (Signed) James Sawyers. Recommendation of Archibald Alexander, £27, current money, as the price of two continental cattle, which were lost, and which I ordered him to sell and make return to me or coll. Sampson Mathews. Given under my hand this 13th December, 1779." (Signed) John Wilson C. P. (B?) S. D.

Robert McMahon vs. William Anderson (son to James).—Writ, 16th March, 1782.

John McMahon vs. Wm. Blair.—March 1784. Abates by plaintiff's death.

Jane Patterson vs. James Patterson, acting executor of Jean Patterson, deceased.—Writ, 26th November, 1772. Chancery. Oratrix, the daughter of Jean Patterson, deceased, who left will dated 1772. Bill for accounting.

August and September, 1784 (A).

James Sawyers' executors vs. Wm. Christian's executors.—To money received by him from the auditors on account of the service of James Sawyers. "Search and see what was allowed in Captain Christian's pay roll to James Sawyers." Captain Christian received for James Sawyers £8, 6, 8 of Thos. Madison, Esq., by the hands of Richard Thomas—Dune Ross." "I do hereby certify that I drew pay for James Sawyers as a volunteer in my Company, from August on the Cherokee expedition in ye year 1776, from the first day of August till the 25th October and no longer. Given under my hand at Staunton, this 21st day of April, 1778. (Signed) W. Christian, Captain." Claim: James Sawyers, for service at the Long Island, Holston. To be further certified by Captain William Christian. James Sawyers is allowed in Major Christian's pay roll 125 days as a soldier certified by me. (Signed) Sampson Mathews.

August and September, 1784 (B).

James Clarke vs. James Clarke, Jr., son and heir of William Clarke, deceased.—Chancery writ, 24th May, 1784.

John Clark vs. Wm. McClintock, Jr.—"Jeremiah Offriel is now going down in the Militia," 16th June, 1781.

James Hill vs. Philip Woolwine and wife and Elizabeth, their daughter, and John Moore and wife.—A and B, 10th July, 1784.

Daniel Joseph vs. Jacob Torn (Dovan).—Writ, 4th June 1783.

October, 1784.

Philip Benezet vs. James Ewing.—Bond dated 10th February, 1761. I, James Ewing of Stanton Town, in Augusta County, in the Province of Virginia, Chapman.

John Brown vs. Jacob Helfer.—Writ, 23d December, 1781. John was son of Mrs. Margaret Brown, who deposed, 11th October, 1784.

Israel Christian vs. Gilbert Christian, son of Major Wm. Christian, deceased.—Writ, 2d October 1784. Not found.

Edward Wilson vs. Dennis Burns.—Writ, 14th January, 1782. Middlebrook Headquarters, June 7, 1777. Dear friends—I have an opportunity to write to you where I am and how I am. We came from Tygars Valley here, as you no doubt have heard long ago, and had a very fatiguing march of it. But, thank God, I have had my health very well through all my fatigues. I have the good news to tell you that our army is very healthy and in good spirits and increases daily. The English never dare to come out from their breastworks. We are within four miles with our main army and our guards in sight of theirs. We have had no battles lately worth mentioning. I sent a watch up from Winchester by Dennis Burns, and a pair of silver shoe and knee buckles. Also one pair of sleeve buttons which I desired him to leave with you. I told him to sell the watch if he could get the opportunity. If he has sold her get the money and keep it until I return. If I never return, it is yours. You may sell the cow when you can this fall and pay Isaac Carson for keeping her and keep the rest. (I sent £3 in money by Dennis Burnes, which you have got, I suppose.) Also some clothes which I almost forgot to tell you of. I hope you will get them if you have not gotten them from him. You may show Isaac Carson this letter and give my compliments to all. From your well wisher (Signed) Edward Wilson. N. B.—Write all opportunities, and direct to the care of Captain Bowyer at Middlebrook, the Jerseys. To Mr. John Young, Middle River, Augusta, Virginia.

MARCH, APRIL, MAY, 1785 (A).

James Peyton (of Botetourt) vs. James O'Neal.—Writ, 28th February, 1782. —— Story was defendant's brother-in-law.

Joseph Reaburn vs. Jacob Doran.—Petition, 22d September, 1784. Defendant removed to Greenbrier.

James Seawright vs. Christopher Graham, Charles Baskins and William McCune.—Writ, 23d August, 1784. Graham and Baskins at Richmond.

APRIL, MAY, JUNE, 1785 (B).

Robert Givens, infant, by Wm. Givens, his next friend, vs. Margaret McLaughlin.—Writ, 18th July, 1781.

James Gardner vs. George Clendennin.—Writ, 25th October, 1784. Not executed, he being on his way to the Assembly, it being sitting. Writ, 22d December, 1784, not executed by reason of his being on his way home from the Assembly. Writ, 17th November, 1784, not executed by reason of his being at the Assembly. Writ, 19th January, 1785, no inhabitant.

James Kerr vs. Thomas Adams.—Writ, 22d April, 1784. Not executed by reason of the defendant being a Senator. Writ, 24th May, 1784, not executed by reason of his being at the Assembly. Writ, 23d June, 1785, not executed by reason of his being a member of the Senate.

Lewis vs. Wiatt and Tankard.—Contract, 8th November, 1783, between John Lewis, of Augusta, 1st part, Wm. Wiatt, of Spottsylvania, and Stephen Tankard, of Henrico, of 2d part, to convey to parties of 2d part Warm Springs Tract (850 acres). 2d tract of 750 acres, adjoining. 3d tract of 36 acres, adjoining. Contract broken by defendants.

AUGUST, 1785 (A).

Samuel Reeve and Jane, his wife, vs. James Hays.—1783.

William Steele vs. John Lewis.—This is to certify I employed Wm. Steele to act in the business of a Sutler in the place of John Frogg, deceased, from the 10th of October, 1774, to the 20th of November next, at the rate of seven and six pence per day. January 19th, 1775. (Signed) John Lewis.

James Spence vs. John Graham.—Writ, 7th September, 1782.—James Graham deposes, 3d January, 1784. He was a son of John Graham.

AUGUST, 1785 (B).

Alexander White of Frederick County vs. David Hanson of Dunmore County.—Contract of rent, 17th September, 1777, for land in Augusta.

MARCH, APRIL AND MAY, 1785 (F).

William Allen vs. Jasper Balenger and James Gardner.—We, Jasper B. and James G., promise to pay to Wm. Allen, £5, collected by me as commissioner, 20th September, 1783. *Qui tam.*

Robert McChesney and Jane, his wife, vs. Thomas Hines.—Slander. 5th February, 1780. Richard Jones deposes, 26th August, 1780. Deponent was indebted last fall to Ro. McChesney, but went to Carolina before it was paid, at which place Andrew Hays produced his note to Ro. McChesney.

Wm. and Samuel Anderson vs. Wm. Young.—On 29th May, 1781, Alexander Blair was so aged and infirm that he could not attend Court. Alexander deposes, 1st August, 1781: About 40 years ago he got the surveyor, Mr. Hume, to survey the land in question for his brother, James Blair and himself. Writ, 16th May, 1780. Grant by George II to James Blair, 10th March, 1756.

John Burnsides vs. Samuel Anderson (son to James).—Writ, 11th May, 1784.

AUGUST, 1785 (C).

Graham vs. Joseph.—Wm. Graham's letter from Rockbridge, June 10th, 1785.

AUGUST, 1785 (D).

Hugh Brown and Rebecca, his wife, vs. Berry Priddie.—Writ, 23d June, 1785.

MARCH, 1786 (A).

John Anderson vs. Adam Backall.—Petition, 22d September, 1785. Letters of Anderson, dated Woodstock, June 20, 1785.

Florence and Joseph Bell, executors of David Bell, vs. Dr. Samuel Irwin (Erwin).—Case, 21st May, 1783. David had a son, David. Doctor's account against David, naming children.

Bell's executors vs. Francis.—Chancery, 1780. Evin Griffith (3d November, 1780) is going in the service to North Carolina. David Bell, Sr., was on a march in service to the Frontier with a company of men in August, 1777 (1778?).

Miller, assignee, vs. Atwater.—Writ, 28th August, 1784.—Robert Anders on bail.

Anthony Mustoe vs. Samuel Steel and Margaret, his wife.—Writ, 8th February, 1785. Margaret said Anthony was a convict.

MARCH, 1786 (B).

Commonwealth vs. Joseph Thompson and Peter Blake.—Defendants, pretending to have power and authority to take up and secure any of the troops or soldiers in the British service, commonly called conventioners, and stationed at the barracks, in the County of Albemarle, did, on 1st September, 1780, take up and seize John Sowers, a yeoman, and one of the said convention troops, and left him in custody until John paid them ransom. Also Henry Vocust, a German.

Commonwealth vs. Robert and Wm. Risk.—In July, 1780, officers attempted to arrest David Risk as a deserter, but the defendants, his brothers, rescued him.

Commonwealth vs. Robert Henderson.—Defendant raised tumults and sedition, and tried to dissuade the militia from serving, 7th November, 1780.

Dickey vs. Hinds.—John Alexander, now in the Cantucky County, is a material witness, 13th April, 1785.

AUGUST, 1785—MARCH, 1786.

Commonwealth vs. Thomas Forst and Sophia, his wife.—For the murder of Wm. McCutchon. Inquisition held 27th December, 1785.

Commonwealth vs. Fleak.—Wm. Jordan, of Augusta, recognized to appear as witness, 22d September, 1785. Peter Fleak was charged with stealing William's horse.

Commonwealth vs. Thomas Griffin.—Wm. McCafferly obtained a judgment against James Patterson, both in Augusta and in North Carolina.

John Wallace vs. Wm. Gilkison.—Defendant was of good character here and below in Pennsylvania.

MARCH, 1786 (C).

Commonwealth vs. Gardner.—Agnes Fisher, wife of George Fisher.

James Hays, of Rockbridge County, vs. Berry.—1780.

George Skillem vs. Charles Tees.—Writ, 22d September 1784 (also 1769). Defendant gone to the new purchase.

Ann Warwick, infant, by John Warwick, her next friend, vs. Mary Moor, daughter of Levy Moor.—Case writ, 19th July, 1781.

MAY, 1786 (B).

Grand Jury presentments.—May 1787. Jack Hanna presented for unlawfully marrying his uncle's wife, to wit, Rebecca Carson, within 12 months, last past.

George Glenn vs. Alexander McClenachan.—*Qui tam*. Defendant, Clerk of County Court, on 27th December, 1785, issued a marriage license to James Glenn, son of George, under age, without consent of George, whereby a marriage was solemnized between James and Margaret Young.

Wm. Kyle vs. Call.—Writ, 19th September 1782. Susanna Call pleads that at the time of issuing the writ she was married and still is married to John Chapman, of Augusta County. Bond by Susanna Call is dated 14th October, 1778. She swears she was married, 8th January, 1781, by Rev. Mr. James Waddell. Kyle replies that on 19th September 1782, John Chapman was a British subject and prisoner and could not marry Susanna, nor could he be impleaded in this Court. At the time of the marriage, John was living in Augusta, with permission of the British officers, and liable to be recalled by them at any time. He was one of Borgain's troopers and had been a prisoner at the barracks in Albemarle.

MAY, 1786 (A to B).

William Anderson vs. Robert Porter and Reice Porter, infants, and Adam Porter, their father.—Writ, 19th November, 1785.

Mathias Benson vs. Samuel Anderson (Long Glade).—Writ, 17th April, 1784.

MAY, 1786 (M to P).

Sampson Mathews and Catherine, his wife, late Catherine Parks, late Catherine North, administratrix of Roger North, deceased, and Philip North, eldest son and heir of Roger North, deceased, vs. Owen Owens and Samuel Lewis.—Writ, 10th December, 1783.

Philip Wolfersperger vs. Jacob Groff (Grove).—Writ, 22d November, 1784. Bond by Jacob Groff and Philip Wolfersparger, of Heidelberg Township, of Lancaster County, Pennsylvania, to Peter Sitz, dated November, 1782.

Young vs. Richey.—23d September, 1785. Not executed by reason of my being at Richmond. (Signed) A. Mustoe.

AUGUST, 1786 (A to B).

James Anderson and Sarah, his wife, vs. Mary Crane.—Writ, 5th July, 1784.

John Beverage and Elizabeth, his wife, vs. Joseph Malcolm.—Writ, 17th November, 1784.

Isabella Burns vs. Stephen May.—Account for board, July, 1784, to May, 1785. He was a school teacher and the account shows drinks and treating for nearly every meal.

Robert Beverley vs. Samuel Merritt and Catherine, his wife, late Catherine Clononger, administratrix of Valentine Clononger, deceased.—Writ, 4th November, 1785.

AUGUST, 1786 (F to K).

Jacob Gabhert and Mary, his wife, vs. Lewis Myers.—Writ, February, 1784.

Hind's administrators vs. Dickey.—Deposition of Martha Dickey, 10th December, 1786, "McIntoshe's campaign."

MARCH, 1787 (D to K).

Robert Farrier vs. Alexander Seawright.—Writ, 20th August, 1783. Wm. and Alexander Seawright were brothers, and came to Augusta from Cumberland County(?), Pennsylvania. Wm. was living in Cumberland County in 1784. John Anderson was a Justice of Cumberland County, Pennsylvania in 1785.

William Jordan, Jr., vs. John Williams.—Writ, 28th January, 1787.

Joseph Irving (Erwin) vs. Philip North (infant).—Writ, 17th May, 1785.

MARCH, 1787 (A to C).

Samuel Anderson vs. William Blair.—Writ, 24th June, 1785. William Blair (Black Tavern). William had a son, James.

Carlisle vs. Alexander McFarling.—Chancery answer, 1787. Defendant was nephew of Alexander Gibson.

MAY, 1787 (D to H).

Alexander Gibson vs. Stophel Howe, Catherine Howe, Jr., Henry Howe, Philip Seyvert.—A and B writ, 19th April, 1786.

Thomas Gregg vs. Arthur Edwards.—Covenant, 30th March, 1784.

Andrew Shown (Shound) vs. George Greenleigh (Greenbe).—Contract of lease by defendant to plaintiff, 25th March, 1786.

Haslop and Blair vs. Hind's administrators.—Bond of John Hind, of Augusta County, to Isaac Hislop to David Blair of Fredericksburg, being dated 4th April, 1777.

MAY, 1787 (K to M).

Lewis vs. Hamilton.—August 27, 1777. By hunting shirt for Saml. Jones, soldier.

McCullock vs. McDonaugh's executors.—Deposition of Jane E. Gragg in Albemarle County, 12th October, 1786.

Samuel and Robert Purviance vs. Samuel and James McChesney.—Writ, 3d April, 1786.

MAY, 1787 (N to Z).

John Price and Judith, his wife, vs. William Anderson.—Slander.

Wm. Patton of Rockingham County vs. Hugh Botkin.—P. C., 24th May, 1784. Not executed, by reason of his being gone to the Northward.

John Davis (Parris) vs. Captain Wm. Long.—April 15, 1780.—To making a brown Regimental coat. Several suits of clothes with furnishings.

John Stephens vs. Xopher Snediger.—John Stephens, of Greenbrier, January 20, 1787. James Stephens was living at the Point in 1787. Joshua Snediger, son of —— Snediger, of Greenbrier, was apprenticed to Jas. Stephens in 1785 by his father, to learn the art and mystery of a hatter.

AUGUST, 1787 (A to D).

William Bell and Samuel Bell vs. Daniel O'Friel and Jas. Cunningham.—Spa. Ch., 12th June, 1780. In November, 1779, Orator William Bell was employed by James Sayers to purchase beef and pork for the barracks in Albemarle. Plaintiffs and defendants were partners and bill is for accounting and settlement. The winter of 1779 was the worst ever known. William Bell and Cunningham were relatives. James C. had a son, Johnny. William Bell was brother of James Bell. Depositions of Thomas Hill and Elizabeth Hill, his wife, 26th August, 1780. James Sawyers was Commissary for Albemarle Barracks. His wife was Hannah. Her deposition, 19th October, 1784.

AUGUST, 1787 (E to M).

Robert Gragg vs. John McDonald.—Plaintiff of Augusta County, 18th August, 1785. On that day plaintiff contracted to sell 37 acres to defendant. Consideration, bar iron and horses.

Thomas Gragg vs. Greene.—Plaintiff of Augusta County, 1786.

Henry King vs. James Brown and Mary, his wife.—Writ, 13th June, 1785. 1787, August, abates by defendant's death.

James Mitchell vs. John, Wm., James and John Brownlee, Jr.—Chancery spa., 23 June, 1785. Not executed by reason of not knowing which family they were.

NOVEMBER, 1787.

John Allison, Jr., vs. John Dickson and Rebecca, his wife.—Writ, 13th June, 1787.

MARCH, 1788 (A to G).

William Anderson vs. Samuel Anderson and Sarah, his wife.—Writ, 6th November, 1788.

George Bozwell vs. John Mackall.—Plaintiff in 1786, December, removed to Kentucky.

MARCH, 1788 (H to Z).

John Shawn and Sarah, his wife, vs. Catherine Shawn.—Writ, 9th March, 1787.

Jacob Swallow and Mary, his wife, vs. Thomas Stevenson.—4th September, 1786.

John William vs. Danl. Joseph and Eve, his wife.—Writ, 5th March, 1787.

MAY, 1788 (A to H).

Commonwealth vs. Joseph Newton.—For giving in fraudulent tax list. Defendant had moved to Greenbrier, September 17, 1787.

Samuel McCune vs. John Fudge.—Samuel had a daughter of age named Ann. 12th July, 1787.

George Huddle and wife, Margaret, vs. Michael Syford and wife, Catherine.—Writ, 26th November, 1787.

MAY, 1788 (I to Z).

Henry King and Elizabeth vs. Wm. Frizby and Ellenor, his wife.—Writ 9th June, 1783.

Michael Bowyer vs. George Smith. Defendant lives in the "Back Battalion."

AUGUST, 1788 (A to G).

John Crane and wife, Esther, vs. Samuel Carlile.—Writ, 22d April, 1788.

Gothard vs. Ingram.—Abraham Ingram, Sr., account vs. him dated Sussex County, Delaware, 1766.

AUGUST, 1788 (H to P).

John Johnston and wife, Mary, vs. George Rymer and Nelly his wife.—Writ, 11th June, 1788.

Captain John Pope vs. John Lewis.—1777, December 16. To cash paid a soldier on your (Captain Pope's) account. See letters to Capt. John Pope, Waggonmaster.

AUGUST, 1788 (R to Z).

James Spence vs. James Graham et als.—Writ, 13th March, 1783. Chancery. James Graham was son of John Graham, and brother of Christopher Graham. Spence was drafted and served at the siege of York. James Graham absconded and went to Kentucky. James Graham went on a tour of duty to Carolina as a substitute for John Patrick, James Gillespy has a brother, John. John Gilespy's wife was Elizabeth.

NOVEMBER, 1788 (A to C).

Wm. Hall and wife, Rebecca, administrators of Robt. Brafford, deceased, vs. Samuel Brafford.—Rebecca married Wm. after 1st May, 1786. Writ, 30th August, 1787.

Adam Bratton vs. Andrew Reid.—Margaret Guy, widow, 25th June, 1788. Ann Bratton, widow of Robert Bratton, and Adam was their son.

NOVEMBER, 1788 (D to Z).

Hollingsworth vs. Charles Cameron.—Writ, 4th May, 1787. Letter of plaintiff to Archibald Stewart, dated 4th March, 1788. E. Randolph and I. Marshall were yesterday elected for the convention. Ennis is to be returned for Williamsburg.

Benjamin Johnston and Lidia, his wife, vs. John Story.—Writ, 9th August, 1787. 7th September, 1787, Elizabeth Story, James Call and Patty, his wife, are about to move out of the State..

Robert Stuart vs. John Patterson.—Writ 24th October, 1786. Debtor, United States, in account with Major Merritt: 1782, to pay as Dragoon, 12 months, $100; 1783, to pay as Dragoon, 10½ months, $84.75; gratuity, $80; total, $167.45. Contra—By certificate, $100; by one horse, $87.77; by 4 months' pay, $33.30; by certificate, $46.28; total, $167.45. A true copy of an account as settled with me while Commissioner for Army Claims. (Signed) A. W. Dunscomb, March 8, 1787. Delivered certificates to Mr. Murchie. One for $100; one for $46.28; total, $146.28, A. D.

William Stuart, infant, by next friend and father, Wm., vs. Robt. Beath.—Slander. Writ, 30th May, 1788.

William Stuart and Margaret, his wife, vs. Joseph Beath.—Slander. Writ, 30th May, 1788.

William Stuart, infant, by father, William Stuart vs. Joseph Beath.—Slander. Writ, 30th May, 1788.

OFFICE JUDGMENTS.

NOVEMBER, 1788.

Rennick's Assignee vs. Poage.—Writ 15th April, 1788. Wm. Rennick of Greenbrier County, 14th February, 1787.

MARCH, 1789.

Richard Mathews vs. Campbell.—John Campbell, merchant in Philadelphia, 1781, but of Drummore Township, Lancaster County, Pennsyylvania, in 1788. Letters of Campbell related to the Mathews (Richard) answer of John Campbell, sworn to before John Kean in Frederick County, 6th August, 1787. Letter from Campbell, Philadelphia, 4th October, 1781. "Mrs. Campbell joins me in love to you and Mrs. Mathews, and all our friends there." Letter from Richard Mathews to John Campbell, dated New Glasgow, 10th October, 1783: "My brother, Joseph—officers certificates, the interest of which is punctually paid annually and warrants on the Treasury are almost the only circulating medium we have here. John Barclay is going to Georgia. Colonel George Mathews and a number of other officers set off to Georgia about 15th November." Some years before 1788, Richard Mathews lived at New Glasgow, in Rockingham County. Letter of Richard Mathews to John Campbell dated New Glasgow, 11th September, 1781—"Our cattle is now in a very ticklish situation, order being just come from the Governor to impress all that can be got. All our friends here are well. Mrs. Mathews joins me in our love to you and Mrs. Campbell and all our friends with you. I hope to have the pleasure of Cousin Jimmy's company this winter. I suppose I may wish you joy of a son or daughter by the time this reaches you."

John Poage vs. Elizabeth and Andrew Borland.—Writ, 28th August, 1787. In 1783, orator bought of Alexander Breckinridge, right to lands in Kentucky at the falls of Ohio.

MARCH, 1789 (A to K).

Michael Garber vs. Jacob Little.—Slander. Writ, 5th March, 1788. Michael came from York, Pennsylvania.

Rudolph Hawp vs. Wm. and David Wilson.—Writ, 6th October, 1787. Defendants are about to move away.

Frances Hamilton, infant, by Audley Hamilton, her next friend, vs. Joseph Hamilton.—Case, 23d February, 1788.

MARCH, 1789 (L to Z).

Thomas Mynes vs. John Brown.—Plaintiff came from New Jersey and was married in this country (county?).

John Poage vs. William Elliott.—In 1772 plaintiff was at Greenbrier and met Walter Drinnen, who claimed he had title to the place on Tyger's Valley which Nicholas Nutt had settled and lived on two years until he was driven away by Indians. Nutt had sold land to Jacob Marlin, father-in-law to Drinnen. Walter was old and infirm.

DECEMBER, 1788, JANUARY AND FEBRUARY, 1789.

Blair vs. Dixon.—Rebecca Dixon was wife of John Dixon. Martha Robertson was wife of Mathew Robertson in 1774.

MAY, 1789.—JANUARY CAUSES.

Samuel Anderson and Sarah, his wife, vs. William Anderson.—Writ, 8th March, 1788.

William Ledgerwood and Rebecca, his wife; William Berry and Rebecca, his wife; Esther Carrothers, by John Moffet, her guardian, and next friend, vs. John Frazier.—Ejectment, 1787. James Frazier's deposition, 19th October, 1790.—brother of John. John Brownlee testifies 14th November, 1788. Was acquainted with James Elder and Robert Moody, his brother, upwards of sixty years ago, and they then passed for brothers and they then lived with their parents, Robert and Isabella Moody, and deponent was acquainted with them during the whole course of their lives. James Moody married Rebecca Wilson, by whom they had issue. Rebecca Moody who married William Ledgerwood, Jr. Isabella Moody, who married James McClery. James and Rebecca lived within four miles of deponent at time of their marriage and they always passed for husband and wife. Margaret Christian, step-daughter of James Moody, deposes, 14th November, 1788. She was acquainted with James, the elder, and Robert Moody, his brother, near sixty years ago, and they always passed for brothers; deponent at age of twelve years was present at marriage of James Moody to Rebecca Wilson; they had issue, Rebecca and Isabella, above, and Esther Moody, who married John Moffett. Sarah Brownlee deposes, 14th November, 1788. Was acquainted with James and Robert about fifty-eight years ago and ever since till their death.

MAY, 1789.—JANUARY CAUSES

James Sproul vs. William and Mary Hunter.—22d November, 1787. Dr. John Jackson lives in Pennsylvania.

Paxton's Executors vs. James McKenny.—We, James Cooper, of Botetourt County, and James McKenny, of Augusta County, are bound to John Paxton, of Botetourt, etc., 31st March, 1777.

OFFICE JUDGMENTS, MAY, 1789.

Thomas Fellows and wife, Ellenor, vs. William Willman.—Writ, 20th November, 1788.

AUGUST, 1789 (A to G).

Hugh Donahue and Joseph Bell vs. Daniel Kidd.—Daniel Kidd lived in Rockbridge, 17th March, 1785.

Andrew Donnolly, of Greenbrier, vs. Hugh Millar.—In October, 1785, the General Assembly appropriated funds to build a road from eastern to western waters and defendant became contractor and plaintiff was his partner. The road was from Greenbrier C. H. to the Kenoway. The people themselves divided the whole county into thirteen districts, and each district elected a parson to form a committee to superintend the business. The committee appointed Hugh Millar foreman to undertake on behalf of the people and went security in the bond for his performance and took bond of him with condition that equal justice might be done to all. The committee divided the road into thirteen parts, that each individual might work out the tax he was in arrears. At the dividing, Colonel Donnelly told the committee he owed the treasury £170 of taxes due for 1782 as sheriff, and that he thought himself included in the law. Committee refused to grant a certificate to Donnelly because he did not make it appear that he was in the law, etc. (a full account of the transactions). At a meeting of the committee of the inhabitants of the county of Greenbrier, held 30th September, 1786, Hugh Miller, William Renick, John Anderson, James Graham, William Morris, William Johnston, Alexander Welch, Thomas Wright, Samuel Williams, Joseph Claypool, John Hutcheson, Hugh Capertin, and Archibald Hauley; Resolved, (Colonel Donnally assigned a district from Capt. Morris district on Bell Creek to 67th mile tree on Rich Creek). A copy. Teste. W. H. Cavendish, Clerk of Committee. Know all men, etc., I, Hugh Millar, of county of Greenbrier, etc., bound to John Anderson, James Graham, William Morris, Hugh Capertin, William Renick, Archibald Hauley, Joseph Claypool, John Hutcheson, Samuel Williams, Thomas Wright, William McCoy, John Byrnside, John Stuart for Alexander McCoy, William Johnston in £10,000, 25th May, 1786. Condition to do justice to all the inhabitants as foreman in the prosecution of the work.

August, 1789 (H to Z).

Alexander Humphreys vs. Michael Graham.—Slander. Writ, 11th June, 1788. On June 9, 1788, defendant speaking of and concerning a certain William Richardson Watson, who was supposed to have been murdered, and of the bones and remains of a negro found in a cave near the town of Staunton, who had been buried and again raised by the students studying physic under the said plaintiff and by them dissected, said plaintiff might have dissected him the said William Richardson Watson after he was murdered, and then he might have put him in the cave.

Alexander Umphreys vs. Samuel Merrit.—Libel for printing in the *Winchester Advertiser*, a supposed copy of an inquest and deposition in above cause.

Sampson Mathews vs. John Kephart (Gabhart).—Plaintiff of Richmond, 1789. Contract of lease by plaintiff to defendant of "Cloverdale."

November, 1789 (A to H).

Isaac Duffield, infant, by Robert Duffield, next friend, vs. John McCoy.—Slander, 1787.

Thomas Hughes vs. Isaac Younghusband.—Certificate of marriage of Thomas Hughes and Sarah Younghusband, according to the rites and ceremonies of the Church of Ireland as by law established on 31st October, 1768. Witnesses: John Reader, clerk; Bryan McDonald, Sidney Hughes.

(Action: Slander, in that Isaac said Thomas had been married in Ireland. Their depositions are interesting.)

Depositions of John Younghusband at Newberry, South Carolina. Depositions of Mary Younghusband, wife of above. In 1763 Thomas Hughes was, by his uncle, William Tesdall, bound to John Younghusband as apprentice in livery business in Ireland. Thomas married Sarah in Dublin. Sarah was full sister to John Younghusband's wife. Bryan McDonald was brother-in-law to Thomas Hughes. Sidney Hughes was full sister to Thomas Hughes. Thomas brought suit in King's Bench, C. P., against John Y. for Sarah's fortune. Within one year after the marriage Thomas took a farm near John Y. at Mary Mount, in Ireland, County Armagh. In 1771-72 Thomas came to America. Sarah lived until 22d September, 1781. Taken at house of John Younghusband, on Hickory Hill, County Newbury, District of 96, on 4th August, 1788.

NOVEMBER, 1789 (I to Z).

Stephenson vs. Irwin.—Alexander Curry is about to leave the county, 5th December, 1787. John Irvine, son of Edward Irvine, Robert Gragg is about to remove to the frontiers of North Carolina 22d October, 1788.

Robert Shaw vs. Alexander Brownlee.—Rockbridge County, April 17, 1779. Bought of Robert Shaw one hay house for four hundred pounds for the use of the legion for which I promise to pay the above sum in full on demand. Given under my hand this 17th April, 1779. (Signed) Alexander Brownlee. N. B.—By order of the General.

James Lockridge, infant, by Andrew Lockridge, next friend, vs. Samuel Carlile.—Writ 19th March, 1788.

James Lamme vs. William Kennerley.—Writ 10th April, 1788.

MAY, 1790 (A to C).

Charles Brown vs. Thomas Dixon. Mary Woods was mother-in-law of Charles Brown.

Commonwealth vs. Sebastian Woolf.—On 8th June, 1787, defendant had a son Jacob and a son Martin, the latter above sixteen and under twenty-four.

John Kenny vs. John McCaslin.—Writ 20th June, 1789. Luke Bowyer has long removed from the State.

MARCH TO JULY, 1790.

Irons vs. Carlyle. Samuel Carlyle and his brother James.

Poage vs. Elliott.—John and Thomas Poage, executors and legatees of the late Father John Poage, deceased, orators. Sometime in 1772 John, senior, purchased of Walter Drinnen land in Tygars Valley, part of Nicholas Nutt's settlement. Nutt was the first settler.

Peter Hall and wife, Rebecca, vs. George Hall.—Writ, 30th August, 1787.

MARCH, 1790 (A to L).

Tully Davitt and Samuel Armstrong vs. Estill's Administrators.—Chancery. In 1772 Davitt bought land in Greenbrier of John Estill, but was dispossessed by James Estill and James Wright. After death of John Estill, his widow, Rebecca, married Zack Estill.

Donnely vs. Hinter.—Andrew Donnely writes from Kanawha, 1792.

Abraham Ingram vs. Zachariah Calloway and Ellenor, his wife.—26th November, 1788.

James Lamme, Assignee of David Lamme, vs. John and Thomas Story.—Writ, 17th June, 1787.

DECEMBER, 1789, JANUARY, FEBRUARY, 1790.

Commonwealth vs. Thomas Clifton, late of Delaware, but now of this county.—26th December, 1789. Found not guilty.

Edwin vs. William Gourdin.—Attachment February, 1790.

Henry Mace vs. Samuel Lamme.—24th November, 1789.

MARCH, 1790 (M to E).

Henry Millar vs. Samuel and Robert Gragg.—Writ, 31st August, 1787. Executed.

MARCH, 1790 (M to Z).

Richard Mathews vs. John Patterson.—William Allen, of Botetourt, is about to remove out of the State, 28th May, 1788. Letter of Richard Mathews dated "Elk Meadow," 2d June, 1787.

OFFICE JUDGMENTS.

AUGUST, 1790.

Elizabeth Brown vs. James Brown.—Margaret Brown deposes 13th March, 1790. The property is hers and she never gave it to Thomas Brown, her son, or Elizabeth Brown, his wife. Elizabeth was executrix of Thomas in 1789.

William Grosse and wife, Margaret, vs. Edward Bryson and wife, Charity. Writ, 3d November, 1788.

Mines vs. Moses Hays.—Moses had been in possession of the land for thirty odd years before suit was brought, i. e., 1788. Land grant by Beverley Randolph, Lieutenant-Governor, to Thomas Mines, dated 12th June, 1787.

John Paris vs. Richard Madison's Administrator.—Writ, 11th March, 1787.

William Grogge vs. Jeremiah Knocher.—Defendant was a soldier in Virginia (Doubtful).

David Laird vs. Hugh Donaghe and John Poage.—Thomas McClung is about to remove, 16th October, 1788.

SEPTEMBER AND OCTOBER, 1790.

Henry Mace vs. James Lamme.

AUGUST, 1790.

John Burns vs. John Steel (Taylor).—Writ, 1st April, 1790.

NOVEMBER, 1790.

Samuel and Robert Purviance vs. Samuel and James McChesney.—Writ, 16th May, 1787. Bond by defendants to plaintiffs 10th July, 1773.

David Laird vs. Hugh Donaghe.—Writ, 3d September, 1788. Depositions of James and John Donaghe and Thomas Davies taken at the house of David Russell, Green County, North Carolina, 15th May, 1789.

Catherine Mathews, by her next friend, Philip North, vs. Sampson Mathews.—Plaintiff married defendant in 1783 and now sues for divorce for cruelty.

MARCH, 1791 (A to L).

Isaac Archer and wife, Sarah, vs. George Lewis.—26th August, 1790.

William Patten and Sampson Mathews, Executors of Margaret Cawley, widow of John Cawley, deceased, vs. Alexander McClennahan and Executor of John Poage, who were executors of John Cawley.—Bill for settlement. Letter by John Poage dated March 5, 1787, to Uncle Patten, addressed to Mr. William Patten at South Fork.

Abraham Evans and wife, Mary, vs. Joseph Burk and Elizabeth Martin.—15th April, 1789. A. and B.

William Heron vs. John Lamb.—Petition, March, 1791.

MARCH, 1791 (A to L).

Peter Heiskell vs. Wm. Kinkead, Crawford and Bengle Andrew.—Writ, 19th May, 1790. Catherine Lowdermilk, wife of Michael L.

John Hogshead, infant, by Ann Hogshead, his next friend, vs. Andrew Bowman.—A and B, 18th May, 1789.

Samuel Kauffman vs. John Fleiger and James Kean.—Plaintiff lived in Lancaster County, Pa., and defendants in the town of Lancaster.

James Kenner vs. Peter Heiskell.—Chancery, Spa, 17th December, 1789.

MARCH, 1791 (M to W).

Catherine Mathews vs. Sampson Mathews.—Petition for plaintiff for alimoney pending suit for divorce. Affidavit of Alexander Humphreys, August

20, 1790, that Catherine told Sampson in his presence that she would return if he would put away Lucy, but he refused her to his attorney. On May 17, 1790, Sampson advertised that he would not pay any contracts of Catherine as she had absconded from his bed and board. Joseph Mathews and Mary, his wife, 1790.

McChesney vs. Keys.—Robert McChesney, Jr., son of James McChesney, 1786.

Richard Mathews vs. John McDougal. James Mathews now residing in Kentucky, 28th June, 1790.

Joseph Malcom vs. Joseph Beith.—John Chesnut and Patience Chesnut are about to remove out of the State, 17th September, 1790.

August, 1791 (A to G).

Cowdon vs. Handley.—Settlement of Samuel Wilson's estate. Ejectment. John Griffin and Elizabeth Griffin, his wife, gave up to Martha Cowdon all the right he had in the land in the right of his wife, Elizabeth. The property was occupied by Martha and Dennis Callahan. Margaret Mathews deposes 9th June, 1791, that some years ago her late husband, Robert Reed, was not willing to accept a title to the land from John Griffin and Elizabeth, his wife, until Mrs. Martha Cowdon would relinquish her dower therein.

Commowealth vs. Edward Broback and Agnes, his wife.

James Dickey vs. Edward Wilson.—In 1779, as one of a district laid off for the purpose of raising a soldier to serve in the armies of the United States, plaintiff agreed to pay his proportion of £1,500 to Edward Wilson for performing that service; Edward Wilson got married soon after this; Alexander Robertson was Commissioner of the Provision Law, 1789. Did Wilson marry a Gambell?

August, 1791 (H to W.)

McNair vs. Mathews.—Order of A. M. McClanachan, A. C. A., to John Spears to go with his wagon to Rockfish Gap on Saturday, 25th August, 1781, to take a load of public hemp to Philadelphia and return with military stores, dated August 18, 1781. Affidavit of John that he performed the service and had received no compensation, 26th August, 1789. George Spears was his brother and performed the service with him. Discharge of George Spears from service dated Albermarle Barracks, October 23, 1781, signed William Allen, W. V. Account of transactions of Richard Mathews with the Commonwealth. William Allen was conductor to the first brigade of wagons, eight in number, to and from Philadelphia. Thomas Lewis was conductor to second brigade of wagons, ten in number. Valentine White with the third brigade.

August, 1791 (H to W).

James Spence vs. John Gray and his son, Alexander Gray, deceased, and his son, John, Jr.—Chancery.

May, 1791.

George Mathews vs. Robert Burns, Executor.—Bill, 15th December, 1789. Answer of Margaret Cunningham Burns, daughter of Robert Burns, deceased, infant, by James Lyle, guardian, filed May, 1791. Robert's will filed. In 1782 he left widow, Isabella, and daughters, Mary, Margaret Cunningham Burns and step-daughter, Sarah Lockhart, son, Thomas Burns; Henry Burns; Mary Burns had married James Curry in 1789, 14th December. Sarah Lockhart had married Asher Waterman in 1789, 14th December.

(Parson) William Wilson vs. William Blair.—Writ, 4th November, 1788. Suit over removal of William Blair from a seat in the Stone Meeting House.

Peter Link and Judy, his wife, vs. Peter Hanger, Jr.—Writ, 24th February, 1791.

SEPTEMBER AND NOVEMBER, 1791.

John Bullitt (Labouner), of Rockingham County, charged with horse stealing.

Richard Mathews vs. Isabella Burns.—Robert Burns died in October after a lingering illness.

Arthur Ringland and Mary, his wife, vs. Edward Brockenson.—Writ, 19th July, 1791.

John Bosong vs. William Wallace.—Writ, 1st February, 1791. Case. John died August-September, 1791.

John McClure vs. Thomas McCullough.—Writ, 10th January, 1788. About 1783 defendant removed to the French Broads.

NOVEMBER, 1791.

Commonwealth vs. Thomas Wells, James Wells and Nancy Wells, their mother.—26th August, 1790.

Elihu Greene vs. Christopher Grabble (Graybill?).—Slander. Writ, March, 1790, Christopher Graham is about to remove to Kentucky, 9th September, 1791. Prior to 1789, Green was living on the French Broad and was brother-in-law of Captain Smith.

James Knowles and John Knowles, his son, vs. William Knowles.—6th March, 1790.

William McCutchen, infant, by David Fulton, his next friend, vs. John McCutchen, Jr.—Slander, 16th June, 1790.

James Rutledge and Ellenor, his wife, vs. John Curry.—Slander, 21st October, 1788. Andrew Erwin's lie bill. Rutledge's wife was Eleanor Ralston.

MARCH, 1792.

Joseph Thompson vs. Hugh Donaghe.—Elizabeth, wife of William Thompson, John Donaghe, son of Hugh Donaghe. Joseph Thompson removed to Botetourt about 1781 on Jackson's River. William and Joseph were brothers.

McNutt vs. Bowyer.—Power of attorney by Alexander McNutt now at Halifax, Nova Scotia, to John McNutt, of Augusta County, 1761.

William Hutcheson (wife Mary), vs. John Burke, Elizabeth, his wife.— Writ, 5th September, 1788. In February, 1788.

William Henry vs. Zachariah Johnston, Jr.—Writ, 26th December, 1789. Slander. Zachariah had a brother James.

William Gillespy vs. George Benson.—Writ, 1790. James Gillespy moved to Kentucky, middle of November, 1788, and died about December last. Orator (?) and his brother, Samuel Gillespy, were appointed executors.

Mary Devericks, infant, by Thomas Devericks, next friend, vs. Jarred Erwin and Elizabeth, his wife.—Slander. Writ, 16th August, 1790.

James McGonegal and Margaret, his wife, administratrix of Fleming, deceased, her late husband, vs. Bailey.—Bond by William Fleming, of Paxton Township, County Lancaster, Pa., to William Bailey, of Yorktown, coppersmith, 19th August, 1774.

August, 1792.

George Lewis and wife, Mary, vs. Isaac Archer.—17th August, 1790.

May, 1792 (A to K).

Agnes Cummins, infant, by Robert Cummins, her next friend, vs. John Rutherford.—Br. Promise. Writ, 21st August, 1790.

Henry Brown and Mary, his wife, late Mary Timberlake, administrator, and Edwin Young, administrator of John Timberlake, deceased, vs. Henry Miller.—Writ, 18th October, 1790.

May, 1792 (L to M).

James Mitchell vs. Samuel Hunter.—Bill filed 1790. In 1780 Andrew Hunsberry enlisted to serve a term of duty, eighteen months in the regular troops of this Commonwealth. Did Andrew desert? John Bright was also a soldier. Andrew called James Mitchell "daddy" and James called him "son." Deposition of Henry Smith taken in Amherst County, 1790. Peter Shipe was a soldier in Captain Lapsley's company in the beginning of the year 1781. Thomas Mitchell was son of James.

David Laird vs. Hugh Donaghe.—Writ, 22d October, 1788. John Donaghe, James Donaghe and Thomas Davis, living in Green County, North Carolina, 17th March, 1789. David Laird had a man, Jones, in his company who deserted. Daivid Laird had a daughter, Anne. Hugh Donaghe had a son, John.

May, 1792 (N to Z).

Thomas Turk, Jr., son of Thomas Turk, Sr., vs. Thomas Turk, Sr.— *Son vs. Father.* Chancery. (Executed bond to.) In 1772 Thomas, Sr., deeded land to Thomas, Jr., condition, love and affection.. Thomas, Jr., married Anne Rhea. Thomas was seventeen years old in 1772.

John Scott, infant, by John Scott, his father and next friend, vs. Jacob Levingston and Lidia his wife.—Writ, 3d December, 1791.

May, 1792 (N to Z).

Peck vs. Bowyer.—Bill to perpetuate testimony.

November, 1792.

John Mills, heir-at-law of Robert Mills (John was a nephew of Robert) vs. Joseph and Florence Bell and William Bell.

Sarah Allison, infant, by John Allison, father and next friend, vs. Hugh Gaul.—Writ, 1st September, 1791.

John Frazier, Ann Frazier vs. Rebecca Ledgerwood, Rebecca Berry and Esther Corruthers, infant.—Spa. Chancery, 16th April, 1787. Oratrix and orator are children of Isabella Frazier. Isabella was sister to Robert Moody, now deceased, who took John Frazier and kept him until Robert's death, when John was forty years old. Robert died December, 1776 (1786?). Robert's nuncupative will 15th December, 1786. James and Robert Moody's father died intestate. Isabella Moody was their mother and administered on their father's estate. The Moodys came from Pennsylvania. John Frazier was brother-in-law of Robert Moody and they came to Virginia shortly afterwards. John Frazier died leaving five small children and a widow. Three of the children took all the land and left nothing for John and Anne, whom Robert Moody took care of. James Moody's wife died and his daughters being all married and he being an old man, he took in his son-in-law, William, and Rebecca Ledgerwood, and shortly afterwards James sold his land to his step son, Robert Willson. Then William and Rebecca took James as long as his money lasted, when they sent him back to Robert naked and destitute. Robert prepared to make a will because he found that his brother James' heirs and the Ledgerwood family in particular would come from Kentucky and take everything he had. James Frazier. 19th July, 1790. Anne Frazier's deposition to same effect, 19th July, 1790. Isabella Frazier's deposition to same effect, 19th July, 1790. Elizabeth Hill's deposition to same effect, 19th July, 1790. Samuel Frazier's deposition to same effect, 19th July, 1790. Rebecca Berry's deposition taken in Fayette County, October, 1789. Zachariah Johnston deposes 5th October, 1790: was born within one mile of Robert Moody's; John Frazier was accidentally killed. Rachel Wilson deposes that her husband bought a plantation from James Moody. Mrs. Mary Wilson went to Kentucky. John Brownlee deposes that he knew old Robert Moody, father of James and Robert Moody and continued intimate with the two sons after their father's death. Sarah Brownlee deposes that when she was a girl James Moody was married to her mother, a widow; James's father died and Robert and his mother kept all the estate and James never received any of the estate. John Frazier died when plaintiffs were very young, intestate, and the oldest son, Samuel, took the land. Rebecca was wife of William Ledgerwood.

February, March, May, and June, 1792.

Joshua Humphreys vs. William Sheels.—Plaintiff and his family, 1789, employed defendant to carry them to Kelly's landing on the Kenawha on their way to Kentucky, but defendant failed to meet his engagement. Writ, November, 1789.

John McRoberts vs. Charles Cameron.—In 1790 plaintiff bought 400 acres from defendant lying in the county of Kentucky, part of 1,000 acres, for which Charles had a certificate on Dick's River, near Logan's Fort, by the name of Dochester's Improvement.

July, August, November, 1792.

Lewis Myers vs. Peter Lamb.—Witness, William Lamb, 14th December, 1791. Writ, 22d June, 1792.

James Edwin vs. John Young.—Writ, 13th April, 1792. Records from Cumberland County, Pa., show judgment vs. James Patrick (James Erwin Special Bail), 1787, 30th July, which James Patrick paid in part. Also judgment by James Irwin vs. John Young, 13th January, 1787.

Thomas Williams vs. William Johnston and wife, Jane.—Writ, 23d March, 1792.

MARCH, 1793.

James Hessant (Essex) and Christianner, his wife, vs. Sebastian Woolf.—Writ, 29th November, 1791.

Jacob Levingston and Lidia, his wife, vs. Benjamin James.—Writ, 1st July, 1792. Assault and battery.

AUGUST, 1793 (M to Z).

North vs. Mathews.—Catherine Mathews, wife of Sampson, was first widow of Roger North, then widow of Edward Park. Roger North died in the fall of 1776, leaving a will which Catherine could not find and she took out administration. Philip is the only surviving heir to Roger North. She married Edward Park in the fall of 1777 and Edward died December (July), 1780. Catherine took out administration on Edward's estate in Henrico County. Roger owned a tan yard. Affidavit by Catherine, 1793. Edward had daughters (sisters?) Polly and Fanny Park. Catherine married Sampson, June, 1783. Edward Park had a nephew, Jonathan Park.

Patrick Ready and Sally, his wife, vs. Thomas Caul.—Writ, 18th April, 1793.

Frances Smith, Spinster, vs. Thomas Jones.—Breach Promise, 1792.

MAY, 1793 (A to L).

Robert Armstrong vs. Daniel Friel.—John Hawkins was agent for the State at Albermarle Barracks October, 1780.

Ann and Rebecca Craig, daughters of Robert Craig, vs. John and Robert Craig.—Robert, the father, died June, 1788. Writ, 30th October, 1790. Family quarrel.

James Campbell and wife, Bridget, vs. Thomas Green and Nancy, his wife.—16th January, 1793.

Commonwealth vs. Francis Eccord and wife, Dolley.—15th January, 1793. Assault on —— Heeder.

Francis Edwin and wife, Elizabeth, vs. Nicholas Wisehart and wife, Rachael.—Writ, 4th September, 1792.

William Flannagan and wife, Elizabeth, vs. Jacob Van Lear.—1st July, 1791. A and B?

Mary Holms, infant, by John Holms, her father and next friend, vs. John Campbell.—Writ, 7th November, 1792.

William Knowls and wife, Mary (Donavan).—14th February, 1792.

NOVEMBER, 1793 (L to Z).

Sampson Mathews vs. Ann Hogshead.—James Anderson and Alexander Kilpatrick were living in Greenbrier in 1789. Sampson Mathews was of the City of Richmond, 1786.

Mynes vs. Jamison.—William McGowan is about to move out of the State, 1793. Edward Harding, same.

Thomas Story vs. William Kelly and wife, Mary.—Writ, 3d September, 1792. A and B.

MAY, 1793 (M to Z).

Miller vs. William Lamb.—Defendant no inhabitant, 1792–3.

David McCoy and wife, Jane, vs. Thomas Beard.—Writ, 14th August, 1792.

George Miller vs. Samuel Runkle.—Slander. Defendant said plaintiff cheated the church out of some subscriptions he was to collect, and that was the worse because he was an elder. Frederick Dull, Montgomery County, Pa., deposes, 1st May, 1792. He was an elder in the Reform Church in Whitpain at the time Mr. Winkhouse was minister of said congregation. When the minister announced there would be a collection for the purpose of erecting a church near Staunton. John William Miller deposes that in 1785 and 1786, September of each year, John George Miller stayed at his house when collecting money to build a church about ten or twelve miles from Staunton. Deponent lent John George a horse to go to see Rev. Mr. Muhlenberg. Deponent knew John George in Germany and came over sea with him. (Signed) Frederick Dull, Casper Schlater, George Flieger, John William Miller. Sebastian Getz lived in the same village in Germany with John George and came over sea with him.

William Patterson vs. Robert Beard.—Deposition of John Craig in Buncombe County, North Carolina, 2d November, 1792.

Peter Rough vs. Jacob Teeford.—Assault and battery on Susanna Rough, daughter of plaintiff, 1791.

William Blair vs. Daniel Donavin.—Writ, 20th December, 1792. I, Daniel Donavin, of Randolph County, Virginia, am bound to William Blair, Sr., of same county and State. Bond dated 18th November, 1788.

Daniel Shorrets and wife vs. William Steele, infant son of John Steele.—Writ, 21st December, 1791.

John Thompson vs. Nicholas Echus and wife, Elizabeth Echus.—Writ, 12th January, 1793.

Smith (yth) Tandy, of Amherst County, vs. Lewis and Phileman Richards.—Contract of lease 27th February, 1790.

AUGUST, 1793 (D to M).

John Dixon vs. James Kerr and Robert Campbell.—Deposition of James Kerr taken in Lexington, Kentucky, second Tuesday in June, 1793. Son of James, defendant John Campbell's deposition at same place. John Dixon was drafted to go into service under McIntosh, but persuaded Kerr to sell him a servant as a substitute.

John Gold, infant, by Robert Gold, next friend, vs. John Scott.—1791.

Frederick Grove and wife, Elizabeth, vs. Margaret Rusk.—Writ, 10th September, 1792.

William Kerr vs. John Dixon.—Trespass on land involving title. John Allison appeared as agent for William Kerr and was William's nephew. William Rankin is about to remove to Kentucky, 16th September, 1789.

William and James Kerr were sons of John Kerr. Jury finds special verdict; patent to Wm. Kerr 2d June, 1760. William Kerr and Martha, his wife, 17th May, 1768. Deposition of Elizabeth McClure, 5th August, 1789. She was the daughter of John Kerr. William Allison, son of John Allison, Sr. See some papers of above suit in the papers Samuel Hunter vs. Torbett and Mitchell.

NOVEMBER, 1793 (A to L).

Mary Holmes, infant, by John Holmes, her father and next friend, vs. Thomas Story.—Writ, 1st November, 1792. November, 1793, abates by plaintiff's marriage.

Samuel Hunter vs. Hugh Torbett and Alexander Mitchell.—Chancery. Spa. 25th July, 1777. Deposition of William Bryan, of Fauquier, taken Friday, 22d August, 1777, aged thirty years. He is son-in-law of David Kaile (Haile?). David Kaile deposes at same time he is sixty years and upwards. James Cunningham deposes, 16th August, 1783, that in May, 1777, Hugh Torbett was selling his land with intention of going to Holston. After Nathaniel Torbett came from Northward. Alexander Mitchell's answer says: In 1771 he and other defendant bought a tract of land from Col. William Campbell, 614 acres, "After the defendants came to Virginia" (1773). Hugh Brawford and Rachel Brawford were son and daughter of Samuel Brawford. Rachel was married to William Wallace before 21st November, 1780, and on that date is about to leave these parts. Susannah Hunter was wife of Samuel.

Ezekiel Hopping vs. Thomas Story.—Thomas Riddle is about to remove to Kentucky, 18th September, 1792.

AUGUST, 1793 (A to D).

John Haggerty vs. Anthony Ingleton and Mary, his wife.—Writ, 4th January, 1793.

Andrew Keith vs. William Kelley and Mary, his wife.—Writ, 18th April, 1793.

NOVEMBER, 1793.

John Young vs. Rankin.—Plaintiff in 1784 married Mary Rankin, daughter of George Rankin. John Rankin was a brother of George. Mary died 1788 leaving one child, a son; John Young is married again 25th May, 1793.

John Collins, and Nelly, his wife, vs. Philip Dyer.—Writ, 8th June, 1793.

Henry King vs. Arthur Connelly and Jane, his wife.—Writ, 14th September, 1792. Mary Kirland is about to move out of the State, 1793. Mary is seventeen years old 29th June, 1793. Mary's sister was Jane, wife of William Johnston.

MAY, 1794 (A to M).

Patrick Brady and wife, Catherine, vs. Edward Brady.—Writ, 18th April, 1793.

Peggy Givins, Margaret Gibbons vs. John Hall, painter.—Writ, 23d February, 1795.

William Knowls and Mary, his wife, vs. Finley.—1793.

Archer's Administrator vs. Archer's Executor.—David Sawyers, administrator of Rebecca Archer. Rebecca died May, 1789; John Archer, her husband, died May, 1771. Bill to make John Archer's Executor pay Rebecca's Administrator the alimony that was decreed to her. Rebecca lived at home with her husband some time after alimony was decreed. John Gardner is about to go to Kentucky, where he expects to remain, September 22, 1790. Rebecca was not in her right mind. Was Rebecca Blair, daughter of John Archer and wife to William Blair? Who was John Blair, a legatee of John Archer?

Rebecca Gardner, widow of Thomas Gardner, Francis Gardner and Samuel Gardner, orphans of said Thomas Gardner, vs. John Brown, Rebecca Brown, widow of Hugh Brown, deceased, Sally Brown and Margaret Brown, infants and orphans of Hugh Brown.—Chancery. Spa. 23d March, 1791. Rebecca Gardner (widow) had married Robert Brown by 1792, September (January) 27. David Trimble deposes that he was in Staunton when Rebecca Gardner, now plaintiff, was on her way to Pennsylvania; and Maj. John Brown, deceased, father to defendant, was present when said John Brown, deceased, told her (Rebecca). Taken September 27, 1792. Did Maj. John Brown and Thomas Coalter own "Coalter's Place" together? Deposition of William Brown taken in Greenbrier 20th December, 1793. Rebecca Gardner fled to Buchanan's Fort for protection from Indians. Thomas Gardner was killed by the Indians. Bill says Thomas Gardner and John Brown in 176– became joint purchasers of Coalter's Place. Thomas died the spring following the purchase, leaving widow Rebecca and sons, Francis and Samuel. Eight or ten years afterwards, John Brown died leaving four sons, Thomas, James, Hugh and John, and one daughter, ——. Hugh is dead, leaving Rebecca Brown, widow, and two daughters, Sally and Margaret. Rebecca Brown, defendant, is not an inhabitant 20th August, 1791, Patrick Buchanan and David Trimble are about to remove from the State, 18th September, 1792.

Mathew Gleaves vs. John Finley.—Mathew was apprenticed to John Finley (Wheelwright) by his guardian, William Gleaves, 24th January, 1775. Mathew was son of Mathew, deceased.

Palmer vs. Chesnut.—Deed by Beverley to William Palmer, of land in Augusta, 25th July, 1740. Recorded in Orange.

William Palmer and wife, Jane, vs. James Chesnut.—Slander. Writ, 2d November, 1792.

Nicholas Spring vs. Robert Bailey and Elizabeth Bailey, late Elizabeth Bosong, Administratrix of John Bosong.—January 25, 1794.

John Stephenson vs. Stephenson.—John and Adam Stephenson were brothers. Adam died intestate, leaving Rebecca Stephenson, his widow. Anne, who married James Waddel; Sarah, wife of John Hair; James Stephenson, William and Rebecca Stephenson were infants. Decree for division.

Jane Connolly, by John Coalter, her next friend, vs. Arthur Connolly.—Chancery. 11th December, 1792. Divorce.

John Donnell and Sarah, his wife, vs. William Mallory.—Writ, 26th August, 1793.

JANUARY, FEBRUARY, 1794.

William Allison vs. Charles Stuart.—Charles contracted to build a fulling mill for William, which he performed and then removed into some of the back counties, but then returned again to Augusta. Charles answers that he went to live in the neighborhood of Col. Samuel Vance, who then lived in Augusta.

OCTOBER, 1794.

Charles Cameron vs. William and Samuel Armstrong.—1794. Abates by death of Samuel.

MAY, 1794.

Susanna King, infant, by Adam King, next friend, vs. Samuel McClintock.—Writ, 2d November, 1793. Breach Promise of Marriage. Susanna was daughter of Mary King. Did Samuel go to Kentucky?

Thomas Green and wife, Nancy, vs. Michael Myers.—Writ, 8th January, 1793.

Hugh Nelson vs. James Spence.—In 1785. Orator bought from defendant 130 acres, giving note for purchase money, afore which defendant sued and got judgment without making title. Bill to enjoin judgment until title made.

Van Swearingen vs. Richardson.—Plaintiff was lessee of the Panther Gap Mill and plantation in Rockbridge, which belonged to Crockett.

NOVEMBER, 1794.

Thomas Rutledge and wife, Deborah, vs. David Henderson, Jr.—15th June, 1794.

William Woods vs. Robert Harrison and William Handley.—28th June, 1794. I, Robert Harrison, of Burburn County, Kentucky, 1793. Harrison no inhabitant.

John Young vs. James Ervin.—In 1785, plaintiff was miller for James in Pennsylvania, but afterwards came to Virginia, where defendant got judgment vs. him on a judgment obtained in Pennsylvania.

AUGUST, 1794.

Donaghe vs. Rankin.—I, Hugh Donaghe, of Green County, North Carolina, to Isaac Rankin, 28th March, 1789.

Gibson vs. Elliott.—James Creswell (Carwell) lives on the French Broad, 24th May, 1794.

MAY, 1795 (M to Z).

Michael Myers and wife, Jane, vs. Thomas Green.—Writ, 8th January, 1793.

Richard Mathews vs. Isabella Burns, Executrix, Robert Burns.—Writ, 14th May, 1788. Peter Hanna deposes 14th October, 1793, that in 1781 he had charge of public stores in Staunton, where he lived, under direction of Thomas Hughes. Spa. for witnesses, 15th October, 1794, returned from Rockingham: "Thomas Harrison not at home, Daniel Harrison and Randolph Given in the army."

James Monce (Moncey) vs. William Blair.—Slander. Writ, 21st November, 1792. James Hetly is aged and infirm and lives in Greenbrier, 23d May, 1794.

MAY, 1795 (M to Z).

Alexander McClenachan vs. Michael Garber.—Trespass, 2d May, 1792. Plea states that McClenachan claims title to the said close under Dr. Alexander Humphreys, who claimed title by virtue of two orders of the Augusta Court, March, 1788, granting leave to Hum— to build an *Elaboratory* on the prison lot, and July, 1791, granting Humphreys leave to lease said house and part of the lot which he had enclosed for a period of eight years in order to indemnify said Humphreys for erecting said buildings. Garber owned a garden adjoining the public lot and he and other citizens have an immemorial right to pass through said lot, and waters flowing from the street during rain passed through the lot. A certain Mrs. Gilham, tenant under McClenachan, built a dam which threw the waters on Garber's garden, which dam Garber cut.

OCTOBER, 1795.

Commonwealth vs. Mathews.—Mathews, corporal in Gibson's Co., 15th October, 1795.

AUGUST, 1795.

Andrew Ervin vs. William Curry and Frances, his wife.—Writ, 11th September, 1793.

Francis and Christian Eccord vs. William Chambers and Anthony Mustoe. Writ, Spa. April, 1789. 1785 to 178– plaintiffs had dealings with defendants as deputy sheriff. Francis was a German and unacquainted with English language. The bill charges serious impositions on Francis by defendants and prays settlement of accounts, etc. Christian was son of Francis.

NOVEMBER, 1794.

Henry Spearing vs. Isaac Rankin.—In 1787 plaintiff lived in Richmond and was a shoemaker. Isaac Rankin persuaded him to come to Augusta and his brother Richard. Writ, 11th April, 1792.

MARCH, 1795 (A to H).

Atkinson vs. Donnelly. —Walter Cunningham, now of Kentucky, March 3, 1795. Letter of Andrew Donnelly dated Kanawha County, 3d March, 1795.

Edward Burk, Administrator, and Robert Bailey and Elizabeth, his wife, late Elizabeth Bosong, Administratrix of John Bosong, deceased, vs. William Wallace.—Writ, 24th May, 1793.

James Dunlop vs. James Spence.—19th February, 1793. William Spence, son of James. Jane Spence makes oath July, 1795, that her husband, James

Spence, etc. Robert Douglas had moved to Campbell County, 1794. George Rust lived in same county. William Kilbreath has lately gone to French Broad.

NOVEMBER, 1795.

John Lamb vs. James Rankin.—Slander. Writ, 6th March, 1793.

Margaret Blair, infant, by William Blair, next friend, vs. Adam Hadesbell.—Slander, 17th April, 1795.

Benjamin Eakle vs. John Tucker and Hannah, his wife.—Slander, 26th June, 1795.

Elizabeth Wilson, infant, by Robert Wilson, next friend, vs. Daniel Fane. Slander. Writ, 27th May, 1795.

William Henry vs. James Johnston and wife.—Thomas Brown deposes, Lexington, Kentucky, January 2, 1792. James Porter is about to remove to Kentucky 14th October, 1790.

Chrisley Lambert vs. William Griffith, infant, by Abel Griffith, next friend. A. and B., 8th November, 1794.

MARCH, 1795.

Samuel Blackwood, William Blackwood, Joseph Blackwood, by Walter Davies, guardian, Ann Blackwood, Eleanor Blackwood, Rebecca Blackwood, Robert Scott and Mary, his wife, formerly Mary Blackwood, vs. Mark Hadden (Hatton).—Spa. Chancery. 7th April, 1793. Orators, etc., are heirs and devisees of William Blackwood, deceased. Their mother, relict of William, married Mark Hadden. Their mother is dead. The marriage took place about 1781, and the mother lived about eleven years. One year after the mother's death, settlement shows: 1781-2, to maintaining and clothing William Blackwood, six years; to maintaining and clothing Eleanor Blackwood four years, to maintaining and clothing Rebecca seven years, to maintaining and clothing Joseph Blackwood seven years. 1782, cash paid James Doak for teaching two of the children; 1783, cash paid Newton Conley for teaching two of the children; 1786, cash paid William Chambers for teaching two of the children; 1789, cash paid John Hagerty for teaching three of the children; 1787, cash paid William Ranson for teaching — of the children; 1791, to maintaining, boarding and keeping Ann Blackwood nine years, to maintaining, boarding and keeping Samuel Blackwood three years, to maintaining, boarding and keeping Mary Blackwood three years. Bill for settlement of William Blackwood's estate.

Joseph Boughman and wife, Elizabeth, late Elizabeth Secaford, relict of Jacob Secaford, deceased; George Boughman and Elizabeth, his wife, daughter and heir-at-law of said Jacob Secaford, vs. William Rusk, Administrator of John Secaford.—Spa. Chancery, 1st March, 1794.

John Fudge vs. Benajah Thompson, of Cumberland County, Va.—Spa. Chancery. 1789, 25th May. Defendant has removed to Georgia and is in low circumstances.

James Johnston and Sarah, his wife, vs. George Peterson.—Slander. Writ, 16th September, 1794.

MAY, 1795 (A to G).

William Caul, infant, by Hugh Caul, next friend, vs. John Allison.—A. and B., 21st May, 1794.

Commonwealth vs. John Dixon.—Trespass for cutting down James Kerr's corner trees 31st May, 1794. John Allison was grandson of John Kerr, deceased, 1794. This suit involves title to land of James Kerr and John Dixon in 1792.

Elizabeth Carden, infant, by Joseph Carden, next friend, vs. Samuel Thomas.—Case, 19th August, 1794.

Curry vs. Rankin.—James Rankin, bond to Henry Gregg, dated 1st August, 1785, assigned by Henry to Thomas Gragg 1st August, 1785, and assigned by Thomas 3d November, 1787.

MAY, 1796.

William Blair vs. Daniel Fane.—Plaintiff's daughter, Margaret, infant, eighteen years old.

James Campbell and wife, Bridget, vs. James Essex and wife, Christian.—Slander. 27th July, 1793.

Alexander Humphreys vs. George McIntosh, George G. McIntosh.—Suit to compel defendant to return to plaintiff's service as an apothecary. Letter from George McIntosh dated Edinborough, February 27, 1793, contracting with plaintiff to come to Staunton and be his apothecary for four years.

Bogan vs. Phifer.—Richard Mathews is about going out of the State, 31st October, 1795.

Margaret Hatton, infant, by Margaret Hatton, her next friend, vs. Jacob Swallow and wife, Mary, and Peter Miller, infant, his servant and apprentice.—Slander. 20th September, 1794.

Elizabeth Miller, infant, by Judith Miller, her next friend, vs. Michael Cowley and wife, Jean.—Slander. Writ, 18th September, 1794. Plea that Elizabeth was married at date of writ.

AUGUST, 1796.

William Samuel, James Anderson and George Glenn (defendants) vs. William Young (orator).—Writ. Chancery, 27th September, 1793. William and Samuel were brothers. Petition by William Young, 1792, states that some years ago he employed George Nicholas to commence and prosecute this cause, that on removal of George from this county the case was entrusted to John Nicholas, who drew and filed the bill, shortly after which John also declined practicing in this court, and left his business to Robert Jouett, Esq., Attorney, who has also declined practicing in this court. Witness is aged and infirm. Petition for rehearing. Ellinor Young, wife of William Young, orator, 1st November, 1793. Samuel Anderson and George Glenn returned no inhabitants, 25th August, 1790. Samuel Anderson's deposition 15th February, 1791, before Benjamin Harrison, a Justice of Bourbon County. Spa. executed on Samuel Anderson, 30th August, 1787.

OFFICE JUDGMENTS.

Thompson vs. Gibson, etc.—*Dehomine Replegiando* writ, 4th May, 1796. Writ to sheriff: you cause to be replevied Archibald Thompson whom Alexander Gibson, Larkin J. Gibson and Reizen Barnett have taken and keep taken unless he was taken for murder, etc., that we may have no more clamor thereupon for want of justice and make return, etc. Agreeable to the within writ to me directed, I have gone to the defendants and demanded the said Thompson. The defendants say that he is legally and lawfully enlisted into the service of the United States of America and that they should not be justifiable in delivering him upon any application contrary to the rules and articles of war, but that they will appear when called on and subject themselves to the decision and directions of the proper authority. (Signed) James Campbell, D. S.

Archibald Thompson vs. Larkin J. Dickinson, Rezin Barnett, Charles Williams, John Johnston, Robert Christian, John Carice (?), John Mindo (?), John Collins, Oliver Blackburn, Thomas Harrington, John White.—False imprisonment. 12th April, 1796. Writ.

Mary Beaton vs. Peter Herolf and wife, Margaret.—Writ, 9th April, 1796. Slander A. and B.

John Ballard and wife, Elizabeth, vs. Catherine Dold.—Writ, 14th April, 1796. Trespass.

William Armstrong vs. Robert Stuart and wife, Mary.—Spa. Chancery. 10th April, 1795. William's father, Robert Armstrong, died 1786, orator was oldest son, but some one took advantage of Robert's age and infirmity and caused a will to be written devising the lands to orator's brother Samuel. Robert was not of sound mind at time of making the will, but Samuel took possession of the lands until year when he died. Robert Stuart inter-married with the widow of Samuel. Bill to set aside the will. Mary says she was not Samuel's widow, but was sister of orator and daughter of Robert Armstrong. Her father died the last day of December, 1786. She had a sister Nancy who was since married. Robert Armstrong was a fuller. Mary married Robert Stuart about 1792–3. Answer sworn to 25th March, 1796. Hugh Meems and Nancy Meems (Nancy Armstrong, sister of orator?) are about to move to South Carolina, 1st July, 1795.

AUGUST, 1796 (K to Z).

William McPheters vs. John Moffett.—Suit about lines of land between plaintiff and defendant settled by arbitration 20th May, 1796.

JUNE, 1796 (A to G).

Isaac Carson, infant, by Abraham Carson, next friend, vs. Alexander Curry.

JUNE, 1796 (H to Z).

Francis Acord vs. Henry Smith and —— Runkle.—Injunction.

MARCH, 1796.

Byers vs. Blair, Jr.—For killing the plaintiff's dog.

Alexander Stuart vs. James Clemens.—Defendant not found, moved to Albermarle 25th November, 1795.

Elizabeth Wilson, infant, by Robert Wilson, next friend, vs. Joseph Byers. Slander. 27th May, 1795.

MARCH, 1796 (F to K).

William Gamble, John Gamble, infants above 16; Joseph Gamble, infant above 11 years; Sarah Gamble, infant above 16; Margaret Gamble, infant above 14; Agnes Gamble, infant above 12; surviving orphans of Joseph Gamble, deceased, by William Gamble, their next friend, vs. William Patton and Isabella Gamble.—In 1779 Joseph Gamble, father of orators and oratrices, died intestate, and William Patton and Joseph's widow, Isabella, administered. William Gamble is elder brother as well as next friend. Bill for settlement, 1792.

Spa. to revive against David Stephenson and Mathew Patton, executors of William Patton, deceased, dated 20th June, 1793. William Patton's answer says, 10th January, 1793: Joseph Gamble in his lifetime prevailed upon William Patton to leave the house of Mrs. Cawley, in Staunton, and go to his plantation to labor for him, which William did about 1st March, 1777. After Joseph's death, William had no desire to remain with Joseph's family, but Isabella persuaded him to remain one year on wages. Joseph Gamble was killed by a stroke of a horse. Hugh Botkin is about to remove out of the State, 23d August, 1792.

Nathaniel Jeffries vs. Robert Throckmorton, Sr.—Chancery. Injunction, 26th May, 1794. Plaintiff boarded with defendant in Martinsburg, Berkeley County, for some time prior to 6th February, 1789. On 30th September, 1799, James Pettigrew swore that Robert Throckmorton, in discharge of a just debt, has removed himself to the Spanish territories, but Robert's wife remains in this County.

James Johnston and Sarah, his wife, vs. Lawrence Lynch and Catherine. his wife.—Slander. Writ, 18th October, 1794.

Dyer vs. Kerns.—Eleanor Young, late Eleanor Keenan.

MARCH, 1796 (A to C).

Buchanan vs. McCutchen.—Deed by Alexander Douglas to Andrew Duncan conveys a tract in Beverley Manor, 233 acres, joining Patrick Campbell's and Charles Campbell's and Brownlee's land, and a tract known as the Pine Run, where Francis Beatty once lived, 230 acres. Dated 16th October, 1746. Witnesses: Robert and John Cunningham.

Suit between Samuel Buchanan and Elizabeth, his wife; David Craig and Mary, his wife; John Edmonson and Jennet, his wife; John McKinny and Jane, his wife; James Brownlee and Florence, his wife, vs. William McCutchen, John McCutchen and John McCutchen, Jr., heirs-at-law of Wm. McCutchen.—Spa. 23d July, 1791. Writ, redocketing, 27th September, 1793. Whereas, I, Andrew Duncan, of Lincoln County, have authorized and given to James Brownlee, Sr., of Augusta County, power of attorney to convey a tract of land on Pine Run, joining Hugh Torbet and William Brownlee and John Shields, which McCutchen claims by caveat from Andrew Duncan, heir by law. 25th May, 1785. Witnesses: Alexander Brownlee, Jr., and John Brownlee. James Brownlee and Florence Brownlee, heirs-at-law of Andrew Duncan, deceased; all the above wives were daughters of Andrew Duncan, deceased, who left also a son, Andrew. Andrew, Sr.'s widow was Jannet. Andrew, Jr., was dead, 1791, intestate. Widow Jannet married William McCutchen. Alexander Douglas bought the land from Francis Beatty. William McCutchen was dead, 1791, as also Jannet. Francis Beatty first improved the land. Francis Beatty, shortly after making his entry, went to Carolina. William McCutchen entered a caveat versus Beatty and obtained judgment in 1769 and a patent in 1773. William Alexander deposes that in 1766, November, he was with William McCutchen at Williamsburg, when William McCutchen told him he had put in a friendly caveat to save the land for Andrew Duncan's children.

AUGUST, 1796 (A to K).

Hite vs. William Scott.—Attachment, 1796. Defendant is a shoemaker and is gone.

Alexander Humphreys vs. Edward Burk.—Dr. Ephraim McDowell is about to remove out of the State, January 1, 1795.

William Hill vs. James Hill.—Trespass on case for suing out attachment unlawfully.

Elizabeth Brown, administratrix of Thomas Brown, deceased, vs. Bowyer.—Writ, April, 1791. Plaintiff, Thomas Brown, died April, 1787.

OCTOBER AND NOVEMBER, 1796.

John McDonald vs. John Fell and wife, Catherine.—Slander, 23d May, 1796. No inhabitants.

MARCH, 1796 (O to Z).

William Wright vs. William Armstrong.—Spa. Chancery, April, 1790. In beginning of year 1785, orator was moving out of the Western County with his family through the County of Augusta, and met William Armstrong, who lived on Christian's Creek, and proposed to orator that orator crop for him that year.

Sebastian Wolfe vs. Lewis Myers.—Case, 15th August, 1793. Robert Carlisle is about to move out of the State, 16th February, 1796.

William Villally (Philally) vs. Samuel Frame.—Ro. and George Blakely are about to remove out of the State, 22d July, 1795.

Richard Rankin vs. Austin & Co. (of Richmond).—Chancery. Spa. Dated 1st June, 1793. Richard had a brother, George, deceased at time of the writ.

JANUARY–FEBRUARY–APRIL, 1796.

James Chesnutt vs. William Palmer.—Spa. Chancery, 12th September, 1794. In year 17— orator came to Augusta and was about to settle near William Palmer, Sr., and met William, Jr., son of William, Sr. William Palmer, Sr., had a daughter, Mary Moore.

MARCH, 1796 (L to N).

Mathews vs. Peter Hog's Administrator.—Great number of accounts and papers of Hog's. He mentions in one of the papers: 12th August, 1768.

"Uncle Patton:" Dear Sir—The boy brings three letters, that for my father be kind enough to deliver to the Captain of the first ship for Glasgow, or leave in the care of Mr. Muzie; that for Mr. Nicholas pray deliver it to himself. * * * (Signed) Peter Hog. 20th June, 1771. To Mr. Sampson Mathews.

MARCH, 1797.

Robert Bailey vs. Edward Brien.—Larkin J. Dickinson and Archibald Thompson are about to leave the State, 2d December, 1796. John Johnston, the same, 4th July, 1796. Young Phillips has enlisted in the U. S. Service, 4th July, 1796.

MARCH, 1797 (A to N).

John Matthews vs. Keder Old, administrator of Edward Parks, deceased. Letter from Edward Parks to John Matthews, written from Richmond, 1795.

Thomas Barry vs. Christian Coiner.—Writ, 18th February, 1796. John Wallace is about to remove out of the State, 27th July, 1796.

APRIL–JUNE–JULY–DECEMBER, 1797.

Archibald Thompson vs. Matthew Patton.—Rezin and Peter Barnett are about to move out of the State, October 15, 1796.

Susannah Huff vs. Nicholas Powlas.—Rosanna Sholly is about to remove from the State, 1st September, '97. Nicholas had a daughter, Polly.

AUGUST, 1797 (M to Z).

James Monce (Moncea–Monsey) and wife, Ann, vs. William Blair.— Slander. Writ, 13th December, 1791. Subpoena to both for Robert, Agnes and Elizabeth Wilson, 31st October, 1795. Joseph Byers is about to remove, 27th August, 1796. David Brown deposes, Hampshire County, 17th May, 1793. Ann Monce and her daughter, Ellinor.

Rush vs. Spence.—(Odd paper.) "Hood's heirs vs. Essex.—Ejectment. Hood died December preceding the dismission of the suit."

Stephen Smith vs. William Breckinridge.—Bond by defendant to Stephen Smith, of Franklin County, dated 1st December, 1795.

AUGUST, 1797.

John Collins and wife, Eleanor, vs. Lawrence Lynch and Catherine, his wife.—A. and B. 20th April, 1797.

Robert Grattan vs. William Donaldson.—Slander. Writ, 18th August, 1796. William Blain is about to remove from jurisdiction of this Court, 1st March, 1797. James Cameron is about to leave the State, 26th October, 1796.

George Mathews, Sr., adversus Margaret Mathews, by Jacob Kinney, next friend.—Spa. Chancery, 27th February, 1796. Not found. (A) Spa. 25th March, 1796. No inhabitant. (P) Spa. 27th June, 1797. Executed July 6, 1797.

Joseph Parks vs. Cornelius Ruddle.—Injunction to judgment.

Wm. Hogshead, infant, by James Hogshead, next friend, vs. John Bing.—Writ, 18th March, 1795.

James McNutt vs. Wm. Sprowl, devisee of Samuel Sprowl.—Writ, 1st August, '95. Notice given by plaintiff to take depositions of Robert Gamble, James Beard and other witnesses of the inhabitants of the Southwest Territory. Depositions of Saml. Henry, James Tedford and James Ewing before David Craig, James Gillespy and James Houston, in Blount County, Territory S. Ohio, October 30, 1795, that they viewed 320 acres and appraised it. Depositions of Robert Gamble and James Beard before Thomas McCullock, James Gillespy and James Houston, in Blount County, Territory S. Ohio, 22d December, 1795, say: James Beard sent the pocket book and papers of Samuel Sprowl, deceased, to his house, and when William Sprowl came out to this Country, Ro. Gamble delivered the whole of the papers of Samuel, deceased, to William Sprowl. Covenant by Samuel Sprowl to convey land to McNutt, in Sevier County, State of Franklin, 18th September, 1787. James McNutt, of County of Augusta, and Samuel Sprowl, of County Sevier, in State of Franklin. The land joins Jacob Alexander.

AUGUST, 1795 (H to M).

David Fulton vs. Samuel McCutchen.—Trespass writ, 14th April, 1795. Samuel McCutchen, Sr., deposes, 26th June, 1797: About 50 years ago, Benjamin Bordan showed deponent a tree as a corner of Borden's land. Samuel, Sr., had a son William and a son Samuel.

Eversole vs. Bell.—Robert Stephenson had a son, Edward.

AUGUST, 1797 (A to M).

John Story and Thomas Story adversus Hugh Donaghe.—Elizabeth Caul deposes, 6th August, 1796: James Stuart, son of John and Mary Stuart, was born in the month of March, and that Thomas Story, son of Thomas Story, Sr., was born in May, and her own son, Hugh Caul, was born 12th June in the same year, and Thomas Story, the present defendant, was 28 years old last May. She had a register of the birth of her own children which was existing when she deposed. Mary Dixon (formerly Mary Stuart) deposes at the same time that her son, James Stuart, was born 16th March, 1768, and Thomas Story was born May following. She was sister-in-law of William Stuart, who died the fall after birth of James. These depositions were taken because Mary and Elizabeth were very old.

William Bell vs. John Fleiger.—15th June, 1796, writ. Received of David Hanna and William Bell, 4 beeves at £14, for the use of the Augusta County militia, now ordered in the service. (Signed) John Flieger, Commissary. September 28, 1794. Same for use of Augusta Cavalry, now ordered into the service. September 28, 1794.

MAY, 1798 (M to Z).

Bolzer Seldomridge vs. Bennia Gregg.—28th August, 1797. Not found.

Shelly vs. Rankin.—I, Peter Shelly, of Washington County, Maryland, to Frederick Rods, of same County and State, 20th December, 1785.

Philip North vs. Keder Old, Administrator Edward Parks.—Writ, 24th February, 1796.

Isabella and Barbara Walker, infants, by Hugh Donaghe, their guardian, vs. Elizabeth and Robert Walker, Arthur Connolly and John Campbell.—Alex. Walker, father of oratrixes, and husband of Elizabeth, and father (?) of Robert, died, 1774, with will. Bill for accounting. Elizabeth Walker's answer, sworn to 10th December, 1790. Spa. in chancery, 2d June, 1787. This suit contains settlement of the estate, with all the heirs, giving names.

November, 1798 (D to M).

Mary Keith, infant, by Lawrence Lynch, next friend, vs. Peter Hall.—Writ, 11th November, 1797.

November, 1798.

James Stuart and Polly, his wife, vs. George Fosnaught.—8th June, 1798.

November, 1798 (A to C).

Brown's Administratrix vs. John Fleiger.—Received of James Brown, 4 beefs for the Militia of Augusta County, now in actual service. John Fleiger, Commry., Sept. 27, 1794.

August, 1799.

Thomas Turk vs. Frederick Steele and son, Andrew Steele.—Orator made entries for land, 10th October, 1762; 20th December, '66; 24th February, 1768.

May, 1799 (C).

John Canote vs. Peter Shally.—Mary Shally, only daughter of Peter Shally, deposes, that about a year ago, her brother Christian, who had some time before been married to a daughter of John Canote, Sr., sister to plaintiff. 24th November, 1797. Mary Shally (Shirley) and Henry Harmon are about to remove, and also Sally Argenbright, November 17, 1797. 4th September, 1797, Christian Shally is about to remove to Kentucky.

March, 1799 (C to Z).

James Hill vs. William Hill.—In 1789 there was a final settlement bill in the hands of Mr. Joseph Bell for benefit of William Hill. There were two men named William Hill, one of whom absconded and the certificate was for the benefit of the other.

Charles Hedrick, Jr., son of Charles Hedrick, of Staunton, binds himself to Adam Bickle, a saddler, 1789.

Joseph Huffman vs. Alexander Gibson.—Leonard Huffman was son of plaintiff.

Lawrence Lynch and Catherine, his wife, vs. Charles Brooks.—13th March, 1799.

John and Jacob Rapp vs. James Seawright.—13th March 1799. John Ward is about to leave the State.

MARCH, 1799.

Leonard Huffman vs. Alexander Gibson.—Writ *de homine replegiando,* 1796. "Leonard Huffman has been duly enlisted and mustered in the service of the United States, has received his bounty, pay, clothing, &c., and is now under orders to march at the shortest notice to the Frontier of Tennessee. I know of no just cause why a demand should be made of him under cover of the Civil Power and do not consider myself justifiable in delivering him up (to the injury of the service) on any pretence whatever, unless directed so to do by the proper authority." (Signed) Alexander Gibson, Captain in the 4th Regiment, United States Army.

MAY, 1799 (H to P).

Richard King and Nancy, his wife, vs. William Jameson.—Slander, 1799.

James Kerr and Robert Kenny vs. John McCune and William Bell.—Debt. Writ, 7th November, 1796. The estate of James Lessley, Jr., deceased, debtor, in 1777. To one year's boarding at school. To one year's schooling of one scholar. To nocalating the same scholar. This scholar was Betsy Lessly. She was a daughter of James. Elizabeth McCune deposes, 1799— her son John. Hat for Polly Lessley.

Peter Lower vs. Hugh Paul.—Edward Bryan died between 1797, 7th December, and 26th March, 1798.

JUNE, 1799 (A to G).

George Andrews vs. Mathew Christian.—"Some time before Mathew left this Commonwealth."

John Bier vs. Jacob Sheetz and wife, Elizabeth, late Elizabeth Bleehon (Bleehern).—26th September, 1797.

MAY, 1797 (A to G).

James Dardis vs. Charles and Hugh O'Neal.—A and B writ, 3d December, 1795. William Telfair is about to go out of the State. 3d December, 1795.

FEBRUARY, 1798 (A to L).

Estill vs. Geiger.—Thomas Ray is about to remove from this County, 27th September, 1797.

MARCH AND APRIL, 1798.

Wheeler vs. Trumper.—Rachel Hamond, mother to William Wheeler, apprentice to Lawrence Trumper.

Henry Teeford vs. Adam Saftly.—Slander. Writ, 20th July, 1796. John Waddell is about to remove out of the State of Virginia, 27th September, 1796.

JANUARY–MAY–JUNE, 1798.

Florence Henderson vs. James Old.—Case writ, 7th June, 1796. Breach promise executed, and Philip Dold, bail. Judgment for plaintiff. Was this Florence Bell? No.

JUNE, 1799 (H to Z).

Kinkead vs. Donnelly.—Thomas Kinkead, in 1771, purchased from Jacob Passinger a tract of land in Greenbrier called Spring Lick, once the property of Christian Sanders, orphan. Christian Pessinger deposes, 1797, that he and Christian Saunders made the first improvement on the land prior to 1751, when it was surveyed.

Blair vs. McKenny's Executors.—William Blair vs. Isabella McKenny, executor of William McKenny, 17th January, 1799. James Mitchell was a shoemaker. William Blair was a tanner near North Mountain Meeting House.

John Fennel vs. George Peevy.—Chancery, 25th May, 1796. George Peevy was father-in-law of James Robinson, 179-. Robinson had run away (to South Carolina?). William Peevy, son of George, had a sister, Jane, living in South Carolina, 15th May, 1797. Jane was married and had a daughter.

AUGUST, 1800 (K to Z).

William Bowyer, Administrator, and Pricilla Madison, devisees of Richard Madison, vs. Thomas Madison, Andrew Lewis and Agatha Madison, Executors of John Madison.—Chancery. Spa. 22d August, 1786. Defendants returned no inhabitants, 27th May, 1788. Richard Madison was son of John Madison. John Madison's will is in Botetourt. Pricilla married William Miller, Agatha Madison answers from Botetourt County. Thomas was also son of John, who died first part of 1784. John's children, Margaret, Lucy and George, were living with him at the time of his death. John had sons, James, Gabriel. John was clerk of Augusta and resigned only upon the express condition that Richard should be appointed and this appointment was considered as an advancement to Richard by his father, John. Pricilla was daughter of William Bowyer. Thomas Madison's answer sworn to in Washington County, 16th September, 1788. Robert Rennick's deposition in Botetourt, 1790. Hugh Crockett's deposition in Montgomery County, 14th October, 1790. Copy of will of John Madison, of Botetourt County, dated 19th December, 1783. Son William, deceased. Son Roisland. Daughter-in-law, Elizabeth, widow of William. Granddaughters, Susanna Smith Madison, and Agatha Strother Madison, daughters of William. Son, George, 2,000 acres Kentucky land. Son, Thomas. Son-in-law, Andrew Lewis. Daughter-in-law, Susanna Madison. Mourning to be purchased and presented to Mrs. Margaret Harvey.

AUGUST, 1800 (K to Z).

Margaret McClenachan vs. Elijah McClenachan.—Margaret was widow of Elijah, Sr., and covenanted to release to Elijah, Jr., defendant here, her dower in consideration of an annuity, which he failed to pay, and Margaret sued. Lettice Ann McClenachan.

William McGarvin and wife, Polly, vs. John Strain and wife, Eleanor.—Slander.

John McMullen and wife, Mary, vs. Edward Lefler and wife, Hannah.—William and Polly McGarvin are about to move out of the County, 18th February, 1799.

John Patton, of Rockbridge County, vs. Levi Bow, late of Rockbridge County.—Attachment, 26th July, 1800. John Patton is a stranger, but a good man, etc., 26th July, 1800. John Coalter.

Eleanor Smith vs. William Risk and wife.—Slander, 17th March, 1798.

OCTOBER, 1799 (L to Z).

Robert McDowell vs. James Anderson, Jr., and Sr.—Both defendants of Greenbrier County in 1799.

James Patton vs. Lusbbon and Williams.

FEBRUARY, 1799 (A to K).

Robert Armstrong and Elizabeth, his wife, assignee of Elizabeth Graham, vs. John Graham.—Elizabeth Armstrong was daughter of Elizabeth Graham, and was married before 10th August 1795.

Frederick Black, of Rockingham, vs. George Fifer.

Commonwealth vs. John Kilkenny, Jr.—Mary King, daughter of Richard King, 2d November, 1798.

OCTOBER, 1800.

Thomas Bell vs. John McClure.—October, 1800, abates by plaintiff's death. Writ, dated 27th September, 1800.

Mickle vs. Fackler.—John Cox is about to leave the State, 31st March, 1798.

Reed vs. Reed.—Collin Reed, son of one of the heirs-at-law of John Reed, deceased, orator. John and Robert Reed, formerly of Augusta, were brothers and now deceased. Robert died intestate, 178-, without direct heirs. Collin is next of kin (half-blood) to Robert. Collin has brought suit in the District Court vs. Margaret Reed, alias Margaret Mathews, widow and relict of said Robert, which suit has been removed to the High Court of Appeals.

Henry Roper vs. Isaac and Charles Hudson.—14th June, 1798.

MARCH, 1800 (H to Z).

John Kilkenny and Sally, his wife, vs. William Short and Mary, his wife.—A. and B.

John Kirk, Daniel O'Friel and John Elliott vs. James Bell's heirs.—In 1784 plaintiffs and defendants, with Samuel Bell entered into partnership to buy land in Kentucky. Robert Henderson was agent. Bill for a division. Answer by Martha, William, John, Agnes and Rachel Bell, relict and heirs of James Bell, to the bill of complaint exhibited against them, and Robert

Bell, Francis, Samuel, Mary Ann Bell, infants. 14,237 acres were located in James Bell's name in Fleming County, on Triplett's Creek, of which O'Friel gets 1,100 acres, John Kirk gets 500 acres, James Bell gets 4,506 acres, John Elliott gets 800 acres. Daniel Phreel.

MAY, 1800.

John Swisher vs. James Powell Cocke.—Deceit, 12th November, 1796.

JULY, 1800 (I to Z).

William Lyons, et al.—Petition for road at Greenville. List of petitioners, 1800.

Benjamin Reiger vs. Benjamin Kennerley.—Writ, 5th July, 1800. July, 1800, abates by defendant's death.

Andrew Young, of Rockbridge, vs. James Hathorn.—Attachment, 13th April, 1797. Defendant has removed. Contract dated 29th February, 1796, of lease between James Howthorn, of Surrey County, North Carolina, and John and Robert Dunlop.

JUNE AND SEPTEMBER, 1800.

Robert Poag's road petition.—Staunton and Lexington Road, near Rockbridge line. List of petitioners.

Andrew Hunter road petition.—From Cornelius Adairs to Joseph Burks, passing Andrew Hunter's Mill. List of petitioners.

David Hogshead's road petition.—To and from Charles Hogshead's Sulphur Spring in Genning's Gap. Petitioners.

James Peevy vs. Samuel Meek.—Attachment, 1799. Meek had removed; wife, Elizabeth.

AUGUST, 1800 (A to I).

Joseph Altoffer vs. Jacob Sheets and Elizabeth, his wife, late Elizabeth Player, Administratrix of Peter Player (Peter Player) deceased.—Settlement of Peter Player's estate in Rockingham, July Court, 1800.

William Bowyer vs. Thomas Mines.—1798, August. 1800 abates by plaintiff's death.

John Hunter vs. Peter Franker.—Peter Franker and his son, John, 1799.

FEBRUARY, 1800.

William Bratton vs. Frederick Shaver.—Petition, 28th November, 1799. Defendant no inhabitant.

Thomas Downing and Polly, his wife, late Polly Robertson, vs. Anthony Whitsel.—3d November, 1799. Note dated 23d September, 1796, to Polly Robertson.

Daniel Fane vs. Joseph Byers.—Attachment, 19th May, 1796. Frances Stuart, widow.

Samuel Miller and John Lewis, Executors of Henry Miller, vs. Peter Whitsel, Sr.—May, 1799. Defendant no inhabitant.

Molley Downey vs. James Lowe and Polly, his wife.—28th August, 1799. A. and B.

John Loftus vs. Joseph Anderson and Daniel Chestnut.—20th September, 1799. No inhabitants.

Jacob Peck vs. Frederick Shafer.—1799. No inhabitants.

MARCH, 1800 (A to G).

James Cochran vs. William Walmsley and C. Bogert.—Defendants lived in Randolph County.

MAY, 1800 (A to G).

James Gillespy vs. Robert Beverley.—Chancery. Writ, 30th July, 1796. Full account of Beverley's made of procedure in regard to the Beverley Manor lands. Gillespy bought a tract in 1773, and now sues for a title. Gillespy removed from the County. Thomas Mynes, of Augusta County. Smith Slaughter and Robert Cockburn, of Berkeley County. Power Attorney.

JANUARY, APRIL, JULY, SEPTEMBER, DECEMBER, 1799.

Laywell vs. Andrew Silling.—Abraham Laywell's apprenticeship to Andrew rescinded, as Andrew is about to move out of the State.

NOVEMBER, 1800 (A to G).

Joseph Bell and Jane, his wife, vs. Peter Smith.—A. and B., 1798.

Isabella Burns vs. George Mathews.—Capias, 11th July, 1797. Action to recover from George, the board, etc., of his wife,, Margaret. Order by Margaret to Mr. Robert Gamble to pay the account to "Sister Burns," 1793. Mrs. Margaret Mathews to Philip Hopkins. 1793, One hat for Grace. One hat for Charles Mathews. Received of Mrs. Isabella Burns the above account in full. Philip Hopkins. 1793. Boarding Mrs. Mathews fifty days. Boarding Miss Peggy. Boarding Miss Jean. Boarding son, George. Boarding son, Charles. Boarding driver, Patrick Donoghe. Boarding servant, Grace. 1797. Order by Isabella dated Harrisonburg.

MAY, 1800 (H to Z).

Peter Hanger vs. Beverley. Poage vs. Beverley. Hill vs. Beverley.—Several other suits for lands in Beverley Manor. Catherine, by Augustine Argenbright, her next friend.

Merritt vs. Samuel Merritt.—Chancery. In 1785 oratrix married Samuel Merritt. She was a widow and possessed of considerable estate by the will of her former husband.

JULY, 1800 (A to H).

Gregory vs. Flieger.—William Brady, a soldier in the United States Army, now near Staunton. The troops are shortly to march to some other State, 28th May, 1800.

Hogshead vs. Hart.—Silas Hart's heirs, viz, Oliver, Silas, Josiah, and Joseph Hart, Edith Hough, John, Betsy and Nelly Thomas and Joseph Gilbert. Spa. 29th December, 1796. All except Gilbert are non-residents.

NOVEMBER, 1800.

McClure vs. Reuben Kennerley.—August, 1800, abates by defendant's death.

Jesse Bennett vs. Peter Hog.—Bennett was a relative of Hog. Dr. Jesse Bennett, of Greenbrier. Alexander Nelson bought a tract of land in Kanawha County on the Ohio ten-mile creek from Peter Hog. Hog repurchased it through Bennett.

John Crawford vs. Timothy and Joseph Green.—Case, 9th June, 1800. No inhabitants.

Robert Gamble vs. William Breckinridge.—24th June, 1800. Debt. No inhabitants.

David Laird vs. Isaac Rankin.—15th July, 1800. 1800, August, abates by plaintiff's death.

Mullen vs. McGuire.—Samuel McGuire was an officer (Lieutenant) in the 4th Regiment, U. S. Army, and under arrest and required to keep his quarters when the sheriff arrested and imprisoned him for debt. Upon habeas corpus he was released.

AUGUST, 1800.

Thomas Butler vs. Jacob Miller.—18th September, 1799. No inhabitants.

George Berry vs. Joseph Gerral, alias Jewell.

Jacob Geiger vs. Thomas Mynes.—5th May, 1800. No inhabitants.

Gamble and Gratton vs. Benjamin Kennerley.—9th November, 1799. 1800, July, abates by defendant's death.

Mustoe and Chambers vs. Christian Mummer.—14th April, 1800. No inhabitants.

Robert McCulloch vs. Thomas Mynes.—6th May, 1800. No inhabitants.

Joseph Paints vs. Simon Hankey.—10th March, 1798. No inhabitants.

NOVEMBER, 1800 (H to Z).

Lewis Myers vs. William Kennerley.—16th February, 1799. 1800, November, abates by plaintiff's death.

Samuel Wilson and wife, Elinor, late Elinor Alexander, vs. Hugh Alexander.—1798.

MARCH, 1801 (M to Z).

Mary Wilds, infant, by Valentine Wilds, next friend, vs. William Cochran.—30th November, 1798. Margaret Craig is about to remove out of the State, 29th August, 1800. Spa. to Rockbridge for Nicholas Reader and wife, Elizabeth.

David Moore, brother of William, vs. William Jolly.—William made a contract with Jolly to build a furnace for William. Jolly engaged himself at the iron works of Mr. Crawford in Greenbrier. Work was negligently done, and Jolly went to Pennsylvania.

JUNE, 1803.

Archer's Executors vs. Poage's Executors.—Single package. Receipt by Edmond Randolph, signature. Many accounts current and receipts, 1780. Account of John Trimble, December, 1778. To cash paid for said Archer for a soldier enlisted. Agreeable to Act of Assembly, as per supperscription, £6 paper money. 19th November, 1782. Received of John Poage, executor of John Archer, £16, the proportion for raising beef and clothing for a District. (Signed) Thomas Bradshaw, Collector. 16th March, 1784. Received of John Poage £3.1.3 on account of the legacy left to my wife by John Archer, deceased. (Signed) Robert vs. Ross. 1774. Account of James Bell, deceased (affidavit by Agnes Bell, September, 1783), for boarding, washing and lodging and trouble of Rebeka, his wife (Archer's wife), from 15th August to 15th May. Sampson Archer (brother of John) and his children mentioned as some of the poor entitled under the will. George Kinkead ditto. John Poage's letter to Sampson Mathews, about deposit of £200 by John Archer with Colonel Dandridge in 1755–56.

MAY, 1804 (A to C).

Burk vs. Parry.—Deposition, 1801, of Joseph Burk, that his brothers, Edward and William.

JUNE, 1803 (I to Z).

Mathew Patton vs. Archibald Thompson.—Defendant, servant of plaintiff, had enlisted as a soldier under Captain Gibson.

James Patton, heir of John Patton, who was only son and heir of William Patton, deceased, vs. Mathew Patton and David Stephenson, Executors of said William Patton.—Chancery. Decree, 27th March, 1802, that complainant is not lawful heir of John Patton. William died about April1, 1793. Affidavit, 10th February, 1797, by James Wallace, of Carickafaden, Parish Donagh, Bowery of Irishowen, County Donegall, Ireland, farmer. Knew William Patton, formerly of Tuluaree, Parish Donagh, but many years ago went to America, and lately died there, leaving will and appendix. David Stephenson and Mathew Patton, executors, son William married to Mary Beatty, still living at Carickafaden, were married in parish of Donagh by Rev. Thomas Shawbridge, dissenting clergyman. Affiant was best man about fifty-six years ago.

JUNE, 1803 (I to Z).

Patton's heir vs. Patton's Executors.—Continued. William, soon after marriage, went to America, leaving issue one son, viz, John Patton, who died about twenty years ago, leaving James Patton, his son, and only issue, who now lives at Carickafaden. Certificate by John Pitt Kenedy, rector of Donagh Parish, that he knows said James Patton, is about twenty-four years old, five feet nine inches high, wears his own hair dark brown, blue eyes and weighty eyebrows, of dark complexion, pretty stout, 29th August, 1801. Elizabeth Caruthers deposes that she was well acquainted with Mary Beatey, wife of William Patton, although she was called Mary Beatey, it being a custom in Ireland among poor people for married women still to retain their maiden names. Heard that William left Ireland when son, John, was infant. Was well acquainted with John. John died, leaving child by Ruth Wallace. Never heard John acknowledge the child, but it lived with him, he treated it as his child and she always understood it' was his. Child lived with grandmother, Mary Beatey, until nine years old, when affiant left Ireland about eight years ago. Complainant now present is said child. 10th February, 1801. Samuel Scott deposes. Is twenty-eight years old and always acquainted with plaintiff, living in same neighborhood. Mary Beatey died December two years ago. John Patton had many relations on his mother's side. 30th May, 1801. Mathew Patton being a non-resident, order publication. Removed to Kentucky. Bill states James is only son and heir of John Patton, who was only son and heir of William Patton, late of Augusta. William left them in Ireland in 1741. Mathew's answer states that William was a distant relative of Mathew.

MARCH, 1801 (H to L).

Habersham, Postmaster General, vs. Vincent Topp, Postmaster at Staunton.—Verdict vs. defendant.

Kennerley vs. John Allison.—Caveat dated 7th April, 1795. Plaintiffs, James and William Kennerley, George Craig, John and Christopher Fowler, Martin Grove. Involves 215 acres on South River, surveyed for John, 13th September, 1794. Claimed by caveators by reason of patent, 1st December, 1740, to William Russell. These 215 acres were decreed to John in caveat proceedings in District Court. Thomas Turk, Sr., deposes about sixty years ago he, Thomas, carried the chain upon survey of a tract for William Russell. Thomas Lawson settled at the Spring now owned by Martin Grove, and James Kennerley ordered him off. Again survey made forty-eight years ago near where deponent now lives and then lived. He has lived sixty-seven or sixty-eight years on land where he now lives. Special verdict finds patent to Russell, 1st December, 1740. Beverley Manor lines. Lands in dispute have been in possession of John and Christian Fanber and Martin Grove and their predecessors for upwards of thirty years. Land was conveyed by Russell to Bloodworth and afterwards became vested in James Kennerley, father of caveators.

OFFICE JUDGMENTS.

AUGUST, 1804.

Charles Massie's death.

AUGUST, 1803 (N to Z).

George Slagle vs. Martin Grove.—Trepass.

OCTOBER, 1803 (A to C).

William Abney vs. Robert Garland. Robert Christian, apprentice to plaintiff, went to Amherst Court, where he lost money and hats of plaintiff, which he was there to sell for plaintiff, at cards to defendant. Christian was afterwards a soldier in United States Army.

AUGUST, 1802 (A to C).

Catherine Baylor, wife of Jacob Baylor, by Alexander Anderson, vs. Jacob Baylor.—Lived faithfully with defendant in Virginia and Pennsylvania, and is now aged and infirm, having raised twelve children.

Campbell vs. Connelly.—William Hinds and Joseph Patterson, witnesses, living in Jessamine County, Kentucky.

MARCH, 1802 (A to L).

Mathew Burnet vs. John Strain and Eleanor.—Slander. Mathew was a school teacher.

OFFICE JUDGMENTS.

MAY, 1803.

James Flack vs. Michael Hannon.—Thomas Chinn had removed to Tennessee.

MARCH, 1802 (M to Z).

George Weir's Orphans vs. James Mitchel, Executor of Thomas Beard.—Arbitration awarded in plaintiff's favor, 1786. Defendant was to pay before oldest child of Jane, daughter of Thomas, came of age.

OCTOBER, 1803 (P to Z).

Mary Swallow vs. Jacob Swallow.—Divorce.

OCTOBER, 1803 (D to M).

Daniel Muse, of Northumberland County, vs. John Monroe, of Richmond County.—Note dated — May, 1794.

AUGUST, 1801 (A to B).

Brownlee vs. Myers.—Original deed by Phinley McClure, of Orange County, to John Brownlee, of same place, dated 26th May, 1742, conveys tract in B. M. Glade, of Hammock's Branch, Cor. Pat. Campbell, Cor. David Mitchell, 444 acres. Test, Shurley Whatley, James Clark, Catlett Conway.

FEBRUARY, 1806 (M).

Mustoe vs. Graham.—Deposition of Charles Arbuckle, 1st November, 1805, in Greenbrier. He possesses a receipt by Jacob Skiles, 6th April, 1792, from George Clendennin for collection from War Department at Philadelphia, pay roll of ninety-two privates, one captain, one lieutenant, two ensigns, four sergeants, also list of rations, allowing each officer and private a ration per day for 153 days. Certificate of ammunition furnished all for service in 1790. George, receipts, 24th April, 1793, for having received the several allowances for services of the Kanawha Rangers. William Clennondon, of Mason County, taken first Tuesday of October, at house of John Vanhever, in town of Point Pleasant, before Justice John Boush and John Henderson. Brother of George Clendenon. Letter of Joseph Graham from Monroe County. Certificate, 1st September, 1791, by George Shaver, Lieutenant, and Andrew Lewis, Ensign, that Joseph Graham has served as a soldier at Kanawha. Deposition of Reuben Slaughter, 14th May, 1805. He negotiated sale of goods by Mustoe and Chambers to the soldiers in Kanawha County in 1791. Col. George Clendenin was considered paymaster. Joseph Graham was a soldier on Kanawha River in 1791 and came down from Greenbrier with George Shaw, who was lieutenant. George died about 1796. Order, 11th May, 1791, by William Miller on Col. George Clendennin for his pay as soldier accepted by George. David Johnson's similar order. Ditto James Robertson, David Johnston, James Spencer, John Sharp.

MAY, 1804 (D to H).

John Dixon vs. George Anderson.—Affidavit, 17th October, 1801, that John Campbell is an inhabitant of Kentucky, and is about to return to that State. Deposition of John states that in 1785 or 1786 he assisted his brother, Robert Campbell, to build a house for defendant. John Patterson and his brother, Thomas Patterson.

Andrew Honeyman vs. Hugh Donaghe.

DECEMBER, 1803 (A to G).

Cochran vs. Hopkins.

OCTOBER, 1807 (M to O).

McCue vs. Mathews, Administrator.—Richard Mathews died 9th October, 1802, at his home in Kentucky.

MAY, 1807 (N to Z).

Stone vs. Woods.—John Yates is about to leave, remove from the State.

JANUARY, 1814.

Hyden vs. Hyden.—Joshua Hyden is brother of Joseph.

MAY, 1811 (F to I).

Fisher vs. Alfred.—Contract, 1809, with George Alfred as schoolmaster, signed by Alexander Nelson, Samuel Lessley, Joshua Hiden, James Johnston, Archibald Griffey, George Tevenbaugh, Daniel Fisher, John Brown,

Jane Crawford, John C. Baskin, Charles Baskin, James Anderson, George Anderson, Thomas Galbreath, James Kelley, Robert Hansberger.

MAY, 1815 (R to Z).

James Williamson vs. Charles B. Rhodes.—Breach of Covenant. Plaintiff, in 1811, was editor of "Spirit of the Press" in Staunton, and engaged defendant as printer.

Peter Moore vs. Rice.—Letter of Peter Moore, February 27, 1815. Peter Moore and John Jenkins were soldiers in War of 1812.

OCTOBER AND DECEMBER, 1813.

Bowyer's Administrator vs. Griffin.—Bill to foreclose mortgage recorded 18th September, 1787. John Griffin and Elizabeth to Bowyer. Original mortgage filed. From 1794 to 1803 John Griffin was residing at German Town, in North Carolina.

Crawford's Orphans vs. Crawford's Administrator.—Charles Surface and Florence, his wife, late Florence Crawford.

JUNE, 1812.

John Campbell, of Kentucky, formerly of Augusta County, vs. John Mills. —Plaintiff and defendant were executors of Martha Burnsides. Bill sworn to in Mason County, Kentucky. James Campbell was nephew of John.

Fleiger vs. Scott's Administrators.—Contract, 14th September, 1797, mentions plantation whereon Christian Gregory now lives.

APRIL, 1806 (H to Z).

Robert Reed, Caton Reed, Hugh Ballantine and Frances, his wife, heirs of Robert Reed, vs. Margaret Reed, widow of Robert, who has married George Mathews.—Suit for accounting. Notice, 30th March, 1799, to take depositions of Ann Gibson, Elizabeth Cavens, Mary Edwin, Margaret Erwin, Samuel McKee and Martha McKee, to be taken in Fayette County, Kentucky.

MAY, 1806 (A to G).

Boswell vs. Boswell.—Plaintiff was Elizabeth Slusher, daughter of Conrad Slusher. Depositions to be taken, 13th July, 1805, in Abingdon, of Robert Kincaid, James and Samuel Vance, Robert E. Cummins, Rev. Charles Cummins, Thomas Moffett, Philip Kesner and wife, Sarah Fink, Bartholomew Baker and wife, Hannah Baker, James Maxwell, John Collins and wife, William King and John Nutty. Depositions of James Maxwell and Grizzy, his wife. Deposition of John Kistner and *Rachael*, his wife. Deposition of Sarah Fink, formerly Sarah Cunningham. Deposition of Sarah Baker, wife of Bartholomew Baker. Deposition of Hannah Baker, daughter of Bartholomew Baker.

August, 1807 (L to Z).

Malcom vs. Hogshead.—June, 1806, notice to take deposition of John Bing, of Gallia County, Ohio. Deposition taken, 11th August, 1806, before Andrew Erwin and Peter Aleshine, Justices of Gallia County.

February, 1804.

Hopping vs. Hines.—Original deed, Ebenezer Alexander and wife to Hinds, 1778. James Bridget, son-in-law of Thomas Hinds.

February, 1804 (H to L).

Lear's Administrators vs. Thornton.—Peter Fleming, Presiding Justice of Bambeau County, Kentucky. Mention of Coate Thornton, Daniel Lear. Lyle vs. Stuart.—Original letter of Owen Owens.

September, 1807 (A to Z).

Graham vs. Risk.—Joseph Graham went to Monroe County about 1800.
John Strain vs. Connelly.—James Strain, father of complainant, died intestate, 1789, leaving land. Descended to his children, Robert, James, Allen, Polly, Jinney, Nancy, Peggy and complainant. Polly married David Connelly and died, leaving Arthur Connelly and James Strain Connelly, infants of five and seven years.
Isaac Rankin.—*Commission de Lunatico inquirendo.*

May, 1806 (A to E).

William Chambers vs. James Lang.—Defendant was inhabitant of Kentucky or Tennessee since 1789.

May, 1816 (M to Z).

West's Administrators vs. Humphrey's Administrators.—Deposition of William Gibson, in Landesburgh, Cumberland County, Pennsylvania.

April, June and July, 1813.

Robert and David Griffith, sons of Abel Griffith, who died in 1812, vs. Magdalene, Caleb and Hiram.—Magdalene was widow, Caleb and Hiram were two infant sons. Bill for partition.
Moore vs. Stockdale.—Robert Stockdale came to America, 1775, and settled on line between Pennsylvania and Maryland, then went to Loudon County, Virginia, thence to Rockingham, thence to Augusta. Was related to Stogdells in Pennsylvania. William Hart deposes that he was born in Hambleton Township, Pennsyvania, and removed to Amherst County, Virginia. James Ellis deposes ditto.

FEBRUARY, 1815 (A to G).

William Black vs. John Bosong's Administrators.—John Bosong died, January, 1793. His widow, Elizabeth, married Robert Bailey. He left two children, William and Polly. Polly married Jesse Minter. William died intestate, leaving children.

Doake vs. Stone.—John Stone, a garnishee, came to live with his father, Gotleib Stone, the defendant, who was a hatter.

Donoghe vs. Duerson.—John Duerson was Donoghe's overseer, 1804.

Givin vs. Fulton.—John Graham no inhabitant, April, 1812.

FEBRUARY, 1811 (H to M).

Robert McDowell vs. William G. Dudley.—Plaintiff kept tavern at Jenning's Gap.

JULY AND SEPTEMBER, 1813.

John Campbell vs. Arthur, John and David Connelly.—John and David are sons of Arthur. Settlement of Walker's estate.

AUGUST, 1813.

Commonwealth vs. Ballard.—Single papers. Capias to hear judgment. Defendant, John M. Ballard, was constable at Waynesboro, and was prosecuted by information for extorting money by color of his office.

MAY, 1804 (R to Z).

Richardson vs. Cupps.—Thomas Sawyers is about to remove out of the State, 28th September, 1801.

MAY, 1812.

Morton vs. Seymour.—Joseph Seymour (Leamer?) is about to remove from State.

AUGUST, 1815 (M to Y).

Hogshead vs. McCue.—Thomas Erwin is about to remove out of State.

MAY, 1816 (A to C).

Campbell vs. Humphreys.—Affidavit, 19th January, 1811, of James Campbell in Green County, Kentucky.

MAY, 1813 (H to Z).

Wilson vs. Shultz.—In 1799 Thomas Wilson kept tavern in Rockbridge. James Alexander, nephew of Hugh Alexander.

AUGUST, 1813.

Bumgardner vs. Thompson.—Single package.

Frederick L. E. Ameling and Sophia, late Sophia Leekemp, administratrix of Albert Leekemp, deceased, vs. Jacob Fackler.

MAY, 1814 (D to I).

Donaghe vs. Headrick.—Andrew Honeyman has removed to the Western County, 25th October, 1809.

MAY, 1814 (K to O).

Benjamin Mosby vs. James Allen and Alexander Nelson.—Deposition, 27th November, 1812, of James Edmonson in Fleming County, Kentucky, migrated to Kentucky in fall of 1809. Capt. James Edmondson. It required from 5th October to 30th October to make journey from Augusta to Fleming County, Kentucky.

MARCH TO DECEMBER, 1814.

Connelly vs. Donoghe.—Sam Blackburn testifies as to sale by George Mathews to Donoghe of 1,000 acres on Ohio River, belonging to James Culbertson. Plat filed shows survey on Miami River for James Wood, 1,000 acres; James Galt, 1,000 acres; James Culbertson, 920 acres; Francis Whiting, 1,000 acres; James Findley. Plat and description of Culbertson tract calls for Ohio River, Turkey Creek, 1,000 acres, survey No. 453. This is suit to recover expenses of making survey in 1799 for Donoghe. See the papers.

AUGUST, 1814 (E to I).

Johnston vs. Orr.—Journal of James Johnston's vendue, 3d December, 1798. Leonard and Isaac Garman are about to remove from State, 12th August, 1806. William and David Orr. David E. Orr was son of William. Robert Patterson, of South Carolina. Samuel Gregory is in service of his country, 22d November, 1813.

Harrow vs. Gardner.

SEPTEMBER, NOVEMBER, DECEMBER, 1815.

Elizabeth Harman, widow of Michael Harman, vs. John G. Flack and Polly, his wife, late Harman, Lewis, Sally, Alexander and Susannah Harman, children and heirs of Alexander.—Michael died, August, 1807.

OCTOBER, 1808 (L to M).

McCue vs. Miller.—Patent by Henry Lee, 13th July, 1792, to Henry Miller, assignee of Adam Stephens, assignee of William Minter, on Mossy Creek, 192 acres. Patent, 23d October, 1788, by Randolph to Samuel McFeeters, assignee of Moses Hall, 213 acres by survey, 11th October, 1768, on drafts of Mossy Creek. Plat, 36 acres in dispute.

..Stuart vs. Moore.—9th May, 1810, Henry McCadden (McAdden, McFadden) will remove to Ohio next Monday.

OCTOBER, 1810 (M to W).

Turk vs. Magill.

MARCH AND APRIL, 1808 (A to D).

Moses vs. Floyd's Administrator.—Deposition, August 19, 1805, in both of Van Swearingen. Thomas Green was schoolmaster in Calfpasture, 1782, his deposition sworn to in Flewanna, 1805. Isabella McGlammery tertifies of Greene's bad character. Letter to Van Swearingen, Jr., January, 1805. John McKenny, son to William McKenny, mentioned. Charles Floyd was blind. Charles had only a wife, Jane, their only child having died.

COUNTY COURT CHANCERY DECREES DECIDED.

1823, 1824, 1825 (I to N).

John Jamison vs. Thomas Todd.—In 1797 plaintiff, while inhabitant of Kentucky, gave his bond to Thomas Todd, of same State. Afterwards, before 3d November, 1805, plaintiff moved to Virginia.

King's Administrator vs. Dennison.—Writ of *Ne Exeat.* 1819, Daniel Dennison is about to remove from the State.

Laird's Executors vs. Hodgson.—1795, received of Master William Hodgson, for his father, Mr. James Hodgson, May, 1803, rule for security for costs, plaintiff, widow Laird, having removed to Kentucky.

Henry Miller and Hannah, late Hannah Crawford, Peter Hanger, Jr., and Patsey, late —— Crawford, vs. James Bourland, et al.—Daughters of George Crawford. George died intestate, leaving six children, viz, the two female plaintiffs, Polly Bourland, who married James Bourland; Nancy Miller, late Nancy Crawford, who married John Miller; Jane McCue, who married Franklin McCue, Peggy Crawford, minor. Bill for petition. Report of Commisisoners filed, 25th December, 1824.

William Moore vs. Elizabeth Boyd.—Elizabeth was widow of John Boyd, deceased, testate, and John Varner (Vernum) was her son. John Boyd was son of Andrew Boyd. Some of her children have gone to Kentucky.

Andrew and John McClure, heirs of James McClure, deceased, vs. Bill for partition. James died, 13th September, 1799, intestate, leaving widow and eight children, viz, Elizabeth McClure, his widow; Andrew, John, Margaret, James, Samuel, Josiah, Eleanor and Elizabeth. His children, Eleanor and Elizabeth, are infants. Josiah died while infant.

John E. McClanahan vs. John Carter Littlepage, Nathaniel Wilkinson, John Oliver.—Involves a lot in town to be laid off at Hot Springs.

CHANCERY CASES REMOVED TO SUPERIOR COURT.

David Miller vs. William, John, Francis (of age), Josiah, Elizabeth and Jane Johnston, infants, heirs of John Johnston, deceased, who was heir of

William Johnston, deceased; Mary Johnston, widow of John; Reuben Shackelford and Rebecca, his wife, late Johnston; Malackia Likes (Lex) and Margaret, late Johnston, devisees of William Johnston, deceased; James Allen, Sr., and George Moffett, executors of William.—Writ, 3d November, 1799. Shackelford and wife no inhabitants. Certain William Johnston died 1786 testate. Will probated devised land to three daughters. After widow's death, executors sold to Dr. John Johnson, who sold to orator, but now deceased. One, John Johnson, son of William, got possession of part of tract and died, 1797, intestate, leaving issue as above.

INQUESTS.

Thomas Boyd (son of Andrew Boyd) died intestate, 10th March, 1800, without issue, and his heirs were the heirs of John White, nephew of Andrew Boyd.

CRIMINAL PROSECUTION PRIOR TO 1795.

1768.

Peter Martin's warrant to arrest Benjamin Kimsey as a common liar and disturber of peace. On complaint of James Bockhannon, David Hase, Arsbald Reah, William Bochannon. Recognizee, with Robert Risk and John Bell * * *

1768.

Writ *ad quad damnum* on petition of John Hinton. Jury as follows: David Ralstone, Andrew Ewin, Henry Ewin, Benjamin Kinley, William Ewin, Jacob Copelin, Thomas Bryan, Michael Waren, Samuel Sampels, John Bryan, John Brown, Cornelius Bryan. Signatures of all and George Skilleron (Skillem).

1768

Augusta County debtor to Robert McClenachan, 1768, to covering and repairing a bridge in Staunton near Mr. Reed's, £8,10,0.

MAY, 1768.

County debtor to James Trimble. Holding inquest on body of Thomas Wright. Signature of James Wright.

Horse of Dewalt Persing impressed to carry prisoner to prison.

Henry Gambill (Cambell), petitions in re Doctor Donaldson, deceased.

NOVEMBER 21, 1768.

Committal of Robert McMahan upon suspicion of murdering Robert Reburn. Recognizance as witnesses and signatures of Jean Reburn, John Reburn, Thomas McMahon, Robert Patterson, James O. Murray, Robert R. Craig.

Francis Smith's account against the County to 428 pounds tobacco due from the Lead Mine Company.

1787.

Committal (and depositions) of prosecution of John McKee for attempted murder of Charles Wall. Signatures of Samuel Vance, John Byrd, Jonathan Humphreys, Philip Inchminger, Charles Wall.

Commonwealth vs. Cavern.—Signatures of Hugh Brown, John Tanner (Johann Danner), James Hopkins, Andrew Wilson, John and Michael Dickey.

1747.

Commonwealth vs. Mathew Young.—Signature of James Patton.

COUNTY COURT JUDGMENTS.

March, 1801 (M to Z).

James Ralston vs. William Hynes and George Skull.—22d May, 1798. Hynes no inhabitant.

Alexander Stewart vs. Samuel McChesney.—In 1773 orator was in City of Leedstown, in County of ——, to purchase servants, and there met Samuel Henning (Herring) and his son-in-law, Samuel McChesney, on the same business. (Was Leedstown in King and Queen?).

VARIOUS OLD PAPERS—1760-1770.

Commission for privy examination of Mary McPheeters, Executrix of Thomas Peevy, deceased, and wife of William McPheeters, as to deed, McPheeters to Samuel McNeb, dated 21st August, 1765. Commission dated 28th August, 1765.

Same as to Margaret, wife of Andrew Hays, deed to John Miscampbel, dated 21st August, 1765.

Same as to Susanna Preston in deed of William Preston to Michael Cloyd, 26th August, 1765.

Same as to Hannah Robinson, in deed James Robinson to Arthur Graham, 20th August, 1765.

Petition for road from Adam Reader's Mines to Isaac Robertson's, from thence to Widow Wright's Mill; thence to Thomas Harrison's in the Great Road to the Court House, 2d January, 1761. Thomas Pickins, Isaac Robertson, James Wright, Tunes Van Pelt, John Chrisman, Lydia Wright, William Munsey, Robert Bellshe, Jacob Gum, Jacob Gum, Jr., John White, Leonard Herring, John Black, Thomas Harrison, William Dunlop, Robert Kearr, Alexander Painter, Jacob Miller, Scidmore Munsey, William Pickins, John Jackson, David Robertson, Henry Mase, James Thomas.

Numerous certificates of hemp weighed.

Commisison for privy examination Susanna Preston.

Deed to Edward Hinds, August, 1765.

CRIMINAL PROSECUTIONS PRIOR TO 1795.

Signatures of Abraham Martin, Jacob Shore, John Johnston, Michael Garber.

COUNTY CLAIMS, 1800–1807.

Coalter's petition regarding a change of market and new Court House street.

1817.

Affidavit of Zachariah Belsha and Jones Henderson, of Montgomery County.

OLD DEEDS, WILLS, INVENTORIES, POWERS OF ATTORNEY, ETC., TO BE FILED.

William Ledgerwood's gift to his daughters, Martha Patterson and Jean Moffett, 15th June, 1782.
Samuel Henderson's original will, 1782.
John Cowardine to John Oliver. Original deed, 1787.
William Wood's will. Original, 1782.
James Coursey to daughter, Joannes Eastham, 1783.
Enos Attwater to Craig. Original bill sale, 1783.
Daniel Kidd to Hugh Donahue. Power Attorney, original, 1783.
John Lewis to Andrew Sitlington, 1785. Original.
William Crawford (Agent for Moses Easty, Crawford, Beach & Co.) to Henry Miller, 3d April, 1785. Original.
There are many other original deeds, bonds, etc., in this package.

ORIGINAL PETITIONS AND PAPERS FILED IN THE COUNTY COURT.

1745–1748.

Samuel William and Thomas Story (Surety), ordinary bond, 10th February, 1745.
Thomas McCollough and Andrew Lewis (Surety), ordinary license bond, 12th February, 1745.
John Hutcheson and William Russell (Surety), ordinary license bond, 12th February, 1745.
Robert McClenachan and David Steward, ordinary license bond, 12th February, 1745.
Deposition of Samuel Brown, witness to will of John Dobekin, Sr., being about to leave the parts, 15th March, 1746, before Peter Scholl.
Petition for road by inhabitants of Craig's Creek from Henry Houlston's (Holstine) to James Montgomery's. Signed Henry Holstine, Sr., Wicklor Welch, Stephen Holstine, George Barber, William Lee, John Shichelve, Walter Welch. Henry Houlston.

Ulrich Kyliner petitions to build a water grist mill on ye narrow passage creek near his house.

Valuation of Christopher Zimmerman's improvements on 400 acres on James River, February 13, 1745.; 137 apple trees planted and carried there, 150 miles, £3; meat and bread carried the same distance and liquor, £1, etc. John Newport and Tim Haldway.

Young's appraisement. James Young and John Young, deceased. 17th March, 1747.

Thomas Grubbs, guardian of Abraham Drake, surety James McCoy. (Signed) Mchard.

Katrin Queen, 10th December, 1746, examined before justices charged with stealing a silver plate belonging to David Kinked and Winefer Kinked, his wife. Witnesses summoned to testify to character of Nell Guin. To be summoned: Margaret Gay, Patrick McDonald and Mary, his wife, and Elizabeth Thompson. Bond by John Tillery, of Albemarle County, brick-layer. David Kinked, of said county, joyner, and William Wright, of Augusta, farmer. John Tillery.

Adam Dickson's petition for a road from forks of Cow Pasture to the mill that formerly belonged to James Carter.

Robert Graham petitions for administration on his father's estate, Christopher Graham.

Abraham Drake, aged seventeen, prays administration of his father's estate (Abraham's), to be given to Thomas Grubbs.

Humberstone Lyon deposeth that James Conoly said Humberstone Lyon stole fifteen red deer skins and also twenty-eight red deer skins which Conoly had left at the house of James Scaggs. Also deposition by Samuel Stolucher, the same. Also deposition by Erwin Patterson. Mary Stern deposes that George Gabriel brought from Jacob Miller's. John Blackwelder.

Robert McClenachan complains that Samuel Wilkins keeps a disorderly house.

Frederick Stern, Sr., and Mary Stern bound to appear as witnesses vs. George Gabriell, 12th February, 1746/7.

1747.

Valentine Sevier petitions for ordinary license. Says he is very much infested with travellers.

William Galeabe, witness to will of John Dobekin, about to leave these parts, 15th March, 1746.

Abraham Drake's hand as guardian of Abraham Drake, orphan of Abraham Drake, 22d May, 1747.

Samuel McGa's recognizance, 11th August, 1747.

Abraham Drake, Sr.'s, bond as administrator of Abraham Drake, 22d May, 1747.

James Young's petition to administer on estate of John Young, his brother and nearest heir, 17th June, 1747.

Andrew Baxter petitions to be superannuated. Is now seventy-seven years old (if not seventy-eight). Has neither son nor daughter, nor servant, to help support him and his wife.

Robert Black, Sr., and Robert Black, Jr., bond for affiance of Elizabeth Anderson, formerly the widow Skilran, 27th January, 1747/8.

Robert Black, carpenter, 13th June, 1748.

Martin Levistone, mason, bond, 5th July, 1748.

1749.

Papers relating to Augusta Levy. Robert McClenachan's account, 1748–9. Credit by John Bruce. Credit by James Dawkins, four levys. Credit by Jacob Miller, two levys. Credit by Sam Wilkins, two levys. Credit by John Wilkins, two levys.

Delinquents for 1748. Long and valuable list.

John Cunningham, jailor. Account. To keeping the following: John McFarlin, a criminal; Adam and Valentine Herman; Thomas Godfrey, a servant; Samuel Farish; William Previe, he broke prison; James Donoly, a criminal, for murder; George Young, William Johnston, Joseph Doabs and Stephen Newcomb.

24th December, 1748, Charles Sinclair killed an old wolfe. Certified by John Buchanan.

Martha Anderson, executrix of Isaac Anderson, bond, 17th May, 1749.

Deposition Edward Partridge, aged fifty-nine, taken before justices in Chester, Pennsylvania, says: On 1st January, 1739, one, John Hindman, came to house of John Fletcher, in township of Boringham, in said County. Hindman said to Fletcher, your wife (Elinor) is my sister. Taken 25th May, 1749. Deposition of Providence Scott, aged sixty years last October, taken 25th May, 1749, in Chester County, Pennsylvania. John Hindman, born in the County of Londonderry, Ireland, was, in 1739, at deponent's house in township of Burmingham, inquiring for Elinor Hindman, by direction of his father, and found her the wife of John Fletcher, and acknowledged her as his sister.

1749

Hugh Duglas sold land to John Brooks, now deceased, and was summoned by Mary Dyer (entitled to the land).

Valuation of improvements on 2,464 acres belonging to William Parks, on Southern Border Potomac, 17th November, 1749, viz: George Mouss, improvements. Hanness Dockell's improvements. John Kerre's improvements. Peter Moser's improvements. Jacob Sifert's improvements.

To the Honorable Court of Augusta. Petition of inhabitants and subscribers of the South Fork of the South Branch of Pattomuck are very much discommoded for want of a road to market and to Court if occation but espetily to market. We have found a very good way for a road: Beginning at John Patton's over the mountain to Cap. John Smith's; we begg that you will take this our petition unto your consideration and grant us a briddle road to Court and a road to market where it will sute most convenient, and will ever pray, etc. Costian Huver, Adam Stroud, Christian Evan, John Evan, Peter Haap. German names follow and paper torn so that names are illegible. John Smith, John Patton, Samuel Patton, Mathew Patton, William

Jinison, William Dayer, Claude Evens, George Donther, Roger Doyer, John Wa(l)ker, Abraham Smith, Benjamin Kinley, Daniel Smith, Isaiah Shipman, Henry Smith, Jacob Gillespy, Gabriell Pickens, John Smith, William Logan, John Melkem, John McCluer.

Francis McBride petitions to administer on estate of his brother, Benjamin McBride, during the non-age of his children.

Weights an measures of Augusta County: 1 strong half-peck measure of brass with handles, £2.14.0. 1 bottle measure of brass with handles, £1.4.0. I quart measure of brass with handles, £0.15.6. 1 pint and ½ pint measure of brass with handles, £1.0.6. 1 brass yard and ell, £1.0.0. I set bell metal weight from 56 pounds to quarter pound, £5.13.0. For engraving same with Augusta County, £1.12.6. 1 large branding iron, engraved with Augusta County, £0.12.0. 1 steel punch, engraved with Augusta County, £0.8.0. 1 steel punch with a crown, £0.5.0. 1 set wooden measures complete with Augusta County neatly carved, £2.2.0. A true copy of the invoice. Fredericksburg, 12th February, 1749. Robert Jackson.

John Trotter's petition vs. Capt. Daniel McAnaire, 4th Tuesday in February, 1749-50. Certificate that John is a very poor man, but had lived honest some years in our neighborhood for what we know. Patrick Martin, John Trimble, Jacob Lockhart, Andrew Pickens, Alexander Crawford.

Francis McCown (Cowen), of etc. William McCanless, John McCowen recognize before Robert Campbell, as justice, 11th April, 1749, that Francis shall appear at the next May Court on 3d Wednesday of the month.

John Givins petitions that he be relieved as constable and one of three be put in his stead, viz, Thomas Story, James Craig, Joshua Stickleman. John Davis, same, and nominates Barnibee Eagon, or Samuel Odle, or Joshua Job.

John Ballfought says he is above sixty-eight years old and has served thirteen years in the army, and begs to be levy free.

Examination of Joseph McFarland, late of Lunenburg County, taken before me, Richard Barton, one of the justices for said county, 27th February, 1747-8. Says that he borrowed a saddle from James Litell, of Lunenburg County, and brought it into this County. Same examination of John McNeese. Endorsed, February 27, 1748-9. Friend, William Woods. I desire you to deliver the writing to the Clerk's Office, and you will oblige your friend. Richard Boston.

Commitment of Valentine and Adam Herman for violent robbery of the goods of Jacob Castlean, the warrant of George Robins, 22d April, 1749.

Francis McCown, charged with stealing four pistoles and twenty-one shillings and six pence in silver out of the pocket of John Lockhart.

Inquisition, 15th April, 1749, on body of Samuel Decker, son of Garret Decker, on the South Branch of Potomac, by Peter Scholl, coroner. Samuel received his death by accident by a penknife. Peter Scholl, coroner; Abram Vanderpool, Able Westfall, Hendrey Scarbrough, James Simpson, Johanes Curtract, Conrad Hoerner, Johann Michael Hoerner, Daniel Hoornbeck, Anthony Logen, George Osborn, John Westfall, Cornelius Curt Right (See Curtract above).

Petition, 18th May, 1749, of inhabitants of North River and Picot (peaked) Mountain for a road beginning at John Man's smithshop on the south side of the Peaked Mountain, thence eastward to John M(W)igard's joining to the mountain road and from the smithshop westward to the Stone Meeting House, joining to the Court House Road, and that Jacob Rodger, Robert Scot and James Berd be appointed to lay it out. Jacob Herman, Feldy Pence, Mathew Shope, Jacob Maler, John Bomgardner, John Lynn, Jacob Rodgers, James Berd, Jacob Perer, Mathew Sharp, —— Man, Jacob Man, William Milburn, Jared Chambers, Robert Scot, Robert Hooks, George Scot, William Craig, John Craig, Mathew Thomson, Mathew Thomson, Jr.

Samuel Ferguson, 17th May, 1749, is over seventy and begs to be relieved from public dues.

Attachment against Jacob Costell and Philip Cable and John Lamme's estate, 17th February, 1748–9. Charged that these three had announced that they were going to the French Dominions on Mississippi, and such desertion would be harmful to the English in the war with France.

William McCanless, aged about thirty-six years, being sworn, says he never saw Francis McCown steal, pick or rob John Lockhart's pocketbook, 11th April, 1749. William Henry, the same.

We petitioners, being the frontier inhabitants of this colony, labor under great inconveniences for want of a road being opened from our settlement towards the landing, and there being (as we presume) a sufficient number of inhabitants to open one, we therefore humbly pray that your worship will be graciously pleased to take our case under your serious consideration and grant an order for a road to be opened from Zachariah Callhouns, on Reedy Creek, and thence to the Buffalo Lick and from thence the nearest and best way to Woods River, at the upper end of a small island below the mouth of the Little River, and thence towards the forks of Meadow Creek, and thence to the top of the dividing ridge between Woods River and the South Fork of Roanoke, and that John Vance and Alexander Sayers be appointed to mark and lay off said road from said Callhouns to Woods River, and that John Stroud and James Conley mark and lay off from thence to the aforesaid dividing ridge, etc. That John McFarland and Joseph Crockett be appointed overseers to open and clear said road from said Calhoun's to Woods River, with the subscribers and the adjacent inhabitants and that William Crispe and William Pellem be appointed overseers from Woods River to the aforesaid dividing ridge, etc., and we, your petitioners, shall pray. Hendery Battan, Jacob Goldman, Jacob Goldman, Frederick Cadock, John Scott, John Combe, Samuel Stonacie, Robert McFarland, John Stead, Mordecai Early, John Downing, Charles Sincler, Wiliam Sayers, William Hamilton, Robert V(N)orris, Samuel Mountgomery, Andrew Lynam, James Macee, James Heris, Robert Miller, John Miller, Robert Allcorn, William Miller, John McFarland, Joseph Crockett, Val. Wilcher, Humberstone Lyon, James Miller, Stephen Lyon, Thomas Barnes, James Willy, John Vance, Alexander Sayers, Jacob Cassall, John Gorman.

Inquisition, 19th May, 1750, at the house of James Greenlee, on James River, before John Mathews, on body of Edward Hogan, late of this County. Found that he was drowned accidentally by the oversetting of a cannow as he was crossing over James River, near the house of James Greenlee, on 13th May, 1750. James Mountgomery, Michael Dougherty, John Hitchins, John Ramsey, Josiah F. Hendon, John Vance, John Poage, Samuel Walker, Joseph Walker, John Mathews, Jr., Joshua Mathews, Mathew Vance.

Examination of John Maxwell and James McDowell, as to the death of Edward Hogan, taken 14th May, 1750. John says: On Sunday, 13th May, 1750, he, with Edward Hogan and James McDowell, being at the house of James Greenlee, went over the main branch of James River in a canoe to a place of James McDowell, and on their return the canoe overset and they fell out into the river. John swam ashore and McDowell stuck by the canoe, and after some time got on its bottom by which he saved himself. John and James stripped themselves and made every effort to save Hogan, but were unable. James McDowell says the same. John Carmichael testifies. James Frazier testifies. John Petter Soling testifies. One, Salix, fetched him the news. William Frazier.

Robert Henry's petition in bankruptcy. He built a mill in Pennsylvania, but by misfortune lost everything. His wife died. He had eight children. He came to Virginia, bringing only one child, leaving the rest, and only one piece of money. His creditors show him no mercy, and he prays for relief.

William Johnson, having dropsy, asked to be relieved from levy.

Charles Dolhouse vs. Abraham Cristwell.—Attachment, 6th August, 1750.

Petition of inhabitants of Little River, in Calfpasture, for road from William Gay's to Robert McCutchen's Mill, from thence to Robert Campbell's. Ask only a bridle road to travel with loads on horseback and oblige themselves to cut it and keep in repair. William Elliott, Thomas Fulton, John Meek, John Gay, William Gay, Thomas Meek, James Gay, John Fulton, James Stenson.

Mrs. Jean Rutledge, 25th August, 1750, declines to administer and nominates Hugh Parker.

To ye worshipful his majesties' justices in Court sitting. The petition of John Harrison humbly prayeth that your worships will please to take unto consideration the following account for as much as the goodness of God (delivered ? torn) unto my hand those that sought my life and my and (torn) goods and whereas I thought it my duty to act towards my fellow creatures as such and not as if ye were altogether brutes and I have been at this charge following which I humbly pray that your worships will please to allow and your petitioner as in duty bound shall pray, etc. The charge of burying ye robbers, £2.0.0. Three shillings for ye man I sent for ye surgeon, £0.3.0. To ye surgeon, £0.15.0. By me, John Harrison, Jr.

1750.

Phoebe Davison, relict of Daniel Davison, petitions to administer, 26th February, 1750–51.

Magdalene Bird, widow of Andrew Bird, and his eldest son, Andrew Bird, petition to administer.

Catren Stewart complains that Christopher Finny has abused her so that she cannot do service to any person, 9th February, 1750–51.

Elizabeth Hodge asks that Asobel Hodge, eldest son, qualify as administrator to her husband, John Hodge, deceased, 9th February, 1750–51.

Letter to vestry, February 20, that David Evans is so leasey that he will not work and provide for his family, for they are almost starved with cold and hunger, and they have no other example but cursing, swearing, lying, and the like bad vice. We think it our duty to acquaint you of this condition.

Mathew Patton, John Smith, William Stevenson, Alexander Crockett, Samuel Patton, John Walker.

Recognizance of Ann Harry, 8th October, 1750, before Thomas Ingles, a justice. Sureties, William Bues and Elisha Isaac. John Ingles complains before Thomas Ingles, a justice, that about 6th May, in the year 32, he had a large roan mare stolen. Found in possession of John Harry and his wife, Ann Harry. To William Ingles, constable.

1751-1752.

Petition, 1752, of inhabitants from Forks of Roanoke to James Neiley's Majority have to travel 25 to 30 miles to work on ye road from Reed Creek to Warwick. Petition to have road laid off into precincts. William Bryan, John Bryan, James Bryan, William Walcker, James Campbell, Alexander Ingram, Robert Bryan, Henry Brown, James Bane, William Bryan, Jr., Joseph Love.

Robert McKay, of this County, deceased, in his will, dated 7th October, 1746, appointed subscriber, Zachariah McKay, together with his older brothers, Robert and James McKay, executors. Petition of Zachariah to have administration given to Robert and James, 17th August, 1752.

John Fleming shows that James Young and Sarah, his wife, detain him as a servant without right, etc., 1752.

James Ladyman complains of Hance Harper and his father, Michael Harper. Says Hance is about to leave with his effects, 1752.

George Parish to Andrew Johnston, account sworn to, 16th June, 1752.

Hugh Martin shows he is an old, decrepted man and has earned not a cake of bread this several years, and begs to be exempted of public levy, 1752.

William Downen, grandson of Elinor Cryler (Tyler), 30th May, 1750.

Valuation, 8th February, 1752, of Robert Renicks's improvements on place formerly known as John Harrison's place.

Valuation of David Cloid's two tracts, both on Bossimarkun, 31st January, 1752.

Petition of Reuben Harrison for change of road through his place. Says there was no Court at the usual time in February nor from that time till May.

Petition of inhabitants between Jennings Branch and North River (Gap of Swift Run), it being the nighest way to the chief of our market places, May 20, 1752. Hands to mark ye said road, Sampson Archer and John Young. Hands to mark from Gap to North River, John Hair and Hugh Camble, and thence to the great road already cut. From Gap to Long Glade, thence to North River, thence to the great road leading to the Gap. Patrick Frazer (rest torn).

John Davies, Sr., is seventy-five years old and prays to be exempted from levy.

Mary Kenmore binds her child, nine months old, to Joseph Culton, 19th May, 1752.

Petition for road from Joseph Kennedy's mill by Francis Beaty's, thence to join the Landing Road and Court House Road above James Cowan's.

John Phillips, overseer of road from Massanutten to dry fork of Smith's Creek leading to Augusta Court House, prays to be released and nominates Zebulan Harrison, William McGee and William Draper.

Samuel Woods deposes, 18th February, 1750-51. Edward Boyle. William Evins, deceased.

Martha Anderson deposes, 10th October, 1750. Mary Moore, wife of David Moore.

Petition of Rees Thomas to build a mill on his place on Brook's Creek. (Signed) James Reed, James Claypole, Jonathon Dugles, Martin Shoomacer, William Smith, Francis Green, William Cleypole, John Miller, Charles Daily, Jacob Gom, Robert Williams, James Cleypole, Jr., Adam Reder, George Bowman.

List of tithables liable to work on road from Sherrendo River to top of Blue Ridge at Swift Run Gap. Petition of Hance Magard (Magot). James Urry, William Burk, Stephen Hansburger, Samuel Thornbill, John Fought, John Furniss, Little Partrick, Charles Cross, George Wanol, Jacob Miller, Henry Lung, Adam Miller, Jacob Coger.

Linvell's Creek petitioners for a road leading from Brock's Creek to ye Market Road by Francis Hughes's and from thence to Fredericksburg: Jonathan Douglas, James Claypoole, Rees Thomas, William Smith, William Claypoole. John Miller, Robert Williams.

I, John Mitchell, son of John Mitchell, and brother of William Mitchell, of the County of Augusta, held and firmly bound to Thomas Wilson, late of Pennsylvania. 14th September, 1752. John, Jr., obtained patent with his father's money and for his father's benefit for 400 acres on a branch of James River, known by the name of Broad Spring Branch, which pond was afterwards sold by John, Sr., to his son, William, and William and wife, Margaret, have sold the same to said Thomas Wilson, indemnity against any claims of John, Jr., or any one under him (not recorded).

John Lowery's improvements of 350 acres on North Branch, James River, June 17, 1752.

Petition for road from Joseph Kennedy's Mill to John Huston's, and from John Huston's to the great road from Timber Grove to Woods Gap: James Hill, Joseph Kenedy, John Wilson, James Eakin, John Handly, William Wardlaw, William Lockridge, John Edenston, William McConnell, Walter Eakin, Robert Stewart, Robert Dunlap, Andrew Duncan, John Huston, Samuel Huston, Robert Alexander, Patrick Hays, John Mountgomery, Andrew Steel, John Stewart.

1751-1752.

Valuation of Samuel Porter's improvements on Buffalo Creek, 22d May, 1751.

Petition for road from John Davis's Mill to Woods's Gap, or to the road now clearing over the mountain near said Gap: Andrew Erwin, Robert Fowler, Edward Erwin, Francis Erwin, Charles Campbell, Michael Dickey, Hugh Diver, John Davies, John Francis, Andrew McCombe, John Magill, Hugh Campbell, Robert Carskadan, William Frame, Robert Campbell, Robert Brown, Charles Diver, Daniel Smith, William Alexander, James Patterson, William Magill, John Erwine, Edward Erwine, Benjamin Erwin, William

Brown, Henry Smith, David McCammis, James Anderson, Robert Gamble, Francis Brown, Gabriel Pickens.

Petition for road from Widow Cobern's Mill, on the South Branch, to John Paton's Mill, on the South Fork, at least 30 miles nearer than the road we formerly traveled. A bridle road asked for: William Stephenson, Mathew Patton, Jeremiah Calkin, George West, Peter Reed, Jr., Samuel Patton, Benjamin Patton, Leonard Reed, John Reed, John Knowles, Alexander Crockett, John Patton, Luke Collins, Jacob Reed, Daniel Richardson.

Petition recites that last fall the Court sent James McKay and Richard Harrill to view a road. They accordingly viewed a road to strike out of McKay's road at Reuben Paget's and so to keep down the River on the east side to the County line. Prays an order to appoint Philip Crum, William Hurst or William Harrill to be surveyor, and order all tithables on Flint Run and its branches and Gowny's run and its branches from Walter Cunningham's down to the County line: Jacob Harrill, Peter Emlie, Anthony Horton, Reuben Paget, Richard Harrill, Sr., William Owens, John Kelly, Howard Gibson, James McCoy, Philip Crame, Joseph Hokens, William Hurst, Thomas Lann, Richard Harrill, William Harrill, Thomas Monmon, William Colbee, Thomas Harrill, John Harrill, John Jones, Joseph Ballinger, James Land, Moses Harrill.

Inhabitants of Bull Pasture and head of Cowpasture petition for a road from Walles Asten's Mill to the road on the head of the Calfpasture: Robert Carrolile, Richard Bodkin, Thomas Wright, John Miller, James Hall, Horcklas Willson, John Carrolile, Samuel Forgerson, Michael Harper, Wm. Price, Philip Phegan, William Carrolile, Loftus Pullen, Mathew Harper, Hance Harper, James Anglen, John Shaw, John Carrolile. Wallas Aston to be overseer.

Petition of inhabitants of the North side of the South River of Shenandore for a road. About 3 years ago it was ordered to open a road from Caleb Job's plantation down the South side of the said North River to James McCoy's plantation, which road is not suitable, and prepare a location on North side crossing the river at a place called the Brush Bottom Ford and so along the river by Henry Speer's plantation. Prayer for survey: Mason Combs, William Hurst, Zachariah Mackay, Stephen Phillips, John Hankins, Charles Thompson, Thomas Parent, Adam Cunningham, John Sollers, Wm. Overall, Terence Corcal, Alexander Gunnel, Benjamin Guden, Josiah Parent, Edmon Bollin, Thomas Grubs, Richard Shirley, Thomas Hues, Wm. Dickerson, Thomas McNeal, Ephraim Leeth, William Parent.

Inhabitants near Capt. John Wilson's petition for a road from Capt. John Wilson's and John McClerey's fields, thence to James Wilson's fields, thence to Capt. John Christian's, and there to join with the road from Col. Patton's Mill to Tunkling Spring Meeting House: Robert Campbell, Mathew Wilson, John Wilson, Jr., James McCutchin, John McCutchin, Nathan Patterson, James Clark, John McClerey, Samuel McCutchan, William McCutchan, John Wilson, Thomas Kirkpatrick, James McClerey, John Clark, Samuel Downey.

Petition of Andrew and Magdalene Bird, administrators of Andrew Bird. James Porteus was their attorney, but now deceased, 1751.

Michael Warring petitions that in his deed from David Johnson, at last May term, consideration (£120) may be inserted.

Certificate of Patrick Crawford that he is willing that John Poage shall get license to marry his sister, Mary Crawford, 30th May, 1751.

Thomas Gordon.

Rebekah Gordon.

John (x) Sytner, late of County of Lancaster, Pennsylvania, certifies that on or about 10th March, 1750/51, my father-in-law, Christopher Francisco, gave me jointly with his son, Christopher Francisco, a power attorney to see his lands in Virginia, and Christopher has since annulled the same and granted another power to another son, Stophel Francisco. John renounces all his right under the first power, 20th August, 1751.

Petition of lower inhabitants of the Cowpasture for a road over the mountain to Burdin's tract, 19th October, 1751: James Scott, James Stimson, James Mountgomery, John Scott, James Frem, Hugh McDovel, William Memory, Robert Mountgomery, William Gillespy.

Petitioners for road from Thorn's Gap to Henry Netherton's: Henry Netherton, Barnebas Agan, Elisha Job, Shadk. Parlour, John Davis, William Bethell, William Whitson, Daniel Stover.

Robert McClenachan's account, 1750–1751: Finding the Court in small beer and candles and keeping the Court House and stables, £1,600.

John Harrison, aged 64 (1751), petitions to be relieved from County levy.

James Connerly, lately died without wife or child, and administration granted to George Breckenridge.

Augusta County, in account with John Madison: Entering order for the Sheriff to employ workmen to make a ducking stool, £25.

James Berry, guardian of children of James Berry, deceased. John Jones married James Berry's widow. Petition, November 28, 1751.

1753–1754 (Part 1).

13th March, 1754. Joseph and David Robinson and Edward McDonald appraised ye improvements and value of the stock on ye four sundry tracts of lands belonging to Joshua Hadley, and his expenses in coming to Virginia and moving his family there. 115-acre tract, called ye Half Moone, £23, 0, 0. 186-acre tract, called Long Bottom, £30, 0, 0. 400-acre tract at mouth of Craig's Creek, £44, 0, 0. 50-acre tract, called ye Pound Bottom, £10, 0, 0. For six weeks' journey in coming to and going from Virginia, at 5 sh. per day, £10, 10, 0. For coming with his wagon, stock and family, six weeks at 20 sh. per day, £42, 0, 0. Total, £159, 10, 0.

March, 18, 1754. Report of viewers on road through Joseph Walker's land that it is satisfactory.

13th March, 1754. Valuation of John Mathew's place in Forks of James River.

19th March, 1754. Commissioners report that of John Moffet's estate, after laying off ⅓ to John Trimble and his wife, there remains in the hands of John, Robert and William Christian, guardians of the children of said Moffett, £260, 14, 1.

14th March, 1754. Report of improvements of tract of land on Bull Pasture, 281 acres, belonging to William Wilson, £108, 0, 0.

20th February, 1754. Jennet Patton, widow of Jacob, nominates her daughter, Susanna Patton, to administer.

County to Israel Christian. To guarding the jail upon Harris, 3 nights. To guarding the jail upon the Indian traders.

Valuation of improvements of William Carravin: First tract, 254 acres on Roanoke, 114 fruit trees, etc. Second tract, 172 acres, on Roanoke, 31 fruit trees, etc.

Inhabitants of North Mountain, at head of Muddy Creek, petition for road from Ephraim Love's to the road from South Branch to Swift Run Gap: Ephraim Love, John Herdman, Jeremiah Hanason, Aaron Oliver, Thomas Campbell, Robert Pattison, John Slaven, Patrick Black, Robert Rallstone, John Negarry, Tomes Shanklin, John Taler, Daniel Harrison, John Foolton, Jesse Harrison, Patrick Cain.

James McNutt's estate, by Thomas Beard, 15th August, 1753: Paid for land bought by Beard's wife before marriage, 1751. Paid quitrents for land for 10 years, 1751. Paid quitrents, 1744. Paid to Mr. David Hays debt before marriage. Paid to Robert Alexander for schooling James and Robert McNutt, one year, 1748. Paid to James Dobbins, same, for Alexander McNutt, 1748.

Petition of William Ramsey to build a mill where Israel Peckens or Galloway's mill was—it being on Mill Creek, near North River, in Burden's land—on land lately bought by Ramsey.

Inquisition on body of Nicholas Grout (Trout), 17th July, 1753. Jurors do say that the said Nicholas Trout, in simplicity, without malice, playing with Peter Hull and seizing a gun in said Hull's hands and pulling its muzzle towards him *she* accidentally went off without any act or knowledge of the said Hull and discharged herself with a ball and two great shots into ye breast of said Trout, of which he died immediately on ye spot, and quit ye gun wherewith ye same was done was entirely in fault for not keeping her bounds, but going off without force or consent. In teste: Peter Scholl, Coroner; John Stevenson, Ledwick Francisco, John Mac Michel, James Bruster, Thomas Wats, Thomas Crawford, Patrick Milican, John Wilson, Jacob Harman, Niclas Noll, Hennery Daly, Jacob Nicholas.

Attachment bond of Samuel Love or Michael Boyle, 13th June, 1753.

On 12th June last, there came to the house of Humberstone Lyon, on Reed Creek, one Patrick Gallahur, and enquired the way to Carolina. A son of Lyon pointed the path to the next inhabitants, and Patrick started, but returned secretly that night, when Lyon's son arrested him, but he escaped, leaving behind him personal property—coats, watch, mare and horse, one buck skin, one coat, partly made, one saddle and bridle, 4 shirts.

Adam Herman has served one year as road overseer between Cutalapo Creek and New River, and nominates William Leeper.

Inhabitants of head of South River petition that they have to keep their roads only ½ mile apart for space of four miles and ask that the three be reduced to one. William Smith, Samuel Steel, Robert Alexander, Robert Steel, Nathaniel Steel, George Breckenridge, Chas. Campbell, Patrick Campbell, John Broundlee, Alexander Broundlee, Hugh Fulton, Patrick Campbell, Jr., John Fulton, John Ward, Samuel Doack, John Campbell, Seth Wilson.

William Murrow was contractor for the Court House, not yet having roof on.

Petition for road from Joseph Long's mill to James Young's mill and by William Hall's, on the North River, and into the Great Road on James

Thompson's plantation. It is our course to meeting, mill and market. John Carr, James Campbell, Robert Young, Joseph Long, Samuel Gibson, Solomon Whitly, John Collyer, William Hall, Gilbert Crawford, George Gibson, John Ruckman, James Barton, William Waddington, William Brown, James Moore, John Hanna, James Hutton, William Todd, James Bates, James Footd, James Young, Patrick Young.

19th March, 1753. William McClain petitions that he has grown very aged and to be relieved from County levy.

Inhabitants of North Branch of Roanoke petition that they be relieved of road work on the road down Cottage Creek. James Garrell, Thomas Ingles, William Ingles, Tobias Bright, George Pearis, William Pepper, Adam Loyday, Elija Isaac, Earick Bright, Thomas Hill, Benjamin Ogle, Jacob Brown, John Robinson.

Recognizance, 14th November, 1752, of William Philby to answer as to killing of Robert Friar (Freer).

Robert Freer charged with stealing from Daniel Richison.

Thomas Stairns petitions that a strolling poor woman, with her child, came to his home, when she was taken sick and died, and he prays to be reimbursed for care and charges of burial.

William McMurry petitions for exemption from levy on account of age.

Inhabitants of Calf Pasture petition for a mill on the place of Andrew Loughridge, who has lately settled there. Thomas Gilham, Samuel Hodge, Andrew Kinkead, Robert Gum, John Kinkead, Robert Gay, Andrew Hamilton, Samuel Vincher, James Cambel, John Cambel, William Wils, William Hodge, Robert McKittrick.

1753–1754, Pt. 2.

Patrick Downey to Adam Lunie, bill sale, 18th March, 1754.

Colnraet and Jacob Goeb petition that they are under a father-in-law and so ill used that they ask to choose a guardian, May, 1753.

Attachment bond, George Taylor vs. Christian Milliron, 6th April, 1753.

Return for constable in Fork James River. John Berriesford, Michael Finney, Stephen Arnold.

Examination of Margaret Mitchell, wife of William Mitchell, and daughter of Ephraim McDowell, 1753. She had a son.

Elizabeth Thomas asks that her husband's estate be committed to herself and her brother, John Jones, May, 1753.

Petitioners for a road from William Wilson's mill, on Jackson's River, to Captain Ashton's mill, in the Bull Pasture, being direct road to market and also convenient for the head of Green Bryer settlers. John Miller, William Wilson, Stephen Wilson, Samuel Gay, Robert Gay, Robert Carlile, John Carlile, Hugh Hicklen, John Hicklin, Lostus Pullin, Thomas Hicklin. May, 1753.

1753–1754, Pt. 1.

To the Worshipful Court of Augusta now sitting: We, the inhabitants of this County, have long felt the smart of the great indulgence the ordinary keepers of this County have met with in allowing them to sell such large quantities of rum and wine at an extravagant rate, by which our money is

441

drained out of the County, for which we have no return but a fresh supply to pick our pockets. We, your petitioners, humbly pray your worship to put a stop to the said liquors, which would encourage us to pursue our laborious designs, which is to raise sufficient quantities of grain which would sufficiently supply us with liquors and the money circulate in this County to the advantage of us, the same. We hope that your worships will discover to us that you have a real regard for the good of the County, and lay us under an obligation to pray for your prosperity. Robert Stevenson, James Hamilton, Alexander Walker, James Robertson, James Stevenson, John Christian, Alexander Blair, Thomas Shiels, Robert Christian, Thomas Stewart, James Allen, Joseph Hanna, Francis Beaty, Mathew Lyle, Archibald Reah, John Walker (?), Samuel Downey, Daniel McAnair (McEvear), Robert Spears (Syers), Daniel Danison, Robert Moffet, Alexander Henderson, Andrew Hamilton, John Finley, Thomas Beard, Archibald Armstrong, William Mackan, James Campbell, John Vance, John Archer, James Reburn, Alexander Gibson, William Lewis, George Scott, Joseph Bell, James Coyl, William Logen, Samuel McCune, John Caruth, Patrick Hays, Robert Sayers, Andrew McCombe, James Montgomery, James Scott, George Crawford, John Allen, Edward Spear, James Brown, John King, John Anderson, William Logan, Patrick Campbell, Jacob Lockhart, Sam Wallace, James Knox, John Carlile, Charles Campbell, Mathew Harper, John Jackson, James Miller, John Hutcheson, William Palmer, Samuel Love, James Miller, John Henderson, Zachariah Bell (Belche), Andrew Ewin, John Thompson, Loftus Pullin, James Gay, Alexander Craig, Thomas Teat, William Wallace, John Wilson, Alexander Ritchey, James McGee, John Thompson, Samuel Calhoon, John Trimble, Alexander Thompson, William Snodon, Newman McGonigle, John Trimble, Archibald Allison, John Brown, William Thomson.

March 14, 1754. James Trimble, Assistant Surveyor, enters 200 acres of account land on the head of the South Branch of Potomac; 200 or more above the Indian Plains on South Branch; 200 at a place called the Indian Camp, opposite to a gap in the mountain, upon the head of the South Branch waters; all these entries are above the Crab Apple Bottom; 400 acres on head of South Fork of Potomac, joining the upper survey of Col. Woods's grant upon Clover Creek Road. James Patton.

Two hundred acres on a branch of Buffalo Creek above Samuel Gibson's three or four miles; 150 acres between South Mountain and the South River above the Narrow Passage; 100 acres joining his own land upon a branch of Buffalo Creek; 100 acres between his own and Michael Finney's. James Patton.

Thomas and Andrew Lewis enter 200 joining Horcklas Wilson on Cowpasture; 400 near John Shaw; 400 near head of Bullpasture; 400 North Side Bullpasture, near Bodkin; 200 joining George Wilson; —— at ye Reed Hole, near Hicklin; 200 at a small meadow between ye Warm Spring and Jackson's land; 200 about five miles from Warm Springs, near the path from said Springs to Holden's land on the mountain; —— on Seeder Run; 200 in Calfpasture joining Samuel Gay; 200 near Dunlops old place, where Meek made some improvements. February 28, 1754. Robert McClenachan.

6th March, 1754. Thomas and Andrew Lewis entered 400 on Bratton's Run, in Calfpasture, which runs through that place of Dunlops, where he last lived; 100 on Little River, between McCutchan and Clendenning's old place; 200 joining south side McCutchan's land below William Smith's; 200 on a branch of ye Great River of Calfpasture near a mile northwest of Samuel Fincher; 200 joining Thomas Gay's land in Cowpasture; 200 on ye Glady land at ye Sulphur Mine, south side Warm Spring Mountain Gap; 100 at foot of Warm Spring Mountain, about two miles from said Spring; 200 joining survey at Warm Springs and down the branch; 200 about two miles from Warm Springs; 200 in Cowpasture, side of Warm Spring Mountain, near James Gay's. Robert McClenachan.

19th January, 1754, Andrew Lewis entered two 400-acre tracts on Petter's Creek, a branch of James River, between Adam Dickinson's and the Indian Path; 200 on Warm Spring Mountain, joining the tract formerly Hurden's; three 400-acre branches of James River, near a survey made for William Warwick, and on some of the head branches of ye Back Creek.

By Thomas Lewis, 200 on Cowpasture, where John Shaw lives; 200 where Huraklas Wilson lives; 200 in Bullpasture, at foot of North Mountain.

27th November, 1753, Andrew Lewis entered 400 acres on head of Petter's Creek, which forks from Dickinson's Meadows, joining on the waters of Greenbrier, called Second Creek, on James River waters.

14th April, 1754, William Preston enters 400 on head of Potts Creek; 400 on ye first large bottom on Potts Creek, above Potts Improvements; 400 formerly entered for Tobias Bright on Craig's Creek; two 400 tracts at the Forks of Johns Creek; 400 on ye next large bottom above Colonel Patton's uppermost survey on Craig's Creek.

Petitioners ask that the following be assigned to work the road from James Young's mill to John Buchanan's mill: John Buchanan, James Clark's tithables, Jacob Lockhart's tithables, Thomas Kirkpatrick's tithables, John Bertly, George Bertly, William Martin, Josias Richards, William McFetters' tithables, John Jameson, James Young, Hugh Young, Robert Young's tithables, William McClintog, William Ledgerwood, John Trimble, Moses A'Friel's tithables, Samuel Wallis, Robert Davis, Robert McClenan's tithables, James Moody's tithables, James Philips, William Eckrey, Corneles Donahow, Alexander Ritchey, to be overseer; Adam Thomson, to be overseer; George Peevy, Adam Thomson's tithables, Thomas Peevy, William McNabe, Robert Scoat, Thomas Reed, Abraham Masha, Francis Dune, Mager Scoat, John Bingham's tithables, John Black's tithables, Samuel Downey, Alexander McFetters, Andrew Cowen, James McCorkell, John Vance, James Gilmor, Alexander Ritchie's tithables, Patrick Martin's tithables.

1753–1754, Part 2.

May 16, 1753. To ye worshipful bench, if I be continued overseer of ye road from John Cambel's field to the town for this year, that you allow me William Ledgerwood, John Bigham, George Cambel, William McNabb, James Peevy, John Cambel, Thomas Peevy, Robert Young, taxable; John Black, taxable; David Stewart, Samuel Sprowl, James Miller, James Miles, Abram Miller; Mr. Wright, taxable; James Brown, Samuel Willson, John Cunningham—all for to keep the said road in repairs for the year 1753. (Signed) John Henderson.

May, 1753. Road established from Brown's bridge to the Glebe land, and Robert Campbell and John Trimble be surveyors, and with James Lusk, they clear and keep the same in order. We do appoint Robert Campbell and John Trimble overseers from John Brown's bridge to the Gleve House and the undernamed persons to clear the same: James Lusk, Robert Roberson, Samuel McCuchen, William Hunter, James Hunter, Robert Campbell's man, Mathew Wilson, William Wilson, John Wilson, Jr., John McCleery, James McCleery, Thomas Kirkpatrick and son, John Peevy, James Clarck, John Clarck, James Clark, Jr., Jacob Lockhart, James Lockhart, John Birtly, Josias Richards, William Marten, George Berry, William McFeeters, John McFeeters, William McFeeters, Jr., John Jameson, Patrick Marten, Joseph Marten, William Ward, Moses O'Freel and his man, Robert Philips, Robert Davis, Thomas Reed, Robert Scott, John Vance, Andrew Foster, William Bell, Alexander McKiney, John Speer, Abraham Mathan (Mashaw), Robert Young, John Young, Samuel Young, Hugh Young and his man, John Campbell, George Peevy, Robert McClenan, William Eackry, James Bell, Andrew Steel and his man, John McKiney, Patrick McCloskey, John McSlenan, John McCuchan, Samuel McCuchan, William McClintock, Thomas Peevy, James McCuchen, Duncken McFarlen.

18th November, 1754. Entered for William Preston, assistant surveyor to Mr. Thomas Lewis, the following tracts of land, viz: 400 adjoining survey made on John's Creek; 200 above the uppermost survey on the South Fork of John's Creek; 200 on North Fork of said creek; 800 between Bradshaw's survey and Adam Looney land; 200 called the Sugar Land; 200 called the Mill Place, joining Jacob Patton's old place; 200 below Henry Holston's, joining Frederick Hartsough's land; 800 between Spreading Spring Draft and George Bindwell's; 200 joining Dayley's land; 200 between John McGowen's land and Nathaniel Evans's land; 800 below Laurel Gap, on Potts Creek; 400 on ye next large bottom; 400 on Purgatory Creek; 200 on ye Long Bottom; 400 between William Hutchison's and James Moore's, on ye Path; 400 between Pricilla Reise's land and James McAfee's; 200 at head spring of Little Catawba.

James Trimble, assistant surveyor, enters for 200 on a branch that runs into the main river at or in Given's place, formerly entered and gave up by Joseph Lang; 200 joining his own land upon a branch of Bufelow Creek that runs through Hugh Lusk's land. May 14, 1754.

1765–1766.

Samuel Newberry and Rosanna Newberry, his wife, "Lie Bill" to Thomas and Elizabeth Foster, 9th August, 1765.

Nathan Gilliland deposes, 22d August, 1765, that John Graham, in the Calfpasture, hired an orphan boy named Thomas May, eight years, again.

Thomas and Andrew Lewis's entries at Warm Springs.

Valuation of John Lewis's improvments, 20th May, 1765.

Various lists of tithables.

1755–6–7.

Inquest, 22d January, 1757, on John McCutchan, before Patrick Martin, acting coroner. Was accidentally killed by a tree falling on him. James Clark, Jr., William Clark, William Fulton, James Risk, Mathew Willson, Patrick Martin, Samuel McCutchan, James McCutchan, John Peny (?),

John Risk, William Berry, James Trotter, Robert Campbell, George Berry, John Clark, James Clark (Sen.?), James McCleery, Hugh Fulton.

Burr Harrison's bond as assistant surveyor, 22d November, 1754. Advertisement. Run away from the subscriber living in Augusta County, on the 16th of this instant, a servant man, named William Ratchford, about thirty years of age, and about 5 feet 9 inches high, with short hair of a dark brown, and his beard of a sandy color, and a dimple in his left cheek; is pretty talkative and speaks with a tone and can speak Dutch tolerable well; had on when he went away an old felt hat, an old brown coat lined with brown linsey with the foreskirt partly torn away, a linsey jaccoat wanting sleeves, a shirt of a seven hundred not whitened, old trowsers, and had shoes tied with thongs. Whoever takes up and secures said servant so that his master may have him again shall have two pistoles reward and reasonable charges paid by me. William Lusk. September 18, Anno Dom. 1755.

Valuation of improvements on the "Naked Farm" on waters of Roanoke, formerly the property of Daniel Evans and now in the possession of Peter Evans, 15th March, 1755, 18 acres cleared and well fenced under corn and rie, also ten acres of clear meadow; 100 fruit trees, £1.0.0; 1 lay house, 15 feet by 10, £1.10.0; 1 corn crib, 15 feet long and 4 feet wide, £0.10.0; 1 spring house, 18 feet long and 12 feet wide, £0.15.0; 5 head of horses and 1 breeding sow, £40.15.0; 1 waggon and gears, 1 ax and grubbing hoe, and 2 plows and gears, £26.0.0; 1 stack rie and 1 stack oats, £11.15.0; 22 head neat cattle, £33.0.0. William Conavin, Neal McNeal, James Bean.

1758.

6th January, 1757. Caleb Harman binds himself servant to Robert Reed for seven years.

Eleanor Sharpe petitions for freedom dues from George Anderson.

John Elliott complains, 4th November, 1758, that he suspects Rosanna Ralston, wife of William Ralston, of having stolen from him.

March, 1758. Account of James Trimble, coroner, for an inquest on the body of John Riely.

1760.

Christian Gotty's will in German and English, 1760. 11th March, 1760. Sister Susannah, Sister Catrine. Witness, John Welsh, Christopher Ermentrout, Elizabeth Stringer.

1761.

William Preston's entries, 18th February, 1761: three tracts of 400 acres each between David Cloyd, James Johnson, William Ralston, a survey for John Mills and David Miller, William Ermstrong and said Preston's land, whereon Rentfro formerly lived; also 400 on a branch of Craig's Creek, above Jacob Patton's old place, known by the name of the Mill Place.

1762.

17th August, 1762. John Poage entered 200 acres of South Branch, opposite to Shelton's tract on Earnhart's Branch.

16th November, 1763. John Poage entered three tracts on a branch of Back Creek, called the Valley, opposite to John Miller's on Jackson's River.

Petitioners to open a road that usually led from a ford of the South River above Joseph Hannah's over Cole's ford on the middle and from thence to Mathew Thompson's, which has been lately stopped by Henry Reaburn, notwithstanding it has been a bridle way for nearly twenty years. Robert Scott, Patrick Frazer, James Bruster, Robert Hook, Robert Hook, John Denniston, William Hook, J. Madison, John Stephenson, Archibald Huston, John Craig, John Davison, John Davison, Jr., Patrick Willson, Robert Shanklin.

Bond of William Hyde for the building of a house in the prison yard with specifications, 15th March, 1762. This was a house for the prison keeper to dwell in.

1763–4, Pt. 2.

23d November, 1762. William Fleming and John Maxwell, recognizee for William's appearance. William was a carpenter.

1768–9.

William Preston entered, 30th December, 1767, 250 between Gilbert Marshall and James Alexander on Back Creek; 400 joining lands of Jasper Torry, James Neely and Andrew Wilson; 400 on Potts Creek, above the Paint Bank Survey.

1779–80.

Jailor's account, 1780. To keeping the following: Will Hinton, confined for treason, 23d March to 30 May, 69 days; William Stonate, confined for desertion; George Lair, confined for desertion; Barnebas Tandy, confined for desertion; John Potter, confined for desertion; Mathias Miller, confined for desertion; William Cook, for desertion; Patrick McCimsy, for desertion; James Bridget, for desertion; Henry Lorance, for desertion; Thomas Moreson, Toryism; Duncan Gullion, treason; Swain Palson, treason; James Care, treason; Nathaniel Buton, treason; Joseph Patterson, desertion; Barnebas Barnbloom, desertion; Francis Simson, desertion; John Hikkey, desertion; Peter Bever, desertion; William Douglas, desertion; Charles Millard, desertion; William Brown, desertion; Zack Price, desertion; Samuel Bates, desertion; William Awty, desertion; Samuel Davis, desertion; Thomas Womsby, desertion; Alexander Nelson, desertion; Elkener Moland, desertion; John Cravin, desertion; Dennis Regin, desertion; Barnebas Ackling, desertion; William Graham, desertion; William Hinton, Toryism; Josiah Cockrin.

5th March, 1780. Inquisition on Barnebas Ryan. He died in drunken stupor.

1781–2.

Petition for road from Levi Moore's, on Nap Creek, to Back Creek and up the Back Creek from William Green's to Crab Bottom, on head of South

Branch Potomac, George Hoff, Ebuhe. Browner, Isaac Gum, Ebraham Ingram, James Patton, Peter Robertson, John Robertson, Back Calleway, James Dunwoddy, William Dunwoddy, John Slavens, Ruben Slavens, William Slavens, Esiah Slavens, Bige Warrin, John Waid, Leonard Waids, John Denston, William Green, John Townsend, James Townsend, Hezekiah Stout, Ephram Bates, James McGlaughlin.

Howard's Creek, June 4, 1782. Hugh McWilliams was committed by John Poage on suspicion of being unfriendly to the State, but now orders his release. Hugh has cousins in Carolina, who are tories of the same name. John Moffett.

Account of Alexander Robertson vs. the State for services as commissioner of the Provision Law.

Staunton, January 21, 1782. County of Augusta to John Gordon, Blacksmith. Iron for rivets and ironing three prisoners. Iron for rivets and ironing one prisoner.

1781-2, Pt. 1.

October 31, 1782. I do hereby certify that James Trotter, Esq., was unanimously appointed to assist as Captain in my room by the company that was formerly commanded by myself. Witness my hand. John Cunningham. The Worshipful Court of Augusta.

Certificate of Sampson Mathews that he had administered to Samuel Hardy, Esq., the oath of a privy counsellor, 19th July, 1781.

Goaler's account: James Riley, suspected deserter; Andrews Chivers, suspected deserter; John Right, suspected deserter; James Murphy, suspected deserter; Mordicai Cloud, and William Furrs, thieves; James Riley, suspected deserter.

John Marshal, of Augusta, to B. Borden. Bond, 17th May, 1751. John had bought 182 acres on Catuba Creek.

1785-6.

ADMINISTRATOR AND GUARDIAN BONDS.

Bond of William Burke, 27th March, 1785, to keep in repair the bridge on the creek near Daniel Kidd's in Staunton.

Received of Rebecca Estill £204 for John Estill's estate, tax for quota troop for Continental service, 9th May, 1781. Samuel Hunter, Colonel.

George Moor, of Augusta County, in re Margaret Dick.

COUNTY COURT JUDGMENTS

March, 1764 (C).

McDonald vs. Sumter.—27th November, 1761. Sergeant Thomas Sumter's (in the Virginia Regiment) bond to Alexander McDonald for £59.9.0, C. M. Va. Test. John Cameron, Lieutenant in the Virginia Regiment; Robert Fillson.

Stewart vs. Smith.—25th May, 1762. John Smith's note to John Given for £2.4.0, C. M. Va. Test. Thomas Branan. Assigned to John Stewart. Endorsed Colonel Smith's note, £2.4.0.

August, 1764 (B).

Looney vs. Looney.—11th May, 1764. John Smith's deposition. He was present when the proposals were made that Robert Looney and wife desired to have confirmed. Some time after Colonel Buchanan was sent for to draw the articles, and Buchanan's statements are punctually true. The articles were lodged with deponent. Shortly afterwards defendant and wife made a demand of Peter Looney (now deceased) and David Looney of the house and land. Peter Looney immediately answered (which David agreed to), "choose the spot for the house and it shall be built, and show the land, and Colonel Buchanan and Colonel Smith shall lay it off." They insisted to have land over the creek, but Peter and David refused because it was contrary to the agreement. Then Robert and wife made a second demand of David Looney. The old woman said she chose to have the land in the orchard, which he agreed to, and further said if they chose to have the house where his barn stood, he would remove the barn. The widow Looney sent off for cattle to winter in consequence of the bargain. The first winter after the bargain David Looney wintered Robert Looney's cattle, and deponent several times saw David drawing firewood to the said Robert, and he saw widow Looney send a hand to cut wood for him. Sworn to before William Preston, Isiah Christian, Benjamin Hawkins. William Lawderdeal says that the second winter after the above agreement, Margaret, the relict of Peter Looney, deceased, sent him to Robert Looney to get and drive what cattle fell to her share to winter, according to the agreement. Robert sent one cow. Thomas Ramsey deposes that Robert Looney was intoxicated with liquor when the articles were written, but was perfectly in his senses when they were signed. John Buchanan deposes plaintiffs are Peter and David Looney, defendants are Robert Looney and John Bowyer. There were proposals between defendants and plaintiffs about the making over his land to them, which bargain was afterwards concluded and deponent was sent for to draw the articles. Both parties repeated to him all particulars of the agreement, which he wrote down. Defendant Robert was drinking spirituous liquors too freely so that he lay down to sleep before writing was concluded. Deponent too(k) the articles home and after some time returned and found Robert awake and in his perfect senses. All executed. Part of the land belonged at that time to Absalom Looney. Deponent mentioned this to Robert, who said that Absalom had ordered his land to be sold, that he would buy it and throw it in with his other land and make it over to plaintiffs. Robert told deponent on Absalom's return from Carolina that he had paid Absalom £10 and he was well pleased with what Robert had done. The agreement was that the plaintiffs were to lay off five acres for defendant anywhere he chose on the premises, a certain rent to be paid yearly.

This bill bindeth me, Alexander Legate, of White Clay Creek Hundred, in the County of New Castle, on Delaware, cooper, in —— sum of £8, current lawful money of Pennsylvania, to be paid to James Broom, of the Hundred and County above named, within six months. Alexander Liget. (Seal.) 3d March, 1756. Test. John McCarty, Joseph Smith. Assigned, 16th December, 1761, to Nicholas Bishop by James Broom. Test. George Thompson, James Wilson.

Upp vs. Stone.—April 7, 1760. Henry Stone, debtor to Frederick Upp. To schooling three children six months and reading in church, as per agreement, £2.16.6. To schooling two children three months in 1761, £0.12.0. To my improvement you bought for £20.0.0. To schooling four children for George Broups six months, £3.17.0. To schooling two children for Thomas Millar six months and reading in church, £1.11.0. To schooling two children for yourself and reading in church, £1.16.0. Total, £30.12.6. Credit by cash, £15.6.0. Frederick Upp. Excepted. Sworn to in Frederick County, 11th June, 1763, before Joseph Langdon.

MARCH, 1765 (A).

Long vs. Huston.—Augusta County. This day came before me, James Lockhart, one of his Majestie's Justices for said County, Captain John Blagg, and made oath that in the year 1761, after Colonel Byrd had discharged James Huston, Armourer, there came up instructions from the General for the Commanding Officer to proceed to the Great Island, on which the said Blagg sent orders for the said James Huston to remain there till further orders and his wagon and tools were detained eight days. And as to the difference of currency he knows the said Huston was not paid Virginia currency, but was paid after rate of Pennsylvania money for him and his men. Likewise he understood that the said Huston did not receive pay for the said eight days. John Blagg. Certified by me, James Lockhart.

JUNE, 1764 (C).

Bowyer vs. Robinson.—James Robinson, dancing master, debtor. 1763, March 13th. To half a piece of nankeen, at 11/3. To 1½ yards brown Holland, 3/6. To 1 small book. To your assumsit for Cowan. Ex's p'r Thomas Bowyer and James McDowell.

AUGUST, 1764 (B).

Upp vs. Stone.—We, this congregation on the Fork in Augusta County, acknowledge that we have an agreement made with Frederick Upp, schoolmaster, to keep school. We promise to pay him for six months school-keeping for one child twelve shillings and one bushel of wheat, and the above bargain we promise to do and stand to which we have with our hands, or marks, under written as many children as we will send to the school in ye year 1760. April ye 7th. Henry Stone, 3 children. George Bush, 3 children. Henry Pickle, 4 children. Mark Swearly, 3 children. Peter Smith, 3 children. Adam (mark) Strout, 2 children. Michael Rine, 1 child. A copy. (Note: Stone promised in the presence of several that in case plaintiff would leave the place he then lived (a plant rented from Jacob Westfall) and come and keep school in the neighborhood, he would warrant 34 children. Upon that plaintiff left his place and crop, consisting of six acres winter grain, one acre of oats, two acres of barley, and four acres of (?)).

NOVEMBER, 1764 (A).

Looney vs. Harmon.—Captain Adam Harman's bond, dated 28th February, 1754, to Lones Loony, of Augusta County, for £10, with lawful interest from 29th July, 1746. Grandchild to the said Adam Harman. Test: John Crockett, Ann Crockett.

AUGUST, 1764 (B).

Cabeen vs. Walker.—Thomas Rutherford's deposition, taken 8th May, 1764, before John Neavill, in Frederick County. He was employed as agent for Messrs. Hoops and Walker, contractors, on the said campaign, in the year of our Lord 1761, and that sometime in the month of July that year (the troops being encamped at Stalnaher's on Holston's River), William Cabeen came to the camp and applied to deponent for employment in said contractor's service, alledging that it was in consequence of some engagement, or promise, he was under to Doctor Walker, but having no letter, or writing, to support what he then advanced, the deponent suspected a cheat, and having then several persons under pay more than the service at that time required, the deponent told Cabeen that he could not employ him under any pretence whatever, but in as much as he was then out on the campaign he might draw his ration, until the deponent should know Doctor Walker's sentiments thereon, which the deponent took the earliest opportunity of doing by writing a true state of the affair, and some time in August Doctor Walker, by letter, signified that as it had so unexpectedly happened, that William Cabeen had, without his knowledge, proceeded so far on the campaign, and that notwithstanding he was well assured the contract could in no wise be advantaged by the said Cabeen's services, but at the same time requested me to employ him as an assistant issuer of provisions, at the rate, as this deponent believed, of five shillings per day, and that the deponent looked upon it as an entire act of charity and good nature in Doctor Walker to employ the said Cabeen at that time, and that the deponent left the said Cabeen in the contractor's service about the 29th, or 30th, of October, when the said deponent came off the campaign.

MARCH, 1765 (A).

The King vs. David McKoskry.—Alexander McKoskey, being first sworn before me, saith that on the 26th instant Samuel Woodward and Mary, his wife, being at David McKoskey's house and in the night time he, rising out of bed, found the door open and missing the said Samuel and his wife out of bed, he also missed his coat, jacot, britches, and hat, and a blanket, and next day, pursuing and on the 28th he found the said Samuel Woodward and wife in Timber Ridge Meeting House and got the above goods in their possession with sundry other of David McKoskey's goods by them, viz: One rifle gun of the value of five pounds, one snafel bridle, and one Indian blanket. Certified under my hand this 31st January, 1765. Samuel McDowell.

This day David McKoskey came before me and proved the same as above to the finding of the door open, and also proved the gun, bridle, and blanket to be his property which the above said Alexander found in possession of the said Woodward and wife. Certified under my hand this 31st January, 1765. Samuel McDowell.

Julian vs. McClenachan.—Bond, dated 30th December, 1762, by Alexander McClenachan, Lieutenant in ye Virginia Regiment, to Charles Julian. Test. Nicholas Smyth.

Gallespie vs. Naught.—William Naught's bond, dated 22d November, 1760, to Allen Gillespy, £58. Test. Rebeckah Armstrong. (Armes) New Castle Co. S. S. Certificate that John Evans is one of the Justices for County of New Castle, 6th January, 1764, by Theodore Maunce, Deputy Prothonotory. Certificate, 6th January, 1764, by John Evans that Rebecca Armstrong swore she saw William Naught sign above bond.

MARCH, 1764 (C).

Account Mays with Fleming. 1763, Jessy May, debtor to sundries, £9.18.10½. Credit by hire of your wife as servant three months, £1.10.0. E. E. William Fleming.

NOVEMBER, 1763 (C).

Lewis vs. Lanlas.—Andrew Lewis sues out an attachment, 18th October, 1763, against estate of Christian Landless. Executed by Hugh Wardlaw. Surety, John Bowyer.

Price vs. Allison.—Deposition of Patrick Henry, Jr., aged 27 years, who, being first sworn, deposeth and saith: That sometime about the 20th day of November, in the year 1758, the defendant came to the store then kept by this deponent in Hanover County, and did take up upon credit sundry goods amounting to 31 shillings, and about the same time did obtain an order from this deponent to one, Charles Crenshaw, on which order the said defendant took up, as this deponent believes, goods amounting to 29 shillings 17½ pence, inasmuch as this deponent paid the said last mentioned sum to the said Crenshaw for the said defendant, etc. P. Henry, Jr. Sworn to before, 22d October, 1763. John Henry.

NOVEMBER, 1764 (A).

Brown vs. Leister's Administrator.—The deposition of Joseph Ray, taken by me, Robert Breckenridge, one of his Majesty's Justices of the Peace for said County, this 25th May, 1762. The deponent being first sworn, sayeth that sometime last summer Thomas Brown came to camp at Stalnaker's with a quantity of shirts, which, after being some days in camp, he desired Mr. James Litsler to take them in his store, and if he had an opportunity, to sell them for him, but Mr. Litsler's reply was that his store had been broke open some nights before and several goods taken out, for which reason he did not care to take the charge of any other person's goods, but if Mr. Brown choose to leave them as his horse was very much fatigued, he was welcome to house room, but they should be at Mr. Brown's own risk, which Mr. Brown agreed to, and farther the deponent sayeth not. Robert Breckenridge.

Dean vs. Martin.—19th January, 1764. Note by Joseph Martin, Pat Martin (Test. Andrew Martin), to Adam Dean.

JUNE, 1764 (C).

Duffield vs. Pullins.—27th December, 1754. Loctus Pullin's note to George Wilson. Test. John Miller.

MAY, 1765 (A).

Jackson's Executors vs. Armstrong.—William Armstrong, Andrew Mc-Coard's bond to Robert Jackson, in Frederick, 4th November, 1747. Test. Richard Savage, George Washington.

MARCH, 1764 (B).

Daniel Ponder vs. William Cabeen.—William Cabeen, debtor to Daniel Ponder. 1759. To wintering nine head pack horses for his Majesty's service per your order, at 35 shillings per head, £16.15.0. One of said horses died in February by eating wheat, discounted the same, £0, 15, 0. Total, £16, 0, 0. Sworn to, 18th November, 1762, before Francis Tyler.

JUNE, 1764 (C).

Cochrane vs. Low (In the Forks of James River).—John Low's note, 22d June, 1763, to John Cochrane. Test. John Robinson, John Blear, 29th May, 1764. Low is not in the County.

NOVEMBER, 1764 (A).

Man vs. Galloway.—The deposition of James Walker, gent, being first sworn on the Holy Evangelist, saith that some time in the fall of the year 1769, being stationed at Fort Young as Lieutenant of a company in the Frontier Battalion, the defendant, Man, acted under him as sergeant, and one day a certain John Isabell, having drove up a young horse that was neither cut, doctored, or branded to the best of this deponent's belief, had got him penned up in the fort with an intent to get him in a halter, and for this purpose had collected all the soldiers then in the fort to assist him to halter the said horse; that afterwards, when they had got him in the halter, this deponent saw him break away with the halter on his head and swim across the river, which being then raised by a fresh, could not be forded, and that the said Isabell applied to this deponent, as commander of the garrison, to offer a bottle of rum to the defendant and his brother, Thomas, to swim across the river to drive the horse back, and if that would not induce them, to order them as their officer, which this deponent communicated to them in such words as to let them know if they did not do it for the reward aforesaid that he should lay his commands on them, as he was apprehensive the horse might be hung in the woods by the halter, and accordingly the said defendant and his brother swam across the river and drove the said horse back again, where he was again caught and delivered to the said Isabell, who told this deponent that he was a stray which he intended to ride down to Staunton, and if he could find the owner he would purchase the horse of him, if not that, he would ride him back again to Fort Young, then turn him out, and that he did accordingly ride him down in a day or two after but never returned to Fort Young, but on the contrary rode him down the country and sold him, as this deponent thinks, he was informed by the said Isabell himself, and further this deponent saith not. James Walker. Sworn before me, one of his Majesty's Justices for the said County, this 24th day of June, 1763. John Poage.

NOVEMBER, 1764 (A).

McCallom vs. Endsworth (Ainsworth).—June, 1745. Samuel Endsworth to Patrick McCallom, debtor. To the carriage of 700 yards of brown linen from Seetarro to Philadelphia, £0.17.6. To cash lent him in Philadelphia, £2.10.0. To the carriage of 1,800 weight of stone goods from Philadelphia to Seetarra, at 5 shillings per hundred, £4.10.0.

MARCH, 1765 (A).

Cowdon vs. Dean.—1761. Debtor Sergeant William Dean to Samuel Cowdon, David Stewart & Co. Sundries as per Captain Blagg's directions, £3.0.0.

JUNE, 1764 (B).

Cowdon vs. Patrick.—The defendant sold unto the plaintiff 80 pair of shoes, which were very bad, and not made in a good and workmanlike manner, but so insufficient that the plaintiff could not dispose of the same in ye camp, and by reason thereof his store got a bad character to his great damage.

MARCH, 1765 (A).

Boyd vs. McDonald.—1763. Mr. James McDonald, in account with Alexander Boyd. July 14th. Mr. James McDonald. Sir: Above is your account with me which I desire you'll pay to the bearer, William Buttler. Pray fail not and oblige. Your obedient servant, Alexander Boyd. Fort Lewis, 13th August, 1764.

MARCH, 1764 (B).

John Warrick Sertify to eight or nine hogs that Sepn. (?) Wilson killed. Evidences names: William Givens, James Gay, William Warrick, Andrew Singleton, John Warrick. This was transacted in ye year 1758. John McCreery for. (Addressed) Mr. John Warrick, these—

MARCH, 1765 (A).

Gilbert vs. Jones (Parson Jones' bond, £5.10.7).—John Jones, minister of the County of Augusta, do promise to pay unto Felix Gilbert ——, 18th August, 1763. John Jones, claimant. Test. John Cambblle.

McDonald vs. McClenachan.—I, Alexander McClenachan, Lieutenant in the Virginia Regiment, do promise to pay to Alexander McDonald 33 pounds Virginia currency, 27th September, 1762. Alexander McClenachan. W. Cuningham, James Hughes.

MAY, 1765 (A).

Estil vs. Skilleren.—Augusta Sc——. This day Benjamin Estil came before me and made oath that about the year 1761, or 1762, William Skilleren gave him a note of hand due said Skilleren from one Henry Long, to endeavor to collect of Long for said Skilleren, and if not collected to return the note of hand to said Skilleren, and that the said note was destroyed by the Indians on the 13th day of September last at the dwelling house of John Trimble, deceased, but that there was no credit on said note nor doth he know that ever he received any part or party of said note, but if ever it shall or can be made to appear, or by any means found out, that any part was received by him, he is willing at any time to discount the same with said Skilleren. Given under my hand this 20th day of March, 1765. John Dickinson.

MARCH, 1764 (B).

1762. Ambros Bryan to James Maze, debtor. June 3, to keeping and feeding your elks two months, at 15 shillings, £1.10.0. To keeping and feeding your elks one month, at 10 shillings, £0.10.0. To keeping and feeding your elks six months, at 5 shillings, £1.10.0. To seven months feeding one elk, at 2 shilling 6 pence, £0.17.6. Total £4.17.6. Credit by sundries, ——. By Mathew Brahen, £0.4.0. Total, £0.16.0. By a balance due, £9.11.16.

Augusta, ss. This day James Mazze came before me, one of his Majesty's Justices for this County, and made oath that the above account is just, and that the balance of three pounds, eleven shillings, and sixpence is now due and owing to him. Given under my hand this 21st day of March, 1764. Felix Gilbert.

MARCH, 1765 (A).

Buchanan vs. Draper.—I, John Draper, of Augusta County, do promise to pay, etc., unto Abraham Hains, etc., 31st day of May, 1754. John Draper. Test. Theodosia Vanso. Assigned (in German) to William Lepport (Wilhelm Lippert). Abraham Haines. Test. Johannes Dey.

OCTOBER, 1765 (A).

Fleming vs. McCutchen.—1763. Samuel McCutchen to William Fleming, debtor. Sundries. Credit by cash to James Trotter, £1.0.0.

NOVEMBER, 1764 (B).

Vail vs. Ligate.—We, Alexander Liggetes and Samuel Steel, of Augusta County, etc., do promise to pay James Gilmore, etc., 4th June, 1760. Alexander Liget, Samuel Steel. Test. William Napier, Alexander Milben (Millen).

Wagner vs. Rhoades.—Fort Nelson, August 20, 1764. Sir: I understand Hall has lodged a note of hand of me in your office in order to bring suite against me. I should have been at this Court in order to have settled it with him, but have ingag'd with Captain Christian in his company of militia, who won't let me attend, which if he persist in the suite please to inform the Court of my ingagement. I am, sir, your umble servant, Thomas Rhoads.

OCTOBER, 1765 (B).

Cowden vs. Cabeen.—1761. Debtor, William Cabeen, to Messrs. Samuel Cowden & Co. July 20, to balance from Fort Chriswell, old ledger, £0.16.0. To do. from new do., £8.16.6. December 15, to do. from new book, £2.17.10. October, to do. from Stalnaker's, £20.1.8. To do. from Fort Chriswell, £2.7.0. November, to do. from Stalnaker's, £2.17.6. Credit, by mistake, £2.7.10. By cash, £10.0.0. By do., £1.0.0.

AUGUST, 1765.

Allen vs. McDonall.—I promise to pay Hugh Allen, 22d May, 1765. Alexander McDonald. Test. Robert Anderson.

Kirkpatrick vs. Hawkins.—To Mr. John Kirkpatrick, Merchant in Alexandria. Favor of Captain Ellzey. Sir: I am owing you some cash, if you would send me an account of the exact sum by Mr. Hugh West at any time, should be glad to pay you — or by any other safe hand. I am, sir, your umble servant, Ben Hawkins. Dumfries, February, 1762.

MARCH, 1764 (B).

Jo Ray vs. Wright.—1759. Mr. Joseph Rea, debtor to Alexander Wright. To cash at Winchester, answered for you to Bryon Bruin before you could get out of town, £3.0.0. Cash at Combs, £0.2.3. Interest for three years I ought to be allowed. November 10, 1763. Errors excepted pr. Alexander Wright. Spotsylvania, S. C. Alexander Wright made oath to the above account of £3.2.3 is just. Certified by me this 30th of November, 1763. Fielding Lewis. If he be run off this is useless, so need not order out.

MAY, 1768 (A).

James Cowdon, debtor to Mathew Reed and Hugh Johnston. Sundries.

1766. James Laughlin to Cornelius Reddick, debtor. Sundries. Sworn to before Robert Breckenridge.

Debtor Simon Dehart to Thomas McFarran. Sundries.

John Wiley, Jr., to John Campbell, debtor. To 4 dressed buckskins, at 12, £2.10.0. Sworn to 15th March, 1768, before Samuel McDowell.

Wm. McClintock, debtor. 1762, November; December 17th, per your daughter; December 30, per your daughter; July 18, per widow Vance; 1764, April. Credit, 1763, December 2d, by sundries; December 17.

Wm. McClintock, debtor. Sundries.

Christian vs. Curry.—William Curry (near Staunton) to Israel Christian, debtor. 1759, July 2; 1761, item by son, William; 1763, 24th February; 1766, to your account at the Stone House with Walter Stewart. Sworn to, 29th December, 1766.

Anderson vs. Flushing.—Mr. William Fleming to William Anderson, debtor. 1767.

Bowyer vs. Carpenter.—1762, July 16th. Solomon and Joseph Carpenter, debtor to John Bowyer. Credit by 6½ pounds beaver skins, at 4/ per pound.

Boyd vs. Morrise.—John Morrise. 1766, February 4th; 1767, March 10th; June 10, cash; September 14th. Sworn to by Andrew Boyd, administrator of Alexander Boyd, 18th May, 1768.

Boyd vs. Levy Smith.—1766. October 15th.

Boyd vs. Peter Stephens.—Sundries. 1766, November 11th, November 20th; 1767, March 4th, April 2d.

Boyd vs. William Dougherty.—Sundries. 1766, February 2d, May 23d, September 30th; 1767, August 1st, to Henry Paulin; August 22. Contra: 1766, September 30th, by 72° ginzang root, 2/6d; 2¾ deerskins, 4/.

Boyd vs. John McFawl, Jr.—Sundries. 1766, March 17, April 4, June 8.

John Crank vs. John Craig.—Account. 1763.

William Crow vs. Joseph Gamble.—Account. Sundries. 1761, November 7; 1762, January 15, February 3; 1763, May 8; 1764, January 28, June 8, August 13, September, October 8, November 22, your part of the goods for the Garle (?) Garde (?); 1765, January 14, January 28, by John Stewart, January 30; 1765, February 20, assumpsit for John Stewart; December 16; 1766, February 10, March 8, per Dr. Donaldson, per William Duncan; April 22; 1767, January 8, to your part of a servant; credit given you instead of your uncle for hauling a load from Fredericksburg.

Israel Christian vs. Abraham Drilian (Dulian), lives at Robert Moady's (Christian's Creek).—Sundries. 1762, February 7; October 6; January 28; credit by one week's work in January, 1763, 10/.

AUGUST, 1767 (C).

George Mitchell vs. Thomas Reeves.—1767, August 4; August 18, August 22, August 26, paid Michael Smith per your order; August 29. Es. exd. per Mr. Geo. Mitchell, per Henry Crutcher. Sworn to in Spottsylvania by Henry Crutcher before John Stewart.

AUGUST, 1768 (C).

Boyd vs. Benj. Polson.—1766, November 14.

AUGUST, 1769 (A).

John Stewart vs. Samuel Cowdon.—1762, June 4, cloth returned from your old account and not settled for; house rent, 4 months 25 days; January 16, seven pairs leather breeches for your brother Walter, £8, 11, 0; April; May 16; April; 1763, May, one coat sold to John Martins; 1764, received by James Ward; 1765, May, one coat for your son; 1766, May, by repairing your house that I rented, £2; 1767, July, one pair breeches in Carolina, £1, 2, 0; cash paid Sheriff in ditto, £3, 4, 10; cash paid Gaoler in ditto, £0, 11, 10; cash lent to buy shoes in ditto, £0, 11, 0; cash paid your expenses coming in from ditto, £0, 9, 0; cash for Robert Garral, £0, 15, 0; cash paid Robert Young, £0, 17, 0; 1760, to five months diet for James Stevenson, £4, 10, 0; November, to cash of suit that I was in prison bounds for you.

Pepper vs. Hannon.—We, James Johnson and Valentine Hannan, do promise to pay unto Samuel Pepper, &c., &c., &c., 15th June, 1767. (Signed) James Johnson, Vallaentin Harman. Test, Anthony Bledsoe, James Smith.

MAY, 1768.

M. Harrison vs. John Alderson.—1766, June 6; 1767, February 25; March 12, to credit Moses Marden; April 6; July 30, to credit Masay Staks.

M. Harrison vs. Wm. McGee.—Sundries. 1766, July 4, July 10, July 23, your note due Mr. Thomas Rutherford.

M. Harrison vs. John Phillips.—1767, June 5, credit by 15 geese—by Wm. Harsh.

AUGUST, 1769 (C).

Andrew Crockett vs. James Scott.—Peter Wylie deposes, 17th June, 1769, before William Preston: That when Peter Cochran was on his journey to Halston River, he stayed some time at the deponent's house, when he observed among Cochran's horses a bay mare with a black list along her back, which Cochran told the deponent he had of James Scott, the present plaintiff, in a swap; that some time afterwards the said Cochran returned to the deponent's house and told him that he had sold the above mentioned mare to Andrew Crockett on his way out, and further sayeth not.

AUGUST, 1768 (C).

William Crow vs. Capt. Walter Cunningham.—Sundries. 1762, 1763, 1764; 1762, March 25, to one pair shoes for your sister Betty; June 19, to your provision account, 174 rations, at £1; 1763; 1764; 1765; 1766, January 21, to cash stopped for James and John Ward; January 23, stopped for Thomas Carpenter, Alexander Tilford, Wm. Daucherty, Archey Handley; 1767, April 10, your assumpsit for David Graham; May 15, to club at Poaking; November 20, to club at Vestry; 1768, April 26, to George; March 15, to cash answered for Captain Lynch. Credits—1766, February 11, by cash at Strother and McPherson's frolic; February 22, by cash answered for your son, £15. (Between the dates above scarcely a day passed without several charges for drinks. I have only noticed a few items of an extraordinarily long account.)

AUGUST, 1769 (C).

John Drake vs. Lanty Armstrong.—Sundries. 1761, cash paid Delaney.

AUGUST, 1768 (C).

James McAfee vs. Peter Cochrane.—I, Peter Cochrane, of Augusta, do hereby oblige myself in the penal sum of £120, lawful of Virginia, to make, or cause to be made, to James McAfee, of said County, &c., &c., a good and sufficient title in fee simple for 32 acres of land, less or more, on James River, joining the land of George Givens, and the said Cochrane's right of an entry upon the hill above the house of 400 acres, &c., &c. 11th March, 1765. (Signed) Pettor (mark) Cochran, Margaret (mark) Cochran. Test, Samuel Lawrence, James Lawrence.

AUGUST, 1767 (C).

McCall vs. Boyd's Administrator.—To Mr. Henry Mitchell, merchant, in Fredericksburg: Alexanderia, 6th September, 1764. Mr. Henry Mitchell. Sir:—The last time I saw Mr. McCaul he told me he was just about leaving the Country, and he having a note of hand of mine amounting to £96, 2, 5, which I could not then discharge any part of, and as you have the direction of his affairs, you'll please receive under cover £10, 15, 0, and two orders, one on Mr. James Mercer for £2, 18, 6, due me by his brother, the Colonel, and another, £20, 0, 0, which I'll receive at the next sitting of the Assembly, it being for two months' pay of Person Cotuners, that was attached, for which I never received. You have likewise another order for £22, 10, 0, and interest, for some years due me from Squire Brown, which Mr. Truble included in with a bond of his, and he promised to pay it at the October Court, and make no doubt of your getting it then, or soon after. The balance of £4, 2, 0, you'll receive (if not already paid) from Mr. William Scott, which he owed me. As Mr. McCaul's account against me is for medies. and billiards, he desired I might not put myself to any kind of inconvenience till it suited me. You may depend, however, that I'll endeavor to contrive the balance as soon as lies in my power. My bad fortune in that way has been of great prejudice to me. When it is convenient your acknowledging the receipt of this by way of Staunton—and direct for me—merchant at Fort Lewis, in Augusta County, will be acceptable. I am, sir, your very humble servant. (Signed) Alex. Boyd.

MARCH, 1769 (A).

The Rev. John Kinkead, debtor to Morris Terrell.—Labor. 1767, credit by one dollar at 6/3.

AUGUST, 1768 (B).

George Paris, debtor to Archibald Fresher (?).—Sundries and labor. To cooking and washing for six months for him and his daughter at 6/. Credit by one wagon body at 6/.

MARCH, 1769 (A).

Harrison vs. Fleming.—Sir:—Be so kind to pay Mr. Edmd. Winston, or order, the sum of five pounds, seven shillings and six pence, cash lent you at Benjamin Mosby's, while I served in the Virginia Regiment, and you will oblige, your humble servant. (Signed) C. H. Harrison. October 18, 1766. To Dr. Fleming, in Staunton. Accepted, 28th May, 1767, Bedford Court House. (Signed) Wm. Fleming.

Moses Moore vs. Samuel Cloyd.—Samuel Cloid be pleased for to pay unto John Risk, my father-in-law, that money that you owe me, which is five pound, nine shillings, for I have impowered him for to do for me in my absence for to recover it, or to look after it for me. Given under my hand this fifth day of February and year 1766. (Signed) Moses Moore, Samuel Cloyd. Test, Robert Risk, Martha Risk.

AUGUST, 1767 (C).

Crow vs. Cowdon.—Samuel and Walten Cowdon, debtor to William Crow. 1759, December 30, cash for James Stevenson, John Givins and Brine Mc-Bride; 1760, December 22, to McAnulty's wages; 1762; 1763, February 10, to cash per Wat in Carolina; 1764, April 10, per George Francisco; April 15, per Edward Long; May 18, per Wm. Robertson, per John Stinson's son; June 7.

MARCH, 1769 (A).

Wilson vs. Christian.—William and John Wilson, debtors to Is. Christian. Sundries. 1756–1757, February 26; 1759, March 22; May 31, cash to Thos. Cassaty; credit by Thomas's Rainging, £2, 2, 0; by John's Rainging, £1, 12, 0; balance due when above notes are received from the Government. 1768, by different accounts settled last Assembly. 1763, February 17, cash for Stephen Wilson.

AUGUST, 1768 (B).

Whitesides vs. Graham.—May 20, 1767, Arthur Graham agrees to confess judgment to William Whitesides. Test, P. Henry, Jr.

Garnishment vs. John Henderson, in behalf of Andrew Boyd, vs. Samuel Pepper.—Henderson deposes, 10th March, 1767, that in 1766 he purchased, through Robert McGee, of George Pearis, a tract of land on North Fork of Roanoke, alias Goose Creek.

Whitesides vs. Crawford.—Bond dated 17th May, 1763, by James Crawford to William Hutchinson. Test, Wm. Preston, Susanna Preston.

Yuille vs. Parrish (George Parish).—1759, March 3. Cumberland S—. Sworn to by Thomas Yuille, 22d February, 1762. (Signed) Wade Nethenland. (See if he can be got at Bedford.)

August, 1765.—Robert Reed, debtor to Robert Cunningham. 1766, February.

William Daven to Stephen Trigg, debtor. 1766, October 27; November 24; December 6. (Signed) Stephen Trigg.

AUGUST, 1767 (C).

George Carpenter vs. William Crow.—Simon Robinson deposes, 21st May, 1767, before John Poage: That he was employed by Capt. Crow to help him to take a drove of cattle towards Pennsylvania, and on their way said deponent saith several strange cattle came into the drove, and particularly below Frazier's some came in, as likewise at Davies Mill, all which he believes was turned out, and had particular orders from Mr. Crow to take care of the drove, and likewise to be careful to turn out all stray cattle, and likewise said Crow did assist himself to turn out cattle at different times and order people where they lodged to detain stray cattle from their drove till they could get clear of. William (mark) English deposes: That passing by Shurley's he saw in his pasture Capt. Crow's drove of cattle, and with them he saw several of Mr. Carpenter's cattle. Next morning, after they were started off out of the field and met several of Mr. Carpenter's cattle on the road coming back. Randal Lockhart deposes, 21st May, 1767: That about four years agone he met with Mr. Crow at Pat. Frazier's with his drove and was desired by said Crow to count his cattle, which he did, and counted 131. He assisted Mr. Crow down the road as far as where John Waddell lived, and helped to turn out some cattle out of the drove, and was desired by said Crow so to do. Some time after Mr. Crow came home. Deponent heard Mr. Carpenter and said Crow discoursing about cattle that Carpenter lost. Crow affirmed that he discovered one stray cow, and no more, in his drove at Robert Wilson's. Some time afterwards Crow went down to speak with Carpenter about cattle that he had lost, who affirmed he had lost two. Crow asked him what price he valued his cattle to. He said £6. Crow said he would set the price on an average, or leave it to two men, if he could prove his cattle were in his drove. They nominated Robert Shanklin and William Beard. The appointment was set, and the time came, but Carpenter did not appear. James Bruster deposes: In October, 1763, deponent went to house of George Carpenter in search of lost cattle, which he suspected Mr. Crow had taken off in his drove, and they went in search of Crow's drove. On their way they came to Michael Shirley's. Mrs. Shirley said Crow had asked her to count the drove, which she did, and found them 141. They proceeded to Alex. Buchanan. Mrs. Buchanan told them that Crow's drove increased damnably. Thence they went to one Heard's. Mr. Heard said Crow offered to sell one heifer. They came to Mr. Crow's house in Staunton. Mr. Crow says: Mr. Bruster, I understand you are like to make me out a cow thief? I never called you a thief, but you acknowledged a stray cow which I dare ventur to say is mine, and I have come to see what you have done with her.

MARCH, 1768 (E).

Brown vs. Boyd.—1764. Dr. Mr. Alexander Boyd, to Robert Brown. Shop account. Medicine account. Henrico Sc.—Dr. Robert Brown made oath before me that Alexander Boyd died indebted to him, etc., 10th September, 1766. (Signed) Philip Mayo.

Dr. David McGee, North Fork, to Estate of Alexander Boyd.

Alexander Forbes, Dr., to Estate of Alexander Boyd.—Credit by Mrs. Margaret Robinson.

Mathew Ralstone, Dr., to Stephen Trigg.—Account, 1766–1767.

Dr. Jacob Brown, North Fork, to Estate of Alexander Boyd.—1767.

MAY, 1767 (C).

Hutchinson vs. Boyd.—Mr. Gabriel Jones, Augusta Court House. Sir: I humbly beg your advice in a matter of consequence, and that is one of my neighbors named Robert Boyd has abused my wife and my mother-in-law in a most scandalous manner and publicly reported that they were both perjured. I shall beg, if you be pleased, to take the affair in hands and execute as far as the law directs in such a case, and beg that you will let me have an answer by Mr. Smith, the Sheriff, for I shall be down the fall Court, and you shall be paid to your full satisfaction. From your most humble servant (Signed), William Hutchinson. P. S.—My mother's name, Margaret Marrow (Morrow?); my wife's name, Ann.

Thompson vs. Hays.—John Thompson, Hugh Hays.

November, 1768 (C).

William Beard, Dr., to Wm. Thornton.—To dressing 40 deer skins @ 2/.

Zaphar Carpenter, Dr., to Israel Christian.—1765, 21st December. To 3 dues harps, 1/6.

Francis Kidd, Dr., to John Howard, 1767, December 14. Credit by making and nailing 80 clap boards, £0, 7, 0. Sworn to by Arthur Campbell, before Samuel Bowyer, 16th November, 1768.

1766. Joseph Skidmore to Dr. William Ginits, Dr. To your subscription for a year's schooling, £5, 0, 0, Hampshire County. Sworn to, 8th March, 1768, by William Ginits, before Jonathan Hath (Heath).

I promise to pay, etc., unto Peter Dinges, etc., 11th February, 1767. Ellis Beane. Test, Jesse Beane. Endorsed—1768, Dr., to James Redick; February 10, Dr., to James Laughlin; Dr., to John Laughlin; Dr., to David Robinson.

13th February, 1768. John Thompson, Bording's Land, Dr. Sworn to by Joseph Scot, 18th August, 1768.

John Robinson (Mill Wr.) to James Reddick, Dr., 1767.

1767. Robert Hooks, Dr. Robert Campbell, 5th November, 1768.

March, 1768 (E).

Dr., Mr. William Hughes, Adjutant, etc. February, 1759, to fee ads. Lord Fairfax, 15/. May, 1764, to a retainer, £1, 1, 6; to fee ads. your boys' mother, £0, 15, 0; to Dr. Johnson's account, £1, 17, 6. Credit by Alexander Love. (Signed) Gabriel Jones.

August, 1767 (D).

Malcolm McCown (widow's son) Dr., to John Taylor. 1766, February 5, to account.

William Gilmore, Dr., to Dr. William Cabell. 1763, April 9, to dressing your daughter Eleanor's eye until the 22d day; Bord; Trouble; about her interment; coffin, etc., £3, 15, 0.

August, the 31st day, 1764. Sir: To Capt. Walter Cunningham, please to pay George Dare seven pound ten shilling as soon as my pay comes in to your hand, without Eney Dout, for it is justly due him, and in so doing you will veray much oblige your humble friend to serve. (Signed) James McElhiney. Test, Robert Gilipe.

August, 1768 (C).

Mr. William Teas. His account with Alex. McCaul, 1767, July 31.

Jacob Argenbright, in account with Isaac Heslap. Sworn to in Spottsyl-vania before Charles Yates.

AUGUST, 1767 (C).

Monteath & Co. vs. Boyd's Administrators.—Mr. Alexander Boyd, Dr , to Glasgow Tanwork Company.

AUGUST, 1769 (D).

William Hill, Dr., to James McKee. Sworn to 22d August, 1768.

MAY, 1768 (C).

Perdue Courtney, to John Thompson, Dr. 1765, May. Sworn to.

MAY, 1768.

Michael Reasoner, Dr., to Andrew Boyd's Estate. 1766, January 15.
September 25, 1761. I promise to pay, etc., unto William Ingles or Cum-paney, etc. (Signed) John Smith. Test, Thomas Coaperd (Coasserd). (Endorsed, "Col. Smith to Wm. English—Bill.")

AUGUST, 1768 (D).

September, 1767. George Rodgers, to John Allison, Dr. (George is de-ceased, February, 1768.)
1763. Mr. Robert Hambleton, Dr., to John Biggs. March, 24, to 4 days getting house logs and covering cabin; to 4 days fencing; to 3 days planting corn; to 6 lbs. tobacco @ 3d.; to 8 days work by son and daughter.
Mr. Wm. McCutchan, Dr., to John Handley. 1760. To 1 elk skin, 10/.
February 14, 1766. William Davis, living in the Forks, Dr., to Joseph Scott. To 1 fine hat, 2 alminicks, 1 alminick.
February 20, 1765. Mary Ann Young, daughter-in-law to William Young, 1 alminick.

NOVEMBER, 1767 (E).

John Rees, Dr., to Hugh Hayes.

NOVEMBER, 1768 (C).

1760, January 9. John King, Middle River, to Wm. Crow, Dr.

MARCH, 1768 (D).

Joshua McCormick (North Fork) Dr., to Boyd's Estate. Account, 1766, 1767.
Francis Stuart, Dr., to Thomas McDowell. 1766.

NOVEMBER, 1768 (C).

May 11, 1767. Thomas Moore, Dr., to Edward Sampson. To 40/ you agreed to give me for schooling two of your children @ 20/ each, and a cravat, £2, 3, 9. Credit by 3 yards coarse linen @ 2/6 and a slate.

Augusta County, to wit: The Grand Jurors, for our Lord the King for the County aforesaid, upon their oaths present that Joseph Bell, of the Parish of Augusta, in the County aforesaid, yeoman, falsely, unlawfully, and wickedly devising, contriving and intending one Anne Wallace, a single woman, and daughter of William Wallace, maliciously and injuriously to aggrieve, oppress, ridicule and to bring her and her parents into discredit and disgrace, on the 9th day of March, 1765, at the Parish of Augusta, in the County aforesaid, did forge, counterfeit with and publish on a certain piece of paper the banns of matrimony between the said Anne Wallace and a certain Edward Sampson, a deformed little tailor, in the words following, to wit: "You are to proclaim the Banns of Matrimony between Edward Sampson and Anne Wallace, March 9, 1765. William Wallace. To Parson Jones, Clerk of Church," which said piece of paper, so written, forged and signed with the name of said William Wallace, the said Joseph Bell, the day and year aforesaid, at the County aforesaid, did give, or cause to be given, to one Simon Robinson, Clerk of the Parish Church, of Augusta, and by that means occasioned the said Ann Wallace and Edward Sampson to be published in the said Church without the knowledge or consent of the said Ann or her father, the aforesaid William, and much against their wills, to their great discredit and grief and also against the peace of our said Lord the King, his Crown, and dignity, etc. A true bill. Elijah McClenachan, Foreman.

Mr. Robert Alsup to John Price, Dr. Account, 1762.

Major Robert Breckenridge, Dr. 1759. To my pay as a soldier, 44 days @ 1/, £2, 4, 0. Robert Hall. I certify that Robert Hall served as a soldier 44 days and now is discharged, this 22d February, 1759. Robt. Breckenridge.

May, 1768 (A).

William Anderson vs. Thomas Hughes.—1767. Sworn to 13th August, 1767. Patrick McCallard, Dr., to Andrew Donnelly, 1767, 16th February.

May, 1767 (D).

Thompson vs. Watterson.—Motion by Patrick Henry, attorney.

May, 1768 (A).

Joseph McMurtrey, debtor to Stephen Trigg. 1766, October —.

William Grahams, debtor to James Redeck.—1766, May.

Elijah McClenachan, Sr., debtor to Wm. Fleming.—Account for 1764, including a journey to Mr. Poage's.

November, 1767 (E).

Edwards vs. McCutchen and wife.—A memorandum of a bargain made between Andrew Duncan and David Edwards: That the above Andrew Duncan, of Augusta County, has bargained with David Edward, clothier, late of the County aforesaid, for him to set up a fulling mill, with all the utensils for to work with belonging to the trade, or mystery, of a fuller, &c., &c.

And said Andrew Duncan is to vittle the said David Edwards during the space of three years, in which the said David Edwards is to enter upon the premises, and said Andrew Duncan is to pay to said David Edwards £60 at the expiration of the time, £30 in money and £30 in cattle. The said David Edwards is to learn the said Andrew Duncan and one of his own family the mystery, or trade, of a fuller in the terms above mentioned, and Edwards is to have a house raised for his wife. (Signed) Andrew Duncan, David (his mark) Edwards. 6th March, 1760. Test, David Syer, James Pollock.

August, 1768 (A).

I, William Hays, do hereby impower and authorize Israel Christian to be my lawful attorney for me, my heirs, &c., to sue for, collect, and receive from George Paris, late of this Colony, but now of Carolina, the sum, &c., &c. (Signed) Wm. (his mark) Hays. 6th June, 1768. Test, Francis Smith, Daniel McNeill. Account above assigned is viz: Bedford County. George Paris to William Hays, debtor. 1761. Sundries. To two lbs. powder and four lbs. lead; to 69 days' waggoning in the campaign at 2/6 per day. Sworn to, 16th May, 1765, in Bedford County. Sworn to, 6th June, 1768, in Augusta.

Dunn vs. Burnsides.—William Dennis, account against James Burnsides.

John Campbell vs. William Anderson.—1767, to malling rails, sawing plank. 1767, credit, by Jerry Edwards, by the schoolmaster, by paying mother, by paying Thomas, by paying John Graham. Received by William.

March, 1768 (D).

William Allison vs. William Fleming, son-in-law of James Ryburn, Augusta. 1763. Account. Sworn to in King George County, 31st March, 1767, before James Buchanan.

Henry Dougherty, debtor to Thomas Wilson.—1764, November. Sworn to in Augusta, 20th November, 1766.

Timothy Roark, debtor to John Hite.—1750. Sundries. 1751. Credits, 1751: September 5, by David Vance; July 28, by George Wright.

Fulton vs. Mann.—Fort Defiance, August 28, 1764. Sir:—Please pay to William Fulton £4, 15, 0, for a rifle gun, and you will much oblige, sir, your humble servant. (Signed) Thomas Mann. To Capt. Walter Cunningham.

May, 1767 (D).

August 8, 1765.—Rene Laforce's deposition (aged about 42). In 1764 he ordered Robert Cauthon to deliver to Joseph Martin an obligation of Mathew Lindsey's, payable to Rene. Before Joseph Woodson and William Miller. August 8, 1765, Agnes Laforce's deposition (aged about 40). August 8, 1765, Robert Cauthon's deposition (aged about 29 years). August 14, 1765, William Ford's deposition (aged about 64 years). August 14, 1765, George Chowning's deposition (aged about 32 years).

Cabell vs. Bowen.—Augusta, ss: This day Malcom Allen came before me, John Dickison, one of his Majesty's Justices of the Peace for the County aforesaid, and on his oath sayeth that he went with Moses Bowen to Dr.

William Cabell, and that he, the said Allen, informed Dr. Cabell that his instructions from said Moses Bowen's father was to make a certain agreement with said Doctor, viz: How much his charge must be if he performed a cure upon said Moses Bowen, and how much his charge will be if he missed making a cure, and said Dr. William Cabell answered and said that as said Moses received his wound in defense of his country and in his Majesty's service, the country would pay him, the said Doctor, and that his, the said Moses's father, nor mother, nor uncle, nor aunt, had nothing to do with it; and I said: Then I had nothing more to do with it, and some time afterwards said Moses came to my house, and I went with him down to the Doctor, and the Doctor then informed me that his charge was £15, some shillings and pence. (Signed) John Dickison. 18th March, 1767. Same witness continues, 19th March, 1767: Moses Bowen informed me in his lifetime that Dr. Cabell yoused him very kindly during his continuance with him, and also that he in that time, by the Doctor's direction, went to the river to wash his wound, but instead thereof he swimmed over, and upon his coming back the waters went into his body, and was in danger, but he was preserved by the help of a canoe. Said Moses was of age when he went first to Dr. Cabell; to the best of knowledge he was of age the April before he went to said Doctor. (Signed) John Bowyer.

August, 1768 (A).

Gore vs. Phillips.—Articles of agreement, and concluded this the 22d day of January, 1766, between Joseph Goare, of Frederick County, of the one part, and the subscribers of the other part. Witness that the said Goare, schoolmaster, for my part, doth covenant and agree to and with the said gent., subscribers, to teach their said children, if committed to my care, according to their capacities in reading, writing and arithmetic and all other Christian principles in my power, and if the said master should lose any of the said term of time within the term of twelve months, commencing, it shall be made up at the end of the year. In consideration, we, the said subscribers, do hereby covenant and agree to and with the said master to give him the sum of £1, 3, 0, per scholar, where we are bound each to either in the penalty of £50, as witness our hands the day and year above mentioned. (Signed) Jos. Goare, An. Bird (2), John Blizard (2), Andrew Huling (4), Robert Oneal (2), John Philips (2), Tim Ororke, Sr. (2), Henry Goare (2), John Blizard (1 more), Andrew Huling (1), John Philips (1).

November, 1767 (E).

Bledsoe vs. Herbert.—1765. The estate of Robert Andrews to Anthony Bledsoe, debtor: January 26, to liquor lost with Shay, charged at store at Dunkard Bottom, viz: Various items. Stone House, November 15, 1766. Sir:—I omitted giving you my account with Andrew, which is justly £6, 10, 0. I judge the step to be taken my advice is to serve a writ on the administrators. I therefore beg you will be so kind as to have a writ served in your hands for that sum if it should be agreeable with the law. Your trouble shall be thankfully acknowledged by, sir, your very humble servant. (Signed) Anthony Bledsoe. To Mr. William Herbert.

465

Edm'd. O'Neal, debtor for your son, Isam O'Neal, to Israel Christian—1766. Account.

1764. Andrew Kline, debtor to Michael Gross—July 18, to half pipe of Teneriff wine, £12, 0, 0. Sworn to in Lancaster County, Pennsylvania, 30th November, 1765.

AUGUST, 1767 (D).

Roanoke, Augusta.—James Carty, debtor, to David Bryan, deceased: To one pair buckskin breeches, £1.10.0. Sworn to, March 19th, 1767, by Elizabeth Bryan, administratrix.

Randal Lockhart, debtor to Mathew Read and Hugh Johnson.—1767. To one pack of cards.

MARCH, 1768 (E).

Jones vs. Hughes.—Winchester, November 11, 1763. Dear Sir:—I have settled with Mr. Heath, but to my great grief have not been enabled to discharge the balance due you on account of the deceased debtor, Johnson. As that money should by no means have been detained, I will take it as a singular favor if you'll be easy in the affair, as it will not be beneficial to the estate and troublesome to you to bring suit, and you may depend I'll have it discharged ere you could recover it by law. I am extremely obliged to you for keeping it secret, as I would by no means have it made public. If you would share (spare) the money to the estate, I'd gladly pay you interest for your money, and most gratefully acknowledge myself unfeignedly, dear sir, your most obliged humble servant. (Signed) Alexander Love (for Alexander Boyd). To Lieut. William Hughes, Winchester.

MAY, 1767 (D).

Skileron vs. Graham.—Mr. William Grymes, debtor to John Skileron. Account 1761–1762. Sworn to in Chesterfield before Peter Johnston.

Archer vs. Wilson.—Ephraim Wilson deposes, 10th April, 1766, in Augusta: That he went to William Wilson's, on Jackson's River, with Mr. John Archer in 1756 or 1757. John Warrick was at the house at the time and employed there.

Thompson vs. Watterson.—In pursuance and by virtue of Act of Parliament made and appointed for the more effectual transportation of felons and convicts out of Great Britain into his Majesty's plantations in America, I do hereby assign unto Cockran and Heart, their heirs or assigns, a convict names Agnes Lyons, within the said statutes, to serve for the term of seven years from 3d day of October, 1763, being the day of arrival in Virginia. (Signed) Capt. Thomas Allong. (Endorsed) John Cockran and Heart to George Earnest. George Earnest to William Watterson. Hanover, September 19, 1764.—Ann Lyon, a convict, servant from London, was imported in the Beverley, Captain Allan, and arrived in Rappahannock River, Virginia, sometime in the latter end of October, 1763. The original convictions and general goal delivery are to be seen in the hands of James Miller, merchant, in Port Royal, but there being only one made out for every separate goal, renders it impossible to send it along with each servant. (Signed) Robert Hart.

Christian vs. Mann.—This, my note, shall oblige me to pay unto Mr. William Mann, at the rate of fifty pounds a year, for whatever time he shall be by me employed to assist in Indian trade, hunting, or whatever service he shall be by me directed to perform. Given under my hand, at Staunton, the 19th day of February, 1762. (Signed) Israel Christian. Test, W. Christian. I do promise that if I keep any hands employed in the above service the whole year, William Mann shall be preferred and kept as long as any other in said service, he complying as well as he can with my directions. (Signed) Israel Christian. February 19, 1762.

Looney vs. Patterson.—Robert Looney, debtor to Irvin Patterson's estate. 1745-46. May 10, to sundry goods to Elizabeth Looney, one looking glass, balance due Robert Looney, per settlement. 1744. Credits: By bond for a horse given this year; by ten years' ferriage, per agreement, at 20/ per annum. Settlement of above accounts, 16th January, 1766, by Benjamin Hawkins, James Rowland.

Kent vs. Love.—Jacob Kent vs. Philip Love.—Hugh Crocket deposes, 3d November, 1768, before William Preston: That before Mr. Love settled at Vanse's the plaintiff agreed with the deponent to winter a number of hogs for him; that the fences on said plantation were in very bad order and not lawful, but that the hogs went there before Mr. Love settled on it; that deponent frequently found Daniel McCoy, a servant man belonging to deponent, hunting said hogs; then a gang of hogs came from there to deponent's father's.

Alexander Herron vs. Patrick Quin.—Ejectment. Daniel Harrison, aged about sixty-six or seven, deposes: That he was present when Col. James Wood, then surveyor of the County of Orange (now Augusta), ran off the lands in dispute, and that the first line run by Thomas Lewis this day extends as far, etc., the corner of Samuel Wilkins, and that of Green & Co., under whom said Wilkins claims he has ever since been well acquainted with the lands, etc.; that the lines were not marked until the patent issued, and the reason Wood gave for it was that when he was about to survey the same, he himself was damned drunk and the rest concerned were in same condition, etc. (Signed) Daniel Harrison. 16th December, 1767. John Craven deposes, same time and place (aged forty-five, or thereabouts): He was present when Col. James Wood surveyed the land in dispute, now upwards of 22 years. William Gregg, aged thirty or thereabouts, deposes, same time and place: Samuel Wilkins is dead. Daniel Smith, gent., aged about thirty-seven years: About 12 years ago he was appointed a processioner with John Harrison. Daniel Harrison's additional deposition, 17th December, 1767: He and Alexander Herron bought 200 acres of Samuel Wilkins. Wilkins, after conveying to Herron, found he did not have 100 acres more for deponent and then cancelled the bargain, for which John Wilkins, son of Samuel, paid Harrison £5. Thomas Lewis deposes: That about 1745, talking with Col. James Wood about the difficulty of finding corners on protracted plots when the survey afterwards came to be made, said Wood told this deponent how lucky he had been in a matter of this kind in a plot that he had made for McCay, Hite and Green, on the waters of Cook's Creek, for that he had only run the lines along the courses of the creek and protracted all the other lines and supposed corners which, where an actual survey was made by him after the patent issued, he found trees agreeable to most of the supposed corners which he had mentioned in the protracted plat, or nearly corresponding thereto, which deponent afterwards found to be the case on a survey made by him to determine a suit formerly depending between the said parties. This day Patrick Quin came, etc., and says that Capt. Daniel Harrison is very ailing; he is afraid that he will soon change his natural life, as he doth believe that he will die very soon. (Signed) Abraham Smith. 18th June, 1767. Elaborate survey and description of the lands by Thomas Lewis

MAY, 1753.

Cockrane and Taylor vs. Henry Taylor.—1749, September. Endorsed: There was one of the name, but he has been deceased two years ago, and his wife denies that ever he had any of the articles, so not executed per me. (Signed) John Lewis. Summons dated 29th November, 1752, and note says "Lower end of County on South River."

MARCH, 1771 (B).

Leister's Administrator vs. Hughes's Administrator.—Chancery. Bill filed 1770. Orator, Samuel Cawdon: Shows that in year 175– James Leister, of Staunton, trader, deceased, bought lot No. ——, in Staunton, from James Hughes, —— holder of Staunton, deceased, for £25. James Leister died intestate before deed made; administration was granted to David Stewart (now deceased), Walter Cawdon and orator. Administration applied to Hughes for a conveyance to them personally to secure to them a debt due by Leister to them, and they paid all the purchase money but £8. Then James Hughes died intestate; Widow Euphemia qualified executrix. James left heirs, Jane and Mary Hughes, his daughters. In February, 1757, David Stewart also departed this life. Administration was granted Lewis and Mathews, who relinquished to orator all David's claim to the lot. He now demands a conveyance from Hughes's representatives.

MAY, 1753.

This bill bindeth us, Ralph (his "R. H." mark) Hughes and Richard ("R. S.") Sherley, both of Augusta County, to pay, or cause, etc., unto Mathias Celzar, etc. 15th March, 1750–51. Test, Peter Scholl, Samuel Newman.

MARCH AND PART OF MAY, 1753.

1751.—Thomas Hughes, debtor by H. Hardine's and T. Hill's recommendation to William Cunningham. October 4, 3½ pewter dishes, 5/10; one leghorn hat, 6/; three yards kersey, at 3/6; ten ells oznabrs., at 1/2.

May, 1762 (B).

Patterson vs. Hughes.—James Hughes's note to George Patterson, 3d March, 1761.

March, 1771 (B).

John Stewart vs. James Lockhart.—1754. Amount of George Brown's account. 1755—From William Williams. To Charles Stringham's account, one coat making for your son, William; one coat making for Randal.

May, 1749.

I promise to pay unto Edward Hughes, or order, the, etc. (Signed) John Flood. 21st October, 1747. Test, Morgan Bryan.

September, 1747.

Hughes vs. Sawyers and Cowan.—We jointly and severally promise to pay William Hughes, etc., for value received January 1, 1746, and when said money is paid, said Hughes is to return to William Sawyers one silver watch which he leaves in his hands to counter secure the aforesaid sum. (Signed) William Sawyers, James Cowan. Test, Andrew Kenny. Received from William Hughes, after the perfection of the above note, Capt. John Smith's note, payable to Patrick Dowdall, deceased, for £1, which sum I promise to pay said Hughes, or order, on demand, or return the said note. Witness my hand. (Signed) William Sawyers. January 1, 1746.

March, 1758.

Valentine Guile vs. Patrick Martin.—Patrick Martin, debtor, to fifteen days' services ranging under your command of my sons, Gabriel, Jacob, and George Guile, at 1/ per day each. (Signed) Valentine Guile.

May, 1761 (A).

Gray vs. Hughes.—I do promise to pay, etc., unto Hugh Gray, etc., £3.7.6 and a good buckskin, current money of Pennsylvania, etc. (Signed) James Hughes. 29th October, 1752. Test, Thomas Hall, who makes affidavit, 24th October, 1758, in York County, Pa.

JUDGMENTS SUFFERED.

August, 1769.

Webber vs. Dailey.—John Dailey. 1741.—Balance due for corn lent you. 1744.—Sundries; to serving warrant on John Barnet. 1747.—for your daughter. Contra: 1747.—By Pottecory's drugs. by Samuel Mosby, 3/; by John Lewis, 11/0; errors excepted, February 16, 1750, by me. (Signed) Augustine Webber. A copy. Test: Valentine Wood, Colonel Curd. 1768. Sworn to before Joseph Pollard, 15th August, 1768, by Margaret Webber.

Lewis vs. Martin.—5th January, 1758. Thomas Young, with consent of father, Hugh Young, binds himself for three years to Benjamin Lewis, shoemaker, to learn cord waining.

AUGUST, 1750.

1737.—James Cathey to Samuel Smith, debtor: September 22. 1736.—October 23, Mr. Adam Thompson, debtor to same, January 18. William Robinson's account, debtor to Samuel Smith, 1739—April 4, one almanac. Richard Wood's ditto, ditto, 1738. Mrs. Margaret McDowell, ditto, 1737—June 14. Mrs. Mary McDowell, ditto, 1737—January 17, three yards ribbon to sister. Mr. Michael Woods, ditto, 1738—October 7, one dozen catechisms. 1739—Credit by six foxes, seven raccoons, and one beaver. John Maxwell, ditto. Samuel Woods, ditto. 1734—11¼ yards masquerade, 31/; 7½ yards sagathee, 32/6. 1735—June 26, credit by 36/ discounted with his son, Richard, by Michael Woods. Michael Woods, formerly of Pextunk, ditto, 1733—February 12; 1734—March 28. Francis Beaty, ditto, 1735—October 16, To 2/4½ in goods more than J. Catherwood's order; 1738—May 1, Credit by William Smiley. John Christian, ditto, 1737—February 22, To James Cook for a gunlock. Robert Christian, ditto, 1733–1734–1735–1736—Account; 1733—Credit by order on Treasury for two wolfs' heads; 1734—August 17, By making a coat and britches, 13/; 1736—Credit, October 13, by cash of John; by James Boyle; 1748-9—February 17, Then Robert Christian paid me £1.13.4 Virginia money in part of above debt. (Signed) William Anderson. Samuel Doak, ditto, balance of account given in. Randall McDaniel, ditto. William Hutchinson, ditto. George Hutchinson, ditto. Robert Cunningham, ditto. Alexander Crawford's note, ditto. Above accounts sworn to, 13th October, 1743, in Philadelphia County, Pa., by Samuel Smith, late of Lancaster County. Thomas Renick deposes: On 1st September, 1750, in Staunton, in cause Smith vs. Beatey, that about eight years ago, at his own house, he saw Smith, the plaintiff, and Robert Buchanan, the then sheriff of Lancaster County, and Smith acknowledged having attached and sold Beatey's effects and received satisfaction.

AUGUST, 1764 (B).

Cresap vs. Walker.—Debtor Dr. Thomas Walker: 1755—March 17, To 54 ells of oznabrigs for bags; paid for making 20 bags, 10/; thread, 1/6. March 19, paid William Ives for carriage of 10 horseloads of flour to Fort Cumberland; paid Notley Pigman for water carriage of 87½ bushels of wheat, weight 5,250 pounds, at 3/. March 21, paid Edmond Martin for carriage of 24½ bushels of wheat, weight 1,400 pounds, at 3/; paid James Hayton for carriage of 40 bushels of wheat, weight 2,400 pounds, at 3/. March 28, paid Daniel Lynn for carriage of 12 casks of flour; paid Daniel Lynn for carriage of 33 pounds wheat; to 21 yards oznabrigs for bags; paid for making of six bags, 3/, thread, 6d.; paid William Ives for carriage of 16 horseloads of flour to Fort Cumberland; paid Nathan Triggs for water carriage of 38 bushels wheat; paid Nathan Triggs for water carriage of 200 pounds of flour; paid William Triggs for water carriage of 35½ bushels wheat; paid William Reynolds for water carriage of 39¾ bushels of wheat. April 7, paid William Wiggins for water carriage of 38 bushels of wheat. April 8, paid Samuel Hayton for water carriage of 30 bushels of wheat; paid Samuel Hayton for water carriage of 2 casks of flour. April 17, paid Zebulon Robinet for water carriage of 6 casks of flour and 19¼ bushels of wheat; paid John Crisp for materials for the flat. April 26, paid Isaac Crumwell per your order. May 7, paid William Williams for water carriage of 58 bushels of wheat; paid Joseph Flint's order on you. May 26, paid Vann Swearingen for wintering 20 wagon horses purchased by Governor Sharp for his Majesty's service; paid William Reynolds for water carriage of 2,388 pounds of flour, at 3/. Maryland, Frederick County, to wit: June 30, 1762. Sworn to by Thomas Cresap, gent, before Thomas Norris. Certificate with seal by John Darnall, clerk, that Thomas Norris "is one of his Lordships the Right Honorable the Lord Proprietory his Justices of the Peace" for Frederick County. Castle Hill, September 30, 1760. Sir: Your favor of ye 30th of August came to hand the other day. The contents thereof surprises me, I suppose, as much as Mrs. Hoops's answer did you. I shall not at present enter into the justness, or reasonableness, of the account, as I presume that is out of the question. You, I make no doubt, are sensible the money ought to have been paid by the Crown, and I should have thought your experience from the year 1755 would have convinced you that it was necessary to apply either before or at the time the Commissioners settled the accounts for the campaign of 1758, as no regard has been paid to any accounts that were not brought in before such settlements of any campaign were finished. As to your seeking justice in Virginia, I presume no Court, or jury, can be of opinion that I am to pay the debts due from the Crown which remain unpaid from the neglect of the creditors. Could I assist you I should with the greatest pleasure, but as I cannot, must leave you to take any method you may think just and most likely to recover your due. I am, your most humble servant, (Signed) Thomas Walker. Col. Thomas Cresap, the Old Town, Maryland. James Heaton's receipt to Thomas Cresap, 21st March, 1755, £3.12.0. Edmond Martin's (mark) receipt to Thomas Cresap, 21st March, 1755, £2.2.0. William Frigg's receipt to Thomas Cresap, 28th March, 1755, £2.12.0. John Crisp's order on Mr. Thomas Walker, Commissary, 13th April, 1755. William Williams's receipt .(Test, Jarvis Hougham.) Isaac Cromwell's order. Notley Pigman's receipt. William Reynold's receipt. William Wigins's receipt. William Ives's receipt. William Reynold's receipt. Zebulon Robinet's receipt. Daniel Linns's receipt. Nathan Trigg's receipt. Joseph Flint's receipt. Samuel Haton's receipt. I do certify that sixty head of beef cattle and fifty head of sheep, bought by the contractors for the use of the forces under the command of Col. George Washington, were grazed upon the plantation of Col. Thomas Cresap, at Old Town, from the 15th of July to the 15th of September, inclusive. (Signed) Joseph Galbreath, assistant to the contractors. Fort Cumberland, September 21, 1758. Attachment against Thomas Walker, addressed to sheriff of Augusta, to answer Thomas Cresap, dated 17th February, in second year of our reign. Daniel Linn's receipt. William Ives's receipt. March 1, 1764.—Van Swearinger, Sr., deposes before Joseph Smith, James Smith, Justices for Frederick County, Maryland, aged seventy years, or thereabouts: That on

25th May, 1755, the deponent attended Dr. Thomas Walker, who, he understood, was the King's commissary, with an account for wintering 20 wagon horses, which horses were sent him by Col. Thomas Cresap, who informed him that the said horses were the King's and were purchased by the Governor of Maryland of Mr. Robert Callender, and ordered by the Governor to him, the said Cresap, to have them wintered. Some time in the spring the said horses, with the wagons, which were ordered away from his house by Dr. Thomas Walker, without acquainting him at the time to whom he was to apply for the payment of his account, on which he applied to Colonel Cresap, as he had sent the horses to him, who went with the deponent to Fort Cumberland on the day and date above mentioned, where was Dr. Thomas Walker, to whom the deponent presented his account, which the said commissary perused and made no objection to any part thereof, but told him they had not cash at that time to discharge it, but that as soon as Colonel Washington came up from Virginia, by whom he expected a sum of money, he would pay the account. The deponent informed them that as he lived at a great distance, and it would put him to considerable trouble to be coming after his money, he should for the future expect his money from Colonel Cresap, who he looked upon to be liable to him for it, upon which Dr. Walker desired Colonel Cresap to pay me the money, the amount of which was £30.17.0, which sum the Colonel payed me the next day. Agreeable to his request for which I gave a receipt and never received anything for the same but from Colonel Cresap. (Signed) Van Swearingen, Sr.

ADVERTISEMENT.

Philadelphia, January 31, 1756. Whereas, Application hath been made to his Excellency, General Shirley, on behalf of the owners of the wagons, teams, carriages, horses, and other things contracted for and employed in his service under the late General Braddock; and his said Excellency, General Shirley, having given orders for the settling and discharging all such accounts as yet remain unsatisfied for the said wagons, teams, horses, etc.; and Edward Shippen, Samuel Morris, Alexander Stedman, and Samuel McCall, Jr., Esqs., being, by the directions of the said General Shirley, commissioned and appointed to audit, adjust, and settle the said accounts in conjunction with Robert Leake, Esq., commissary to his Majesty's forces in North America; notice is hereby given that the said Robert Leake, with the said commissioners, will attend at Lancaster, from the third until the thirteenth day of February next, both inclusive, for the settling, adjusting, and discharging all accounts and demands relative to the said wagoners, horses, and other things. When and where all persons concerned are hereby required to appear with their several accounts and contracts (and their proofs and vouchers) relating to the premises, in order to have the same settled and paid by Robert Leake, commissary. Lancaster, 13th February, 1756. The said commissioners and commissary will attend at Philadelphia, where all persons are desired to come immediately who have any demands as above. (Signed) R. Leake, commissary.

November, 1767 (B).

Daniel Pierce and wife, Ketren, vs. George Bowman's Estate.—1764, account.

Thomas Fulton vs. Vallintine Sevier.—November, 1756–1757. June 30, two bales bumbo and two nips bumbo.

MAY, 1767 (B).

We, John (mark) Roberts and Robert (mark) Brown promise to pay to William Mathews, sadler, etc., 23d September, 1765. Test, Fanney Mathews.

Robert Looney debtor to estate of Irwin Patterson.—1745–1746, May 10, Elizabeth Looney. 1744—Credit by 10 years' ferriage at 20/ per year.

NOVEMBER, 1767 (B).

William Simpson and Betty, his wife, administrators of Malcom Campbell, deceased, debtor to Mary McDonald, administratrix of Edward McDonald. 1748–1752–1753—Tanning and currying leather.

Captain Payne's order on Lieutenants Farrar and McClenachan.—Mr. Abel Farror, debtor to John Payne, to one mare (mair), £10.0.0. Mr. Ellix. McClenachan, to one coat, £3.17.6. August 15, 1760. Gent: As I am not intended out on the expedition I shall not have an opportunity of seeing either of you. Should esteem it a favor, very particular, if you'll be kind enough to pay the above accounts to Captain Merridith. His receipt shall be your discharge from yours, etc., (Signed) John Payne.

Pritt vs. Powell.—October the 19th day, 1763. An agreement made between Honorius Powell and Robert Prit, the said Robert Prit is to have one plantation, joining the William Riddle, for forty shillings, or four hundred pounds of good tobacco. The said Robert Prit is to have no part of the peach orchard, but eating peaches, and to dry for his one family's use; and to keep all creatures from harming the orchard; and is to build one good cabin to live in, twenty feet long and sixteen feet wide, upon his own cost and charge. Witness our hands. (Signed) Honorius Powell, Robert (mark) Prit. Test, James Beazley, John (mark) Ogg.

Col. David Stewart, deceased, debtor to Mathew Read and Hugh Johnston. 1764, September 28. 1765, February 1, per daughter; June 14, per son, John. 1766, April 21, per son, John.

Tatham vs. Darr.—George Inglebird, creditor to John Tatham: To making a table with four divisions in the drawer, £0.15.0; to making a bedstead, £0.7.6; to mending a chest, £0.1.0. Augusta, 23d October, 1767. John Tatham makes oath before William Preston of justness of above account and that credit ought to be given on his note to George Inglebird.

James Leatherdale to Stephen Trigg, debtor.— 1766, June 6, to assumed for your son, James.

Payne vs. McClenachan.—Sir: Please to pay Captain Meridith for the match coat you received of me at the Dunkers' Bottom. (Signed) Alexander McClenachan. To Captain Nathaniel Gist.

Augusta County, to wit: Whereas, Complaint has this day been made to me by the Rev. John Kingkade that on Wednesday, the 22d day of this instant, about twelve of the clock at night, when he and his family were in bed and asleep, they were awakened by a noise out of ye house, upon which Mrs.

Kingkade rose up and looking out saw two men which, to the best of her knowledge, she says was Robert Nox and William Hamilton, dressed in women's clothes, on which she asked what they wanted, they making no answer, ran against the door and made several attempts to beat it open, but finding they could not, they pulled a table cloth out of the window, or hole in the house, and after tearing it to pieces, went off. As the said John Kingkade and wife, fearing they did intend some harm to their estate, or lives, and will still pursue their intended wickedness, these are, in his Majesty's name, to command you to take the said Robert Nox and William Hamilton and bring them before me, or some other justice of the peace for this County to answer the said complaint. Fail not to execute this warrant at your peril, and make due return thereof. Given under my hand this 21st day of April, 1766. (Signed) William Bowyer. To any sworn officer to execute and return.

MARCH, 1767.

Thomas Dun, debtor to John Brown.—Living at John Draper's on head-waters of Peek Creek.

Campbell vs. Kinkead.—The Rev. John Kinkead, debtor to John Campbell. March 1, 1766, Sundries; cash lent to Mrs. Kinkead.

Reed and Johnson vs. Jones.—Rev. John Jones, debtor. 1765–1766. John Henderson's Estate, debtor to William Fleming.—1764.

MAY, 1763 (B).

Felix Gilbert, debtor to John Bowyer. To the Board of your storekeeper, Thomas Bowyer, from the 1st December, 1758, to the 1st of August, 1760, being one year and eight months, at £15. To three months do. of your other storekeeper, James McDowell, at £15 per annum.

NOVEMBER, 1767 (B).

1764.—Michael Harper, debtor to William Christian. August 23, to James Bodkin; August 27, to Abram Hempenstall; to David Fraime; to Vance and Doake; to Lieut. William McCutcheon; to Edward Hynds; August 30, to Lieut. William McCutcheon; to James McCutcheon; to John Millar; to Thomas Rhoads; to William Black; September 4, to Jean Graham; to Francis Evick for funeral expenses. Contra: 1764, September 4, by 42 days in service, at 1/6; by part of John Miller's order rejected; by part of Rhoads' order rejected; by part of William Black's order rejected; by part of Jean Graham's order rejected; by bounty.

MAY, 1767 (B).

Findley vs. Lewis.—Col. John Lewis to Robert Findlay, debtor. 1752, December 13, sundries to ye Dutchman, to yourself, per Mrs. Peggey, per self, to Mr. John, to ye boy, per Mrs. Peggey, at Mr. Cunningham's, at Mr. Williams's, at Mr. Brown's, at Mr. Cunningham's, your assumtion for John Stoffelmier, your assumtion for George Baer, one satikis, cash lent at Mr. Long's. Contra: By 1800 of said (8d) nails.

Quarles vs. Thompson.—To Mr. John Thompson, Tinkling Springs. Sir: I would very freely, according to your request, have sent you the money for the proven account if I had had it, but I have it not at present, but as soon as I possibly can get it, depend on it I'll bring, or send, to you. This from your friend and humble servant. (Signed) Edward Thompson. December the 21st, 1765.

Hill vs. McCormack.—Sir: Please to pay Appleona Wall three pounds ten shillings when my pay comes to your hand, and oblige, your humble servant. (Signed) Daniel (?) McCormick. To Capt. David Robinson. August 11, 1764.

Stephenson vs. McClenachan.—We promise to pay to John McVea, etc., to be paid against the time I receive the first of my pay for ranging, etc. (Signed) Josias (mark) Fugett, George Anderson. 23d April, 1764. Assigned, 23d April, 1764, to Adam Stephenson. Received of Alexander McClenachan £1.5.3 in part of ye within this 4th day of December, 1765. Alexander McClenachan, debtor. To your assumption to pay me out of Josiah Fugett's pay £3.15.0. Credit, by cash in part, £1.5.

NOVEMBER, 1767 (B).

Harper vs. Christian.—Capt. William Christian, debtor to Mathew Harper, administrator to Michael Harper. To his bounty as a soldier, £2; to his pay as a soldier, £0.19.0. Credit, by cash paid Francis Evick for funeral charges, £1.5.0.

NOVEMBER, 1764.

Crawford vs. Cassety.—Deposition in Rowan County, North Carolina, of George Felton, relating to a contract in 1761 of James Huston and James Crawford, to rent a plantation in Augusta from Jonas Henderson. They engaged Thomas Cassety to crop it, which he failed to do. Dated, 15th October, 1764.

Herron vs. Harrison (Samuel Harrison vs. Alexander Herron).—Alexander Herron's answer says: That complainant removed from the province of —— at the time and for the purpose mentioned in his bill, and moved to Virginia and settled on Linville's Creek, where he took up 400 acres. Some time afterwards defendant came to Virginia, and hearing of complainant, proceeded to that settlement, thinking that as they were acquainted in the government from which they removed, complainant could direct him to a convenient tract of land. Complainant allowed him to take up an entry of his own of 200 acres, adjoining his own land. At that time the best lands on the creek could be purchased for £3 per hundred acres. That at the time of Braddock's defeat complainant took it into his head to remove to Carolina. Robert Harrison was complainant's nephew.

JUNE, 1764 (B).

Fillbrick vs. Bullett.—1762, July 15. Capt. Thomas Bullett, in account with Henry Fillbrick, debtor. To serving in your company as a soldier from this date till the 8th day of December, being 146 days, at 8d per day, £4.17.4; to a suit of regimental clothes, with a hat, shirt, shoes, and stockings. E:

Excepted. (Signed) Henry Fillbrick. Augusta County, to wit: Henry Fillbrick complains of Thomas Bullett, gent, etc., for that whereas the said defendant on the —— day of ——, 1762, at the County aforesaid, was indebted to the plaintiff, etc., for certain work, labor, and services by the plaintiff in the vocation and employment of a soldier, etc., under the command and by the special appointment and direction of the said defendant, as Captain of the company in the Virginia Regiment, into which the plaintiff was duly enlisted, and being so indebted, etc. And whereas, the said plaintiff, on the 17th day of May, 1762, at the County aforesaid, was duly enlisted as a soldier to serve in the Virginia Regiment, and was drafted into the company commanded by said Bullett as Captain, by virtue whereof and by the laws and customs of the army and the particular establishment and regulations of the said regiment, he, the said Thomas, became bound to pay unto the said plaintiff, at the rate of eight pence for each day that he served in his company as a soldier, and also to give and deliver unto him one complete suit of clothes, or wearing apparel, according to the uniform of the same regiment. Plaintiff says he served from —— to ——. Defendant failed to pay and is sued.

NOVEMBER, 1762 (A).

Kenny vs. Smith.—Col. John Smith to John Kenny, debtor. 1760, to my wages four months under your command, £4. Sworn to by John Kenny, 26th May, 1762.

NOVEMBER, 1762.

Cowdon & Co. vs. Grant.—1761. Debtor, William Grant, late of the Virginia Regiment, to Samuel Cowdon & Co., June to July, account for rum, punch, bumbo, julip, whiskey, sangoree, £2.17.6.

Margaret Woods vs. Thomas Loyd.—Attachment on ground that Thomas has privately removed himself out of this County, or so absconds, etc. 3d September, 1762, executed on medicines; on Loyd's estate in land of James Hargrave.

NOVEMBER, 1762 (A).

Ball vs. Hamilton.—This bill bindeth me, John Hamilton, of Augusta, in Virginia, trader, etc., unto William Ball, of Philadelphia.

NOVEMBER, 1762.

Sayers vs. Baskins.—William Baskins to Alexander Sayers, debtor. To your pay as soldier in my company at Fort Ligonier from December till 1st March, 90 days, £4.10.0, paid you twice. (Signed) Alexander Sayers. Augusta, 18th February, 1762.

AUGUST, 1762.

Stuart vs. Lusk.—17th June, 1757. Received of James Hall, £2.5.0, part of County dues, 1753 and 1754. 25th November, 1754, received of Robert Hall, on account of his father's quit rents for year 1754.

Davis vs. Cowdon.—1761. Mr. Samuel Cowdon & Co. to Thomas Davis, debtor. To ferrying twelve wagons twice at New River, 24 times at 5/9 per time, £6.18.0; to one man and three horses twice, £0.5.0; to James Leister one horse four times, £0.3.4; to Samuel Cowdon one horse six times, £0.5.0.

AUGUST, 1762.

Robert Stevenson, Calfpasture, debtor to John Given.—1757. To sundries at Lafferty's Fort.

Herring vs. Fulton.—(Letter) To Mr. John Madison, These. Sir: As to a school in our neighborhood, it is entirely over. We did all we could, but every project has failed. We could get scholars, but no one would board save William Henderson, and he was not willing to take my son, although I kept his son since fall. I am sorry for our disappointment. If we could have kept Mr. Dalhouse one year longer, perhaps my son could supply his place. The offer you made him as to his wages he does not stand upon so much as the boarding of brother, which he will have to go whither he will. Sir, I wish you could agree with Mr. Dalhouse. I hope you are satisfied in ye progress in learning your son has made while here. You know the charge and inconvenience of sending children abroad. But I am not to persuade you to anything. As to my charge for keeping your son, it shall be as small as you please. He knows his entertainment was mean, but we did the best we could. Pray let me have answer by the bearer. I am in haste; the boys (?) are waiting. Sir, your very humble servant. (Signed) Edward Hall. April, 1762.

Smith vs. Leister's Administrator, James Leister, debtor.—1759. To ye half of three months and half's work at 40/, £3.10.0; to ye use of my horse and saddle from Cristeen to Staunton ye half, £1.0.0; to lining your coat and jacket by my wife, £0.4.6. Credit, by four pans of glass, at 1/, £0.4.0.

MAY, 1763 (B).

Heath vs. Blagg.—Henry Heath vs. Capt. John Blagg.—1761, to Daniel Mingus, per Robert Flude, per John Martin; per servant; to Larey; your order to Edw. Larry; to Margaret; to Sergt. Creaugh per verbal order; to your order to Edw. Larry; sent by John Cain. 1761, to your order to Jos. Hix; to your order to Benj. Norwood; to credit Sergt. John Creaugh; to your order to Jude Ellson; to your order to Bonny and McIntire; to your order to Wm. Brumley; to your order to Abram Childers; to your order to Edward Childs; to rum to the butchers; per Cain; by Jas. Butler; by John McVicker; by Scot; per token of your keys; by Brown; per Butler to fishermen; per token of your keys; per Brown; per Mr. Long's order. Credit Nancy Warrener per verbal order; to butchers; to Sukey; to Sukey; to Sukey; per Nancy Warrener per token of snuffbox; per Jonas; to Sukey; delivered by John Murray; delivered by same; to Sukey; per Mr. Alex. Love; to Lieut. Bonner per verbal order; Club for yourself and Lieut. John Lawson; per Cliffton; to Kane; to club with Lieut. William Fleming; to your assumption for Thomas Drummer. 1762, for Sukey; per Hannah; to cash paid Widow

Tosh for you; for Sukey; for Sukey; on Mr. William Murray's caty. night. To your account at Winchester: To sundry orders to the soldiers, viz: 1762, July 15, to your order to William Adams for half pint rum; to Bradburry, Minzie, and Richardson, half pint rum each; to your order to John Kane. July 24, to your order to Serg. John Creaugh; to your order to Jenkins and Null. July 27, to your order to James Bradbury; to your order to Thomas Hall. July 29, to your order to Edmond Larrey. July 31, to your order to John Grant; to your order to Abram Childers. August 2, to your order to Callan and Harrington; to Thomas Hall; to your order to John Gahagan. August 3, to your order to John Jenkins; to your order to John Gahagan. August 5, to your order to John Reeves (twice); to your order to John Caine. August 7, to your order to Samuel Shaw and Reeves; to your order to Thomas Neill. August 10, to your order to Edmond Larrey. August 15, to your order to Joseph Hix. August 20, to your order to Edward Childers; to your order to Harrington, Richardson and Jones. August 22, to your order to Edward Childs. August 29, to your order to Daniel McIntire and Childs. August 30, to your order to Jenkins and Neill; to your order to Jeremiah Harrington, to your order to George Reed; to your order to Terrall and Robertson; to your order to William Thorp; to your order to William Brock; to your order to Jenkins and Neill; to your order to Norwood, Brumley and Caine. August 31, to your order to Abram Shaw, ditto William Wright; (From Wright's name the date is 1761, but should be 1762.) to your order to Joseph Hughes, ditto William Broke (twice); to Samuel Jackios; to your order to Terrence Sweeney. September 1, to your order to Robert Stewart, ditto Ann Thomas; to your order to Edward Carter. September 2, to your order to Elizabeth Callson, ditto William Cliffton; to your order to William Brock, ditto Robert Sinkfield; to your order to William McAnulty. September 3, to your order to Brumley and Thorp. September 4, to your order to Jonathan Hawkins; to your order to Daniel McIntire; to Harrington and Cullon; to your order to Robert Sinkfield, do. Edward Childs; to your order to James Williams, do. John Wilson; to your order to John Arnold, do. George Hill; to your order to Wentworth Allden; to your order to Henry Cowden; to your order to Thomas Harden; to your order to Cole, Gahagan, Bonney and Mingus. September 5, to your order to Benjamin Norwood. September 6, to your order to Nathaniel Barret and William Thorp. September 7, to your order to Thomas Hardy. September 8, to your order to Michael Gill. September 9, to your order to Thomas Hall, Thomas Thorp, and Barret; to your order to Bradburry and Mingus; to your order to William Cole, William Colson, Emanuel Anthony. September 10, to your order to Jude Ellson. September 11, to your order to Col. Moore's man. September 12, to your order to James Lowery. September 13, to your order to Wentworth Aldin, Norwood and Hughes; to your order to Joseph Hix, Lowery, and Robertson. September 14, to your order to James Williams, Lowery, and Bryan; to your order to Henry Emberson, Charles Travis; to your order to Richardson and Norwood, Joseph Hix; to your order to William Thorp, Daniel McIntire. September 15, to your order to Daniel McIntire and Robertson. September 16, to your order to Bryan and Cole, Elizabeth Colson. September 17, to your order to Bat Rann, Norwood and Ellston; to your order to Wright and Harrington, Robertson and Cole. September 20, to your order to Joseph Hix, Austen Brumley; to your order to

Abot and Norwood. September 21, to your order to Wright and Richardson, Bat Rann. September 22, to your order to Brumley and Harrington; to your order to Daniel McIntire, Lowery and Callan; to your order to Bat Runn, McVicker and Robertson; to your order to Rann and Norwood. September 24, to your order to Thomas and Austin Brumley, William Brumley. September 26, to your order to Hughes, Ellston, Harrington; to your order to Thorp and William; to your order to Abot and Wright. September 27, to your order to Richardson Austin, and Thomas Brumley; to your order to Calan and Harrington. October 2, to your order to Joseph Hix. October 29, to your order to James Butler. October 30, to your order to Joseph Hix, Robert Burns, John Callan; to your order to Thomas Thorp, John Cotter, Robert Burns. October 31, to your order to Reeves Jackaway and Brock, Lowery and Childs; to your order to Stephen Conner, John Callan; to your order to Edward Gills; to your order to James Downey, William Calston; to your order to Jonathan Hawkins; to your order to Colonel Waddle's man, John Cotter; to your order to Grant Harrington and Wright. The deposition of Mr. David Long, before William Preston, 25th February, 1763: That at Fort Lewis, at the return of the regiment after the campaign of 1761, Captain Blagg sent for the deponent, who came to where Captain Blagg was settling an account with John Skelton, clerk, to the said Henry Heath, for his (Captain Blagg's) mess. By which settlement it appeared that said deponent's part in said mess amounted to £5.10.0, which he desired Skelton to charge to him and that he would settle with him for it, which Skelton agreed to. After which the deponent always looked upon himself accountable to Mr. Heath for the charge, and that Captain Blagg did not charge said deponent with the above sum in his accounts on their settlement, and further saith not. (Signed) David Long.

NOVEMBER, 1762.

On demand we, the subscribers, of Augusta County, do promise to pay William Stamps, of Bedford County, the sum of seventeen shilling and seven pence, etc., 14th July, 1762. (Signed) James Mere (Mese), John Lewis. Test, Francis Thorp.

Jacob Kinney's account for the courthouse bell, Richmond.—1796, February 12. Mr. Jacob Kinney to John Taylor, debtor. A large bell for the use of the courthouse, Staunton, weighing 143 ton, at 3/, £21.9.0; oak head stock and letting the Crown into the same, £0.12.0; bolts, screws and other iron work to mount the same, £2.2.0; total, £24.3.0. Carriage, 11/. Received payment by the hands of Gamble and Temple. (Signed) John Taylor.

Printed circular, dated Richmond, January 20th, 1796: John Taylor, coppersmith, from Liverpool, returns his sincere thanks to a generous public for the very great encouragement given him in the making of his strong copper stills (and describes their advantages).

COUNTY COURT.

ORIGINAL PETITIONS AND ORDERS.

Bundle marked "Old papers not belonging to the office—Old patents, deeds, etc."

24th September, 1793.—Between Nathaniel Wilkinson, John Carter Littlepage and John Oliver, of first part, and John Hanger, of second part. Parties of first have sold to second (consideration, £10) one ticket, No. 52, for a lot of half an acre in the town of Hot Bath, established by an Act of Assembly at the Hot Springs, in Bath County. Drawing took place, 14th July, last, and John Hanger drew lot 38. Test: James William Mathews, Charles Tyler, Elijah Tenny, Benjamin Dickenson, Simon Gillespey.

Old papers, etc., vid p. 74 supra.

Arbitration bond between Joseph Byers, William Long, and Jane Blair, dated 1796. Report of Commissioners dividing land sold by Robert McCutchan to John Blair, and by him devised to his three sisters, Elizabeth, Mary and Jane. Elizabeth married Joseph Byers, Mary married William Long.

Jacksonville, Ill., 7th January, 1833. Letter by Nancy W. Horn, recommending Rev. Reddick Horn, whose daughter married Abram N. Mills, who has another wife in Virginia.

Letter of John George Butler (1800).

Grant to George Young, private, 1786, of land for military service, by the Supreme Executive Council of the Commonwealth of Pennsylvania, transferred by George to James Seawright.

John Culbert, of County Donegal, Ireland, to Andrew Erwin.—Power of Attorney to collect from James Lockhart, executor of William Buchanan.

Agreement between David Long and John Brown, cordwinder and servant of David, 1758. John agrees to make 200 pairs shoes (men's and women's) and six pairs boots, and to serve in any company of rangers.

Letter of Andrew Lewis, 1755.

Bundle marked "Old deeds, wills, etc.," County Court. Alexander Elliott and Ann Conway, his wife, to William Anderson, power of attorney to make deed and settlement with James Brent.

Bundle marked "Deeds not fully proved," County Court, 1710.—Carter, Peter Randolph, and Munford Beverley, agreement.

Bundle of old papers unmarked, County Court.—Sarah, wife of Ezekiel Gilliam. Margaret, wife of Samuel Davidson. Ann, wife of —— Barnet. Rebecca, wife of Joseph Forgay. Ruth, wife of John Davidson. Mary, wife of —— McKnight. Rachel, wife of —— McKnight.

Bundle of old papers unmarked, County Court.—John Alor and Mary, of Alethorp County, Georgia. John Hannan and Barbara, of Wilkes County, Georgia. Henry Poss (Pass) and Catharine, of Wilkes County, Georgia. Christian Poss and Susanna, of Wilkes County, Georgia. George Groan and Mardalene, of Wilkes County, Georgia. Lawrence Groan and Mary, of Wilkes County, Georgia.

Children and legal representatives, heirs and coporceners of Anthony Aylor, of Augusta County, deceased, to Phillip Zimmerman, of Lincoln County, Georgia, power of attorney, dated 1802.

Capt. James Frazier's return of officers.—To ye Worshipful Court of Augusta County: At the last regimental court martial, held at Mr. Peter Hanger's, where I resigned my commission, I received orders from that Court to divide my company, which consisted of one hundred and twenty men, rank and file. I had appointed a day for that purpose, and when ye people was convened, we proceeded to divide ye list into two companies, which was done, and each company did proceed to choose their officers by ballot. Ye party belonging to ye South River, etc., have chosen: Alexander Hall, captain; Andrew Fulton, lieutenant; Andrew Steel, junior ensign. And ye other party, consisting of ye Long Meadow and Chritian's Creek, in ye same manner elected their officers. Ye persons chosen for that purpose is as follows: Thomas Calbreth, captain; Robert Graham, lieutenant; Patterson Thomson, ensign. The above persons are recommended to this Worshipful Court of Augusta County, now sitting, so if it may consist with your wisdom to recommend ye above commissions. (Signed) James Frazier Captain. This 16th of December, 1794.

DECEMBER, 1790.

List of present justices. George Moffett, William Bowyer, Elijah Mc-Clenachan, Alexander St. Clair, Alexander Robertson, Thomas Hughart, Joseph Bell, John Tate, David Stephenson, Richard Mathews, Robert Porterfield, John McKemy, dead, James Ramsey, Robert Douthat, James Searight, James Berry, William McPheeters, James Steel (refused to act since he was sheriff), Samuel Vance, in Bath County; John Wilson, in Bath County; Charles Cameron, in Bath County; Robert Gamble, Richmond; Alexander Crawford, Rockbridge County; Alexander Gibson, Alexander Nelson, Joseph Bell, Jr., William Moffett, James Poage, Kentucky.

A list of the names and order of the Justices of the Peace for the County of Augusta, as they stand in the commisison dated, March 24, 1778, viz: Thomas Adams, John Poage, Alexander McClenachan, Alexander Robertson, John Lewis, William McPheeters, Peter Hanger, John Dickinson, George Moffett, William Bowyer, Thomas Hughart, Alexander St. Clair, James Steel, Samuel Vance, John Christian, Sampson Mathews, Michael Bowyer, Elijah McClenachan, John Kinkade, James Tate, John McCreery, James Bell, John Wilson. Additional commission, dated 28th April, 1785: David Stephenson, James Crawford, Jr., Jacob Warrick, Robert Gamble, Robert Porterfield, Richard Mathews, James Davis, John McKeeny. Additional commisison, dated 3d November, 1788: Alexander Nelson, James Searight, John White, John Lewis, Robert Douthat, William Moffett, James Berry, Joseph Bell, Jr., James Poage, John Peebles. Additional commission, 13th June, 1786: Zachariah Johnston, James Ramsey, James P. Cocke, James Stephenson, Alexander Gibson, Moses Hinkle.

Inquisition from Escheator of Rockingham. This indenture of an inquisition taken and made in pursuance of an Act, entitled an Act concerning Escheators at the Court House of Rockingham County, on Tuesday, the 26th day of July, in the year of our Lord, 1796, of and concerning a certain piece, etc., of land commonly known and called by the name of the late Rev. Thomas Jackson, deceased, containing 230 acres, etc., in Rockingham County, on the waters of Linwell's Creek and Muddy Creek, which was first granted by patent, dated 27th June, 1764, to William Sample and by him conveyed to said Thomas Jackson by deeds, 15th May, 1770. Between Mathew Gambill, Escheator, and James Curry, William Herring, Benjamin Harrison, John Rice, Reuben Harrison, John Herdman, George Baxter, Richard Ragan, Samuel McWilliams, Jonathan Shipman, Benjamin Smith, James Burgess, George Sittes, Thomas Shanklin, John Lincoln, William Cravens, jurors, who, etc., do say that the aforesaid Thomas Jackson was, in his lifetime, and the time of his death, seized, etc., of the aforesaid tract, etc. That he died intestate and no person has claimed the land either as lineal or collateral heir and it is escheatable. Signed by all the jurors.

Copy of the will of Samuel Woods, dated 8th January, 1781. I, Samuel Woods, of the County of Amherst, Rockfish Settlement. To wife, Sarah, land purchased of Thomas Patton. To eldest son, James, 350 acres in Albemarle, joining Henry Kerr and Alexander Fretwell. To son, William (infant), two tracts in Amherst, joining Rockfish Meeting House, formerly the property of William Patton and William Crow; and mill property, formerly belonging to Robert and Edward Stephenson, David Black (Clack, Clark?), William Clark, and Langsdon Depriest. To three youngest daughters, to be schooled. To five daughters. Executors, Gabriel Penn, Francis Merriweather, James Brooks, James Woods, Jr., and William Woods. Leaves Jane, Hannah, Elizabeth, and William Dunon(Drenon), to his wife. Test: James Brooks, Alexander Reid, Jr., William Small, John Davis, Joseph Smith. Proved in Amherst, 5th February, 1781.

Rockingham County, 12th September, 1801. By order of Rockingham County Court, surveyed for Benjamin Harrison, 1,129½ acres on both sides of Cook's Creek (including the spring of the main branch of said creek), including the ten following tracts, viz: 83½ acres, part of 100 acres, part of 1,264 acres, patented, 26th March, 1739, to McKay, Hite, Duff and Green, and conveyed by deeds, 18th June, 1749, to Robert McKay, Jost. Hyte, Robert Green, and Robert Green, sole heir of the will of William Duff to Samuel Wilkins, and by him to Daniel Harrison, 27th February, 1749; —— acres patented to —— Harrison, 25th September, 1746; —— acres patented to Daniel Harrison, 10th September, 1755. These three tracts willed by Daniel Harrison to said Benjamin Harrison by will, 8th June, 1767. 165 acres patented to John Edwards, 20th September, 1768, and by him willed to Benjamin Harrison, 31st October, 1775. 130 acres patented to Thomas Gordon, 19th August, 1758, and by him deeded to Benjamin, 20 January, 1793. 32½ acres, new survey, dated 21st February, 1801, as assignee of Alexander Herring, of George Lang, Jr., of George Picket, part of said Picket's warrant for 3,000 acres, dated 13th August, 1763. 38¾ acres, a new survey, dated 21st February, 1801, for 16 acres as assignee of Alexander Herring, of William Russell, part of said Russell's warrant for 1,000 acres, dated 13th February, 1782, and for 23¾ acres as assignee of Jacob Bare, part of his warrant for 1,000 acres, dated 27th June, 1783. 16½ acres, a new survey, as to 11½ acres, assignee of John Harrison, part of his exchange warrant for 750 acres, dated 29th May, 1800. One acre, new survey, by warrant for 3,000 acres, dated 13th August, 1783, assignee of Alexander Herring, of George Lang, Jr., of George Picket. 421 acres, new survey, dated 20th March, 1801, by these warrants, for 50 acres he is assignee of Alexander Herring, of William Oliver, of William Russell, part of his warrant, 13th August, 1783; for 371 acres he is assignee of John Harrison, part of his warrant, 8th May, 1800. 41 acres surplus bond by warrants, viz: For 29 acres he is assignee of John Harrison, part of his warrant for 752 acres, dated 8th May, 1801. For 12 acres he is assignee of Alexander Herring, of George Lang, Jr., of George Pickett, part of his warrant for 3,000 acres, dated 13th August, 1783. Of the whole, plat and metes and bounds.

DISTRICT COURT EXECUTIONS.

September, 1794 (A to I).

Gregg vs. Hinkle.—Sir:—I understand that you are much dissatisfied about the land that I surveyed for Abraham Teter, on the north side of Seneca, joining his own land, saying I promised to send you word before I surveyed it. I remember of promising not to survey it before Andrew Johnson would return from Rockingham, who was to bring your entry, and Andrew returned and brought no entry; and, moreover, old George Teter searched Lewis's records and found no such entry as you spoke of, and the widow Teter demanded the surveying of the same, and as Abraham had the oldest entry by warrant, I thought myself in duty bound to survey it, neither saw I any occasion to send for you, when I knew you had no entry for the land, and yet had time to procure it, and, furthermore, it is uncertain whether old entrys are prolonged on the Eastern waters or not, for Mr. Lewis wrote to me that he knew that they were prolonged on the Western waters, but not on our waters. But if your right is good, my surveying of it will not hinder you from obtaining it, for I don't mean to make the plot till you are satisfied about it. I am ready, at your demand, to survey 100 acres for you on Seneca, above Abraham Teter's land, for your entry is now made by warrant, for I lately obtained a warrant for you from Colonel Hamilton. I desire that you be moderate in your censures, and, whether or not, I am your hearty well-wisher and obsequious, M. Henkle. To Mr. Wm. Gragg. (Addressed) Mr. William Gragg, Sr., On Seneca.

The Commonwealth of Virginia.—To George Moffett, Gent. Greeting: Know you that from the special trust and confidence which is reposed in your fidelity, courage, activity and good conduct, our Governor, with the advice of the Council of State, and on the recommendation of the worshipful Court of the County of Augusta, doth appoint you, the said George Moffett, County Lieutenant of ye Militia of the said County of Augusta, to take rank as such from the nineteenth day of November, 1783. In testimony whereof, these our letters are made patent. Witness: His Excellency, Benjamin Harrison, Esq., our said Governor, at Richmond, this sixth day of April, 1784. (Signed) Benj. Harrison. (Registered.) Seal.

Commission to Zachariah Johnston, George Poage, Thomas Hughes and Thomas Rankin, as Justices for Augusta County, signed by Thomas Jefferson, Governor, at Charlottesville, 29th May, 1781.

Brock's Gap, 20th February, 1758. Sir:—Pay to George Anderson, or order, the sum of four pounds, ten shillings, currency, to be deducted out of my pay for the months of May, June and July, as the same shall become due, for value received of him, from your humble servant. (Signed) William Burke. To Capt. Peter Hog.

List of wolf scalps, beginning 1774: To James Loskey, Joseph Newton, William Porter, Levin Benson, William Rhea, Peter Hoover: 1777, December 16, to John Clemons, George Baxter; 1778, May 21, to Jacob Barrier, Thomas Cartmell, John McEwin, Thomas Mynes, Jonathan Hicklin, Anthony Huston; 1784, November, to John Snider, George Puffenberry, Isaac Mayze, Joseph Newton, Henry Every, Samuel Haws; 1785, March, to John Owfull; November, to Wm. Lansdale, Henry Casebolt, Henry Gragg, Moses Moore,

Senior and Junior, and Jacob Elsworth, Wm. Bennett and John Armogast; 1787, December, to Thomas Galfour, Thomas Frennen and Michael Arbecost; 1788, December, to James Brindle and William Nottigam; 1789, December, to John Portlock and Levin Nicholas; 1790, December, to William Portlock, William M. Jordan and Sylvanus Odle; 1791, December, to Hugh Keenon, Fred Troughbough, Jonathan Inchremiger (?); 1792, December, in all 106,900 pounds tobacco.

COUNTY COURT JUDGMENTS.

MAY, 20, 1762.

Montgomery vs. Lewis.—August, 1758. Sir:—I expected you at this Court and to brought some money to me, but I see that you do not ( ) to pay till you be put to trouble. My mahan (man?) has made complaint to me you have taken two cows in —— of ye land that I was —— which you give your bond to Col. Robison and me, and —— brought good security to me for ye piece of land, which we are willing to take for ye good of ye children, so I require you on sight to deliver ye said cows and I will deliver ye bond that you give for ye said lands. I expect you out in a few days, or mark what will follow, which is all at present. (Signed) John Lewis.

SEPTEMBER, 1763 (A).

A. P. Henry, Jr., vs. J. Oliver.—Account for merchandise, 1759. Sworn to by P. Henry, Jr., in Hanover, before John Henry, 7th October, 1760, and acknowledged to be just to John Hughes, 20th July, 1761, by James Oliver.

MARCH, 1758 (B).

Wood vs. Vanse.—Know all men, &c., we, Ephraim Vanse (Vause?) and George Robinson are held, &c., to Col. James Wood, of Frederick County, &c., &c. Dated 23d September, 1747. Test, Robert Rutherford, John Robinson.

April 28, 1756.—This day Mathew Edmoston, Constable, made oath before me, Patrick Martin, &c., &c., that by virtue of an execution, &c., &c., versus the estate of John Young, &c., he seized the goods of said John Young and by violent force they were forceably taken and rescued from him by Robert Young, Sr., and his wife, Agnes. (Signed) Pat. Martin.

Patrick Conningham, debtor to John Hamilton and William Thomson, for 76 gallons rum at *Pitchbarg*, 1760.

AUGUST, 1764 (B).

Stringer adversus Morrow.—First day of July, 1749. Bond by Daniel (his "O") Stringer, of Followfield Township, County of Chester, and Province of Pennsylvania, yeoman. Am held, &c., to James Ortan, of same place, &c. Condition: To pay £10 in 1751. Test, Wm. Morrow, Walter Hood. Bill for injunction, as follows: To the Worshipful Court of Augusta, Sitting in Chancery: Orator Daniel Stringer, late of Chester County, Pennsylvania: That some time in 1748, or 1749, he purchased a plantation near Buckley's Mill, in said County, of one James Orton, for £100, and executed eight bonds. Orton had bought from William Morrow, but being unable to make the payments, he sold to orator, and Morrow took assignment of the eight bonds. Orator, intending to come to Virginia, sold to Robert Turner for £150, and then set off on his journey to Virginia. Morrow went to orator's wife, persuaded her Turner was insolvent and to give up the bonds to Morrow, which she did, and on his representation that it was necessary, she went to Philadelphia with Morrow—55 miles—where he desired her to tarry at a barber shop till he returned from waiting on the Secretary. After some time he returned and told her she might go home for he had attended to the business without her. Morrow told her that the Secretary gave Morrow a warrant to John Taylor, Surveyor of the County, and she might get home as she could, and left her to walk home on foot. The day after she got home, Morrow came and told her one thing more was necessary to give him possession of the land, by putting out her fire and kindling one in his name, which she also performed, and asked him to give up her husband's bonds, which he agreed to do if she met him at John Taylor's mill that evening. She met him there and found him so drunk that he did nothing but abuse her and her two brothers-in-law who went along with her. Orator shows that on his way home from Virginia a certain Hans Hamilton, then Sheriff of York County, came to the house where he lodged, about two miles on this side of Yorktown, and learning orator's name, asked him if he was not indebted to Morrow, and arrested him at the suit of Morrow, assignee of orator, &c., &c., and carried orator forty miles back to Hamilton's house, where he was forced to remain a prisoner two weeks (as he could procure no one to be his bail in a place where he was a stranger), and then to deliver his two horses (value £40) to the Sheriff as a pledge for his appearance. When he got home he was informed by his wife of her agreement with Morrow, whom orator upbraided. Morrow went with orator to Yorktown, where Hamilton arrested orator at suit of another person, and on his agreeing to go to Hamilton's house to make up with that other person who lived near, Morrow said he must return home, but would come to Hamilton in a few days and settle all matters, and he would carry home orator's mare, which he then rid (worth £11) out of friendship; on which Morrow took the mare, saddle and bridle, together with a wallet in which was a new shirt and 3/ in money. Orator waited eleven days for Morrow's return, and was then compelled to swap a stallion, one of the horses formerly left in the Sheriff's hands, to a mare of the Sheriff's to carry him home; but was obliged to leave nine pounds (the boot which he was to receive in the swap of the said horses), together with the other horse, in the Sheriff's hands. Since which time orator has never seen or met Morrow. Morrow has sued orator in Augusta. Orator never received any of his articles. Sworn to 16th May, 1761, before Daniel Smith.

MARCH, 1764 (B).

Lewis & Robinson vs. Pearis & Co.—Capt. Robert Pearis & Co. to Mr. David Robinson & Co., debtor: 1762, November 9, to 15,113 lbs. beef @ 28/ per hundred, P. C., £211, 11, 7. Contra: 1762, November 9, by George

Elder's pay as manager at the slaughter house, 6 days, at 5/; by William Bills, a butcher, 6 days, at 3/9 per day; by William Marshel, assistant butcher, at 1/3 per day; by Stephen Allinger, assistant butcher, at 1/3 per day; by a corporal and four privates, at /6 per day, six days; by cash at Hoit's; by cash at Fort Pitt; by cash paid John Fleming's expenses; by cash paid Thomas Small's expenses; by cash advanced at Staunton. Capt. William Thomson, pay the bearer hereof, Mr. Charles Lewis, the sum of one hundred and thirty-eight pounds, Pennsylvania money, which we stand indebted to him, and place the same to the account of your humble servant. (Signed) Robert Pearis. Test, John Stewart.

MAY, 1763 (B).

Wright vs. Carpenter.—This day Mr. Solomon Carpenter swore before me that at the time of Mr. Joseph Carpenter giving a warrant to Peter Wright to apprehend two deserters at Fort Young said Wright gave ye warrant to Thos. Fitzpatrick to read and said he could not make out some words, and he read it out over in public, and begun it again, when said deponent went off, and he further sayeth yt ye deserters were not far off at ye time. Given under my hand this 17th April, 1763. (Signed) John Dickinson.

AUGUST, 1762 (B).

McClenachan vs. Augusta Vestry.—Warrant signed by Ben. Waller to arrest Robert McClenachan, late Collector of Augusta Parish Levy, to appear at General Court to answer the Church Wardens. Dated 6th May, in 29th year of reign. Declaration: John Archer and John Christian, Church Wardens, complain of Robert McClenachan, late Collector, &c., in 1748, collected in 1749 levies which he has not paid over. General issue pleaded April, 1757. November 3, 1757, trial by jury, viz: Richard Bland, John Ruffin, Christopher Chamney, John Leaeve, Thomas Knox, Charles Coppidge, Charles Anderson, Clement Read, William Taite, Andrew Munroe, John Lovell and Nathaniel Venable. Verdict for plaintiff, £20. A copy. Test: Litt. Savage, for Ben. Waller, Cl. Crer. Set-off filed by defendant. To delinquents in Montgomery's list: Gilbert Strahorn, Samuel Martin, Peirce Coslie, John Dickson, Stephen Halston, Cornelius Towlin, John Martin, John Welsh, Nicholas Welsh, Silas Staus (Stans).

MAY, 1763 (B).

Bingaman vs. Smith.—January ye 2d day. Received of John Bingamin 861 weight of beef for the use of my Company and the Cherokee Indians at the rate of 10/ per C., £4, 6, 3½, and more to cash upon the same account 18/ per me. (Signed) John Smith.

1762.

Memorandum of ye weight of bacon bought from Jacob Petter, 361, at 4½ = £6, 15, 4½. April ye 12th, 1756. Received from Jacob Petter 287½ pounds of bacon for the use of Capt. Israel Christy's men. I say.

Received by us more eight pounds and three-quarters. (Signed) George Bigham, Robert Armstrong. To Capt. Israel Christy, or Lieut. Alexander Wright. (Endorsed.) Capt. Christian says he has paid the above.

August, 1759.

Carlyle vs. Estill—Carolile vs. Bowd Estill.—Richard Prior, Sr., deposes, 21st May, 1759: That in August, 1757, the deponent being at Fort George, in Bull Pasture, saw two horses in Wallace Estill's cornfield, one belonging to John Carolile and the other to Capt. Preston; that Bowd Estill and several other young men went into the field to drive out the horses; that said Estill and all the others that were with him called dogs and set them on the horses to drive them out, and that the men followed the dogs and horses, making a great noise, but this deponent does not know whether the noise was to encourage the dogs to follow, or to get them off, as he was at a great distance, but he observed all the men turn homeward as soon as all the horses jumped the fence and got out; that after the horses got out of the field they took round the Bottom below the Fort, and as the men were returning the deponent saw a great many dogs break off from the Fort and make straight for the noise where the other dogs were; that after some time a number of the dogs came back, and several of them were bloody, but he is not certain which party of the dogs were bloody or part of both; that soon after the deponent and several other men went down the river and found John Carolile's horse lying dead in the river, and all of them believed he was killed by the dogs, and further sayeth not. Sworn before me this 21st day of May, 1759. (Signed) Robt. Breckinridge.

November, 1763 (C).

Know all men by these presents: That I, Lieut. John Sallard, am held and firmly bound unto Alexander McDonald, &c., &c. 23d March, 1762. Test: Alexander Stewart, Robert Fillson.

November, 1766 (A).

Clendenin vs. Cunningham.—This day Samuel Crocket made oath before me that the return he made to Capt. Walter Cunningham was just and yt John Clendenon was one in the return. Given under my hand this 1st April, 1766. (Signed) John Dickinson. As a soldier, &c., and yt ye time he was in Greenbrier he allowed good, &c.

October, 1765 (D).

Cotton vs. Christian.—Debtor, Mr John Christian to James Cotton: 1764, June 13, to a subscription for four children of your own for five months and twenty-six days at 20/ per annum each; to a subscription for your brother, Capt. William Christian, for one child; to a subscription for William Dean, by your order, for one child; to three bushels of wheat. (Signed) James Cotton. Christian's Creek, September 21, 1765. Joseph Robinson deposes, 15th October, 1765, before John Buchanan: That he was present at an agreement between Mr. James Cotton and some persons about a school that he was then about to begin at Robert Armstrong's, on Christian's Creek, on the 11th day of June, 1764, and that the said Cotton had a liberty given him by the employers to give up the school at any time during the year at his pleasure, and that they were to pay him according to the time the school was kept, and that Mr. John Christian positively ordered me, the deponent, to subscribe a scholar for William Dean, and that said Dean had ordered him to do for him as though he were there present, and further this deponent sayeth not. Arbitrators give plaintiff £3.

NOVEMBER, 1766 (A).

Burnsides vs. Edwards.—Sir:—Please to pay unto James Burnsides fourteen shillings and three pence, cash, when my pay shall come into your hands, and this, my note, shall be your receipt for so much, from your humble servant. (Signed) Joseph (mark) Edwards. To Capt. Charles Lewis.

August 27, 1764.—Sir:—Please to pay unto James Burnsides the sum of eight pounds, five shillings, and nine pence, cash, when my pay shall come into your hands, and this note shall be your receipt for so much, from your friend and soldier. (Signed) Joseph Edwards. To Capt. Charles Lewis. July 5, 1764.

PETITIONS TO MAY COURT, 1767.

May 14th, 1767.

To the Worshipful Court Next Sitting for Augusta:

I, your petitioner, humbly seweth that whereas a wagon road hath been by order opened along ye South Fork of ye South Branch of Potomac, which road is very hurtful to my plantation, I, your petitioner, beg that your worships would appoint two men to view and make report of another road which I shall shew them, and, when granted, will open another sufficiently at my own expense. And I, your petitioner, shall, as in duty, ever pray.

JOHN BENNET.

P. S.—This is to certify, your worships, that ye above petitioner is under a necessity of troubling your worships, as the road is greatly to his disadvantage. Certified by us: Jeremiah Osborn, John Davis, William Davis, James Davis, James Dyer, Charles Woolson, Joseph Woolson, Isaac Woolson, Jacob Regart, John Roreback, John Garner, David Wilson, Charles Smith, Matthew Patton.

Heth vs. Love.—1761. Debtor, Mr. Philip Love to Henry Heth: To your club in the mess on ye campaign with Col. Andrew Lewis, Capt. Fleming and others, as settled by the two former, £3, 11, 3.

MAY, 1765 (C).

Greer, Assignee of Boyd, vs. Blagg.—We, or either of us, do promise to pay to Samuel Boyd, or order, &c., &c., for a certain bay horse that said Boyd sold to William Grant, Sergeant, of the Virginia Regiment, &c., &c, 22d day of January, 1760. (Signed) Wm. Grant, John Blagg. Test: John Heath.

1765.

William Ingles vs. Joseph Ray.—1760. Mr. Joseph Ray to William Ingles, debtor. January 14, to cash lent you at Fort Lewis; to your account from the Bedford book. July 24, to one pair gloves, rum and bumbo. Sworn to, 1765, before Daniel Smith.

MAY, 1765 (C).

Cloyd vs. Dooley.—Attachment. Attachment 30th January, 1765, by David Cloyd, Sr., against James Dooley, and attachment bond signed by David Cloyd, Sr., and David Cloyd, Jr.

NOVEMBER, 1764 (A).

Hugh (mark) Botkins. Bond dated 19th September, 1761, to Handry Picket, conditioned to making deed to 174 acres, comprehending the place John Kare sold to Richard Botkin, joining Robert Reburn and John Strain, on the east; Robert McMahan and John Botkin, on the west; John Richey and James Orrey and Edward Beard, on the north. Test: John and Mary Botkin.

MAY, 1765 (B).

Cunningham vs. Sawyers.—Capt Alexander Sawyers to William Cunningham, debtor. 1758, June 20, for Thomas Baker, for Henry Dooley; August 22, for John Burk; August 29, for Dennis O'Brian; November 3, to one deerskin for Andrew Johnson; November 14, pumps for John Foy; November 16, for John Donally, for James Asque; November 20, for Thos. Welsh, for Israel Young; November 23, for Joshua McCormick, for Abraham Thompson, for Samuel Hamilton, for John Cunningham; to one horse of my own; to my pay for 202 days' service in your Company, £20, 4, 0. Contra: By cash, per Joseph Ray, John Davis, at May Court. (Signed) David Sawyers.

PETITION.

To the Worshipful Court of Augusta County:
We, your humble petitioners, pray that your worships would be pleased to grant a road to be cleared from Adam Reader's Mines to Isaac Robertson's, from thence to Widow Wright's Mill, from thence to Thomas Harrison's, on the great road to the Court House, which will be the covenants' road to travel either north or south, to mill or to market. May ye second day, year 1767. Your favor will oblige your humble petitioners. (Signed) Thos. Pickins, James Van Pelt, Lydia Wright, Jacob Gum, Leonard Herring, Wm. Dunlop, Wm. Blear, Francis Munsey, John Jackson, Adam Kinder, Isaac Robertson, John Chrisman, Wm. Munsey, Jacob Gum, Jr., John Black, Robert Kearr, Scidmore Munsey, Wm. Pickins, David Robertson, Mathias Kinder, James Wright, Timothy Warren, Robert Bellshe, John White, Thomas Harrison, Jacob Miller, Alexander Peanter, James Thomas, Henry Maze.

Michael Bowyer's account as Jailor allowed for insolvent fees for 1769: Chas. Fred. Sivert, in goal for debt, 20 days; Robert McMahon, in goal for felony, 24 days; Joseph Eaton, in goal for debt, 20 days; Wm. Cunningham, in goal for felony, 8 days; Richard Smith, in goal, runaway, 28 days; Andrew Caseday, in goal, runaway, 10 days; John Smith, in goal, madman, 62 days; Patrick Lacey, in goal, good behavior, 6 days; Jonathan Douglass, in goal for debt, 20 days; Robert Phillips, in goal for debt, 6 days; William McNeil, in goal for debt, 20 days; William Simson, in goal for debt, 20 days; James Blan, in goal for debt, 20 days; James Blan, same; Joseph Ray, in goal for debt, 10 days; Nathaniel Lyon, in goal for debt, 20 days; Charles Harris, in goal for debt, 20 days; Christopher Finney, in goal for debt, 20 days; Christian Strickler, in goal, madman, 21 days; David Whiticher, in goal, runaway, 36 days; John Dun, in goal for felony, 1 day; John Munks, in goal, suspicious, 10 days; William Guin, in goal for debt, 20 days; a negro man, in goal for felony, 7 days; James Dinniston, in goal for felony, 11 days; John Price, in goal for debt, 20 days; John Reece's two negroes, in goal 3 months and 16 days, from Carolina; to finding wood for the jail; to finding wood and keeping the Court House.

August, 1765.

John Hamilton vs. Col. John Smith. Writ, 28th August, 1764. Col. John Smith, debtor to John Hamilton, for goods for his soldiers at the Dunkard Bottom and himself—September, 1760: Col. John Smith, himself; Lieut. Hansley, John Smith (bowman), John Lukis, John Hamilton, Stamp Evins, Richard Dodd, Richard Newport, Thomas Deigs, John Cotrel. Said John Smith assumed to pay said accounts in presence of Lieut. Richard Hickman (in Albemarle).
Wm. Givens and Wm. Thompson (both in this County).

August, 1766 (A).

Blackwood vs. Callison.—Know all men, &c., that we, James Callison and Richard Moris, both of Augusta, stand indebted to William Blackwood, &c., &c. 16th September, 1762. Test: Robert Conningham, Samuel Cloyd.

November, 1766 (A).

Capt. Walter Cunningham, debtor, to my pay as a soldier from ye 29th November, 1763, to ye 20th March, 1764, being 111 days, at 1/6 per day. (Signed) E. E., per John Clendenning.
This day Samuel Crockett came before me and made oath that he, the said Samuel Crockett, served as Sergeant at Capt. John Dickinson's, on the Cow Pasture River, under the command of Capt. Walter Cunningham, and further declares that John Clendennen served as a soldier from the twenty-seventh of November to the 20th of March in the said Company, and the said John Clendennen, being neglected from the former to the latter date of being returned in the pay-roll and was out of his pay. Given under my hand this 9th day of July, 1764. (Signed) John Dickinson.

John Hopes (Hapes) vs. Daniel Harrison.—Chancery. Spa. issued September, 1763. Bill states that orator was some years ago employed as Deputy Sheriff under Robert McClenachan, and continued so for two years. Thomas Harrison, Daniel Harrison and John Cravens were his securities. As the end of orator's term drew near he became fearful that he would be behind in his accounts, and withdrew himself to Carolina, leaving his Sheriff's books and effects for the satisfaction of his bondsmen. His effects were immediately attached by Daniel Harrison, who was appointed Deputy Sheriff in orator's place. After some time orator returned to Virginia and sold a tract of land for £47, which he paid to his securities, expecting to have an account rendered to him by defendant, but orator waited a long time for an accounting, and then applied for one, but has never gotten one yet. Prayer for accounting.

Daniel Harrison's answer states that: Claims that orator is still in his debt. Account follows: Downes's fees—William Carrel, David Johnson, James Scott, John Dunbar, William Longin, Mathy Thomas, John Griffeth, John Megil. Adam Bracen Righ's book (boock)—Alen Sculps, Alen Jackson. John Bumgardner's book—Jonathan Duglis, Aorgin Jones, John Crage, Thos. Dwode, Ben Inman Gouge, John Harrison, Henry Netherentine, Samuel Lonard, Renell Macdannel, Jeremiah Orsburn, Jr., Samuel Pattron, James Rutledge, Samuel Samples, Edward Shankling, Hugh Duglis, Wm. Ewing, David Crage, John Griffeth, James Gray, Reuben Harrison, Samuel Henderson, Francis MacBred, Richard Marling, John Phillips, John Pattron, Valentine Seveor, Mathew Ship, John Walker, Thomas Holing, Mung Price, Hugh Camel, John Davis, Jacob Glashe, John Holmes, Joell Hornback, Thomas Loin (Lain), Peter Mate, John Orsburn, Josiah Parrent, Edward Rutledge, James Scot, Mathous Sulcer, Richard Tictum.

COUNTY COURT JUDGMENTS.

OCTOBER, 1765 (C).

Crow vs. Bell.—Elizabeth Hog deposes, 18th October, 1765, before Alex. McClenachan, of lawful age: Sayeth that at the time when the first Fair was held in Staunton, about three years ago, this deponent was standing in the door of Francis Tyler, in Staunton, in company with Miss Priscilla Christian, since deceased, when she was asked by Miss Priscilla if she would not go down to Mr. Crow's store and get a fairing, on which this deponent answered she would not go, and presently Thomas Crow, standing in the store door of his brother William, waived his hand for this deponent and the other to come over to the store, which they did, and as they were going into the store the said Thomas Crow walked out, being called by his sister-in-law, to the best of this deponent's rememberance, and as he passed by them Miss Priscilla asked him if he was not going to give them a fairing, to which he answered: Stay till I come back; on which they went into the store, and Miss Priscilla made the same demand of a fairing from the defendant, Bell, who was then within the counter, and made no reply for some time, but at last he took from the shelves two pieces, or bolts, of ribbon, and told her to take her choice, which she did, and then he cut off a yard and gave it to her, when the said Miss Priscilla asked him if he would not also give this deponent one, to which he answered, yes, and delivered another yard to this deponent, and soon after Miss Priscilla asked the said Bell if he would not give them a fairing for Thomas Crow, to which he answered, yes, and then gave this deponent and the other a yard each from another bolt of ribbon, and some time after, when this deponent went to pay off her account with the plaintiff, William Crow, on hearing the articles read over with which she stood charged, she found a yard of ribbon, to which she objected, as she knew she never had bought any in the store, and on observing it was charged at the same time with the yard of linen which she bought from the said Bell, she told the plaintiff, Crow, that the defendant, Joseph, was wrong in charging her with a yard of ribbon when he had made a present of a ribbon to her and Miss Priscilla Christian at the same time, and she supposed had not charged Miss Priscilla, on which the said Crow looked if the other ribbon was charged to the said Miss Priscilla, but found no account, and then he looked into the said Bell's account and told this deponent that he found no ribbon charged of that date to the said Bell, and further sayeth not. (Signed) Alex. McClenachan.

August, 1766 (A).

Christian vs. King (the Middle River Miller).—Capias dated 28th August, 1765, returned, "He will not be taken." Attachment of his property, dated 24th October, 1765. Account runs through years 1757-8-9, 1760-61-62-63-64. 1757, April 4, four lottery tickets; 1758, May 6, by your sister; May 6, by John Gentry; June 23, by wife; 1759, July 4, by your mother; July 25, by wife; 1761, January 31, bum. and sugar charged Mossey Creek John. Contra: By patroling under Col. Preston, by allowed for going to Sivers's Fort, by making 13 soldiers' shirts, by Hugh Lusk.

Urley vs. Christian.—To Mr. James Cloid, in Augusta County. Fort Lookout, August 13, 1764. Dear Sir:—If Mr. John Willy brings my note for two pounds and orders amounting to five pounds, none, and six pence, sir, you will be so good as to pay him them and keep ye orders and note till we meet, and, sir, you will oblige your humble servant—nuse we have none. I am, sir, your friend and well-wisher. (Signed) Alex. Sayers. To Ensign James Cloid.

I protest the above order. (Signed) James Cloyd.

August, 1765 (A).

Howell vs. Steel.—(This paper is only a wrapper.)—Augusta, September 23d, 1760. Sir:—I came here today in order to meet with you, but your not being here occasions me to write, viz: John Guy came to my plantation and took from me a young horse in value ten pounds. I am sure I can prove the horse my property, so please to order a writ immediately out for him in such a method as is proper, and let it be for ninety pounds, and *apper* in ye *cick*, and I will pay you your fee, and I will employ another attorney to assist with ye evidences I will give you the first opportunity. This from your humble servant. (Signed) W. Wilson.

Joseph Ray vs. William Chandler.—Articles of agreement, &c., 6th Aug., 1760, between William Chandler, of Bedford County, and Joseph Ray, of the said County. Chandler is to deliver to Ray at the Dunkard Bottom, on the New River, £100 worth of such goods as Ray thinks proper as soon as Chandler conveniently can, which said Ray is to sell at 6 per cent out of what he sells for his trouble of selling and the goods remaining unsold Chandler obliges himself to take. For performance of which Ray, with John Smith, John Sutton, Peter Lowney, his sureties, bind themselves. (Signed) Wm. Chandler, Joseph Ray, John Smith, John Sutton, Peter Luney. Test: John Bedel, Moses Hamilton.

Plaintiff charges that Chandler did not comply, and sues for damages. In March, 1765, Sutton was in Carolina.

Col. John Smith deposes: That in August, 1760, being at Fort Lewis, he heard Chandler sell to the plaintiff Ray £100 worth of goods, to be delivered, &c., &c., make payment for ye same. At ye breaking up of ye campaign under Col. Byrd, then carrying on against ye Cherokees, and accordingly ye plaintiff Ray applied to deponent and Luney to become his securities, &c. The goods were not delivered at the time agreed, or any time during the campaign. Ray might have disposed of a still larger quantity of goods to advantage on that campaign. (No date.)

Capt. John Blag deposes: That in 1760, whilst he had a Company of the Virginia Regiment under his command stationed on the frontiers of this County, Joseph Ray applied to him for liberty to supply this deponent's Company in goods and such necessaries as they should want; the deponent answered he was satisfied, and therefore should depend upon him, but after waiting some time, was disappointed, and obliged to apply to another, as this deponent understood that Mr. Ray had met with disappointment with some man he had bought goods of; the deponent further sayeth that he believes he should have taken and wanted about one hundred and fifty pounds worth of goods at that time from Mr. Ray, and further sayeth not. October 24, 1765. (Signed) John Blagge.

March, 1767 (A).

McClung vs. Fleming.—This day Mr. Jas. Knox came before me as a garnishee for the estate of John Flimon, soldier, formerly of Capt. Lewis's Company, and declared that he has no part of said Flimon's estate in his hands, nor hasn't had since said Flimon left the County. Sworn before me this 29th October, 1766. (Signed) John Dickinson.

May, 1765 (C).

Articles of agreement, &c., between Robert Luney, of one part, and Peter Luney and David Luney, of the other part.—Robert Luney, in consideration, &c., but especially of a sufficient support and maintenance to him and his wife, Elizabeth, during their natural lives, &c., (conveys) to his two sons, Peter and David, tract whereon Robert now dwell (except the part lying on the South Side of the Creek, where his son Daniel now lives) ; also the tract where Peter now lives. Peter and David agree to build a good and commodious house for their father and mother wherever Robert choses. Three cows reserved by Robert; rest to be divided between Peter, John and David Luney. Horses he gives to son John, except two which he gives to son Daniel. Dated 11th October, 1759. (Signed) Robert (mark) Luney, Peter Luney, David Luney. Test: John Smith, John Buchanan, Thomas Ramsey.

AUGUST, 1765 (A).

Bowyer vs. Robert Reed.—1757, December 30, to cash; 1758, March 2, to Thomas Hucklin for taylor work for Caleb Harmon; March 2, to Gilbert's account versus Harmon; May 23, to cash; March 2, to one pair stockings for Caleb. Contra: 1757, by Caleb Harmon's pay as a soldier in my Company from 22d June till 29th November, 1757, being 161 days, £8, 1, 0; by your account for ammunition, £2, 5, 0; by your account against the Cherokees, £0, 15, 6; by Mathew Reed's account against Cherokees, £2, 3, 0; by Thomas Saunders, per order on me, £5, 14, 0; by Caleb Harmon's pay as a soldier from the 30th November till the 1st May, 1758, @ 1/ per day; by Harmon's pay in May and June; by ammunition for my Company; 1760, December, by cash. (Signed) E. (Accepted) per William Preston.

Robert Reed, debtor to ye estate of Caleb Harmon, deceased: To cash you received of Col. Preston, being the pay of the said Harmon while a soldier under his command, £18, 14, 0. (Signed) E. E., per John Bowyer, administrator.

Caleb Harmon, debtor to Robert Reed: 1756-1757, sundries; to cash paid David Long for washing when at the Fort; 1756, to cash paid Capt. McNeill for you.

OCTOBER, 1765 (D).

Christian vs. Hamilton.—1759, Dr. Robert Hamilton, debtor to Is. Christian; August 16, to sundries; to 720 lbs. tobacco for Robert Read's attendance on your trial at Williamsburg, 1755.

Johnson vs. Via.—1760, Mr. David Via in account with Thomas Johnson, Jr.: To quit rents of 124 acres; 1761, to paid William Davis, John Lea, David Hill, John Woodgar, John Ogg; 1762, to cash at Albemarle Court. Contra: 1761, by Louisa County. Sworn to, 12th November, 1764, in Louisa County, by Thomas Johnson, Jr., before Nicholas Johnson.

Church Wardens vs. Ward and Preston.—Know all men by these presents, that we, William Ward and William Preston, are held, &c., to Sampson Archer and John Mathews, Church Wardens, in behalf of the parish, in the penal sum of £120, &c., &c. — day January, 1761. Condition: William Ward has undertaken to build a house on the Glebe of said parish for the sum of £60 by the first day of November next. The house to be twenty-four feet long and eighteen feet wide in the clear, and one-story-and-a-half high; the logs to be squared on two sides, and six inches thick, and well duftailed; the sleepers, or lower joists, to be framed in the ground log, which is to be nine inches thick; the joists to be well squared and plained, or moulding struck on each, and to be eight inches by five square. The house to be covered with lap shingles, clear of the sap, and fourteen inches to the weather. The gable ends clapboarded. An upper and under floor to be laid of good plank, well seasoned and lathed. A partition across the house of punch and pennel work, with a wainscoat door in the same. A stair case to be raised with facing and a door. A front door to the house wainscoated, and all the doors hung with iron hinges, and a lock to the front door. One sash window of six panes in the room, and one of the same size opposite to the front door, both well glazed. The floors and shingles to be nailed with good double tens. The vacancies between the logs to be daubed or filled with good mortar in both sides, as well above stairs as below. The house to be underpinned where necessary. A good outside stone chimney to be built, seven feet between the jambs and well pointed with lime. The roof to be made long enough to cover the chimney. The whole job and every part of it to be finished and completed in a workmanlike manner. The undertaker to find everything necessary for carrying on the said job, except timber and stone, which they are to have off the glebe land. (Signed) William Ward, William Preston. Test: George Skillern.

The above is a true copy from the original bond, which is lodged in my hand as Clerk of the Vestry. (Signed) William Preston.

Verdict for defendant.

NOVEMBER, 1766 (A).

Carpenter vs. Fonts (Fotch).—Chancery. Writ dated 24th November, 1763. Complainants are George Carpenter and Ann, his wife; Stephen Hantsberger and Ursilla, his wife; Matthew Hearce and Francis, his wife, daughters and co-heirs of John Shitley, deceased; that John Shitley was an inhabitant of the German Empire, where he died, having a small personal estate, leaving behind him your oratrices, then very young, and ——, his wife, mother of oratrices, and one of the defendants, who by the laws and customs of the empire, possessed herself of the small fortune of her husband. Shortly after the father's death, the widow, thinking to benefit herself and children, transported herself to America, bringing with her your oratrices and what remained of John Shitley's estate, amounting to near £100, Virginia currency, and some time after her arrival married John Fotch, the other defendant, who took possession of all the effects. That as your oratrices grew up, they intermarried (as above) and their husbands frequently applied to the said John Fotsch and wife for the parts due their wives, but obtained only £20 Pennsylvania Currency, £7 Virginia Currency, and 2 horses, worth £14, for which they gave receipt to Fotsch, expecting to receive the remainder in a short time, but now so it is, he refuses to pay them anything more.

John Fotch's answer: He married the widow of John Shitley in Germany and not in America, and that on her passage to America she died at Plymouth. He never possessed himself of any part of Shitley's estate, for he died insolvent, except a few trifling bed clothes made use of by his children on shipboard, but he says the grandfather of oratrices, Malchia Shitley, left them goods and chattels which this defendant, marrying their mother, possessed himself of, and before he came to America sold for as much money as came to £67 Virginia Currency, of which defendant expended £8 for oratrices for provisions and carriage from Switzerland to Holland, where they took shipping, almost 300 miles. He also paid for their passage to America the sum of 16 pistoles, and provisions growing short on shipboard, he was obliged to expend 30 shillings. Having landed in Maryland and intending to settle at Tulpahocken in Pennsylvania, he spent £3, 15 for provisions and carriage to that place. That he left Germany in 1744, and about 2 or 3 years after he came to this country he advanced to oratrices £25 in Virginia Currency, and two mares of the price of £14, 10.

That lately, on 31st March, 1762, he and complainants came to a final settlement and defendant agreed to settle with them £42.

Augustine Price deposes before Felix Gilbert: That is March, 1762, in company with George Carpenter, John Fotch and others, Carpenter and Fotch agreed to leave their dispute to Jacob Pershinger, Jacob Nicholas and Daniel Price, but they could not agree, when they came to an agreement themselves, the only question remaining whether Virginia or Pennsylvania Currency.

Daniel Price deposes the same.

Jacob Miller deposes: That being at the house of John Fotch some time in March, 1749, he heard George Carpenter ask three Gerles, that were heirs to the estate of ——, if they were satisfied with what they had received.

Jacob Pershinger deposes like Augustine Price.

Barbary Miller deposes, that being in company with Usley Shutling in 1750, Usley said she had received a mare and some clothes, and was well satisfied.

John vs. Samples.—Know all men, &c., I, Robert Samples, of Augusta, farmer and holder, &c., unto William English, of Augusta, bricklayer, &c., 17th December, Annoque Domini, 1763. Conditioned to pay in horses, mares or cattle, £17, 10. Test: Samuel Hull, Samuel Sample. Endorsed, 17th May, 1766, to Andrew Johnston. (Signed) William (mark) English.

AUGUST, 1766 (A).

Briggs vs. Joseph English.—I do promise to pay, &c., to Mr. Joseph Langdon, &c., 14th March, Ano. Dom., 1765. (Signed) Joseph English. Test: Archibald Huston, William Hoak. Assigned in Frederick County, 9th October, 1765, to David Briggs by Joseph Langdon.

Cock vs. Ingles.—I, William English, &c., promise to pay to William Cock ——, 16th May, 1764. (Signed) W. Ingles.

NOVEMBER, 1766 (A).

Moore vs. Fleming.—William Fleming, late of Pennsylvania, debtor. To sundries, diets and lodgings, £1, 4, 4; to sundries, clubs for drinking, £0, 14, 4; to freight for saddles from Wilmington, £0, 6, 0; to passage for yourself and rum, seven days, £0, 12, 0; to one mare lent, which you killed by riding, £14, 0, 0; to cash lent, £0, 6, 8.

North Carolina, Bladen County.—This day came Alexander Moore before us, Justices for County of Cumberland, and made oath (to above account), 1st May, 1765. (Signed) Thomas Burnside, Robert Mackel.

N. B.—Sd. Fleming is son to Samuel Fleming, of New London, and assisted in building a house for William Magomerey in Salisbury.

1757. Sergeant John Nash to estate of Robert Finley, deceased, debtor.—September 19, 1758, linen, buttons, thread, linen handkerchiefs, ribbon; April 22, neck cloth, penknife, garters.

OCTOBER, 1765 (C).

McClenachan vs. Crawford.—James Crawford, debtor, to James Simpson. To the balance of accounts (except my wages) on settlement, £0, 15, 0. To my wages as your storekeeper for a year in 1760 and 1761, £24. (Signed) E. E., per Robert McClenachan.

MAY, 1765 (C).

Looney vs. Looney.—Chancery. Col. John Smith deposes that in 1753 or 1754 Robert Looney sent for his son, Absalom, to come from Blue Stone to James River with his family. That before he came in Robert Looney proposed to his son Daniel that he would give him (Daniel) the land over the Creek for his land in the Draft to settle his son Absalom on, to which Daniel agreed, and when Absalom came in he settled on the land and Daniel Looney took possession of the land over the Creek. That some time afterwards Daniel Looney made the said Absalom a title to the same. That Daniel never got any title from his father that the deponent knows of, though he often afterwards heard the said Robert Looney acknowledge the bargain, and that when the said Robert Looney made over his other lands to his sons, he excepted and reserved the land over the Creek for his son Daniel.

Col. John Buchanan deposes: Of the original agreement he knows nothing, but that in 1755 Daniel Looney was in possession of the land over the creek, and that Robert often told deponent he had given his son Daniel the land over the creek in lieu of the land in the draft whereon Absalom Looney then lived, and that Daniel Looney repeatedly told deponent the same thing. That when Daniel was on his death bed he sent for deponent, and, among other things, it was mentioned that the land whereon he then lived was his, and the said Daniel then desired that after his death it might descend to his daughter, which his father, Robert Looney, said nothing against, though he was present.

COUNTY COURT.

PAPER FOUND BETWEEN LEAVES OF ORDER BOOK XI, PAGE 90.

To the Worshipful Court of Augusta County the Petition of the Inhabitants of Reedy Creek Humbly Sheweth:—

That whereas we, your petitioners, for some time past have been debarred settling and improving and cultivating our patent lands on the Western Waters, the reason whereof is best known to our legislators, but by virtue of the late treaty held to the northward, we hope we may, without offense, petition your worships to give orders that there may be alterations and amendments made on the old road leading from Capt. Ingle's Ferry to

James Davis's, on the head of the Holston River, and appoint such surveyors as you in your wisdom shall think fit, and your petitioners, as in duty bound, will pray. (Signed) Joseph Black, James Holice, John Montgomery, Robt. Montgomery, James Montgomery, George Breckenridge, Alexander Breckenridge, Robert Breckenridge, Robert Campbell, Robert Doack, William Doack, William Sayers, Arthur Campbell, William Davis, James Hays, Samuel Hopes, William Leftwich, Gasper Gender, George Gender, Jacob Kinder, William Phips, John Houncal, Barnet Small, John Smith, John Bets, Robert Buchanan, Robert Davis, Samuel McAdam, James Davis, Nicholas Buchanan, Alex. Buchanan.

MAY, 1762 (B).

Crow vs. Hoops.—Carlisle, ye 19th January, 1761. Received from Mr. Adam Hoops the sum of four hundred and seventy-two pounds, eighteen shillings and four pence, Pennsylvania currency, in full for 82 head of beef cattle, purchased by Mr. Arthur Hamilton and John Metcalf for the use of his Majesty's troops under the command of the honorable Brigadier General Monckton. (Signed) William Crow.

This certifies that James Arbuckle and two sons have served as soldiers in my Company of Militia four months and sixteen days, exclusive of what time they have received pay for. (Signed) Alex. Sayers. 21st April, 1759.

MAY, 1762 (A).

Finley vs. Christian.—Debtor, Mr. Israel Christian, in account with Robert Finley. 1757, September, to your assumption for sundry orders drawn on you by the Militia at Fort Dinwiddie amounting to £19, 14, 5½; to your assumption for Thomas Herbert, £1, 10, 0; to same, for Capt. Walker, £0, 13, 6; to the pay of B—— Scott and McFeeters as soldiers in the Militia assigned to me and received by you, 19 days each; to my pay as a soldier under Col. Stewart, received by you, 7 days; to balance in my favor on the return of goods, cash and book debts, £0, 15, 8½; to cash paid for cattle bought for your use, £33, 8, 3; to cash paid expenses in driving them, £0, 18, 3; to cash paid Michael Kelly, wages, for driving said cattle 20 days, £1, 15, 0; to the hire of my horse while purchasing provisions on your account, 101 days; to my wages for one year in your service, per agreement, £25, 0, 0; to my commission on the sale of your goods, amounting to £8, 1, 3, at 2/ per lb., £0, 16, 1. (Signed) Robert Finley. Dated 18th December, 1760.

AUGUST, 1762 (B).

Sproul vs. Bratton.—Sundry accounts which Dunlop assumed to Sproul to be used in the suit of Sproul against Ro. Bratton's Administrator, viz: Capt. James Dunlap, debtor, for the undernamed persons, viz: Thomas Vance, Halbert McClure, James McElhaney, John Low, Edward Howard, James Milliken, Thomas Smith, William Elliott, Alex. Sutherland, James Hamilton, John Gay and Capt. Dunlap.

COUNTY COURT JUDGMENTS.

JUNE, 1763 (B).

Wright vs. Carpenter.—James Graham deposes, 7th April, 1763, before John Dickinson: That at ye time of Mr. Joseph Carpenter, Sr., giving a warrant to Peter Wright which he brought from John Dickinson to apprehend John Humphreys and Joseph Garrit, two deserters, he saw said Carpenter give ye warrant to said Wright, and he, the said Wright, looked on it for some time and then gave it to Thomas Fitzpatrick to read, and he read a part of said warrant over out in public, when said Wright took it out of the other's hands and put it up; the deponent further sayeth that he verily believed, and still thinks, said Wright did not do it, or divulge it in order, or with any intention of giving notice to said deserters; the deponent sayeth this, &c., &c., &c.

FEBRUARY, 1763 (A?).

Low vs. Bratton.—This is to certify that John Low entered himself on my duty roll the 1st day of March, and he has served on duty under my command two hundred and thirty-one days, and is now discharged, this 2d day of November, 1757, and he allows me for pay what debt he contracted at my Fort when I receive his pay. Given under my hand this 2d of November, 1757. Paid to the 8th of June by public proportion. (Signed) James (Samuel) Dunlap.

Mr. Sproule: Be pleased to let William Elet have as much linen cloth as will make him a shurte, and in so doing you will oblige your friend and humble servant. (Signed) James Dunlap. April 5, 1757. To Mr. William Sproule.

FEBRUARY, 1763 (A).

Hugart vs. Bratton.—January 25th, 1758. Capt. Dunlap. Sir:—Please to pay unto Thomas Hugart my pay when it comes into your hands, both my old time and new, and also three pound, twelve, that you were to stop in your own hand, and take his receipt, which I shall acknowledge, as, sir, you are not to fail to pay him, for I had money of him to the full value of my time. Sir, your compliance will very much oblige your friend and very humble servant. (Signed) Josias Wilson.

May, 29th day, 1747.—This day I received of Samuel McClure, in full for two hundred and eighty akers of land for part as quit rents for six years and survey, I say, received by me. (Signed) Benj. Borden. Nathaniel McClones.

MARCH, 1764 (B).

Gilbert vs. Bright.—Peter Hog's bond, 30th January, 1764, upon attachment by Felix Gilbert, versus Samuel Bright, who, Peter Hog says, is run off.

To Capt. Daniel Smith—Stantown, September 25th, 1760. Sir:—This day we begin to gather our cattle, and it is our desire to have all yours upon the Fork as soon as possible, for I intend to start from there next week with all your company's stock, which I expect will amount to sixty or seventy. In order to drive to Pittsborg as for the rest that we have bought between the mountains, I think Mr. Lewis will be obliged to go to Pennsylvania with them, for there is no market at Winchester. I hope you will not disappoint me in driving your cattle to the Fork as soon as possible, for the year is far spent. This, sir, is from your humble servant. (Signed) William Crow.

SEPTEMBER, 1763 (B).

McClenachan vs. Calmer.—I promise to pay, &c., unto John McClenachan, &c., £9, 16, 7, Virginia currency, &c. 29th December, 1761. (Signed) D. Calmer. Test: Alex. Love. This day came the plaintiff, by his attorney, and the defendant being called and not appearing, Alex. Boyd, gent., a garnishee in this cause, appeared and on oath declared that at the time of serving this attachment in his hands there was due from the Country to the defendant, as Chaplain of the Virginia Regiment, two months' pay, amounting to £20, but that on settling his accounts with the Commissioners appointed for that purpose he was ordered not to pay it, whereupon the plaintiff produced the defendant's note of hand for £9, 16, 7. Judgment is therefore granted the plaintiff versus the said defendant for the same and costs. And it is ordered that the aforesaid sum of £20 in the hands of the garnishee, Boyd, be condemned, and it is further ordered that the Sheriff sell (one sword and see particulars) in the hands of Robt. McClenachan, a garnishee formerly sworn in this cause, who also made oath that the defendant was indebted to him £8, 10, 0, and that after paying the said Robt. McClenachan his debt aforesaid he pay the remainder, if any, to the plaintiff in part satisfaction of his judgment and costs, and that he have executed versus the garnishee, Alex. Boyd, for the residue.

FEBRUARY, 1763 (A).

Israel Christian vs. George Wilson.—Israel complains that George said of him, "You are a liar and you have this day been made a public liar, etc. I will prove you one." And whereas the said plaintiff was a Burgess of the said County in the General Assembly of this colony, begun and held at the Capitol in Williamsburg on the 14th day of September, in the 32d year of his late Majesty's reign. and during the several sessions thereof justly and faithfully, sincerely and uprightly, served as such Burgess to the time of the dissolution of the said Assembly, and during all that time performed the duty of his trust and office as a representative for the County aforesaid, by means whereof the said plaintiff afterwards, to wit, on the — day of May, 1761, at the County aforesaid, at a General Election of Burgesses for the County, and in pursuance of a writ under the seal of the Colony directed to the sheriff of the said County for the electing of two Burgesses to serve as representatives of the same County in the then approaching Assembly, to be held at the Capitol in Williamsburg, on the — day of —, in the first year of his present Majesty's reign. was elected by a great majority of the freeholders of the said County as Burgess for the same County in the said Assembly. Defendant, on the — day of October, 1761, at a general muster, having a discourse of and to the plaintiff as a Burgess and of an concerning and writing, or paper (which a certain William Preston had ordered to be read in the public Muster Field in vindication of his draughting the militia to serve on the frontiers as Colonel of the said County, to confute a report that prevailed to his disadvantage and which he alleged had been raised by the said plaintiff), in the presence and hearing, said, "You are a public liar and you impose upon the public; you endeavor to raise and support yourself at the expense of others and the prejudice of the public."

This day Andrew Greagh came before us and upon oath sayeth that on ye 18th night of this instant that he was present at Francis Tyler's ordinary and saw the within-mentioned John Boyers playing at a game called Seven and Eleven for money. (Signed) Andrew Greer. Archibald Alexander, Is. Christian, Justices.

This day came before us Saml. McDowel and upon oath sayeth that on the 18th night of this instant that he was present at Francis Tyler's ordinary, where he saw the within-mentioned John Boyers playing at Seven and Eleven for money. (Signed) Samuel McDowel. Archibald Alexander, Is. Christian.

Augusta County, to wit: Whereas John Boyers, gent, on the night of the 18th instant, was, upon our own view, found gaming at an unlawful game, called Haszard, or Seven and Eleven, in the house of Francis Tyler, ordinary keeper in the Town of Staunton, contrary to the Act of Assembly in that case made and provided, these are therefore in his Majesty's name to summon the said John Boyers to appear to answer the said complaint. (Signed) Is. Christian, Archibald Alexander. 19th August, 1762. To the sheriff of the County, or any constable of the County.

To Mr. William Bowyer, Merchant in Staunton: Richmond, 16th February, 1775. Dear Sir:—I have sent you sprecks of tobacco (which in truth I was obliged to steal from Mr. Coutts, for I don't chew now). I hope, however, you'll find it good, but I will tell him of it, and as its for you I am sure of no complaint. I shall endeavor to get your white head and samp black and send it by next opportunity, but at present its out of my power. I have your favor to Mr. Coutts with 29 casks butter, which shall be shipped on your account and risk. Annexed you have a note of things delivered the bearer. We really had not the salt, nor is there a sack in town, or believe me your wagon should not have gone empty, for I am really much distressed to see Augusta wagons go home empty. I wonder what their mad associations will come. I am giddy when I think about the dispute, it is too ardous a matter almost to think of. I wish they had taken more complacent methods. I am, sir, your most obedient servant. (Signed) James Watt.

Hamilton vs. Cunningham.—Hampshire County, to wit: John McCollough, of the said County, being first sworn, deposeth and saith: That he went to Pittsburg the latter end of July in the year 1760, where (when) Patrick Cunningham, of the County of Augusta, kept store for Messrs. Thomas Semen and Philip Bush and that ye current price of rum at that time was sixteen shillings, Pennsylvania money, per gallon in the wholesale way, but this deponent saith that all the spring before he arrived the current price as settled per the General's orders was twenty-four shillings of the same currency per gallon, and that he, this deponent, disposed of as much rum as came to upwards of eighty pounds at the rate of 24 shillings per gallon and as much more after July as came to £5.15.0 at the rate of 16 shillings per gallon. (Signed) John McCullough. 13th November, 1762. Sworn to before me, Jonathan Heath.

MAY, 1763 (B).

Bowyer vs. Gilbert.—The deposition of Thomas Bowyer, taken before me, Francis Tyler, one of his Majesty's Justices of the Peace, etc. Deponent says that at the time he went up to John Bowyer's to keep store for the defendant (Felix Gilbert) he told him he would be glad he would agree with the plaintiff (John Bowyer) for his board, upon which the defendant told the deponent he might agree himself with the plaintiff, upon which the deponent told the plaintiff Mr. Gilbert would pay him any reasonable charge for the deponent's board. Some time after Mr. Gilbert came up the deponent told Mr. Gilbert before the plaintiff to make a bargain about my board, upon which they had some words about it, the defendant told the plaintiff he might make his own charge, for he would leave it to himself. (Signed) Francis Tyler. Sworn to before me this 25th August, 1762.

MARCH, 1764 (B).

Frame vs. Hooks.—Sir:—Margaret Frame complains to me that you have taken advantage of her son in a bargain of gun swapping. I find there was a little deceit used, for you refused to stand to your agreement, for if you had not known you had the best of ye bargain, you would have been willing to have taken your own again. But I desire you will take your own without giving the widow any more trouble, or you may depend that I will take care to do both you and her justice. From, sir, your, (Signed) John Poage. This 10th February, 1763. To Mr. Robert Hooks.

Elphinstone vs. Blagg.—Captain John Blagg, debtor to Peter Elphinstone. 1761.—To sundries at Reed Creek, Stalnaker, and Long Island; sundry orders deliverd you which you promised to pay. (Signed) E. E. Peter Elphinstone. Sworn to in Frederick County, 10th April, 1762, before John Greenfield.

Donaho vs. Lomax.—1763.—The Stone Meeting House Congregation, debtor to William Lomax. For making on pulpit, £14.0.0. Contra: By cash, £6; by cash, £3; by cash, £0.11.0; by cash, £0.9.0.

JUNE, 1763 (B).

Alexander vs. Berrier.—August 22. David Bell to Philip Berrier. To wagon driving on campaign; to 4 days of a horse; to 6 months' wages; to cash on ye campaign; to one saddle.

AUGUST, 1764 (A).

Grimes vs. Bullitt.—1762, February 12. I do certify I paid Mr. Grimes no more than £2.4.0. Whoever had the other part of his butter is to pay Mr. Grimes for it. (Signed) John Bullitt. (On the back of above is a fragment, viz: Now lets deliver our silver to consider and raise up an army those villians to fight. O, we will covret them and all that protect them; we will teach them such manners as they never knew; we'll send some away back and others to Quebeck, and all their proceedings we'll make for rue.)

Paper endorsed: John Roller's last will. A copy. I, John Roller, of the County of Shenandoah. Some of children of very tender age. All real estate to be sold by executors and proceeds divided between all the children, viz: Jacob, Casper, Catharine Roller, Mary ——, John, Barbara, Rachel, Paul, Andrew, George, Margaret, Sarah, Michael, David, Peter. All to share alike, except my son, Paul Roller, whose share is to be $200 less than any of his brothers or sisters. This deduction I make from his share in consequence of his disobedience to me and —— of before he come of age and taking up with a woman of profligate character. Sons to be put to learn trades. Executors: Casper Roller and Andrew Zirkle, Jr. Dated, 7th June, 1806. (Signed in German. Test: John Crondson, James Anderson, Jane Allen, James Allen. Proved in Rockingham County, April Court, 1816, by Anderson, and at June, 1816, by Crondson. Executors refused to execute. Widow refused to administer. Administration granted George Roller. Test: S. McWilliams, clerk. Test: H. J. Gambill, C. R. C. A copy.

Samuel Gray vs. Thomas Rowland, administrator of Robert Rowland.— Superior Court of Law at Staunton. James Breckenridge deposes, 7th September, 1811, in Botetourt County, before Mathew Harvey, William Anderson: That shortly after the death of Robert, Thomas informed deponent that he had lost a considerable quantity of gunpowder, perhaps about five hundred weight, which he said belonged to Robert's estate, and had in his lifetime been made and packed perhaps for the plaintiff, to discharge a debt due to him which was payable in that article; that he apprehended it had been stolen by negroes in the neighborhood and desired this deponent to collect at the Court House such as he suspected for the purpose of examining them, which was done immediately. This happened shortly after the insurrection among the negroes in the neighborhood of Richmond was discovered. Deponent had no reason to believe that any quantity of gunpowder was stolen. Botetourt County records prove that defendant was convicted of slandering Paxton. John Smelzer was convicted in Sweet Springs District Court of slandering Joseph Ghent. Joseph Ghent is known to deponent since Joseph's infancy and is entitled to credit. On defendant's complaint many negroes were brought to the Court House and regularly examined, but nothing transpired to excite in deponent's understanding the least suspicion of their guilt.

A copy of the will of Walter Crow. Fee, 70 cents, paid in the office by W. Roalston. H. J. Gambrill. I, Walter Crow, of Rockingham County. To wife, Ann. To eight children, viz: Mary Harnsberry, James, John, William, Benjamin, Jacob Crow, Nancy Gregg, Rachel Harnett. Executors, wife Ann, and William Crow, third son of testator. "A certain obligation which John Crow obtained from William Crow at Lewis (Levines) Ferry, on James River, which John assigned to his father, Walter Crow, amounting to £20 principle, interest from August, 1784, if John shall pay some to Anne, etc.," otherwise the amount is to be deducted from John's share. Signed, sealed, etc., 6th August, 1789. Test: William Dunlap, Hannah (mark) Roadecap and lie for, etc. (Signed) William Ewen, C. R. C. Proved in clerk. 28th September, 1789, Rockingham County. Proved by Hannah Roadecap and lie for, etc. Signed) William Ewen, C. R. C. Proved in

Rockingham, 26th October, 1789, by Elizabeth Roadecap. Administration granted widow, Anne; other executor failed to appear. By the Court. (Signed) William Ewen, C. R. C. A copy. Test: H. J. Gambill, D. C. R. C.

To the Worshipful Court of Augusta. The humble petition of Elizabeth Lamb sheweth: That your petitioner, by reason of a piece of writing made by one, George Taylor, in the County of Augusta, and executed before a single magistrate, is obliged to serve and be a servant during the term and time of four years and a half. Therefore, your petitioner humbly prayeth that your worships will consider the case of your petitioner and give her to know what she must do, as she is not satisfied to serve by a piece of writing drawn in the country. Your worships will be able to judge when you see the writing whether it is an indenture or no. Therefore, in consideration of what is above written your petitioner hopes your worships will be pleased to do that which is right and justice shall appertain. And your petitioner shall pray for you. March 21, 1775.

PETITIONS, OCTOBER COURT, 1778.

To the Worshipful Court of Augusta County:

Gentlemen: As I had on ye fourth of July last convened my company by order of Col. Sampson Mathews, Christopher Graham, my first lieutenant, let me know that he intended soon to remove to the County of Hanaraco, Richmond town. On laying this before the company, they proceeded and by free and voluntary choice, chose Charles Baskin first lieutenant, James Gibson second lieutenant, James Graham ensign, to which choice each of them fell in by seniority. I hope it will also meet with your concurrence by recommending them for commissions according to the Act of Assembly. I am, gentlemen, with esteem, your humble servant. (Signed) Zechariah Johnston. October ye 9th, 1778.

19th March, 1787. Adolph Spindle, Clergyman's bond (with Philip Engleman, Frederick Hanger) to celebrate matrimony.

Commonwealth vs. Miller.—Proceedings. Augusta County. This day John Poage, Esq., came before me, Sampson Mathews, a Justice of the Peace for the said County, and made oath that he received a letter signed Alexander Miller, M. A., which he believes to be the handwriting of Alexander Miller, formerly a Presbyterian minister. Said letter was dated April 19th, 1777, and as it appears in the said letter that the said Alexander Miller has maliciously and advisedly, in open defiance of the Act of Gen'l Assembly of the Commonwealth of Virginia, passed the 7th day of October, 1776, for punishing certain offenses, he has endeavored by the words and sentences in the said letter to support, maintain, and defend the power, authority, and jurisdiction of the King of Great Britain within the Commonwealth of Virginia, contrary to the said Act and contrary to the safety, peace, and good order of the people of the said Commonwealth, as also a letter wrote by the said Miller to Col. Abraham Smith to the same effect. These are, therefore, in the name of the Commonwealth of Virginia, I command you to take the said Alexander Miller and bring him before me on Tuesday next, ye 26th instant, in order that he may answer to the said complaint, and this you shall in no way omit at your peril. You are hereby authorized to summon such guard as may be necessary for the safe conducting of the said Miller. Given under my hand and seal this twenty-second day of August, 1777. (Signed) Sampson Mathews (Seal). To John Erwin, constable, to execute and make return. You are required to summon Benjamin Erwin and John Christian, son of Robert, on behalf of the Commonwealth against the said Miller. Given under my hand ye 22d August, 1777. Executed 26th August, 1777. (Signed) John Erwin, constable.

Sir:—I congratulate you on your success at ye election, in ye words of Mordecia to Esther, 4, 14, "who knows but thou art come, for such a time (of calamity) as this and hope ye will make ye precept Exod. 23, 2, yet constant comparison in ye distressing crisis."

I write (as I proposed) to you with great cheerfulness, confidence, and freedom from a persuasion, yet I have to speak to a man of penetration and honesty, one who has ye fear of God before his eyes, and I hope and pray that you may have courage to appear for ye common good, as under ye inspection of ye God who stands and presides in ye Assemblies of ye Mighty.

I doubt not by year's time many, nay, contradictory, plans have been proposed to you and many wants complained of. I think I will complain to you of only two wants, viz: Peace and safety. Other wants will in time be rapidly supplied if these are obtained. You will say, how are these to be obtained? I answer, I think neither by war nor claiming independence; in war, unless by a miracle, we are unfit to conflict with Britain; and to claim indepencence appears to me evidently wrong, for ye following reasons, viz:

1. What deprives others of their property is unjust and useless; but independency deprives Britain of her property, therefore claiming independency is unjust and unlawful; ye first is true, property is by divine appointment, and to invade it is forbid by ye 8th Commandment. Therefore unjust and unlawful the second is thus proven, yet Britain has a property is allowed by common language, "British America," "British colonies,," our patents and ye consent of ye powers concerned in ye late pacification, but independency deprives Britain of her territories, i. e., of her property, therefore unjust and unlawful.

2. What is imprudent and unprofitable is a civil evil and loss to a people, but independency is imprudent and unprofitable, therefore evil and loss. Ye agreement is proven, thus civil prudence consists in increasing the wealth, in lowering taxes, in securing ye safety of ye people; ye opposites to these are imprudent and unprofitable. But independency stops our trade, increases our taxes, and exposes us to ye vengeance of Great Britain for attempting to rob her of her property, all which is evident; therefore independency is evil and loss.

3. What will be condemned by friends and enemies, expose a people to general disregard and to be deserted and opposed, nay exposed, to all ought not to be done; but claiming independency will produce all these evils, therefore claiming it ought not to be done. Thus is proven by ye first reason we will be condemned for perfidy and ingratitude to our founders and protectors, and suspected by friends and enemies for ye future. And as our claim is only by force and strength, a stranger may treat us as pirates and take per strength what we hold, and we can't complain of injustice done us, therefore independency ought not to be claimed.

4. What subjects men to ye divine displeasure and punishment ought to be avoided in conduct, but violating oaths to civil persons is such: Ezek. 17, 12 to 22. Independency is inconsistent with out allegiance to Britain. You see what will follow—either to avoid claiming independency or be subjected to ye divine displeasure and punishment. If, then, independency be unjust and unlawful, evil and loss; if it exposes to general condemnation and to be treated as pirates by any who can and will; if it subjects to ye divine displeasure and punishment; surely it will not, nor ought not, be claimed by any wise, honest, and Christian people. To these I could add more, but think these sufficient at present. You will ask, seeing peace and safety can't be obtained by war or independency, how then shall it be obtained? I answer: If we have done evil, let it be escaped from and not persisted in any longer; if we persevere in shedding more blood and prolonging ye calamities of war, we thereby increase ye guilt and misery of ye people. Shall ye continue to do what —— and at first ought not to be done? Our distress is great, but our rash folly has made it so. Our way and our doings have procured these things to ourselves, Jer. 4, 18. You have now an equal right and privilege with any other member to reason and even repeal all or anything hitherto done by conventions or congresses. I think it would be needful to inquire of ye people, ye commissioners of ye committees, whether it was their instructions to you to enter into war with and independence on Britain? And if these men, viz committees, etc., have exceeded ye powers ceded to them by their constituents, they and not ye people ought to suffer. To treat with Lord Howe for peace and safety is ye best plan you can fall upon to save ye lives and estates of your constituents. Great is ye trust now reposed in you and much good or injustice may and will result from your determinations. May God direct and strengthen you to do ye first and prevent you from being accessary to ye last is ye prayer of yours in sincerity,

April 19, 1777. ALEXANDER MILLER, M. A.

P. S.—If you desire it, I will send you some of my thoughts on ye bill of rights and plan of government; if you do, let me know by a line. 'Tis reported there has been an engagement to ye northward and yet ye Americans were not able to keep ye ground. As ye press is and ought to be open, if you see cause and think it will assure any good end, you may put this in a paper by ye following title, viz: A letter to a gentleman on his being elected a Burgess.

At a Court of Commissioners, held for Augusta County, the 16th day of July, 1776, and continued by adjournment to the 17th of July, 1776, at the Court House of the said County, agreeable to a commission from the late the Honorable the Committee of Safety of Virginia. Present: Samuel McDowell, gent; Michel Bowyer, gent; Sampson Mathews, gent.

The Commonwealth of Virginia against Alexander Miller, defendant.—Upon considering the charges against Alexander Miller, the defendant, as well as the evidence adduced in support of the same, and also the verdict of the jury, we, the Court, are of opinion that the matter, as far as it relates to aiding and giving intelligence to the enemy, comes within the ordinance of Convention, and therefore give judgment: That the said Miller be confined to the bounds of the plantation whereon he now lives, in this County, till the end of the present war with Great Britain, and that he do not in any manner aid, abet, correspond, or converse with the enemies of America, nor argue nor reason with any person or persons whatsoever on any political subject relating to the dispute between Britain and Amercia, or until he be thence discharged by the Executive Power, or General Assembly, of the Commonwealth of Virginia; and in the meantime he, the said Miller, be kept in safe custody until he shall enter into bond himself in the sum of one hundred pounds and two good securities in the sum of fifty pounds each. And that the whole of the costs of this prosecution be levied on the estate of the said Alexander Miller, viz: To Thomas Smith and James Hill, they finding themselves and horses for going 120 miles to William Hutchison's, on Indian Creek, in Botetourt County, each at the rate of 4 pence per mile, and for returning the same distance with the prisoner, at the rate of 4 pence per mile each. To Robt. McFarland, summoned by the officer; to assist, for going 50 miles, at 4 pence per mile. To the witnesses for attending one day each, 25 pounds of tobacco, or two shillings and one penny, viz: William Ewing, Silas Hart, Mary Erwin, James Montgomery, William Givens, Robert McFarland, Thomas Smith, and James Hill. To the clerk, for attendance two days, twenty shillings. To the sheriff, for attending the Court and summoning a jury, twenty shillings. To Daniel Kidd, for summoning the witnesses, in which he rode 150 miles, at four pence per mile. And that the clerk issue executions for the above sums, respectively, when required thereto by the claimants. (Signed) Samuel McDowell. A true copy. Test: William Cunningham, Clerk.

We of the jury do find the defendant guilty of the charge mentioned in the warrant, and do assess a fine of one hundred pounds and two years' imprisonment. (Signed) Jos. Humphreys.

Recognizance of Col. Abraham Smith, John Poage, Esq., Capt. David Bell and Mr. Benjamin Erwin to appear as witnesses, to be held for this County, on 3d Tuesday in September next by 10 o'clock in the forenoon, against Alexander Miller, M. A. Dated 26th August, 1777.

Bond, 22d July, 1776, by Alexander Miller, M. A.; John Miller, Alexander Long, conditioned according to the judgment of the Commissioners' Court, passed 17th July.

Letter addressed to Mr. James McChesney, Sorrey Cunty, North Carolina: Rockbridge County, July ye 27, 1788. Dear Cousin: This is the second time I wrote to you and have not heard of you or received a line from you. But I hope this will find you and your Mamey and your brothers and sisters well as we are at present. Joanna would be fond to see you all. I have heard that you were all in a notion of moving to Nolson or Frnch Broad, and I expect that either or Kentucky is better than where you live. I intend selling all the land I have and move, but I cannot sell that little place until you come and make me a deed, and if you comeI will give you a horse for your Mamey, I allow the best for you. He will be a horse that will carry you or your Mamey home again freely. Perhaps your Mamey will come with you. I would be fond to see you this fall, because as I —— off I would sell all together and I can have a deed made here by a lawyer. But it would be costly. No more at present, but give my respects to your mother, your brothers and sisters in general. Affectionate friend. (Signed) Samuel McChesney. Excuse haste.

Mem. for Mr. Williams: Enquire after Elliot Rutherford, executor to his brother, Thomas Rutherford, who died about 20 years ago. Spencer Hill married Mary Rutherford, daughter of Thomas Rutherford, deceased. Her fortune is in the hands of Elliot Rutherford, who lives about a mile from Rockingham Court House. Enquire what the fortune is, and how it is to be got.

N. B.—Suit must be brought in the name of Spencer Hill. The fortune is supposed to have been about £30 pounds at first.

This shall oblige me, my heirs and assigns to deliver unto Major William Long a warrant for one thousand acres of land for his service as a captain in ye Continental service. Given under my hand this 4th day of December, 1783. Witness: T. Madison. Assigned, 23d March, 1784, by William Long to Andrew Sutlington. (Signed) Alex. McClenachan. Test: Wm. Scott,

Dear Sir: I received a few lines from you while in Richmond concerning the money that my brother, Thomas', estate is indebted to you. I have your money ready if we could meet in Staunton. I shall be down at my brother, Michael Bowyer's, at General Washington's birth night if you can make it convenient to be up at Staunton about that time and bring the bond. I will pay the principal and interest, but my brother, in his lifetime, let your son, Stranther, have some money in camp. Shall be glad if you can get the amount from him, as you promised to discount it out of the bond. If you cannot be at Staunton at the time before mentioned, you will please to let my brother know when you can attend there and I will meet you. I am, dear sir, your most humble servant. (Signed) John Bowyer. 19th December, 1789. To Gabriel Jones, Esq.

DISTRICT COURT JUDGMENTS.

APRIL, 1790.

Adams vs. Bowyer.—Richmond, October 28, 1785. Sir:—The order of Court, directing payment to be made for the averages (?) of labor in the Clerk's Office of Augusta, out of Mr. Madison's estate, seems to me to be unwarranted by law, for it ought to have been the effect of an agreement between Mr. Madison's representatives and them. Nor do I conceive that you can maintain an action in your own name for what you have done, because there is no privity between you and Mr. Madison's estate. I therefore rather advise that a suit be instituted in the name of the justices against Mr. Madison's administrators by way of a special action in the case. The charges against Mr. Madison must be for breach of duty, and the amount of the damages will probably be equal to what you have desired for bringing up the records. I am, sir, your most obedient servant. (Signed) Edm. Randolph.

Augusta Sec.—Inquisition at Staunton the 19th of May, in the thirteenth year of the Commonwealth, before Joseph Bell, gent, one of the coroners. Upon the view of the body of a person unknown in a cave, discovered by Michael Grove, John Robeson, Robert Jacobs, —— dead and much consumed and upon oaths of (the jurors who sign below) —— do say that he was a white man, and it appears to them from circumstances to be the body of a certain William R. Watson, who was an inhabitant of Staunton about November last, and that the said person has been murdered wilfully by some person or persons unknown to us. (Signed) Joseph Bell, coroner; John Griffen, foreman; Michael Garber, Samuel Merritt, William McDowell, Michael Sivert, Herman Lovingood, Owen Owens, James McLaughlin, Abraham Groves, Francis Huff, John Gorden, Henry Hauk, Robert Astrop, Hugh McDowell, Michael Cawley, James McGongal, Daniel Donavan.

Augusta Sec.—On the 9th day of June, 1788, called before me Joseph Bell, coroner for said County, the subscribers being a majority of the within jurors, to take up the said matter from finding further testimony was to be had in the matter, caused to come before us Alexander Humphreys and William Wardlaw. After being sworn, Alexander Humphreys deposeth and sayeth: That about March last that his students, William Wardlaw and James McPheeters, did take from the place of burial a negro and dissect him for their information and that he understood they sewed him up in a bag and put him in the cave within mentioned, and further deposeth that after a negro lays some time in his grave the odds cannot be known between him and a white person as to color. Mr. Wardlaw deposeth and sayeth: That about March Court last him and James McPheeters opened a negro grave and took therefrom the body, in order to dissect the same for their insight in their business, and after doing so, did sew him up in a crokass bag and put him in the cave within mentioned. But sayeth when they took him up he appeared of an ash color and that, while they had him in custody, his color did not change as well as he recollects and further sayeth not. (Signed) Joseph Bell, coroner; Michael Garber, Daniel Donovan, Hugh McDowell, Michael Syvert, Hermon Lovingood, Samuel Merritt, John Garden, James Megongal Francis Huff, Owen Owens, James McGlachlin.

Commonwealth vs. Wm. Hinton, Martin Gryder, John Gryder.—Augusta Sec.—This day David Harned and John Owens, before me, that on Wednesday, the 13th of this instant, William Hinton came to the house of the said David Harned, with an armed force, and declared himself in the favor of the Crown of Great Britain and that General Howe might as well go home with his men, for he could raise men enough to subject the country and that he would do it yet; and also inquired for Captain Hite and Joseph Smith, and swore that if he could catch them he would strip them and tie them to an apple tree and whip them till they would be willing to enlist into his service and swear to be true to him; and spoke very disrespectful of General Washington and of his troops in general. That the country belonged to the King and that the King would keep it yet, and that he would go as Captain and raise better men than the country could; and that the above conversation was repeated sundry times, and further these deponents saith not as witness our hands this 16th day of August, 1777. (Signed) David Harned, John Owens. Sworn before me. Daniel Smith.

Sir:—I have received information by the deposition of David Harned, etc., that a certain William Hinton has openly appeared in defense of George the Third, King of Great Britain, and in open violation against the United States of America, and has enlisted men in behalf of the King of Great Britain. These are therefore to request you, in the name of the Commonwealth, to raise any number of volunteers or as many as you will think necessary without the loss of time. You are to march your men to Smith's to apprehend the said William Hinton and all his abettors and all those concerned in behalf of the said King and in violation against this Commonwealth. You are to bring them to Staunton and have them secured under a proper guard until proper proceedings can be had on them, and I expect they will receive their proper reward of their deserts. You are to be reinforced by Capt. David Bell, Thomas Hewit, Capt. William Anderson, Captain Hopkins and Capt. Daniel Smith. Herein fail not. Given under my hand this 19th August, 1777. (Signed) Abraham Smith. To Capt. Patrick Buckhanon. Endorsed: "By virtue of the within order, I have taken Martin Groeder and Henry Groeder, and John Groeder, William Hinton, Peter Hinton, and Elisha Nox, and brought them before Sampson Mathews, William Bowyer and Alexander St. Clair. (Signed) Patrick Buchanan. August 21, 1777.

August County, Sec.—To the sheriff, or goaler, of the County ——. We send you herewith the bodies of William Hinton, Martin Groeder and John Groeder, taken and brought ——. by warrant —— of Abraham Smith, Esq., County Lieutenant, upon information made upon oath before Daniel Smith, Esq., by David Hernot and John Owens of being guilty of a breach or coming under the Act of Assembly made in this State for punishing certain offenses and after learning sundry evidences, viz: David Harnet, John Owens, Thomas Alderson, Joseph Smith, John Conner, Joseph Burgess, Jacob Falkner, George Keller, Peter Grass, John Bright, we are of opinion that the said William Hinton, Jr., Martin Groeder, and John Groeder have been guilty of a breach of the Act aforesaid. You are therefore required to receive them —— until they shall from thence be discharged by order of the Justices of our said Court, to be held on the Third Tuesday in September next, and this shall be your warrant. Given under our hands and seals this 23d day of August, 1777. (Signed) Sampson Mathews (seal), William Bowyer (seal), Alexander Sinclair (seal).

Spa for witnesses for defence, viz: Robert Harrison (son of Thomas), Jonathan Haynes, James See (?), Catharine Keisell, Daniel Smith, Sr., William Vance, Elizabeth Scothran, Isaiah Harrison, Thomas Lookey, Abraham Bowyer, William Russell, Thomas Moore. Verdict of Guilty vs. John Groeder, fined £2 and two years' imprisonment. Verdict of guilty vs. Martin Groeder, fined £50 and three years' imprisonment. Verdict of guilty vs. William Hinton, fined £400 and four years' imprisonment.

(On back of the papers is an abstract of the evidence in handwriting of the clerk, evidently jotted down for his own amusement):

Joseph Smith—reputed Tory and drinking the King's health. Capt. Hite intended to take him and desired Smith to go with him. Went to Hinton's mill. Found and seized him. Resisted. Got away. Stoned them. Called to them and told them, you will be all hanged yet. Followed them. With stones. Two recruits. Offered them ye money (?) and would not go with d—— scoundrel. Willing to go before. Several suspected Tories. Johnson, whom Hinton called out to assist him and damned him for not complying with his sworn word. A barbeque that night when open war was to be declared. Arnet, Owens and Alderson.—Hinton followed Hite and Smith. Where the d—— Tory catchers. If here I would tie to apple tree and would whip till I made them enlist in my service. I am Tory. The King has a right to the country and shall have it. Have no occasion to come here, for I can raise men enough to take the country and I will do it, for I am Captain of better men than they. Whipped two of their officers today and served them in ye same manner as how did Washington. See Howe drive them as stray sheep. Mrs. Scothern.—Had sworn two into his service. Who are they? Phillips and Williams, who had before entered into our service. (Proved by Alderson.) Bright.—Damned him for giving information to take up Tories and turned his pistol towards him. Burgess.—Last fall heard him declare himself a King's man, and that the King had a right to the country. Heard some good news. What it was—Howe driving General Washington through the Jersey. Do you call that good news? Yes.

Commonwealth vs. John Archer.—Similar to above.

PETITIONS.

March, 1775.

This day Mary Gregory came before me and made oath that the Indians came to her house and took from her four hogs and one cow of the value of eleven pounds, ten shillings about five years ago. Given under my hand this 22d March, 1775. (Signed) John Poage. They said they were Mingoes. Mr. Gregory lives on the head of Greenbrier.

Augusta County to the Worshipful Court of aforesaid: Whereas my husband, David White, was killed in last expedition and his affairs were unsettled, I not being able to come to Court, humbly pray that your honors will see for (supor?) my father, Jacob Eaverman, to administer on his estate. Witness my hand this 15th of March, 1775. (Signed) Cateren (mark) White. Robert Minnes, Andrew Skidmore.

13th September, 1839, personally appeared Elizabeth Balsley, aged 79 years, made the following declaration, act of 7th July, 1836: That she is the widow of Christian Balsley, who was a private in the war of the Revolution, and who was placed upon the pension roll on the 4th of March, 1831, and which will appear by his pension certificate hereto annexed. She was married 9th August, 1778, in County of Cumberland, Pennsylvania. That she was not married to him prior to his leaving the service. Christian died, 22d June, 1837, in Augusta County.

Certificate, 19th June, 1788, that Joseph Maze, aged about 32 years, late a private of the militia of Augusta County, was disabled in the service of this Commonwealth by a wound in his right leg. Is allowed eight pounds yearly from 1st January, 1786. (By) Edmund Randolph.

31st October, 1793.—Gov. Henry Lee certifies that said Joseph Maze is continued on pension list. 13th December, 1791.—Same certifies that John Wheeler, late a private in the State Line and disabled in the service of this Commonwealth, is put on the pension list at £8 yearly from 1st January, 1792. 22d August, 1791.—John Burton's assignment to James Johnson four years of his pension for 1791-92-93-94. Test: John Craig, who deposes, 1st April, 1793, that on the 14th of last February, John Burton was alive at his house in Boncom County, North Carolina. 31st October, 1793.—Henry Lee certifies that John Burton, formerly a private in the Old Virginia Regiment, in year 1760, and disabled in service of this Commonwealth, continued a pensioner at £5 yearly.

Bath County, to wit: This day John Dickinson made oath that he has been so indisposed in body for more than three months past that he has not been able to travel to Staunton Court to look after his pension warrant. (Signed) Samuel Shrewsbury. 14th April, 1794.

I do further hereby certify that above deponent has for better than three months been the greatest part of the time dangerously ill with sickness, pains and a swelling in his body and often attended with high fevers, but is now on the mending hand, but not yet fit to ride any distance about his own plantation. (Signed) Samuel Shrewsbury. 14th April, 1794.

7th December, 1790.—Beverley Randolph certifies that John McKinney, about 33 years of age, late a private in the troop raised for an expedition against the Indians in the year 1774, and disabled by several wounds at the battle of Point Pleasant in the service of Virginia, is continued pensioner at £15 annually, commencing 1st January, 1790.

22d October, 1789.—Same certifies to same. John was disabled by two balls, which passed through the thick muscles of his left thigh and tore and lacerated them in a great degree. Endorsed, with certificate, Fayette County Court—July Court, 1790—that John McKinney proved himself to be the person mentioned in above certificate.

CIRCUIT COURT CAUSES ENDED—OLD STYLE.

No. 5.

Browning vs. Swearingen.—In year 1736 John Browning purchased of Jorst Hite 1,200 acres on the Potomac. John died testate, devising the lands to sons, George and Nicholas. George died testate and devised to Joshua Browning. Nicholas died testate, devising to John Wrightson Browning. Oratrix Rosamon married Wm. Keating. Anthony Turner deposes: That he came into this State, now Berkeley County, with his father, Anthony Turner, deceased, on May, 1740. He was then eight years old. He lived there until fall of 1752, when he removed to New Castle County; removed from there August, 1762, to Carolina; made frequent removes but returned to Berkeley County in December, 1773. John Van Unter (Nuter) deposes: He was born in Berkeley County and on 6 March, 1798, was in sixty-second year of age.

No. 17.

Acklin vs. Walker.—Settlement of the Wolf Hill tract with list of the settlers in Washington County: Samuel Biggs, James Craig, Samuel Evans, David Gitgood, John Vance. Affidavit of Alexander Breckinridge, of Bourbon County.

No. 18.

Buchanan vs. Dorsey.—From Ohio County, November, 1796. John Vance made a settlement of the same land on which John Black had settled on

Middle Wheeling Creek and transferred his right to Walter Buchanan. Deed by John Black, of Washington County, Pennsylvania, to Jos. Dorsey, of Washington County, Pennsylvania, 1796. Test: Henry and John Perviance.

Bowyer vs. Smith.—Deed, dated 27th October, 1794, by David Smith and wife, Mary, Christian Smith and Catherine, his wife, of Rockingham County, to Jacob Bowyer, of same County.

No. 19.

Caldwell vs. Campbell.—John Campbell, of Berkeley County, sold to Caldwell land on northwest side of Ohio River, part of 1,250 acres belonging to John, who was heir-at-law of Archibald Campbell, deceased (1796), in whose name 6,000 acres were located.

Madison vs. Lewis.—William Madison and Col. James Barnett were soldiers in the battle of Guilford in 1781. John Thompson's answer to bill filed against him, together with Joseph and James Thompson, by James M. Marshall, in the High Court of Chancery of Virginia. His father, William Thompson, removed from Maryland to Virginia in 1747. Soon afterwards Fairfax issued a proclamation encouraging those persons who had settled upon his lands to continue thereon, and that they should have 400 acres for each settlement. The alarm the dispute between Fairfax and the Crown had excited amongst the people was his reason for this means being taken to quiet them. William remained upon his settlement until 1793, when he died intestate, having six lawful children, viz: John, Joseph, James, William, Henry Sarah (now wife of Jacob Hidener, of Hardy County). Sworn to in Frederick County by John Thompson, 27th July, 1799.

No. 23 (or 22?).

Kinkade vs. Cunningham.—Bill filed 1803. Thomas Kinkade was a very ignorant and illiterate man. Walter Cunningham bought the land from Andrew Donnelly and is now living in Kentucky. Margaret Reid, who married George Mathews, is aunt, or near relative of Walter Cunningham. John Beard deposes: That in 1762-3 he worked a crop with William McClenachan on a plantation on Spring Creek, called Spring Lick plantation. An improvement had been previously made by Christopher Landiss. Andrew Donnelly testifies: That in 1753 John and Robert Fulton planted four acres of corn on a plantation now (1802) owned by William Reenick, called Cave Place. The Fultons lived there with their families and deponent lived there with them for the purpose of digging quisang. Boughman's fort was broken up by Indians in 1754. William Kincaid was son of Thomas. James Burnsides was an early settler. Eve Johnston deposes: That she lived on Potts Creek in 1782, and several years before she lived within a mile of Christopher Landiss (Landers) in 1753-54. Christopher Persinger deposes: That he, with Landers, first improved the land.

No. 8.

Fry vs. Hunter.—Petition shows that Benjamin Rush and John Moffett purchased the shares of Bullett and Wilfut (feet). Bill filed 1796. Spa.

1797, to Botetourt for Moses Hunter and wife, Andrew Lewis, Alexander Love and wife. Spa. to Norfolk County, 1797, for Alexander Love and wife returned executed.

Fox vs. Throckmorton.—Bill, 1788. Orator and oratrix are John Fox and wife, Grace. Grace was daughter of John (William?) Young, who died intestate. John Throckmorton, of Gloucester County, administered and was appointed guardian of Grace. Throckmorton died testate, in Berkeley County. John Fox dates a notice "Louisa County, 1793."

No. 22.

Jones vs. Tomlinson.—Orator is David Jones. In 1772 David Jones made a settlement on Grave Creek, in Ohio County. Joseph Tomlinson obtained a settlement certificate for himself and Charles McLean. In 1770 David Owings made settlement near Jones, which was confirmed by law of 1799. Settlement made in 1771 on land of Joseph Coving, land claimed by Jones, by Nathaniel Tomlinson, who transferred to Joseph. In 1772 Nathaniel sold to Campbell and Talin. Benjamin Biggs was a justice of Ohio County, and Silas Hedges was sheriff in 1785. The Commissioners to settle unpatented lands in 1781 were: James Neal, Charles Martin, and William Haymond (Hayward); William McClung was chairman. Charles McClean deposes, in Fayette County, Pennsylvania, 1804: He first went to Grave Creek Flats in 1772, where he saw George R. Clarke, who surveyed the Flats into various tracts. Plaintiff acted under the Indiana Company. Charles McClean moved with his family to Grave Creek Flats in December, 1773, and settled at McClains's Spring. He left in May, 1774, in consequence of the breaking out of Dunmore's war. Morgan Jones deposes, in Jueen County, Pennsylvania: He first visited the Flats in 1772. Plaintiff had employed George Rogers Clark to survey the Flats into tracts. The first tract was laid off for Morgan Jones. Second for Joseph Tomlinson. Third for David Jones, plaintiff. The line passed over one of the little *graves*. Charles McDonald was also one of the settlers.

No. 13.

Noble vs. Taylor.—In 1785 Mahlon Taylor, of New Jersey, sold land in Frederick County to Noble—Mahlon afterwards married and moved to Albany. On May 15, 1800, Mahlon Taylor, administrator of Mahlon Taylor, late of New York, answers: Deed, dated 24th January, 1791, by Mahlon Taylor and wife, Mary, of Hunterdon County, New Jersey.

No. 182.

Taylor vs. Taylor's Administrator.—Suit begun 1805 by John Taylor, of Augusta County, vs. John Taylor, son of Nathaniel Taylor. Nathaniel died in Jefferson County, September, 1804, intestate, leaving orator and nine other children. Thomas Taylor, brother and orator, qualified administrator. Nathaniel, Jr., was another brother. Orator's sister married William Fig. Orator's sister, Nancy, married George Bozewell and moved to Kentucky. In division of estate by order County Court of Jefferson, 1806, these heirs named: Thomas Taylor, Elizabeth Figg, Fanny Taylor, James Taylor, John Taylor, William Taylor. Figg's wife was Mary.

514

Taylor vs. Tate and Campbell.—John Taylor married Elizabeth, daughter of Charles Campbell, prior to 1774. Charles's daughter, Jean, married Thomas Tate. Margaret married Arthur Campbell. James, John M. C., Mary M. C., Allen Taylor were relatives.

PENSION LISTS—PRINTED—FILED IN COUNTY COURT OFFICE.

Pensioners belong to following corps:
7th Va. Regt.—Lee's Legion, Buford's Detachment.
15th Va. Regt.—2d State Regt., Militia, 1st Regt. Dragoons.
12th Va. Regt.—2d Regt. Dragoons, Heth's Detachment.
4th Va. Regt.—10th Va. Regt., 2d Va. Regt.
Roger's Regt.—9th Va. Regt., 2d Regt. Militia.
11th Va. Regt.—Corps of Invalids, Campbell's Detachment.
8th Va. Regt.—Thruston's Volunteers, 3d Dragoon Regt.
1st Dragoon Regt.—6th Dragoon Regt., 6th Va. Regt.
3d Va. Regt.—1st State Regt., Grayson's Regt., 3d Regt. Dragoons.
1st Regt. Artillery.—1st Regt. Dragoons, 2d Regt. Dragoons.
Harrison's Regt.—Haw's Detachment, 1st State Regt.
Kentucky Militia.—Stephenson's Regt., 5th Va. Regt.
9th Va. Regt.—Hazen's Regiment, 13th Va. Regt.
1st Regt. Militia.—Morgan's Rifle Corps, 14th Va. Regt.
Gaskin's Regt.

COUNTY COURT RECORDS.

Mutilated letter with notes endorsed on it. No name. No date:
Honorable Sir:
    you'l obse
a considerable Body
a Fort on
was erected by som
likewise on the su
at a place known by the name of
which was Garrison
belonging to Capt.
Jas. Dunlap it
with the poor

_____

are from House
Drafted for wa
obeyed as this un
ants into so great a
are about to re
you with this Malon

P. S.—There was a detachment from Captain Hog's Fort, at Brock's Gap, sent to the assistance of Captain Dunlop, which we suppose have fallen into the hands of the enemy as they have not yet been heard of, which has reduced Captain Hog's Rangers to the number of about twenty.

Endorsement:—Unless you can fall on some speedy method for the protection of the inhabitants, especially those between this Court House and Frederick County (the southern parts being protected by several ranging companies), one other inrode of those savages will effectually depopulate at least that part of the County.

I, Thomas Lyons, of Greenville, in Augusta County, and State of Virginia, under apprehension of approaching death, do make this my last will and testament. It is my will that my brother, William Lyons, of the Town, County and State aforesaid, shall, after paying all my just debts, receive and possess all my estate, real and personal, wheresoever it may be found. Given under my hand and seal in the Chickasaw Nation this 8th day of July, 1806. (Signed) Thomas Lyons. Test: John McKee, Samuel Mitchell, Malcom (mark) McGhe. Proved, 19th July, 1806, before Samuel Mitchell, agent for the United States to the Chickasaw Nation in the Chickasaw Agency, by John McGee and Malcom McGee. Recorded, 19th July, 1806, in the book of the Chickasaw Agency. A true copy of Thomas Lyons's will, 16th August, 1806. Test: Jefferson L. Edmonds, M. T. Stribling (Stirhling).

To the Worshipful Court of Augusta, Greeting: We, the subscribers hereof, having taken the oath of fidelity to this State, looked upon the aforesaid oath to be sufficient unless we had been found faulty in giving in of our property, which we never kept back, nor have we refused to pay our public debts, but are willing to act as true sustainers of this State, for us to appear at Court looks like murder, to leave our families to the ravages of a savage enemy and hope you will in your wisdom consider us, &c., &c. (Signed) Charles Fornalson, Jonathan Boffanton.

October, 1851.—Order: That satisfactory evidence has been adduced to the County Court of Augusta that Thomas Yorkshire was a pensioner of the United States at the rate of $8 per month; was a resident of the County of Augusta, in the State of Virginia, and died in said County and State in the year 1837, on the 24th day of February; that he left no widow but two children, Nancy and John. This day, 27th October, 1851, Joseph Smith made oath that he was well acquainted with Thomas Yorkshire (as above).

Corporation of Staunton, to wit: 26th April, 1823.—Smith Thompson deposes: He was well acquainted with Samuel Bell, and that he served in the Virginia Line on Continental establishment during the Revolution as an ensign in Captain McGuire's Company, attached to the 16th Regiment, commanded by Col. William Grayson; that he was afterwards promoted to a lieutenancy and attached to Capt. Thomas Bell's company in the same regiment, the said McGuire having resigned. The said Samuel Bell was at the battles of Brandywine, German Town, Guilford Courthouse, and Hot Water, in which (last) he was wounded in eight or nine places and taken prisoner, and afterwards taken by the enemy to Williamsburg and paroled and continued in the army to the end of the war as a supernumerary officer. Said Bell died in the town of Staunton in year 1788.

Jackson's River, May ye 15th, 1755. Dear Brother:—I have been stopping here several days in purchasing of provisions. I have purchased as much grain as will serve three months, but will have a great deal of deficiency in getting of meat. I propose to march in ye Narrows towards Greenbrier.

I think I shall get to Marlings in two days, where I purpose to construct a small fort. I hope you will be so kind as to remind Mr. Jones to bring pay for my company from Colonel Wood as often as he has an opportunity, which he promised to do. I have nothing that is new to aquaint you of. I am, dear brother, your most affectionate and very humble servant. (Signed) Andrew Lewis.

P. S.—If you see Mr. McNeal, pray hasen him to me.

19th March, 1793.—James Brownlee deposes: That John Brownlee, aged about 78 years, is a material witness.

ORDERS OF COURT.

Augusta, 1758.

To Mr. John Madison, in Augusta.—November 2, 1758. Dear Sir:— I wrote you last night by Mr. McMahon. I have nothing to add but that I have sent you, per Ned, as many peaches as cost 6/3, beside what is in a bag. You will readily know by the color of them that they were bought of persons of the same hue. I hope Mrs. Madison will excuse the bad choice, as my cousin, Ned, gave me but an hour to provide for him. Those in a small bag and the apples my wife compliments your children with. I wish them safe to hand and have ordered Ned to make two days' journey home. I think the peaches are too heavy for his horse to carry them home in one day. I hope you will approve of the orders. I am, with the same respect as usual, yours, &c. (Signed) James Madison.

P. S.—I am too lazy and lame to go to the other house at this time of night for more paper—30 past 8 precisely.

To Thomas Walker, Esq.—Old Town, August 30th, 1760. Dear Sir:— The answer given me by Mr. Hoops, to my account, pasturage of cattle in 1758, greatly surprises me. He tells me the account is out of time, the charge is exorbitant, and that he don't believe that the pasturage was had. It is very extraordinary that a man of his forbearance should be cut out of his money. As to the rate charged, it is the same paid me daily, and as to the number of cattle and sheep charged, it is not a fourth part of what were pastured that year by me, Mr. Galbraith only signing a certificate for those last taken away, without allowing anything for what were killed the whole summer for the garrison at Fort Cumberland. As I always looked on you as a gentleman of an established good character, I cannot think you will agree to an act of injustice. Therefore hope you will order the payment of this account and prevent my giving you any trouble, that on its not being discharged I must, in justice to myself, do, and which would be very disagreeable to me. At the time the cattle were brought to my plantation, there was above 60 acres of meadow fit to mow, as good as ever scythe was put into, besides 60 acres of exceeding good pasture, and they had the full swing of the whole plantation. If I am obliged to make use of any means to right myself, which may not be agreeable to you, hope you will excuse me, as I choose rather to seek justice in Virginia than in Pennsylvania. I am, sir, your most humble servant. (Signed) Thomas Cresap.

To the Worshipful the Justices of Augusta: The humble petition of Terrence Carbarry sheweth: That your petitioner was brought a servant into this County from Pennsylvania by John Risk, who sold him to Francis Beattey, and was again sold by said Beattey to James Rosebrough with whom he served last of his time, and is now likely to be defrauded out of his freedom dues. May it therefore please your worships the premises to consider and to appoint unto your petitioner such freedom as ye law directs, either against Francis Beattey, or John Rosebrough, and your petitioner (as in duty bound) shall pray.

AUGUST, 1780 (A).

To the gentlemen of the committee in the respective companies of Augusta County. Gentlemen: From some late occurrences it has been judged necessary to call a convention of delegates from the various counties and burroughs of this colony to meet at Richmond, in the County of Henrico, on the 20th of March next, and it is become a question whether the right of electing such delegates is vested in your committee, or in the freeholders of this County in general. You are requested to assemble the respective companies to which you belong and deliberate whether it will be most convenient for the freeholders to assemble to make such election themselves, or refer it to the judgment of the committee, who are hereby requested to meet in Staunton on Wednesday, the 22d instant, to make report of the determination of the respective companies on this head, and consider of such other matters that then may be laid before them. (Signed) Thomas Lewis, Sampson Mathews, William Lewis, Alexander McClenachan, Michael Bowyer. February 2, 1775.

Bohannon vs. Martin.—Copy of Proceedings. Writ, dated 21st December, in 31st year of reign. By John Buchanan, gent., vs. Patrick Martain.— Account of what militia was under command of Capt. Patrick Martain since the 2d of May:

Name.	When Entered.	Days on duty.	When Discharged.	Pay per die
Capt. Patrick Martain	Aug. 4th	36	9 Sept.	10/
Adam Thompson	Aug. 4th	28	1 Sept.	1/
Samuel Black	Aug. 4th	36	9 Sept.	1/
David Stuart, Serg.	Aug. 4th	36	9 Sept.	1/4
John Perrie	Aug. 4th	36	9 Sept.	1/
Patrick English	Aug. 4th	34	7 Sept.	1/
John Vance	Aug. 4th	36	9 Sept.	1/
William Hodge	Aug. 4th	36	9 Sept.	1/
Charles Erwin	Aug. 4th	36	9 Sept.	1/
Edward Hinds	Aug. 4th	36	9 Sept.	1/
John Trimble	Aug. 4th	12	16 Aug.	1/
John Beard	Aug. 16th	24	9 Sept.	1/
Gabriel Guile	Aug. 23rd	15	7 Sept.	1/
Archibald Gilkeson	Aug. 16th	24	9 Sept.	1/
Jacob Guile	Aug. 23rd	15	7 Sept.	1/
George Guile	Aug. 23rd	15	7 Sept.	1/
John Jameson	Aug. 26th	8	3 Sept.	1/
William Martain	Aug. 26th	8	3 Sept.	1/

Sworn to 16th December, 1756, by Capt. Pat. Martin. Receipt, 16th December, 1756, by Capt. Pat. Martin for above.

The Country, debtor to provisions expended per Capt. Patrick Martin and company, when on duty in his Majesty's service: To 300 lbs. flour from Samuel Black at 10/ per 100, £1, 10, 0; to 16 lbs. butter from Michael Harper at 4d., 2/; to ¼ lb. salt from George Capler, 3/; to 1 cow from Valentine Guile, £1, 1, 6; to ¼ lb. salt from George Capler, 3/; to 42 lbs. mutton from Val. Guile, 5/3; to 183 lbs. flour from Michael Brock, 18/3¾; to 277 lbs. beef from Val. Guile at 10/ per 100, £1, 7, 8; to wild meat from John Vance, 2/6; to carcas venison from John Garden, 1/6; to 35 lbs. flour from Val. Guile, 3/6; to 4 bushels potatoes from Val. Guile, 4/6; to two horses, with driver, four days, at 4/6 per day, 18 shillings; to one horse at mill, 1/6; to same, 1/6; to four lbs. butter, 1/10½; to impressed from John Givens 32 head (lead), £1; to provisions from William Hoger, 7/0. October 22, 1756. Sworn to 16th December, 1756, by Capt. Pat. Martin. Receipt, 16th December, 1756, by Capt. Pat. Martin. Declaration in asst. against Pat. Martin for above amounts.. A copy. (Signed) John Madison.

April 24, 1823.—Joseph Bell, Jr., deposes to same effect as Smith Thompson, *supra*, as to his brother, Samuel Bell. Samuel entered the Army 8th day of March, 1777. Samuel died in Staunton in 1788, leaving Sarah, Thomas, John Bell and affiant as his legatees. Said Thomas Bell died testate in Albemarle County; that said John also died testate in Augusta County. Order entered by the Court in accordance with above facts, and further that Thomas Bell left William Love, Robert Washington Bell, Sally Jefferson Bell and Mary Wills his legatees.

DISTRICT COURT RECORDS.

JUDGMENTS.

1796 (A to K).

Rebecca McPheeters vs. Woods.—Jane McPheeters deposes, 11th September, 1795, that: She was with her sister, the plaintiff, at John Campbell's some time in May, 1794, being the night before the said Campbell set off for Greenbrier. Polly Notly–Patterson Thompson.

SEPTEMBER, 1802 (A to G).

Court of Rockbridge versus Steele.—List of delinquents and insolvents in the County Levy for 1796 in the Northeast District, by J. Purris, D. S. for S. Keys, S. R. C.: Abednego Casteel, runaway; William Campbell, removed to Amherst; Torence Doran, removed; John Donnaho, Jr., Botetourt; Peter Horn, removed; James Martin, removed to Kentucky; Samuel Paxton, Sr., removed to Amherst; Samuel Raneck, removed to Kentucky; Robert Simpkins, removed; Simpson Sturgeon, removed to Tennessee; Peter Sumbro, removed to Augusta; Thomas Tongate, Amherst.

APRIL, 1793 (A to Q).

We, the undernamed jurors for the Commonwealth of Virginia, present that Alex. Sproul did, on the 18th day of January last, in the County aforesaid, unlawfully make a forcible entry into the house and possession of George Almarode, with arms, of which he was then possessed, and does continue to keep out the said Almarode, to his hurt and damage. In witness whereof the undernamed jurors have hereunto set their hands and seals this 13th day of February, 1792. (Signed) Francis Hull, John Summers, Robt. Morris, Robert Cooper, Samuel McCutchan, Andrew Donaldson, Thomas Boyd, John McCoskry, David Humphreys, James Cunningham, George Everts, Jacob Wehrly, John Cunningham, Robert Hanna, John McCutchan, Henry Venus, Ro. Tate, Hugh Dougherty, Henry Minger, William McCutchan, John Foulwidder, John Logan, Mexard Berryhill, James Henry.

SEPTEMBER, 1802 (A to G).

Court of Rockbridge vs. Steel.—List of delinquents in County Levy with the District of Hawkins Windell, Commissioner, for the year 1796: Lasty F. Ayten, Frenchbroad; Eden Bales, Kentucky; James Bales, Kentucky; James Buckerage, Cumberland; John Cowan, Cumberland; James Curry, removed; John Collins, Holsteen; John Duff, Tennessee; Samuel Aires, Bath County; Mark Biggs, runaway; John Brown, Botetourt; Caleb Beggs, Botetourt; Jacob Collier, Pennsylvania; Samuel Corwen, Botetourt; James Caul, removed; Jesse Dolter, Augusta; Adam Dickey, dead; George Gabbert, Greenbrier; Cutlip Gabbert, Augusta; James Henton, Rockingham; John Hamilton, Kentucky; Joseph Hanmin, Botetourt; James McGill, Roanoke; Jacob Oyler, Botetourt; George Rule, Botetourt; Joseph Snodgrass and Benjamin Snodgrass, Kentucky; Henry Standoff, Bath County; Anthony Watson, Tennessee; John Miller (shoemaker), runaway; Humphrey Ellis, Botetourt; Armstrong Ellis, Botetourt; William Gill, Botetourt; Jean Henry, Clinch; David Henry, Pennsylvania; John Jinkins, runaway; Mark Morris, Jr., Roanoke (Botetourt); Wm. Reid, runaway; James Sewell, Kentucky; Wm. Stuart, removed; Nicholas Lusong, Tennessee; John Varner, Botetourt; Jacob Way, runaway; Robert Shields, Tennessee.

SEPTEMBER, 1802 (N to Z).

Minmo vs. Knowles.—Deed dated 27th November, 1797, between Thomas Douthat, of Augusta, of first part, and William Nemmo, next friend to Mrs. Jane Douthat. Witnesseth: Separation and misunderstanding have taken place between Thomas and Jane, and Thomas is sensible of his imprudent conduct towards the said Jane, and having resolved to reform and become a good and friendly husband towards Jane, and bound in honor to make a liberal support for his wife, conveys 200 acres, purchased of James Guy in 1794, on head of Great Calf Pasture; also a tract bought of James Hodg, 30 acres, and personal property, to stand seized for nine months, for benefit of Jane and her son, Robert. Thomas agrees for the nine months to conduct himself with temperance, sobriety and honesty, and will become a reformed man, and will not during the said term disturb his wife, or knowingly come where she is, without her free consent (then upon his reformation being certified by five gentlemen, she will live with him again; otherwise the property to remain hers). Recorded in General Court, 18th June, 1798.

MUNROE'S LETTER, 1790.

CHARLOTTESVILLE, November 19, 1790.

DEAR SIR:

Being appointed by the Assembly to the Senate of the United States, I have thought it my duty to comply with the wishes of my country by accepting that appointment. I shall sit out immediately to enter on the duties of the office on the first of December. What effect this may produce on my professional pursuits depends on the experiment to discover. My friends assure me the Congress will adjourn in March, so that they will never interfere. It is my most earnest wish to carry them on together and if possible shall attend the Courts as usual. In any event, I must request of you to put my business in the utmost forwardness, so that the friend who may act for me may have no trouble and my clients no cause of complaint.

I enclose you the bond of Howard L—— to Butler, upon which you will be pleased to issue a writ. I think you are acquainted with my causes. I beg you, however, to write me on that subject to Philadelphia and I will give you further information respecting them.

You will be so obliging as to give the above information to such of my clients as you see, as I decline a public advertisement until I shall make an experiment of this trust and determine how far it will suit me. I send you a receipt for Mr. Stuart, to whom you will please make my respects, as also to William (?) Bowyer.

With real esteem, I am, dear sir, sincerely yours,

JAS. MONROE.

P. S.—I send you Baskins's will, which was, contrary to my expectations, rejected by the Judge. You will please issue a writ against the person who recovered the judgment immediately, provided you receive this so as to do it within three months from the judgment, that, I believe, being the time allowed by law.

To James Lyle, Esq., Clerk of the District Court at Staunton.

SEPTEMBER, 1795 (A to K).

Wilson to Bowyer.—Contract between John Bowyer, of Rockbridge, and Henry Williams, of same place. Williams has undertaken to build a brick house for Bowyer upon the top of the hill where said Bowyer shall direct—following dimensions: 56 feet in length and 20 wide; foundation to be 3 feet above ground at the lowest part; first story to be 12 feet high between the ceiling and the lower floor; second story to be 10 feet between the second floor and the ceiling; as many doors and windows as said Bowyer shall think fit; bricks round the windows and doors to be rubbed and made smooth; a brick wall each side of the passage, one brick thick in the lower story; four fireplaces, two below and two above, of the size Bowyer shall direct; chimneys to extend four feet at the lowest (above the top of the house);

the whole to be done and finished in the strongest and best manner that such work is usually done, and to be finished by the first of October next. Bowyer is to pay £190, half before 1st July next; remainder when work is done. Dated, 19th March, 1793.

N. B.—The *hith* of the house is to be 26 feet, of brick work.

CHARLOTTESVILLE, November 15, ——.

DEAR SIR:

Permit me to present to your acquaintance the bearer, Mr. Hansford, a young gentleman who intends to practice in your Court, and whom you will find remarkably well read in the law, and in other respects a very sensible, worthy young man. I shall thank you to present him to any of your acquaintance of the Court, that he may become known, as he deserves. I wrote you lately and requested you to file for me declarations in the cases of Long vs. Turk, and Garber vs. Humphreys. If you have not been able to render me this service, he will do it himself.

I am, dear sir, very respectfully yours,

JAS. MONROE.

J. Lyle, Esq., Clerk of Staunton District Court. By Mr. Hansford.

CHARLOTTESVILLE, 8th August, 1790.

DEAR SIR:

The Justices of Pendleton County are desirous to remove their Clerk from office on account of his misconduct. The gentleman who bears this being in a hurry, and some of my Acts of the Assembly being loaned out and not able to command them, I have been able to find nothing on the subject but the clause in the Act of Government, page 35, putting the inspection of their conduct under the General Court and the District Court law, whereby it is transferred to the Districts. Perhaps there is nothing else on it. The mode of process is not designated, whether by motion or otherwise, but presume there can be no other, and in that case, whether notice is to be given by those who made it, or a citation to be issued by the Clerk, citing him to appear to defend himself against a motion to that effect, stating the charges. As this is written within your line, shall thank you to attend to it and take such steps as you may think proper.

Respectfully, I am,   JAS. MONROE.

Mr. Lyle, Clerk of the District Court at Staunton.

CHARLOTTESVILLE, 29th June, 1792.

DEAR SIR:

You were so obliging as to undertake to speak to some suitable person in Staunton to make for me a light wagon, for two horses, for plantation use, on your return, may I request of you to drop me a line for Charlottesville informing whether you have been able to engage one, the terms, and the time it will be finished; such as are used in the Northern States to carry the produce of a farm in, and not such as we employ to carry tobacco, &c., to market, is the kind I want. It should, however, for the kind, be strong, sound, well formed and the ironwork good.

Very respectfully, I am, dear sir, your very humble servant,

JAS. MONROE.

James Lyle, Esq., Staunton.

DEAR SIR:

Tell Stuart I congratulate him on his marriage.

JAS. MONROE.

Patent to Jacob Stover, 5,000 acres in Spottsylvania. Dated 15th December, 1733: In St. Mark's Parish, on West Side of the Great Mountains, and bounded: black walnuts and a hickory on Shenandoah River, two sycamores, to foot of a naked mountain at upper end of a large island, white oak, Spanish oak, three pines, a red oak, three locust trees. Consideration: The importation of one hundred persons to dwell within our Colony and Dominion of Virginia, whose names are: Jacob, Catherine, Abraham, Christian, Isaac, Jacob, Joseph, Mathew, Sarah, Catherine, Ann, Susanna, Barbary, Dorothy, Rachel *Miller*, Jacob, Anna, Isaac, Abraham, John, Jacob, Joseph, Peter, George, Calkins, Christopher, Anna, Rachel, Catherine, Sarah, Susanna, Barbary, Dorothy, John, Anna, Jacob, John, Abraham, Isaac, Rosina, Susanna, Catherine, Ragley *Mire* (Nure?), Henry, Catherine, Henry, John, Isaac, Catherine, Anna, Rachel *Sowder*, Henry, Christiana, Jacob, Henry, Paul, Rudy, Joseph, Peter, Isaac, John, Hamudy, Stophar, Susanna, Rachel, Barbara, Claplir, Margaret ,Elizabeth *Hain*, John, Barbel, Rudy, Chr., John, Mathew, Joseph, Isaac, Peter, David, William, Anna, Christiana, Frenley, Robby, Dorothy *Funk*, Jacob, Frina, Christian, John, Isaac, Rudy, Mathew, Stopher, Peter, Joseph, David, Jacob, Jane, Dorothy, Christiana *Sowder*.

Miss Sarah Price, to the Major William Price, Richmond:

DEAR SISTER:

Enclosed is a statement of your brother, William, yours and my accounts, wherein his estate is indebted to you £250, 11, 7, and I am £157, 8, 5½, amounting to £408, 0, 0, with interest from January 12, 1797. When Mr. Talliaferro was here I showed the settlement with your brother William in his handwriting. I believe he has them. We are all well, and joins me in love to everybody.

I am your affectionate brother,

RO. DOUTHAT.

N. B.—If it was possible I would go down, but that is out of the question. I expect to be down early in May for you and sister Jane, that (?) I hope Major and Mrs. Price and sister Lucy will come also.

This day 26 years I left Ireland.

R. D.

March 1st, 1810.

APRIL, 1802 (M to Z).

Piper vs. Hartley.—This may certify that on complaint being made to me, as a member of the Abolition Society, &c., that a certain Negro Tom was illegally held in slavery by a certain Peter Piper, of Franklin Township, York County. I attended, and on viewing the writings given to Peter Piper by Peter Hartley respecting the sale of the said negro, I found that they had originated in Maryland, and that of course the boy had been brought from Maryland to the State of Pennsylvania, which is contrary to the laws of Pennsylvania, and by which means the said Negro Tom obtained his freedom and is now a free man. Certified this fourteenth day of December, 1799, by me.

BENJAMIN WRIGHT,

A Member of the Abolition Society for the relief of free negroes unlawfully held in bondage.

To whom concerned.

STATE OF PENNSYLVANIA,
  Adams County, ss:

Personally appeared before me, Abraham Russell, Peter Piper, who being duly sworn, saith that about the month of January, 1787, he purchased from Peter Hartley a negro boy named Tom as a slave for life, for the sum of £50 and a fat hog valued at £2. Received a bill of sale from Hartley, which is mislaid, and that through the interference of Benjamin Wright the said negro boy was liberated from slavery in the beginning of the year 1792.

PETER (mark) PIPER.

Sworn to 16th August, 1800.—A. RUSSELL.

Certificate that Russell is a Justice of the Peace.

ADAMS COUNTY, PENNSYLVANIA.

15th August, 1800. Benjamin Wright deposes upon his solemn affirmation (being conscientiously scrupulous against making oath) that being one of the Incorporation Society for the Relief of Negroes Held in Slavery Contrary to the Laws of Pennsylvania, and having had information that Peter Piper held a negro boy called Tom as a slave contrary to law, called on said Peter Piper, who informed this affirmant that he had purchased the boy from a Peter Hartley as a slave, and showed him the bill of sale that Peter Hartley had executed to him, the said Peter Piper. This affirmant then told Peter Piper that he could not hold the boy in slavery by the bill of sale, the law not being complied with in recording the boy, and in order to liberate the boy this deponent proceeded to search the records of Cumberland County (in which County the said negro boy was born), and found he was not recorded there, and on returning to the County where the boy was held, said affirmant effected the liberation of the said negro boy, according to the laws of Pennsylvania, and farther saith not.

BENJAMIN WRIGHT.

Sworn to, 15th August, 1800, before William McLean, John Dickson, Walter Smith.

DISTRICT COURT.

List of deeds recorded in Orange County executed by Benjamin Borden, 1734–1745:

To John Patterson, 26th November, 1741; same, same date; Robert Poage, 13th October, 1742; William Smith, 17th September, 1742; William

Fearnley and wife, 25th November, 1742; John Steavenson, 11th April, 1743; John Buchanan, 6th April, 1743; Alexander Walker, 14th April, 1743; James Walker, 14th April, 1743; John Walker, 15th April, 1743; James Moore, 13th April, 1743; James Robinson, 15th April, 1743; Elizabeth Hunter, 10th May, 1743; William Hall, 8th April, 1743; Andrew Baxter, 15th March, 1742; William Evans, 13th March, 1742; Daniel Lyle, 8th April, 1743; Richard Consort, 14th March, 1742-3; John Carr, 7th July, 1743; Charles Dohoney, 11th February, 1741-2; William Guin, 7th July, 1742; Robert Culton, 6th May, 1742; John Buchanan, 15th July, 1742; Joseph Colton, 6th May, 1742; Charles Hays, 1st June, 1742; George Henderson, 1st June, 1742; John Lowery, 16th August, 1742; John Moore, 16th August, 1742; James Eakins, 26th June, 1742; Samuel Dunlap, 16th August, 1742; Samuel McCutchan, 3d August, 1742; Patrick Hays, 16th August, 1742; William Lockridge, 25th June, 1742; William Porter, 16th August, 1742; Robert Dunlap, 25th June, 1742; William Cowden, 10th July, 1742; Mathew Lyle, 3d August, 1742; Alexander McClary, 7th June, 1742; James Trimble, 2d August, 1742; John Mathews, 7th June, 1742; John Shields, 2d August, 1742; John Patterson, 21st August, 1742; James Martin, 20th July, 1742; William McCanless, 16th August,, 1742; Henry Kirkham, 26th July, 1742; James Young, 17th June, 1742; Richard Wood, 17th June, 1742; Samuel and William Wood, 6th July, 1742; Gilbert Campbell, 6th July, 1742; Joseph Lapsley, 6th July, 1742; John Gray, 6th July, 1742; Robert Heastane, 6th July, 1742.

1781 or 1782.

To the Worshipful Court of Augusta County, the petition of the sundry inhabitants in the bounds of Captain Long's Company of Militia humbly showeth:

That your petitioners, while headed by Captain Christian, and since headed by Captain Long, then enjoyed the greatest tranquility, but now likely to be clouded by the loss of so noble an officer by a mere delusion.

The most of us can, and will (if called upon), undertake to declare on oath that Captain Long behaved himself at the Battles of Hot Water and Jamestown as a good soldier and a noble officer. As to his conduct at York we cannot pretend to say farther than from the most authentic accounts that we could collect he had not that fair play that a true citizen ought to have had. From which motives induces us to believe, and truly hope, your worships will, when you come to look at the affair, reinstate him in his post, that we may continue our old rank, as we have ever been faithful subjects, contributed every thing in our power for the benefit of the States, turned out cheerfully our quota of men on every occasion.

Therefore, as your worships is the only door we are to go through to justice, humbly hope you will recommend him to his Excellency, the Governor, which will prevent us from falling from our old rank, to wit, the second in the Battalion to the youngest, and your petitioners shall, as in duty bound ever pray, &c &c.

(Signed) Jas. Davis, John Christian, Jr., Rich'd Shires, Saml. Blackwood, John Brooks, Jr., Robert Scott, Samuel Brooks, John Black, William Black, Joseph Bell, Ensign; Thomas Rutledge, Gill. Christian, James Bert, Gilbert

Christian, Giles Brooks, W. Christian, William Davis, Thomas Kear, Benjamin Carr, James Wright, John Bell, Edward Rutledge, Samuel Armstrong, Neal O'Dear, Joseph Kerr, Robert Christian, Francis Best, Charles Donely, Jonathan Brooks, Jacob Gabert, Anthony Black, Alexander Wright, William Shields, William Brown, Robert Christian, Lieutenant; Gabriel Alexander, James Bready, Jacob van Lear, John Christian, Mathew Alexander, John Bready, Joseph Colter, John Alexander, John Bready, George Marshall.

At the battle of Jamestown I can assist, as per witness. (Signed) Michael Coalter, then Lieutenant under him. Capt. Samuel McCutchan, Capt. Patrick Buchanan, Richard Thompson, Col. William Grahams James.

1781–2 (Part 2).

The Commonwealth of Virginia, debtor to John Black, Sr., for sundry expenses exhibited on John Davis, a soldier in the Western Battalion, being wounded on the 26th day of November, 1780, and had his leg taken off at the said John Blacks, on the South River, Augusta County, Virginia, viz: To eight days for surgeon and said Davis and a man to attend at 40 dollars per·day each (960 dollars), £288; to 27 days' board for surgeon's mate, a man to attend, and said Davis, at 40 dollars per day each (3,240 dollars), £972; to five days' boarding for the surgeon's mate and attendant during their time of settling business and preparing for their March, at 40 dollars per day per man (400 dollars), £120; to seven yards of a six hundred at £12 per yard, £84; to hire of a man and horse for one day at 50 dollars, £15; to damaging a bed, £100; to washing bandages and sundry linens, £100; to a coffin, £100; to digging a grave, £40; to four lbs. of candles, £14, 8, 0; to funeral expenses, £50. Sworn to in Court, 15th May, 1781.

OLD PAPERS.

I do certify that William Slaven was chose Ensign in my Company of Augusta Militia in the room of Jonathan Humphries, who hath resigned his commission, and he is recommended to the Court of said County for a commission.   CHARLES HAMILTON, *Captain.*
October 8, 1782.

To the Worshipful Court of Augusta:

We have appointed Thomas Cartmell, Ensign for the Company in Greenbrier. Desires he may be sworn to his commission. Given under my hand this 17th day, November, 1781.   GEORGE POAGE.

1781–2.

RICHMOND, 10th May, 1782.

To the Worshipful Court of Augusta County.

GENTLEMEN:—Inclosed you'll receive the commissions containing the names of the gentlemen recommended.

I beg leave to observe that I have received a letter from Thomas Hughes, Esq., of your Court, wherein he informs me that the Court has reinstated Capt. Francis Long (who was broke for cowardice) in his former commission. If so, I humbly conceive that the Court have exceeded their power, for they have only power by law, or the Constitution, to recommend, and I am persuaded (should that be the case) that it is without precedent that any officer that has had a legal inquest by a court-martial and broke for cowardice should be recommended as fit to take command of a Company. I need not observe the ill consequences that will attend such a precedent, and therefore request, should such a proceeding have taken place, that the Court will please reconsider the matter and recommend some other fit person.

I am with all due respect, gentlemen, your humble servant,

SAMP. MATHEWS.

I, Sampson Mathews, a magistrate for the County of Augusta, do hereby certify that I have administered the oaths prescribed by law to be taken by a Governor unto Thomas Nelson, Jr., Esq.

Given under my hand at Staunton this 19th day of June, 1781.

(A copy.)   SAMP. MATHEWS.

Return of patroling done by the patrol of Staunton from May 24 until June 26, 1782: Patrolled June 2, at night, viz: William Blair, Francis Mora, Anthony Mustoe, David Greiner, Dennis Calaghan; June 6th and 8th, Blair, Mora, Mustoe; June 18th and 26th, Blair, Mora, Mustoe and Greiner. Sworn to by Capt. William Blair, 28th June.

Return of the patrol of Staunton from April 20, 1782: April 20th, Wm. Blair (Captain), Francis Mora, Anthony Mustoe, Dennis Callaghan; April 24th, 28th, 30th, Blair, Mora, Callaghan, Mustoe; May 4th, 8th and 12th, Blair, Mora, Mustoe; May 22d, Blair, Mora, Mustoe and David Greiner. Sworn to by Blair, May 24.

Following paper in package marked 1755–56–57—it is apparently a fragment—on the back is written:

"A Copy.   JOHN RANDOLPH, C. H. B."

Paid in Northampton:

To the County... 7070

To:
Paid in Hampshire, in part................................. 597
Paid in Lunenburg, in part................................. 770
To Robt. Brackenridge, Sheriff............................. 680
To David Stewart... 120
To John Brown.. 160
To Geo. Robinson, Geo. Rowland, Geo. Horbinson, James Humphries, Matthew Sheddon, Mr. Moore, Jeremiah Green, Philip Watkins, John McAfee, Andrew Gaughagan, Peter Farr and George *Duck*, each 140 1680

Paid in Brunswick to the County, in part........................ 3195
To Wm. Hugart, John Hamilton, Samuel Hamilton, Robert Gillaspy,
George Douther, James Burnsides, Jos. Milehan, John Lewis,
John (——), James Jackson, James Miller, David Howell, Robt.
Gillaspey, Corporal Samuel McMary, Eldad Reade, Topher Car-
penter, Henry Lawless, Robt. Gay, John Stevenson, John Weems,
John Taylor, Wm. Kinkead, John Kinkead, James Clements,
James McKnight, Wm. Mann, Thomas McMullin, each 300.... 8100

(Endorsed.) We, the undersubscribers, do acknowledge we have sold our part of the within tobacco to Israel Christian, and desire the tickets for it may come out in his name, as witness our hands. (Signed) John Trimble, William Preston, John Madison, Henry Murray, William Kinkead, William Preston (signed for James Patton), Robert Patrick, William Man, and John Brown.

OLD PAPERS.

Mathias M. Youcam, of Bedford County, to William Thompson—power of attorney to convey 267 acres whereon Mathias formerly dwelt, joining land lately possessed by James Campbell, on Roanoke River, to Alex. Boyd, Paymaster to the Virginia Regiment. Dated, 16th November, 1760.

MISCELLANEOUS PAPERS.

County Court Order Book 42:
April 28, 1829.—The County Court of Rockingham County is requested to return the Augusta County Surveyors' Book for 1761 to 1779.

Alexander Kilpatrick's (jailor) account, 1781: Keeping the following: William Hinton, for Toryism, from November 17, 1780, to May 20, 1781; William Wood, for desertion, from November 17, 1780, to December 17; John Wood, for desertion, from November 25, 1780, to December 17; John Wilphong, for murder, from December 3, 1780, to February 26, 1781; William Douglass, for desertion, from December 8 to December 17; James O'Neal, for desertion, from 21st to 22d December; George Stewart, for desertion, from December 29, 1780, to January 13; John Hairs, for deser-tion, from December 29, 1780, to January 13; William Douglass, for deser-tion, from February 12 to March 6; Rob. Hughes, for desertion, same; David Wilson, for desertion, from April 13 to April 21; Robert Dobin, for desertion, from April 14 to 21; Robert Dobin, reconfined, from August 19 to 21; nineteen Continental deserters, confined, and released by Capt. Thomas Martin; nineteen prisoners brought from the Richmond public jail; five negroes and six prisoners of war; Samuel Powell, confined as vagrant, from October 18 to November 6; James Richards, confined for felony, from October 23 to November 16; Edward White, confined for felony, from October 16 to November 20.

COPY OF NEW HAVEN LOTTERY TICKET.

New Haven Lottery.—This ticket in New Haven Lottery, No. 21, shall entitle the owner to such lot in said town as shall be drawn against its number, agreeable to the scheme of said lottery. (Signed) Alex. St. Clair, John Wayt, Wm. Chambers, Ashur Waterman, Managers. Staunton, August 24th, 1801.

This ticket in Morgantown Lottery, No. 143, shall entitle the holder to such lot in said town as shall be drawn against its number, agreeable to the terms of said lottery. (Signed) Jacob Kinney, William Wirt, John Coalter, Managers. June 2d, 1800.

(On the reverse is):

Scheme of a Lottery.

(Morgantown, in Albemarle County.)

May 30, 1800. GIDEON MORGAN.

79 Town Lots—50 ft. front; 120 ft. back.

SINGLE PAPER.

To All Head Boroughs and Constables Within His Majesty's Colony and Dominion to Whom These Presents Shall Come:

Whereas, Robert Bratton and James Kirk, inhabitants of ye Calf Pasture, have this day, being the 7th of this instant, September, made oath before me, one of his Majesty's Justices of ye Peace for Augusta County, that they were last night robbed of two black horses and a sorrel mare having a star and snip and a yearling colt with her, one orange-colored sitting gown, a pale china gown, one striped blue and white cotton gown, one single petticoat, one light-colored broadcloth coat, two beaver hats, one black velvet cap, one old hunting saddle, one woman's saddle of buckskin, one blue jacket of home-made cloth, one hat of Bermuda platt with a red ribbon band, shifts, shirts, table linen, sheets, women's head cloths, four pairs of men's shoes, three pairs of women's shoes, two bridles and a halter, a curb and a snaffle, a rifle gun (double tricked), and a plaid gown. The servant man is well set, with black curled hair, pockfretted, having a scar on ye right side of his face, to a scar on his jaw blade. The woman is tall, has curled hair and is pockfretted. Both of them native Irish. Whoever secures said servants, so as that they shall be brought to their master, shall have six pistoles for a reward and reasonable charges besides, paid by Robert Bratton and James Kirk. Therefore, in his Majesty's name, I charge and command you and every (one) of you in your several precincts to search diligently for ye said persons, by whom the said robbery was committed, and to make hue and cry after them from town to town and from county to county, as well by horsemen as footmen, and if you find them, that then you apprehend and bring them before a Justice of ye Peace of ye County where they shall be taken, to be dealt with as ye law directs.

Given under my hand and seal ye 7th of September, 1747.

WILL JAMESON.

Augusta County, to wit.—On the oath of Robert Renoxe it appears to me that Mathew Young did beat and abuse Michael Bready with the butt end of his musket to that degree that his life is in danger, which appears to me in view as also the opinion of Dr. Flood, who is ordered to attend him.

I, therefore, in his Majesty's name, command you to apprehend and inclose the said Mathew Young in close prison until it appears that the said Bready is in a way of recovery, and that he, the said Young, be discharged by due course of law.

You are likewise to apprehend and inclose one John Walker, who appears to vindicate the above Young in his desired murder, &c.

Given under my hand and seal, this first day of September, 1747.

JAMES PATTON.

To the High Sheriff of this County.

Executed by me, John Edward, 2d September, 1747. Mathew Young's bond (with Nathan Lusk (Loosk) and James (mark) Asebury) for appearance at next Court. Signed, sealed and acknowledged before us: James Paton, John Buchanan, John Willson.

Mr. Jones: Sir:—I understand by Mr. Lockhart, my servant boy has complained to the Court that I did not give him such learning as he expected, and that there is not any cause for him to expect anything but what I have already done for him. I could easily make appear. However, I do hereby freely and entirely give up all my right and title to him, as I understand he has a mind to choose a master and go to a trade, &c. I am, sir, your humble servant. (Signed) James Cotton. Monday, November 21, 1768.

Note dated 25th March, 1820, by Henirick Jordan (signed in German) to John Gochenour.

Having sew I, Constable one year, do now return Seth Rodger, Thos. Petterson, and John Allison for the ensuing year. (Signed) John Dickson.

Commitment to jail by Richard Woods of two negroes, George and Pall, for robbing the house of William Hall, together with George Henricks. 22d November, 1768.

Sir:—I understand that there is a law suit pending between me and Daniel Kidd. I know nothing of it, for I have nothing against him. Therefore I desire that it may be dismissed. (Signed) John Jones. June 19, 1764.

FORT NELSON, December 29th, 1764.
This certifies that Majorwood Timberlake was duly enlisted to serve in Capt. Christian's Company the space of one year from the 13th of June last, and is now discharged by order of Colonel Lewis, having served 200 days. £15. (Signed) Jos. Ray, Ensign. Assigned: 5th April, 1764, to James McAgavock.

Dr. John Wood, doctor to Samuel Pritchard. January 29, 1766.

Affidavit to account by Mathew Gellesapey, in Granville (Greenville) County, South Carolina, 1767, before John Pickens.

10th July, 1784.—Power of attorney by Elizabeth Kinkead to David Kinkead, of Fayette County, Virginia, to make a deed to Joseph Guin, of Augusta County.

20th May, 1771.—Order by Robert Anderson to Mr. Daniel Kidd, dated Charlottesville.

23d March, 1795.—Jacob Vanfossen's list of taxable property, two tithables, viz: himself and son Abraham.

16th December, 1780.—John Poage gives this public notice: That the following persons propose making inclusive surveys, viz: Leonard Bell, round the land where he lives in the Cow Pasture; Jacob Doran, round the land he got of Ludwick Shaddow, near William Mathews; John Archer, round the land where he lives on north side Middle River; Samuel Henderson and James Crawford, joining the land formerly Thomas Stevenson's.

Archer's Executors vs. Poage's Executors.—Single package. Receipt, 28th May, 1781, by William Blair to Robert Armstrong, for £4, 3, 6, in full of legacy to William's daughter, by John Archer.

Returns of an election held by John Boyd and James Mitchel, Lieutenants, show that James Shields beat Ensign Wilson by two votes—15th December, 1783. Thomas and Robert Tate, Windel Grove, and George Shoultz write under date of December 12, 1783, that they belong to the Company formerly Captain Tate's, and being abroad and so unable to vote at the last election for Captain, now desire Ensign Wilson should be promoted.

Inquisition dated March 3, 1783, before Coroner John McCreery, on the body of John Mitchell. Verdict: He died a natural death at David Frame's stillhouse.

Letter from Thomas Hughes, dated August 21, 1783, certifying that Peter Hane is entitled to compensation from Virginia for services as scaleman.

Account of Alexander Killpatrick against the County, dated October, 1780, for riding express for the law for the Commissioners of the Specific Tax, one day.

James Hogshead, son of John Hogshead and grandson of James Hogshead, is the only heir of William Hogshead, to whom was granted fifty acres in 1756.

July 6, 1800.—John Holmes, Sr.'s will (of Augusta County): To wife *Meelsee,* all estate, and to live in the new house he built on Mr. Bernhard's land. Executor, George Bernhard, Sr. Test: David Nickey. Proved by him, 27th October, 1800.

June 18, 1788.—John Wiley's will: To sons Thomas and William and to all children, viz: William, Thomas, Elizabeth, Sarah, Mary. Test: David Humphreys, Rd. Tate, James Henery. September, 1792. Proved by one witness: Humphreys.

June 19, 1799.—John Burke's will: To wife; to daughter, Polly Huston four lots in Greenville; to daughter, Rachel Hoop, two lots in Greenville; to son John; to daughter Betsy Martain; to son Joseph—executor. Test: Adam Hawpe, James Shields, William Steele, Wm. H. Rayburn. 25th October, 1802. Proved by Rayburn.

April 16, 1802.—John Swisher's noncupative will—not established: To children, two daughters, sons. Made 11th April, 1802—the day before his death. John Pence and Jacob Spots and testator's son John to be executors. Test: Mathew Hunter, Catherine Hunter. To four eldest sons, among them John and Jacob. He had two daughters and six sons.

Account of sales of Edward Braden, deceased. Elizabeth Braden, widow and relict, relinquishes her right to administer in favor of her son, George Braden, and son-in-law, Peter Jones. 23d December, 1805.

July 19, 1795.—William Douthat's will—certified copy. To wife Ann, fulling mill near Staunton, in Col. William Bowyer's meadow; also a lot in Pattonsburg; also a house and lot in Fincastle, now occupied by Joel and Luke Bott. To Brother Robert; to Polly Douthat, wife of Robert. Test: Joel Bott, John and Jane Lewis.
October Court, 1795.—Order that witnesses be summoned from Botetourt.
October 25, 1798.—Receipt for the original by Hugh French and wife, Ann French, late Ann Douthat, the widow.

September 26, 1780.—Will of John Gay, of Rockbridge—going to war: To stepson, David Moore; to Brother Thomas; to Brother Robert, estate in Pennsylvania; to Brother Archabal, share of Joseph's estate; to bound boy, John Winden; to wife Elizabeth. Test: John Frazer, Henry Gay. No certificate of proof.

May 26, 1788.—Francis ("F. H.") Huff's will—farmer: To wife Catherine, land he lives on on Jenning's Branch; to children Francis Huff, Samuel Huff, Catherine Feny, Jacob Huff, Susanna Huff, Henry Huff. Executors: Sons Francis, Samuel, Jacob. Test: Wm. Edmundson, Wm. Heron. 15th June, 1790. Proved by Edmundson.

Package marked "Old Copies of Records."—Record of Christian, *qui tam*, vs. Bell—1756. Gabriel Jones was attorney for plaintiff. Defendants did not appear. Clerk makes off the record and sends to Jones. On back is this (in writing of Clerk): "Dr. Gab. look over the fees John brings and also this record. Should ye Jud. be also as well vs. Def. as (   ) or have

I done it right long plages me so I know not what I am doing." Under above (in Jones's handwriting) is this, viz: "I think ye Judgm't ought to be agt. the Deft. only —— consequently the sher. had no occasion —— and his doing it was not ex officio but non officio, if I may be allowed to make Latin that knows no more of it than Mother McClenaghan does polite writing, or her —— modesty. What ye D—— do you imagine I can look over your d—— old notes, when I am preparing for the grave. I have 3 parts finished my ( ) and am going over to make up ye loss by assisting to make a Christian —— Pray God make it a good one. You see I ( ) like a parson."

Record in John Moffett vs. John Graham, otherwise called John Graham, of Nantmill, in Chester County, Pennsylvania, 20th year of George II. On bond dated 22d September, 1743, by John Graham, of Nantmill, &c., to John Moffett, of Augusta. Test: Thomas and Andrew Lewis.

Plat of Adam Spitler's 196 acres on south side Christian's Creek, corner Ingboten—Zumbro's corner—corner Van Leer's land.

Archer's Administrator vs. Archer's Executor.—Copy of bill. Rebecca Archer died in May, 1789, and John Archer, her husband, died May, 1771.

Plat of David Miller's 103 acres, on a bend of Middle River, known by name of Brushy Neck—formerly conveyed by William Beverley to William Johnston.

Package marked "Papers—1780 to 1790."—This is to certify that I, Robert Gewn (signed Gwinn) and William Forknor, executors, and uncles to James Neal's orphans, are desirous that there should be an order to bind Samuel Neal to Lanty Graham, and James to Robert Gewn. October, 1778. (Signed) Robert Gwinn, William Forknor.

Package marked "Papers of No Particular File."—January 6, 1804. This writing is to certify that I, James Miller, having intermarried with Fanny Lindon, daughter of Molly Lindon, deceased, who was sister to Elizabeth Hodge, wife of Francis Hodge, also sister of Charles Clack: the said Fanny being sister to Joseph Lindon, late of Augusta County, who ran away upwards of eleven years ago from said County, being then about eleven or twelve years old, and has never been heard of since by any of his relations, and is therefore supposed to be dead, and there being a legacy belonging to the said Joseph if living, or if dead, as is supposed, to the said Fanny and the undersigned, as heirs of the said Joseph, said legacy issuing out of the estate of George Matlock, deceased, of the County of Louisa (relinquishes to James Brooks his right to administer on Joseph's estate). (Signed) James Miller.
Polly Vines deposes, 27th November, 1804, in Botetourt County, before John Todd: That Joseph Lindon went from Augusta upwards of ten years ago; Joseph was her cousin; he has but one sister, Fanny Miller; Joseph was son to Molly Lindon, formerly Molly Clack, who was sister of Elizabeth Hodge, wife of Francis Hodge, and sister of Charles Clack.

December 23, 1799.—Jane Todd, widow of James Todd, deceased, relinquishes her right to administer in favor of her son, George Todd.

February 24, 1800.—Mary Woods relinquishes her right to administer on the estate of her son Jacob Woods in favor of her son William Woods.

November 28, 1814.—Catherine Morrison, widow of William Morrison, relinquishes administration to her brother, George Marshall, Jr.

Package marked "Promiscuous Papers—Federal Court."—Trimble vs. Cargo—Bill filed 23d June, 1831, addressed to Hon. Alexander Caldwell, Judge of the U. S. Court holden at Staunton. By Alex. G. Trimble and —— Trimble, infant, by Alex. G. Cargo, her next friend, lawful issue and heirs of Elizabeth Trimble, formerly Elizabeth Cargo: That about 1804 Alex. Gibson, uncle of Elizabeth Cargo, died testate, will recorded in District Court devising to his nephew, Daniel Gibson, but if he died without issue, then to Samuel Alex. Cargo and Elizabeth Cargo, children of Alexander's sister. Daniel took possession of 520 acres about two miles southeast of Staunton. Daniel has died, leaving no legal issue. Shortly after Alexander's death complainant's mother, Elizabeth, married —— Trimble and removed to Tennessee, and subsequently to Mississippi, where she died, leaving husband and complainants—husband is since dead. Samuel A. Cargo, nephew of Alex. Gibson, and co-devisee of complainant's mother, still lives, in Alabama. Samuel A. Cargo sold the land to Silas H. Smith. It was found in a former suit that Elizabeth Trimble had died without heirs. Prayer for partition.

1823–1824–1825.

File No. 926.—Robert Hemming, assignee of Fountain Maury, vs. Jacob Kinney and Alex. St. Clair, executors of Hugh McDowell and John, Robert and Mary McDowell, infants—heirs of Hugh McDowell—by Kinney and McDowell, their guardians. Spa. dated 18th April, 1799. Hugh's will dated 26th July, 1793. Bill to subject Hugh's property to a judgment.

File No. 926.—Frazier, &c., vs. Paul and wife. John Watkins Frazer, James Frazer, Isabella Frazer, Samuel Craig Frazer and Polly Frazer, children and heirs of Samuel Frazer, complain no one has taken out letters of administration, but their mother, Isabella (who has since married James Paul), has continued in possession. Prayer to have dower assigned and estate settled.

File No. 926.—Calvert vs. Kennerley. Ross (Rolls?) Calvert and Charles Harper complain that on 19th September, 1794, George Calvert purchased of James Kennerley, since deceased, a tract in Culpeper County—325 acres. George assigned the title bond to orators on 29th March, 1806. Kennerley died testate. Will recorded in Staunton District Court, but died intestate as to this land. James Kennerley's son, Benjamin, has died intestate and without issue. James left other issue, viz: Sons James, Thomas, Samuel; Mary Lockhart, then wife of Patrick Lockhart, but now sole; Elizabeth Poindexter, wife of Joseph Poindexter; William and Reuben; Kitty Craig, wife of George Craig. William and Reuben and James have made a deed to orators, but were without title. The heirs reside partly in Virginia and partly in other parts. Thomas resides in Kentucky. Spa. dated 23d August, 1810.

File No. 926.—Fowler vs. Poage's executors. Andrew Fowler complains that for his services in Braddock's war he was entitled to 400 acres on Big Sandy, in this State, for which John Poage, deceased, agreed to give him 200 acres, originally entered by George King, between the 14th and 16th mile trees, in Jennings Gap, and by King assigned to Poage, and by Poage to complainant, on 14th July, 1775. Poage obtained the 400 acres, but gave Fowler no title to the 200, but he has sold it to another, leaving Fowler to the charity of a generous Country, or the exertions of a son. Orator lost his two sons in the war.

Copy of the entry—4th July, 1769—by James (George) King, 200 acres, between the 14th and 16th mile trees, in Jennings Gap. Assigned to John Poage, 22d June, 1772.

William McPeeters deposes, 6th September, 1802, that in 1783 Andrew Fowler had his leg broke and cut off.

Isabella McGlammery deposes, 6th September, 1802, she is daughter of Robert McKitrick.

File No. 926.—Hays vs. Trout. William Hays, son of Moses Hays, infant, complains that on 2d May, 1760, John Risk made an entry for 200 acres between John Wilson and Robert Campbell and the Mountain, which entry he afterwards gave to his son, David Risk. David made improvements, but shortly enlisted and was called forth against the armies of Great Britain. During David's absence, Thomas Mines made an entry and obtained patent for the land. On David's return, David assigned his rights to orator, who had survey made and has received patent dated 1789. David Trout has purchased from Mines. Spa. dated 21st September, 1791.

File No. 926.—Henry vs. Henry's executors. Mary Henry, widow and relict of James Henry, who died testate in Augusta, will dated 31st October, 1806, complains that she has not received her part of the estate. James's daughter Sarah has married James Poage and moved to Ohio. James's daughter Nancy has married Charles Henry and moved to Tennessee. Spa. dated October 23, 1812.

File No. 926.—Herron's Administrator vs. Patterson. Thomas Herron, administrator of William Herron, complains that William was a schoolmaster and taught one and a half years by agreement dated 31st July, 1798. Among the subscribers was Mary Patterson. Mary refuses to pay, and common law suit cannot be brought because one party is dead and other cannot testify. Bill for discovery. Mary answers that William spent one-quarter of his time with her, from 6th August, 1799, when he began school, until December come a year afterwards. Contract dated 31st July, 1798. Spa. dated 29th June, 1801.

File No. 926.—Lockridge's widow vs. Lockridge's heirs. Elizabeth Lockridge, widow of Samuel Lockridge, who died December, 1812, leaving fourteen children; he left in Augusta 425 acres, 125 of which he bought from John Montgomery, but has received no title for. Montgomery administered on Samuel's estate. The heirs are, viz: Eleanor, Polly, Catherine, Samuel, Savannah and Allen Lockridge, all infants; and Alice, wife of Andrew Guyto; Nancy, wife of Thomas Kincaid; Jane, wife of William Fulton—who have all moved to Ohio; and these adults, viz: Andrew Lockridge; Betsey, wife of Thomas Gwynn; Sally, wife of Robert Gwynn; Rebecca, wife of William Kincaid; also a grandchild, Guy Hamilton Kincaid, son to daughter Peggy, who was wife to Robert Kincaid, who survived her. Spa., 1814.

File No. 926.—Leonard vs. Leonard. Daniel Leonard complains that his father, Adam Leonard, Sr., died intestate, leaving widow Susannah and children, viz: Orator, David, George, Elizabeth, Susannah (wife of John Hildebrand), Adam, Jacob, Catherine, John, Margaret, Samuel—the last five being infants.

File No. 926.—Brookes vs. Brookes. William and John Brookes, infants, by Thomas Marshall, guardian, and Susanna, David and Elizabeth Brookes, infants, by Joseph Parks, their guardian—all children and heirs of Samuel Brookes, of Augusta, who died intestate, leaving three (3) other children, viz: Jonathan, James Moffett and Nioma Brookes—also infants—and widow Mary. Bill for partition. Spa. before 1806.

File No. 926.—Fisher vs. Fisher. Jacob and John Fisher complain that their father, Daniel Fisher, died in January, 1817, leaving Widow Ann and children, viz: Margaret, wife of Benjamin Ransbarger; William, Polly, Henry, Andrew, Samuel, Sarah Fisher (Samuel and Sarah, infants), and Daniel, who has already received his share, and ——. Bill to allot dower and partition.
Another bill filed by William Fisher says Daniel left ten (10) children, viz: William, Jacob, John, Adam, Henry, Andrew, Peggy, wife of Benjamin Ransbarger; Polly, Samuel, Sally.
Division decreed and plot land on Christian's Creek.

File No. 926.—Montgomery vs. Montgomery. John Montgomery, Jr., and William H. Montgomery complain that on —— February, 1818, their father, John Montgomery, Sr., died, leaving Widow Agnes and children, viz: Thomas, Hetty, Isabella, Hughart, Rebecca E. Montgomery, and orators. Isabella, Hughart and Rebecca are infants. John died intestate, excluding those of his children who had received anything from their grandfather, Thomas Hughart. Bill for division.

File No. 926.—Turk vs. Kennerley.—Thomas Turk complains that on 24th February, 1768, he entered 400 acres near his own and James Kennerley's land in Augusta. James Kennerley, Sr., claimed the land, and now James Kennerley, Jr., holds it, and also holds up the will of James, Sr., refusing to probate it.

File No. 927.—Thompson vs. Connolley. Writ dated 20th December, 1798. Deed by Daniel McClean, of Fayette County, Kentucky, to Robert

Thompson, dated 24th September, 1792, conveys tract in Randolph County, on West and North side of Tyger's Valley River, adjoining Henry Delay, William Westfall. Recorded in Randolph County, 24th September, 1792. Robert Thompson complains that in 1782 he bargained for a piece of land from Daniel McClain.

Deed dated 22d April, 1793, between Robert Thompson, of Bath County, to Jacob Warde, of Randolph County. Tract in Randolph County, on Tygar's Valley River, adjoining Henry Delay and William Westfall. Recorded in Randolph County.

Deed dated 28th August, 1792, between John Hamilton, Isabel Barker, the late wife of James Stuart; Ralph Stuart, William Westfall, Henry Delay, of one part, and Daniel McClean, of other. Whereas above have purchased of John McClenachan 1,000 acres on Monongahela River, in Tyger's Valley, part of 3,000 acres granted to James Walker for military services in the French war, conveys 180 acres. Recorded in Randolph.

File No. 927.—Miller vs. Bourland.—Henry Miller and wife Hannah, late Crawford, Peter Hanger, Jr., and Patsey, his wife, late Crawford, complain that George Crawford owned valuable land on Middle River. Crawford died testate, leaving six children, viz: female plaintiffs, Nancy, wife of John Miller; Jane, wife of Franklin McCue; and Peggy Crawford, a minor.

File No. 927.—Moore vs. Boyd. Copy of will of John Boyd, dated 8th December, 1792.

File No. 927.—McClure vs. McClure. Andrew and John McClure, heirs (sons), of James McClure, complain that James died 13th September, 1799, intestate, leaving widow and eight children, viz: Widow Elizabeth, orators John and Andrew, and Margaret, James, Samuel, Jonah (Josiah), Eleanor and Elizabeth. (Eleanor and Elizabeth, infants.) Josiah died an infant. Bill for partition.

File No. 927.—Fauber vs. Palmer's Widow. David Fauber and Barbara, his wife, complain that Jacob Palmer, father of Barbara, died, leaving land. Leaving Widow Barbara and children, viz: Oratrix, George, Jacob Gabbart Palmer, Hannah, wife of John Grove; Peter S. Palmer, Philip O. Palmer, Polly, wife of George Teaford; Elizabeth Palmer, Julian Palmer, Margaret Palmer, David Palmer. (Three last infants.) Bill for partition sworn to 23d June, 1828.

File No. 927.—Stuart vs. Black. Robert Stuart complains that Samuel and James Black claim his land. Robert is son of Thomas Stuart, who received conveyance from Beverley, 1st March, 1749. Beverley conveyed to John Black, ancestor of defendants, 30th May, 1749.

William Black deposes, 16th November, 1801, at house of John Black, in Montgomery County: Remembers the line (?) trees, when he was a small boy, 20 years ago. Deponent is son to Samuel Black.

John Black, aged 45 years, deposes, 16th November, 1801, at house of John Black in Montgomery County: Is son to Samuel Black. Deponent and Robert Stuart attended I. Cunningham's school.

Receipt, viz: "July ye 15th, 1742. Received of John Black, ye quit rent of 738 acres of land in Mannor Beverley, due for four years last past, viz: A. D., 1738; A. D., 1739; A. D., 1740; A. D., 1741.

per John Hart, D. S. O. C."

Samuel McCutchen identifies Hart's handwriting above.

Samuel and James Black (son of Samuel Black) answer: Their land is part of 738 acres surveyed for John Preston, 19th and 23d April, 1738, and sold to Samuel and James's grandfather, John Black, by Beverley, 31st May, 1749.

Cornelius Adair deposes on the premises, 19th December, 1801: About 30 years ago he was shown the stumps, &c., by father of the complainant, Robert, who told him they were the corner of Patton's land (now Swisher's).

Joseph Coalter deposes, same time and place: Some time ago he was informed by a certain Mary Donnally, then an old woman, now deceased, who had lived in Patton's family, that said Patton had at first made a large survey, perhaps about 1,700 acres.

William Black deposes, same time and place: That a considerable time ago his brother, Samuel Black, showed him the corner. Deponent is now about 62 years old, and has known the corner since he can remember, and it was a corner on the Manor line and his father's tract. Mr. Stuart died, 1788.

John Black deposes, on premises, 19th December, 1801: That in 1755 he helped repair the fence of his uncle, John Black, grandfather to defendant. Two years after Braddock's defeat he was taken on the muster roll, at the age of 16.

File No. 927.—Backenstoe vs. Backenstoe. Elizabeth Backenstoe, widow of Frederick Backenstoe, complains, 24th September, 1826, that Frederick died intestate, 18—, leaving infant children, viz: George, John, Margaret, Frederick, Mary.

File No. 927.—Scott vs. Scott. John Scott complains that William Scott, formerly of Augusta County, and late of Lincoln County, now in Kentucky, being indebted to John Adams, executed his bond, dated 1st September, 1785, shortly thereafter left this State and hath gone to parts unknown, having first sold his land to James Ewen, now deceased.

File No. 927.—Scott vs. Clinebill. William Scott complains, 1st March, 1802, that several years ago he laid off a town on his lands known by name of Middle Brook. George Clinebill drew lot 28.

END OF VOL. I.

INDEX

INDEX

The spelling in the original manuscript has been followed throughout this publication.

[The "Honor Roll" of Subscribers will be continued in the Second Volume.]

Abbot (Abot, Abbit, Abett).
Abett, Benj., 213.
Abbit, Ishmael, 105.
Abbott, James, 176, 321.
Abbot, Jeremiah, 324.
Abbot, Nathan, 90.
Aberman, Catherine, 184.
Aberman, Jacob, 178, 179, 184, 198, 199.
Aberman, John, 182.
Aberman, Mary, 182.
Aberman, Michael, 176, 180, 182.
Abney, Isabella, 258.
Abney, John, 159, 189, 194, 258, 261, 379.
Abney, Wm., 265, 272, 276, 283, 421.
Abner, John, 189.
Abraham, Levi, 251.
Acord (Eccord), Francis, 407.
Ackling, Barnebas, 446.
Acres (Akers), Jacob, 287.
Acres, Simon, 16, 18, 299.
Acres, Thomas, 42, 61.
Acres, Uriah, 42, 61, 98, 129, 143.
Acres, Wm., 42, 61, 378.
Acton, Thomas, 174.
Adair (O'Dear).
Adair, Cornelius, 416, 538.
Adair, John, 166, 366.
Adair, Mary, 366.
A'Dair, Robert, 72, 91, 100.
Adair, William, 296.
Adams, Agnes, 341.
Adams, Elizabeth, 137, 376.
Adams, Francis, 65.
Adams, George, 137, 150, 341, 478.
Adams, John, 137, 538.
Adams, Mary, 115.
Adams, Thomas, 197, 200, 202, 210, 212, 240, 376, 378, 382, 481.
Adams, William, 115.
Agan, Barnaby, 58.
Agan (Barnabas), 439.
Agen, Bernard, 41.
Agnew, James, 255.
Ailor (Aler Alor, Aylor).
Ailor, Anthony, 182, 200, 236, 480.
Aires, Samuel, 520.

Airron, Alex., 157.
Akerling (Ekerling), Samuel, 357.
Akry, James, 52.
Akry, Wm., 57, 69.
Alor, John, 480.
Alor, Mary, 480.
Albright, Charles, 248.
Alcorn, Robert, 40.
Alderson, John, 457.
Alderson, Thomas, 194, 510.
Alderman, James, 190.
Alderman, Richard, 190.
Alemback, Peter, 171.
Aler, Jacob, 182.
Aleshine, Peter, 424.
Alexander, Agnes, 44.
Alexander, Andrew, 177, 251, 253.
Alexander, Archibald, 46, 107, 167, 169, 177, 183, 188, 189, 196, 200, 381, 501.
Alexander, Cornelius, 239.
Alexander, Ebenezer, 424.
Alexander Elinor, 418.
Alexander, Evan, 290.
Alexander, Francis, 113, 148, 374, 317.
Alexander, Gabriel, 54, 141, 214, 274, 526.
Alexander, George, 44.
Alexander, Hugh, 291, 418, 425.
Alexander, Jacob, 411.
Alexander, James, 14, 36, 44, 54, 68, 79, 83, 97, 146, 247, 267, 297, 298, 368, 425, 446.
Alexander, John, 180, 209, 247, 276, 384, 526.
Alexander, Joseph, 145, 173, 177, 245.
Alexander, Martha, 251.
Alexander, Mary, 44.
Alexander, Matthew, 253, 526.
Alexander, Rachel, 247.
Alexander, Robert, 343, 437, 440.
Alexander, Thomas, 120.
Alexander, Wm., 44, 145, 177, 180, 189, 278, 343, 409, 437.
Alfall, John, 215.
Alfred, George, 422.
Alford, William, 179.
Alkier, Mones, 55.
Allcorn, Robert, 434.

Allden, Wentworth, 478.
Allen, Benjamin, 14, 17.
Allen, **Daniel, 307.**
Allen, David, 251.
Allen, Francis, 195.
Allen, George, 273.
Allen, Hugh, 98, 118, 137, 141, 163, 183, 184, 368, 376, 455.
Allen, James, 29, 46, 64, 72, 137, 175, 179, 183, 184, 201, 220, 251, 261, 271, 272, 278, 279, 286, 288, 317, 318, 368, 426, 428, 442, 503.
Allen, Jane, 184, 376.
Allen, John, 271, 279, 280, 442, 503.
Allen, Malcom (Malcolm, Malcome), 71, 98, 132, 156, 317, 324, 345, 350, 464, 465.
Allen, Martha, 150.
Allen, Mary, 132, 186, 251.
Allen, Robert, 27, 136, 138, 139, 144, 150, 152, 154, 251, 316, 328, 380.
Allen, Reuben, 105.
Allen, Samuel, 211.
Allen, Thomas, 186.
Allen, Wm., 225, 229, 374, 383, 393, 395.
Allet (Aylet, Elliott), John, 319.
Allford, John, 124.
Allinger, Stephen, 486.
Allison, Alex., 67.
Allison, Archibald, 442.
Allison, Charles, 135, 143, 329.
Allison, James, 21, 25, 311, 314.
Allison, Jannet, 67.
Allison, John, 29, 62, 135, 143, 240, 298, 314, 387, 398, 400, 401, 405, 406, 419, 462, 530.
Allison, Martha, 16.
Allison, Robert, 144.
Allison, Samuel, 62.
Allison, Sarah, 398.
Allison, Wm., 197, 354, 371, 400, 403, 464.
Allong, Thomas, 466.
Allsup (Alsup), Robert, 353, 463.
Almarode, George, 520.
Alsberry, Charles, 96.
Alsberry, Thomas, 139.
Altoffer, Joseph, 416.
Ameling, Frederick L. E., 426.
Ameling, Sophia, 426.
Amherst, Jeffry, Gen'l, 208.
Anders, Robert, 383.
Anderson, Andrew, 179, 201, 215, 216, 222, 225, 255, 264, 265, 272, 273.
Anderson, Alex., 69, 103, 104, 235, 272, 275, 277, 278, 421.
Anderson, Barbara, 89.
Anderson, Calvert, 294.
Anderson, Daniel, 249.
Anderson, George, 13, 18, 20, 53, 81, 95, 97, 100, 126, 202, 205, 213, 219, 235, 251, 252, 326, 335, 336, 337, 339, 343, 350, 361, 370, 422, 423, **445, 475, 483.**
Anderson, Isaac, 15, 17, 303, 432.

Anderson, Elizabeth, 140, 163, 301, **315,** 343, 364, 432.
Anderson, Jacob, 144, 148, 155.
Anderson, James, 44, 140, 152, 153, 163, 270, 301, 302, 335, 343, 347, 359, 360, 361, 364, 372, 377, 383, 385, 299, 406, 414, 423, 438, 503.
Anderson, John, 13, 14, 29, 31, 33, 46, **63,** 77, 95, 103, 107, 136, 137, 149, 150, 152, 160, 187, 209, 293, 315, 338, 347, 361, 367, 368, 372, 373, 374, 383, 386, 391, **442.**
Anderson, Joseph, 417.
Anderson, Margaret, 78, 196.
Anderson, Martha, 432, 437.
Anderson, Robert, 225, 229, 232, 277, 322, 326, 340, 361, 369, 455, 531.
Anderson, Samuel, 187, 240, 272, 372, 383, 385, 386, 387, 390, 406.
Anderson, Sarah, 385, 387, 390.
Anderson, Thomas, 187, 295.
Anderson, William, 21, 25, 33, 80, 139, 187, 193, 196, 199, 205, 215, 225, 235, 295, 340, 361, 372, 373, 377, ·379, 381, 383, 385, 386, 387, 390, 456, 463, 464, 470, 480, 503., 510.
Anderdell, James, 372.
Andrews, Adam, 61, 300.
Andrews, George, 413.
Andrews, John, 117, 119, 167.
Andrews, Robert, 130, 465.
Aneer, Daniel, 307.
Angely, Alex., 146.
Angely, Isabel, 146.
Angely, Peter, 146, 170.
Anglen, James, 44, 70, 438.
Angleman, Peter, 189, 216.
Annan, James, 68.
Anthony, Emanuel, 478.
Arbocoast, Michael, 161, 484.
Arbuckle, Charles, 421.
Arbuckle, James, 105, 111, 315, 336, 498.
Arbuckle, Margaret, 315.
Arbuckle, Matthew, 134.
Arbuckle, Rachel, 111.
Archbold, Bartholomew, 186.
Archer, Isaac, 394.
Archer, John, 21, 26, 48, 77, 107, 137, 139, 142, 155, 157, 158, 159, 194, 219, 226, 325, 359, 364, 365, 366, 372, 374, 402, 412, 418, 442, 466, 486, 510, 531, 533.
Archer, Joseph, 397.
Archer, Rebecca, 219, 365, 376, 402, 419, 533.
Archer, Robert, 156.
Archer, Sampson, 21, 74, 83, 90, 365, 418, 419, 436, 494.
Archer, Sarah, 394.
Argenbright (Archenbright), Augustine, 253, 254, 272, 417.
Archenbright, Jacob, 144, 155, 462.
Argenbright, John, 192.

Argenbright, Martin, 182.
Argenbright, Sally, 411, 412.
Armogast, John, 484.
Armentrout (Harmentrout), Elizabeth, 83, 320.
Armentrout, Frederick, 113, 360.
Armentrout, John, 179.
Armentrout, Stophel, 113.
Armentrout, Susanna, 113, 323.
Armor, Thomas, 320.
Armstrong, Ann, 109, 122.
Armstrong, Archibald, 174, 185, 250, 330, 337, 343, 380, 442.
Armstrong, Elizabeth, 280, 281, 285, 415.
Armstrong, James, 20, 22, 31, 36, 42, 58, 85, 95, 106, 111, 142, 293, 295, 300.
Armstrong, Jane, 95, 111.
Armstrong, John, 126, 379.
Armstrong, Lanty, 344, 355, 457.
Armstrong, Lydia, 95.
Armstrong, Margaret, 337.
Armstrong, Mary, 336.
Armstrong, Matthew, 48.
Armstrong, Nancy, 407.
Armstrong, Paul, 111.
Armstrong, Phebe, 379.
Armstrong, Rebeckah, 451.
Armstrong, Robert, 14, 18, 21, 48, 54, 58, 74, 91, 95, 105, 120, 137, 138, 147, 157, 164, 269, 320, 336, 349, 352, 399, 407, 414, 487, 488, 531.
Armstrong, Samuel, 257, 393, 403, 407, 526.
Armstrong, Sarah, 85, 277, 366.
Armstrong, Thomas, 58, 68, 75, 109, 122, 253, 305, 307, 326.
Armstrong, Wm., 39, 61, 66, 106, 120, 249, 255, 257, 272, 278, 285, 302, 374, 403, 407, 409, 452.
Arnett, Thomas, 154.
Arnold, John, 478.
Arnold, Stephen, 60, 61, 62, 127, 441.
Artus, John, 344.
Asebury, James, 530.
Ashley, William, 222.
Ashton, Wallace, 28.
Askins, Elenor, 189, 204, 239, 240.
Askin, John, 116, 166, 186, 208.
Askins, Philemon, 114, 330.
Asque, James, 489.
Asten, Walles, 438.
Astrop (Aistrop), Anne, 291.
Astrop, Robert, 248, 257, 291, 509.
Attwaters, Ann H., 226.
Atwater (Attwater), Enos, 226, 430.
Atkins, John, 64, 68, 105.
Atkinson, John, 355.
Atkinson, Rebecca, 355.
Aulford, Henry, 122.
Austin, Richardson, 479.
Awty, William, 446.
Ayler, William, 25.

Aylett, William, 25, 33.
Ayten, Lasty F., 520.

Backall, Adam, 383.
Backenstoe, Elizabeth, 538.
Backenstoe, Frederick, 538.
Backenstoe, George, 538.
Backenstoe, John, 538.
Baer, George, 474.
Baffenbarger (Buffenberry, Puffenberry), George, 41.
Bags, John, 87.
Baggs, Robert, 219.
Bags, Thomas, 87.
Bailey, Barnabas, 285.
Bailey, Charlotte, 285, 292.
Bailey, Elizabeth, 273, 402, 404.
Bailey, John, 193, 285.
Bailey, Marsa, 193.
Bailey, Robert, 273, 274, 402, 404, 410, 425.
Bailey, William, 285, 397.
Bain, Alex., 322, 362.
Bainbridge, James, 157.
Baker, Elizabeth, 236.
Baker, Bartholomew, 423.
Baker, George, 132.
Baker, Hannah, 423.
Baker, Hester, 134.
Baker, Humphrey, 23, 56, 61, 132, 144.
Baker, Joseph, 180.
Baker, Josias, 62.
Baker, Lewis, 22.
Baker, Sarah, 423.
Baker, Thomas, 236, 489.
Bakon, Ludwick, 41.
Baldwin, James, 115.
Balenger, Jasper, 383.
Bales, Eden, 520.
Bales, James, 520.
Baley, Edward, 61.
Baley, James, 61.
Ball, William, 476.
Ballard, John, 407.
Ballard, John M., 425.
Ballor, John, 340.
Ballentine, Francis, 423.
Ballentine, Hugh, 423.
Ballfought, John, 433.
Ballinger, Joseph, 438.
Balsley, Christian, 286, 288, 511.
Balsey, Elizabeth, 511.
Bamier, John, 142.
Bandsgrove, Edward, 176.
Bandy, John, 86.
Bane, James, 61, 95, 436.
Banister, Mark, 187.
Banks, William, 233.
Barber, George, 430.
Barclay, Andrew, 311.
Barclay, John, 34, 389.
Barefield, William, 146.
Bare, Jacob, 482.

543

Barker, Edward, 234.
Barker, Elias, 184.
Barker, Israel, 537.
Barker, Joel, 107.
Barker, Thomas, 125, 351.
Barnard, Patrick, 87.
Barnbloom, Barnebas, 446.
Barkley, Joseph, 181.
Barnes, Ann, 284.
Barnes, Elizabeth, 233.
Barnes, George, 233.
Barnes, Margaret, 284.
Barnes, Mary, 284.
Barnes, Thomas, 139, 434.
Barnes, William, 284.
Barnet, Ann, 480.
Barnett, Alex., 230.
Barnett (Barnet).
Barnett, Benjamin, 60.
Barnet, Hugh, 363.
Barnett, James, 513.
Barnet, John, 469.
Barnett, Joseph, 347.
Barnet, Patrick, 88, 147.
Barnett, Peter, 410.
Barnett, Reizen (Rezin), 406, 407, 410.
Barnett, Richard, 60.
Barnett, Thomas, 147, 363.
Barnhart, George, 287.
Barrel, Dominick, 68, 75.
Barren, Jane, 94.
Barret, Domnick, 80, 274.
Barret, Hannah, 267.
Barret, Luke, 257.
Barret, Nathaniel, 478.
Barrier, Casper, 173.
Barrier, Jacob, 173, 200, 274, 282, 483.
Barrier, Margaret, 143.
Barrier, Philip, 135, 348.
Barrier, Susanna, 282.
Barry, George, 219.
Barry, Thomas, 410.
Barton, James, 441.
Barton, Richard, 433.
Bartley, John, 20, 21, 57.
Baskins, Andrew, 55.
Baskins, Chas., 202, 223, 228, 382, 423, 504.
Baskins, John, 132.
Baskin, John C., 423.
Baskins, Wm., 13, 30, 48, 52, 72, 92, 142, 147, 329, 476.
Basseman, Christopher, 289.
Baites, James, 146, 147, 441.
Bates (Beats, Baites), Ephriam, 250, 447.
Bates, Samuel, 446.
Bates, Thomas, 335.
Bates, William, 21, 156.
Batley, James, 47.
Battersby, William, 59.
Battan, Hendrey, 434.
Batton, Henry, 40.
Bates,, James, 57.

Baughman, Anna M., 79.
Baughman, Henry, 79, 328.
Baumgartner, J. Godfrey, 318.
Baxter, Andrew, 25, 431, 525.
Baxter, George, 134, 157, 481, 483.
Baxter, Jerman, 105.
Baxter, John, 245.
Baxter, Joseph, 62, 309.
Baxter, William, 245.
Bay, Thomas, 177.
Bayard, James, 303.
Baylor, Catherine, 421.
Baylor, Jacob, 421.
Beal, Thomas, 357.
Beane, Ellis, 461.
Bean, Isaac, 26.
Bean, James, 24, 445.
Beane, Jesse, 461.
Bear, Jacob, 87, 353.
Bear, John, 161.
Bear, William, 144.
Beard (Berd), Beedon, 288.
Beard, Charles, 175, 180.
Beard, David, 164, 175, 180, 378.
Beard, Edward, 93, 175, 308, 324, 489.
Beard, Hugh, 108.
Beard, James, 26, 28, 29, 37, 67, 71, 72, 73, 93, 140, 214, 315, 411, 434.
Beard, Jane, 93, 421.
Beard, John, 137, 209, 513, 518.
Beard, Mary, 93.
Beard, Robert, 400.
Beard, Thomas, 21, 116, 219, 362, 400, 421, 440, 442.
Beard, Wm., 91, 107, 120, 138, 197, 331, 332, 351, 460, 461.
Bearling, John, 152.
Beath, Joseph, 389.
Beath, Robert, 389.
Beaton, Mary, 407.
Beatey (Beaty, Beety), Francis, 23, 135, 298, 304, 408, 409, 436, 442, 470.
Beaty, John, 39, 299.
Beaty, Mary, 418, 419, 420.
Beazley, James, 473.
Beck, Stephen, 214.
Bedel, John, 493.
Bedford, William, 143.
Bee, George, 77.
Beech (Beach), John, 226, 266.
Beesley, Jeremiah, 196.
Beggs, Alexander, 61.
Beggs, Caleb, 520.
Begley, Henry, 355.
Beith, Joseph, 395.
Bell, Agnes, 415, 419.
Bell, David, 138, 150, 152, 176, 193, 199, 209, 214, 215, 236, 245, 262, 270, 292, 309, 311, 348, 383, 502, 507, 510.
Bell, Elizabeth, 118, 119.
Bell, Florence, 245, 270, 383, 397.
Bell, Francis, 276, 278, 279, 416, 518.

Bell, James, 13, 19, 20, 21, 26, 54, 60, 80, 85, 120, 139, 143, 157, 172, 180, 209, 211, 216, 237, 246, 278, 279, 289, 305, 306, 307, 317, 331, 345, 357, 387, 415, 416, 418, 419, 444, 481.
Bell, Jane, 80, 417.
Bell, John, 132, 211, 263, 289, 305, 307, 415, 428, 519, 526.
Bell, Joseph, 55, 63, 78, 79, 80, 82, 83, 84, 98, 133, 134, 140, 175, 188, 192, 194, 196, 197, 199, 202, 207, 208, 212, 213, 215, 216, 219, 222, 223, 226, 227, 231, 236, 240, 243, 245, 252, 262, 265, 266, 268, 271, 272, 277, 278, 352, 369, 383, 390, 397, 412, 417, 442, 463, 481, 491, 492, 508, 509, 519, 525.
Bell, Leonard, 178, 201, 217, 254, 531.
Bell, Liard, 174.
Bell, Margaret, 46, 82, 95.
Bell, Martha, 415.
Bell, Mary A., 80, 416.
Bell, Rachel, 80, 415.
Bell, Robert W., 519.
Bell, Robert, 311, 416.
Bell, Sally J., 519.
Bell, Samuel, 89, 137, 232, 256, 265, 278, 328, 386, 415, 516, 519.
Bell, Sarah, 519.
Bell, Thomas, 189, 400, 415, 516, 519.
Bell, Wm., 30, 48, 55, 65, 66, 77, 120, 171, 176, 221, 245, 249, 250, 255, 262, 266, 270, 272, 274, 320, 328, 335, 351, 372, 386, 387, 397, 411, 412, 413, 415, 444.
Bell (Belche, Bellshe, Belsha, Belshire, Belsher), Robert, 97, 153, 429, 489.
Belsha, Zachariah, 430, 442.
Bence, Mary, 119.
Bend, Frances, 325.
Bendall, Elizabeth, 65.
Bender, Johannes, 298.
Benezet, Philip, 337, 381.
Bengle, Andrew, 394.
Benjamin, Christian, 350.
Bennet, Benjamin, 107, 134, 372.
Bennett, Catherine, 134.
Bennett, Jesse, 418.
Bennet, John, 192, 488.
Bennett, Joseph, 176, 374, 379.
Bennett, Martha, 372.
Bennett, Richardson, 372.
Bennett, William, 484.
Benson, John, 124, 317, 242.
Benson (Benston), George, 198, 207, 371, 397.
Benson, Levin, 483.
Benson, Margaret, 124, 174, 317, 342, 377.
Benson, Matthias, 260, 372, 377, 385.
Benton, Richard, 62.
Bernard, John, 76.
Bernhard, George, Sr., 532.
Berrall, Dominick, 15.

Berrier, Philip, 502.
Berrisford, Ann, 112.
Berrisford, Agnes, 341.
Berrisford, Catherine, 341.
Berrisford, Frances, 341.
Berrisford, Jennet, 341.
Berrisford, John, 50, 60, 112, 330, 341, 441.
Berrisford, Lydia, 112, 341.
Berrisford, Margaret, 341.
Berrisford, Mary, 330, 341.
Berry, Charles, 17, 231, 285, 286.
Berry, George, 64, 148, 152, 285, 286, 418, 445.
Berry, Isham, 248, 251.
Berey, Jacob, 247.
Berry, James, 47, 49, 64, 79, 277, 278, 280, 439, 481.
Berry, John, 47, 57, 79, 127, 145, 208, 228, 257, 260, 290.
Berry, Rebecca, 390, 398.
Berry, William, 172, 390, 445.
Berryhill, Mexard, 520.
Bert, James, 525.
Bertly, George, 443.
Bertly, John, 443.
Best, Christopher, 128.
Best, Francis, 526.
Best, James, 237.
Bethell, Wm., 47, 57, 58, 69, 439.
Beton, Richard, 61.
Bets, John, 498.
Beus, William, 24, 26, 45.
Bever, Peter, 446.
Beverage, Elizabeth, 385.
Beverage, John, 385.
Beverly, Munford, 480.
Beverly, Robert, 385, 417.
Beverly, Wm., 73, 98, 295, 533.
Bibee, John, 327.
Bibee, Thomas, 327.
Bickle, Adam, 250, 262, 275, 291, 412.
Bickle, Mary, 291.
Biche, Stephen, 250.
Bier, John, 413.
Biggs, Benjamin, 514.
Biggs, Edward, 152.
Biggs, James, 14, 19.
Biggs, John, 353, 462.
Biggs, Mark, 520.
Biggs, Samuel, 512.
Bigham, George, 62, 84, 116, 299, 348, 374, 487.
Bigham, Jane, 236.
Bigham, John, 57, 112, 137, 143, 177, 216, 236., 348, 443.
Bigham, Sarah, 115.
Bilbo, Absalom, 90.
Bills, William, 486.
Bindwell, George, 444.
Bing, John, 181, 203, 411, 424.
Bingaman, Christian, 74, 160, 361.

Bingaman, Henry, 74.
Bingman (Bingamon), John, 53, 56, 74, 103, 486.
Bingham, George, 487.
Bingham, John, 443.
Binnell, Moses, 172.
Bird, Abraham, 83, 88, 101, 320.
Bird, Andrew, 88, 101, 107, 132, 157, 164, 366, 435, 438, 465.
Bird, John, 75, 81, 218.
Bird, Magdalene, 435, 438.
Bird, Sarah, 81.
Bird, Thomas, 48.
Birdwell, George, 128.
Birdwell, Sarah, 113.
Bishop, Edward, 61.
Bishop, Nicholas, 449.
Bishop, William, 40, 67, 74.
Black, Alexander, 54, 116.
Black, Andrew, 160.
Black, Anthony, 36, 54, 92, 164, 526.
Black, David, 160, 482.
Black, Elizabeth, 92, 160.
Black, Frederick, 415.
Black, Gawin, 313.
Black, James, 160, 371, 537, 538.
Black, John, 14, 23, 36, 46, 54, 57, 58, 79, 136, 140, 142, 143, 152, 158, 160, 164, 170, 192, 209, 220, 237, 250, 345, 371, 429, 443, 489, 512, 513, 525, 526, 537, 538.
Black, Mary, 192.
Black, Mathew, 312.
Black, Joseph, 498.
Black, Patrick, 440.
Black, Rebecca, 190, 250.
Black, Robert, 34, 227, 237, 432.
Black, Samuel, 29, 46, 68, 79, 117, 142, 143, 180, 190, 202, 237, 518, 519, 537, 538.
Black, Thomas, 15, 17, 18, 28, 39, 143, 149, 319, 361,.
Black, Wm., 116, 142, 143, 178, 189, 201, 212, 215, 237, 425, 474, 525, 537.
Blackburn, Archibald, 227.
Blackburn, Benjamin, 230.
Blackburn, Oliver, 407.
Blackburn, Samuel, 286, 426.
Blackly, John, 322, 324.
Blackmore, John, 158.
Blackmore, Henry, 257.
Blackmore, Samuel, 259.
Blackmore, William, 256.
Blackwelder, John, 431.
Blackwood, Ann, 405.
Blackwood, Eleanor, 405.
Blackwood, Joseph, 263, 405.
Blackwood, Mary, 405.
Blackwood, Rebecca, 263, 405.
Blackwood, Samuel, 153, 405, 525.
Blackwood, Wm., 263, 348, 490.
Blagg, John, 97, 126, 335, 340, 343, 350, 356, 449, 477, 488, 493, 502.

Blain, Joseph, 132.
Blain, Wm., 410.
Blair, Alex., 118, 383, 442.
Blair, Elenore, 190.
Blair, Elizabeth, 252, 480.
Blair, David, 386.
Blair, James, 145, 176, 190, 215, 241, 248, 362, 364, 369, 379, 383, 386.
Blair, Jane, 480.
Blair, John, 142, 209, 215, 248, 345, 369, 480.
Blair, Joseph, 190, 196, 210, 216, 230.
Blair, Margaret, 215, 379, 405.
Blair, Mary, 372, 480.
Blair, Rebecca, 402.
Blair, Wm., 209, 222, 223, 228, 240, 252, 291, 372, 379, 381, 386, 396, 400, 402, 404, 405, 406, 410, 414, 527, 531.
Blake, John, 170.
Blake, Peter, 384.
Blakely, George, 409.
Blakely, John, 320, 324.
Blakely, Robert, 409.
Blakemore, Adam, 239.
Blakemore, Samuel, 250.
Blakemore, Sarah, 250.
Blan, James, 490.
Bland, Richard, 486.
Bland, Thomas, 154.
Blane, George, 305.
Blankenship, Josiah, 195.
Blanton, Samuel, 306.
Blanton (Blantin), Wm., 105, 141.
Blaze, Conrad, 182.
Bleameat, Anthony, 247.
Blear, John, 452.
Blear, Wm., 489.
Bledsoe, Anthony, 132, 138, 157, 158, 356, 363, 457, 465.
Bleehon, Elizabeth, 413.
Bletcher, Abraham, 83.
Blizard, John, 465.
Blizzard, Thomas, 170, 193.
Bloodworth, Mary, 295.
Bloodworth, Russell, 420.
Blowin, Lewis, 290.
Bly, Samuel, 24.
Blyth, William, 307.
Blythe, Samuel, 29.
Bocock, John, 96.
Boddy, Charles, 162.
Bodkin (Botkin).
Bodkin, Diana, 377.
Bodkin, Hugh, 213, 386, 408, 480.
Bodkin, James, 185, 213, 248, 377, 474, 489.
Bodkin, John, 120, 146, 213, 335, 374, 489.
Botkin, Mary, 489.
Bodkin, Richard, 42, 44, 139, 320, 438, 489.
Boff, Conrad, 338.
Boff, Mary, 338.
Boffanton, Jonathan, 516.
Bogard, Anthony, 42, 43, 103.

547

Bowyer, Priscilla, 414.
Bowyer, Samuel, 461.
Bowyer, Teresa, 246.
Bowyer, Wm. C., 288.
Boyd, Adam, 308.
Boyd, Alexander, 96, 128, 129, 157, 158, 322, 331, 332, 335, 338, 354, 362, 453, 456, 458, 460, 462, 466, 499, 500, 528.
Boyd, Andrew, 128, 144, 151, 362, 427, 428, 456, 459, 462.
Boyd, Christian, 157.
Boyd, Eleanor, 377.
Boyd, Elizabeth, 427.
Boyd, Esther, 118, 119.
Boyd, John, 130, 150, 191, 195, 427, 531, 537.
Boyd, Patrick, 166, 189.
Boyd, Robert, 41, 118, 377, 460.
Boyd, Samuel, 323, 488.
Boyd, Thomas, 130, 428, 520.
Boyer, Benjamin, 285.
Boyer, James, 199.
Boyr, John, 23.
Boyers, John, 501.
Boyles, Charles, 152.
Boyl, Dudley, 135.
Boyle (Boil), Edward, 17, 18, 293, 437.
Boil (Boyle), Hugh, 21.
Boyle, James, 470.
Boyle, Michael, 440.
Boil, William, 61, 288.
Boyter, Christian, 26.
Bozwell, George, 387, 514.
Bracenrigh, Adam, 491.
Brackfield, Isaac, 87.
Bracking, Matthew, 112.
Bradbury, James, 478.
Braddock, Gen'l, 472.
Braden, Edward, 532.
Braden, Elizabeth, 532.
Braden, George, 532.
Bradford, Samuel, 136.
Bradley, Margaret, 134.
Bradshaw, Elizabeth, 206.
Bradshaw, Thomas, 122, 129, 134, 148, 208, 419.
Bradshaw, Wm., 62.
Brady, Catherine, 401.
Brady, Edward, 201, 401.
Brady, James, 347.
Brady, Michael, 31.
Brady, Patrick, 401.
Brady, William, 21, 417.
Brafford, Robert, 388.
Brafford, Samuel, 388.
Bragg, Thomas, 59.
Brahen, Mathew, 454.
Braiding, Bryan, 371.
Braiding, John, 371.
Branan, Thomas, 448.
Branch, Elizabeth, 180.
Brandes, Henry, 222.

Brand, James, 277, 278.
Brand, Susanna, 281.
Bramham (Branham), John, 27, 28.
Brannon (Branan, Branham), Thomas, 97, 112, 123, 448.
Brannon, Timothy, 183.
Brannon, William, 188.
Bratton, Adam, 172, 178, 185, 201, 388.
Bratton, Ann, 54, 67, 298, 388.
Bratton, George, 215, 216, 225.
Bratton, James, 188, 198, 201, 215, 221, 223, 272, 276, 278.
Bratton, John, 188.
Bratton, Peter, 284.
Bratton, Robert, 30, 33, 49, 51, 54, 67, 72, 120, 123, 134, 148, 178, 298, 335, 368, 388, 498, 529.
Bratton, Thomas, 221.
Bratton, William, 281, 416.
Brawford, Hugh, 400.
Brawford, Rachel, 400.
Brawford, Rebecca, 222.
Brawford, Robert, 222, 281.
Brawford, Samuel, 254, 400.
Bray, Matthew, 123.
Brady, James, 526.
Bready, John, 526.
Bready, Michael, 530.
Brealy, Daniel, 21.
Breasline, William, 250.
Breckenridge (Brackenridge, Breackenridge), Adam, 79, 301, 305, 306, 307.
Breckenridge, Alexander, 133, 295, 297, 305, 307, 319, 346, 389, 498, 512.
Breckenridge, Ann, 35, 39, 77.
Breckenridge, George, 35, 39, 77, 133, 293, 294, 298, 301, 303, 305, 306, 307, 346, 439, 440, 498.
Brackenridge, James, 294, 305, 307, 503.
Breckenridge, Jest, 357.
Breckenridge, John, 244.
Brackenridge, Lettice, 32, 136, 369.
Breckenridge, Mary, 306.
Breackenridge, Robert, 32, 33, 42, 45, 46, 48, 52, 53, 69, 70, 72, 77, 80, 83, 97, 107, 132, 136, 146, 147, 300, 305, 306, 307, 311, 322, 327, 336, 343, 354, 358, 451, 455, 463, 487, 498, 527.
Breckenridge, William, 410, 418.
Breedin, Edward, 80.
Breedin, Mary, 80.
Breeding, Brian, 209.
Breeding, James, 177.
Bredley, Mary, 138.
Breeze, Susanna, 281.
Breezley, Elizabeth, 263.
Breezeley, Mary, 263.
Breezley, Patrick, 252.
Brent, James, 237, 480.
Brent, John, 351.
Brewer, William, 154.
Briant, John, 34.

Briant, Morgan, 17.
Brice, John, 31.
Bridget, James, 424, 446
Brien, Edward, 288, 410.
Dilen, Susanna, 288.
Brig, Hybert, 193.
Briggs, David, 360, 369, 496.
Briggs, Samuel, 131, 140.
Bright, Earick, 441.
Bright, George, 24.
Bright, John, 191, 194, 397, 510.
Bright, Samuel, 499.
Bright, Tobias, 23, 24, 48, 62, 441, 443.
Brindle, James, 484.
Bringenham, James, 74.
Brinster, James, 118, 135.
Briscoe (Brisco), William, 169, 179.
Britt, John, 174.
Broback, Agnes, 395.
Broback, Edward, 275, 395.
Brock, Effie, 42.
Brock, Michael, 519.
Brock, Nicholas, 18, 47.
Brock, Rudy, 42.
Brock, William, 18, 478.
Brockenson, Edward, 396.
Brookbank, Edward, 209.
Brook, Catherine, 81.
Brooks, Charles, 413.
Brookes, David, 536.
Brookes, Elizabeth, 536.
Brooks, Giles, 526.
Brooks, James, 242, 261, 482, 533, 536.
Brooks, John, 101, 218, 236, 432, 525, 536.
Brooks, Jonathan, 263, 277, 278, 279, 526, 536.
Brookes, Mary, 536.
Brookes, Nioma, 536.
Brooks, Samuel, 525, 536.
Brookes, Susanna, 536
Broups, George, 449.
Broyle, Adam, 159.
Brown, Abraham, 60, 67, 115, 140, 147.
Brown, Alice, 87, 90.
Brown, Anne, 45, 64, 362.
Brown, Andrew, 103, 108.
Brown, Benjamin, 192.
Brown, Catherine, 94.
Brown, Charles, 392.
Brown, Cornelius, 255, 260, 276.
Brown, David, 410.
Brown, Elizabeth, 246, 271, 393, 409.
Brown, Esther, 77, 98, 338, 344.
Brown, Francis, 44, 136, 438.
Brown, George, 308, 469.
Brown, Henry, 24, 61, 64, 65, 77, 87, 90, 313, 344, 397, 436.
Brown, Hester, 191.
Brown, Hugh, 212, 265, 370, 383, 402, 429.
Brown, Isabella, 122, 334, 341.
Brown, Jacob, 24, 37, 62, 63, 354, 362, 441, 460.

Brown, James, 32, 43, 45, 47, 49, 64, 142, 177, 191, 195, 211, 256, 257, 258, 284, 290, 347, 370, 387, 393, 402, 412, 442, 443, 449.
Brown, Jane, 103, 284, 370.
Brown, John, 13, 15, 20, 24, 37, 40, 41, 54, 56, 65, 68, 71, 74, 77, 80, 81, 118, 120, 130, 139, 141, 142, 148, 161, 163, 185, 190, 220, 224, 228, 229, 231, 265, 269, 271, 274, 286, 321, 322, 347, 348, 363, 364, 370, 381, 389, 402, 422, 428, 442, 444, 474, 480, 520, 527, 528.
381, 393, 402.
Brown, Margaret, 229, 265, 271, 321, 364, 381, 393, 402.
Brown, Mary, 38, 90, 190, 387, 397.
Brown, Morgan, 38.
Brown, Rebecca, 212, 265, 266, 269, 370, 383, 402.
Brown, Richard, 39.
Brown, Robert, 26, 44, 129, 130, 154, 269, 298, 319, 354, 365, 370, 402, 437, 460, 473.
Brown, Samuel, 24, 37, 257, 430.
Brown, Sally, 265, 402.
Brown, Squire, 458.
Brown, Thomas, 96, 120, 141, 152, 174, 191, 245, 246, 258, 265, 271, 393, 402, 403, 405, 409, 418, 451.
Brown, Wm., 28, 44, 57, 81, 89, 122, 133, 135, 143, 190, 191, 208, 334, 341, 402, 438, 441, 446, 526.
Brown, Windell, 41.
Browner, Ebrthe, 447.
Browning, George, 512.
Browning, John, 512.
Browning, John W., 512.
Browning, Joshua, 512.
Browning, Nicholas, 512.
Browning, Rosamon, 512.
Brownlee, Alex., 181, 185, 198, 202, 302, 392, 408.
Brownlee, James, 260, 387, 408, 517.
Brownlee, John, 33, 69, 260, 387, 390, 398, 421, 517.
Brownlee, Rebecca, 170, 318.
Brownlee, Sarah, 390, 398.
Brownlee, William, 249, 387, 408.
Broundlee, Alexander, 440.
Broundlee, John, 440.
Bruback, Madlena, 323.
Bruce, Charles, 274.
Bruce, George, 327.
Bruce, James, 274.
Bruce, John, 33, 298, 432.
Bruin, Bryon, 455.
Bruister, James, 76, 182, 440, 446, 460.
Brumley, Austen, 478, 479.
Brumley, Thomas, 479.
Brumley, William, 477, 479.
Bruner, Peter, 77.
Brunton, Robert, 327.

Brush, Blakely, 110, 352.
Brush, James, 189.
Brush, Richard, 110.
Bryon, Alice, 68.
Bryan, Ambros, 454.
Bryans, Ann, 92.
Bryce, Archibald, 327.
Bryan, Christopher, 380.
Bryan, Cornelius, 47, 428.
Bryan, David, 24, 112, 135, 165, 331, 466.
Bryan, Edward, 413.
Bryan, Elizabeth, 135, 165, 358, 466.
Bryans, George, 140.
Bryans, James, 128, 133, 358, 436.
Bryan, John, 47, 61, 151, 371, 428, 436.
Bryan (Bryon), Joseph, 68, 69.
Bryan, Margaret, 174.
Bryan, Martha, 144.
Bryan, Morgan, 298, 469.
Bryan, Robert, 436.
Bryan, Sarah, 267.
Bryan, Thomas, 47, 428.
Bryan, Wm., 40, 61, 119, 123, 132, 139, 400, 436.
Bryant, James, 358.
Bryce, Archibald, 92.
Bryson, Charity, 393.
Buchanan, Agnes, 89.
Buchanan, Alex., 229, 460, 498.
Buchanon, Archibald, 89, 91, 358.
Buckanon, Andrew, 150.
Buchanan, David, 222, 232, 252, 272, 277, 278, 285, 290.
Buchanan, James, 77, 84, 107, 142, 143, 231, 342, 362, 370, 428, 464.
Buchanan, Jane, 204.
Buchanan, John, 13, 15, 16, 19, 20, 21, 30, 31, 46, 53, 56, 57, 62, 69, 82, 93, 105, 107, 110, 116, 124, 134, 136, 138, 141, 144, 156, 158, 159, 171, 194, 263, 314, 323, 325, 359, 383, 432, 443, 448, 487, 494, 497, 518, 525, 530.
Buchanan, Margret, 30, 136.
Buchanan, Mary, 124.
Buchanan, Maryan, 298.
Buchanan, Nicholas, 498.
Buchanan, Patrick, 142, 193, 195, 198, 200, 222, 230, 235, 244, 402, 510, 526.
Buchanan, Rebecca, 27.
Buchanon, Richard, 229, 242.
Buchanan, Robert, 124, 204, 304, 470, 498.
Buchanan, Ruth, 27.
Buchanan, Samuel, 136, 142, 222, 408.
Buchanan, Sarah, 231.
Buchanan, Thomas, 322, 323.
Buchanan, Walter, 127, 358, 513.
Buchanan, Wm., 84, 202, 219, 263, 428, 480.
Bucher, George, 192.
Buckerage, James, 520.
Buckley, Robert, 96.
Buchman (Baughman), Henry, 328.
Buckner, Mordecai, 346.

Buckthorn, Sarah, 151.
Buff, George, 129, 350.
Buffenberry, George, 83, 229.
Buffington, Jonathan, 213.
Bulgier, Daniel, 303.
Bullitt, John, 266, 274, 396, 502.
Bullitt, Thomas, 153, 333, 339, 475, 476.
Bullock, James, 24.
Bumgardner, Christian, 78.
Bumgardner, Godfrey, 207, 325.
Bumgardner, John, 300.
Buntin, Andrew, 165.
Buntin, James, 97.
Burback, Adam, 238.
Burford, St. Lawrence, 20.
Burgess, Elizabeth, 269.
Burgess, James, 268, 269, 481.
Burgess, Joseph, 194, 510.
Burgess, Robert, 269.
Burkin, John, 114.
Burley, George, 189.
Burley, Horden, 98.
Burnet, Jacob, 28.
Burnet, Jane, 17.
Burnet, Mathew, 421.
Burke(Burk), Andrew, 256.
Burk, Ann, 224.
Burke, Betsy, 256.
Burk, Catherine, 270.
Burk, Charles, 17, 26.
Burk, Edward, 268, 404, 409, 418.
Burke, Elizabeth, 396.
Burk, Francis, 144.
Burke, Henry, 248.
Burk, Isham (Isem), 268, 270, 271, 275, 289.
Bourk, James, 24, 26, 28.
Burk, 47, 58, 256.
Burk, John, 102, 209, 263, 291, 396, 489, 532.
Burk, Joseph, 394, 416, 418, 532.
Burk, Lucretia, 58.
Burke, Mary, 191.
Burke, Nancy, 256.
Burk, Patrick, 31.
Burke, Philip, 256.
Burke, Samuel, 256.
Burk, Thomas, 26, 35, 326.
Burk, Wm., 26, 33, 50, 60, 209, 218, 224, 226, 235, 237, 246, 256, 326, 360, 418, 437, 447, 483.
Burns, Bartholamy, 62.
Burns, Dennis, 381, 382.
Burns, Elizabeth, 52.
Burns, Henry, 396.
Burns, Isaac, 143, 266, 348.
Burns, Isabella, 264, 385, 396, 403, 417.
Burns, James, 119.
Burns, John, 71, 74, 266, 394.
Burns, Margaret C., 264, 395, 396.
Burns, Mary, 396.
Burns, Peter, 196.

Burns, Richard, 257.
Burns, Robert, 227, 264, 395, 403, 479.
Burns, Thomas, 396.
Burnsides, James, 96, 141, 150, 181, 464, 488, 513, 528.
Burnsides, John, 127, 137, 207, 280, 374.
Burnsides, Martha, 423.
Burnsides, Rachel, 323.
Burnside, Thomas, 496.
Burt, William, 62.
Burton, John, 251, 252, 256, 264, 273, 276, 511, 512.
Burton, Richard, 19, 25, 46, 74.
Burton, Thomas, 57.
Burwell, Lewis, 45.
Bues, William, 436.
Buse (Bruce), Alex., 140.
Bush, Agnes, 109.
Bush, Catherine, 184.
Bush, George, 107, 449.
Bush, James, 355.
Bush, John, 97, 287.
Bush, Michael, 184.
Bush, Philip, 501.
Bush, William, 185.
Busheers, William, 242, 356.
Bushon, Elizabeth, 51.
Buster, John, 213.
Buster, Paul, 184.
Buzzard, Peter, 190.
Butt, Amos, 219.
Butt, Henry, 250.
Butcher, Nicholas, 169.
Butcher, Valentine, 96, 169.
Butler, John, 46, 48.
Butler, John G., 480.
Butler, James, 477, 479.
Butler, Patrick, 248.
Butler, Thomas, 418.
Buttler, William, 453.
Buton, Nathaniel, 446.
Byers, Joseph, 284, 408, 410, 416, 480.
Byers, William, 62.
Byrd, Col., 213, 214, 343, 449, 493.
Byrd, C. W., 208.
Byrd, John, 429.
Byrd, William, 209, 234.
Byrnside, John, 391.

Cabeen, Wm., 324, 325, 333, 450, 452, 455.
Cabell, Wm., 345, 351, 461, 465.
Cable, Philip, 434.
Cachill, James, 51, 52.
Cadock, Frederick, 434.
Cafferty, Ann, 166.
Cafferty, Mary, 22.
Caghey, James, 158.
Cain, Cornelius, 94.
Cain, Daniel, 87.
Cain, Jacob, 262.
Cain, John, 84, 477, 478.
Cain, Margaret, 369.

Cain, Patrick, 76, 313, 440.
Calbreath, Thomas, 262, 264, 278, 481.
Calbraith, William, 223, 224.
Caldwell, Alex., 534.
Caldwell, Ann, 107.
Caldwell, Catherine, 287.
Caldwell, David, 42, 177.
Caldwell, Elizabeth, 227, 287.
Caldwell, George, 20, 31, 32, 68, 103.
Caldwell, James, 36, 48, 51.
Caldwell, John, 108, 117, 142, 143, 160, 205, 237, 245, 287, 310.
Caldwell, Rob., 29, 57, 227, 280.
Caldwell, Samuel, 107, 127, 142, 227.
Caldwell, Sarah, 205, 237.
Caldwell, Thomas, 279.
Caldwell, William, 280, 298.
Calhoun, James, 341, 362.
Calhoun, John, 362.
Calhoun, Patrick, 341.
Calhoun, Samuel, 442.
Calhoun, Zachariah, 434.
Calkin, Jeremiah, 438.
Call (Caul), Elizabeth, 411.
Call, Hugh, 405, 411.
Call, James, 247, 249, 388, 520.
Call, John, 308.
Call, Betty, 388.
Call, Patty, 388.
Call, Susannah, 247, 249, 358.
Caul, Timothy, 144.
Caul, Thomas, 399.
Caul, William, 405.
Callan, John, 479.
Callachen, Charles, 152, 176.
Callahan (Callaghen, Callachan), Dennis, 201, 227, 228, 395, 527.
Callahan, Edward, 192.
Callahan, Martha, 395.
Callihan, Owen, 64.
Callender, Robert, 472.
Calley, Christian, 113.
Calley, John, 113.
Calleway, Back, 447.
Calloway, Elinor, 393.
Calloway, James, 113.
Calloway, Zachariah, 393.
Callison, Daniel, 250.
Callison, James, 48, 53, 141, 142, 147, 174, 306, 348, 490.
Callson, Elizabeth, 478.
Calmers, D., 500.
Calmer, Davis, 335, 338, 499.
Calston, William, 479.
Calwell, Elizabeth, 86.
Calwell, Margaret, 317, 342.
Calwell, Robert, 317, 342.
Calvard, Benjamin, 174.
Calvert, George, 534.
Calvert, Ross, 534.
Calvie, Margaret, 342.
Calvin, Andrew, 152.

Calvin, James, 318.
Camble, John, 228.
Cameron, Charles, 187, 220, 221, 223, 234, 240, 242, 251, 273, 388, 398, 403, 481.
Cameron, Christian, 172.
Cameron, George, 187.
Cameron, James, 172, 410.
Cameron, John, 314, 331, 447.
Cammerlon, John, 191.
Camp, Ichabod, 340.
Campbell, Archibald, 513.
Campbell, Arthur, 357, 461, 498, 515.
Campbell, Alexander, 123, 280, 293, 307, 311, 343, 365.
Campbell, Andrew, 31, 300, 304, 308, 343, 376.
Campbell, Bridget, 274, 399.
Campbell, Catherine, 282.
Campbell, Charles, 40, 44, 50, 53, 54, 67, 107, 111, 124, 127, 138, 139, 150, 189, 190, 192, 193, 196, 199, 364, 367, 379, 380, 408, 437, 440, 442, 515.
Campbell, Collin, 285.
Campbell, Daniel, 307, 311, 377.
Campbell, David, 136, 141, 324.
Campbell, Donald, 357.
Campbell, Elizabeth, 50, 107, 112, 138, 162, 332, 335, 347, 351, 354.
Campbell, George, 33 ,72, 80, 141, 239, 443.
Campbell, Gilbert, 27, 80, 122, 525.
Campbell, Henry, 140.
Campbell, Hugh, 41, 44, 154, 206, 255, 291, 376, 436, 437, 491.
Campbell, Isaac, 227.
Campbell, Isabella, 107.
Campbell, Jacob, 129.
Campbell, James, 24, 27, 36, 42, 53, 57, 61, 66, 69, 116, 124, 125, 129, 144, 146, 182, 216, 237, 315, 342, 374, 376, 399, 406, 407, 423, 425, 436, 441, 442, 528.
Campbell, Jean, 514.
Campbell, John, 20, 28, 36, 39, 42, 46, 47, 53, 56, 57, 72, 74, 107, 134, 137, 144, 151, 154, 177, 182, 183, 190, 194, 205, 216, 219, 225, 232, 241, 244, 253, 254, 255, 264, 265, 272, 273, 277, 298, 331, 340, 350, 351, 367, 374, 376, 377, 379, 389, 399, 412, 422, 423, 425, 440, 441, 443, 444, 453, 455, 464, 474, 513, 519.
Campbell, Joseph, 46, 181, 371, 377.
Campbell, Lettice, 80.
Campbell, Malcolm, 45, 61, 104, 107, 112, 138, 332, 347, 351, 473.
Campbell, Mary, 42, 238, 239.
Campbell, Mary A., 27, 296.
Campbell, Maryan, 298.
Campbell, Margaret, 71, 134, 315, 515.
Campbell, Mathew, 317, 322.
Campbell, Moses, 41, 307.
Campbell, Patrick, 33, 50, 54, 298, 408, 421, 440, 442.
Campbell, Prudence, 27.

Campbell, Richard, 147, 151.
Campbell, Robert, 13, 44, 46, 50, 80, 97, 100, 119, 126, 154, 171, 172, 193, 196, 206, 238, 248, 255, 262, 331, 340, 376, 400 422, 433, 435, 437, 438, 443, 444, 445, 461, 498, 535.
Campbell, Sarah, 172, 368.
Campbell, Thomas, 303, 440.
Campbell, Wm., 83, 85, 137, 141, 144, 162, 166, 184, 298, 330, 401, 519.
Camell Morgan, 296.
Canady, William, 85.
Cancill, Conrad, 83, 324.
Cancill, Margaret, 83, 324.
Candler, John, 112.
Candler, William, 112, 325.
Cannon, Isaac, 187.
Cannon, John, 183.
Cannon, Patrick, 39.
Canote, John, 412.
Canterall, Joshua, 81.
Cants, John, 113.
Cape, William, 21.
Capertin, Hugh, 391.
Caphart, Daniel, 271.
Caphart, Peter, 209.
Capler, George, 519.
Caplinger, Dorothy, 168.
Caplinger, George, 171.
Caplinger, Jacob, 87.
Caplinger, Samuel, 168.
Carbarry, Terrence, 517.
Carden, Elizabeth 406.
Cargo, Alex. G., 534.
Cargo, Elizabeth, 534.
Carden, Joseph, 406.
Cargo, Samuel, 247.
Cargo, Samuel A., 534.
Carice, John, 407.
Carlile, Agnes, 378.
Carlile, Elizabeth, 57, 378, 380.
Carlile, Esther, 323.
Carlile, James, 57, 392.
Carlile, John, 42, 44, 101, 156, 166, 211, 256, 261, 380, 441, 442.
Carlile, Mary, 101.
Carlile, Nancy, 378.
Carlisle, Robert, 42, 44, 225, 256, 323, 350, 371, 378, 409, 441.
Carlisle, Samuel, 250, 259, 372, 388, 392.
Carlisle, Wm., 44, 71.
Carlock, Conrad, 61.
Carlock, David, 61, 92, 328.
Carlock, Frederick, 40, 61, 298.
Carlock, John C., 41.
Carlock, George, 61.
Carlton, Esther, 338, 344.
Carlton, William, 338, 344.
Carmickle, James, 96.
Carmichael, John, 27, 296, 311, 435.
Carmichael, Ruth, 27.
Carn, Michael, 121.

552

Carns, Archibald, 63.
Carpenter, Ann, 342, 495.
Carpenter, Catherine, 224.
Carpenter, George, 135, 138, 342, 359, 459, 460, 495, 496.
Carpenter, John, 102.
Carpenter, Joseph, 48, 63, 68, 116, 130, 162, 326, 338, 339, 456, 486, 499.
Carpenter, Michael, 201.
Carpenter, Nathaniel, 130.
Carpenter, Nicholas, 224.
Carpenter, Solomon, 130, 456, 486.
Carpenter, Thomas, 130, 326, 338, 354, 361, 457.
Carpenter, Zopher, 130, 461, 528.
Carr, Benjamin, 158, 526.
Carr, Dabney, 116.
Carr, Gilbert, 139.
Carr, Henry, 41, 55.
Carr, James, 51, 88, 446.
Carr, John,, 57, 191, 441, 525.
Carr, Thomas, 141.
Carr, William, 29, 96.
Carraby, Terrence, 51.
Carraven, William, 61, 440.
Carren, William, 156.
Carrick, Johnston, 331.
Carrick, Samuel, 245.
Carrigan, Patrick, 315.
Carroll, Elizabeth, 164.
Carroll Joseph, 305.
Carroll, Torrance, 44, 58.
Carroll, William, 17, 28, 30, 38, 221, 491.
Carrolile, John, 438, 487.
Carrolile, Robert, 438.
Carrolile, William, 438.
Carsall, Jacob, 114.
Carscaden, Robert, 42, 44, 437.
Carson, Abraham, 233, 250, 380, 407.
Carson, Henry, 43, 49.
Carson, Isaac, 232, 233, 250, 380, 382, 407.
Carson, John, 294.
Carson, Rebecca, 232, 384.
Carson, Susannah, 43, 49.
Carson, Thomas, 30, 31, 296.
Carter, Edward, 478.
Carter, James, 13, 21, 26, 32, 431.
Carthrae, John, 192.
Cartner, Peter, 47.
Cartmill, Henry, 141.
Cartmill, James, 350.
Cartmill, John, 34, 137, 218, 350.
Cartmill, Samuel, 136.
Cartmill, Thomas, 180, 222, 247, 483, 526.
Cartwright, Henry, 57.
Cartwright, Sarah, 115, 119.
Carty, James, 132, 466.
Caruthers, Robert, 324.
Caruthers, Elizabeth, 420.
Caruthers, Jane, 120.
Caruthers, John, 175, 180, 193, 203, 282.
Carruthers, Rebecca, 209.

Caruthers, Robert, 180, 182, 186.
Caruthers, Samuel, 180.
Carruthers, William, 181.
Carrothers, Esther, 390, 398.
Caruth, John, 442.
Carvin, William, 331.
Casaty, James, 136.
Casaty, John, 136, 140, 144.
Casaty, Neil, 136, 140, 151.
Casaty, Patrick, 136.
Cassaty, Peter, 151.
Cassaty, Thomas, 459, 475.
Case, William, 302.
Casebolt, Henry, 239, 483.
Caseday, Andrew, 490.
Cassall, Jacob, 434.
Cassidy, Neal, 55.
Castlean, Jacob, 433.
Castleberry, David, 319.
Castleberry, William, 319.
Casteel, Abednego, 519.
Casteel, William, 245.
Castey, John, 135.
Castle, Jacob, 23, 38, 40, 102.
Catchey (Carthrae), James, 105.
Catherwood, J., 470.
Cathey, George, 16, 20, 22.
Cathey, James, 56, 304, 470.
Cathey, Richard, 470.
Caton, John, 150.
Caton, Thomas, 324.
Cave, James, 40.
Cavens, Elizabeth, 423.
Cavin, John, 135.
Cavit, Moses, 150.
Cawdon, Samuel, 468.
Cawden, Walter, 468.
Cawley, John, 143, 167, 185, 343, 351, 394.
Cawley, Margaret, 185, 343, 351, 394.
Cawley, Michael, 509.
Cawley, John, 351.
Cawthorn, Robert, 345, 464.
Canthorn, William, 71, 311.
Celzar, Mathias, 468.
Chadwick, Uriah, 23.
Chambers, Ann, 291.
Chambers, James, 251.
Chambers, Jared, 434.
Chambers, John, 92, 96.
Chambers, William, 131, 252, 253, 260, 272, 275, 287, 288, 291, 343, 404, 405, 424, 529.
Chamnee, Christopher, 486.
Champe, John, 360.
Chandler, William, 121, 343, 356, 493.
Chapman, Henry, 100.
Chapman, John, 347, 385.
Chapman, William, 299.
Charlton, William, 158.
Chestnut, Daniel, 417.
Chestnut, James, 402, 409.
Chesnutt, John, 244, 395.

Chestnut, Patience, 395.
Chestnutt, Sophia, 255.
Chestnutt, William, 255.
Chew, Samuel, 32, 304.
Chew, Thomas, 13, 16, 17, 21, 28, 324.
Childers, Abram, 477, 478.
Childers, Edward, 478.
Childers, Joseph, 378.
Childs, Edward, 477, 478.
Childs, Nancy, 164.
Chiles, Micajah, 149.
Chinn, Thomas, 421.
Chisum, John, 373.
Chiswell (Chizwell), John, 107, 157, 158, 310.
Chittam, Elizabeth, 99.
Chittam, Philip, 32, 304.
Chittam, Mary, 65.
Chivers, Andrew, 447.
Chowning, George, 345, 464.
Ciler, Abraham, 41.
Chrisman, John, 140, 173.
Christman, Abraham, 154.
Christian, Anthony, 323.
Christian, Catherine, 39.
Christian, Gilbert, 84, 230, 276, 277, 381, 525.
Christian, Gill, 525.
Christian, Isaiah, 448.
Christian, Israel, 38, 65, 68, 71, 72, 78, 79, 82, 88, 89, 98, 99, 100, 104, 107, 110, 123, 127, 128, 136, 138, 141, 203, 230, 265, 309, 323, 325, 334, 337, 348, 350, 352, 353, 357, 365, 381, 440, 456, 459, 461, 464, 466, 467, 486, 487, 494, 498, 500, 501, 528.
Christian, John, 13, 19, 36, 78, 99, 102, 107, 117, 139, 152, 169, 177, 178, 183, 186, 188, 189, 196, 200, 201, 202, 203, 211, 216, 223, 229, 230, 243, 251, 259, 297, 304, 319, 325, 429, 438, 439, 442, 470, 481, 486, 487, 488, 489, 505, 525, 526.
Christian, Mathew, 413.
Christian, Pat., 142.
Christian, Priscilla, 341, 491, 492.
Christian, Robert, 36, 120, 139, 143, 155, 200, 201, 215, 216, 259, 272, 277, 297, 304, 319, 421, 439, 442, 407, 505, 526.
Christian, Sampson, 137, 150, 355.
Christian, William, 31, 34, 36, 45, 55, 68, 80, 84, 85, 120, 130, 132, 137, 142, 143, 147, 156, 157, 158, 163, 165, 188, 248, 317, 338, 341, 344, 345, 351, 355, 359, 364, 370, 381, 439, 467, 474, 475, 487, 526.
Christler, John, 199.
Christwell, Henry, 20, 26, 64, 120.
Church, William, 187, 190.
Churchill, Henry, 79.
Churn, Peter, 158.
Clack, Charles, 533.
Clack, Molly, 533.

Claiborne, Richard, 379, 380.
Claine, Michael, 23.
Clarke, Adam, 286.
Clark, Agnes, 106.
Clark, Daniel, 157.
Clarkson, David, 250.
Clark, George, 107, 148.
Clark, George R., 514.
Clark (Clerk), James, 20, 24, 57, 80, 132, 142, 150, 278, 355, 381, 421, 438, 443, 444, 445.
Clark, John, 63, 105, 143, 149, 152, 156, 173, 210, 344, 373, 381, 438, 444, 445.
Clark, Margaret, 127, 150, 158, 355, 364.
Clarke, Mary, 125.
Clark, Robt., 84, 143, 147, 153, 171, 192, 222.
Clark, Samuel, 142, 167.
Clark, Walter, 173.
Clark, Wm., 127, 365, 381, 444, 482.
Clase, Henry, 244.
Claxton, David, 368.
Claxton, Sarah, 368.
Claypole, James, Jr., 50, 437.
Claypoole, Jane, 92, 146, 168.
Claypool, Joseph, 391.
Claypoole, Wm., 50, 92, 146, 168, 437.
Clearey, Nathaniel, 41.
Cleaver, William, 204.
Cleghorn, Wm., 53.
Clements, Abram (Abraham), 33, 298.
Clements, Catherine, 273.
Clements, Jacob, 85.
Clements, James, 272, 528.
Clements, John, 261, 263.
Clemmons (Clemons), Caspar (Gaspar), 201, 202, 205.
Clemons, Christian, 136.
Clemons, Isabella, 101.
Clemons, Jacob, 101.
Clemons, James, 99, 407.
Clemons, John, 148, 197, 483.
Clemons, Ruth, 101.
Clendenning (Clendenin, Clendennon), Ann, 108.
Clendenning, Archibald, 100, 108.
Clendennin (Clendenning), Charles, 21, 117, 295.
Clendenning, Esther, 74.
Clendenning, George, 241, 382, 422.
Clendennin, John, 156, 342, 349, 486, 490.
Clenebill, George, 538.
Clennondon, Wm., 422.
Clerk, James, 14.
Clerk, Jones, 198.
Clifford (Clifton), Thomas, 260.
Clifton, Thomas, 393.
Cliffton, William, 478.
Cline, John, 276.
Clofford, Thomas, 154.
Clononger, Catherine, 385.
Cloninger (Clonegar, Clononeger), Valentine, 167, 171, 184, 209, 230, 241, 385.

Cloyd, David, 49, 86, 129, 131, 140, 330, 344, 348, 436, 445, 489.
Cloyd, James, 107, 132, 136, 138, 141, 148, 492.
Cloyd, John, 86 136, 139.
Cloyd, Joseph, 121.
Cloyd, Mary, 86.
Cloyd, Michael, 138, 344, 429.
Cloyd, Mirian, 159.
Cloud, Mordecai, 447.
Cloyd, Samuel, 60, 91, 348, 355 357, 459, 490.
Coager, Michael, 68, 127, 184.
Coager, Nicholas, 68.
Coalter, John, 141, 263, 264, 274, 402, 415, 529.
Coalter, Joseph, 538.
Coalter, Michael, 174, 526.
Coalter, Thomas, 402.
Coaperd (Coasserd), Thomas, 462.
Coats, Elizabeth, 181.
Coats, John, 141, 293.
Coats, Joshua, 181.
Cobb, Esther, 357.
Cobb, John, 86.
Cober, Jacob, 24.
Cober, Moses, 147.
Coburn, James, 29, 37.
Coburn, Jonathan, 37, 177.
Cockburn, Robert, 417.
Cockmill, John, 26.
Cocks, John, 102.
Cock, Gabriel, 180.
Cocks, James P., 246, 253, 259, 416, 481.
Cocke, Sally (Sarah), 376.
Cock, William, 496.
Cockendale, Mathew, 371.
Cockran, Andrew, 310.
Cockrain, Dennis, 173.
Cochran, Elenor, 197, 206.
Cockrain, Elizabeth, 158.
Cockrain, James, 158, 164, 275, 290, 417.
Cockrane, John, 76, 112, 123, 155, 158, 163, 223, 340, 264, 452, 466.
Cochraine, Margaret, 356, 458.
Cockrain, Mary, 158.
Cockran, Peter, 124, 306, 355, 356, 457, 458.
Cockrain, Robert, 158, 223, 261.
Cockran, Susanna, 123, 136, 364.
Cockran, William, 418.
Coe, Timothy, 61.
Cofer, Sylvester, 187.
Coffey, Benjamin, 179.
Coffey, Hugh, 26, 28.
Coffman, Martin, 28, 29.
Coffman, Henry, 161, 162.
Coger, Conrad, 149.
Coger, Michael, 182, 191.
Cohiren, Margaret, 315.
Cohoon, James, 310.
Cohoon, Thomas, 28.
Coile, Gabriel, 349.

Coile, James, 00.
Coile, Valentine, 115.
Coil, William, 215.
Coiner, Christian, 410.
Coiner, John, 284.
Coiner, Margaret, 280.
Coiner(s), Michael, 286, 288.
Colbee, William, 438.
Colberson, Robert, 315.
Cole, Alberdina, 250.
Cole, Catherine, 25, 30.
Cole, David, 245, 250.
Cole, Jacob, 218, 252.
Cole, James, 253.
Cole, John, 116.
Cole, Patsy, 223.
Cole, Richard, 223.
Cole, William, 478.
Coleman, Ann, 229.
Coleman, Catherine, 41, 42, 300.
Coleman, Esther, 229.
Coleman, Samuel, 166, 376.
Coleman, Thomas, 23.
Coleman, Wiat, 166.
Colhoon, Ezekiel, 23, 40.
Colhoon, George, 23.
Colhoon James, 23, 28, 43, 53, 56, 58, 60, 64, 310.
Colhoon, Patrick, 23.
Colhoon, William, 23.
Collet, Joseph, 64.
Colley (Colly), John, 41, 90, 336.
Collier (Collyer), Alex., 99.
Collier, Jacob, 520.
Collier, Moses, 138, 153, 327.
Collier, John, 57, 99, 317, 441.
Collins, Ann, 237.
Collins, Eleanor, 409.
Collins, John, 175, 185, 356, 401, 407, 409 423, 520.
Collins, Luke, 41, 60, 69, 438.
Collins, Richard, 237.
Collony, John, 306.
Colmer, David (Davis), 96, 100, 328.
Colony, Thomas, 209.
Colquhoon, James, 119.
Colson, Elizabeth, 478.
Colson, William, 478.
Colter, Joseph, 526.
Colting, Elias, 294.
Colton, Joseph, 525.
Colven, Joseph, 358.
Colville, George, 17.
Combe, Andrew, 44.
Comble, John, 434.
Combs, Mason, 44, 438.
Conavin, William, 445.
Conkin, George, 244.
Conkin, Joseph, 244.
Conley, James, 434.
Conley, John, 40.
Conley, Newton, 405.

Connell, William, 246.
Connelly (Connolly), Arthur, 171, 208, 380, 401, 402, 412, 424, 425.
Connelly, David, 424, 425.
Connelly, James S., 424.
Connelly, Jane, 401, 402.
Connely, Jean, 380.
Connelly, John, 177, 306, 425.
Connelly, Thomas, 140, 145.
Connolly, Darby, 204.
Conoly, James, 431.
Conner, Ann, 120.
Conner, Charles, 59.
Conner, Hugh, 94, 121.
Connor, John, 177, 510.
Conner, Stephen, 479.
Connerly, Arthur, 225, 227.
Connerly, Darby, 196.
Connerly, Dennis, 184.
Connerly, James, 25, 47, 48, 439.
Conerly, Robert, 85.
Connerly, Thomas, 150, 194.
Conrad, Hance, 82.
Conrad, Hannah, 130.
Conrad, Jacob, 130, 179.
Conrad, John, 140, 290.
Conrad, Owley, 250.
Conrad, Stephen, 140, 143, 189.
Conrad, Wolrick (Woolrick), 82, 97, 213.
Conrad, Woolbeck, 377.
Constable, Sarah, 214.
Consort, Richard, 525.
Contz (Countz, Counts), Elizabeth, 83.
Conway, Ann, 480.
Conway, Catlett, 421.
Cook, Ellinor, 242.
Cook, Honor, 242.
Cook, James, 470.
Cook, Jane, 56.
Cooke, Mary, 106, 318.
Cooke, Patrick, 21, 56, 106, 340.
Cook, Thomas, 251.
Cook, Walter, 232, 233, 242.
Cook, William, 233, 446.
Cooper, Jacob, 41, 108.
Cooper, James, 145, 273, 280, 390.
Cooper, John, 280.
Cooper, Robert, 520.
Cooper, Thomas, 97, 170, 273.
Copland, Benjamin, 316.
Copelin, Jacob, 428.
Coppidgs, Charles, 486.
Corbee, William, 288.
Corbett, Ann 209.
Corbit, Mary, 28.
Corbin, Joseph, 358.
Corcal, Terence, 438.
Cordell, George, 258.
Corlock, Heorndkis, 55.
Corn, Michael, 118.
Cornet, Mortain (Martin), 76, 79.
Corrigan, Pat., 130.

Corry, Samuel, 318.
Corwen, Samuel, 520.
Cosho, Benoni, 263.
Coslie, Pierce, 486.
Costell, Jacob, 434.
Costley, Pierce, 60.
Cotner, Thomas, 22, 29.
Cotril, John, 341, 490.
Cotter, John, 479.
Cotton, James, 134, 152, 487, 488, 530.
Cotuners, Person, 458.
Coudon, James, 132.
Coulter, James, 300.
Coulter, John, 237, 286, 370.
Coulter, Michael, 144, 156, 176, 219.
Coulton, Andrew, 264, 267.
Coulton, James, 32.
Coulton, Joseph, 15, 54.
Counts, Elizabeth, 195, 320, 321.
Counts, John, 88, 195, 199, 320, 321.
County (Counce), Martin, 61.
Counts, Teterick, 88.
Countzman, Elizabeth, 118.
County Court Chancery Decrees, 427.
County Court Judgments, 292, 306, 429.
County Court Order Books, 13.
County Court Records, 515.
Coursey, Brush, 99.
Coursey, James, 99, 218, 430.
Courtney, Perdue, 353, 462.
Coursey, William, 379.
Coutts, John, 179.
Coutts, Patrick, 198.
Courts, John F., 67, 71, 74.
Coving, Joseph, 514.
Cowan (Cowen), Andrew, 53, 57, 120, 126, 362, 443.
Cowan, David, 362.
Cowen, Edward, 128.
Cowan, James, 139, 151, 362, 436, 469.
Cowan, John, 520.
Cowen, William, 128.
Cowarden, John, 135, 196, 338, 373, 430.
Cowardin, Mary, 164.
Cowardin, Robert, 164.
Cowden, Elizabeth, 326.
Cowden, Henry, 478.
Cowden, James, 326, 353, 358, 455.
Cowdon, Jennet, 43.
Cowden, John, 207.
Cowden, Martha, 206, 207, 395.
Cowdon, Samuel, 126, 322, 329, 335, 349, 355, 358, 363, 453, 455, 456, 459, 476, 477.
Cowden, Walter, 195, 456, 459.
Cowdon, William, 142, 147, 525.
Cowder, James, 85.
Cowder, Walter, 335.
Cowger, John, 250.
Cowley, Jean, 406.
Cowley, John, 206.
Cowley, Michael, 406.

Daggett, Rhoda, 330.
Daggett, Richard, 330.
Daggy, Jacob, 250.
Dair (Dare), George, 81, 461.
Dale, Alex., 132, 140, 155, 170.
Dale, John, 133.
Daley (Dailey), Charles, 35, 437.
Daily, John, 98, 112, 137, 165, 262, 330, 339, 340, 355, 361, 440, 469.
Dalhouse, Charles, 300.
Dalhouse, John, 223, 229, 243.
Dallis, Charles, 36.
Dalton, William, 148.
Dandridge, Col., 418.
Daniel, John, 42.
Danison, Daniel, 442.
Dansie, Thomas, 47.
Dardis, James, 413.
Darlington, William, 323.
Darnell, Jacob, 35.
Darnall, John, 471.
Darr, George, 158.
Darrel, Sampson, 291.
Dart, Ananias, 71.
Daucherty, William, 457.
Daven, William, 459.
Davenport, James, 354.
David, James, 103, 132.
Davidson, Andrew, 201, 202, 204, 207, 211, 223.
Davidson, Daniel, 90, 130.
Davidson, John, 199, 201, 202, 203, 207, 211, 223, 480.
Davidson, Josiah, 90, 169, 173, 177, 183, 192, 196.
Davidson, Margaret, 480.
Davidson, Ruth, 480.
Davidson, Samuel, 109, 480.
Davis, Benjamin, 85.
Davis, Daniel, 356.
Davis, David, 14, 15, 27, 48, 293.
Davis, Edward, 43, 49.
Davis, Eleanor, 27, 35.
Davis, Elithorn, 85.
Davis, Elizabeth, 27.
Davis, Francis, 190.
Davis, Hannah, 323.
Davis, Henry, 377.
Davies (Davis), James, 14, 30, 49, 61, 62, 132, 141, 223, 240, 245, 255, 293, 294, 481, 488, 498, 525.
Davis, Jane, 122, 132.
Davis (Davies), John, 20, 23, 25, 28, 37, 41, 44, 47, 51, 67, 75, 89, 111, 116, 135, 139, 141, 150, 152, 153, 180, 183, 326, 370, 386, 433, 436, 437, 439, 482, 488, 489, 491, 526.
Davis, Judith, 116.
Davis, Philip, 314.
Davis, Robert, 20, 21, 26, 51, 56, 57, 59, 176, 191, 194, 196, 221, 297, 378, 443, 444, 498.

Davis (Davies), Samuel, 17, 27, 32, 132, 140, 293, 294, 319, 323, 332, 333, 446.
Davis, Thomas, 52, 81, 122, 212, 394, 397, 477.
Davis, Walter, 45, 82, 143, 172, 203, 263, 405.
Davis, Wm., 35, 141, 170, 252, 305, 352, 364, 462, 488, 494, 498, 526.
Davison, Daniel, 435.
Davison, James, 62.
Davison, John, 47, 140, 327, 446.
Davison, Josiah, 373.
Davison, Phebe, 312, 435.
Davison, Samuel, 43.
Davitt, Tully, 146, 185, 215, 227, 393.
Dawkins, James, 432.
Dawson, Andrew, 184.
Day, Edward, 260.
Day, Johannes, 454.
Day, Joseph, 221.
Day, Thomas, 171.
Dayer, William, 433.
Deack, Nicholas, 316.
Deal, Alex., 144.
Dean, Adam, 105, 138, 149, 174, 330, 452.
Dean, Agnes, 165, 241.
Dean, John, 81, 140, 158, 179, 241.
Deane, Mary, 340.
Dean, Thomas, 236.
Dean, Wm., 105, 106, 118, 123, 139, 181, 332, 340, 453, 487.
Deary, Jacob, 274, 277.
Deavitt, Tully, 155.
Decker, Garret, 433.
Decker, Hermanus, 53.
Decker, Samuel, 433.
Deer, Francis, 180.
Dehart, Simon, 455.
Deigs, Thomas, 341, 490.
Delap, Samuel, 28.
Delay, Henry, 527, 537.
Delwood, William, 116.
Denham, Joseph, 307.
Dening, Walter, 304.
Deniston, Daniel, 22, 28, 30, 75.
Deniston, James, 99, 102, 159, 215.
Dennison, Daniel, 13, 30, 34, 427.
Dennison, John, 77, 226, 446.
Denniston, Robert, 207.
Denny, Patrick, 161, 348.
Dennis, William, 464.
Denston, John, 447.
Denton, Jane, 49.
Denton, John, 19, 45, 57, 59, 69.
Denton, Jonas, 19, 49.
Denton, Robert, 40.
Depriest, Langsdon, 482.
Dever, Elizabeth, 359.
Dever, Hugh, 173, 174, 359.
Dever, James, 359.
Dever, John, 193.
Devine, John, 274.

Devine, Nathaniel, 274.
Devine, Sarah, 272, 274.
Devine, Selina, 272.
Devitt, Charles, 307.
Devericks, David, 397.
Devericks, Mary, 397.
Dew, Samuel, 355.
Dewey, Stephen, 20.
Dice, George, 164.
Dice, Mary, 164.
Dice, Mathew, 193.
Dice, Mathias, 380.
Dick, Abraham, 171.
Dick, Charles, 368.
Dick, Margaret, 447.
Dick, Mary, 275.
Dickens, Henry, 26, 47.
Dickey, Adam, 520.
Dickey, John, 211, 216, 429.
Dickey, Martha, 385.
Dickey, Michael, 44, 139, 143, 144, 395, 429, 437.
Dickinson (Dickenson, Dickerson), Adam, 13, 22, 25, 26, 46, 48, 98, 293, 295, 296, 369, 443.
Dickenson, Benjamin, 480.
Dickenson, John, 58, 65, 72, 78, 94, 97, 98, 107, 134, 139, 152, 169, 171, 173, 177, 180, 183, 189, 193, 196, 197, 202, 210, 213, 223, 230, 248, 249, 252, 256, 264, 268, 272, 276, 279, 283, 286, 288, 291, 334, 342, 346, 356, 369, 374, 454, 481, 486, 487, 490, 493, 499, 511, 512.
Dickenson, Joseph, 356.
Dickinson, Larkin J., 407, 410.
Dickinson, Martha, 134.
Dickenson, William, 44, 438.
Dickson (Dixon), Adam, 431.
Dickson, Archibald, 170, 180, 227.
Dickson, John, 120, 152, 233, 377, 387, 390, 400, 406, 422, 464, 465, 486, 524, 530.
Dickson, Mary, 411.
Dickson, Rebecca, 387, 390.
Dixon, (Dickson), Robert, 323.
Dixon (Dickson), Roger, 329.
Dixon, Thomas, 392.
Dicktour, Joseph, 141.
Diddle, John, 273.
Dill, John, 24.
Dill, Peter, 24.
Dillen, Catherine, 170.
Dillen, James, 348.
Dillen, William, 170.
Dills, John, 301.
Dinges, Peter, 461.
Dinguid, William, 112.
Dinniston, James, 490.
Dinwiddie, Governor, 234.
Dinwiddie, John, 356.
Dinwoody, John, 242.
Dinwoodie, William, 245.

District Court, 524.
District Court Records, 519.
Diver, Charles, 44, 71, 437.
Diver, Hugh, 44, 176, 437.
Divier, James, 261.
Doabs, Joseph, 432.
Doage, David, 120.
Doage, Robert, 157, 158.
Doak, David, 144.
Doak, James, 274, 405.
Doak, John, 245, 289, 294.
Doak, Robert, 248, 272, 498.
Doak, Samuel, 30, 66, 294.
Doack, William, 498.
Dobbin, James, 180, 440.
Dobikin, John, 17, 28, 298, 430, 431.
Dobin, Robert, 528.
Dobson, James, 245.
Doby, Robert, 132.
Dockell, Hanness, 432.
Dodd, Alex., 281.
Dodd, Philip, 414.
Dodd, Richard, 341, 490.
Dodson, Jacob, 126.
Dodson, Thomas, 41.
Doggett, Rhoda, 102, 112, 135, 325, 330, 342.
Doggett, Richard, 102, 112, 135, 325, 342.
Doghead, Richard, 126.
Dohoney, Charles, 525.
Dold, Catherine, 407.
Dold, Philip, 414.
Dalhouse, Charles, 435.
Dolphin, John, 42.
Dolson, Garrett, 250.
Dolter, Jesse, 520.
Domnark, John, 109.
Donahu (Donahow), Cornelius, 57, 443.
Donaho (Donaghe), Hugh, 117, 118, 140, 145, 160, 181, 240, 356, 390, 394, 396, 397, 403, 411, 412, 422, 430.
Donaghe, James, 397.
Donahu, John, 24, 396, 397, 519.
Donald, Robert, 79, 323, 358.
Donald, William, 149.
Donaldson, Andrew, 520.
Donaldson, Joseph, 100, 123, 127, 129, 350.
Donalrson, Robert, 238.
Donaldson, William, 410.
Donally, Hugh, 300.
Donerly, John, 26, 28, 105, 308, 311, 314, 489.
Donley, William, 65.
Donnally (Donaly, Donnelly, Donily, Donnerly), Andrew, 243, 391, 393, 404, 463, 513.
Donnally, Charles, 134, 147, 156, 201, 217, 241, 243, 247, 315, 370, 526.
Donnally, Mary, 538.
Donnell, John, 399, 403.
Donnell, Sarah, 399, 403.

Donnelly, Euphemia, 378.
Donnerly, Dennis, 182.
Donoly, James, 432.
Donovan, Mary, 399.
Donavin (Donavin), Daniel, 256, 400, 509.
Dooley, Henry, 138, 146, 342, 489.
Dooley, James, 489.
Dooly, Thomas, 199.
Doran, Jacob, 169, 213, 382, 531.
Doran, Torence, 519.
Dorrick, John, 50.
Dorsey, Joseph, 513.
Doughaty, Ann, 293.
Doughaty, Jacob, 293.
Doughert, Mary, 15.
Dougherty, Charles, 108, 148.
Dougherty, Elizabeth, 323.
Dougherty, Henry, 464.
Dougherty, Hugh, 520.
Dougherty, Michael, 30, 310, 434.
Dougherty, Rebecca, 108, 148.
Dougherty (Dowerty), Wm., 26, 53, 141, 323, 353, 456.
Douglass, Alex., 300, 408, 409.
Douglass, Hugh, 13, 300.
Douglas, John, 148, 190.
Douglas, Jonathan, 50, 57, 98, 143, 357, 372, 490.
Douglas, Robert, 405.
Douglas, Thomas, 177.
Douglas, Wm., 446, 528.
Douthat, Ann, 532.
Douthat, Jane, 520, 523.
Douthat, Lucy, 523.
Douthat, Polly, 532.
Douthat, Robert, 248, 252, 253, 259, 278, 286, 292, 481, 520, 523, 532.
Douthat, Thomas, 520.
Douthat, William, 282, 532.
Douther, George, 433, 528.
Dove, George, 41.
Dove, Jane, 165.
Dove, Thomas, 41, 311.
Dover, William, 170.
Dowdall, Patrick, 469.
Dowley, Henry, 332.
Dowling, Robert, 174.
Dowman, Sarah, 188.
Downen, William, 436.
Downey, James, 479.
Downey, John, 300.
Downey, Martha, 175.
Downey, Molly, 417.
Downey, Patrick, 441.
Downey, Samuel, 136, 141, 173, 438, 442, 443.
Downing, John, 40, 305, 434.
Downing, Patrick, 72.
Downing, Polly, 416.
Downing, Samuel, 57.
Downing, Thomas, 416.

Downing, William, 379, 380.
Downs, Henry, 13, 14, 18, 19, 20, 21, 26, 34, 37, 49.
Doyle, Michael, 169.
Doyer, Roger, 433.
Drady, Daniel, 64, 79, 84, 87.
Drady, Elizabeth, 84.
Drady, Ezekiel, 101.
Drady, Thomas, 84.
Drady, William, 87.
Drake, Abraham, 25, 28, 299, 431.
Drake, John, 355, 457.
Draper, Abraham, 290.
Draper, Eleanor, 38, 306.
Drapier, Elizabeth, 90.
Draper, George, 23, 28, 38.
Draper, James, 290.
Draper, John, 38, 132, 351, 454, 474.
Draper, William, 52, 437.
Drapier, John, 90.
Drening, Walter, 309, 310, 326.
Drilian (Dulian), Abraham, 456.
Drinnen, Thomas, 166.
Drinnen (Drenning), Walter, 337, 390, 392.
Dryden, David, 42.
Dryden, Eleanor, 42.
Dryden, Thomas, 145, 215, 376.
Drumer, Mary, 99.
Drummer, Thomas, 477.
Dubs, Jost, 300.
Duck, George, 527.
Dudley, Wm. G., 425.
Duel, Charles, 26.
Duerson, John, 425.
Duff, Arthur, 38.
Duff, John, 520.
Duff, William, 298, 482.
Duffy, James, 185.
Duffev, Patrick, 101, 119.
Duffield, Ann, 263.
Duffield, Isaac, 391.
Duffield, Isabella, 263.
Duffell (Duffield), Robert, 97, 129, 263, 391.
Duglass, Alex., 21.
Duglass, George, 55.
Duglas, Hugh, 432, 491.
Dugles, Jonathan, 437, 491.
Dull, Frederick, 400.
Dunbar, Andrew, 334.
Dunbar, David, 305.
Dunbarr, Frances, 214.
Dunbarr, John, 40, 54, 323, 491.
Dunbarr, Jonathan, 230.
Dunbarr, Thomas, 182.
Duncan, Andrew, 253, 260, 346, 408, 409, 437, 463, 464.
Duncan, James, 97, 131.
Duncan, Jane, 253.
Duncan, Janet, 97, 215, 409.
Duncan, John, 97, 131, 266.

Evans, David, 43, 298, 299, 435.
Evans, Ezekiel, 129, 352.
Evans, Griffith, 232, 379.
Evans, James, 309.
Evans, Jane, 91, 307.
Evan, John, 432, 451.
Evans, Mark, 15, 24.
Evans, Mary, 124, 394.
Evans, Moses, 126.
Evans, Nathaniel, 124, 136, 140, 444.
Evans, Patrick, 142.
Evans, Peter, 118, 445.
Evans, Rhoda, 102, 112, 135, 325, 330, 342.
Evans, Robert, 343.
Evans, Samuel, 512.
Evins, Stamp, 341, 490.
Evans, Susanna, 154.
Evans, Uriah, 24.
Evans, Wm., 189, 303, 437, 525.
Eavenman, Jacob, 511.
Evert, Christiania, 156.
Everts, George, 520.
Evert, Windlu(e), 156.
Every, Henry, 483.
Evick, Christian, 102.
Evick, Francis, 474, 475.
Ewin, Andrew, 428, 442.
Ewen, James, 538.
Ewin, Wm., 428, 503, 504.
Ewing, James, 98, 104, 120, 146, 206, 338, 355, 367, 373, 374, 381, 411.
Ewing, John, 246, 249, 280.
Ewing, Mary, 65.
Ewing, Robert, 65.
Ewing, Robert Fulton, 272.
Ewing, Samuel, 370.
Ewing, William, 491, 507.
Eyers, William, 258.
Eyness, Henry, 155.

Fackler, Jacob, 426.
Fackler, John, 288, 290.
Fagan, Philip, 95.
Failey, John, 145.
Fairbern, Robert, 250.
Faires, Edward, 128.
Fairfax, Lord, 461.
Fairies, John, 239.
Falkner, Jacob, 510.
Fallingash, Charles, 184.
Fane, Daniel, 405, 406, 416.
Fane, Margaret, 406.
Fancy, Henry, 41.
Faris, John, 251, 343.
Farish, Samuel, 432.
Farlie, James, 104.
Farr, Peter, 527.
Farrell, John, 83.
Farrell, Margaret, 99.
Farrell, William, 83.
Farrier, Robert, 386.
Farris, James, 132.

Farris, Margaret, 132.
Farris, Wm., 108, 132, 250.
Farror, Abel, 473.
Farrow, Abraham, 325.
Fauber, Barbara, 537.
Fauber, Christian, 420.
Fauber, David, 537.
Fauber, John, 419.
Fauntleroy, Moore, 215, 227.
Fearis, Robert, 209.
Fearnley, May, 318.
Fearnley, Wm., 318, 525.
Feemster, Elizabeth, 122.
Feemster, Thomas, 105, 120, 122.
Fell, Catherine, 409.
Fell, John, 409.
Fellows, Ellenor, 390.
Fellows, Thomas, 390.
Felps, Samuel, 194.
Felton, George, 475.
Felts, John, 127.
Fennel, John, 414.
Feny, Catherine, 532.
Feoris, Robert, 180.
Ferguson (Farguson, Forguson), **Henry,** 102, 326.
Ferguson, John, 21.
Ferguson, Samuel, 36, 44, 97, 141, 320, 325, 434, 438.
Farrell, Barbara, 83.
Ferren, Patrick, 234.
Ferrill, Robert, 245.
Fewell, Anthony, 130, 137.
Fields, Henry, 128.
Fieler, John, 130.
Fifer, George, 415.
Figare, Edward, 60.
Figare, John, 60.
Figg, Elizabeth, 514.
Figg, Mary, 514.
Fig, William, 514.
Files, John, 93.
Fillbrick, Henry, 107, 333, 339, 475, 476.
Fillson, Robert, 329, 447, 487.
Fimster (Fimester), Thomas, 317.
Fincher, Samuel, 443.
Findley, David, 232.
Findley, James, 110, 122, 126, 131, 426.
Findley, John, 99, 131, 142, 177, 200, 215.
Findley, Robert, 110, 126, 159, 474.
Findley, Wm., 131, 138, 178, 216, 248, 357.
Fink, Sarah, 423.
Findley (Finla), David, 232, 260, 268.
Finley, Elizabeth, 366.
Finla, James, 21.
Finla (Finley), John, 13, 18, 120, 123, 148, 154, 183, 268, 297, 319, 402, 442.
Finley (Finla), Patrick, 33, 34, 259.
Finley, Robert, 29, 83, 333, 348, 497, 498.
Finley, Samuel, 285, 301.
Finley, Wm., 16, 55, 213.
Finny, Christopher, 435, 490.

Finey (Finney), Michael, 19, 25, 28, 60, 61, 441, 442.
Finn, Catherine, 73.
Fisher, Adam, 536.
Fisher, Agnes, 384.
Fisher, Andrew, 536.
Fisher, Ann, 536.
Fisher, Archibald, 140, 345, 351, 353.
Fisher, Daniel, 422, 536.
Fisher, George, 384.
Fisher, Henry, 536.
Fisher, Jacob, 536.
Fisher, James, 309.
Fisher, John, 536.
Fisher, Margaret, 536.
Fisher, Polly, 536.
Fisher, Samuel, 536.
Fisher, Sarah, 536.
Fisher, Susanna, 345, 351, 353.
Fisher, Wm., 536.
Fitzgerald, Wm., 325, 330.
Fitzhugh, Daniel, 324.
Fitzhugh, Thomas, 314.
Fitzjarrel, Cornelius, 170.
Fitzjarrell, Frederick, 49.
Fitzjarrell, Wm., 113, 114.
Fitzpatrick, Alex., 171.
Fitzpatrick, Andrew, 137, 167.
Fitzpatrick, Anthony, 365.
Fitzpatrick, Cornelius, 176.
Fitzpatrick, Patrick, 87, 88.
Fitzpatrick, Susanna, 114.
Fitzpatrick, Thomas, 37, 72, 102, 315, 323, 486, 499.
Fitzwater, Cornelius, 173.
Fitzwater, John, 54, 82, 112, 194, 196.
Flack, James, 290, 421.
Flack, John G., 426.
Flack, Peter, 243.
Flack, Polly, 426.
Flanagan, John, 35.
Flannagan, Elizabeth, 399.
Fleak, Peter, 384.
Fleck, Benjamin, 235.
Fleiger (Flieger), John, 394, 411, 412.
Fleisher, Henry, 201, 202, 221.
Flesher, John, 213, 215, 376.
Flesher, Peter, 161, 208.
Fleming, Elizabeth, 170, 225.
Fleming (Flimon), John, 53, 56, 74, 317, 320, 322, 333, 343, 358, 436, 486, 493.
Fleming, Margaret, 225, 232, 379.
Fleming, Peter, 424.
Fleming, Samuel, 342, 496.
Fleming, Wm., 107, 117, 121, 131, 134, 170, 208, 210, 214, 215, 219, 222, 225, 232, 309, 317, 342, 350, 354, 355, 357, 397, 446, 451, 454, 456, 458, 463, 464, 474, 477, 496.
Fletcher, Christ, 103.
Fletcher, Eleanor, 320, 432.
Fletcher, Joab, 176.

Fletcher, John, 82, 320, 432.
Fletcher, Robert, 97, 103, 148.
Flieger, George, 400.
Fling, Nancy, 199.
Flinn, John, 121.
Flinn, Tiadey, 131.
Flint, Joseph, 471.
Flood, John, 87, 308, 469.
Flower, Samuel, 121.
Flower, Elizabeth, 230.
Floyd, Charles, 118, 214, 237, 427.
Floyd, Jane, 427.
Floyd, Samuel, 163.
Floyd, William, 163.
Flude, Robert, 477.
Fogle, Catherine, 212.
Fogle, John, 212, 264.
Folley, Mary, 97.
Fomelson, Charles, 213.
Fonelson, Joseph, 213.
Foolton, John, 440.
Foolwiller, Leonard, 235.
Footd, James, 441.
Forbes, Alex., 460.
Forbes, David, 145.
Forbes, George, 130.
Forbes, Wm., 255, 257, 290.
Forbise, Robert, 325.
Forbush, George, 33, 35, 294.
Forbush, Olive, 33.
Ford, William, 464.
Forehand, Darby, 206.
Forehand, Elenore, 206.
Forgay, Joseph, 480.
Forgay, Rebecca, 480.
Forish, John, 129.
Forkner, Wm., 149, 343, 533.
Forman, John, 40.
Fornalson, Charles, 516.
Fornice, John, 50.
Forris, Elizabeth, 195.
Forst, Sophia, 384.
Forst, Thomas, 384.
Forster, James, 245.
Forster, Thomas, 240.
Forsythe, Benjamin, 189.
Forsnaught, George, 412.
Foster, Andrew, 68, 221, 229, 444.
Foster, Elizabeth, 366, 444.
Foster, Henry, 366.
Foster, James, 255.
Foster, John, 282.
Foster, Joster, 255.
Foster, Thomas, 444.
Foster, Wm., 112, 114, 138, 209, 256, 261, 347.
Fotch (Fotsch), John, 342, 495, 496.
Fought, Andrew, 29, 30, 103, 136, 148, 300.
Fought, Elizabeth, 103.
Fought, Gaspar, 245.
Fought, John, 50.
Fought, John J., 84, 437.

Foulwidder, John, 520.
Founton, David, 318.
Foutch, John, 304.
Fowler, Andrew, 117, 213, 535.
Fowler, Christopher, 419.
Fowler, Elisha, 305.
Fowler, James, 25, 89, 142, 301.
Fowler, John, 89, 130, 196, 341, 344, 356, 419.
Fowler, Margaret, 341, 356.
Fowler, Robert, 37, 44, 142, 145, 154, 437.
Fowler, Wm., 160, 339, 369.
Fox, Grace, 514.
Fox, James, 274.
Fox, John, 514.
Foy, John, 489.
Foyle, Elizabeth, 303.
Foile (Foyle), Robert, 22, 32, 34, 50, 62, 303.
Frain, James, 36.
Frame, James, 43, 48, 78, 139, 326, 337.
Frame, John, 337.
Frame, Margaret, 337, 502.
Frame, Mary, 155.
Fr..me, Samuel, 409.
Frame, Thomas, 78, 173, 199, 200, 208, 243, 250.
Frame, Wm., 44, 373, 437.
Frames, David, 96, 155, 201, 247, 335, 337, 474, 531.
Francis, Ann, 78.
Francis, George, 142.
Francis, John, 24, 44, 78, 120, 245, 250, 367, 437.
Francis, Mary, 367.
Francis, Thomas, 355.
Francis, Wm., 78, 230, 245, 253, 256.
Francisco, Christopher, 439.
Francisco, Geo., 98, 99, 104, 350, 360, 459.
Francisco, John, 104, 140, 143, 360.
Francisco, Ludwick, 24, 60, 69, 135, 360, 440.
Francisco, Stiffell, 26, 49.
Francisco, Stophel, 439.
Franker, John, 416.
Franker, Peter, 416.
Franklyn, Borlingham (Beringham), 326, 338.
Franklin, Eastham, 298, 301.
Franklin, Edward, 14, 301.
Franklin, Reuben, 29, 301.
Franster, Andrew, 38.
Fraser, Margaret, 298.
Frazier (Frazer, Frazure), Ann, 398.
Frazier, David, 370.
Frazier, Isabella, 398, 534.
Frazier, James, 61, 62, 115, 193, 202, 248, 251, 272, 274, 278, 373, 390, 398, 435, 480, 481, 534.,
Frazier, John, 36, 118, 138, 151, 170, 214, 234, 335, 370, 390, 398, 532.
Frazier, John, W., 534.

Frazzier, Patrick, 46, 109, 138, 436, 446, 469.
Frazer, Polly, 534.
Frazier, Robert, 26, 30, 80, 136.
Frazier, Samuel, 148, 218, 398, 534.
Frazer, Samuel C., 534.
Frazier, Thomas, 214.
Frazier, Wm., 114, 115, 360, 435.
Freedley, Ann Mary, 37, 47.
Freedley, John Lewis, 37.
Freedly, Ludwick, 32.
Freedley, Magdalene, 32.
Freehold, Wm., 251.
Freeland, Margaret, 121.
Fregg, John, 206.
Friedley, Barbara, 179.
Friedley, Israel, 179.
Frem, James, 439.
French, Ann, 532.
French, Hugh, 532.
French, Mathew, 352.
Frennen Thomas 484
Fresher, Archibald, 458.
Fretwell, Alex., 482.
Friar (Freer), Robert, 441.
Fridley, Jacob, 192.
Fridley, Ludwick, 192.
Friel, Catherine, 208.
Friel, Daniel, 208, 399.
Friend, Jonas, 140, 194, 198, 201, 202, 204, 211, 2223.
Frits, Frederick, 83, 103.
Frits, Janet, 83.
Frizby, Ellenor, 387.
Frizby, Wm., 387.
Fragg, Agatha, 183, 262.
Fragg, Arthur, 162.
Frogg, John, 151, 162, 168, 169, 177, 183, 213, 233, 372, 383.
Frothingham, John P., 50.
Frow, James, 169.
Fudge, Christian, 196.
Fudge, Conrad, 114.
Fudge, John, 144, 196, 387, 405.
Fugett, Josias, 475.
Full, Andrew, 102.
Fuller, Henry, 61, 62, 70.
Fullerton, Alexander, 45, 46, 49.
Fulsh, Conrad, 114.
Fulscher, Widow, 26.
Fulton, Andrew, 248, 272, 278, 481.
Fulton, David, 398, 411.
Fulton, Elizabeth, 105, 115.
Fulton, Hugh, 120, 251, 440, 445.
Fulton, James, 222, 307.
Fulton, John, 115, 142, 213, 315, 317, 435, 440, 513.
Fulton, Mary, 222.
Fulton, Robert, 256, 280, 333, 513.
Fulton, Thomas, 96, 105, 112, 113, 115, 118, 119, 125, 140, 148, 174, 181, 301, 335, 349, 435, 473.

Gay, Samuel, 13, 19, 31, 33, 34, 35, 36, 37, 93, 292, 380, 441, 442.
Gay, Sarah, 265, 315.
Gay, Thomas, 443, 532.
Gay, Wm., 78, 100, 145, 242, 336, 435.
Gee (McGee), Wm., 183.
Geiger, Jacob, 272, 274, 418.
Geiger, Thomas, 74.
Gender, George, 498.
Gender, Jasper, 498.
Genewine, Peter, 270.
Gentry, John, 492.
Geoffey, Abel, 265.
George, Thomas, 146.
Gernor, Francis, 95.
Gerrall (Jewell), Joseph, 418.
Getty, Dennis, 114, 123, 138.
Getz, Sebastian, 400.
Ghent, Joseph, 503.
Ghest, George, 147.
Gholston, Anthony, 214.
Gibbin, George K., 301.
Gibboney, Alex, 296.
Gibbons, James, 293.
Gibbons, Jane, 293.
Gibbons, Margaret, 401.
Gibbon (Gibbons), Nicholas, 300, 313.
Gibbons, Samuel, 189.
Gibson, Alex, 21, 30, 52, 62, 136, 156, 172, 185, 229, 244, 246, 247, 280, 286, 300, 386, 406, 413, 442, 481, 534.
Gibson, Ann, 423.
Gibson, Daniel, 52, 534.
Gibson, David, 21, 205, 229.
Gibson, Elizabeth, 52.
Gibson, George, 57, 115, 153, 178, 335, 348, 441.
Gibson, Howard, 438.
Gibson, Isabella, 115.
Gibson, James, 202, 504.
Gibson, John, 177, 183, 256.
Gibson, Larkin J., 406.
Gibson, Mary, 62, 231, 280.
Gibson, Rachel, 169.
Gibson, Robert, 22, 32, 231.
Gibson, Samuel, 57, 140, 441, 442.
Gibson, Smith, 256.
Gibson, Wm., 229, 424.
Gifford, Thomas, 214.
Gilbert, Felix, 88, 93, 107, 114, 135, 139, 141, 155, 161, 164, 169, 170, 182, 183, 188, 190, 196, 301, 330, 331, 335, 453, 454, 474, 496, 499.
Gilbert, Joseph, 418.
Gilham, Elizabeth, 226.
Gilham, John, 236.
Gilham, Thomas, 54, 85, 441.
Gilham, William, 209, 226.
Gilipe, Robert, 461.
Gilkeson, Archibald, 143, 518.
Gilkason, Robert, 21, 152.
Gilkison, William, 246, 384.

Gill, Edward, 178, 479.
Gill, James, 18, 294, 341.
Gill, Wm., 520.
Gillaspy (Gillespy), Alex, 213, 329.
Gillespy, Allen, 451.
Gillespy, Daniel, 219.
Gillespy, Elizabeth, 218, 388.
Gillespy, Jacob, 168, 433.
Gillespie, James, 273, 388, 397, 411, 417.
Gillespy, John, 177, 218, 246, 388.
Gillespy, Mary, 315.
Gillesapey, Mathew, 531.
Gillespy, Robert, 315, 528.
Gillespy, Samuel, 397.
Gillespy, Simon, 480.
Gillespie, Thomas, 159, 260.
Gillespy, Wm., 208, 218, 315, 397, 439.
Gilliam, Ezekiel, 480.
Gilliam, Sarah, 480.
Gilliland, Nathan, 53, 116, 120, 172, 444.
Gillison, John, 33.
Gilmer, John, 144.
Gilmer, Wm., 166.
Gilmore, Ann, 379.
Gilmore, Eleanor, 461.
Gilmore, James, 57, 85, 108, 111, 138, 139, 140, 150, 153, 329, 379, 443, 454.
Gilmore, John, 43, 85, 108, 155, 168, 181, 193, 329.
Gilmore, Martha, 111.
Gilmore, Peachy R., 144.
Gilmore, Thomas, 93, 108, 168, 329.
Gilmore, Wm., 108, 181, 199, 461.
Ginits, Wm., 353, 461.
Gist, Nathaniel, 473.
Gist, Samuel, 133, 347, 350.
Gitgood, David, 512.
Givin (Givins), Daniel, 175.
Givin, David, 220, 221.
Givens, George, 112, 251, 458.
Givin, Hugh, 235.
Givens, Isabella, 251.
Givens, James, 20, 55, 58, 136, 137, 146, 293, 301, 369.
Givins, John, 55, 94, 182, 193, 196, 240, 241, 251, 263, 316, 327, 433, 448, 459, 477, 519.
Givin, Joseph, 215.
Givens, Martha, 89, 91, 99.
Givins, Peggy, 401.
Given, Randolph, 404.
Givin, Robert, 18, 28, 216, 218, 260.
Givens, Samuel, 20, 25, 55, 89, 91, 99, 189, 316, 324.
Givens, Sarah, 316.
Givens, Wm., 91, 114, 166, 177, 322, 330, 331, 343, 382, 453, 490, 507.
Glasgow, Wm., 88.
Glashe, Jacob, 491.
Glaspy, Alex, 303.
Glaspy, Matthew, 353.
Glass, Samuel, 128.

Greedy, John, 114, 330.
Greer, Andrew, 356.
Green, Ann, 378.
Green, David, 226.
Greene, Elihu, 396.
Green, Elinor, 19, 312, 317.
Green, Ellen, 396.
Green, Elsa, 322.
Green, Francis, 121, 437.
Green, Garrett, 176.
Green, Hugh, 90.
Green, James, 110, 312.
Green, Jeremiah, 527 .
Green, John, 264, 312, 322.
Green, Joseph, 418.
Green, Mary, 145.
Green, Moses, 312.
Green, Nancy, 399, 403.
Green, Robert, 19, 298, 312, 317, 361, 482.
Green, Richard, 294.
Green, Thomas, 378, 399, 403, 427.
Green, Timothy, 418.
Green, Wm., 226, 317, 349, 446, 447.
Green, Zachariah, 255.
Greenfield, John, 502.
Greenlee, Mary, 103, 106, 193, 194, 195, 198, 303.
Greenlee, James, 13, 17, 22, 41, 71, 74, 104, 106, 146, 198, 303, 350, 359, 434, 435.
Greenlee, John, 106, 109, 125.
Greenleigh, George, 386.
Greenwood, Josiah, 226.
Greer, Absalom, 288.
Greer, Alex, 329.
Greer (Greagh), Andrew, 87, 99, 117, 119, 126, 142, 143, 154, 157, 326, 335, 346, 366, 501.
Greer, John, 66.
Greer, Joseph, 214.
Greever, David, 214.
Gregg, Bennia, 411.
Gregg, Henry, 406.
Gregg, John, 87, 318.
Gregg, Margaret, 144, 321, 338.
Gregg, Nancy, 503.
Greeg, Robert, 136, 209, 319.
Gregg, Thomas, 386.
Gregg, Wm., 93, 308, 318, 321, 338, 347, 366, 368, 467.
Gregory, Christian, 423.
Gregory, James, 109, 145, 164.
Gregory, John, 232, 233, 242.
Gregory, Joseph, 178.
Gregory, Mary, 99, 510.
Gregory, Naphthalum, 51, 99, 100, 328.
Gregory, Samuel, 426.
Greiner, David, 213, 253, 259, 262, 280, 527.
Grems, John, 48.
Grenby, John. 136.
Grider, Benjamin, 44.
Grieder (Krieder), Peter, 353.

Griffey, Arch'bald, 422.
Griffin, Elizabeth, 395, 423.
Griffin, John, 189, 207, 222, 245, 395, 423, 509.
Griffin, Thomas, 243, 384.
Griffith, Abel, 187, 209, 424.
Griffeth, Benjamin, 112.
Griffith, Caleb, 424.
Griffeths, Charles, 110.
Griffeths, Daniel, 14.
Griffith, David, 424.
Griffiths, Edward, 307.
Griffith, Evin, 383.
Griffith, Hiram, 424.
G. iffith, John, 112, 307, 491.
Griffeths, Lucretia, 47, 58.
Griffith, Magdeline, 424.
Griffiths, Mary, 347.
Griffiths, Mathuselah, 24.
Griffeth, Morris, 112.
Griffith, Robert, 424.
Griffith, Sarah, 109.
Griffith, Wm., 94, 337, 405.
Grigsby, Ann, 180.
Grimes, see Graham, 364.
Grimes, Jane, 337.
Grimes, John, 185.
Grimes, Lanty, 185.
Grimes, Martha, 194.
Grimes, Robert, 337.
Griner, David, 194, 200, 228.
Gripping, Wm., 186.
Grissem, William, 248.
Griver, David, 205.
Groan, George, 480.
Groan, Lawrence, 480.
Groan, Mardalene, 480.
Groan, Mary, 480.
Grieder (Groeder), Henry, 510.
Grieder (Groeder), John, 510.
Groeder, Martin, 510.
Groff (Grove), Jacob, 385.
Grogge, Wm., 394.
Gross, Barbara, 197.
Grosse, Margaret, 393.
Gross, Michael, 466.
Grosse, Wm., 393.
Grove (Groves), Abraham, 267, 509.
Grove, Easter, 365.
Grove, Elizabeth, 365, 400.
Grove, Frederick, 400.
Grove, Hannah, 537.
Grove, Jacob, 244.
Grove, John, 305, 537.
Grove, Martin, 419, 420.
Groves, Mathew, 365.
Grove, Wm., 365.
Grove, Windel, 531.
Grover, Margaret, 374,
Grover, Philip, 374.
Grub, Benjamin, 306.
Grub, Hannah, 306.

Grub, Peter, 356.
Grubbs, Francis, 44.
Grubbs, Thomas, 25, 26, 28, 431, 438.
Gryder, Martin, 509.
Grymes, Christopher, 375.
Grymes, David, 93.
Grymes, Elizabeth, 185.
Grymes, Francis, 141.
Grymes, James, 69.
Grymes, Jane, 347.
Grymes, John, 14, 51, 93, 372, 509.
Grymes, Robert, 51, 347.
Grymes, Wm., 93, 106, 110, 466.
Guinn, David, 199, 204.
Guinn, Jane, 132.
Guinn, John, 307.
Guinn, Joseph, 201, 221, 229, 377.
Guinn, Robert, 132, 202, 212, 310, 533, 536.
Gwynn, Thomas 536.
Gwinn, Wm., 167.
Guden, Benjamin, 438.
Guest, Christopher, 69.
Guffee, John, 187.
Guile, Gabriel, 469, 518.
Guile, George, 469, 518.
Guile, Jacob, 469, 518.
Guile, Valentine, 469, 519.
Guinn, Daniel, 184.
Guin, Joseph, 531.
Guin, Nell, 431.
Guinn, Samuel, 185.
Guin, Wm., 490.
Gullet, John, 216.
Gullet, Wm., 216.
Gullion, Duncan, 446.
Gum, Isaac, 447.
Gum, Jacob, 429, 489.
Gum, John, 47, 178, 188, 204, 221, 266, 277.
Gum, Joseph, 197.
Gum, Robert, 196, 441.
Gum, Wm., 525.
Gunn, Jacob, 310.
Gunn, Norton, 171, 175.
Gunnel, Alex, 438.
Gunnod, Alex, 44.
Gurn, John, 176.
Guthery, Adam, 211.
Guthrey, John, 287.
Guy, Henry, 25, 322.
Guy, James, 277, 520.
Guy, John, 25, 50, 246, 492.
Guy, Margaret, 388.
Guy, Martha, 322.
Guy, Robert, 317.
Guy, Samuel, 50.
Guy, Wm., 17, 28, 50, 250, 266.
Guyto, Andrew, 536.

Haap, Peter, 432.
Habercham, Postmaster General, 419.
Hackett, Bozwell, 242.

Hackett, Mary, 238, 239.
Hackett, Thomas, 165, 173.
Haddon (Hatton), Mark, 405.
Haddon, Wm., 96, 180.
Hadesbell, Adam, 404, 405.
Hadley, Joshua, 439.
Hadley, Richard, 62.
Hadley, Simon, 310.
Haffenstall, Abraham, 122.
Haggert, Thomas, 207.
Haggerty, John, 400, 401, 405.
Hain, Barbara, 523.
Hain, Christiana, 523.
Hain, Claplir, 523.
Hain, Elizabeth, 523.
Hain, Hamudy, 523.
Hain, Henry, 523.
Hain, Isaac, 523.
Hain, Jacob, 523.
Hain, John, 523.
Hain, Joseph, 523.
Hain, Margaret, 523.
Hain, Paul, 523.
Hain (Hane), Peter, 241, 523, 531.
Hain, Rachel, 523.
Hain, Rudy, 523.
Hain, Stophar, 523.
Hain, Susanna, 523.
Haines, Abraham, 151, 332, 371, 454.
Hair (Hairs), John, 276, 402, 436, 528.
Hair, Matthew, 127.
Hair, Patrick, 63.
Hair, Sarah, 276, 402.
Haislip, Robert, 177.
Halderman, Jacob, 82.
Haldman, Daniel, 293.
Haldman, Thomas, 302.
Haldman, Wm., 138.
Haldway, Timothy, 431.
Hale, George, 378.
Hale, Peter, 378.
Hale, Robert, 378.
Halefor, John, 65.
Haling, Andrew, 145.
Hall, Alex, 251, 248, 262, 272, 275, 278, 481.
Hall, Andrew, 128, 145, 146, 334.
Hall, Edward, 30, 32, 41, 54, 68, 303, 305, 477.
Hall, Francis, 189, 311.
Hall, George, 15, 19, 393.
Hall, Henry, 172, 189, 259, 260, 266, 277, 281.
Hall, Isabella, 85, 112, 137, 332.
Hall, James, 44, 113, 150, 230, 281, 438, 476.
Hall, Jane, 27.
Hall, John, 127, 136, 140, 141, 145, 170, 182, 259, 401.
Hall, Mary, 268.
Hall, Moses, 110, 426.
Hall, Nancy, 280.

Hall, Peter, 293, **412**.
Hall, Rebecca, 388, 393.
Hall, Richard, 44, 48.
Hall, Robert, 85, 112, 137, 213, 242, 261, 352, 354, 372, 463, 476.
Hall, Susanna, 113.
Hall, Thomas, 236, 469, 478.
Hall, Wm., 24, 27, 57, 127, 145, 149, 317, 388, 440, 441, 525, 530.
Halliday, James, 300.
Hallingsworth, Elizabeth, 260.
Hallingsworth, Margaret, 260.
Halman, Wm., 341.
Halstin, Henry, 354.
Halston, Stephen, 486.
Ham, Mary Ann, 274.
Ham, William, 275.
Hamel, George, 279.
Hamel (Hansel?), Margaret, 279.
Hamilton, Agnes, 123.
Hamilton, Alexander, 124, 370.
Hamilton, Andrew, 13, 18, 98, 101, 120, 141, 154, 183, 201, 261, 441, 442.
Hamilton, Archibald, 28, 29, 48, 111, 140, 250, 253, 348.
Hamilton, Arthur, 498.
Hamilton, Audley, 85, 387.
Hamilton, Charles, 221, 226, 526.
Hamilton, Darkis, 373.
Hamilton, Frances, 389.
Hamilton, Hans, 485.
Hamilton, Hugh, 135.
Hamilton, Isaiah, 61.
Hamilton, James, 36, 40, 117, 225, 243, 244, 253, 257, 311, 442, 498.
Hamilton, Jesse, 180.
Hamilton, John, 58, 95, 101, 109, 123, 153, 158, 193, 314, 332, 340, 341, 349, 380, 441, 476, 484, 485, 490, 520, 528, 537.
Hamilton, Joseph, 250, 389.
Hamilton, Margaret, 78, 100, 124, 336.
Hamilton, Mary, 285.
Hamilton, Moses, 104, 126, 314, 493.
Hamilton, Patrick, 204.
Hamilton, Robert, 66, 140, 155, 314, 349, 353, 462, 494.
Hamilton, Samuel, 141, 323, 489, 528.
Hamilton, Thomas, 62, 228, 245, 379.
Hamilton, Taylor, 314.
Hamilton, Wm., 40, 41, 90, 98, 100, 161, 167, 178, 184 196, 213, 232, 314, 336, 374, 434, 474.
Hamm, Valentine, 240.
Hammel, John, 284.
Hammer, George, 97.
Hammer, Nicholas, 103.
Hammond, John, 21.
Mamond, Rachel, 413.
Hanason, Jeremiah, **440**.
Handley, Archey, **457**.
Handley, Grissell, 114.

Handley, John, 101, 114, 137, 315, **320**, 437, 462.
Handlin, John, 318.
Handlin, Mary, 176.
Handlin, Wm., 318.
Handlow, Wm., 23.
Handly, Marty, 358.
Handly, Wm., 320, 403.
Hane, Peter, 323.
Hanger, Frederick, 251, 278, **279**, 504.
Hanger, Jacob, 292.
Hanger, John, 480.
Hanger, Pat., 202.
Hanger, Patsy, 427, 537.
Hanger, Peter, 194, 196, 197, 210, **223**, 225, 251, 275, 396, 417, 427, 481, 537.
Hankey, Simon, 418.
Hanley, John, 50.
Hanley, John S., 32.
Hanley, Sigismund, 294.
Hanna, Brice, 364, 365.
Hanna, David, 242, 411.
Hanna, Isaac, 249.
Hanna, Jack, 384.
Hanna, John, 57, 65, 128, 141, 150, **153**, 186, 324, 356.
Hannah, Joseph, 96, 107, 273, 337, **442**, 446, 520.
Hanna, Peter, 403.
Hanna, Robert, 520.
Hanna, Wm., 369.
Hannan, John, 480.
Hannan, Michael, 421.
Hannan, Valentine, 457.
Harmon, Valentine, 457.
Hansberger, Robert, 289, 423.
Hansburger, Stephen, 437.
Hanson, David, 383.
Hantsberger, Stephen, 50, 495.
Hantsberger, Ursilla, 495.
Hansford, Theodosius, 259.
Hara, Patrick, 97.
Harbeson (Horbeson), Wm., 46, **47**.
Harbold, Nicholas, 326.
Hard, Rudy, 41.
Harden (Hardin), Benjamin, 18, **296**, 298, 301, 308, 312.
Harden, John, 60, 177, 323.
Harden, Thomas, 478.
Hardine, H., 468.
Harding, Edward, 400.
Harding, George, 258, 260.
Harding, Henry, 26, 301.
Harding, Mary, 400.
Hardy, Samuel, 447.
Hardy, Thomas, 478.
Hare, John, 51.
Harger, John, 50, 61, 62.
Hargrave, James, 476.
Harie, Richard, 380.
Harland, John, 309.

Harmentrout, Elizabeth, 321.
Harmentrout, John, 321.
Harmless, Thomas, 271.
Harmon (Hermon), Adam, 23, 25, 38, 41, 53, 69, 110, 432, 433, 440, 450.
Harman, Alex, 426.
Harman, Barbara, 480.
Harmon, Caleb, 82, 84, 104, 334, 445, 494.
Harmon, Catherine, 290.
Harmon, David, 128.
Harmon, Elizabeth, 426.
Harmon, Ernest, 189.
Harmon, George, 23, 189.
Harmon, Henry, 73, 116, 335, 411, 412.
Hermon, Jacob, 23, 26, 31, 53, 73, 81, 308, 434, 443.
Harmon, James, 106.
Harmon, John, 26, 32, 47, 63, 308.
Harmon, Lewis, 426.
Harmon, Mary, 123.
Harmon, Michael, 282, 284, 426.
Harmon, Peter, 172, 290.
Harmon, Polly, 426.
Harmon, Sally, 426.
Harmon, Stophel, 189.
Harmon, Susannah, 426.
Harmon, Valentine, 23, 432, 433.
Harned, David, 194, 509.
Harness, Conrad, 57.
Harness, Michael, 29, 58.
Harnett, Rachel, 503.
Harnsberry, Mary, 503.
Harper, Charles, 534.
Harper, Elizabeth, 54.
Harper, Hans (Hance). 42, 44, 54, 105, 142, 436, 438.
Harper, Jacob, 124.
Harper, John, 124.
Harper, John, 240, 341.
Harper, Mathew, 42, 44, 118, 329, 344, 351, 438, 442, 475.
Harper, Michael, 44, 54, 88 129, 344, 351, 436, 438, 474, 475, 519.
Harper, Nicholas. 202, 208 .
Harper, Phillip, 87, 179.
Harper, Robert, 28.
Harper, William, 243.
Harplore, Nicholas, 119.
Harpole, Nicholas, 173, 180, 187.
Harrell (Harrill, Harrold), Jacob, 35, 438.
Harrill, John, 438.
Harrill, Moses, 438.
Harrill, Richard, 438.
Harrill, Thomas, 438.
Harrel (Harrold), Wm., 26, 46, 438.
Harrington, Ann, 218.
Harrington, Charles, 218.
Harrington, Grant, 479.
Harrington, Jeremiah, 478.
Harrington, Thomas, 407.

Harris, Charles, 490.
Harris, Henry, 55.
Harris, James, 40, 135, 151, 231.
Harris, John, 212, 347.
Harris, Robert, 193, 194, 195, 288.
Harris, Sherwood, 198.
Harrison, Benjamin, 90, 101, 153, 157, 187, 364, 371, 406, 481, 482, 483.
Harrison, Burr, 371, 373, 445.
Harrison, C. H., 355, 458.
Harrison, Catherine, 124.
Harrison, Cuthbert, 263.
Harrison, Daniel, 31, 40, 45, 49, 53, 65, 68, 69, 75, 92, 122, 302, 305, 309, 313, 324, 334, 340, 343, 347, 349, 350,,352, 357, 358, 364, 368, 404, 440, 467, 468, 482, 491.
Harrison, David, 129, 140.
Harrison, Elizabeth, 183.
Harrison, Gideon, 90.
Harrison, Isaiah, 40, 510.
Harrison, James (alias Harris), 371.
Harrison, Jeremiah, 13, 19, 31, 101, 124, 357.
Harrison, Jesse, 109, 440.
Harrison, John, 16, 40, 43, 48, 50, 65, 90, 109, 110, 111, 143, 157, 176, 297, 301, 315, 324, 328, 334, 344, 435, 436, 439, 467, 482, 491.
Harrison, Joseph, 40, 299..
Harrison, M., 457.
Harrison, Mary, 101, 334.
Harrison, Mathew, 157, 158, 160, 169, 173, 177, 183, 348, 355, 368.
Harrison, Nehemiah, 182.
Harrison, Randolph, 404.
Harrison, Reuben, 50, 193, 343, 361, 369, 436, 481, 491.
Harrison, Robert, 40, 45, 93, 98, 305, 312, 313, 326, 340, 343, 403, 475, 510.
Harrison, Samuel, 101, 301, 312, 340, 475.
Harrison, Sarah, 121, 364.
Harrison, Thomas, 13, 19, 31, 63, 121, 134, 183, 293, 298, 304, 404, 429, 489, 491, 510.
Harrison Wm., 296.
Harrison, Zebulon, 142, 298, 361, 437.
Harry, Ann, 436.
Harry, David, 14.
Harry, John, 14, 436.
Harsh, Wm., 457.
Hart, Aaron, 61.
Hart, Charles, 23.
Hart, Jacob, 206.
Hart, James, 206, 269.
Hart, John, 364, 370.
Hart, Joseph, 418.
Hart, Josiah, 418.
Hart, Mary, 276.
Hart, Miles, 61.
Hart, Oliver, 418.

Henderson, Alex, 36, 55, 279, 442.
Henderson, Daniel, 167, 168, 170, 220, 359.
Henderson, David, 36, 198, 199, 201, 202, 210, 216, 226, 229, 238, 239, 246, 272, 378, 403.
Henderson, Florence, 414.
Henderson, George, 99, 110, 121, 122, 303, 305, 307, 525.
Henderson, James, 75, 86, 116, 117, 141, 142, 190, 235, 241, 247, 263, 268, 277, 279, 377.
Henderson, Jane, 160.
Henderson, John, 20, 85, 99, 122, 126, 127, 134, 135, 168, 173, 185, 206, 238, 241, 323, 329, 332, 350, 355, 379, 422, 442, 443, 459, 474.
Henderson, Janes, 215, 250, 430, 475.
Henderson, Joseph, 143 ,179.
Henderson, Margaret, 170.
Henderson, Michael, 315.
Henderson, Robert, 384, 416.
Henderson, Ruth, 170.
Henderson, Samuel, 36, 41, 55, 59, 84, 91, 99, 100, 101, 121, 134, 136, 142, 144, 145, 160, 170, 230, 324, 331, 430, 491, 531.
Henderson, Sarah, 170.
Henderson, Suasannah, 241, 247.
Henderson, Wm., 14, 15, 48, 103, 111, 116, 140, 193, 210, 211, 241, 247, 249, 268, 274, 296, 369, 477.
Henderson, Valentine, 72, 318.
Hendley, Archibald, 325.
Hendon, Josiah F., 434.
Hendrick, Charles, 275.
Hendricks, George, 154, 356.
Hendrix, Henry, 126.
Henkle, M., 483.
Henley, John S., 296.
Henley, Sigismund, 296.
Henning, Robert, 534.
Henning (Herring), Samuel, 429.
Henricks, George, 530.
Henry, A. P., 484.
Henry, Carter, 355.
Henry, Charles, 535.
Henry, David, 520.
Henry, Henry, 41.
Henry, James, 520, 532, 535.
Henry, Jean, 520.
Henry, John, 337, 451, 484.
Henry, Mary, 535.
Henry, Nancy, 535.
Henry, P., Jr., 337, 459.
Henry, Patrick, Jr., 127, 329, 338, 353, 451, 463.
Henry, Robert, 435.
Henry, Samuel, 171, 229, 250.
Henry, Sarah, 535.
Henry, Wm., 27, 159, 396, 405, 434.
Henshaw, Moses, 203.

Henson, Peggy, 73.
Henson, Wm., 73.
Henton (Hinton), George, 191.
Henton, James, 520.
Henton, John, 187.
Heorce, Frances, 342, 495.
Heorse, Martin, 342.
Heorce, Mathew, 343, 495.
Herbert, Thomas, 498.
Herbert, Wm., 130, 137, 158, 465.
Herd, John, 97.
Herdman, John, 97, 157, 182, 190, **440,** 481.
Herdman, Thomas, 149.
Heris, James, 434.
Herndon, Edward, 295.
Herndon, John, 376.
Herndon, Joseph, 102, 360.
Hernet, David, 510.
Herolf, Margaret, 407.
Herolf, Peter, 407.
Herrin (Herring, Herron), Abigail, 119.
Herrin, Alexander, 19, 31, 40, 48, 73, 101, 119, 149, 340, 347, 467, 475, 482.
Herring, Barthwell (Bethwell), 173, **174.**
Herring, James, 67.
Heren, John, 109, 329.
Herring, Joseph, 67.
Herring, Leonard, 429, 489.
Herring, Samuel, 67.
Herron, Thomas, 535.
Herren, Wm., 157, 394, 481, 532, **535.**
Hervey (Hewey), James, 16.
Heslep, Andrew, 74.
Heslap, Isaac, 462.
Hessam, Jacob, 399.
Hessent, James, 238.
Hest, Isaac, 329.
Hetrick, Adam, 321, 336, 360.
Hetrick, Caspar, 360.
Hetrick, Elizabeth, 321.
Hetrick, John, 360.
Hetzell, Thomas, 174.
Hettly, James, 372, 404.
Hewit, David, 510.
Hewit, Thomas, 187, 193, 196, 240.
Hibler, Wm., 261.
Hickey, Catherine, 79.
Hicklin,, Henry, 265.
Hicklin, Hugh, 51, 54, 217, 323, **441.**
Hicklin, James, 221, 263.
Hicklin, John, 97, 441.
Hicklin, Jonathan, 483.
Hicklin, Thomas, 122, 128, 137, 161, 196, 212, 221, 380, 441.
Hickman, Joshua, 33.
Hickman, Richard, 490.
Hicks (Hix), Henry, 128.
Hicks, Joseph, 132, 152, 477, 478, **479.**
Hicks, Thomas, 111.
Hide, Wm., 99, 101, 118.
Hider, Adam, 83.

Hidener, Jacob, 513.
Hidener, Sarah, 513.
Higgins (Higins), Daniel, 85, 153.
Higgins, John, 153.
Higgins, Mary, 153.
Higgins, Michael, 153.
Highlands, Catherine, 140, 148.
Highlands, Henry, 140, 148.
Hikkey, John, 446.
Hiland, Dominick, 123.
Hildebrand, John, 536.
Hill, Ann, 301.
Hill, David, 494.
Hill, Elizabeth, 210, 387, 398.
Hill, George, 478.
Hill, James, 125, 131, 142, 143, 195, 209, 210, 218, 239, 373, 381, 409, 412, 437, 507.
Hill, John, 26, 142, 157, 302.
Hill, Johnston, 89, 90, 92, 328, 336.
Hill, Neomi, 90, 97, 98, 338.
Hill, Robert, 92, 368.
Hill, Samuel, 301.
Hill, Spencer, 508.
Hill, T., 468.
Hill, Thomas, 105, 140, 170, 387, 441.
Hill, William, 302, 409, 412, 462.
Heindricks, Peter, 241.
Hinds (Hind, Hines), Ann, 213.
Hinds, Edward, 213, 429, 518.
Hind, John, 55, 209, 224, 226, 260, 300, 328, 386.
Hinds, Mary, 114.
Hind, Samuel, 110, 137, 151.
Hinds, Thomas, 383, 424.
Hinds, Wm., 30, 34, 55, 67, 139, 224, 241, 247, 260, 421.
Hindmen, Alex, 179.
Hindman, Elinor, 432.
Hindman, John, 31, 302, 325, 432.
Hinkle (Hinckle), Benjamin, 262.
Hinkle, Isaac, 194, 196.
Hinkle, Joseph, 206.
Hinkle, Moses, 246, 247, 255, 481.
Hinsher, John, 250.
Hintle, Abraham, 192.
Hinton, Henry, 327.
Hinton, John, 70, 313, 428.
Hinton, Peter, 510.
Hinton, Wm., 176, 194, 446, 509, 510, 528.
Hislop, Isaac, 386.
Hitchins, John, 434.
Hite, Abraham, 88, 101.
Hite, Jacob, 135.
Hite, John, 22, 294, 464.
Hite, Joseph, 310.
Hite, Jost., 18, 295, 298, 312, 512.
Hite, Rebecca, 88, 101.
Hix, Ann, 171.
Hix, John, 195.
Hoak, Wm., 496.
Hob, Peter, 204, 215.

Hobleman, Wm., 90.
Hodge, Asabel, 43, 52, 435.
Hodge, Elizabeth, 43, 52, 435, 533.
Hodge, Francis, 533.
Hodge, Hannah, 52.
Hodge, Jacob, 52.
Hodg, James, 529.
Hodge, John, 25, 154, 176, 201, 435.
Hodge, Jonathan, 52.
Hodge, Rachel, 52.
Hodge, Samuel, 122, 145, 441.
Hodge, Wm., 82, 441, 518.
Hodgson, James, 427.
Hodgson, Wm., 427.
Hoerner, Conrad, 433.
Hoerner, Johann M., 433.
Hoff, George, 447.
Hoffmans, George, 143.
Hoffman, Hannah, 130.
Hog, Elizabeth, 341, 349, 491.
Hog, P., 368.
Hog, Peter, 86, 104, 113, 184, 188, 197, 203, 205, 209, 226, 318, 320, 344, 372, 409, 410, 418, 483, 499.
Hog, Thomas, 184, 198, 291.
Hogan, Edward, 434, 435.
Hoger, Wm., 519.
Hogg, Wm., 310.
Hogshead, Ann, 221, 246, 294, 399.
Hogshead, Charles, 281, 282, 416.
Hogshead, David, 152, 211, 416.
Hogshead, Margaret, 291.
Hogshead, Elizabeth, 288.
Hogshead, James, 17, 18, 28, 140, 166, 200, 202, 211, 246, 288, 411, 531.
Hogshead, John, 21, 48, 53, 67, 151, 166, 221, 247, 291, 294, 531.
Hogshead, Margaret, 291.
Hogshead, Michael, 85.
Hogshead, Nancy, 288.
Hogshead, Rebecca, 291.
Hogshead, Robert, 246, 288.
Hogshead, Thomas, 277.
Hogshead, Wm., 21, 288, 291, 411, 531.
Hokens, Joseph, 438.
Holdman, Daniel, 14, 22, 108, 109
Holdman, William, 60, 61, 93.
Holdway, Timothy, 14.
Hole, George, 226.
Hole, Peter, 220, 221.
Holice, James, 498.
Holing, Thomas, 491.
Holland, Elizabeth, 259, 260.
Holland, Hannah, 230.
Holles, James, 94.
Holliday, Wm., 253.
Hollowback, George, 97.
Holly, William, 354.
Hollyback, George, 58.
Holmes, David, 276.
Holmes, Hugh, 261.
Holmes, Isaac, 245.

Holmes, James, 291.
Holmes, Jane, 291.
Holmes, John, 21, 23, 30, 275, 289, 300, 301, 399, 400, 401, 491, 531.
Holmes,, Mary, 271, 275, 399, 400, 401.
Holmes, Meelsee, 531.
Holmes, Thomas, 55.
Holse, Hugh, 179.
Holston (Holstine), Henry, Jr., 63, 430, 444.
Holston (Holdston), Stephen, 30, 431.
Holt (Hoult), Peter, 59.
Holton, Wm., 102.
Homan, John, 23.
Honeyman, Andrew, 215, 422, 426.
Honeyman, Henry, 215.
Hony, James, 28.
Hood, George, 279, 281.
Hood, John, 22, 311.
Hood, Tunis, 295.
Hood, Walter, 484.
Hoofman, Philip, 95.
Hook, George, 234, 237.
Hook, Joseph, 279.
Hook, James, 101, 234.
Hook, Jane, 168.
Hook, Michael, 61.
Hook, Robert, 26, 81, 168, 195, 309, 434, 446, 461, 502.
Hook, Wm., 234, 262, 366, 466.
Hoop, Rachel, 532.
Hoops, Adam, 327, 498.
Hoopwood, Wm., 35, 39,
Hoornbeck, Daniel, 433.
Hope, George, 107.
Hope, John, 349.
Hopes (Hapes), John, 491.
Hopes, Samuel, 498.
Hopkins, Archibald, 100, 145, 179.
Hopkins, James, 429.
Hopkins, John, 85, 97, 110, 145, 152, 180, 182, 193, 317.
Hopkins, Philip, 277, 417.
Hopping, Ezekiel, 400, 401.
Horbert, Wm., 157.
Horbinson, George, 527.
Hord, Joseph, 132.
Horless, Philip, 158.
Horloes, Philip, 308.
Horn, Nancy W., 480.
Horn, Peter, 519.
Horn, Reddick, 480.
Hornback, Joel, 41, 46, 55, 491.
Hornberrier, Jacob, 156.
Horner, James, 108.
Horse, Henry, 41, 112.
Horse, Peter, 41, 76.
Horshman, Woolrick, 127.
Horton, Anthony, 438.
Hough, Edith, 418.
Hougham, Jarvis, 471.
Houncal, John, 498.

House, George, 290.
House, Hannah, 81.
House, Henry, 81, 290.
House, Peter, 290.
Houston, Archibald, 182.
Houston, James, 24, 411.
Houston, Rebecca, 182.
Hover (Hoover), Boslen, 101.
Hover, Michael, 173.
Hover, Peter, 483.
Hover, Postley (Pastle), 41, 141.
Hover, Sebastian, 97, 167, 218.
Hoverstick, Adam, 177.
How (Howe), Catherine, 244, 386.
How, Henry, 244, 386.
How, John, 323.
How, Joseph, 40, 158, 352, 358.
How, Peter, 79, 360.
How, Stephen, 244.
How, Stophel, 386.
How, Stuffe, 205.
Howard, Ignatius, 369.
Howard, Henry, 179.
Howard, Edward, 498.
Howard, John, 461.
Howard, Mordicai, 335.
Howell, David, 528.
Howell, James, 338.
Howell, Samuel, 123, 327, 338.
Howlam, Wm., 227.
Hubbard, Ephriam, 108, 325, 326.
Hucklin, Thomas, 494.
Huddle, George, 387.
Huddle, Margaret, 387.
Hudson, Charles, 278, 279, 415.
Hudson, Isaac, 415.
Huett, Thomas, 190, 191.
Huff, Catherine, 532.
Huff, Francis, 244, 261, 509, 532.
Huff, Henry, 532.
Huff, Jacob, 532.
Huff, Samuel, 532.
Huff, Susanna, 409, 410, 532.
Huffman, Andrew, 262.
Huffman, Elizabeth, 162.
Huffman, George, 189.
Hufman, Henry, 250.
Huffman, Honecle, 87.
Huffman, Leonard, 413.
Huffman, Joseph, 413.
Huffman, Mary, 162.
Huffman, Nicholas, 162.
Hugart, James, 28, 116, 248, 333.
Hugart (Hughart), Thomas, 123, **142**, 154, 160, 169, 176, 177, 178, 185, **186**, 188, 189, 192, 196, 197, 202, 203, 215, 216, 217, 219, 220, 222, 223 225, **240**, 245, 350.
Hugart, Wm., 162, 528.
Hughes (Hughs, Hues), Aaron, 137, **157**, 169, 175.
Hughes, David, 77.

Hughes, Edward, 20, 21, 22, 77, 469.
Hughes, Euphemia, 133, 144, 154, 209, 346, 359, 363, 468.
Hughes, Francis, 42, 44, 46, 50, 212, 437.
Hughes, George, 39.
Hughs, Halph, 52.
Hughs, James, 71, 72, 75, 79, 80, 82, 83, 84, 85, 86, 87, 88, 89, 133, 144, 154, 205, 243, 284, 290, 346, 359, 363, 454, 468, 469.
Hughes, Jane, 144, 154, 346, 359, 363, 468.
Hughes, John, 87, 93, 148, 152, 169, 484.
Hughes, Joseph, 478.
Hughes, Mary, 144, 154, 346, 359, 363, 468.
Hughes, Neel, 187, 379.
Hughes, Priscilla, 108.
Hughes, Ralph, 468.
Hughs, Rosemond, 38.
Hughes, Robert, 528.
Hughes, Samuel, 66.
Hughes, Sidney, 392.
Hughes, Thomas, 44, 183, 217, 219, 222, 226, 229, 232, 240, 245, 392, 404, 438, 463, 468, 483, 527.
Hughes, William, 26, 47, 245, 302, 354, 461, 466, 469.
Huling, Andrew, 149, 199, 352, 465.
Hull, Francis, 520.
Hull, Peter, 440.
Hull (Hulls), Samuel, 38, 131, 496.
Humble, Conrad, 181.
Humble, Martin, 87, 181, 193.
Humble, Uriah, 87, 88, 323.
Humphries, Alex., 253, 265, 266, 268, 278, 284, 391, 394, 404, 406, 409, 509.
Humphreys, David, 520, 532.
Humphreys, Hannah, 306.
Humphries, James, 527.
Humphries, John, 499.
Humphreys, Jonathan, 199, 215, 218, 227, 429, 526.
Humphreys, Joseph, 202, 507.
Humphreys, Joshua, 194, 195, 196, 197, 205, 207, 223, 398.
Humphrey, Wm., 31.
Hunt, Charles, 215.
Hunt, Roger, 295, 296.
Hunt, Thomas, 315.
Hunter, Alex., 229.
Hunter, Andrew, 416.
Hunter, Catherine, 244, 532.
Hunter, Dinah, 271.
Hunter, Elizabeth, 26, 271, 525.
Hunter, James, 244, 324, 371, 444.
Hunter, John, 26, 68, 101, 137, 151, 179, 181, 182, 214, 257, 416.
Hunter, Mary, 282, 390.
Hunter, Mathew, 532.
Hunter, Moses, 510.
Hunter, Samuel, 111, 116, 160, 185, 219, 220, 221, 251, 253, 397, 400, 401, 447.
Hunter, Susannah, 400, 401.

Hunter, Wm., 26, 149, 217, 255, 261, 299, 390, 444.
Hunsberry, Andrew, 397.
Huntsberger, Stephen, 342.
Huntsberger, Ursilla, 342.
Huntsman, Lawrence, 95, 109.
Hursh (Hurst), Wm., 26, 44, 46, 438.
Hurt, Moses, 126.
Hurstman, Alrick, 116.
Huston, Anthony, 483.
Husten, Archibald, 60, 65, 118, 136, 160, 165, 172, 324, 350, 446, 496.
Huston, James, 57, 111, 174, 292, 304, 340, 356, 358, 449, 475.
Huston, John, 437.
Huston, Mathew, 147.
Huston, Polly, 532.
Huston, Samuel, 74, 103, 437.
Hutchinson, Ann, 461.
Hutcheson, George, 42, 77, 84, 93, 110, 289, 297, 304, 319, 470.
Hutcheson, James, 42, 84, 119, 331.
Hutchinson, John, 14, 20, 24, 37, 42, 61, 80, 83, 125, 206, 342, 352, 391, 430, 442.
Hutcheson, Mary, 396.
Hutcheson, Polly, 284.
Hutcheson, Robert, 250.
Hutcheson, Sarah, 237, 241.
Hutcheson, William, 13, 19, 77, 81, 84, 93, 142, 149, 171, 224, 261, 304, 323, 331, 342, 349, 353, 372, 396, 444, 459, 461, 470, 507.
Hutchings, John, 62.
Hutton, James, 335, 441.
Hutton, Samuel, 100, 335.
Huver, Costian, 432.
Huy (Huey), James, 26, 33, 35, 60, 72.
Hyard, Landred, 41.
Hyde, Charles, 206.
Hyde, John, 206.
Hyde, Joseph, 137.
Hyde, Wm., 153, 446.
Hyden, Joseph, 422.
Hyden, Joshua, 422.
Hynd, James, 354.
Hynds, Edward, 150.
Hyndman, John, 320.
Hynes, Ann, 195.
Hynes, Thomas, 195.
Hynes (Hynds), Wm., 429.
Hyte, Jost., 482.

Iax, Thomas, 42.
Inchminger, Philip, 429.
Inchremiger, Jonathan, 484.
Inglebird, George, 473.
Ingleman, Philip, 252, 274, 275.
Iugleman, William, 249.
Ingler, John, 92, 436.
Ingles, Thomas, 436, 441.
Ingles, W., 349.
Ingles, Wm., 119, 157, 158, 436, 441, 489.

Kennerly, James, 144, 153, 173, 200, 291, 371, 419, 420, 534, 535, 536.
Kennerly, John, 185, 187, 198.
Kennerly, Mary, 187.
Kennerly, Reuben, 418, 534, 535.
Kennerly, Samuel, 534.
Kennerly, Thomas, 138, 534, 535.
Kennerly, Wm., 392, 418, 420, 534, 535.
Kenney, Chesley, 280.
Kenney, Jacob, 280.
Kenny, Andrew, 469.
Kenny, Bryan, 364, 372, 378.
Kenny, James, 231, 375.
Kenny, John, 329, 392, 476.
Kenny, Joseph, 231.
Kenny, Mathew, 179, 223, 237, 284.
Kenny, Robert, 145, 188, 195, 201, 202, 205, 218, 243, 413.
Kenny, Sarah, 378.
Kenon, Felix, 115.
Kensley, Conrad, 81.
Kensley, Katrine, 81.
Kensley, Savina, 81.
Kent, Jacob, 132, 147, 467.
Kent, Samuel, 140.
Kentner, George, 168.
Kentner, Michael, 168.
Kepels, George, 130.
Kephart, Elizabeth, 378.
Kephart (Gabhart), John, 391.
Kephart, Peter, 378.
Kerkham, Elizabeth, 74.
Kerkham, Hannah, 74.
Kerkham, Jane, 74.
Kerkham, John, 122.
Kerkham, Martha, 74.
Kerkham, Michael, 18.
Kerkham, Robert, 18, 74.
Kerkendolls, Abraham, 206.
Kerkley, Francis, 66, 74, 84.
Kern, Nicholas, 174.
Kerr, Andrew, 95, 323.
Kerr, David, 374.
Kerr, Henry, 39, 482.
Kerr, James, 13, 14, 28, 160, 188, 246, 328, 336, 382, 400, 401, 406, 413.
Kerr, Jane, 300.
Kerr (Carre) John, 13, 14, 94, 110, 160, 167, 174, 187, 300, 322, 401, 406, 432.
Kerr, Joseph, 526.
Kerr, Martha, 401.
Kerr, Rachel, 95.
Kerr, Richard, 61.
Kerr, Samuel, 171.
Kerr, Thomas, 142.
Kerr, Wm., 110, 137, 172, 377, 400, 401.
Kersey, Martin, 350.
Kervine (Kerwin), Wm., 15, 16, 18.
Keslinger, Christian, 191.
Keslinger, Jacob, 191.
Kesner, Philip, 423.
Kettle, Mary, 167.

Keys, Benjamin, 142.
Keys, John, 261.
Keys, Roger, 16, 22, 95.
Keys, S., 519.
Kibbeath, Thomas, 210.
Kidd, Daniel, 84, 119, 181, 187, 209, 390, 430, 447, 507, 530, 531.
Kidd, Francis 461.
Kidney, Daniel, 26.
Kilbreath, Wm., 405.
Kile, Alexander, 132.
Kilkenny, John, 415.
Kilkenny, Sally, 415.
Kilpatrick, Alex., 209, 211, 214, 218, 221, 227, 399, 528, 531.
Kilpatrick, Charles, 120.
Kilpatrick, George, 30.
Kilpatrick, James, 215.
Killpatrick, John, 110.
Kilpatrick, Lettice, 168.
Kilpatrick, Roger, 140.
Killpatrick, Thomas, 20, 59, 110, 125, 144, 168.
Kimberland, Jacob, 123.
Kimberland, Mary M., 123.
Kinsey, Benjamin, 428.
Kincaid, Guy H., 536.
Kincaid, Robert, 423, 536.
Kincaid, Thomas, 536.
Kincaid, Wm., 513, 536.
Kinder, Adam, 489.
Kinder, Betsy, 251.
Kinder, Catherine, 39.
Kinder, Jacob, 498.
Kinder, Mathias, 489.
Kinder (Kender), Peter, 39, 300.
Kinder, Sarah, 39.
King, Catherine, 48.
King, Eleanor, 153.
King, Elizabeth, 48, 387.
King, George, 535.
King, Henry, 155, 156, 163, 220, 235, 239, 242, 262, 364, 387, 401.
King, James, 67, 71, 184, 535.
King John, 16, 42, 44, 61, 78, 87, 111, 237, 244, 348, 442, 462.
King, Joseph, 118, 153, 244.
King, Mary, 415.
King, Nancy, 413.
King, Nicholas, 153.
King, Richard, 413, 415.
King, Robert, 25.
King, Susanna, 155, 163, 235, 364, 403.
King, William, 13, 14, 19, 20, 290, 295, 423.
Kingkade, Borough, 43, 108.
Kingkade, Jane, 473.
Kingkade, John, 52, 344.
Kingkade, Joseph, 53.
Kingkade, Robert, 102, 128.
Kingkead (Kinkade), Andrew, 366, 441.
Kinkead, Ann, 108.

Kinkead, Anna H., 128.
Kinkead, Elizabeth, 531.
Kinkead, David, 28, 47, 345, 431, 531.
Kinkead, George, 270, 418.
Kinkead, James, 223.
Kinkead, John, 189, 191, 196, 197, 202, 210, 212, 215, 225, 226, 229, 239, 241, 343, 350, 351, 441, 458, 473, 474, 481, 528.
Kinkade, Joseph, 142, 179.
Kinkead, Mathew, 188.
Kinkead, Patrick, 350.
Kinkead, Robert, 142.
Kinkead, Samuel, 20, 71.
Kinkead, Thomas, 170, 172, 212, 242, 310, 373, 378, 414, 513.
Kinkead, Wm., 175, 183, 201, 211, 212, 310, 346, 394, 528.
Kinkead, Winifred, 28, 142.
Kinkead, Winefor, 431.
Kinley, Benjamin, 313, 323, 358, 428, 433.
Kinneer, Susanna, 228.
Kinneer, Andrew, 228.
Kinney, Jacob, 264, 270, 271, 283, 284, 289, 410, 479, 529, 534.
Kinney, Mathew, 156.
Kinsley, Benjamin 102.
Kinsley, Maundling, 90.
Kinsley, Phillipina, 90.
Kirk, Alexander, 209, 248.
Kirk, George, 263.
Kirk, James, 120, 183, 263, 265, 529.
Kirk, John, 142, 221, 232, 263, 415, 416.
Kirk, Robert, 257, 377.
Kirkham, Elizabeth, 315.
Kirkley, Francis, Jr., 76, 186, 324.
Kirkham, Hanna, 315.
Kirkham (Kerkham), Henry, 15, 18, 68, 122, 359, 525.
Kirkham, Jane, 315.
Kirkham, Michael, 136, 145, 359.
Kirkham, Robert, 315.
Kirkham, Samuel, 358, 360.
Kirkland, Samuel, 274.
Kirkley, Elizabeth, 186.
Kirkpatrick, James, 207.
Kirkpatrick, John, 455.
Kirkpatrick, Robert, 217.
Kirkpatrick, Thomas, 57, 431, 443, 444.
Kirland, Jane, 201.
Kirland, Mary, 401.
Kirtley, Francis, 107, 172, 248.
Kirtley, Thomas, 248.
Kisling, Christiana, 177.
Kisling, Christopher, 177.
Kistner, John, 423.
Kistner, Rachael, 423.
Kline, Andrew, 128, 130, 342, 349, 466.
Knave, Henry, 57.
Knave, Leonard, 79.
Knight, Andrew, 90.
Knight, Charles, 343.
Knocker, Jeremiah, 394.

Knowles, James, 396.
Knowles, John, 41, 396, 438.
Knowles, Mary, 401.
Knowles, William, 396, 399, 401.
Knox, James, 14, 40, 122, 442, 493.
Knox, John, 100.
Knox, Robert, 75, 103, 356.
Knox, Thomas, 486.
Koch, Alex., 174.
Kuykendall, Abraham, 329.
Kuykendall, Mathew, 366.
Kuykendall, Tees, 366.
Kyar, Augustian, 267.
Kyhner, Ulrich, 25.
Kyle, Anthony, 264.
Kyle, Gabriel, 97.
Kyle, John, 304.
Kyle, William, 209, 215, 247, 249, 385.
Kyler, Sarah, 237.
Kyliner, Ulrich, 431.
Lacey, Patrick, 115, 116, 118, 250, 490.
Lacey, James, 204, 213, 217.
Lackey, Thomas, 18.
Ladd, Edward, 234.
Ladd, Priscilla, 115.
Ladlers, John, 183.
Ladyman, James, 436.
Laferty, Esther, 365.
Laferty, Thomas, 365.
Lafferty, Ralph, 248.
Laforce, Agnes, 345, 464.
Laforce, Rene, 345, 464.
Lair, Catherine, 149, 334.
Lair, Ferdinando, 149.
Lair, George, 149, 446.
Lair, Margaret, 149.
Lair, Mathias, 149, 169, 334.
Laird, Anne, 397.
Laird, David, 118, 140, 154, 172, 175, 242, 250, 254, 397, 397, 418.
Laird, James, 107, 146, 148.
Lamb Conrad, 87.
Lamb (Lamme), Elizabeth, 184, 504.
Lamb, John, 394, 405, 434.
Lamb, James, 269, 372, 393, 394.
Lamb, Margaret, 360.
Lamb, Peter, 398.
Lamb, Wm., 26, 360, 398, 400.
Lambert, Christy, 405.
Lambert, Jane, 177.
Lambert, John, 177, 197, 250, 253, 374.
Lambert, Mathias, 374.
Lame, Wm., 150.
Lamme, David, 393.
Lamme (Lamb), Robert, 366.
Lamme, Samuel, 393.
Lamon (Lamor), Jacob, 268.
Lamon (Lamor), Mary, 268.
Lance, Bernard, 246.
Lance, Barneth, 221.
Land, James, 438.
Land, Momus, 60.

Land, Thomas, 26.
Landcisco, Henry, 41, 58.
Landis, Christopher, 513.
Landless, Christian, 451.
Landrunn, Thomas, 31, 132, 133.
Lane, John, 23.
Lane, Joseph, 25.
Laney, John, 100.
Lang, David, 119.
Lang, George, 482.
Lang, Henry, 363.
Lang, James, 424.
Lang, Joseph, 363, 444.
Lang, Samuel, 363.
Langdon, Joseph, 57, 449, 496.
Langdon, Thomas, 57.
Lange, Charles, 361.
Langsby, James, 176, 209, 218.
Langsdale, Wm., 185.
Lankford, John, 87.
Lankford, Thomas, 87.
Lann, Thomas, 438.
Lansdale, Wm., 483.
Lapsley, James, 103, 132.
Lapsley, John, 122, 324.
Lapsley, Joseph, 15, 17, 18, 23, 49, 60, 116, 136, 525.
Lapsley, Wm., 95, 96, 324, 328.
Larkin, Henry, 108, 136, 148.
Larney, Andrew, 144.
Larry, Edward, 477, 478.
Lattimore, Mathew, 174, 232.
Laughlin, James, 138, 455, 461.
Laughlin, John, 461.
Laughten, Henry, 187.
Laverty, Jane, 347.
Laverty, Ralph, 26, 34, 120, 229, 296, 314, 322, 347, 369.
Law, Elizabeth, 185.
Law Emmanuel, 277
Law, Michael, 371
Law, Robert, 185.
Lawderdeal, Wm., 448.
Lawler, Mary, 295.
Lawler, Michael, 295.
Lawler, Momus, 61.
Lawless, Henry, 528.
Lawrence, Daniel, 103.
Lawrence, Henry, 82, 180, 208.
Lawrence, Jacob, 240.
Lawrence, James, 136, 142, 326, 458.
Laurence, Jasper, 180.
Lawrence, John, 26, 42, 103, 334.
Lawrence, Samuel, 142, 147, 458.
Lawrence ,Wm., 142, 326, 328.
Lawson, Hugh, 41.
Lawson, James, 102.
Lawson, John, 477.
Lawson, Mary, 149.
Lawson, Richard, 138.
Lawson, Thomas, 419.
Laywell, Abraham, 244, 252, 284, 417.

Laywell, Andrew, 252, 274, 284.
Laywell, Hannah, 274.
Laywell, Peter, 251, 252.
Laywell, Samuel, 252.
Lea, John, 363, 494.
Leaeve, John, 486.
Leahe, John, 129.
Leahe, Robert, 339.
Leahorn, Nicholas, 147.
Leake, Robert, 472.
Lear, Daniel, 424.
Leas, Jacob, 276, 283.
Leathe, Barbara, 53.
Leathe, Ephriam, 41, 44, 53, 59.
Leath, George, 25, 41.
Leath, John, 28.
Leatherdale, James, 140, 351, 473.
Ledderdale, James, 141.
Ledfords, The, 24.
Ledford, John, 105.
Ledgerwood, Rebecca, 390, 398.
Ledgerwood, Wm., 32, 57, 398, 390, **430, 443.**
Lee, Bridget, 94.
Lee, Henry, 426, 511, 512.
Lee, Wm., 430.
Leebow, John, 307.
Leech, Ephriam, 26.
Leekemp, Albert, 426.
Leekemp, Sophia, 426.
Leeper, Andrew, 86.
Leeper, Gawin, 141, 144.
Leeper, James, 47, 107, 121, 133.
Leeper, John, 182, 200.
Leeper, Joseph, 130.
Leeper, Margaret, 47, 107, 121, 133, **144.**
Leeper, Nicholas, 47.
Leeper, Susanah, 200.
Leeper, William, 69, 440.
Leese, Henry, 241.
Leescomb, Wm., 186.
Leeth, Ephriam, 438.
Lefler, Edward, 415.
Lefler, Hannah, 415.
Leftwich, Wm., 498.
Legate, Alex., 448.
Legan, Beverly, 266.
Lehdown, Ludwick, 182.
Lein, Solomon, 179.
Leister, James, 96, 98, 468, 477.
Lemley, John, 349.
Lemmon, Joseph, 193.
Lemon, George, 287.
Leo, Martin, 180.
Leonard, Adam, 536.
Leonard, Catherine, 536.
Leonard, Daniel, 536.
Leonard, David, 536.
Leonard, Elizabeth, 536.
Leonard, George, 536.
Leonard, Jacob, 536.
Leonard, John, 536.

Leonard, Margaret, 536.
Leonard, Samuel, 536.
Leonard, Susannah, 536.
Leopold, Wm., 62.
Lepport (Lippert), Wm. (Wilhelm), 454.
Lesley, Betsey, 413.
Lesley, James, 13, 30, 413.
Lessley, Agnes, 188.
Lessley, Betsy, 413.
Lessley, Elizabeth, 188.
Lessley, Hanna, 204.
Lessley, Jacob, 287.
Lessley, James, 140, 175, 185, 188, 217.
Lessley, Mary, 188, 204, 380.
Lessley, Polly, 413.
Lessley, Rachel, 188.
Lessley, Samuel, 422.
Lessley, Sarah, 188, 217, 270.
Letch, Thomas, 295.
Lettimore, Jane, 95.
Letsler, James, 329.
Levasey, Thomas, 143.
Levin, Nicholas, 484.
Levingston, Jacob, 397.
Levingston, Lidia, 397.
Levinstone, John Martin, 294.
Leviston, James, 253.
Leviston, John, 13.
Leviston, Robert, 13.
Leviston, Thomas, 13.
Levistone, Martin, 432.
Lewell, Andrew, 212, 229.
Lewell, Margaret, 212.
Lewell, Rebecca, 205.
Lewis, Alexander, 299.
Lewis, Andrew, 14, 18, 29, 38, 45, 46, 48, 50, 51, 54, 62, 65, 69, 87, 107, 108, 116, 119, 136, 139, 145, 154, 183, 253, 254, 299, 312, 333, 349, 414, 422, 430, 442, 443, 444, 451, 480, 488, 514, 517, 533.
Lewis, Anthony, 180.
Lewis, B., 342.
Lewis, Benjamin, 470.
Lewis, Charles, 105, 107, 121, 140, 156, 157, 158, 162, 166, 168, 210, 211, 327, 333, 339, 349, 486, 488.
Lewis, David, 68, 80.
Lewis, Fielding, 324, 455.
Lewis, George, 18, 30, 76, 114, 238, 306, 309, 311, 315, 329, 330, 332, 342, 394, 397.
Lewis, James, 79.
Lewis, Jane, 532.
Lewis, John, 13, 15, 16, 19, 33, 34, 37, 39, 44, 45, 47, 50, 95, 99, 166, 174, 176, 184, 189, 190, 196, 197, 202, 204, 210, 224, 233, 241, 247, 262, 293, 294, 296, 299, 307, 308, 309, 315, 323, 329, 335, 382, 383, 388, 410, 430, 444, 468, 469, 474, 479, 481, 484, 528, 532.
Lewis, Margaret, 16.

Lewis, Mary, 397.
Lewis, Mathias, 332.
Lewis, Peggy, 121.
Lewis, Samuel, 240, 385.
Lewis, Sarah, 333, 339.
Lewis, Thomas, 13, 19, 22, 46, 50, 78, 87, 95, 144, 162, 175, 179, 351, 442, 443, 444, 467, 468, 518, 533.
Lewis, Wm., 30, 65, 76, 218, 294, 395, 442, 518.
Lewis, Wm. T., 345.
Lewis, Zachariah, 361.
Lewis, Zachary, 322.
Lickings, Dorothy, 168.
Lickings, John, 168.
Lidderdale, James, 297, 315.
Liddle, Thomas, 96.
Liget, Alex., 449.
Liggetes, Alex., 454, 455.
Lightfoot, John, 305.
Likes (Lex), Malackia, 428.
Likes, Margaret, 428.
Lilley, John, 174, 218.
Linam, Andrew, 40.
Lincoln, Abraham, 193, 370, 372.
Lincoln, Isaac, 171.
Lincoln, John, 481.
Linday, John, 309.
Linden, James, 195.
Linden, Mary, 195, 209.
Linderbach, Jacob, 199.
Lindley, Hannah, 296.
Lindley, Thomas, 295, 296.
Lindon, Benjamin, 165.
Lindon, Fanny, 533.
Lindon, Joseph, 115, 165, 248, 533.
Lindon, Molly, 533.
Lindsay, Matthew, 116, 143, 144, 328, 464.
Lindsay, Samuel, 99, 152.
Lingle, Jacob, 74.
Lingle, John, 169.
Lingle, Peter, 172.
Lingle, Philip, 191.
Link, Jacob, 285.
Link, James, 227.
Link, Judy, 396.
Link, Mathias, 215.
Link, Peter, 396.
Linkorn, John, 380.
Linn, John, 307.
Lion, Joseph, 94.
Linsey, Mathew, 335.
Linville, Thomas, 18, 30, 293, 295.
Linwell, Thomas, 296, 298.
Linwell, William, 14, 17, 298.
Litell, James, 433.
Little, Andrew, 86, 95.
Little, Jacob, 389.
Little, John, 41, 114.
Little, Patrick, 50.
Littlepage, James, 94, 106, 320, 321, 325, 327.

McAuley, Spence, 390.
McBride, Benjamin, 42, 433.
McBride, Brine, 459.
McBride (McByrd), Francis, 40, 42, 49, 54, 323, 433, 491.
McBridge, James, 113, 332, 340.
McBridge, Joseph, 121, 128.
McBride, Mary, 116, 121.
McBride, Rosanna, 121.
McBride, Thomas, 128.
McBride, Wm., 40, 121, 128, 133, 136, 146, 191.
McCadden (McAdden, McFadden), Henry, 427.
McCafferty, William, 243, 384.
McCain, James, 140, 147.
McCaleb, Enos, 287.
McCall, James, 56, 62.
McCall, Samuel, 339, 472.
McCallock, Thomas, 145.
McCallom, Patrick, 84, 331, 453, 463.
McCallough, John, 501, 502.
McCames, Nancy, 279.
McCamey, Wm., 125, 173.
McCammis, David, 438.
McCampbell, James, 144.
McCandless, John, 139.
McCandless (McCanless), Wm., 15, 136, 305, 307, 433, 434, 525.
McCann, Agnes, 284.
McCann, Chrisman, 217.
McCann, James, 284.
McCapen, Elizabeth, 314.
McCapen, John, 314.
McCarkrey, Cormick, 117.
McCarty, John, 273, 449.
McCarty, Martha, 273.
McCartney, Andrew, 265.
McCaslin, Andrew, 212.
McCastle, John, 188.
McCatlin, John, 113, 392.
McCathrey, James, 105.
McCaul, Alex., 461.
McCaumus, James, 167.
McCaveis, David, 135.
McCawrins, David, 106.
McCawrins, Margaret, 106.
McChesney, George, 255, 256.
McChesney, James, 217, 255, 256, 386, 394, 395, 507.
McChesney, Jane, 383.
McChesney, Robert, 380, 383, 395.
McChesney, Samuel, 176, 386, 394, 429, 507.
McCimsy, Patrick, 446.
McCitrick, Robert, 105.
McClain, Alex., 373.
McClain, Francis, 178.
McClain, Wm., 441.
McClalen, Wm., 153.
McClallan, Joseph, 37.
McClanahan, John E., 427.

McClary, Alex., 28, 525.
McClary, John, 120.
McClean, Charles, 514.
McClean, Daniel, 536, 537.
McClean, Wm., 33.
McCleaster, Neal, 79.
McCleery (McClerey), James, 222, 390, 438, 444, 445.
McCleery (McClerey), John, 192, 215, 438, 444, 445.
McClelan, Abraham, 335.
McClelan, Alexander, 831.
McCleland, Jane, 293.
McCleland, Joseph, 293.
McClehill, James, 295.
McClelhill, Jane, 295.
McClelhill, Joseph, 20, 25, 34.
McClellan, Robert, 20, 56.
McClelland, Thomas, 292.
McClellon, Wm., 144.
McClemun, Alex., 123.
McClanachan, A. M., 393, 395.
McClenachan, Alexander, 98, 108, 109, 121, 156, 160, 162, 165, 169, 177, 183, 187, 188, 189, 196, 197, 202, 209, 210, 223, 238, 242, 258, 265, 266, 270, 277, 282, 327, 331, 346, 376, 380, 384, 394, 404, 451, 454, 473, 475, 481, 491, 492, 508, 518.
McClenachan, Ann, 182.
McClenachan, Elijah, 88, 117, 160, 169, 172, 177, 183, 188, 189, 192, 196, 197, 199, 202, 203, 207, 217, 219, 223, 226, 240, 246, 251, 255, 463, 481.
McClenachan, John, 72, 108, 119, 125, 134, 150, 153, 157, 158, 160, 163, 165, 166, 169, 177, 182, 183, 185, 187, 198, 209, 210, 287, 499, 537.
McClenachan, Letticia, 414.
McClenachan, Lettitia W., 287.
McClenachan, Margaret, 414.
McClenachan, Margaret A., 185.
McClenachan, Reuben, 226.
McClenachan, Robert, 20, 24, 25, 31, 32, 33, 45, 46, 47, 48, 50, 51, 54, 58, 63, 69, 70, 72, 78, 79, 82, 85, 100, 102, 111, 117, 126, 175, 182, 187, 210, 258, 261, 283, 285, 287, 288, 294, 301, 313, 314, 321, 328, 349, 428, 430, 431, 432, 439, 442, 443, 486, 491, 497, 500.
McClenachan, Sarah, (?)
McClenachan, Wm., 120, 141, 154, 181, 182, 195, 200, 365, 369, 513.
McClenen, Joseph, 302.
McClenon (McClenan), Robert, 57, 443, 444.
McClenery, Samuel, 49.
McClewrath, John, 26.
McClewer (McClure), David, 48.
McCleve, Hugh, 67.
McClintin, John, 28.
McClintock, John, 206, 275.

McClintock, Martha, 267.
McClintock, Robert, 183.
McClintock, Samuel, 253, 254, 403.
McClintock (McClintog), William, 20, 56, 57, 206, 240, 267, 353, 381, 443, 444, 455, 456.
McClones, Nathaniel, 499.
McCloskey, David, 249.
McCloskey, Patrick, 444.
McClune, Mary, 89.
McClune, Nathaniel, 89.
McClung, James, 27, 136, 341.
McClung, Jennet, 69.
McClung, John, 69, 144, 248.
McClung, Joseph, 142.
McClung, Mary, 27.
McClung, Thomas, 394.
McClung, Wm., 230, 514.
McClure, Agnes, 27.
McClure, Andrew, 173, 293, 295, 307, 427, 537.
McClure, Arthur, 152, 348.
McClure, Eleanor, 289, 427, 537.
McClure, Elizabeth, 401, 427, 531, 537.
McClure, Halbert (Herbert), 29, 36, 136, 140, 145, 146, 348, 364, 376, 498.
McClure, Hugh, 234, 371.
McClure, James, 91, 127, 145, 234, 236, 293, 364, 366, 427, 537.
McClure, John, 54, 91, 115, 120, 136, 139, 140, 141, 143, 234, 313, 365, 396, 415, 427, 433, 537.
McClure, Jonah (Josiah), 537.
McClure, Josiah, 427.
McClure, Margaret, 145, 146, 376, 427, 537.
McClure, Mary, 128, 143, 330, 364, 376.
McClure, Michael, 377.
McClure, Moses, 15, 27, 145, 146, 300.
McClure, Nathan, 16, 28, 83, 312.
McClure, Nathaniel, 128, 140, 145, 348, 364.
McClure, Phinley, 421.
McClure, Samuel, 60, 61, 90, 128, 146, 147, 178, 323, 330, 427, 449, 499, 537.
McClure, Thomas, 140.
McClure, Wm., 91, 137.
McCochran, James, 66.
McCollan, Patrick, Patrick, 333.
McColley, John, 62.
McCollom, John, 116.
McComb, Andrew, 254, 437, 442.
McComb, Jane, 254.
McCommus, Jane, 258.
McCommey, John, 220.
McConkey, Samuel, 240.
McConnell, Elizabeth, 310.
McConnell, Wm., 437.
McCoole, Andrew, 297.
McCord, Andrew, 14, 16, 43, 45, 48, 296, 452.
McCord, James, 45, 48, 322.

McCord, Samuel, 113.
McCorkle, Alex., 61, 62.
McCorkle, Benjamin, 273.
McCorkle (McCorkell), James, 20, 49, 53, 57, 356, 443.
McCorkle, Mary, 273.
McCorkle, Pat (Patrick), 61, 163.
McCorkle, Robert, 53.
McCorkle, William, 280.
McCormick, Adam, 96.
McCormick, Daniel, 330, 340, 475.
McCormick, David, 61.
McCormick, Joshua, 61, 139, 330, 344, 462, 489.
McCormick, Martha, 131, 139.
McCormick, Maxwell, 66.
McCormick, William, 257.
McCoskry, John, 520.
McCoumas, David, 103.
McCown, Agnes, 155.
McCown, Catherine, 155.
McCown, Francis, 15, 18, 38, 45, 48, 93, 155, 172, 322, 433, 434.
McCown (McCowen), George, 135, 161, 172.
McCown, James, 30, 104, 107, 144, 323.
McCown (McCowen), John, 25, 26, 28, 139, 155, 225, 345, 433.
McCown, Jane, 124.
McCown, Malcolmn, 139, 163, 351, 461.
McCown, Margaret, 18, 93, 107.
McCown, Moses, 73, 124.
McCowing, Francis, 298.
McCoy, Alex., 206, 373, 391.
McCoy, Daniel, 68, 114, 119, 467.
McCoy, David, 400.
McCoy, Duncan, 68.
McCoy, James, 431, 438.
McCoy, Jane, 400.
McCoy, John, 110, 184, 186, 194, 202, 216. 391.
McCoy, Mary, 168.
McCoy, Robert, 59, 298, 312.
McCoy, Sally, 363.
McCoy, Wm., 391.
McCoy, Zachary, 299.
McCrachy, James, 155.
McCreary, James, 141, 144.
McCreary, John, 54, 123.
McCreery, Robert, 193, 202, 218.
McCreery, Elizabeth, 371.
McCreery, John, 141, 153, 156, 191, 196, 197, 199, 202, 208, 216, 220, 221, 225, 226, 229, 239, 247, 299, 371, 433, 481, 531.
McCreery, Wm., 220, 221.
McCroorey, James, 154.
McCroskie, Alex., 28.
McCroskie, Elizabeth, 27.
McCue, Franklin, 427.
McCue, Jane, 53, 427.
McCuley, John, 61.

McCullough, James, 267.
McCullough, John, 183, 326.
McCulloch, Mary, 35.
McCullough, Robert, 248, 252, 253, 267, 271, 418.
McCulloch (McCullough), Thomas, 15, 18, 22, 33, 107, 150, 261, 299, 396, 411, 430.
McCullow, Patrick, 48.
McCummins, David, 44.
McCune, Ann, 387.
McCune, Elizabeth, 413.
McCune, Francis, 21.
McCune, James, 14, 18, 20, 21, 104, 249.
McCune, John, 18, 20, 202, 413.
McCune, Samuel, 36, 88, 214, 242, 387, 442.
McCune, Wm., 184, 378, 382.
McCurdy, Archibald, 156.
McCurry, John, 66.
McCurry, Wm., 70.
McCutchin (McCutcheon, McCutchen, McCuchan), James, 438, 444, 474.
McCutchen, Jane, 253.
McCutcheon, John, 171, 176, 199, 236, 249, 250, 252, 253, 254, 272, 276, 278, 285, 323, 396, 404, 438, 444, 520.
McCutcheon, Robert, 30, 36, 50, 343, 435, 480.
McCutcheon, Samuel, 120, 156, 179, 193, 194, 202, 213, 217, 224, 323, 326, 411, 438, 444, 454, 520, 525, 526, 537.
McCutcheon, Wm., 120, 131, 132, 142, 145, 147, 158, 244, 245, 253, 373, 384, 396, 408, 409, 411, 438, 462, 474, 520.
McDaniel, Bryan, 112.
McDaniel, Edward, 60, 69.
McDaniel, Mary, 330.
McDaniel, Randal, 187, 304, 470.
McDaniel, Wm., 62.
McDaniels, John, 354.
Macdannel, Renell, 491.
McDavid, Patrick, 206, 209.
McDavitt, Wm., 269.
McDonagh, Diana, 242.
McDonagh, Edward, 242.
McDonagh, John, 242, 258, 261.
McDonald, Alex., 103, 176, 329, 331, 447, 454, 455, 487.
McDonald, Bryon (Bryan), 138, 392.
McDonald, Charles, 514.
McDonald, Edward, 61, 351, 439, 473.
McDonald, Elizabeth, 62, 105.
McDonald, Henry, 166.
McDonald, Isaac, 98, 105, 330.
McDonald, James, 61, 65, 167, 453.
McDonald, Jennet (Janet), 77, 111, 337, 341, 356.
McDonald, John, 90, 164, 330, 409.
McDonald, Joseph, 61, 105.
McDonald, Mary, 323, 351, 431, 473.
McDonald, Patrick, 34, 36, 323, 431.

McDonald, Randolph, 356.
McDonald, Samuel, 166.
McDonall, Elizabeth, 113.
McDonall, Francis, 113.
McDonnall, Hugh, 48, 113.
McDonnall, James, 42.
McDonall, Jane, 34, 37.
McDonall, John, 113.
McDonall, Mary, 113.
McDonall, Rebecca, 113.
McDonall (McDonald), Randolph, 34, 37, 77, 111.
McDonall, Samuel, 113.
McDonall, William, 113.
McDonell, Randolph, 341.
McDonnald, Randal, 295.
McDonnell, Bryan, 299.
McDonnell, Mary, 325.
McDonough, Edward H., 230.
McDonough, John, 189, 195, 206.
McDougal, John, 200, 395.
McDovel, Hugh, 439.
McDowell, Elizabeth, 165.
McDowell, Ephriam, 16, 409, 441.
McDowell, Frances, 116.
McDowell, Hugh, 248, 257, 277, 283, 509, 534.
McDowell, James, 68, 71, 84, 102, 108, 116, 122, 130, 139, 143, 144, 145, 160, 165, 178, 298, 302, 318, 359, 435, 449, 474.
McDowell, Jean, 293.
McDowell, John, 15, 38, 293, 285, 293, 295, 303, 305, 307, 333, 387, 534.
McDowell, Magdalene, 259, 303, 305.
McDowell, Margaret, 304, 470.
McDowell, Mary, 125, 304, 470.
McDowell, Randall, 293.
McDowell, Robert, 248, 257, 284, 291, 415, 534.
McDowell, Samuel, 68, 84, 85, 90, 107, 108, 125, 143, 145, 152, 160, 165, 166, 169, 171, 177, 178, 183, 188, 190, 196, 198, 305, 335, 355, 450, 451, 455, 501, 506, 507.
McDowell, Sarah, 198, 277, 291.
McDowell, Thomas, 462.
McDowell, Wm., 194, 196, 227, 234, 235, 248, 509.
McElhaney, James, 498.
McElhenny, James, 138, 331, 340.
McElhenny, John, 137.
McElhenny, Wm., 125, 170, 172.
McElhiney, James, 461.
McElroy, Alex., 323.
McElvane, Moses, 335.
McElvenay, Samuel, 315.
McElwain, Moses, 153.
McElwrath, John, 135, 151.
McElwrath, Robert, 151.
McEvoy, Hugh, 219.
McEwen, John, 483.

McFadden, Edward, 290.
McFarland (McFarlin, McFarling), Alex., 185, 254, 256, 265, 268, 276, 279, 386.
McFarland, Daniel, 185.
McFarland (McFarlend), Duncan, 58, 153, 444.
McFarland, Eleanor, 185.
McFarland, Isabella, 185.
McFarland, James, 185.
McFarland (McFarlin), John, 40, 55, 185, 432, 434.
McFarland, Joseph, 433.
McFarland, Mary, 185.
McFarland, Wm., 58, 179, 285.
McFarlin (McFarland), Robert, 54, 55, 439, 507.
McFarron, Agnes, 89.
McFarron, James, 89, 91.
McFarron, Thomas, 125, 153, 455.
McFawle, John, 150, 456.
McFeeters, Randolph, 426.
McFerrin, Samuel, 344.
McGa, Samuel, 431.
McGachlin (McLaughlin), James, 509.
McGarry, Edward, 68, 89, 91, 92.
McGarry, John, 313.
McGarry, Robert, 91, 92, 97.
McGarrock, Hugh, 52.
McGarvin, Polly, 415.
McGarvin, Wm., 415.
McGavock, James. 158, 434.
McGaw, James, 15.
McGaw, John, 66.
McGaw, Samuel, 14, 16, 30, 31.
McGee, David, 144, 148, 354, 460.
McGee, James, 442.
McGee, John, 516.
McGhe (McGee), Malcom, 516.
McGee, Philip, 329.
McGee, Richard, 348.
McGee, Robt., 105, 121, 332, 340, 459.
McGee, Wm., 83, 157, 323, 329, 355, 437, 457.
McGeery (McGarry), Edward, 321, 343.
McGill, Edward, 293.
McGill, James, 101, 121, 141, 145, 365, 520.
McGill, John, 44, 119.
McGill, Margaret, 39, 45.
McGill, Wm., 24, 39, 44, 45, 102.
McGinas, Rebecca, 64.
McGinas, Sarah, 64.
McGinness, Edward, 60.
McGinnis, Catherine, 57, 73.
McGinnis, Francis, 124.
McGlammery, Isabella, 427, 535.
McGlammery, John, 275.
McGlauchlin, Jane, 170.
McGlauchlin, Wm., 170.
McGlaughlin, Edward, 203.
McGlaughlin (McGlauchlin), Hugh, 166, 167, 170.

McGlaughlin, James, 167, 477.
McGomerie, James, 15.
McGongal, James, 509.
McGonegal, James, 223, 235, 379, 397.
McGonegal, Margaret, 232, 397.
McGonagle (McGonigle), Newman, 68, 442.
McGowen, John, 444.
McGowen, William, 274, 400.
McGown, John, 63, 66.
McGraw, Barnabas, 246.
McGraw, Charles, 196.
McGraw, James, 211.
McGraw, Mary, 246.
McGraw, Sarah, 196.
McGrawger, James, 119.
McGray, Agnes, 203.
McGregor, Thomas, 109, 210, 244.
McGinnes, Daniel, 250.
McGinney, John, 50.
McGuire, Francis, 177.
McGuire, John, 71.
McGuire, Samuel, 418.
McGuire, Terrence, 85.
McIntire, Daniel, 478, 479.
McIntosh, George, 406.
McIntosh, George G., 283, 406.
McKain, James, 137, 138, 141.
McKamy, John, 93.
McKannie, Francis, 360.
McKarney, John, 120.
McKarney, Wm., 120.
McKay, Alex., 26.
McKay, Andrew, 35.
McKay, Jas., 26, 42, 44, 46, 53, 436, 438.
McKay, Margaret, 19.
McKay, Moses, 26, 53.
McKay, Robert, 19, 53, 436, 482.
McKay, Zachariah, 436.
McKay (McCay), Zachery, 26, 44, 53, 58.
McKeachy, James, 94, 378.
McKee, Alex., 380.
McKee, Charles, 248.
McKee, James, 65, 83, 144, 462.
McKee, John, 65, 144, 249, 429, 516.
McKee, Martha, 423.
McKee, Samuel, 135, 137, 423.
McKee, Wm., 108, 142, 145, 150, 378.
McKem, John, 101.
McKemy, James, 57.
McKemy, John, 229, 230, 240, 252, 481.
McKemy, Wm., 237.
McKendrick, Patrick, 65, 66, 71.
McKendrick, Sarah, 66.
McKeney, William, 355.
McKenless, Wm., 305.
McKenny, Alex., 63, 82, 150.
McKenny, Eleanor, 270, 288.
McKenny, Isabella, 414.
McKenny, James, 270, 273, 287, 390.
McKenney, John, 20, 21, 187, 194, 198, 241, 268, 270, 287, 427.

McKenny, Margaret, 288.
McKenny, Wm., 270, 414, 427.
McKensey, Alex., 189.
McKibbon, John, 210, 261.
McKiney, Alex., 444.
McKings, Christmass, 211.
McKinlay, Alex., 311.
McKinlay, Wm., 311.
McKinney, James, 358.
McKinny, Jane, 408.
McKinny (McKinney), John, 220, 243, 254, 264, 274, 276, 408, 444, 512.
McKittrick, Jane, 326.
McKittrick, John, 221, 225, 229.
McKittrick (McKettrick), Robert, 71, 171, 173, 186, 326, 377, 441, 545.
McKnight, Andrew, 238.
McKnight, James, 528.
McKnight, John, 124.
McKnight, Mary, 196, 480.
McKnight, Rachel, 480.
McKnight, Wm., 119.
McKown, John, 304.
McKoskry, Alex., 450, 451.
McKoskry, David, 450, 451.
McKoy, James, 322.
McLain, John, 211.
McLamor, Thomas, 113.
McLamore, Timothy, 247.
McLaughlin, James, 509.
McLaughlin, John, 250.
McLaughlin, Margaret, 382.
McLean, Charles, 514.
McLean, Daniel, 315.
McLean, Wm., 524.
McMahon, Abraham, 192, 193.
McMahon, Elizabeth, 192.
McMahon, John, 81, 94, 100, 148, 182, 199, 201, 210, 213, 235, 237, 324, 377, 381.
McMahon, Joan, 35.
McMahon, Julian, 94.
McMahon, Margaret, 160.
McMahon, Robert, 20, 25, 36, 63, 81, 94, 150, 154, 157, 235, 296, 320, 324, 381, 428, 489, 490.
McMahon, Samuel, 63.
McMahon, Thomas, 428.
McMahon, Wm., 193.
McMary, Samuel, 528.
McMasters, John, 21, 296.
MacMichel, John, 440.
McMollen, Wm., 108.
McMorry, Samuel, 315.
McMordie, Robert, 63.
McMullin, Edward, 162.
McMullen, John, 415.
McMullen, Mary, 415.
McMullen, Torance, 26.
McMullin, Archibald, 34.
McMullin, Edward, 130.
McMullin, John, 130.

McMullin, Turence, 299.
McMullin, Thomas, 528.
McMullin, Wm., 344.
McMurdie, James, 69.
McMurdo, Robert, 311.
McMurray, Samuel, 343.
McMurry, Alexander, 56.
McMurry, John, 56.
McMurry, Wm., 48, 79, 130, 441.
McMurty, Alex., 84.
McMurty, Joseph, 138, 142.
McMurty, Samuel, 84, 116.
McMurtrey, Joseph, 463.
McNabb, Andrew, 16, 27.
McNabb, Baptist, 25, 145.
McNabb, Catherine, 27.
McNabb, James, 145, 372, 375.
McNabb, Martha B., 372.
McNabb, Samuel, 330, 344, 372, 375, 429.
McNabb, Wm., 53, 57, 120, 167, 365, 372, 443.
McNaire, Daniel, 127, 158, 266.
McNamara, Hugh, 79.
McNamara, Timothy, 235, 254, 257, 266.
McNaught, Tiddy, 374.
McNaught, Wm., 126.
McNeal, James, 26, 41, 44, 58.
McNeal, John, 271.
McNeal, Neal, 61, 91, 181, 445.
McNeal, Thomas, 271, 438.
McNeeley, David, 374.
McNeill, Daniel, 141, 464.
McNeill, John(114, 115, 119.
McNeil, Wm., 490.
McNeiley, Hannah, 167.
McNeese, John, 433.
McNight, Robert, 106.
McNulty, John, 79, 92.
McNutt, Agnes, 164.
McNut, Alex., 69, 261, 265, 396, 440.
McNutt, Francis, 164.
McNutt, George, 206.
McNutt, Isabella, 164.
McNutt, James, 164, 181, 236, 290, 411, 440.
McNutt, John, 151, 164, 396.
McNutt, Robert, 440.
McNutt, Samuel, 411.
McPeeters, Wm., 535.
McPharron (McFarron), John, 15, 17, 30, 91, 302.
McPheeters)McFeeters), Alex., 48, 57, 141, 443.
McPheeters, James, 509.
McPheeters, Janes, 519.
McPheeters (McFeeters), John, 80, 120, 445.
McPheeters, Margaret, 200.
McPheeters, Mary, 429.
McPheeters, Rebecca, 519.
McPheeters, Samuel, 140, 170, 200, 426.

McPheeters (McFeeters), Wm., 15, 20, 32, 56, 57, 68, 75, 80, 138, 148, 155, 191, 196, 197, 202, 210, 212, 216, 219, 220, 223, 226, 229, 240, 243, 252, 256, 320, 407, 429, 443, 444, 481.
McRoberts, John, 188, 344, 398.
McRoberts, Samuel, 138, 146, 152.
McSlenan, John, 444.
McSpadden, Archibald, 173.
McSwine, George, 44, 62.
McVea, John, 475.
McVey, James, 167.
McVicker, John, 477.
McWiller (McWillen), Alex., 151.
McWilliams, Hugh, 447.
McWilliams, S., 503.
McWilliams, Samuel, 481.
Maccrow, James, 323.
Mace, Henry, 172, 287, 357, 393, 394.
Mace, Nicholas, 357.
Macee, James, 434.
Mack, Jacob, 193.
Mack, Margaret, 193.
Mack, Randolph, 16.
Mack, William, 304.
Mackall, John, 387.
Mackan, Wm., 442.
Mackay, Zachariah, 438.
Mackel, Robert, 496.
Mackey, John, 172.
Macom (Macomb, Maycomb), John, 24, 29, 33.
Madison, Agatha, 90, 239, 372, 414.
Madison, Agatha, S., 414.
Madeson, Andrew, 414.
Madison, Catherine, 160.
Madison, Elizabeth, 414.
Madison, Gabriel, 414.
Madison, George, 117, 414.
Madison, Humphrey, 55, 70, 160.
Madison, J., 446.
Madison, James, 331, 414, 517.
Madison, John, 13, 20, 49, 51, 76, 79, 90, 104, 108, 130, 136, 146, 160, 188, 202, 233, 265, 321, 330, 366, 367, 414, 439, 477, 513, 517, 519, 528.
Madison, Joseph, 513.
Madeson, Lewis, 414.
Madison, Lucy, 414.
Madison, Priscilla, 241, 414.
Madison, Richard, 187, 188, 189, 193, 198, 199, 202, 203, 204, 209, 219, 220, 229, 233, 234, 235, 238, 239, 241, 393, 414.
Madison, Richardson, 205.
Madison Roisland, 414.
Madison, Sarah, 513.
Madison, Susanna, 414.
Madison, Susanna S., 414.
Madison, T., 508.
Madison, Thomas, 128, 130, 133, 370, 414.
Madison, Wm., 234, 414, 513.
Madison, Wm. S., 160, 164.

Magill, Archibald, 267.
Magill, Charles, 244.
Magill, James, 171, 172, 191, 313, 340.
Magill, John, 154, 437.
Magill, Wm., 14, 172, 437.
Magert, Catherine, 185.
Magert, David, 162.
Magert, Wm., 185.
Maggit, Daniel, 304.
Maggit, John, 304.
Magomery, Wm., 496.
Magot (Magard, Maggot), Hance, 50, 69, 155, 351, 437.
Maggot, John, 28.
Maggott, Samuel, 135, 144.
Mahon, Francis, 260.
Mahon, John, 260.
Mahanee, Julian, 75.
Mahoney, Julian, 88.
Malcom, George, 91, 135.
Malcome, John, 64, 92, 165.
Malcolmn, Joseph, 140, 176, 385, 395.
Malcome, Mark, 92.
Malcolm, Samuel, 203.
Malcolm, Sarah, 91.
Maleer, Valentine, 169.
Mallan, Michael, 324.
Maler, Jacob, 434.
Maloney, Dennis, 274.
Mahoney, John, 288.
Mallard, Michael, 87.
Mallory, Roger, 18.
Mallory, Wm., 403.
Mallow, Adam, 170.
Mallow, Barbara, 191.
Mallow, George, 249.
Mallow, Mary, 170.
Mallow, Michael, 97, 98, 169, 170, 191.
Mamsley, William, 244.
Mann, Damis, 116.
Mann, Jacob, 434.
Mann, John, 44, 46, 116, 145, 331, 433.
Man, Nathan, 250.
Mann, Thomas, 44, 108, 338, 452, 464.
Mann, Wm., 89, 103, 120, 153, 175, 201, 206, 338, 352, 467, 528.
Mansening, Henry, 185.
Mantle, Stophel, 271.
March, Michael, 71, 74.
Marden, Moses, 97, 457.
Mark, Wm., 299.
Marke, John, 50.
Markle, Charles, 248, 250.
Marlen, Rosanna, 128.
Marlin, Jacob, 301, 390.
Marlin, Thomas, 221.
Marling, Richard, 491.
Marlow, Charles, 109.
Marmeon, Thomas, 167.
Marr, Gideon, 13.
Marron (Morrow), Margaret, 461.
Marshall, Ann, 146.

Marshall, George, 526, 534.
Marshall, Gilbert, 446.
Marshall, I., 388.
Marshall, James M., 513.
Marshall, John, 378, 447.
Marshall, Thomas, 536.
Marshall, Wm., 182, 486.
Martin (Martain), Abraham, 281, 430.
Martin, Alex., 234, 243, 244, 252, 257.
Martin, Andrew, 452.
Martain, Betsy, 532.
Martin, Charles, 514.
Martin, David, 123, 173, 186, 237, 346.
Martin, Edmond, 470, 471.
Martin, Elizabeth, 394.
Martin, George, 93, 273.
Martin, Hugh, 14, 53, 127, 436.
Martin, James, 320, 321, 324, 519, 525.
Martin, Jane A., 237.
Martins, John, 456, 477, 486.
Martin, Joseph, 68, 161, 445, 452, 464.
Martin, Margaret, 161.
Martin, Patrick, 15, 20, 46, 53, 56, 57, 73,
    77, 79, 107, 123, 139, 151, 152, 161, 323,
    433, 443, 444, 452, 454, 469, 518, 519.
Martin, Peter, 428.
Martin Phebe, 285.
Martin, Samuel, 486.
Martin, Thomas, 528.
Martin, Wm., 56, 57, 103, 127, 180, 285,
    321, 322, 443, 518.
Mase, Nicholas, 102, 182.
Masey, John, 197.
Masha, Abraham, 57, 443, 444.
Massie, Charles, 120.
Mason, James, 378.
Mason, John, 24, 94, 101.
Masters, Margaret, 190.
Masterson, Peter, 266.
Mate, Peter, 491.
Mateer, Elizabeth, 284.
Mateer, James, 120.
Mateer, Wm., 175, 185, 201.
Mathards, Hugh, 301.
Mathers (Mather), Wm., 110, 317.
Mathews, Alexander, 25.
Mathews, Andrew, 206.
Matthews, Ann, 357.
Mathews, Archer, 119, 143, 162, 164.
Mathews, Archibald, 352.
Mathews, Catherine, 385, 394, 399.
Mathews, Charles, 417.
Mathews, Edward, 357.
Mathews, Elizabeth, 140, 357.
Mathews, Fanney, 473.
Mathews, G., 372.
Mathews, George, 94, 111, 112, 115, 127,
    140, 149, 157, 158, 159, 160, 162, 169,
    175, 177, 183, 184, 196, 197, 209, 357,
    359, 365, 367, 389, 395, 410, 417, 423,
    426, 513.

Mathews, Grace, 417.
Matthews, Hiram, 53.
Mathews, James, 395.
Mathews, James W., 480.
Matthews, Jane, 357.
Mathews, Jean, 417.
Mathews, John, 15, 17, 46, 48, 50, 56, 61,
    62, 69, 78, 88, 111, 112, 125, 139, 155,
    304, 357, 409, 434, 439, 494, 525.
Mathews, Joseph, 218, 269, 274, 389, 395.
Matthews, Joshua, 77, 111, 113, 140, 149,
    168, 322, 357, 434.
Matthews, Lettice, 357.
Mathews, Margaret, 395, 410, 417.
Mathews, Martha, 149, 155, 168, 357.
Mathews, Mary, 111, 209, 395.
Mathews, Peggy, 417.
Mathews, Richard, 61, 62, 202, 240, 389,
    393, 395, 396, 403, 406, 422, 481.
Mathews, S., 372.
Mathews, Sampson, 61, 62, 86, 94, 96, 112,
    121, 122, 139, 140, 154, 164, 168, 169,
    173, 175, 177, 179, 183, 184, 188, 190,
    192, 196, 197, 202, 209, 211, 217, 219,
    232, 233, 237, 240, 253, 283, 324, 357,
    359, 364, 367, 381, 385, 391, 394, 395,
    399, 410, 418, 419, 447, 481, 504, 505,
    506, 510, 518, 527.
Mathews, Samuel, 320.
Mathews, Thomas, 171, 176, 366.
Mathews, Wm., 139, 159, 473, 531.
Mathewson, Alex., 75.
Mathewsoi, Mathew, 250.
Matlock, George, 533.
Maunce, Theodore, 451.
Maupin, Daniel, 100.
Maury, Fountain, 534.
Maury, John, 107, 159.
Mausume, Daniel, 99.
Maxwell, Alex., 134, 204, 206.
Maxwell, Grizzy, 423.
Maxwell, James, 423.
Maxwell, John, 20, 42, 53, 60, 62, 86, 107,
    114, 124, 125, 157, 158, 172, 181, 295,
    304, 317, 435, 446, 470.
Maxwell, Mary, 42, 124.
Maxwell, Robert, 135.
May, Caleb, 145.
May, Jesse, 112, 451.
May, John, 160.
May, Joseph, 178.
May, Stephen, 385.
May, Thomas, 444.
Mayer, Jacob, 174.
Maies (Mayes, Maze), James, 28, 40,
    44, 55, 75, 161, 314, 329, 454.
Mayes (Maze), Joseph, 66, 87, 230, 253,
    254, 261, 264, 271, 275, 279, 283, 308,
    511.
Mayes, Richard, 156.
Mayes, Robert, 273.
Mayfis, John, 23, 294.

Maynard, Joseph, 95, 358.
Mayo, Philip, 460.
Mayze, Isaac, 483.
Maze, Henry, 182, 429, 489.
Maze, Wm., 136.
Mazer, Joseph, Sr., 265.
Mazer, George, 324.
Mead, John, 286.
Mead, Wm., 121.
Means, Hugh, 60, 61, 320, 359.
Means, James, 100.
Means, Jennet, 69.
Means, Robert, 69.
Means, Wm., 133.
Meecans, Chrismass, 203.
Meechant, Stephen, 236.
Meek, Agnes, 275, 277.
Meek, Daniel, 277.
Meek, Elizabeth, 146.
Meek, James, 95, 364.
Meek, Jane, 95, 161.
Meek, John, 91, 161, 328, 368, 435.
Meek, Martha, 95.
Meek, Mary, 95, 368.
Meek, Samuel, 416.
Meek, Thomas, 91, 275, 343, 368, 435.
Meek, Wm., 91, 95, 368.
Meeks, James, 359.
Meeks, John, 215.
Meeks, Wm., 139.
Meeley, John, 73.
Meems, Hugh, 407.
Meems, Nancy, 407.
Megill, John, 491.
Meigham, Theobald, 92.
Meissner, Jacob, 287.
Melkem, John, 433.
Melly, John, 114, 158.
Memory, Agnes, 315.
Memory, Wm., 315, 439.
Meneers, John, 294.
Mercer, James, 458.
Mere (Mese), James, 479.
Meredith, John, 189.
Merriot, Obadiah, 14.
Merritt, Catherine, 385.
Merrit, Samuel, 385, 391, 417, 509.
Merriweather, Francis, 482.
Merry, Thomas, 73.
Metcalf, John, 498.
Metter, Thomas, 201.
Michael, John, 285.
Michael, Nicholas, 190.
Mickle, Peter, 181.
Middleton, John, 206.
Mihills, Richard, 75.
Milben (Millen), Alex), 455.
Milburn, Wm., 434.
Mildeborger, Nicholas, 109.
Milehan, Joseph, 528.
Miles, Abraham, 346, 363.
Miles, Ann, 213.

Miles Elizabeth, 346, 363.
Miles, George, 290.
Miles, James, 58, 62, 443.
Milican, Patrick, 440.
Millard, Charles, 446.
Millor, Abraham, 245, 249, 296, 443, 523.
Miller, Adam, 14, 17, 18, 24, 28, 29 ,50, 68, 279, 437.
Miller, Alex., 137, 139, 143, 163, 194, 311, 346, 363, 380, 504, 506, 507.
Miller, Andrew, 128, 146,, 330.
Miller Ann, 54, 523.
Miller, Barbara (Barbary), 29, 496, 523.
Miller, Catherine, 150, 523.
Miller, Christian, 296, 523.
Miller, Daniel, 208, 154, 266.
Miller, David, 28, 61, 63, 105, 150, 308, 427, 445, 533.
Miller, Dorothy, 523.
Miller, Elizabeth, 208, 249, 406.
Miller, Francis, 187.
Miller, George, 400.
Miller, Hannah, 27, 97, 427, 537.
Miller, Henry, 216, 220, 393, 397, 416, 426, 427, 430, 537.
Miller, Hugh, 136, 391.
Miller, Isaac, 523.
Miller, J., 333.
Miller, Jacob, 50, 64, 147, 150, 171, 291, 299, 303, 312, 325, 418, 429, 432, 437, 489, 496, 523.
Miller, James, 21, 40, 51, 53, 62, 223, 315, 346, 434, 442,, 443, 466, 528, 533.
Miller, John, 21, 34, 40, 44, 50, 54, 67, 92, 97, 106, 120, 128, 129, 133, 187, 251, 290, 299, 343, 380, 427, 434, 437, 438, 441, 446, 452, 474, 507, 520.
Miller, John G., 400.
Miller, John M., 33.
Miller, John W., 400.
Miller, Joseph, 523.
Miller, Judith, 275, 406.
Miller, Lawrence, 347.
Miller, Margaret, 132.
Miller, Mark, 75.
Miller, Martha, 106.
Miller, Mary, 92, 254.
Miller, Mathew, 523.
Miller, Mathias, 446.
Miller, Nancy, 427, 537.
Miller, Opopheone, 75.
Miller, Patrick, 136, 212, 251.
Miller, Peter, 216, 406.
Miller, Rachel, 523.
Miller, Robert, 40, 132, 330, 434.
Miller, Samuel, 286, 416.
Miller, Sarah, 523.
Miller, Susanna, 523.
Miller, Thomas, 192, 360, 431, 449.
Miller, Williams, 19, 25, 40, 61, 63, 175, 299, 302, 308, 414, 422, 434, 464.
Milligan, Martha, 33.

Millicon, Charles, 61.
Milligan, James, 100.
Milligan, Joseph, 33.
Milliken, Charles, 298, 299, 300.
Milliken, Hugh, 117.
Milliken, James, 498.
Milliron, Christian, 441.
Milliron, Christian G., 111.
Millroy, Alexander, 95.
Mills, Agnes, 62, 65.
Mills, Abram N., 480.
Mills, Elizabeth, 65.
Mills, Hugh, 102.
Mills, James, 20, 21, 98.
Mills, John, 15, 46, 47, 49, 62, 141, 150, 298, 351, 397, 423, 445.
Mills Lawrence, 112.
Mills, Nicholas, 64.
Mills, Richard, 316.
Mills, Robert, 245, 397.
Mills, William, 20, 49, 173, 314.
Milsap, Elianor, 92.
Milton, John, 327, 336.
Mindo, John, 407.
Mines, Thomas, 217, 373, 393, 416, 535.
Minger, Henry, 521.
Mingus, Daniel, 477.
Minnis, Robert, 151, 180, 184, 511.
Minter, Jesse, 425.
Minter, Wm., 105, 426.
Mire, Abraham, 523.
Mire, Anna, 523.
Mire, Barbary, 523.
Mire, Calkins, 523.
Mire, Catherine, 523.
Mire, Christopher, 523.
Mire, Dorothy, 523.
Mire, George, 523.
Mire, Isaac, 523.
Mire (Mires), Jacob. 61, 353, 523.
Mire, John, 523.
Mire, Joseph, 523.
Mire, Peter, 523.
Mire, Rachel, 523.
Mire, Ragley, 523.
Mire, Sarah, 523.
Mires, Susan, 24.
Mire, Susanna, 253.
Mires, Wm., 24.
Mish, Thomas, 69.
Missinger, Conrad, 253.
Miscampbell, Andrew, 144.
Miscampbell, John, 429.
Mitchell, Alex., 400, 401.
Mitchell, Andrew, 31, 32, 33, 298.
Mitchell, David, 32, 145, 323, 421.
Mitchell, Euphemia, 233.
Mitchell, George, 456.
Mitchell, Henry, 458.
Mitchell, James, 61, 65, 67, 96, 138, 191, 198, 215, 233, 249, 272, 274, 280, 282, 387, 397, 421, 531.

Mitchell, John, 20, 26, 32, 65, 66, 141, 152, 186, 229, 232, 437, 531.
Mitchell, Margaret, 306, 437, 441.
Mitchell, Mary, 31.
Mitchell, Matthew, 17.
Mitchell, Robert, 179.
Mitchell, Samuel, 516.
Mitchell, Thomas, 250, 280, 397.
Mitchell, Wm., 167, 179, 232, 282, 283, 287, 306, 437, 441.
Moady, Robert, 456.
Moberry, Robert, 70.
Moffett, George, 73, 85, 86, 90, 92, 107, 120, 139, 143, 144, 145, 160, 168, 169, 170, 177, 178, 183, 188, 189, 193, 196, 197, 198, 199, 200, 202, 207, 209, 211, 218, 221, 222, 225, 229, 233, 240, 258, 305, 312, 428, 481, 483.
Moffett, James, 141, 256, 259.
Moffett, John, 21, 55, 86, 141, 209, 212, 220, 294, 297, 390, 407, 439, 447, 513, 533.
Moffett Jean, 430.
Moffett, Mary, 55, 316.
Moffett, Robert, 39, 442.
Moffett, Thomas, 16, 294, 423.
Moffett, Walter, 184.
Moffett, Wm., 86, 256, 261, 263, 267, 481.
Mogommery, Wm., 342.
Moiser, Henry, 280.
Moland, Elkener, 446.
Monce, Ann, 410.
Monce, Ellinor, 410.
Monce (Moncea, Monsey), James, 404, 410.
Mommon, Thomas, 438.
Monroe, James, 521, 522, 523.
Monroe, John, 421.
Monsey, Francis, 106.
Monsey, Samuel, 94, 153, 299.
Monsey, Scidmore, 99, 136.
Montague, John M., 144.
Montgomery, Agnes, 536.
Montgomerie, Ann, 82, 315.
Montgomery, Alex., 314.
Montgomery, Carpenter, 314.
Montgomerie, Daniel, 88.
Montgomerie, Francis, 376.
Montgomery, Hetty, 536.
Montgomery, Hugh, 372.
Montgomery, Hughart, 536.
Montgomery, Isabella, 536.
Montgomerie, James, 17, 19, 20, 24, 26, 48, 49, 76, 82, 129, 131, 136, 138, 146, 147, 148, 177, 179, 201, 296, 308, 315, 344, 366, 430, 439, 442, 498, 507.
Montgomery, John, 109, 140, 141, 157, 158, 212, 322, 323, 369, 380, 434, 437, 498, 536.
Montgomery Mary, 93, 321, 366, 367.
Montgomery, Rebecca E., 536.

Montgomerie, Robert, 28, 48, 101, 103, 439, 498.
Montgomerie, Samuel, 40, 347, 434.
Montgomery, Thomas, 343, 536.
Montgomery, Wm., 120, 137, 344.
Montgomery, Wm. H., 536.
Montier, James, 121.
Moody, Elizabeth, 240.
Moody, Esther, 390.
Moody, Isabella, 390, 398.
Moody, James, 53, 57, 101, 390, 398, 443.
Moody, Mary, 240.
Moody, Rebecca, 390.
Moody, Robert, 36, 390, 398.
Mooney, Margaret, 274.
Mooney, Patrick, 155.
Moore, Alex., 131, 159, 181, 342, 363, 364, 496.
Moore, Andrew, 177, 182, 193, 303.
Moore, Ann, 140.
Moore, Barnard, 167.
Moore, David, 57, 68, 85, 131, 142, 247, 302, 306, 318, 357, 418, 437, 532.
Moore, Edward, 61.
Moore Elizabeth, 57, 336.
Moore, Francis, 217, 222.
Moore, George, 447.
Moore, Isabella, 64.
Moore, Jacob, 174.
Moore, James, 57, 138, 165, 233, 343, 441, 444, 525.
Moore, John, 26, 46, 56, 60, 73, 80, 93, 97, 125, 144, 157, 175, 235, 305, 307, 324, 330, 381, 525.
Moore, Joseph, 156, 268.
Moore, Levi, 226, 378, 384, 446.
Moore, Mary, 179, 306, 357, 384, 410, 437.
Moore, Moses, 82, 95, 180, 233, 241, 355, 357, 459, 483.
Moore, Peter, 41, 423.
Moore, Phebe, 66, 130, 312.
Moore, Philip, 55.
Moore, Quantin, 305, 307.
Moore, Reuben, 243.
Moore, Richard, 151, 158.
Moore, Robert, 43, 60, 73.
Moore, Samuel, 57, 93, 329, 331.
Moore, Susanna, 378.
Moore, Thomas, 14, 19, 28, 66, 74, 98, 130, 151, 157, 164, 250, 312, 324, 366, 462, 510.
Moore, Wm., 13, 16, 105, 147, 153, 235, 354, 373, 419, 427.
Mora, Francis, 28, 527.
Moral, Samuel, 180.
Moreman, John, 237.
Moreson, Thomas, 446.
Morgan, Benjamin, 88.
Morgan, David, 294.
Morgan, Eleanor, 95.
Morgan, Gideon, 273, 529.
Morrow, Henry, 52.

Morgan, Lewis, 29, 60.
Morgan, Lucus, 25.
Morgan, Luther, 287.
Morgason, Benjamin, 373.
Morgert, Samuel, 163.
Morley, Cornelius, 307.
Morley, Daniel, 37.
Morley, Richard, 298.
Morlen, Jacob, 122, 316.
Morrice, Wm., 148.
Morris, Isaac, 174.
Morris, Mark, 520.
Morris, Richard, 348, 490.
Morris, Robert, 520.
Morris, Samuel, 339, 472.
Morris, Wm., 151, 316, 373, 391.
Morrise, John, 456.
Morrison, Catherine, 534.
Morrison, Isaac, 168.
Morrison, William, 14, 15, 534.
Morrow, Benjamin, 315.
Morrow, Thomas, 371.
Morrow, Wm., 339, 372, 484.
Morton, Hugh, 315.
Morton, Robert, 264.
Morton, Wm., 315.
Mosby, Benjamin, 355, 426, 458.
Mosby, Samuel, 469.
Moseley, Robert, 97.
Mosely, Wm., 168.
Moser, Adren, 23.
Moser, Elizabeth, 121.
Moser, Peter, 432.
Moses, Marcella, 378.
Moses, Samuel, 378.
Moura, Henry, 218.
Moura, Peter, 218.
Mowgainey, Good, 323.
Mouse, Catherine, 91.
Mouse, Daniel, 91.
Mouse, Elizabeth, 120.
Mouse, Fred., 87.
Mouse, George, 87, 120.
Mouss, George, 432.
Moyer, Jacob, 156.
Muldrough (Maldrough), Andrew, 26, 28, 79,83.
Muldrough, Jane,, 148.
Mulhlolland, John, 50, 305, 307, 309.
Muhlenberg, Rev. Mr., 400.
Muler, George, 224.
Mullen, Mathew, 144, 351.
Mummer, Christian, 418.
Munks, John, 159, 490.
Munroe, Andrew, 486.
Munsey, Francis, 489.
Munsey, Skidmore, 329, 429, 489.
Munsey, Wm., 429, 489.
Murdock, James, 149.
Murley, Catherine, 88.
Murley, Cornelius, 68, 299, 322.
Murley, Daniel, 68, 88, 322.

Murphy, Daniel, 56.
Murphy, Hugh, 352.
Murphy, James, 63, 61, 447.
Murphy, John, 109, 148, 174, 258, 326.
Murphy, Mark, 170.
Murphy, Mary, 190.
Murphy, Nancy, 258.
Murphy, Robert, 336.
Murphy, Wm., 215, 235.
Murphy, Zachariah, 170.
Murray, Adam, 142, 208.
Murray, Ann, 310.
Murray, Benjamin, 310.
Murry, Eleanor, 35.
Murray, Elizabeth, 155, 211, 357.
Murray, Henry, 66, 74, 76, 95, 100, 118, 302, 323, 333, 528.
Murray, James, 237, 299, 300, 322.
Murray James O., 428.
Murray, John, 131, 138, 139, 140, 143, 148, 155, 211, 355, 357, 477.
Murray, Richard, 140, 148.
Murray, Sally, 333, 339.
Murray, Thomas, 94.
Murray, Wm., 54, 63, 208, 311, 322, 478.
Murrow, Wm., 440.
Murty, Joseph, 156.
Muse, Daniel, 421.
Muse, George, 41.
Mustoe, A., 385.
Mustoe, Anthony, 209, 228, 235, 249, 250, 255, 259, 260, 263, 384, 404, 527.
Mynes, Alice, 255.
Mynes, Isaac, 255.
Mynes, Thomas, 389, 417, 418, 483.
Myers, Jane, 403.
Myers, Lewis, 286, 385, 398, 409, 418.
Myers ,Mary, 268.
Myers, Michael, 403.
Myers, Thomas, 282, 418.
Myrtin, Andrew, 15.

Nahan, Mary, 140.
Nail, David, 259.
Nail, Thomas, 259.
Nailer, Wm., 118.
Nalle (Naule), Martin, 172, 179, 184.
Nalle (Naull), Wm., 172, 184, 191, 193, 196.
Nanby, John, 213.
Napier, Wm., 455.
Napper, John, 378.
Nash, John, 126, 348, 497.
Naught, Wm., 451.
Neal (Neill), James, 202, 240, 514, 533.
Neal (Neil), Judith, 120, 132.
Neal, Samuel, 202, 263, 533.
Neale, Wm., 310.
Nealle (Neill), Thomas, 245, 374, 478.
Nealey (Neilley, Neely), James, 48, 61, 106, 110, 112, 119, 132, 159, 353, 436, 446.

Nealey (Neilly, Neely), John, 60, 149, 159, 310, 344, 350, 369.
Neavill, John, 450.
Needham, John, 176, 191.
Needham, Siner, 191.
Neelly, Alex., 353.
Neely, Andrew, 153, 344.
Neeley, Robert, 117.
Neese, Michael, 124.
Negarry, John, 440.
Neiff, Leonard, 42.
Neighdebour, Jacob, 216, 217.
Neigley, Sebastian, 167.
Neill, George, 60.
Neil, Peter, 198.
Nelson, Alexander, 253, 263, 278, 418, 422, 426, 446, 481.
Nelson, Daniel, 179.
Nelson, David, 123, 130.
Nelson, Elizabeth, 219.
Nelson, Hugh, 216, 403.
Nelson, John, 123, 152, 153.
Nelson, Johnston, 170.
Nelson, Thomas, 215, 219, 250, 527.
Nemmo, Wm., 520.
Netherland, Wade, 355, 459.
Netherentine, Henry, 491.
Netherton, Henry, 41, 44, 47, 439.
Nevitt, Thomas, 303.
Newbanks, John, 105.
Newberry, Rosanna, 444.
Newberry, Samuel, 136, 444.
Newby, John, 191.
Newby, Whaley, 380.
Newcom, Jonas, 72.
Newcom, Jonathan, 51.
Newcomb, Stephen, 432.
Newcll, James, 132.
Newgally, Samuel, 56.
Newly, Isaac, 193.
Newly, Rachel, 193.
Newly, Wm., 193.
Newman, Andrew, 78.
Newman, John, 290.
Newman, Samuel, 468.
Newman, Sarah, 94.
Newport, John, 14, 17, 27, 431.
Newport, Richard, 341, 490.
Newton, Joseph, 387, 483.
Newton, Wm. J., 250.
Nickel, John, 138, 144, 205.
Nickey, David, 532.
Nickle, Andrew, 216.
Nickle, Elizabeth, 216.
Nickle, Joseph, 216.
Nichols, John, 14.
Nicholas, Jacob, 123, 130, 139, 141, 155, 336, 496.
Nicholas, George, 176, 205, 213, 225, 242, 406.
Nicholas, John, 16, 253, 406.
Nicholas, Simon, 158.

Orrey, James, 489.
Orsburn, Jeremiah, Jr., 491.
Orsburn (Osburn), John, 42, 491.
Orton, James, 339, 484.
Orum, Elizabeth, 118.
Orum, Letitia, 118.
Osborn, George, 42, 55, 433.
Osborn, Jeremiah, 42, 55, 103, 488.
Ott, John, 281.
Ott, Michael, 277, 281.
Overall, Wm., 41, 44, 438.
Overshine, Philip, 279.
Overton, Claugh, 231, 280.
Owe, Stophel, 259.
Owells, John K., 39.
Owens, David, 514.
Owen, James, 379.
Owens, John, 194, 509, 510.
Owens, Owen, 189, 195, 200, 234, 385, 424, 509.
Owens, Wm., 438.
Owler, Mary, 127.
Owler, William, 54, 127.
Oyle, Benjamin, 24.
Oyler, Jacob, 520.
Ozburn, Wm., 148.

Pace, Nicholas, 254.
Pacer, George, 355.
Page, Alexander, 132.
Page, Charles, 267.
Page, James, 379.
Page (Poage), Nathan, 363.
Paget, Reuben, 438.
Pain, Joseph, 61.
Painter, Adam, 176, 178.
Paintef, Alexander, 69, 113, 124, 429.
Painter, Barbara, 174.
Painter, Catherine, 113.
Painter, Christian, 174.
Painter, John, 174, 175, 290.
Painter, Margaret, 174.
Painter, Mary, 174.
Painter, Mathias, 174.
Paints, Joseph, 418.
Paintree, John, 163.
Palmer, Barbara, 537.
Palmer, Cornelius, 284.
Palmer, David, 537.
Palmer, Elizabeth, 537.
Palmer, George, 537.
Palmer, Hannah, 537.
Palmer, Jacob, 286, 537.
Palmer, Jane, 402.
Palmer, John, 284.
Palmer, Julian, 537.
Palmer, Margaret, 537.
Palmer, Polly, 537.
Palmer, Peter S., 537.
Palmer, Philip, 537.
Palmer, Robert, 232.
Palmer, Wm., 20, 103, 148, 402, 409, 442.

Palson, Swain, 446.
Parell, John, 189.
Parent, Josiah, 41, 44, 438, 491.
Parent, Thomas, 44, 438.
Parent, Wm., 44, 438.
Paris (Parris), George, 352, 458, 464,
Paris, John, 221, 341, 393.
Parish, George, 355, 436, 459.
Park, Fanny, 399.
Park, Jonathan, 399.
Park, Polly, 399.
Parker, George, 88, 176.
Parker, Hugh, 42, 326, 337, 435.
Parks, Catherine, 374, 379, 385.
Parks, Edward, 225, 283, 374, 379, 409, 411, 412.
Parks, George, 71, 312.
Parks, James, 239.
Parks, John, 144, 154.
Parks, Joseph, 410, 536.
Parks, Wm., 39, 432.
Parlour, Shaldk., 439.
Parman, James, 51.
Parris, Wm., 187.
Parry, David, 247, 272, 278, 287, 289, 290.
Parry, Joshua, 243, 244, 267.
Parsenger, Jacob, 104, 124, 139, 142.
Parsons, Charles, 179, 369.
Parsons, Thomas, 328.
Partridge, Edward, 432.
Patterson, Agnes, 38.
Patterson, Benjamin, 227.
Patterson, Edward, 61, 71.
Patterson, Elianer, 88.
Patterson, Erwin (Irwin), 16, 17, 35, 45, 50, 61, 80, 88, 90, 92, 100, 112, 431, 467, 473.
Patterson George, 469.
Patterson, James, 33, 42, 44, 136, 149, 193, 198, 203, 381, 384, 437.
Patterson, Jane, 381.
Patterson, Jean, 381.
Patterson, Jennett, 175.
Patterson (Pattison), John, 15, 17, 30, 35, 37, 38, 39, 144, 149, 175, 245, 299, 302, 305, 366, 388, 393, 422, 491, 524, 525.
Patterson, Joseph, 205, 225, 421, 446.
Patterson, Margaret, 92, 100.
Patterson, Mary, 175, 337, 341, 356, 535.
Patterson, Martha, 430.
Patterson, Mathew, 146.
Patterson, Nathan, 23, 438.
Patterson, Robert, 29, 38, 48, 73, 79, 293, 300, 313, 337, 370, 426, 428, 440.
Patterson, Samuel, 146, 354.
Patterson, Sarah, 193.
Patterson, Thomas, 152, 351, 422.
Patterson, Walter, 60.
Patterson, Wm., 55, 136, 233, 249, 282, 341, 356, 400.
Patton, Benjamin, 438.

Patten, George, 191.
Patton, Hance, 248.
Patton, Henry, 32, 318.
Patton, Jacob, 61, 62, 303, 439, 444, 445.
Patton, James, 13, 15, 17, 19, 21, 22, 23, 32, 34, 38, 45, 50, 53, 54, 56, 58, 60, 64, 67, 68, 69, 70, 293, 297, 300, 302, 305, 307, 310, 319, 322, 347, 361, 370, 414, 418, 420, 429, 442, 447, 528, 530.
Patton, Jennet, 439.
Patton, John, 39, 41, 43, 56, 307, 308, 415, 418, 419, 420, 432, 438.
Patton, Margaret, 147.
Patton, Matthew, 41, 70, 81, 98, 107, 138, 149, 284, 361, 408, 410, 418, 419, 420, 432, 436, 438, 488.
Patton, Robert, 333.
Patton, Samuel, 41, 312, 432, 436, 438, 491.
Patton, Sarah, 191.
Patton, Stephen, 418.
Patton, Susannah, 62, 439.
Patton, Thomas, 104, 149, 184, 482.
Patton, Wm., 120, 136, 148, 212, 386, 394, 408, 419, 420, 482.
Patrick, Charles, 68, 178.
Park, Edward, 399.
Patrick, James, 399.
Patrick, John, 87, 117, 141, 170, 199, 207, 388.
Patrick, Little, 437.
Patrick, Robert, 22, 55, 528.
Pasenger (Passinger), Catherine, 182, 337.
Pasenger (Passinger), Jacob, 182, 326, 337, 414.
Paul, Audley, 66, 67, 125, 128, 348.
Paul, Hugh, 288, 413.
Paul, Isabella, 534.
Paul, James, 534.
Paul, John, 180, 195.
Pauling (Paulin), Henry, 156, 456.
Paxton, Elizabeth, 348.
Paxton, James, 346.
Paxton, John, 50, 60, 67, 71, 74, 146, 155, 320, 348, 490.
Paxton, Joseph, 77, 356.
Paxton, Samuel, 51, 60, 61, 108, 348, 373, 519.
Paxton, Sarah, 27.
Paxton, Thomas, 27, 50, 51, 82, 91, 107, 136, 322, 348, 356.
Paxton, William, 61 .
Payne, John, 473.
Payne, Richard, 198.
Payton, John, 180.
Peace, Joseph, 206.
Peachman, Henry, 216.
Peanter, Alex., 489.
Pearce (Pearse), Joseph, 163, 366.
Pearce, Silas, 150.

Pearis, George, 114, 126, 134, 355, 441, 459.
Pearis, John, 137.
Pearis, Richard, 323, 325.
Pearis, Robert, 325, 485, 486.
Peary, George, 53, 57.
Peary, Jacob, 274.
Peary, James, 53, 56, 57, 259.
Peary, John, 31, 141.
Piery (Peary), Thomas, 20, 56, 57.
Peartree, Matthew, 131.
Peartree, Rebecca, 326.
Pebbles, Ann, 213.
Peck, Andrew, 254.
Peck, Jacob, 186, 189, 192, 194, 197, 205, 248, 250, 264, 379, 380, 417.
Peck, John, 262.
Pecken, Israel, 440.
Peebles, John, 201, 481.
Peerie, John, 122.
Peerie, Thomas, 101, 122.
Peerson, George, 270.
Peery, Ally, 240.
Peery, Jane, 240.
Peevy, George, 414, 443, 444.
Peevy, James, 416, 443.
Peevy, Jane, 414.
Peevy, John, 444.
Peevy, Thomas, 429, 443, 444.
Peffer, Samuel, 132.
Peggs, Matthew, 85.
Peggs (Pegg), Samuel, 64, 125, 147.
Peircy (Percy), Sarah, 237.
Peircy (Percy), Thomas, 237.
Pellam (Pellem), Wm., 40, 434.
Pence, Adam, 96, 100, 148, 156, 336.
Pence, Barbara, 87.
Pence, Catherine, 96, 104, 326.
Pence, Feldy, 434.
Pence, Gabriel, 330.
Pence, George, 193, 336.
Pence, Jacob, 26, 87, 96, 100, 142, 321, 326, 336, 337.
Pence, John, 87, 195, 532.
Pence, Nicholas, 96.
Pence, Valentine, 26, 336, 360.
Pendleton, Benjamin, 14.
Peninger, Henry, 97, 99, 175, 179.
Penn, Gabriel, 323, 482.
Pension Lists, 515.
Penticost, Dawsey, 177, 182, 183.
Peny, John, 444.
Peoples, George, 206.
Peoples, Jacob, 182.
Peoples, John, 157, 186, 194, 229, 373.
Peoples, Nathan, 144.
Peoples, Wm., 93.
Pepper, Samuel ,139, 152, 155, 158, 355, 457, 459.
Pepper, Wm., 441.
Peyton, James, 382.

Percey, John, 200.
Pere, Wm., 62.
Perer, Jacob, 434.
Perkins, Eliza, 51, 315.
Perkins, Utis, 33, 34, 35, 43, 50, 302, 315.
Perry, David, 94, 235, 237, 332.
Perry, James, 268, 380.
Perry (Perrie) John, 71, 518.
Perry, Joshua, 225, 233, 235, 237.
Perry, Mary, 16.
Pershinger, Jacob, 496.
Persing, Dewalt, 428.
Persinger, Christopher, 513.
Persinger, Jacob, 135.
Perviance, Henry, 513.
Perviance, John, 513.
Pessinger, Christian, 414.
Peteet, John, 62.
Peters, Jacob, 41, 328.
Peters, Martin, 41.
Peterson, George, 405.
Peterson, Jacob, 116, 119.
Petter, Jacob, 486.
Petterson, Thomas, 530.
Pettigrew, James, 408.
Peyton, Edward, 130, 131.
Peyton, James, 382.
Peyton, John, 174.
Pharis (Pheris), John, 343, 350.
Phegan, Philip, 44, 49, 122, 438.
Phelan, Garet, 228.
Philby, Wm., 441.
Phillips, James, 20, 21, 36, 56, 57, 148, 200, 373, 443.
Phillips, John, 137, 142, 369, 373, 437, 457, 465, 491.
Phillips, Robert, 36, 324, 444, 490.
Phillips, Steven (Stephen), 41, 44, 306, 438.
Phillips, Wm., 357.
Phillips, Young, 410.
Phipps, Nathaniel, 75.
Phips, Wm., 498.
Phogle, Anthony, 208.
Phogle, Philip, 208 .
Pickens, Andrew, 13, 14, 15, 20, 433.
Picken, Ann, 309.
Pickens, Gabriel, 44, 97, 312, 313, 433, 438.
Pickens, John, 13, 15, 29, 30, 34, 48, 58, 90, 295, 296, 305, 307, 309, 312, 320, 322, 531.
Pickens, Margaret, 334, 340.
Pickens, Thomas, 142, 429, 489.
Pickens, Wm., 22, 97, 309, 321, 329, 489.
Pickens, Zerubiah, 97.
Picket, Henry, 163.
Picket, Handry, 489.
Picket, George, 82.
Pickett, Jane, 109.
Pickle, George, 280.
Pickle, Henry, 97, 156, 181, 369, 371, 449.

Pickle, Jacob, 281.
Pierce, Daniel, 131, 472.
Pierce, Ketren, 472.
Pierce, Wm., 14, 20.
Piercy, Allen, 292.
Piercey, George, 292.
Piercey, John, 292.
Pierie, Wm., 32.
Pigg, Matthew, 67.
Pigman, John, 149, 151.
Pigman, Notley, 470, 471.
Pilsher, Richard, 36.
Pilson, Richard, 55, 174.
Pilson, Samuel, 176.
Pindle, William, 256.
Pinkerton, David, 236, 240.
Pinkerton, James, 240, 282.
Pinkerton, John, 77.
Pinkerton, Joseph, 236.
Piper, Peter, 523, 524.
Place, Wm., 169.
Player, Elizabeth, 416.
Player, Peter, 416.
Pleasants, John, 312, 315.
Pleasants, Thomas, 315.
Plucket, James, 318.
Plumer, Daniel, 68.
Plumer, Robert, 68.
Plumer, Wm., 34.
Plunkett, John, 213.
Poage, Ann, 363.
Poage, Elizabeth, 16.
Poage, George, 116, 124, 125, 142, 146, 152, 220, 221, 224, 226, 229, 239, 240, 483, 526.
Poage, James, 222, 224, 250, 256, 363, 481, 535.
Poage (Poge), John, 30, 46, 53, 77, 84, 102, 107, 122, 142, 160, 169, 177, 183, 184, 188, 189,196, 197, 200, 202, 203, 210, 218, 222, 223, 224, 226, 229, 234, 238, 239, 244, 245, 247, 257, 280, 389, 390, 392, 394, 418, 419, 434, 439, 445, 456, 447, 453, 459, 481, 502, 504, 507, 511, 531, 535.
Poage, Rachel, 124, 272.
Poage, Robert, 13, 16, 29, 51, 64, 68, 77, 94, 111, 200, 215, 216, 305, 307, 416, 524.
Poage, Seth, 305, 307.
Poage, Thomas, 114, 120, 201, 209, 231, 251, 392.
Poage, Wm., 146, 151, 201.
Poake, Mary, 306.
Poffenbarger, Michael, 279.
Poindexter, Elizabeth, 534.
Poindexter, Joseph, 170, 207, 372, 534.
Pointer, Thomas, 93.
Pollard, Joseph, 469.
Poller, John, 186.
Pollock, Ann, 152.

Pollock (Pollick), James, 90, 121, 152, 179, 464.
Polson, Benjamin, 456.
Ponder, Daniel, 111, 146, 333, 452.
Ponder, Jeremiah, 111.
Pope, John, 388.
Porter, Adam, 385.
Porter, Daniel, 223.
Porter, James, 405.
Porter, John, 93.
Porter, Mary, 220, 223.
Porter, Reice, 385.
Porter, Robert, 385.
Porter, Samuel, 437.
Porter, Thomas, 133.
Porter, Wm., 220, 246, 257, 483, 525.
Porterfield, James, 245.
Porterfield, Patrick, 51.
Porterfield, Robert, 240, 241, 481.
Porteus, James, 13, 18, 20, 29, 30, 36, 301, 438.
Portlock, John, 484.
Portlock, Wm., 484.
Porton, John, 62.
Posey, Benjamin, 42.
Posey, Thomas, 184, 372.
Poss, Catherine, 480.
Poss, Christian, 480.
Poss (Pass), Henry, 480.
Poss, Susanna, 480.
Potter, Abraham, 299, 309.
Potter, James, 230.
Potter, John, 446.
Potts, John, 84, 125, 138, 156, 334, 338.
Powell, Ambrose, 230.
Powell, Gabriel, 174, 357.
Powell, Honarius, 351, 473.
Powell, Samuel, 528.
Powell, Simon, 147.
Power, Walter, 146.
Power, Susanna, 113.
Powlas, Nicholas, 251, 409, 410.
Powlas, Polly, 410.
Poulson, Anderson, 106.
Pousman, Henry, 231.
Purkins, Elizabeth, 311.
Pratt, Lilley, 153.
Prentice, Daniel, 361.
Preston, Agnes, 89.
Preston, Anne, 17.
Preston, Cald., 334.
Preston, Elizabeth, 17, 34, 80.
Preston, Lettice, 17.
Preston, John, 17, 20, 23, 29, 33, 34, 35, 294, 298, 299, 310, 538.
Preston, Margaret, 17.
Preston, Mary, 89.
Preston, William, 17, 56, 73, 75, 79, 82, 84, 85, 106, 107, 108, 138, 146, 210, 212, 291, 325, 334,, 335, 359, 429, 443, 444, 445, 446, 448, 457, 459, 467, 473, 479, 494, 495, 501, 528.

Preston, Susanna, 429, 459.
Previe, Wm., 432.
Price, Augustine, 53, 81, 101, 113, 124, 141, 496.
Price, Calem, 191, 193.
Price, Catherine, 193.
Price, Daniel, 308, 496.
Price, Elizabeth, 81.
Price, Evan, 163.
Price, Henry, 308.
Price, Isaac, 228, 233, 234.
Price, James, 26, 58.
Price, John, 81, 136, 149, 174, 217, 218, 224, 233, 234, 261, 272, 386, 463, 490.
Price, Judith, 386.
Price, Judy, 198.
Price, Mary, 191, 218, 224, 233.
Price, Michael, 307, 308.
Price, Mung, 491.
Price, Philip, 173.
Price, Rice, 42.
Price, Samuel, 286.
Price, Sarah, 286, 523.
Price, Thomas, 209, 377.
Price, Wm., 44, 81, 300, 438, 523.
Price, Zack., 446.
Priddie, Benj., 383.
Pringle, Samuel, 184, 193.
Prior, Richard, 123, 333, 487.
Priore, Wm., 30.
Prit, Robert, 351, 473.
Pritchard, Sarah, 174, 352, 530.
Pritherock, Wm., 44.
Pritherock, Thomas, 44.
Props, Michael, 41, 97, 182.
Provence, Thomas, 310.
Pryor, Richard, 332.
Puckett, Jeremiah, 344.
Puff, George, 281.
Puff, Jacob, 280.
Puffenberry, George, 216, 483.
Puffenbier, George, 86.
Pullen, Samuel, 263.
Pullin, Loctus, 452.
Pullin, Loftus (Lofty), 21, 42, 44, 120, 201, 212, 315, 438, 442,
Pullin, Losters, 441.
Purris, J., 519.
Purris, Wm., 195.
Purviance, Robert, 386, 394.
Purviance, Samuel, 336, 338, 386, 394.
Purviance, Wm., 306, 347.

Quails, Charles, 31.
Quarles, John, 311.
Queen, Katrin, 431.
Quin, Catherine, 25, 26, 34, 57, 59, 63, 64, 73.
Quin, Jane, 341, 356.
Quin, John, 13, 16, 21, 293.
Quin, Patrick, 110, 341, 356, 357, 467, 468.

Rabint, Edward, 175.
Raburn, Joseph, 140.
Raburn, Robert, 353.
Raddon, Mary, 196.
Rafferty, Wm., 285.
Ragen, Jeremiah, 112, 142.
Ragan, Richard, 481
Ragland, Nathan, 157.
Ralph, Thomas, 210.
Ralston, Barbara, 37.
Ralston, David, 41, 428.
Ralston, Eleanor, 396.
Ralstone, James, 128, 214, 429.
Ralston, Jane, 214.
Ralston, Margaret, 128.
Ralstone, Mathew, 460.
Ralstone, Robert, 21, 30, 41, 73, 324, 326,
   334, 440.
Ralston, Rosanna, 82, 445.
Ralston, Sarah, 128.
Ralston, Wm., 41, 61, 82, 123, 136, 324,
   445.
Rambo, Swain, 37.
Ramey, Daniel, 81.
Ramsey, Alex., 236.
Ramsey, Andrew, 177, 241.
Ramsey, George, 236.
Ramsey, Isabella, 137, 332.
Ramsey, James, 166, 192, 233, 246, 481.
Ramsey, John, 20, 26, 28, 37, 49, 53, 55,
   56, 59, 65, 75, 77, 82, 87, 101, 113, 140,
   170, 177, 208, 209, 233, 309, 315, 322,
   323, 324, 371, 372, 434.
Ramsey, Josiah, 158.
Ramsey, Margaret, 51, 56, 166, 324.
Ramsey, Rosanna, 204.
Ramsey, Robert, 28, 32, 46, 85, 112, 137,
   309, 332.
Ramsey, Thomas, 330, 448, 494.
Ramsey, William, 50, 233, 378, 440.
Randal, James, 117.
Randal, Mildred, 160.
Randal, Rachel, 160.
Randal, Richard, 179.
Randals, John, 177.
Randolph, Azariah, 241.
Randolph, Beverly, 393, 512.
Randolph, E., 388.
Randolph, Edmund, 418, 508, 511.
Randolph, James, 65.
Randolph, John, 527.
Randolph, Sir John, 295.
Randolph, Peter, 480.
Randolph, Peyton, 20.
Randolph, Richard, 295.
kaneck, Samuel, 519.
Rankins, George, 67, 401, 409.
Rankin, Isaac, 403, 404, 418, 424.
Rankin, James, 205, 242, 245, 246, 267,
   272, 278, 405, 406.
Rankin, John, 251, 261, 267, 401.
Rankin, Mary, 251, 267, 401.

Rankin, Richard, 271, 409.
Rankin, Thomas, 198, 199, 205, 213, 251,
   261, 483.
Rankin, Wm., 400, 405.
Rann, Bat., 478, 479.
Ransbarger, Benjamin, 536.
Rapp, Jacob, 413.
Rapp, John, 276, 413.
Ratchford, Wm., 69, 445.
Raveling, John, 116.
Ray, Fergus, 303.
Ray, James, 356.
Ray, John, 109, 126, 139.
Ray, Jo., 455.
Ray, Joseph, 98, 121, 132, 136, 200, 209,
   245, 325, 343, 451, 489, 490, 493, 530.
Ray, Rebecca, 327.
Ray, Thomas, 175, 413.
Rayburn, Wm. H., 532.
Rayreigh, John, 155.
Rea, Charlotte, 167.
Rea, Joseph, 333, 455.
Reaburn, Adam, 142, 145.
Reaburn, Edward, 108.
Reaburn, Henry, 73, 105, 108, 370, 446.
Reaburn, James, 62, 105, 108, 142.
Reaburn, Joseph, 163, 361, 382.
Reaburn, Margaret, 81, 320, 324.
Reaburn, Robert, 154, 178.
Read, Alexander, 107, 108.
Read, Clement, 486.
Read, John, 279.
Read, Mathew, 361, 466, 473.
Read, Richard, 331.
Read, Robert, 361.
Reade, Eldad, 528.
Reader (Reder), Adam, 134, 171, 193, 429,
   437, 489.
Reader, Anthony, 193.
Reader, Elizabeth, 418.
Reader, John, 392.
Reader, Mathias, 175.
Reader, Nicholas, 418.
Ready, Patrick, 274, 399.
Ready, Sally, 399.
Reager, Burket, 41.
Reager, Michael, 349.
Reaglen, Nathan, 239.
Reah, Alex., 190.
Reah, Archibald, 155, 442.
Reah, Arsbald, 428.
Reah, Hugh, 190.
Reah, John, 190.
Reah, Wm., 168, 190, 379.
Reasoner (Reasner), Michael, 149, 462.
Reburn, James, 442.
Reburn, Jean, 428.
Reburn, John, 428.
Reburn, Robert, 428, 489.
Reddick, Cornelius, 455.
Redman, John, 179, 201, 379.
Redman, Sarah, 188.

Redpoth, John, 154, 167, 261.
Redick, James, 461, 463.
Ree, Wm., 296.
Reece, John, 490.
Reece, Joseph, 366.
Reed, Adam, 103, 169.
Reed, Alex., 142, 249, 274, 292.
Reed, Andrew, 294.
Reed, Barbara, 103, 243.
Reed, Caton, 423.
Reed, Collin, 415.
Reed, George, 478.
Reed, Jacob, 438.
Reed, James, 437.
Reed, John, 186, 209, 415, 438.
Reed, Leonard, 438.
Reed, Margaret, 252, 356, 360, 415, 423.
Reed, Martha, 200.
Reed, Mathew, 143, 199,, 200, 263, 326, 356, 415, 455, 494.
Reed, Peter, 42, 55, 244, 250, 438.
Reed, Robert, 82, 117, 122, 152, 158, 252, 272, 273, 303, 334, 356, 363, 395, 415, 423, 445, 459, 494.
Reed, Thomas, 66, 133, 156, 443, 444.
Reenick, Wm., 513.
Rees, Thomas, 50, 57.
Reese (Rees), John, 123, 462.
Reese, Wm., 191.
Reeves, Brewer, 372.
Reeve, Jane, 382.
Reeves, John, 478.
Reeves, Samuel, 231, 382.
Reeves, Thomas, 217, 372, 376, 456.
Regart, Jacob, 488.
Reger, Anthony, 42.
Regin, Dennis, 446.
Reglan, John, 250.
Reglar, John, 222.
Regular, Rachel, 267.
Reid, Agnes, 303.
Reid, Alex., 240, 482.
Reid, Andrew, 388.
Reid, Catherine, 243.
Reid, John, 353.
Reid, Joseph, 17.
Reid, Margaret, 513.
Reid (Read), Mathew, 357.
Reid, Robert, 251, 376.
Reid, Wm., 520.
Reiger, Benjamin, 416.
Reily, John, 232.
Reily, Nancy, 232.
Reise, Priscilla, 444.
Reiny, Michael, 368.
Renalds, Richard, 140, 170.
Renich, Robert, 322.
Renick, Sarah, 365.
Renick, Thomas, 304.
Renick, Wm., 391.
Rennick, Robert, 272, 285, 414.
Rennick, Wm., 389.

Renix, Robert, 14, 21, 26, 39, 48, 53, 64, 76, 77, 115, 256, 294, 414, 436.
kenix, Thomas, 33, 115, 208, 299, 300, 470.
Renix, Wm., 134, 153.
Renold, James, 35.
Renolds, James, 136.
Renolds, Mary, 136.
Renoxe, Robert, 529.
Rentfro,, Margaret, 107, 112.
Rentfro, Peter, 23, 28.
Rentfro, Steven, 61, 327.
Rentfroe, Margaret, 327, 333.
Reyburn, James, 354.
Reynolds, Wm., 471.
Rhea, Ann, 397.
Rhea, Walter, 483.
Rhea, William, 248.
Rhodes, Alice, 288.
Rhodes, Charles B., 423.
Rhoades (Rhoads), Thomas, 131, 139, 141, 142, 143, 167, 189, 195, 210, 214, 228, 231, 238, 252, 265, 288, 333, 455, 474.
Rhyne, Michael, 42.
Rice, David, 139, 143, 346.
Rice, George, 155.
Rice, John, 154, 481.
Rice, William, 272.
Richards, Jacob, 87.
Richards, James, 528.
Richards, John, 87, 132.
Richards, Josiah, 38, 57.
Richards, Josias, 443, 444.
Richards, Lewis, 400.
Richards, Owin, 334.
Richards, Philemon, 400.
Richards, Robert, 147.
Richards, Wm., 206.
Richardson, Daniel, 18, 41, 46, 55, 306, 438.
Richardson, Ephriam, 180.
Richardson, Ezekiel, 107.
Richardson, Holt, 90, 321, 322.
Richardson, James, 222.
Richardson, Joseph, 150.
Richardson, Mary, 107, 150.
Richeson, Aaron, 203.
Richison, Daniel, 18.
Richeson, Ephriam, 203.
Richison, Daniel, 441.
Richey, Alexander, 53.
Richey, Hugh, 265, 377.
Richey, James, 223.
Richey, John, 222, 237, 245, 489.
Richey, Mary, 265.
Richey, Patience, 280, 282, 285.
Richey, Wm., 308.
Ricketts, Zachariah, 246.
Ritchey, Alex., 443.
Ritchie, Hugh, 376.
Ritchie, John, 130, 335.
Riddle, Thomas, 270, 400, 401.

Riddle, Wm., 413.
Rider, Anthony, 194, 196.
Rider, Mathias, 135.
Ridgway. Josiah, 109.
Riely, James, 252.
Riely, John, 445.
Riffle, Francis, 229.
Right, John, 447.
Rigland, Nathan, 155.
Riley, Alice, 330.
Riley, Barney, 68.
Riley, James, 447.
Riley, Michael, 58.
Riley, Wm., 44.
Rine, Michael, 449.
Rinehart, Catherine, 50.
Rinehart, Christian, 50.
Rinehart, Daniel, 50.
Rinehart, Ludwick, 50.
Rinehart, Matthew, 50.
Rinehart, Michael, 50.
Rinehart, Philip, 110.
Riney, Michael, 128.
Ringland, Arthur, 396.
Ringland, Mary, 396.
Rinkens, Wm., 47.
Risk, David, 384, 535.
Risk, James, 110, 180, 367, 444.
Risk, Jane, 180.
Risk, John, 16, 17, 18, 66, 120, 142, 188, 268, 355, 357, 367, 445, 459, 518, 535.
Risk, Margaret, 110.
Risk, Martha, 459.
Risk, Robert, 384, 482 ,459.
Risk, Wm., 384, 415.
Rissner. John, 185.
Ritchey, Alex., 442, 443.
River, Peter, 255.
Roadecap, Elizabeth, 504.
Roadecap, Hannah, 503.
Roahk, Michael, 178.
Roalston, W., 503.
Roark, Timothy, 464.
Robb, John, 283, 291.
Robb, Wm., 36.
Roberson, Robert, 444.
Roberts, Benjamin, 285.
Roberts, David, 138, 199.
Roberts, Eliamer, 93.
Roberts, John, 473.
Roberts, Joseph, 49.
Roberts, Nicholas, 306.
Roberts, Rebecca, 90.
Robertson, Albert, 206.
Robertson, Alexander, 160, 169, 177, 183, 188, 189, 192, 193, 195, 196, 197, 199, 200, 201, 202, 207, 212, 220, 226, 229, 233, 236, 240, 241, 243, 244, 279, 395, 447, 481.
Robertson, David, 167, 175, 429, 489.
Robertson, Elizabeth, 370.
Robertson, Isaac, 429, 489.

Robertson, James, 16, 30, 157, 158, 188, 356, 358, 422, 442.
Robertson, John, 332, 447.
Robertson. Lettice, 364.
Robertson, Margaret, 151.
Robertson, Martha, 390.
Robertson, Mathew, 150, 173, 186, 278, 390.
Robertson, Polly, 416.
Robertson, Wm., 64, 140, 141, 184, 192, 193, 204, 268, 348, 359, 361, 364, 370, 447, 459,
Robeson, John, 508.
Robinet, Zebulon, 471.
Robins, George, 433.
Robinson, Ann, 362.
Robinson, Annabella, 146.
Robinson, David, 57, 61, 96, 123, 141, 144, 146, 157, 328, 335, 439, 461, 475, 485.
Robinson, Elizabeth, 84, 93, 96, 321, 328, 336, 362, 367.
Robinson, Esther, 69.
Robinson, George, 13, 16, 19, 20, 24, 28, 63, 69, 70, 73, 80, 105, 131, 139, 188, 299, 314, 353, 362, 363, 367, 484, 527.
Robinson Hannah, 120, 429.
Robinson, Isaac, 134, 135, 145, 147, 181, 342, 369.
Robinson, Isabella, 144.
Robinson, Israel, 24, 116.
Robinson, James, 17, 18, 28, 37, 48, 54, 69, 84, 123, 131, 134, 139, 148, 153, 328, 335, 353, 360, 362, 367, 414, 429, 449, 525.
Robinson, Jane, 23, 188.
Robinson. Jean, 296.
Robison (Robinson), Jennet, 305.
Robinson, Joel, 369.
Robinson, John, 16, 36, 58, 63, 69, 80, 96, 98, 110, 135, 137, 141, 144, 146, 295, 307, 308, 321, 325, 328, 329, 332, 335, 336, 338, 350, 362, 367, 374, 441, 452, 461, 484.
Robinson, Joseph, 48, 49, 61, 156, 439, 487.
Robinson, Margaret, 122, 130, 141, 157, 165, 356, 358, 360, 363, 460.
Robinson, Martha, 105, 131, 139.
Robinson, Mary, 366, 367.
Robinson, Mathew, 84.
Robinson, Michael, 347.
Robinson. Samuel, 131, 139, 344, 362.
Robinson, Sarah, 126.
Robinson, Simon, 98, 459, 463.
Robinson, Thomas, 328, 336, 367.
Robinson, William, 36, 59, 70, 95, 106, 119, 122, 130, 144, 157, 165, 304, 329, 330, 338, 344, 351, 356, 358, 360, 362, 363, 367, 470.
Robison (Robinson), James, 305.
Robottom, Mathew, 133.
Robson, Wm., 192.

Robton, John, 26.
Rock, John, 227.
Rock, Mary, 227.
Rodcap, Barbara, 97.
Rodcap, Catherine, 97.
Rodcap, Elizabeth, 97.
Rodcap, Hannah, 97.
Rodcap, Jacob, 97.
Rodcap, Peter, 97.
Rodgers, Agnes, 214.
Rodgers, George, 149, 356, 462.
Rodger, Jacob, 434.
Rodgers, Robert, 135, 144.
Rodgers, Seth, 171, 229, 530.
Rodgers, Thomas, 257, 263, 348.
Rodgers, Wm., 231, 263.
Rods, Frederick, 411, 412.
Rogers, George, 361.
Rogers, James, 86.
Rogers, Robert, 86.
Roland, James, 141.
Roleman, Christian, 168.
Roleman, Jacob, 168.
Roler, Mary, 282.
Roller, Andrew, 503.
Roller, Barbara, 503.
Roller, Casper, 593.
Roller, Catherine, 503.
Roller, David, 503.
Roller, George, 503.
Roller, Jacob, 503.
Roller, John, 503.
Roller, Margaret, 503.
Roller, Mary, 503.
Roller, Michael, 503.
Roller, Paul, 503.
Roller, Peter, 503.
Roller, Rachel, 503.
Roller, Sarah, 503.
Rook, John, 318.
Roork, Elinor, 18.
Roots, George, 220.
Roper, Henry, 415.
Roreback, John, 488.
Rose, Alex., 314.
Rose, Anne, 314.
Rose, John, 314.
Rose, Robert, 44, 314.
Rosebraugh, James, 51, 323, 518.
Rosebraugh, John, 518.
Rosemond, John, 39, 120.
Ross, David, 248.
Ross, Duncan, 381.
Ross, Elizabeth, 259, 263.
Ross, Hugh, 55, 71, 85.
Ross, James, 246, 287, 309.
Ross, Jane, 71.
Ross, John, 248.
Ross, Robert, 213.
Ross, Ruth, 276.
Ross, Sarah, 248.
Ross, Wm., 219.

Rotherback, Adam, 103.
Rothgap, Anne, 58.
Rothgap, John J., 58.
Rough, Peter, 400.
Rough, Susanna, 400.
Roughenough, Peter, 28.
Roundtree, Noah, 161.
Row, John, 36.
Rowland, George, 527.
Rowland, James, 467.
Rowland, Robert, 107, 112, 503.
Rowland, Thomas, 152, 503.
Roy, Robert, 60.
Rucker, Samuel, 220.
Ruckman, John, 57, 441.
Ruddell, Stephen, 330, 339.
Ruddle, Archibald, 57.
Ruddle, Cornelius, 57, 105, 152, 263, 323, 410.
Ruddle, Isaac, 323.
Ruddle, John, 17, 19, 25, 46.
Ruddle, Stephen, 303.
Ruffhead, John, 258.
Ruffhead, Margaret, 258.
Ruffin, John, 486.
Ruffner, Peter, 308.
Rule, George, 520.
Runkle, Peter, 148, 199.
Runkle, Samuel, 208, 252, 400.
Runnion, Henry, 173.
Rush, Benjamin, 513.
Rush, Charles, 169.
Rusk, Margaret, 400.
Rush, Michael, 183.
Rusk, James, 160.
Rusk, John, 13, 142.
Rusk, Samuel, 293.
Rusk, Wm., 217, 405.
Russell, Abraham, 524.
Russell, Andrew, 17, 20, 28, 48, 103, 140, 173, 176, 192, 230.
Russell, Ann, 325.
Russell, Brice (Bryce), 47, 86.
Russell, Caleb, 181.
Russell, David, 394.
Russell, James, 325.
Russell, John, 230.
Russell, Joseph, 18.
Russell, Joshua, 176, 218, 275.
Russell, Margaret, 192.
Russell, Moses, 275, 312.
Russell, Robert, 172, 192, 218.
Russell, Wm., 13, 28, 64, 82, 295, 318, 374, 419, 430, 482, 510.
Rust, Abraham, 250.
Rust George, 405.
Rutherford, Elliott, 163, 508.
Rutherford, Ellis, 199.
Rutherford, Elizabeth, 151, 160, 163.
Rutherford, Harrison, 368.
Rutherford, John, 117, 397.
Rutherford, Joseph, 91, 111, 151, 163, 182.

Rutherford, Mary, 163, 508.
Rutherford, Reuben, 163.
Rutherford, Robert, 163, 348, 484.
Rutherford Samuel, 91.
Rutherford, Thomas, 151, 160, 163, 326, 450, 457, 508.
Rutledge, Deborah, 403.
Rutledge, Edward, 174, 182, 263, 277, 278, 328, 366, 491, 526.
Rutledge, Eleanor, 277, 299, 396.
Rutlidge George, 36, 277, 374.
Rutledge James, 39, 42, 46, 277, 293, 301, 304, 306, 319, 396 491.
Rutledge Jane, 264.
Rutledge, Jean, 42, 435.
Rutledge, Edward, 174, 182, 263, 277, 218, 374.
Rutledge, Sarah, 366.
Rutledge, Thomas, 36, 63, 264, 403, 525.
Rutledge, Wm., 156.
Ryan, Barnabas, 446.
Ryan, Eleanor, 287.
Ryan, Jeremiah, 168.
Ryan, John, 252.
Ryan, Joseph, 62.
Ryan, Martha 131, 168.
Ryan, Mary, 168.
Ryan, Timothy, 168.
Ryburn, James, 464.
Ryley, Alice, 117.
Ryley, Judith, 124.
Ryley, Patrick, 106 117, 330.
Ryley, Philip, 177.
Rymer,, George, 253, 254, 388.
Rymer, Nelly, 388.

St. Clair, Alexander, 165, 166, 167, 189, 196, 197, 198, 199, 202, 203, 204, 207, 210, 216, 220, 223, 227, 240, 244, 253, 257, 258, 261, 277, 238, 286, 379, 481, 510, 529, 534.
Saftly, Adam, 414.
Salix, Wm., 161.
Saller, John, 305.
Sallers, John, 44.
Salling, George, 61, 62, 99.
Salling, John P., 23, 24, 61, 62.
Sallis, Nicholas, 211.
Sallard, John, 116, 329, 487.
Sallow, John, 110.
Sally, John P., 293, 311.
Sally, Mary E., 311.
Sample, Wm., 481.
Samples, Robert, 496.
Samples, Samuel, 88, 428, 491, 496.
Sampson, Edward, 119, 133, 352, 366, 462 463.
Samuel, Wm., 406.
Sancion, Daniel, 61.
Sanders, Alex., 280.
Sanders, Mary, 153.
Sandford, Wm., 42.

Sansile, Richard, 72.
Sarch, Mathias, 61.
Saulsbury, Mary, 71.
Saulsbury, Wm., 171.
Saunders, Jesse, 86.
Saunders, Thomas, 494.
Savage, George, 222.
Savage, Litt, 486.
Savage, Patrick, 205.
Savage, Richard, 452.
Sawyers, Alex., 158, 332.
Sawyers, David, 402, 489.
Sawyers, Hannah, 234, 236, 329.
Sawyer, James, 154, 203, 210, 233, 234, 236, 381.
Sawyers, John, 210.
Sawyers, Sampson, 174, 212.
Sawyers, Thomas, 233, 425.
Sawyers, Wm., 347, 469.
Say, Simon, 41.
Sayers, Alexander, 40, 54, 56, 62, 102, 106, 107, 117, 121, 122, 123, 127, 132, 329, 332, 335, 336, 340, 358, 370, 434, 476, 489, 492, 498.
Sayers, David, 74, 75, 97, 124, 367.
Sayers, Hannah, 74, 75, 365, 387.
Sayers, James, 124, 137, 151, 365, 387.
Sayers, Rebecca, 365.
Sayers, Robert, 54, 71, 74, 75, 123, 124, 132, 159, 340, 358, 367, 370, 442.
Sayers, Wm., 40, 56, 106, 434, 498.
Scaggs, James, 431.
Scarbrough, Hendry, 433.
Scarbrough, Robert, 72.
Scathorn, Joseph, 368.
Schlater, Casper, 400.
Scholl, Peter, 13, 14, 16, 19, 20, 45, 50, 51, 52, 53, 54, 69, 112, 308, 430, 433, 440, 468.
Scholl Wm., 55.
Schooley, Isaac, 62.
Schutterle, John, 348.
Scidmore, James, 127.
Scidmore, John, 137.
Sciler, Jacob, 218.
Sciler, Jeremiah, 60, 69.
Sciler, Philip, 194, 204.
Scoat, Majer, 443.
Scoat, Robert, 443, 444.
Scone, John, 52.
Scone, Nicholas, 66.
Scotborn, Wm., 184.
Scothorn, Elizabeth, 194, 510.
Scott, Alex., 46, 58, 195, 222, 246.
Scott, Andrew, 28, 29, 68, 90, 186, 209, 218, 308.
Scott, Ann, 309.
Scott, Archibald, 225, 245.
Scott, Benjamin, 58, 63, 369.
Scot, David, 99.
Scot, Elizabeth, 322, 325.
Scott, Francis, 164.

Scott, George, 26, 41, 334, 434, 442.
Scott, Isabella, 164.
Scott, Jacob, 111, 116.
Scot, James, 26, 40, 48, 58, 99, 116, 164, 296, 315, 355, 366, 379, 439, 442, 457, 491.
Scott, Jane, 85, 321, 379.
Scott, Jean, 164, 329.
Scott, John, 48, 63, 98, 99, 110, 111, 116, 164, 285, 303, 397, 400, 434, 439, 538.
Scott, Joseph, 99, 116, 364, 462.
Scot, Judith, 63.
Scot, Major, 57, 67.
Scott, Margaret, 134.
Scott, Mary, 138, 238, 321, 405.
Scott, Matthew, 164, 181.
Scott, Nathaniel, 164.
Scott, Providence, 432.
Scott, Rachel, 164.
Scott, Robert, 16, 19, 26, 54, 57, 110, 139, 199, 237, 241, 263, 309, 405, 434, 446, 525.
Scott, Samuel, 24, 26, 33, 97, 136, 309, 321, 420.
Scott, Sarah, 237, 241.
Scott, Thomas, 16, 41, 210, 218, 236, 246.
Scott, William, 16, 28, 61, 62, 65, 67, 101, 164, 220, 290, 322, 325, 409, 458, 508, 538.
Scull, John, 300.
Sculps, Alen, 491.
Scyler, Christian, 286.
Scyler, Margaret, 286.
Sea, Frederick, 46, 112.
Sea, George, 39, 41, 46, 55.
Sea, John, 46.
Seaborn, Nicholas, 126.
Seahorn, Nicholas, 139.
Sealey (Seeley), Jeremiah, 73, 110, 318, 331, 339.
Searight, Alex., 235.
Searight, Ann, 379.
Searight, George, 234, 237, 379.
Searight, Gilbert, 235.
Searight, James, 137, 236, 237, 256, 481.
Searight, Jane, 234.
Searight, John, 237.
Searight, Margaret, 237.
Searight, Wm., 235.
Seaton, Augustine, 332.
Seawright, Alex., 386.
Seawright, George, 379.
Seawright, James, 382, 413, 480.
Seawright, Jane, 228, 379.
Seawright, Wm., 386.
Seborn, John, 178.
Seborn, Nicholas, 178.
Secaford, Elizabeth, 405.
Secaford, Jacob, 405.
Secaford, John, 405.
Sedusky, Anthony, 205.
See, James, 73, 510.

Seegar, Frederick, 342.
Seewright, James, 148.
Seewright, John, 121, 141, 144, 150.
Seldomridge, Bolzer, 412.
Seiler, John, 124.
Sellers, George, 296.
Selling, Andrew, 417.
Selling, Laywell, 417.
Seltzer, Mathias, 18, 19, 46.
Selzer, Henry, 373.
Semen, Thomas, 501.
Sempil, Abagail, 324.
Semple, John, 66, 324.
Settleton, Andrew, 95.
Severt, Charles F., 122.
Seviar, John, 99, 122, 138, 147, 151, 154, 372.
Sevear, Valentine, 18, 20, 28, 29, 31, 35, 37, 39, 40, 45, 49, 55, 61, 67, 123, 151, 296, 324, 371, 431, 473, 491.
Sevior, Joanna, 174.
Sewell, James, 520.
Sexton, Wm., 250.
Seyers (Sayers), Robert, 15.
Seyford, Michael, 265.
Seymore, Felix, 328.
Seymour, Joseph, 425.
Seyvert, Nicholas, 202.
Seyvert, Philip, 244, 386.
Shaddon, Mathew, 123, 345, 351, 353.
Shaddon, Susanna, 123, 345, 351, 353.
Shadow, Ludwick, 169, 213, 531.
Shack, Alex., 171.
Shackelford, Rebecca, 428.
Shackelford, Reuben, 263, 428.
Shafer, Frederick, 417.
Shaggs, James, 23.
Shall, Robert, 189.
Shally, Christian, 412.
Shally (Shirley), Mary, 412.
Shally, Peter, 412.
Shalpman, Fenix, 97.
Shanie, Peter, 122.
Shankland, Edward, 121, 130.
Shankland, Richard, 106.
Shanklin, John, 152.
Shanklin, Robert, 89, 92, 173, 324, 446, 460.
Shanklin, Thomas, 272, 481.
Shanklin, Tomes, 440.
Shankling, Edward, 491.
Shankling, Thomas, 270.
Shanks, Wm., 234.
Shannon, Samuel, 244, 261.
Sharp, Gov., 471.
Sharp (Sharpe), Edward, 136, 350.
Sharp (Sharpe), Eleanor, 81, 445.
Sharp, John, 285, 422.
Sharp, Mary, 368.
Sharp, Matthew, 26, 434.
Sharp, Sarah, 149.
Sharp, Wm., 161, 180, 247.

Simson, Wm., 490.
Simston, Richard, 51.
Sinclair, Alex., 187, 510.
Sinclair, Charles, 40, 56, 432.
Sinclair, Charles, 434.
Singleton, Andrew, 453.
Singleton, Manoah, 207, 233.
Sinkfield, Robert, 478.
Sithington, Andrew, 145, 430.
Sittes, George, 481.
Sitz, Peter, 385.
Siver, Francis, 158.
Siver, Francis P., 158.
Siver (Sivers), Jacob, 41, 82.
Siver, Margaret, 158.
Siver, Mary, 158.
Sivers, Windle, 82.
Sivert, Barbara, 158.
Sivert, Charles F., 158, 490.
Sivert, Michael, 509.
Sixby, John, 21.
Skaggs, Henry, 132.
Skean, John, 92, 105.
Skeleron, Elizabeth, 302.
Skelleron, William, 302.
Skelton, John, 39, 129, 145, 343, 356, 358, 359, 479.
Skidmore, Andrew, 511.
Skidmore, James, 341, 356.
Skidmore, John, 169, 171, 177, 179, 183, 194, 196.
Skidmore, Joseph, 197, 199, 324, 352, 353, 461.
Skidmore, Sarah, 341, 356.
Skiles, Jacob, 421.
Skillem, Eliza, 315.
Skillem, Elizabeth, 364.
Skillem, George, 330, 335, 364, 384.
Skillem, Wm., 364.
Skillern, Elizabeth, 34, 301.
Skillern, George, 51, 55, 85,, 117, 121, 125, 127, 143, 156, 158, 495.
Skillern, Wm., 34, 51, 85.
Skilleron (Skillern), George, 428.
Skileron, John, 466.
Skilleron, Wm., 454.
Skillran, Elizabeth, 432.
Skoot, Alex, 41.
Skoot, Benjamin, 41.
Skout, Hermanns, 42.
Skoot, James, 41.
Skoot, John, 41.
Skoot, Samuel, 41.
Skull, George, 429.
Slack, Randal, 181, 205.
Slaven, John, 259.
Slack, Sarah, 205.
Slagle, George, 420.
Slater, Elizabeth, 289.
Slaughter, Reuben, 422.
Slaughter, Smith, 417.
Slaughter, Wm., 164.

Slaven, John, 101, 440.
Slaven, Wm., 526.
Slavens, Esiah, 447.
Slavens, John, 447.
Slavens, Reuben, 447.
Slavens, Wm., 447.
Slavey, Christian F., 288.
Sleet, John, 131.
Sloan, John, 35.
Sloane, James, 28.
Sloven, Wm., 227.
Slover, Abraham, 115.
Slover, Jacob, 115.
Slusher, Conrad, 423.
Slusher, Elizabeth, 423.
Small, Barnet, 498.
Small, Thomas, 486.
Small, Wm., 482.
Smallbridge, Samuel, 178.
Smallman, Thomas, 177, 182, 183.
Smallwood, John, 348.
Smelzer, John, 503.
Smelzer, Pelzer, 357.
Smiley, Alex., 36.
Smiley, Andrew, 150.
Smiley, John, 61, 165, 356, 364.
Smiley, Mary, 36.
Smiley, Walter, 53, 73, 137.
Smiley, Wm., 470.
Smith, Abraham, 65, 72, 76, 78, 80, 83, 85, 107, 115, 133, 134, 144, 169, 170, 177, 183, 189, 192, 196, 228, 312, 349, 367, 433, 468, 504, 507, 510.
Smith, Adam, 370.
Smith, Agnes, 333.
Smith, Alexander, 142.
Smith, Amey, 112.
Smith, Andrew, 94, 99, 168.
Smith, Anna, 159.
Smith, Barbara, 351.
Smith, Barten, 213.
Smith, Benjamin, 481.
Smith, Betty, 128.
Smith, Catherine, 41, 513.
Smith, Charles, 212, 488.
Smith, Christian, 513.
Smith, Dal., 82.
Smith, Daniel, 44, 74, 77, 84, 85, 92, 98, 101, 103, 104, 107, 122, 141, 164, 165, 193, 196, 313, 321, 329, 360, 362, 368, 385, 369, 433, 437, 467, 489, 499, 509, 510.
Smith, David, 513.
Smith, Eleanor, 415.
Smith, Elizabeth, 41, 98.
Smith, Esther, 64.
Smith, Francis, 105, 143, 146, 150, 153, 159, 182, 225, 344, 399, 429, 464.
Smith, George, 209, 244, 256, 316, 388.
Smith, Henry, 44, 53, 76, 79, 92, 112, 250, 313, 330, 331, 349, 397, 407, 433, 438.
Smith, Hugh, 342, 349.

Smith, Isaac, 00.
Smith, James, 203, 367, 457, 471.
Smith, Jane, 180, 236.
Smith, John, 18, 27, 28, 33, 39, 41, 47, 50,
    55, 58, 61, 62, 63, 76, 78, 79, 82, 85, 102,
    110, 118, 123, 131, 158, 161, 175, 190,
    193, 194, 210, 245, 293, 295, 297, 302,
    309, 313, 323, 325, 329, 333, 341, 343,
    349, 350, 361, 362, 364, 367, 432, 433,
    436, 448, 462, 469, 476, 486, 490, 493,
    494, 497, 498.
Smith, Johnny, 128.
Smith, Jonathan, 134, 146, 158, 178, 197,
    367.
Smith, Joseph, 62, 194, 449, 471, 482, 509,
    510, 516.
Smith, Lawrence, 264, 265.
Smith, Levy, 126, 132, 353, 456.
Smith, Margaret, 323, 364.
Smith, Mary, 123, 190, 333, 513.
Smith, Mathew, 228, 231.
Smith, Michael, 117, 346, 456.
Smith, Nancy, 260.
Smith, Nicholas, 54, 64, 128, 346, 451.
Smith, Peter, 213, 417, 449.
Smith, Paul, 369.
Smith, Philip, 24, 31, 41.
Smith, Richard, 490.
Smith, Robert, 26, 36.
Smith, Samuel, 304, 470.
Smith, Sarah, 192.
Smith, Silas, 534.
Smith, Stephen, 410.
Smith, Thomas, 49, 51, 93, 121, 129, 132,
    163, 165, 167, 171, 174, 175, 178, 181,
    182, 184, 193, 199, 200, 201, 209, 210,
    212, 214, 233, 235, 260, 261, 265, 335,
    351, 374, 498, 507.
Smith, Tobias, 49, 61.
Smith, Walter, 524.
Smith, Wm., 14, 15, 50, 54, 86, 98, 102, 178,
    182, 189, 236, 241, 316, 367, 437, 440,
    443, 524.
Smith Zachariah, 88, 118.
Smithers, Andrew, 335.
Smithers, Archibald, 200, 374.
Smithers, Cecolin, 200.
Snediger, Joshua, 386.
Snediger, Xopher, 386.
Snider, Jacob, 250.
Snider, John, 213, 483.
Snoddon, George, 249.
Snodgrass, Benjamin, 520.
Snodgrass, Joseph, 520.
Snowden, Jacob, 379.
Snowdon, Wm., 116, 118, 308, 442.
Snyder, John, 221.
Sollace, Nicholas, 136.
Sollas, James, 172.
Sollas, Margaret, 172.
Sollas, Nicholas, 154, 172, 173.
Sollers, John, 438.

Solles, Nicholas, 141.
Soling, John P., 435.
Sommerville, Samuel, 278.
Son, Elizabeth, 219.
Son, Michael, 219.
Sorrell, Mary, 84.
Sorrell, Richard, 30, 84.
Sorrell, Walter, 30.
Sorrels, Sarah, 269.
South, Isaac, 77.
Southerland, John, 157.
Sowder, Anna, 523.
Sowder, Catherine, 523.
Sowder, Christian, 523.
Sowder, Christiana, 523.
Sowder, David, 523.
Sowder, Dorothy, 523.
Sowder, Frina, 523.
Sowder, Henry, 523.
Sowder, Isaac, 523.
Sowder, Jacob, 523.
Sowder, Jane, 523.
Sowder, John, 523.
Sowder, Joseph, 523.
Sowder, Mathew, 523.
Sowder, Peter, 523.
Sowder, Rachel, 523.
Sowder, Rudy, 523.
Sowder, Stephen, 523.
Sowell, John, 36.
Sowers, John, 384.
Sumersalt, Andrew, 222.
Sparks, Edward, 184.
Speakhard, Jacob, 268.
Spear, Edward, 442.
Spear, George, 161.
Spearing, Henry, 404.
Spearing, Richard, 404.
Spearman, Lewis, 238, 254.
Spears, George, 395.
Spears (Spear), Henry, 19, 32, 41, 44.
Spears, Hugh, 20.
Spears, John, 20, 21, 28, 29, 56, 85, 395.
Spears (Syers), Robert, 442.
Speat, John, 32.
Speer, Frederick, 168.
Speer, Henry, 438.
Speer, John, 444.
Speere, Hugh, 315.
Speers, Wm., 86.
Spence, James, 383, 388, 395, 403, 404.
Spence, Wm., 291, 404.
Spencer, James, 422.
Spencer, Thomas, 120.
Spindle, Adolph, 250, 504.
Spiller, Wm., 325, 358.
Spitler, Adam, 533.
Spittler, John,
Spots, Jacob, 532.
Spotts, George, 208.
Sprigg, Nicholas, 218.
Spring, Nicholas, 265, 402.

Stewart, Benjamin, 338.
Stewart, Catren, 435.
Stewart, David, 139, 188, 296, 311, 323, 345, 363, 365, 375, 443, 453, 468, 473, 527.
Stewart, Elizabeth, 347, 361, 362.
Stewart, Francis, 141, 142, 214.
Stewart, George, 528.
Stewart, James, 26, 78, 95, 109, 136, 157, 198, 299, 336, 343, 361, 396, 372.
Stewart, John, 135, 137, 139, 145, 155, 160, 198, 301, 310, 319, 320, 321, 322, 324, 325, 327, 341, 346, 347, 357, 358, 360, 362, 363, 364, 365, 366, 369, 437, 448, 456, 469, 473, 486.
Stewart, Mary, 336.
Stewart, Ralph, 180, 183, 193, 204, 208.
Stewart, Robert, 343, 437, 478.
Stewart, Samuel, 321.
Stewart, Sarah, 94.
Stewart, Sebina, 372.
Stewart, Thomas, 338, 343, 442.
Stewart, Walter, 358, 456.
Stewart, Wm., 153, 174, 183, 359.
Stickleman, Joshua, 433.
Stiffey, Christian, 95.
Stiffey, John, 95.
Still, Jacob, 242.
Stinson, James, 439.
Stinson, John, 13, 22, 459.
Stinson, Thomas, 14, 21, 24, 34.
Stoakes, Capt., 247.
Stockdale, Robert, 424.
Stockdon, Richard, 94.
Stockton, Thomas, 146.
Stodghill, Ambrose, 331.
Stoffelmier, John, 474.
Stokes, David, 41.
Stokes, Margaret, 372.
Stokes, Mitford, 290.
Stolucher, Samuel, 431.
Stonacie, Samuel, 434.
Stonate, Wm., 446.
Stone, Catherine, 112.
Stone, Christian, 221.
Stone, Gotleib, 425.
Stone, Henry, 97, 112, 140, 156, 449.
Stone, John, 425.
Stoner, Jude, 36.
Stophelmine, John, 353.
Storey, Ann, 197.
Storn, Thomas, 75.
Story, Elizabeth, 388.
Story, John, 394, 307, 388, 393, 411.
Story, Thomas, 13, 56, 65, 94, 105, 137, 197, 227, 304, 393, 400, 401, 411, 430, 433.
Stout, Hezekiah, 447.
Stover, Daniel, 25, 439.
Stover, Elizabeth, 343.
Stover, Jacob, 312, 523.
Strahorn, Gilbert, 486.

Straen, David, 285.
Strain, Allen, 424.
Strain, Eleanor, 415, 421.
Strain, James, 271, 424.
Strain, Jinney, 424.
Strain, John, 109, 271, 415, 421, 424, 489.
Strain, Nancy, 424.
Strain, Peggy, 424.
Strain, Polly, 424.
Strain, Robert, 424.
Strange, Archibald, 241.
Stratton, Seriah, 174, 179.
Strawbridge, Thos., 418.
Strean, James, 283.
Strean, Robert, 283.
Street, John, 356.
Stribling (Strihling), M. T., 516.
Strickley, Christian, 57.
Strickler, Abraham, 16.
Strickler, Christian, 490.
Strickling, Levi, 277.
Stride, John, 40.
Stringam, Charles, 65, 67, 77.
Stringer, Daniel, 48, 332, 339, 484.
Stringer, Elizabeth, 445.
Stringham, Charles, 469.
Strother, Joseph, 187.
Strother, N., 325.
Stroud, Adam, 155, 432.
Stroud, John, 23, 68, 434.
Stroud, Michael, 41.
Stroud, Peter, 369.
Stroup, Martin, 39.
Strout, Adam, 449.
Strutsenocker, Henry, 169.
Stuart, Agatha, 262.
Stuart, Alexander, 95, 174, 267, 268, 279, 282, 284, 287, 372, 407.
Stuart, Archibald, 36, 55, 72, 84, 224, 256, 263, 278, 378.
Stuart, Benjamin, 141.
Stuart, Charles, 86, 403.
Stuart, David, 20, 21, 25, 28, 30, 45, 47, 50, 54, 56, 65, 67, 69, 76, 79, 80, 82, 106, 112, 133, 364, 372, 518.
Stuart, Edward, 253, 263.
Stuart, Elizabeth, 144, 365.
Stuart, Francis, 147, 149, 280, 416, 462.
Stuart, Isabella, 167.
Stuart, James, 146, 167, 270, 328, 411, 412, 537.
Stuart, John, 77, 95, 98, 125, 126, 142, 143, 145, 149, 164, 196, 217, 232, 246, 288, 316, 357, 377, 391, 411.
Stuart, Margaret, 255, 389.
Stuart, Mary, 328, 407, 411.
Stuart, Polly, 288, 412.
Stuart, Ralph, 95, 178, 537.
Stuart, Rebecca, 537.
Stuart, Robert, 14, 85, 95, 215, 248, 257, 388, 407, 527, 538.
Stuart, Samuel, 17, 299, 304.

Teat, Thomas, 442.
Teater George, 109.
Tebout, Cornelius, 294.
Tedford, Alev. 169, 180.
Tedford, David, 170, 180.
Tedford, James, 411.
Tedford, Jeremiah, 169.
Tedford, John, 169.
Tedford, Robert, 71, 180.
Tedford, Henry, 414.
Tedford Jacob, 400.
Teel, John, 34.
Tees, Jane, 199.
Tees, John, 279.
Tees, Joseph, 30, 300.
Teeter, Paul, 180, 194.
Telfair, Wm., 413.
Telford, Alex. 138.
Telford, James, 151.
Telford, Jeremiah, 142.
Templeman, Wm., 360.
Templeton, James, 154.
Tencher, Samuel, 99, 100.
Tencher, William, 100.
Tennent, Charles, 320, 324.
Tenney, Elijah, 480.
Tern, Jacob (Dovan), 381.
Terrald, John, 26.
Terrell, Morris, 458.
Terrell, Timothy, 347.
Terry, Jasper, 61.
Terry, William, 61, 158.
Tesdall, Wm., 392.
Teter, Abraham, 483.
Teter, George, 483.
Teter, Paul, 146.
Tevenbaugh, George, 422.
Thomas, Ann. 478.
Thomas, Betsy, 418.
Thomas, Catherine, 120.
Thomas, Elizabeth, 53, 312, 441.
Thomas, Evick, 101.
Thomas, Griffith, 19.
Thomas, Jacob, 312.
Thomas, James, 40, 189, 198, 200, 210, 429. 489.
Thomas, John, 24, 134, 157, 158, 191, 196, 301, 361, 418.
Thomas, Levi, 250.
Thomas, Mathy, 491.
Thomas, Nelly, 418.
Thomas, Rees, 437.
Thomas, Richard, 381.
Thomas. Samuel, 195, 211, 217, 406.
Thomas, Wm., 155, 209, 486.
Thompson, Abraham, 489.
Thompson, Adam, 53, 57, 67, 71, 304, 328, 336, 338, 470, 518.
Thompson, Alex., 138, 143, 158, 172, 198, 442.
Thompson, Andrew, 234.
Thompson, Ann, 325.

Thompson, Anthony, 62, 348.
Thompson, Archibald. 406, 407, 410, 418, 419.
Thompson, Benijah (Benajah), 261, 405.
Thompson, Benjamin, 69.
Thompson, Billy, 358.
Thompson, Charles, 438 .
Thompson, Christopher, 115.
Thompson, Edward, 114, 142, 250, 320, 322, 475.
Thompson, Eleanor, 100, 203.
Thompson, Elizabeth, 71, 396, 431.
Thompson, George, 449.
Thompson, Henry, 513.
Thompson. Hugh, 24, 86, 87, 95, 100.
Thompson, James, 57, 97, 100, 101, 144, 170, 172, 184, 441, 513.
Thompson, Jane, 97, 101, 114.
Thompson. Jeremiah, 315.
Thompson, John, 138, 139, 142, 143, 144, 149, 156, 166, 168, 177, 179, 338, 348, 353, 355, 358, 400, 442, 461, 462, 475, 513.
Thompson, Joseph, 248, 384, 396, 513.
Thompson, Margaret, 127.
Thompson, Mary, 115, 170, 188, 202, 209.
Thompson, Matthew, 26, 38, 68, 107, 446.
Thompson, Moses, 293, 308.
Thompson, Naome, 328, 336, 338.
Thompson, Patterson, 278, 519.
Thompson, Richard, 526.
Thompson, Robert. 68, 138, 140, 172, 178, 193, 202, 203, 206, 213, 218, 239, 240, 275, 348, 355, 527, 537.
Thompson, Smith, 204, 277, 288, 516, 519.
Thompson, Susanna, 358.
Thompson, Thomas, 37, 69, 80, 86, 105, 114, 320.
Thompson, William, 13, 14, 20, 29, 144, 177, 182, 188, 197, 242, 277, 278, 312, 317, 372, 396, 490, 513, 528.
Thomson, Adam, 443.
Thomson, Alexander, 14, 16, 20, 23, 24, 29, 30, 48, 54, 68, 83, 103, 165.
Thomson Hugh, 13.
Thomson, John, 36, 83, 93, 102, 103, 127, 131, 331, 354.
Thomson, Martha, 301.
Thomson. Mathew, 301, 434.
Thomson, Moses, 199.
Thomson, Patterson, 481.
Thomson, Thomas, 331.
Thomson (Thompson), William, 16, 17, 19, 20, 21, 24, 28, 32, 46, 68, 103, 106, 110, 119, 442, 484.
Thorn, Sarah, 43.
Thornbill, Samuel, 437
Thornhill, Samuel, 50, 77, 114.
Thornton, Albneazer, 268.
Thornton. Coate, 424.
Thornton, Ebenezer, 283.

Turk, Elizabeth, 366, 368
Turk, James, 147, 174, 366, 368.
Turk, Margaret, 313, 365.
Turk, Mary, 365, 466.
Turk, Robert, 29, 292, 297, 301, 366.
Turk, Thomas, 34, 141, 236, 246, 272, 273, 313, 359, 365, 366, 368, 372, 397, 412, 419, 420, 536.
Turkey (Turley), Ignatius, 270.
Turnbull, James, 308.
Turner, Anthony, 512.
Turner, Robert, 339, 485.
Turpen (Turpin), Solomon, 95, 152.
Tutt, Wm., 112, 119.
Tyler, Charles, 480.
Tyler, Francis, 107, 324, 325, 334, 452, 491, 501, 502.

Uff, Frederick, 122.
Uly, Wm., 154.
Umphries, John, 130.
Underwood, Elizabeth, 74.
Underwood, James, 98, 109.
Underwood, John, 74.
Underwood, Joseph, 74.
Underwood, Mary, 74.
Unermerman, Isaac, 271.
Unemerman, Stephen, 271.
Upp, Frederick, 339, 449.
Upton, Edward, 347.
Urie, James, 335.
Urquhart, W., 169.
Urey (Urry), James, 50, 69, 437.
Usher, Ann J., 14, 40.
Usher, Loves, 203.
Uter, Matthew, 42.
Utt, Catherine, 73.
Utt, Caspar, 73.
Utter, Mary, 71.
Utter, Valentine, 71.

Vachob, John, 201.
Vachub, John, 343.
Vachub (Wauchub), Joseph, 107, 108, 120, 343.
Vahab, John, 213.
Valentine, Michael, 127.
Vallendegham, George, 183.
Vaminon, Peter, 180.
Vance, David, 464.
Vance, George, 20, 36.
Vance, James, 56, 273, 423.
Vance, John, 40, 57, 77, 161, 225, 226, 273, 434, 442, 443, 444, 512, 518, 519.
Vance, Martha, 226, 273.
Vance, Mathew, 62, 434.
Vance, Samuel, 179, 191, 194, 196, 197, 199, 202, 207, 216, 218, 220, 221, 224, 228, 239, 240, 244, 251, 378, 403, 423, 429, 481.
Vance, Thomas, 135, 498.
Vance, Wm., 510.

Vanderpool, Abraham, 42, 308, 316, 433.
Vaneman, Peter, 87, 106, 140, 141.
Vanfossen, Abraham, 531.
Vanfossen, Jacob, 531.
Vanhever, John, 422.
Vare, Ann, 106.
Various Old Papers, 429.
Van Law, Jacob, 175.
Van Lear (Van Lears), Jacob, 82, 230, 399, 526.
Van Matre, Jacob, 177.
Van Pelt, James, 489.
Van Pelt, Margaret, 103, 339.
Van Pelt, Tunis, 335, 429.
Vanscoy, Aaron, 171.
Vanse, Ephraim, 484.
Vansell, Edmund, 132.
Vanso, Theodosia, 454.
Van Unter (Nuter), John, 512.
Varner, John, 427, 520.
Varner, Samuel, 109.
Vasteen, William, 274.
Vaub, John, 364.
Vaught, Catherine, 309.
Vaught, John Paul, 309.
Venable, Nathaniel, 486.
Venus, Henry, 520.
Verden, Egenier, 101, 121.
Verner, John, 356.
Vernold, Samuel, 103.
Vernon, Elizabeth, 198.
Via, David, 129, 149, 175, 494.
Via, Francis, 175.
Via, Robert, 149.
Viare, John, 62.
Viers, David, 154.
Viers, Elizabeth, 154.
Viers, Francis, 144, 161.
Viers, Gideon, 154.
Viers, Mildred, 154.
Viges, Francis, 134.
Viges, Wm., 134.
Villelly, William, 249, 409.
Vincher, Samuel, 441.
Vineman, Peter, 179.
Vines, Polly, 533.
Viney, Andrew, 40, 67.
Vinyard, Christopher, 127, 140.
Vocust, Henry, 384.
Vohub, Joseph, 154.
Vorris (Norris), Robert, 434.
Voss (Vause, Vance), Ephriam, 24, 58, 62, 69, 81.
Vought, Caspar Paul, 309.
Vought, Elizabeth, 309.
Vought, John P., 300.
Vowter, Wm., 131.

Wacheb (Wachub, Wahub), Joseph, 185, 266, 370.
Wachtel, Henry, 285.

Warrick, Jacob, 178, 240, 481.
Warrick, Wm., 453.
Warrin, Bige, 447.
Warring, Michael, 152, 438.
Warrington, James, 103.
Warrington, Mary, 347.
Warwick, Ann, 384.
Warwick, Christopher, 188.
Warwick, Jacob, 180, 191, 199.
Warwick, John, 49, 135, 145, 280, 215, 384.
Warwick, Wm., 95, 180, 443.
Washington, George, 452, 471, 472.
Waters, Wm., 215.
Waterman, Asher, 264, 396, 529.
Waterman, Sarah, 264.
Waters, Elizabeth, 94.
Waters, Matthew, 76.
Waters, Thomas, 320, 325.
Waters, Richard, 41.
Waters, Thomas, 48, 86.
Watterson, Mary, 322.
Waterson, Thomas, 29, 34, 71, 205.
Watterson, Wm., 142, 150, 153, 164, 175, 352, 356, 466.
Watkins, Alice, 29.
Watkins, John, 197, 361, 366.
Watkins, John S., 153, 171.
Watkins, Philip, 344, 527.
Watkins, Wm., 29, 138.
Watling, John, 41.
Wats, Thomas, 322, 440.
Watson, Alexander, 278.
Watson, Anthony, 520.
Watson, Benjamin, 125.
Watson, Elizabeth, 28, 314.
Watson, James, 138.
Watson, John, 28, 186.
Wason, Joseph, 28, 358.
Watson, Richardson, 117.
Watson, Wm. R., 391, 509.
Watt, James, 501.
Watts, Arthur, 31.
Watts (Watt), George, 71, 110, 130, 132.
Watts, Wm., 149.
Waugh, Isaac, 271.
Waugh, James, 379.
Waugh, Mary, 202, 209, 379.
Way, Jacob, 520.
Wayt, John, 290, 590.
Weaver, Christiana, 241, 260.
Weaver, George, 118, 142, 171, 241.
Weaver, John, 260.
Weaver, John G., 260.
Weaver, Peter, 241.
Webb, Joseph, 156.
Webb, Julius, 135.
Webber, Augustine, 469.
Webber, Margaret, 469.
Weems, John, 528.
Weems, Thomas, 64, 66.
Weer, George, 138.
Weer, Joseph,, 170.

Weer, James, 170.
Weer, John, 138.
Weer, Samuel, 151.
Wees, Jacob, 119.
Weir, Francis, 205.
Weir, George, 421.
Weir, Samuel, 191.
Wehrly, Jacob, 520.
Welch, Alex., 391.
Welch, John, 234.
Welch, Sarah, 234.
Welch, Thomas, 340.
Welch, Walter, 430.
Welch, Wicklor, 430.
Weldon, George, 210.
Welfong, Michael, 171.
Wells, Ann, 206.
Wells, James, 396.
Wells, Nancy, 396.
Wells, Thomas, 206, 396.
Welsh, John, 257, 386.
Welsh, George, 87.
Welsh, Henry, 284.
Welsh, John, 150, 213, 445, 480.
Welsh, Mary, 347.
Welsh, Nicholas, 120, 150, 386.
Welsh, Thomas, 489.
Weltshire, John, 102.
Wendon, Sarah, 211.
Weorly, John, 287.
West, Alexander, 117.
West, George, 42, 438.
West, Gowan, 90, 92.
West, Henry, 268.
West, Hugh, 355.
West, John, 41.
West, Thomas, 87.
West, Wm., 143, 155.
Westcoat (Westcourt), Ebenezer, 17, 53.
Westfall, Abel, 42, 433.
Westfall, Abraham, 130.
Westfall, Daniel, 204, 205.
Weltfall, Delay, 537.
Westfall, Euric, 58.
Westfall, George, 197.
Westfall, Henry, 527.
Westfall, Jacob, 42, 55, 202, 217, 449.
Westfall, Joel, 178, 202.
Westfall, John, 433.
Westfall, Wm., 55, 194, 202, 527, 537.
Westfall, John, 29, 42, 55, 130.
Wetherall, George, 343.
Whatley, Shirley, 421.
Wheeler, Garrat, 204.
Wheeler, John, 272, 276, 511.
Wheeler, William, 273, 289, 413.
Whitaker, Charles, 55, 310.
White, Alexander, 120, 383.
White, Bryant, 23.
White, Cateren, 511.
White, Catherine, 93.
White, David, 183, 184, 264, 511.

White, Edmund, 222.
White, Edward, 528.
White, Gordon, 264.
White, Henry, 310.
White, Isaac, 29, 54, 136, 143, 225, 264.
White, James, 264.
White, Jane, 225, 264.
White, John, 81, 84, 93, 136, 137, 140, 141, 170, 205, 407, 428, 429, 481, 489.
White, Joseph, 65, 91.
White, Robert, 244, 262.
White, Solomon, 161.
White, William, 17, 19, 65.
White, Valentine, 228, 237, 239, 395.
Whitely, Lilley, 156.
Whiteside, Anne, 325.
Whitesides, James, 367.
Whiteside, Mary, 71, 74.
Whiteside, Moses, 175.
Whiteside, Wm., 71, 74, 325, 330, 367, 459.
Whiticher, David, 490.
Whiting, Francis, 426.
Whitley, Catherine, 345, 352.
Whitley, Lilley, 150.
Whitley (Whitly), Jonathan, 74, 136, 150, 345, 352.
Whitley, Paul, 150, 376.
Whitlev, Robert, 144.
Whitley, Solomon, 57, 441.
Whitman, Catherine, 145.
Whitman, Charles, 145.
Whitman, Hurson M., 145.
Whitman, Jacob, 145.
Whitsel, Anthony, 416.
Whitsell, Martin, 87, 224.
Whitsel, Peter, 416.
Whitson, Wm., 439.
Whitton, John, 180.
Whitzell, Mary, 377.
Whooley. Peter, 130.
Whooley, Wm., 130.
Wiatt, William, 241, 382.
Wicks, John, 77.
Wier, Francis, 180.
Wigard, John, 433.
Wiger, David, 220, 223.
Wiger, Sarah, 220, 223.
Wiggins, Wm., 471.
Wilcher, Val., 434.
Wild, Mary, 418.
Wilds, Valentine, 418.
Wiley, Alex., 265.
Wiley, Elizabeth, 150, 153, 532.
Wiley, George, 40.
Wiley, James, 127.
Wiley, John, 40, 270, 455, 532.
Wiley, Margaret, 265.
Wiley, Martha, 127.
Wiley, Mary, 532.
Wiley, Robert, 42, 170, 215.
Wiley, Sarah, 532.
Wiley, Thomas, 532.

Wiley, Wm., 532.
Wilfong, John, 218.
Wilfong, Michael, 216.
Willfunk, George, 343.
Wilkey, Peter, 316.
Wilkins, John, 42, 432, 467.
Wilkins, Samuel, 13, 14, 19, 26, 31, 32, 40, 309, 431, 432, 467, 482.
Wilkins, Sarah, 40.
Wilkinson, Nathaniel, 427, 480.
Willbey, James. 40.
Willey, John, 144.
Williams, Abby, 107.
Williams, Ann, 96.
Williams, Catherine, 106, 270.
Williams, Charles, 407.
Williams, Christopher, 141, 148.
Williams, David, 130, 249, 272, 278, 279.
Williams, George, 101.
Williams, Henry, 81, 521.
Williams, James, 130, 258, 478.
Williams, John, 80, 109, 183, 270, 289, 386, 387.
Williams, Michael, 101.
Williams, Moses, 116, 139.
Williams, Philip, 81.
Williams, Remembrance, 106.
Williams, Richard, 107, 333.
Williams, Robert, 50, 262, 369, 437.
Williams, Samuel, 391, 430.
Williams, Thomas, 237, 256, 309, 399.
Williams, Wm., 13, 38, 46, 68, 77, 85, 469, 471.
Williamson, Abbey, 161.
Williamson, Charles, 44, 190.
Williamson, David, 190.
Williamson, James, 423.
Williamson, Peneripy, 190.
Williamson, Richard, 161, 190.
Williamson, Roger, 190.
Willis, Henry, 324.
Willis, Stephen, 106, 110.
Willis, Wm., 139, 142.
Willman, Wm., 390.
Willott, Allden, 151.
Willson, George, 328.
Willson, Horcklas, 438.
Willson, John, 147, 530.
Willson, Mathew, 444.
Willson, Patrick, 446.
Willson, Robert, 398.
Willson, Samuel, 320, 443.
Willson, Wm., 363.
Willy, James, 434.
Willy, John, 492.
Wilmoth, John, 191.
Wilmoth, Thomas, 175.
Wilpert, John D., 44, 79, 318, 327, 328.
Wilphong, John, 528.
Wils, Wm., 441.
Wilsby, Mary, 120.
Wilshire, Nathaniel, 40.